Travels of Boris Savinkov in Europe, Pre-1914 Borders (Left)

① London
② Paris
③ Geneva
④ Nice
⑤ Genoa
⑥ Antwerp
⑦ Berlin
⑧ Prague
⑨ Rome
⑩ Warsaw
⑪ Verzhbolovo

⑫ Vilnius
⑬ Riga
⑭ Oslo
⑮ Helsinki
⑯ Murmansk
⑰ Saint Petersburg
⑱ Arkhangel
⑲ Minsk
⑳ Mogilyov
㉑ Mozyr
㉒ Bucharest

㉓ Kiev
㉔ Moscow
㉕ Yaroslavl
㉖ Vologda
㉗ Kharkov
㉘ Sevastopol
㉙ Tambov
㉚ Rostov-on-Don
㉛ Nizhny Novgorod

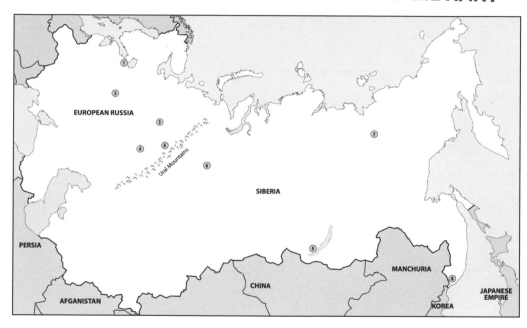

Savinkov in Eastern Russian Empire (Above)

① Saint Petersburg
② Moscow
③ Kazan
④ Samara
⑤ Ufa

⑥ Omsk
⑦ Yakutsk
⑧ Vladivostok
⑨ Irkutsk

TO BREAK
RUSSIA'S CHAINS

TO BREAK RUSSIA'S CHAINS

BORIS SAVINKOV AND HIS WARS AGAINST
THE TSAR AND THE BOLSHEVIKS

VLADIMIR ALEXANDROV

PEGASUS BOOKS
NEW YORK LONDON

TO BREAK RUSSIA'S CHAINS

Pegasus Books, Ltd.
148 West 37th Street, 13th Floor
New York, NY 10018

First Pegasus Books edition September 2021

Interior design by Maria Fernandez

Library of Congress Cataloging-in-Publication Data is available.

ISBN: 978-1-64313-718-6

10 9 8 7 6 5 4 3 2 1

Printed in the United States of America
Distributed by Simon & Schuster
www.pegasusbooks.com

For Sybil

CONTENTS

Few men tried more, gave more, dared more
and suffered more for the Russian people.
—Winston Churchill

There is no more sometimes than the trembling
of a leaf between success and failure.
—W. Somerset Maugham

CONVENTIONS

All dates for events in Russia prior to 1918 are given in the Old Style (OS), or Julian, calendar that was used until the beginning of that year and that was thirteen days behind the New Style (NS), Gregorian, calendar used in the West during the twentieth century. During the nineteenth, it was twelve days behind. Occasionally a double date is given for clarity in connection with events that were also important in the West: e.g., Bloody Sunday on January 9/22, 1905, which means January 9 according to the OS calendar and January 22 according to the NS calendar.

There is no single system for transliterating Russian that accomplishes everything one could wish. In the body of the book, I use a system that helps the reader approximate Russian pronunciation. However, in the references I use a system that is conventional in scholarly bibliographies. As a result, the names of some individuals and places appear in two variants, but their equivalence should be obvious (e.g., Moiseyenko = Moiseenko). Well-known names of people and places are given in their most familiar forms—thus Nicholas II, not Nikolay II; Saint Petersburg, not Sankt-Peterburg. I also preserve the transliterations of names as used by authors themselves and in references.

Traditional Russian naming practices for people consist of first names, patronymics (derived from the father's first name), and surnames. For the sake of simplicity, I leave out most patronymics.

Estimates of what different sums of money from the past would be worth in today's dollars are determined by calculators at http://www.measuringworth .com/uscompare.

AUTHOR'S NOTE

This is the story of a remarkable man who became a terrorist to fight the tyrannical Russian imperial regime, and when a popular revolution overthrew it in 1917 turned his wrath against the Bolsheviks because they betrayed the revolution and the freedoms it won. If any of the extraordinary plots he hatched against the Bolsheviks had succeeded, the world we live in would be unrecognizable.

Boris Savinkov was famous, and notorious, during his lifetime both at home and abroad because of the major roles he played in *all* the cataclysmic events that shook his homeland during the first quarter of the twentieth century. The story of his life has an epic sweep and challenges many popular myths about the Russian Revolution, which was arguably the most important catalyst of twentieth-century world history. Although now largely forgotten in the West, Savinkov is still a legendary figure in Russia, and a controversial one—so much so that many documents about him remain locked away in the secret archives of the FSB, the security agency that succeeded the KGB.

It is hard to believe Savinkov's life because of all the triumphs, disasters, twists, and contradictions that filled it. Neither a Red nor a White, he forged his own path through history. He chose terror out of altruism, although what he did bears no resemblance to what "terrorism" means today. He closely supervised teams of terrorists and agonized over the morality of his actions, but never killed anyone himself. He was a cunning conspirator, but fell victim to the greatest deception in the annals of Russian political skullduggery. He spent years evading the tsar's police, but became a government minister during the revolutionary year 1917. He could be as hard as stone and instilled fear and loathing in his enemies, but was admired by international statesmen and became close friends with world-famous artists. He yearned for family life and strived to be a loving husband and father, but sacrificed his personal happiness for political goals.

He sent men and women to their deaths, but could recite Romantic poetry for hours and wrote novels and memoirs that are read to this day. He believed in the inviolable rights of human beings, but concluded that only a dictator could guarantee them during periods of great national upheaval. He was fiercely loyal to his comrades-in-arms, but decided to deceive them when he took an immense final gamble in his fight against the Soviet regime. Trying to understand Savinkov's beliefs and the choices he made often forces one to think what might have seemed unthinkable.

Savinkov's life also refracts two issues that remain critically important today: the character of the Russian state and its role in the world. All his efforts were directed at transforming his homeland into a uniquely democratic, humane, and enlightened country—one in which the people control not only their government but also the economic system under which they live, one that welcomes self-determination for all its nationalities, and one that seeks harmonious relations in the international community. The support Savinkov got for his goals from numerous countrymen during his career suggests that the paths Russia took during the twentieth and twenty-first centuries—the tyranny of the Soviet period, the authoritarianism of Putin's regime—were not the only ones written in her historical destiny. Savinkov's goals are a poignant reminder of how things in Russia could have been and how, perhaps, they may still become someday.

Boris Savinkov's life is also an exceptionally good story—too good to be left untold any longer. All that follows really happened, and everything that is between quotation marks comes from a memoir, a letter, or another historical document.

CHAPTER ONE

THE PERSONAL IS ALWAYS POLITICAL IN RUSSIA

T he doorbell rang shortly after 1 A.M., shattering the quiet just when everyone in the Savinkov household had gone to bed.

"Police!" a commanding male voice answered the maid's anxious question; then, before she could even start unlocking the door, the voice added angrily, "Hurry! Open up!"

What better time than late at night to ensure that everyone is home and so disoriented by sleep that they cannot resist or even argue effectively? The Gestapo and KGB would perfect the method in the twentieth century, making the dreaded nighttime knock or ringing doorbell the subject of countless nightmares and the herald of millions of disappearances. But in the more innocent nineteenth century, even in the notoriously autocratic Russian Empire, the practice was still too rare for the average person to feel anything but shock and surprise.

It was December 23, 1897, and Boris Savinkov, aged eighteen, and his brother Alexander, twenty-three, had come home for Christmas to the family's apartment in Warsaw earlier that day. Both were university students in the imperial capital, Saint Petersburg—Boris was studying law, Alexander mining engineering—and had not seen their parents and four siblings since the beginning of the school year. They had all just spent a wonderfully warm family evening together, talking excitedly, happy to see one another again, the parents filled with delight, marveling at how much their sons had matured in just several months, and very proud of their passionate desire to do something good and important for their country.

When Sofia Alexandrovna, their mother, heard who was at the door, she hurried to their room. Even though the family's life had flowed peacefully until then and no one had ever had any problems with the police, her instinct told her that her sons were involved. Both were already up and dressing hurriedly, with their father, Victor Mikhailovich, standing by, looking anxious.

A moment later, in a uniform with epaulettes, a saber at this side, and the spurs on his boots ringing, Colonel Utgof of the gendarmes, the Russian imperial political police, strode into the room. A dozen other people—policemen, official witnesses, the building's custodian—crowded in after him.

"Excuse me," the colonel began with a formal bow as he brought his heels together in an elegant foot scrape. "By order of the authorities, I must carry out a search."

The parents looked at each other with horror. Victor Mikhailovich was a well-known and respected justice of the peace in the Russian imperial court system in Poland. To have police search an official's home in those years was almost unheard of.

Over the next four hours, the police dug through everything in the large, high-ceilinged apartment, dumping clothing and books on the floor, scrutinizing photographs, riffling through documents, reading letters, ripping open furniture upholstery, and leaving filthy footprints everywhere amid the chaos. It was sickening to see strangers' hands do whatever they wanted with the family's most intimate and cherished possessions. The youngest son and the three daughters were also roused from their beds, and their mattresses, pillows, and bedding prodded and groped. Boris and Alexander were thoroughly frisked as well. No one in the family would ever forget the stinging humiliation they felt that night.

The number of police and the effort they expended might have been appropriate if they had been searching for a cache of guns or explosives, or even an illegal printing press. However, what they were looking for was far more innocuous, and the colonel and his minions found it in Boris's wallet and in a basket that Alexander had brought with him and had not even unpacked yet—nineteen envelopes containing copies of a protest by students in Saint Petersburg against imperial policies in Poland, and part of a student organization's bylaws. Their oldest sister, Vera, also surrendered two additional envelopes that she had torn in half and tried to hide under her pillow.

In the eyes of the police, this little pile of paper was damning evidence of sedition.

"Say goodbye to your parents," the colonel commanded Boris and Alexander. "You're coming with me!"

The parents could not believe what was happening. Their eyes filled with tears, and Sofia felt sobs rising in her throat as they rushed to embrace their sons. The young men had turned pale but seemed calm.

Acting as if he had completed a social call, and adding another surreal note to his rude violation of a family's peace and privacy, the colonel once again went through his bowing and foot-scraping routine; then, letting the young men go first, the entire pack of police and officials trooped out.

The brothers were taken by carriage to the Alexander Citadel, which the Russian authorities had built on the northern edge of Warsaw to fortify the city after suppressing a rebellion, and locked up in its notorious Tenth Pavilion, where dangerous political prisoners were kept.

In Russia, History Is Never the Past

This event triggered a change in Boris that would define his life. For the first time, he had been confronted—not in the abstract and not at second hand—with the implacability of the Russian imperial regime, which loomed overhead like a mountainside ready to give way at the slightest touch. All he had done with his brother was raise a small voice of protest against Russia's heavy-handed policies in Poland, but this was enough to trigger police retribution that demonstrated he was less a citizen of his country than an abject subject.

What drove Boris and his fellow students was a desire for justice. But what drove the imperial regime was a fear of history repeating itself.

o—+—o

The relations between Russia and Poland were long, convoluted, and bloody, and had entered their current phase over a century earlier. In 1772, during an event that became known as the First Partition, Russia, Austria, and Prussia—Poland's stronger neighbors—seized parts of its territory (because they could). There was a Second Partition in 1793, when Prussia and Russia took even more. Finally, in 1795, after defeating Polish armies led by Tadeusz Kościuszko, a hero of the American Revolution and friend of Washington and Jefferson, Russia and

Prussia split what was left in the Third Partition. Russia got the lion's share, and Poland disappeared as an independent state from the map of Europe for the next 123 years.

But although the Poles had lost their country, they remained a proud people and nation. Many fought on Napoleon's side when he invaded Russia in 1812. Poles rose unsuccessfully against Russian imperial rule in 1830 and again in 1863, with numerous insurrectionists killed, hanged, and sent to Siberia. Russia tightened her grip after this and began barbaric programs to suppress Polish secular and Catholic religious identity. In 1879, Russian was proclaimed the only language of instruction in Polish territories.

It does little to mitigate Russia's miserable behavior in Poland—although it helps explain it—to point out that analogous policies existed in Polish territories that Prussia had seized. (And as is usually the case between neighboring states whose relative strength varies over time, the pendulum of history had swung the other way in the past, when the Poles occupied Moscow and attempted to take over the Russian throne in the early seventeenth century.) Even more broadly, the end of the nineteenth century was a bad time for smaller peoples and weaker states everywhere as European and American imperialism marched across Asia, Africa, the Pacific, the Caribbean, and Latin America. Think of just the United States grabbing Hawaii, Puerto Rico, Cuba, Guam, and the Philippines in the 1890s, or the widespread prohibitions against Native American languages and religious practices on reservations and in boarding schools that lasted well into the twentieth century.

Because of the recurring uprisings in the nineteenth century, the long history of Russian oppression was never far out of mind among Poles. But just three months before Boris and Alexander were arrested, an event occurred that inflamed all the old passions on both sides. It also made the historical past into a living present for Boris and prompted him to act.

On October 3, 1897, in Vilnius, which is now the capital of independent Lithuania but was then an important city in Russian Poland, the cornerstone was laid for a monument to Count Mikhail Muravyov-Vilensky, the Russian governor-general who put down the Polish uprising in 1863 (and who received his title of nobility and the second, honorific part of his surname—which means "of Vilnius"—as rewards). Liberal Russians and nationalist Poles reviled him as "The Hangman" because of the number of people he executed, especially in Vilnius itself, which was the seat of the uprising. To nationalist Russians, however, he was a heroic figure who suppressed a mutiny against legitimate order and defended Russian and Orthodox Christian interests against Catholic Poles in the northwestern region of the empire.

That anyone would even think of erecting such a monument incensed students at Warsaw University. (An American analogy might be the monument to Confederate general Nathan Bedford Forrest, the first grand wizard of the Ku Klux Klan, which was erected in Selma, Alabama, in 2000, although it did not last very long.) The students' outrage increased when six of their professors sent a telegram to Vilnius supporting this tribute to a man who, as they put it, "freed the northwestern region [of the Russian Empire] from the Polish-Catholic yoke and confirmed the truism that it was and is purely Russian." Believing that their sycophantic teachers had betrayed them, the Polish students sought to widen their protest by appealing to peers elsewhere in the empire. They received a strong positive response from university students in Saint Petersburg. And the primary organizers of the Russian student protest against the Warsaw professors were Boris and Alexander Savinkov. The batch of letters they had brought home and that the police had seized criticized the six professors and was supposed to be mailed to other members of the faculty in Warsaw University.

A Childhood in Russian Poland

It is hard to imagine Boris behaving any differently, given his childhood and youth, although by itself his family background could not have predicted all the phases of his tempestuous future life.

He was born on January 19, 1879, in Kharkov, a historic city that was then in the Kiev Governorate of the Russian Empire and is now in northeastern Ukraine. His parents were ethnic Russians and belonged to the country's hereditary minor nobility, which was a social status at the time that provided some privileges but by itself did not usually imply wealth. Boris had five siblings: in addition to his older brother, Alexander, he had a younger one named Victor, an older sister named Vera, and two younger sisters, Nadezhda and Sofia. Shortly after Boris's birth, his father received a new judicial appointment, and the family moved to Warsaw. That is where Boris grew up, and this influence proved seminal.

Boris's parents were unusually liberal for Russians of their class, even if their lives had not been openly political before their sons' arrest. As Boris's mother recalled in her memoir, poignantly titled "Years of Sorrow," prior to that event they lived the way any fairly prominent government official's family did—without any special cares, social interests, or questions, except for the everyday. She and her husband raised their children in a close-knit atmosphere of cultured gentility. They indulged but did not spoil them and guided them toward practical and socially useful occupations. For example, and as was typical for their class, they sent their firstborn, Vera, to a school in Kharkov that was called the Institute for Well-Born Young Women and stressed French and deportment. Despite its finishing-school flavor, however, the school also prepared its charges for careers as teachers, and Vera would show genuine grit later in life by becoming a seasoned frontline nurse during the Russo-Japanese War.

The Ministry of Justice paid Victor Mikhailovich a good salary, which allowed him to provide his family with a comfortable if not lavish lifestyle. A well-educated and enlightened man, he was very sensitive about interpreting the law fairly. He also tried to be lenient and never distinguished among those who appeared before him—whether they were Russian, Polish, or Jewish, educated or not, rich or poor. As a result, he quickly became popular with the region's intimidated population, to the extent that locals would address him to his face as "*zacny sędzia*" ("honorable judge" in Polish); even more significantly, they also did so behind his back. Victor Mikhailovich took pride in the fact that during his twenty-year career in the Polish territories, he never compromised his conscience or yielded to his superiors' pressure, a stance that earned him the reputation of being "difficult" and a "red" among other Russian officials. He feigned indifference to these characterizations in public. But in private, he complained often and bitterly to his wife about the police brutality he witnessed and how ashamed this made him feel that he was Russian.

Sofia Alexandrovna, Boris's mother, had a rebellious streak that would resurface in her children. Her father was a general in the Russian army, staunchly conservative and fervently loyal to the imperial throne and the Orthodox Church, and her parents arranged her marriage when she was only seventeen and had just left finishing school. It was her great good fortune that the man chosen to be her husband proved to be loving, humane, and liberal, even if significantly older. Sofia Alexandrovna quickly turned against her family's traditions. An intelligent, strong-willed, and idealistic woman, she became an agnostic, developed progressive views, and took an interest in literature and philosophy; she also did some writing herself, in addition to her memoir. Her marriage to Victor

Mikhailovich was very close, and Sofia dedicated herself to her six children and their education, tutoring them in French and German, and encouraging them to learn Polish, despite the imperial regime's attempts to discourage the language.

Boris's parents enrolled him in Warsaw's First Gymnasium, an elite institution comparable to an American prep school that was attended by the children of Russian officials and Russophilic Poles (collaboration with foreign occupiers was not just a twentieth-century phenomenon), from which he graduated in the spring of 1897. Boris left few recollections about his childhood, and what he said about his schooling does not suggest it had a positive or even a formative role in his youth, even though he got good grades.

The gymnasium was run by ex–military officers who tried to instill a martial spirit in their pupils, and the boys wore uniforms every day, including regulation peaked caps. The early years were filled with the gray tedium of rote memorization and grinding intimidation by eccentric teachers who did not hesitate to give stinging fillips to the boys' ears when they failed to answer correctly. In the middle school years, the boys suffered through translations from Greek and Latin, struggled with algebra while fighting off sleep, and relished the occasional romp of quasi-military drills in the countryside on warm spring days. When the boys were older, predictable adolescent preoccupations took over: planning for a formal ball with girls from their sister school, sneaking cigarettes and beer in the hallways when no one was looking, and maneuvering in class to distract teachers from homework assignments or to escape hard questions on oral exams. Boris's disparaging recollections of the gymnasium were likely colored by his distaste for the school's mission, which was intended to foster intense loyalty toward official Russian imperial ideology.

Despite this, Boris did form friendships at school, and one in particular would be the most important in his life—Ivan Platonovich Kalyaev. The future notorious terrorist was born in Warsaw to a retired Russian police officer and the daughter of a ruined Polish nobleman. His years in the First Gymnasium ensured that he would be fluent in Russian, to the extent that he would write accomplished poetry in the language (Boris nicknamed him "The Poet"), but he always spoke Russian with a Polish accent. The young men became close friends despite their differences. Kalyaev practically lived in the Savinkov apartment and was treated like a son by the parents.

If Boris was buttoned up and somewhat shy as a youth, Kalyaev was the opposite. He wore his heart on his sleeve and seemed ready to open himself up to anyone with whom he felt rapport. There was also something otherworldly about him: people remembered especially the pallor of his thin face and the innocent and sorrowful expression of his enormous eyes, as if he were partially lost in some other dimension of being. Boris always found this very moving in his friend, even though his own character was more down to earth.

By the time he graduated from the gymnasium Boris had acquired a worldly polish—he was intellectually sophisticated, ambitious, well dressed, a charming conversationalist, well mannered, and even an elegant dancer. He was also good-looking in a somewhat feral way, with a sensuous mouth and a quizzical expression in his slanting eyes set into a narrow, high-cheekboned face.

Boris's mother also influenced his education by giving him her love for literature. In addition to classic Russian writers—Pushkin, Gogol, Tolstoy, Dostoyevsky—he liked the romantic works and tales of adventure by Lord Byron, Sir Walter Scott, Alexandre Dumas, Victor Hugo, Mayne Reid, Robert Louis Stevenson, and Jack London. For a high school pupil in late imperial Russia, these were all entirely orthodox tastes, and Boris's avid reading would have a lasting effect on him.

Another important influence on him and in the Savinkov household generally was Sofia's brother, Nikolay Yaroshenko. His ideological path was similar to his sister's, and he also rebelled against their father, albeit in a curiously hybrid way. He began by embarking on a military career—he would rise to the rank of major-general—before committing himself to art and became a leading member of the influential Wanderers group, who were famous for realistic paintings with socially conscious themes. Several of his canvases, which are now in the collections of major Russian museums, became iconic condemnations of tsarist inequities: *The Stoker* (1878) depicts a powerfully muscled worker illuminated by a lurid red light from a furnace, suggesting the degradation and potential revolutionary strength of the working class; *The Prisoner* (1878) shows a man in a dark cell peering out of a small high window, a visual metaphor for life in Russia; *Life Is Everywhere* (1888) portrays a peasant family with a young child framed by the barred window of a prison railway car, but done in the style of Renaissance paintings of the Holy Family. There was even a painting called *The Woman Terrorist* (1881, repainted), inspired by Vera Zasulich, a heroine of the Russian revolutionary movement, who in 1878 tried to kill General Fyodor Trepov, the governor-general of Saint Petersburg (and who, coincidentally, had distinguished himself during the suppression of Polish rebellions in 1830 and

1863). It is one of the paradoxes of Russian imperial society—and a reflection of the sometimes contradictory forces at play in it—that a highly ranked career army officer could also dedicate himself to a critical and politicized art with impunity.

Nikolay Yaroshenko was close to his sister and her family, especially his nephews Boris and Alexander. When the boys were ten and fifteen, he took them on a trip to the fashionable spa town of Kislovodsk in the Caucasus Mountains, in the south of Russia, a region that Russians associated with freedom, picturesque landscapes, exotic native tribes, and romantic adventures, rather like the West was for Americans. The uncle did not hesitate to speak freely in front of them about his admiration for the student revolutionaries of Zasulich's generation or for their present-day heirs.

Uncle Nikolay also introduced several of his famous friends into the Savinkov household, including the writer Gleb Uspensky, who wrote with great sympathy about the plight of Russian peasants and was the model for the man in the painting *The Prisoner* (Boris would later marry his daughter), and the writer Mikhail Saltykov-Shchedrin, who bitterly satirized imperial Russian society and whose works Boris later eagerly absorbed. Another visitor was the internationally celebrated chemist Dmitry Mendeleyev, creator of the periodic table of elements. Boris would have little interest in science, but the progressive and humanitarian ideals of his uncle and the legacy of the uncle's writer friends would resonate throughout his life.

These influences had a formative effect on the young Boris. Another, less liberal uncle and his wife remembered how during his visits to their country house Boris would demonstratively shake hands with all the servants when he walked into the dining room, an action that underscored his democratic beliefs but shocked the couple. Boris's strong opinions also impressed his younger cousins, who adored him and followed his lead in everything. When he declared that he had decided to become a vegetarian and that it is immoral to eat animals, they immediately followed suit and avoided eating the meat on their plates by hiding it in napkins.

⚊

Warsaw itself, which was the center of Polish cultural and economic life, left an imprint on Boris as well. It was a busy, flourishing, and cosmopolitan place that looked far more Western European than Russian—with broad squares, grand colonnaded buildings, royal palaces, and imposing Catholic cathedrals. The numerous Russian officials and officers who lived in Warsaw and the Orthodox churches that had been built for them—to the annoyance of Poles—gave it a partially Russian veneer. There were many Jews, too, more than a third of the population, most of them poor and all discriminated against by imperial policies. In light of this, it is notable that Boris never shared the blight of anti-Semitism that was widespread among Russians; indeed, many of his closest revolutionary comrades would be Jews.

But despite the Russian overlay, Warsaw was still a resolutely Polish city. Upper-class Poles preserved a culture of personal behavior and style that marked them to such an extent, and so differently from Russians, that Baedeker's famous early twentieth-century tourist guide to the Russian Empire tried to prepare potential visitors to Warsaw: "The contrast between the lower classes and the noblesse is very striking, the latter being physically and in character refined to an almost excessive pitch of elegance. Polish women are renowned for their grace and beauty." Boris's own courtliness and urbanity, which some of his political enemies would later characterize as pretentiousness, more likely reflected conventional upper-class Polish (and Russian) social norms and etiquette.

As a result of his family's liberalism and because of where he grew up, Boris developed a deep affection and respect for Poles. He sympathized with their national aspirations, admired their culture, and learned to speak Polish fluently with a Warsaw accent, all of which would have a decisive effect on his life decades later. He also became aware of Poland's fraught relations with Russia early in life. He claimed that he felt deep indignation at the sight of a monument facing the city's main Catholic cathedral that was dedicated to "Poles who remained loyal to the tsar during the uprising." He was indignant as well that he and his fellow pupils were prohibited from speaking Polish in school. He was indignant that officially Poland did not exist at all but that, as imperial political geography would have it, there were several "provinces on the Vistula River populated by Russians of the Catholic faith." And most importantly, he was indignant that people could be arrested and "left to rot" in the city's Citadel or exiled to Siberia simply because they loved their country.

In the Hands of the Imperial Police

When Boris and Alexander arrived in the Warsaw Citadel's prison they were questioned by a different officer of the gendarmes—one Colonel Motov. Both denied they were members of a secret organization, declined to say anything about others involved in the plan to mail the protests, and claimed they did not remember the names of the professors in Warsaw to whom they had already sent letters. Boris also lied that the student organization whose bylaws had been found on him was merely a study group.

Back in the apartment, Sofia Alexandrovna wandered, despondent and angry amid the disorder and ruin left by the police. She noticed with horror that her husband, who looked older than his fifty-eight years, had turned deathly pale and started clutching at his chest because he had difficulty breathing. She quickly put him to bed and sent for a doctor, who succeeded in calming him. But she was far too upset to go to bed herself and sat down to dash off a blistering letter to Warsaw's governor-general about the violence that had been done to her family; she then rushed outside to post it herself.

Results followed with surprising speed. Perhaps it was because Victor Alexandrovich was a judge and thus not without influence in the city administration; perhaps it was because the governor-general, Prince Alexander Bagration-Imeretinsky, proved to be relatively humane for a man in his position. Whatever the cause, he quickly summoned the city's chief prosecutor and the commanding general of the gendarmes to explain themselves. He also sent an adjutant to the Savinkov apartment to convey his apology. Three days later Boris and Alexander were freed.

They spent the Christmas and the New Year holidays at home, trying to forget what had happened. But they could not; the outrage was too great, and their mother watched apprehensively as they kept rehashing the details of their arrest, their eyes burning with hostility. Their father had taken the blow especially hard, and Sofia began to worry about the long-term effect on his health. When the parents accompanied their sons to the train station for the trip back to Saint Petersburg, they could see that the affair was far from over.

⌒—⊶

And they were right. Just two months later, in February 1898, Boris telegraphed that Alexander had been arrested. Sofia immediately left for Saint Petersburg.

This was her first descent into the nightmare world of tsarist police bureaucracy, and its inhumanity produced an impression that she never forgot: rude officials who avoided her or gave her the runaround; officers who either refused to identify Alexander's supposed crime or threatened appalling punishments for his unnamed offense; interminable waits in squalid anterooms with other petitioners who searched in vain for encouragement in one another's frightened eyes.

The dark and bewildering world she entered was a shocking contrast to the magnificent outward appearance of this severely beautiful northern capital. Founded by Tsar Peter the Great to "cut a window through to Europe" and to give landlocked Russia access to the seas and oceans of the world, Saint Petersburg radiated the grandeur of imperial ambition and achievement. Unlike Moscow, with its often-crooked streets, medieval Kremlin, and many old onion-domed churches, Saint Petersburg looked Western and modern, with vast ministries encased in rhythmic stone façades, extensive parks and squares, imposing multi-hued palaces, granite-lined canals, and broad, straight boulevards. There were churches everywhere, too—this was Russia, after all—but the biggest, Saint Isaac's Cathedral, was built in the style of European Neoclassicism, and Kazan Cathedral on the city's main thoroughfare, Nevsky Prospect, was modeled on Saint Peter's Basilica in Rome.

The empire's military power was everywhere on display as well, and martial music was integral to the city's soundscape. Bands playing bravura marches accompanied infantry and cavalry as they passed through the streets on the way to parades and drills, their serried rows of bayonets, helmets, and cuirasses flashing in the sun. The imperial ideals of authority and discipline seemed imprinted everywhere on the city's male population, nearly one-tenth of whom wore uniforms of one kind or another—military officers, civilian officials, even students and schoolboys.

Sofia Alexandrovna spent two months navigating the police labyrinth in Saint Petersburg before she was finally allowed to visit Alexander, and even then, it was for just twenty minutes twice a week. He had been in solitary confinement the entire time and looked terrible, his face pale and swollen. But there was nothing she could do for him, and she had to leave him as he was, because her husband and four younger children, some of whom had fallen ill, needed her back in Warsaw. She never did find out what the charges against Alexander were.

Then things got even worse. Because of their son's troubles, Sofia and her husband's old acquaintances in Warsaw's official circles began to look askance at them. Four months later the parents were shocked to hear that the police had searched Boris's room in Saint Petersburg, but fortunately they had not arrested him. A month later came yet another blow: Sofia received a message that Alexander's health had deteriorated to the point that she needed to do everything possible to have him freed. Again, she rushed to the capital, and this time succeeded, thanks to a more humane director of the police department, Alexey Lopukhin (ironically, he would play a crucial role in upending Boris's life years later, but in a way no one could have predicted). Because of his prison ordeal Alexander now looked like an invalid—thin, hunched over, and so pale there was a greenish tint to his cheeks. Sofia brought him home, but her joy would be brief.

Youthful Fire

Early in 1898, after returning to Saint Petersburg University from his home visit and arrest in Warsaw, Boris threw himself into student protests. At first his focus was limited to reforming the antiquated curriculum and defending students' civil rights. His childhood friend Ivan Kalyaev was also a student at the university, and together they took on leading roles by joining the student Organizing Committee. But the imperial regime and its ministry of education resisted change in this as in everything else, passions on both sides inevitably flared, and students began to go into the streets to demonstrate. From the regime's perspective, such protests were a disruption of public order and an additional provocation. However, for many Russian students at the time, this dynamic of escalation became a well-trodden path to more serious forms of rebellion. Indeed, there were few revolutionaries of any political stripe who came to prominence during the next two decades who had not been radicalized while at university.

As the student protests began to morph into something approaching a revolutionary movement, Boris became progressively more active. He also began to develop into a passionate and effective advocate, one who could persuade people—or at least win arguments, which is not the same thing—via the force of his eloquence and personality.

A fellow student, Mark Gorbunov, whose revolutionary career began in the same student circles but who would later become a Bolshevik and a poison-tongued defamer of Boris's legacy, recalled a memorable encounter they once had in the room of a mutual acquaintance, an attractive young woman. The subject was the People's Will Party, which had assassinated Alexander II in 1881. Boris found the terrorists of the past and their tactics not just fascinating but appealing, while Gorbunov questioned their political effectiveness. The two were arguing so intensely that the young woman—Vera Glebovna Uspenskaya, the daughter of the famous writer who had visited the Savinkovs in Warsaw—looked frightened and enthralled at the same time: she turned pale and wrapped herself in a big shawl as she watched, her large dark eyes open wide.

Boris did most of the talking during the encounter with Gorbunov, which had become typical for him. He was quick, witty, and self-confident; his style was never to defend, but always to attack. He also had an excellent memory, which allowed him to ornament his arguments with apt quotations, including long passages from the satirist Saltykov-Shchedrin, another of his uncle's friends who had visited the Savinkovs in Warsaw. Gorbunov was powerless to stop the flood of Boris's arguments, he recalled, and said that he felt like a man on horseback who was losing his balance during a headlong gallop.

At the same time, Boris revealed a trait that dampened Gorbunov's admiration for him somewhat—his tendency at times to get carried away with a deftly turned phrase, and then to pause, together with his listeners, as if admiring what he had just said. Boris's motivation seems to have been a mix of self-assertion and a touch of theatricality as much as the ideas themselves. This is hardly a sin in a young man, especially if he has an admiring female audience, and Gorbunov's recollection is tinted by his later animosity. But the "theatricality" of Savinkov's nature would become one of the hallmarks of how his enemies described him in the future as well.

However, none of this put off the young woman—quite the contrary. Vera was two years older than Boris, tall, slender, and not so much pretty as handsome, with clear-cut features, dark hair, and large, determined eyes set into an oval face whose matte pallor made it seem well scrubbed. She eschewed any makeup and pulled her hair back into a somewhat unruly chignon, as if proclaiming that she did not believe in doing anything to enhance her appearance because it would have been frivolous in light of her dedication to progressive ideas and radical politics. But Vera was also a passionate woman and easily excitable. She tended to speak fitfully when agitated, although the sweet expression on her small, mobile face softened the awkwardness.

Boris and Vera's growing closeness did not stop their involvement in the student protest movement in Saint Petersburg. Boris was especially active, although he proved to be more effective as a speaker and polemicist in small private settings than at big public meetings because his skills were more intimate and not oratorical in the classical sense. The demonstrations kept increasing in size and intensity. In March 1899, one large gathering near the grand Kazan Cathedral, just a half mile from the Winter Palace, the tsar's residence, was broken up by mounted, knout-wielding Cossacks and police. Vera and Boris tried to help a young woman and were beaten themselves: Vera's coat was torn and her hand was badly swollen from a blow, and he had been struck on the head. Over 600 students, men and women, were arrested.

Later in the spring of 1899 the protests reached a climax. After students in the capital organized a nationwide strike against police brutality, many hundreds were arrested throughout the empire, including one-third of the entire student body of Saint Petersburg University. Most escaped prison and were quickly remanded into the custody of their parents, which was a surprisingly mild punishment. But for some, like Boris, the consequences were more serious. He had given an inflammatory speech during a student meeting, and a prosecutor in the Saint Petersburg regional court, Maximilian Trusevich, singled him out for special punishment. Because Boris's official home was in Warsaw, he, like other students who did not live in the capital, was expelled, and enrollment in any other Russian university was now closed to him as well. It could have been even worse, however: the imperial regime would soon start conscripting unruly students into the army.

Without any other alternatives in Russia, Boris decided to try to finish his education abroad. But first he and Vera cemented their relationship in a traditional Orthodox Church wedding in the summer of 1899.

On the one hand, given their commitment to radical politics, this is somewhat surprising because the Russian ceremony is very elaborate and "high church"— icons and frescoes on the walls, the priest garbed in gold brocade vestments, a choir, chanting and singing in Old Church Slavonic, groomsmen holding crowns, processions, incense, candles—and neither the bride nor the groom evinced any interest in the church or in organized religion later in their lives. But on the other hand, their choice reflects the mores to which they subscribed and which they did not see as contradicting their desire to transform Russian society. These could be called "Victorian" and were widespread among others of their set in Russia—personal loyalty and respect, rectitude, politeness, prudence, commitment to family and children, and concern for their educational and moral development. From this point of view, a church wedding was the proper thing to do. More radically inclined revolutionaries often saw things very differently.

Boris's parents and siblings welcomed Vera very warmly into their tight-knit family. Not only was the wedding a joyous occasion, but it was also a relief from the ceaseless thrum of anxiety caused by Boris's and Alexander's risky political activities. Vera became especially fond of her gentle, aging father-in-law and characterized spending time with him as a "genuine pleasure." She even began to prefer his company to that of her own mother, who was prone to painful neurotic episodes during which she spent "entire days grumbling at everyone" and complaining that "everything is a burden to her." The life of Vera's own family had been darkened for the past decade because her father suffered from a progressive mental illness that led to his being institutionalized in a psychiatric clinic in 1892.

After the wedding, Boris left Vera in Saint Petersburg, where she had family and friends, and went to Germany and France with a Polish friend from his Warsaw days in the hope of continuing his education. He first tried attending the University of Berlin for several months and then moved to the University of Heidelberg, but neither experiment went well. Boris remained unseduced by the intellectual prominence of either institution or by the picturesque charms of Heidelberg, whose university dated to the fourteenth century and was one of the oldest in Europe. Moreover, despite the modernity of German society as a whole, he found its materialism distasteful. Things did not go any better for him in Paris.

While he was abroad, Boris also did not focus on his studies as much as on gauging both countries in terms of their potential for revolution. This too proved a disappointment. He found the German socialists to be politically timid and repulsively chauvinistic. He was further disillusioned by the open cooperation between the German police and the Russian Okhrana—the imperial political police (the word means "protection") that operated at home and abroad—who monitored the subversive activities of Russian students and émigrés. The students themselves were far too timid for his taste, as he did not hesitate to proclaim at a meeting he attended, and needed to be more "revolutionary."

What Boris did enjoy during his European sojourn was the contacts he began to make with various Russian revolutionaries who were living and plotting in Germany and France. French agents employed by the Okhrana in Paris kept an eye on him while he was there and reported that although he identified himself as a student, he spent "very little" time in the universities, consorted with politically "suspect" Russians, and went to all the Russian émigré meetings.

The Judas

However, the French agents who shadowed Russian revolutionaries in the streets of Paris, lurked around their meeting halls, and bribed maids for the contents of their wastepaper baskets were not the Okhrana's only source of information. The police had another weapon that was far more important and effective—a secret informant at the heart of one of the most important Russian revolutionary groups, a man who had been providing the Okhrana with details about the revolutionaries' rosters, meetings, movements, and plans since 1893, when Boris was still a schoolboy in Warsaw. During the previous half-dozen years, this informant's value to the Okhrana kept increasing as his stature among the revolutionaries also grew and he became privy to increasing amounts of secret information. The fees the Okhrana paid him grew accordingly, as did their trust in his loyalty to the imperial regime.

But he was something other than the double agent the imperial police believed him to be, as his activity over the course of the next decade would demonstrate, which was also when Boris Savinkov's life became inextricably tied to his. Even in the crowded field of larger-than-life figures populating Russia at the turn of the twentieth century—some grotesque and outlandish, others noble and heroic, yet others criminally negligent or pathetically misguided—he loomed over the historical landscape like a monstrosity.

His name was Evno Fishelevich Azef, and his humble origins could never have predicted his diabolical career. He was born on July 11, 1869, to a very poor Jewish family in Lyskovo, a small town in the Grodno Governorate of Russian Poland, which was part of the empire's notorious Pale of Settlement. This was the region bounded by what had been independent Poland's borders in the eighteenth century, and it was the ancestral home of Poland's Jews. When the region was incorporated into Russia, its Jewish population was required to remain where they had lived before. By the turn of the nineteenth century this amounted to some five million people. Few ever managed to leave, and those that could did so only with great difficulty.

Because Jews were not allowed to own farmland in the Pale, they lived mostly in semiurban villages, or shtetls, where most men worked as small artisans, craftsmen, or businessmen. Poverty was rampant, families were large, and religious traditions strong. There was no love lost between the Jewish population and their Russian overlords, or between the Jews and their Russian, Polish, and Ukrainian neighbors in the Pale. Anti-Semitic policies were part of the empire's legal and social fabric, and Russia had become notorious around the world for its discrimination and the bloody pogroms that erupted in its territory with depressing regularity. There had been a wave in the early 1880s; worse was to come in 1903–1906. It is hardly surprising that shtetls became a breeding ground for resentment and that Jews would gravitate to Russian revolutionary movements.

Evno's father, Fishel, was a tailor who struggled to provide for his wife and six other children. When Evno was five years old, the family managed to move to Rostov-on-Don, a rapidly developing commercial city near the Sea of Azov in southern Russia. Despite the father's efforts in starting a business, they remained poor. Nevertheless, the move caused a dramatic change in Evno's life because he was exposed to a bustling urban center with a varied population where Jews were a small minority. Even more important is that his father set him on a secular path by enrolling him in a technical high school, thus breaking with the Jewish tradition of having young men pursue a purely religious education centered on the Torah and the Talmud.

The cost of schooling was high for the poor family, and the father's inability to pay fees in a timely manner forced Evno to prolong his studies. He graduated only in 1892, when he was twenty-one, several years older than his peers. It was a degrading experience that was probably aggravated by the fact that the majority of students were Christian and that Evno's relations with them were hostile. It also did not help that he was strikingly ugly—heavily built, with a puffy yellow face, thick lips, and a squeaky high voice—which led some of the pupils to abuse him by calling him "a fat pig."

Evno's resentments had multiplied in high school, and that is where he also first came into contact with Russian radical circles. He fell in with some other pupils who were reading and disseminating antigovernment literature and had ties to revolutionaries in the city. But when he learned that a number of them had been arrested and that he could be next, he decided to flee. By then, he had already concluded that even with a high school diploma his prospects for good employment in Russia were very dim, and that, as a Jew, it would be difficult for him to gain admission to a Russian university. He resolved to seek a higher education abroad.

This required money, and Evno got it through theft, thereby beginning what could be called the theme of "dirty money" in his life. A merchant had hired him as a traveling salesman for a consignment of butter. When Evno sold it for 800 rubles (equivalent to perhaps $10,000 today), he pocketed the money and fled to Germany. He first enrolled in a polytechnic institute in Karlsruhe, a small provincial city in the southwest of the country, which is where he also became involved in Russian émigré revolutionary circles. However, his interest in radical ideology, which was never strong to begin with, was soon eclipsed by a desire to improve his own lot by any means necessary. And when his stolen Russian money ran out, he hit on the idea of informing on his fellow students in Germany and his old revolutionary acquaintances in Rostov.

The procedure he followed was remarkably simple: on April 6, 1893, he wrote a letter to the gendarmes headquarters of Rostov-on-Don to offer his services. Four days later he wrote in the same vein to the head of police in Saint Petersburg. The police quickly bit, and when, a month later, Azef asked for a monthly salary of fifty rubles, they agreed. The success of this initiative allowed Azef to transfer to Darmstadt, where he studied electrical engineering at one of Germany's best technical colleges. In 1899 he passed his examinations and, after working for firms in Germany, was posted to Russia.

From that point on, he systematically climbed the steps of a career that proved to be duplicitous or even "triplicitous," to coin a word (standard terms fail to capture his grotesque exceptionalism), as he shuttled back and forth across Russia's frontier whenever his machinations required. On the one hand, he kept rising ever higher in the Okhrana's esteem because of the value of the information he provided. But on the other, and although he never showed any genuine commitment to revolutionary ideology, his reputation among the revolutionaries kept rising as well. They valued him as a hardheaded pragmatist and, especially, as an expert on the practical and technical aspects of terrorism, for which he was exceptionally well equipped by virtue of his scientific training.

By 1901, Azef had handed the Okhrana a major coup when he revealed the location of an underground printing press in Russia used for publishing revolutionary materials, which was seized, and the personnel operating it were arrested. Simultaneously, the revolutionaries had begun to think of him in a leadership role.

But this was just the beginning of his astonishing career, and many people on both sides of the revolutionary struggle would die as a direct result of his actions. Boris would meet Azef for the first time in 1903.

From Rebellion to Revolution

By the time Boris Savinkov returned from Europe to Saint Petersburg in 1901 (the exact date is uncertain), he had made a fateful decision about his future: he would become a full-time revolutionary and dedicate himself to overthrowing the imperial regime. In light of the catastrophic social, political, and economic problems besieging Russia, student grievances were simply too limited a concern.

At the turn of the twentieth century, not only rebellious students and revolutionaries but many moderate liberals believed that Russia was in a perilous state. As they saw it, a thick pall of stagnation, reaction, and hopelessness had blanketed the country for two decades, ever since the assassination of Alexander II in 1881 ended a period of tepid, albeit promising reforms. The current tsar, Nicholas II, was, like his father, Alexander III, an absolute monarch who was constrained not by laws or governmental institutions but only by historical traditions, by advisers who served at his pleasure, and by his own limited imagination. He was not a cruel man, but he was weak-willed, conservative, pious, and easily swayed, especially by his narrow-minded and credulous wife, the German-born Tsaritsa Alexandra. All power across the entire empire, which was the largest country in the world and spanned a dozen time zones, flowed from the throne down. Without the tsar's agreement, no one anywhere could do anything to initiate political change from the ground up. The only institutions that allowed an individual to effect very limited social change were either strictly local or charitable, and the imperial bureaucracy could always override any initiative even on this level.

This imperial system was paternalistic by inclination and tried to act benevolently, but its long-term practical effects were dire for the majority of its subjects. The peasants, who made up 80 percent of the population and whose labor was the backbone of the empire's predominantly agricultural economy, lived largely in archaic poverty and ignorance; the workers in Russia's developing industries were exploited and impoverished; the educated classes were disenfranchised and often disillusioned. And as Savinkov knew well, everyone was at the mercy of the regime's reactionary whims.

"What is to be done?": the eternal question—the despairing howl—of Russian history resounded over the country seemingly without an answer, until the revolutionaries, for the most part socialists and Marxists of different stripes, decided that the time to do something was now and took matters into their own hands.

⚬—⊢—⚬

However, this was not the whole story of Russia before the early 1900s, and one did not need to be a reactionary or a monarchist to see that there were still glimmers of hope and not just unequivocal reasons for despair.

Like an old mansion that still has sturdy timbers and walls even though parts of the foundation and roof have been attacked by rot, the Russian Empire also had areas of strength. It had experienced a decade-long period of promising, even if patchy, economic growth at the end of the nineteenth century. Government revenues had doubled, the length of the railway system had increased by 50 percent, foreign investments had flooded in, and hundreds of new corporations and companies had been established. For much of this period Russian credit was high and the ruble was stable. By 1902, Russia had become the fifth-largest steel producer in the world and was emerging as an industrial power.

Even with the disheartening signs of economic weakness toward the end of the decade—a series of crop failures in the late 1890s and 1901 hit the peasantry hard; this was followed by an economic depression that spread throughout the country—it was not a foregone conclusion that Russia was doomed to descend in a downward spiral. By 1910, a new economic boom was underway. The country had enormous, largely untapped wealth in its natural resources. There were some strong and talented men with vision who could provide leadership in a time of great turmoil. Moscow, the old capital, was leading the country in growth. It had become a major transportation hub, an industrial and trade center, and one of the biggest cities in the world. Its energetic and independently minded business elites played a major role in the local government and poured money into social improvements and cultural initiatives, even in the face of systematic resistance by the imperial bureaucracy in Saint Petersburg. These civic-minded businessmen and their city provided models for what could have spread across the country. But there were other forces at play that would prevent it.

⚬—⊢—⚬

Initially, before Savinkov found his footing, he briefly embraced Marxism and its cardinal belief that the future belonged to the industrial working class, which was destined to revolt against its bourgeois oppressors and establish a socialist state. Because the labor movement in Russia was relatively poorly developed in the late 1890s—the country's industrialization was still far behind Western Europe and the United States—Savinkov, like many other former students who had joined the revolution's ranks, committed himself to awakening factory workers to their plight and rallying them to the coming revolution.

Savinkov now also had a deeper and more personal stake in the country's future because he recently had become a father. On April 26, 1900, while he was still abroad, Vera gave birth to a daughter, Tatyana. His absence had been hard for Vera because there were some health complications initially, although in the end mother and the baby were fine.

Vera also fully shared Boris's commitment to the revolutionary cause, and after he returned, the young family settled in a scruffy district on the outskirts of Saint Petersburg, where he organized a propaganda circle for a group of factory workers, giving lectures and leading discussions. There were risks in such a life, and Savinkov could not have had any illusions about them. The police had files on him from his two arrests. They were also doing everything they could throughout the empire to uncover and stamp out sparks of revolution, no matter how small. To avoid detection, Savinkov began to develop his skills in clandestine operations. Eva Broido, who worked with him at the time and who would later become a prominent revolutionary herself, remembered him as "a born conspirator, a master of dodging the police." He regularly used disguises that combined a theatrical flair with attention to detail: whenever he went to meet his workers he put on a shabby worker's coat, a paint-stained cap, and smeared paint or whitewash on his hands and face.

This is also the time when Savinkov began to write, as he would continue to do in a variety of genres for the rest of his life. His first piece was published in 1900, when he was only twenty-one, and has the sober title "The Petersburg Movement and the Practical Tasks of the Social Democrats." It is noteworthy for several reasons, including the fact that it got the attention of Vladimir Lenin, the future Bolshevik leader and one of the most influential political figures in twentieth-century history.

Savinkov's essay appeared in a Russian émigré political journal published in Geneva and was based on his experiences with the factory workers. As would become typical of him both in his life and in his writings, he focused not on ideological questions but on practical methods—specifically, how a revolutionary movement should be organized and what individual members should do in it. His argument was simple: there were not enough people agitating among the workers, and those involved were not sufficiently conspiratorial. As a result, he explained, individuals had to carry out several revolutionary functions at once, and this made it easy for the police to arrest entire groups.

Lenin commented on Savinkov's piece in his 1902 brochure "What Is to Be Done?" (whose title repeated the primary existential question of Russia), which became famous in the annals of international communism because it contributed to the fateful split in the Marxist Russian Social Democratic Party that gave rise to the Bolsheviks. As such, Lenin's brochure is one of the most influential documents in twentieth-century revolutionary history.

Lenin singled out for praise Savinkov's argument that there were not enough leading figures in the revolutionary movement. This resonated with Lenin's own belief that a "vanguard" of committed revolutionaries was essential to spread Marxism among workers, an idea that also foreshadowed his own future authoritarian behavior. However, such agreements between Savinkov and Lenin would not be repeated. When they met in 1917, it would be at daggers drawn.

Prison

The concern that Savinkov expressed in his essay about inadequate secrecy among revolutionaries was prescient because his disguises failed to shield him for very long. On April 18, 1901, the police arrested him for possessing illegal literature. A more thorough investigation resulted in a second, more serious and accurate charge being added later—that he was engaged in antigovernment propaganda among workers in Saint Petersburg.

Savinkov was no longer merely a self-proclaimed revolutionary: he had been canonized as one by the ultimate authority—the imperial police. The new dossier they started on him would grow very thick over the coming years. In light of his future career, it is noteworthy that at this early stage during questioning by the police he proudly acknowledged his socialist worldview but rejected violence: "The use of force . . . from my point of view, is impermissible under any circumstances and for any reasons."

Vera hurried to inform Sofia, who got the news just when it seemed that the worst was finally behind her: only one week after she had brought her oldest son, Alexander, home to convalesce from his prison ordeal. Vera was pregnant again, but she managed to sound chipper and brave in her letter. She tried to persuade Sofia not to come to Saint Petersburg because even she was not allowed face-to-face visits with her husband. Sofia agreed, and for the time being decided not to mention Boris's arrest either to Alexander or her husband, who was becoming increasingly distraught and whose health was deteriorating under the blows that kept falling on the family.

⚬—⚬

Savinkov spent a total of ten months in two prisons in Saint Petersburg while his case crept through the judicial system. The same prosecutor who had played a role in his expulsion from Saint Petersburg University, Trusevich, also had a hand in his imprisonment, as he would in several other dark moments later in his life. Vera was eventually allowed to visit him with their baby daughter, to deliver parcels with clothing and books, and to write to him.

Savinkov kept these letters for the rest of his life, as he would several hundred others she sent him over the next dozen years. The fact that the letters survived at all is nothing less than remarkable in light of how unsettled his life would be in Russia and abroad during the next quarter of a century. And that he saved them in spite of how his relationship with Vera would change is also very revealing.

From the first, Vera sounds as if she is buffeted by alternating gusts of hope and despair. This duality is captured even in the physical appearance of the letters, all of which have ugly yellow streaks across the pages—signs that they had been tested for secret writing by prison censors.

It is only a few weeks after Boris was arrested and Vera begs him not to worry about her, even though she admits that she is miserable without him; she tries to cheer him up, as well as herself, by reminding him that they "are still young" and by assuring him that she is "deeply convinced" the future will bring them happiness. She of course never mentions his revolutionary activities, but they are implied in her hopes. She laments that during a visit to the prison she was allowed only to glimpse him through a grate in a dimly lit room and "couldn't even squeeze your hand." She praises "Tanyurka"—an affectionate and humorous Russian diminutive for "Tatyana"—because she "conducts herself very nobly" for a one-year-old, and assures him that they are both "hale and hearty women who know how to wait until you are released, whole and unharmed." Boris had worried that the prison's dark and depressing appearance might frighten the little girl and emotionally scar her, but Vera assures him that this cannot happen because she is too young.

Later Vera writes that even though their families and friends are of course upset about what has happened to him, she still feels quite alone because no one can share fully the depth of her yearning: "if you only knew how much I miss you, you wouldn't judge me for crying sometimes"; and then, to soften her lament, she adds: "but this happens rarely." She reports that she corresponds frequently with his parents, "who are very caring about me," especially his father, who writes often. She continually revels in their daughter, who is "such a wonderful little girl that it's simply a marvel," and includes a photograph of her: curly-haired, dimpled, and poised in a crisply ironed dress.

The last letter in this series comes six months later and is dated October 26, 1901. Vera writes that it is 5 A.M. and that she is leaving for the hospital. She insists that she is not at all afraid and urges him not worry about her or Tanya. Boris would once again miss the birth of his child. Their son must have been born the same day or soon after—the actual date is not known—and they named him Victor, after Boris's father. In the family, his diminutive would be Vitya.

A Revolutionary Finishing School

In the spring of 1902, Boris Savinkov unexpectedly received a temporary respite. Because he had not committed a capital crime, he was released from prison and exiled to Vologda, a provincial city 350 miles to the east of Saint Petersburg, to await his final sentence.

The change was very timely. Savinkov's psychological constitution was stronger than his brother's, and he had not been broken by the ordeal of imprisonment the way Alexander had, but it still took a toll on him. He now looked older than his twenty-three years—thinner, pale, jittery—and had developed a slouch. He had also lost a lot of his hair, and what was left he cut very short, but he compensated for this with a thin, spreading moustache, the ends of which he curled jauntily up.

Savinkov's treatment as a political prisoner was not unusual in imperial Russia. In the late nineteenth century, hundreds and then, as the twentieth century unfolded, thousands of revolutionaries were exiled to Vologda and other provincial cities for varying periods of time. Because of its "convenient" location in relation to Saint Petersburg—convenient from the point of view of the police—Vologda became known unofficially as "Siberia-by-the-Capital." The actual Siberia began a thousand miles farther east, and that is where the likes of Vladimir Lenin, Lev Trotsky, and Joseph Stalin were sent when their turns came.

But for all the brutality with which the imperial regime treated political prisoners, it was also surprisingly and paradoxically humane at times in the conditions it imposed on exiles, although this could vary greatly depending on the location and the zeal of the local police and administration. Before he was sent to Vologda, Savinkov was allowed to visit his parents in Warsaw for three days with his wife and children.

Even more surprising from a contemporary standpoint is that after being settled in Vologda for a while, Savinkov was free to bring Vera and the children to live with him; moreover, he could live wherever he chose. Initially, Savinkov found an apartment to rent in a building that also housed the city's Catholic chapel, which had been established in this unlikely location because of the numbers of Polish political exiles who had been sent to Vologda over the decades. The presence of the church and the Poles, with whom Savinkov quickly established friendly relations, was a poignant reminder of his first act of rebellion against the empire.

◦———◦

Vologda itself was a backwater of some 20,000 souls in the flat Russian north amid endless dark forests under a vast empty sky and consisted mostly of weather-beaten, one-story wooden houses scattered over a wide area on both sides of the meandering Vologda River. There were a few factories, some industry and trade, mostly in decline—an exception was the famous local butter, which was even exported to Europe—and a number of notable old churches. For most of the exiles, it was an unappealing place to be stuck away from the political action, even if it was an enormous improvement over prison. But the landscape's brooding cold beauty, with its thin, silvery light and spectacular crimson sunsets, did have its admirers—and it still does. Savinkov kept a notebook in Vologda and included in it some appealing sketches of the area's scenery.

In addition to living where they wished, exiles were also free to occupy themselves pretty much as they pleased, provided they had the money to pay for their comforts. For someone with an education, employment was relatively easy to find, even if you were politically suspect. To help make ends meet, Savinkov, who appears to have been helped financially by his parents at this time, got two jobs—as a secretary in the local court and as a document copier for a lawyer. Because he had begun to study law in Saint Petersburg, he had some relevant training.

With extra time on his hands, Savinkov also continued to write, although in a new vein. He produced a swarm of book reviews that appeared anonymously in a well-known and respected left-liberal journal, *Russian Wealth*, which published articles on an eclectic array of subjects. Savinkov reviewed mostly books about Russian literature, but also a memoir, a travelogue, and some new works of fiction, including, most notably, Andrey Bely's experimental debut publication in 1902, *The Second Symphony*, which he (appropriately) panned. Over the course of the next decade, Bely would emerge as a major poet and one of the greatest Russian novelists of the twentieth century.

Savinkov also turned to writing fiction himself. His first efforts—only some have survived, unfortunately, because not all the newspapers in which they appeared have been preserved—were several short stories drawing on his life in Warsaw. In addition, he also produced "The Night," an imitation of a satirical work about the transitory nature of authorial fame by Maxim Gorky, an immensely popular, radically oriented contemporary writer.

Pleased with what he had written and full of self-confidence, Savinkov sent "The Night" and a second (lost) story to Gorky himself, seeking his approval and hoping that he would help get them published. But when the famous writer's response finally arrived, it could not have been more discouraging. Gorky advised Savinkov to take up any other craft than literature. "Writing," he explained condescendingly, "is a difficult matter and not everyone is up to it."

Savinkov was not used to being rebuked and spent the entire day with his face as dark as a "cloud of stone," according to a friend who was there. But a pleasant surprise was coming. Despite his disparagement, Gorky wanted to help beginning writers and sent Savinkov's stories to a Moscow newspaper, *The Courier*, which had a literary section edited by another very popular writer, Leonid Andreyev, who specialized in gloomy and despairing portrayals of contemporary Russian society. Andreyev accepted "The Night," which Savinkov had signed with the pseudonym "V. Kanin," and it appeared in the September 5, 1902, issue, thus marking Savinkov's debut as an author of fiction. The news caused jubilation in Vologda, and Savinkov's friends organized a celebration that lasted late into the night and included his reading the story out loud.

"The Night" is written in the then-popular "decadent" style and is full of naïve and clumsy atmospheric effects meant to suggest the frightening mysteriousness of existence (a howling wolf, a shivering horse, an enormous fiery moon that sheds no light). The small, nasty devil who appears in the story tells the narrator that human existence is sordid, vain, and empty, and then announces what sounds like Savinkov's own sense of things: "in a century hardly one of you is born who loves himself sufficiently to be able to love others. And all the others only mutter unnecessary and incoherent phrases because they hate others and don't love themselves." In the context of Russian literature—and Savinkov was very well read—such ideas inevitably recall Dostoyevsky's famous character Raskolnikov in *Crime and Punishment*, who tries to combine his egotistical idea of being an "extraordinary individual" with altruism. For Dostoyevsky, a devout Russian Orthodox Christian, this combination was anathema. Savinkov apparently saw things differently, although he used Dostoyevsky as a literary touchstone later as well.

Because of the numbers of like-minded radicals and the freedom they had to gather, Vologda became something like a revolutionary clubhouse or training camp. One of the exiles even jokingly nicknamed Vologda the "Athens of the North," and it would indeed be Boris Savinkov's final university in all subjects revolutionary.

There was no shortage of intellectual stimulation. The Savinkovs and others regularly received new books and magazines containing the latest best-selling works by left-leaning writers who sympathized with the revolutionaries, Gorky and Andreyev among them. Illegally published revolutionary literature must have reached them easily as well.

Boris and Vera were also hospitable and organized regular gatherings in their home that were attended by exiles who would have made even socially conscious hostesses in Moscow or Saint Petersburg proud, including Alexey Remizov—on the verge of becoming an important writer—and Nikolay Berdyaev—a major philosopher then moving from Marxism to Christian spirituality. Boris assumed a prominent role on these occasions, and people remembered him because of his individualism, although some resented his self-assured manner.

Because of the lackadaisical attitude that often typified the Russian imperial bureaucracy, the police in Vologda were also astonishingly lax. Once an exile arrived and registered with the governor's office, they were effectively free from close surveillance. Many exiles quickly realized that it would be foolish not to exploit the opportunity. Savinkov took advantage of it shortly after he arrived and made a round trip to Saint Petersburg for his father-in-law's funeral in March 1902, which is when he brought Vera and the children back with him. The gendarmes in Vologda noted his absence but did nothing about it. The erratic benevolence of the imperial regime even extended to allowing a three-day visit to Vologda by Boris's mother and his brother Alexander, who had just been released from yet another imprisonment in Moscow and was on his way to a much harsher exile in eastern Siberia. Sofia and Alexander parted from Boris with deep sorrow. The brothers did not know it, but they would never see each other again.

Marxists vs. Socialist Revolutionaries

Savinkov's time in Vologda was transformative because that is where he decided to become a terrorist. Even before he arrived, when he was still in prison, he had lost faith in the political program on behalf of which he had tried to mobilize factory workers in Saint Petersburg. Grassroots agitation was too slow, too limited in scope, and too ineffective against the crushing power of the imperial regime. Savinkov had also concluded that Marxism did not address the "agrarian question," which was of fundamental importance for Russia. But even more important was his growing attraction to the heroic assassinations carried out by the People's Will Party in the 1880s. In an individual act of terrorism, the personal and the political fuse into a unique affirmation of vengeance, justice, and the self.

Given Savinkov's inclinations, there was only one movement in which he could find an ideological home within the spectrum of Russian radicalism during the early years of the twentieth century—the Russian Socialist Revolutionary Party, usually called just Socialist Revolutionaries or SRs for short. They were the primary rivals of the Marxist Russian Social Democrats, the party out of which the Bolsheviks emerged in 1903 when they split from their rivals, the Mensheviks.

⚬━━⚬

"Bolshevik" and "Menshevik" derive from the Russian words for majority and minority, and although the Bolsheviks were not in fact the majority in the Social Democrats, Lenin kept the name to make it seem as if his branch was more numerous. In addition to personal animosities between Lenin and his Menshevik counterpart, Yuly Martov, the branches of the party differed in principles of organization, with Lenin insisting on members' obedience to a central authority, while Martov welcomed a looser structure. As a participant and close observer put it, the SRs and the Marxists of either faction fought one another with almost the same passionate intensity as they fought the imperial regime, albeit without bloodshed (at least prior to 1918, one should add).

The conflict between the parties was based on profound differences in how they understood history, economics, society, ethics, and even human nature. Savinkov's shift from one camp to the other reflected a major change in his world outlook and self-conception.

Like all Marxists, the Russian Social Democrats based their revolutionary plans on the "industrial proletariat class" and viewed the peasantry as "petty bourgeois" proprietors (their worst term of opprobrium), no matter how small and insignificant their individual plots of land were. The Marxists also viewed history in terms of inevitable "class warfare" that would destroy the bourgeoisie and establish the "dictatorship of the proletariat."

From the Socialist Revolutionary perspective, however, the Marxists were blinded by the ideology that they had imported from the West and ignored the crucial fact of Russian reality—that peasants were four-fifths of Russia's population and therefore should be the primary focus of revolutionary liberation.

By all objective measures, the situation of most Russian peasants was in fact frightful. At the beginning of the twentieth century, their agricultural labor gave them only between one quarter and one half of what they needed to live on. To make up the rest, they had to hire themselves out as laborers or seek seasonal work in cities. This made them hungry for more land and receptive to agitation for radical social change. The primitive conditions under which they lived are starkly illustrated by child mortality. In 1913, the death rate among peasant newborns under the age of one ranged from 28 to 39 percent, depending on the region. The rates in western European countries were roughly half: 14 percent in Britain, 17 in France, 20 in Germany, and 21 in Austria-Hungary.

The plight of industrial workers was in many ways even worse than that of the peasants. Over 50 percent of workers' children died before their third birthday, and, according to some estimates, over 80 percent were undernourished. Conditions were worse in Moscow than in Saint Petersburg.

Accordingly, the Socialist Revolutionaries conceived of themselves as the party of peasants and workers, with an emphasis on the former. As socialists, the SRs advocated destroying capitalism and the privileges of the bourgeoisie, including transferring land ownership to the peasantry and control of factories to the workers. But they eschewed "class warfare" and welcomed anyone into their fold who embraced their democratic and socialist ideals, without regard to the "class" to which they had belonged. The Bolsheviks would eventually appropriate the SR platform of socialized land reform as well as several other ideas. But fundamental ideological differences between the two parties would never be bridged, including the Bolshevik transformation of "class" into a category as indelible as "race."

The tactics the parties used created a pronounced divide between them as well. The Marxists believed that a revolution could only be made by mass movements of workers who were organized and led by trained party leaders. The Socialist Revolutionaries also carried out extensive grassroots agitation, in their case among peasants as well as workers. But unlike the Bolsheviks, the SRs were resolutely anti-authoritarian. They did not put their faith in top-down party leadership—the formula that would eventually lead to Bolshevik tyranny—but in inspiring the masses to rise up.

And for this they developed their distinctive and notorious tactic of "central terror"—the assassination of government officials who had key roles in maintaining tsarist despotism. The SRs believed that eliminating such figures would demonstrate the regime's vulnerability, which, in turn, would catalyze the masses to fight for radical political and social change. The SRs felt compelled to resort to this method because there was no peaceful way to change the government in Russia. And, as a result, they condemned the use of terrorism in countries that had elections and democratic institutions.

By contrast, Lenin and other Marxists condemned terrorist assassinations as expressions of individualistic bourgeois values and as evidence that terrorists mistrusted the masses. The Bolsheviks would go so far as to deny the Socialist Revolutionaries any legitimacy by claiming that they were neither truly "revolutionary" nor "socialist," and Lenin labeled them mere "adventurers." Nonetheless, because they focused on the peasantry, and despite, or because of, the role that terror played in their tactics, the Socialist Revolutionaries were far more popular and numerous than the Bolsheviks before and during the revolutionary year of 1917.

"Moral" Terror

The SR assassins called themselves "terrorists" proudly, but what they meant by this bears no resemblance to what the word means now.

Today the word makes people recoil with revulsion and fear because it denotes random slaughter by religious, nationalist, or racist fanatics intent on avenging what they perceive as injuries to their own kind. Today's terrorists usually do not even attempt to target those individuals who are specifically responsible for their injuries, such as politicians and generals, and can attack almost any national, social, or cultural group, chosen by chance and engaged in any pastime, with the more victims the better—be it American office workers, French theatergoers, Black parishioners, Sunni worshippers, Turkish pedestrians, Russian vacationers, Israeli commuters, Afghani schoolgirls. The list goes on and on.

Had the Socialist Revolutionaries known of such events, they would have condemned them as unequivocally criminal, just as they condemned political assassinations in countries with free elections. In fact, the SRs actually went to extraordinary lengths to avoid injuring innocent bystanders during their terrorist assassinations.

Nevertheless, it is impossible to escape a fundamental paradox at the heart of the Socialist Revolutionary ethos. On the one hand, they believed they were justified in killing individuals who were in power because they were combatting the evil that those individuals abetted. But on the other, most of the SR terrorists were highly moral individuals and agonized over their actions, which they sought repeatedly to justify to themselves and their comrades. As a prominent member of the party characterized it, their attitude toward terrorism was "almost reverential." He recalled how a factory worker who wanted to take part in an assassination decided that he was "unworthy" because he had previously led a drunken, dissolute life, and "for this sort of thing you need to go in wearing a clean shirt." Striking evidence of the difficulty the SR terrorists had in reconciling their actions with their conscience is that most of them saw their own deaths during the assassinations or after being captured as just punishment for their transgression.

⸻

The actual catalyst for Savinkov's decision to join the Socialist Revolutionaries was his meeting a charismatic member of the earlier, heroic period of the Russian revolutionary movement, the legendary Ekaterina Breshko-Breshkovskaya, nicknamed "Babushka [Grandmother] of the Russian Revolution" because of her decades-long commitment to the cause. Born in 1844 into a nobleman's family and an active revolutionary since 1873, her stages of the cross included over twenty years in Siberian prisons and exile. When she was finally released in the amnesty that a hopeful regime granted to political prisoners in 1896 on the occasion of Nicholas II's coronation, she still did not stop. Early in 1902, Babushka became one of the founders of the Russian Socialist Revolutionary Party and of its secretive Combat Organization, the militant wing that actually carried out terrorist assassinations.

A tireless agitator and organizer, she immediately started a series of trips to provincial cities in Russia to recruit new members; the numerous political exiles there were an especially promising pool. Proceeding cautiously because the police were suspicious of her motives, but managing to evade their surveillance by virtue of her advanced age and modest dress, she enlisted Kalyaev in Yaroslavl, a historic city some 150 miles northeast of Moscow. In turn, he told her about his old friend Boris Savinkov in Vologda, with whom he had stayed in touch and even visited in exile.

Babushka's attention was flattering to the young men she approached, all of whom knew her reputation. Her manner was also very persuasive. An old comrade characterized her as "a preacher, an apostle who convinces with words and even more by active example. Young souls were always drawn to her because she believed in them, and her faith compelled them to rise above themselves." Plump and silver-haired, with a childlike smile on her soft round face and only the shadows around her eyes betraying the suffering she had known, she spoke in a low, sweet, cultured voice about the need to organize, to fight, and to kill tyrants so that the people would be free.

Many would heed Babushka. Many others of varying political persuasions would advocate and carry out terrorist attacks as well, with the result that during the first decade and a half of the twentieth century some 17,000 people became victims throughout the Russian Empire, from government ministers to rank and file policemen to civilians. A high-ranking minister, Count Sergey Witte, would characterize Russia as "one vast madhouse."

Savinkov joined the Socialist Revolutionaries in the fall of 1902. So did his friend and future comrade-in-arms Boris Moiseyenko, a taciturn, cool-headed, ex-university student who was also in Vologda and lived on the same street. Both had been greatly impressed by the assassination carried out the previous spring by the SR Stepan Balmashov, a former university student. On April 2, he entered Minister of the Interior Dmitry Sipyagin's office in Saint Petersburg disguised as a military adjutant. He waited calmly until Sipyagin arrived, then walked up to him, announced that he had brought important papers, and fired two poisoned bullets into him at point-blank range. Following this, he shouted: "That's how one must act with these people!" The minister died an hour and a half later. Balmashov was one day short of his twenty-first birthday.

At his trial, he acknowledged that he had faced a moral quandary because although he considered terrorism "cruel and inhuman" it was also "regrettably" the only possible method in the fight against autocracy. Sentenced to death, he refused to petition Nicholas II for clemency and was hanged on May 3.

For idealistic young men like Savinkov and Moiseyenko, Balmashov's theatrical assassination and noble death were very seductive.

Several months later Babushka made another visit to Vologda. Coincidentally, a second gust of inspiration arrived soon after—news that Grigory Gershuni (the conspiratorial name of Isaac Gersh) had been arrested in Kiev on May 13, 1903. The Socialist Revolutionaries revered Gershuni as the "tiger of the Revolution": he cofounded their party, was the first head of its Combat Organization, and organized Minister Sipyagin's assassination.

That news clinched it for Savinkov. The tactical efficacy of terrorism mesmerized him, and the appeal of heroic action became irresistible. He resolved to escape and to join the Combat Organization. So taken was he with the idea that he even began to persuade a woman acquaintance who visited him in Vologda that she should join as well, stressing that it suited her "temperament." She concluded that terrorism for its own sake had eclipsed all other considerations for Savinkov.

Escape

In late spring 1903 the news Boris Savinkov dreaded finally arrived. He had been sentenced to five years' exile under police supervision in Eastern Siberia; the term had even been increased from the original three years. He wrote to inform his mother, once again upsetting the relative calm she had enjoyed the previous winter.

Shortly thereafter Sofia got an additional shock—Boris's letters from Vologda suddenly stopped. She wrote to him repeatedly and sent telegram after telegram, but there was no response.

Boris had begun by sending Vera and the children to stay with his parents in Warsaw. He then worked out the details of his escape with the help of the SR network of members and sympathizers in Vologda, and on or around July 10, 1903, made his move.

There was a standing order from the Vologda police chief forbidding exiles from going to the city's railroad station and its river landing. But following in the steps of other escapees, Savinkov simply ignored the toothless prohibition and took a train to Archangel, a major port on the White Sea 400 miles to the north that was a center of shipbuilding and international trade.

He had a local contact, and shortly after he arrived, the contact informed him that a Russian merchant vessel was about to leave for Norway in just one hour. The opportunity was too good to miss. Savinkov did not have enough time to return to the train station for the luggage he had left in the check room, which included his passport in one of the bags. He also could not afford to linger in Archangel and wait for another suitable ship, because the police might start looking for him. (In fact, his disappearance from Vologda would be discovered by the authorities only several days after he escaped, on July 14.) So he abandoned all his belongings, and trying to be as inconspicuous as possible boarded the *Imperator Nikolay I* with a second-class ticket to Vardø in the extreme northeast of Norway.

One might have thought the Russian police would keep an eye on a busy port that could be used by political escapees from the region. But no one stopped

Savinkov to see his papers. Gendarmes would certainly have done so at regular land border crossings, such as the major one for train travelers at Verzhbolovo between Russia and Germany. In fact, the Russian Empire was notorious in Europe at that time because of its stringent border controls: passports and visas were required to enter the country, and if you wanted to leave, you needed police authorization. By contrast, other European countries allowed free travel between them without passports.

The slow-moving *Imperator Nikolay I* made a number of stops along the way and took six days to cover 700 miles along the bleak, low-lying Russian coastline before it dropped anchor in Vardø's harbor. Now that Norwegian soil was within sight, Savinkov's next challenge was how to get to it without documents. But this also proved surprisingly simple. When customs agents came on board, Savinkov pretended that he was a fish merchant on business and climbed down into the launch heading for shore. Fifteen minutes later he was a free man.

Some days later his mother in Warsaw received a postcard from Norway with a single word on it, "Greetings." She recognized her son's handwriting and understood.

But her relief was short-lived, because in August 1903, or less than a month after getting the postcard from Boris, she got more bad news about Alexander. His sentence had been changed from exile in Irkutsk, a sizeable city in central Siberia, to a much harsher exile in Yakutia, a remote area in the northeastern corner of Siberia that is one of the coldest places on earth. Sofia realized that she would have to keep this shocking news from her husband, who was collapsing under the strain of what was happening to his older sons. She invented an entire story for his benefit about how Alexander was actually carrying out a plan of his own to work as a geologist in the provinces. In order to make this more persuasive, she even composed reassuring letters that she pretended were from Alexander and read them to her husband. Fortunately, for the time being, he believed them. For long periods, however, they would not know where Boris was, what he was doing, or even if he was alive; neither would Vera.

Once Savinkov was out of Russia, travel without a passport was easy. Languages were also not an obstacle because he was fluent in French, the lingua franca of the age. From Vardø he went by ship to Trondheim and then Oslo in Norway, and from there to Antwerp in Belgium. By August he had made it to Switzerland, which had a long tradition of granting political asylum to foreign revolutionaries. Geneva was also where the Socialist Revolutionary Party leadership made its home.

Terror Central

Although officially directed by its Central Committee, in 1903 the Socialist Revolutionary Party was effectively run by just one of the committee members—Mikhail (Moishe) Rafailovich Gots, a man with impeccable revolutionary credentials. The son of a rich and successful Jewish tea merchant in Moscow, he had begun to study medicine at Moscow University in 1885, which is when he also became a member of the People's Will Party. The following year he was arrested for involvement in revolutionary activity and exiled to Siberia. His participation in armed resistance by a group of political prisoners protesting abuses, during which he was seriously wounded, led to a trial by a military tribunal and a lifelong sentence of hard labor. But after six years this was reduced to exile because of his health problems. And in 1900, a year after being granted clemency and allowed to return to European Russia as his health continued to deteriorate, he moved abroad, first to Paris, then Geneva.

The imperial regime would pay a heavy price for its humane treatment of Gots inasmuch as he would live for another six years and become its most implacable opponent. Gots was one of the founders and chief theoreticians of the Socialist Revolutionary Party and Combat Organization, as well as its foremost ideologist of terror and editor of the leading SR journal. His apartment in Geneva became the Party's headquarters, and he dedicated most of his considerable personal wealth to the Party's needs.

Gots produced a powerful impression on Savinkov when they first met. At thirty-seven, he was a dozen years older than his visitor and already a legendary figure. He was slender and slightly built, with a curly black beard framing a pale face, and his lively eyes seemed filled with youthful fire. This was all the more striking because Gots spent much of his time as a chair-bound invalid. He suffered from a progressive paralysis of his legs that doctors had tentatively diagnosed as polyarthritis, but none of the traditional treatments worked, and the condition was so painful that he could not sleep without morphine.

Despite his frailty, Gots spent all his time on revolutionary work and lived like an ascetic. His apartment, which he shared with his wife, was furnished as sparsely as a student's, and in a gesture toward the SR Party's democratic populism he always wore a traditional Russian-styled blouse with a side-fastened collar that was decorated with a bit of simple embroidery along the edges. His manner was unpretentious and hospitable. But he prided himself on being very observant and a keen judge of people, and his gaze was riveting.

He quizzed Savinkov about why he wanted "to participate," as he put it, "only in terror" and "not in general work." Savinkov made an accommodating reply befitting his status as a raw recruit: although he attached the greatest importance to terror, he was willing to place himself completely at the disposal of the central committee and to engage in any of the party's activities.

Gots listened carefully, then paused. He had decided to put Savinkov off for the time being: "I can't give you an answer yet," he replied. "Wait a while—and stay in Geneva."

Gots had actually taken to Savinkov right away and would quickly develop a paternal, even a tender affection for him, referring to him as "our Benjamin"—an allusion to the youngest and best-loved son of Jacob and Rachel in Genesis 35:18. But Gots was also wary and wanted Savinkov to be vetted by the new leader of the Combat Organization, who had replaced Gershuni when he was recently arrested. And this new leader was none other than Evno Azef, who had risen to a position of central authority in the most feared and effective terrorist organization in Russia.

⊶

Geneva was, and still is, a dignified-looking city of stone and brick, comfortably situated between two mountain ranges on the shore of a beautiful lake from which an iconic white fountain jets to an impressive height. There was a considerable contrast in 1903 between its law-abiding burghers and prosperous outward appearance—it was already famous for its watches and jewelry—and the Russian revolutionaries conspiring below the surface of its large foreign colony.

While Savinkov waited for an assignment from Gots, he roomed together with Boris Moiseyenko, his friend and fellow exile from Vologda, who had also recently escaped and wanted to join the Combat Organization. Moiseyenko had brought the welcome news that Ivan Kalyaev was planning to come to Geneva as well. When he did, they would have the core of a formidable terrorist cell cemented by close personal friendship.

In the meantime, the two young men kept largely to themselves and to a small circle of like-minded revolutionaries. An occasional visitor from the outside was the venerable Babushka, who had been spirited out of Russia because of a renewed threat of arrest and came by to check on her recruits. To raise money and spread the word about the struggle for justice in Russia, she would soon go on a very successful lecture tour of the United States—including large and enthusiastic audiences of American sympathizers and Russian expatriates in New York (several thousand at Cooper Union), Boston (3,000 in Faneuil Hall), Philadelphia (2,000), Chicago, and elsewhere.

⊙━━⊙

Many of the other young Russian revolutionaries in Geneva whom Savinkov met had also been university students, and with time and freedom on their hands they often gathered to talk. Savinkov impressed, and was remembered by, all who met him, although not everyone liked the impression he made. He stood out because of his individualism, which extended even to his appearance. The other young men were largely indifferent to how they looked and, in keeping with their commitment to revolutionary struggle and solidarity with the masses, wore nondescript clothing. It was also rare for any of them to have very much money. But Savinkov always dressed carefully and even looked dandyish with his elegantly tailored suits, stylish cravats, and groomed moustache. He also tended to keep somewhat aloof from the others, producing the impression that he was unwilling to share everything he thought and felt. However, when he chose, he could also be a charming conversationalist and brilliant storyteller.

Victor Mikhailovich Chernov, the goateed, cerebral Socialist Revolutionary theorist and member of its Central Committee, got to know Savinkov well. He found him to be original, strong, and passionate, but also secretive, extravagant, and something of a "fantasist," as he put it—someone who longed for a life filled with brilliance and flash.

An annoying trait in Savinkov was his apparent indifference to the theoretical concerns that Chernov had worked out laboriously himself. Once, at a gathering in Geneva and within Chernov's earshot, Savinkov had confided to someone else with a chuckle:

Well, in matters agrarian, you'll have to forgive me, I'm hardly a specialist. How many *desiatins* of land a peasant needs and according to what formula—in such things I'd rather rely on Victor Mikhailovich here. His department doesn't concern me. Everything that the Party says about this I accept and will not utter a word against it; and I advise you not to as well.

Chernov never forgot or forgave Savinkov the perceived slight or his attitude toward the "agrarian question," which he seemed to view as hopelessly boring and prosaic despite its centrality in the SR Party platform. For Chernov, this early impression of Savinkov presaged his future "extreme subjectivism" and "Mephistophelian" contempt for people (although it is clear that Chernov's memoir of Savinkov as he was in his early days was also colored by their fraught relations over the course of the next dozen years). Paradoxically and deplorably in Chernov's view, these were the same traits that would later allow Savinkov to "conquer the hearts and minds" of his followers.

Sometimes the common ground Savinkov found with other revolutionaries had nothing to do with their dangerous profession and even transcended political differences. Nikolay Valentinov-Volsky was a committed Marxist, but although in theory this made him Savinkov's ideological enemy, they both shared a love of Russian poetry, which allowed them to spend a delightful evening together when they happened to meet in Kiev after both had left Geneva.

When they began, Savinkov took a loaded revolver out of his pocket and put it by his side, in case of a police raid. They then turned to talking about the works of Russia's greatest poets—Pushkin, Lermontov, Tyutchev, Fet—and about well-known poets of the second rank—Maykov, Apukhtin, Polonsky. They pulled the poets' books off the shelves of their host's well-stocked library and read favorite poems out loud. Volsky recalled that "Savinkov knew a great many poems by heart and recited them splendidly, with a noble simplicity, and without that unpleasant affectation and unbearable theatricality which is for some reason customary in reciting poetry."

As the evening wore on, Savinkov made a confession that completely disarmed Volsky. Not only did he love poems by the second-raters, but even by Semyon Nadson, a long-haired, handsome romantic who died tragically young (of consumption, of course) and had been a favorite of sentimental provincial young ladies a decade earlier. Savinkov could recite him from memory too, and

Volsky never forgot how this future terrorist, with slender hands "like a young woman's," tenderly mouthed lines about the loveliness of "first timid words" and the "trembling of a maidenly-pure soul."

The Chief of Terror

Several weeks passed while Savinkov waited in Geneva for his assignment. To fill his time, he returned to writing and produced at least one short story, "In Twilight. A Sketch," which a Socialist Revolutionary journal published in November 1903. In it, Savinkov imagines how a young terrorist, torn between self-doubt and revolutionary elation, manages to escape police surveillance in Saint Petersburg and stabs one of his pursuers to death on the eve of a major public demonstration. The detailed descriptions of the terrorist's state of mind, his wanderings through the city, and the assassination do credit to Savinkov's imagination. But he was not even close to anticipating what actually lay ahead for him.

Then, one morning in late September or early October 1903, when Savinkov was sitting alone in the room he shared with Moiseyenko and not expecting anyone, there was a knock on the door. When he opened it a strikingly ugly man stood before him: tall and top heavy, with a slouching, obese torso perched on skinny legs; a thick, short neck; and a round head with a low forehead and closely cropped brown hair. His fleshy, dark-complexioned face, with big, widely spaced brown eyes, a skeptically cocked left eyebrow, and fat lips, was fixed in an impassive, stony expression. He looked to be in his early thirties and dressed modishly, which jarred with his grotesque physique.

"Evgeny Filippovich Azef," the visitor introduced himself and extended his hand.

Savinkov recognized immediately who he was—the new head of the Combat Organization. He had used a Russified first name and patronymic instead of the Jewish "Evno Fishelevich."

Azef walked in and sat down. Acting as if he were bored, which seemed strange under the circumstances, and speaking slowly, he asked Savinkov in an unpleasantly high-pitched voice: "I've been told that you want to work in terror? Why specifically in terror?"

Savinkov repeated politely what he had told Gots earlier. He also volunteered that at the present moment he considered the assassination of Minister of the

Interior Vyacheslav von Plehve to be the most important task facing the Combat Organization.

Azef listened with the same lethargic expression. He seemed to weigh everything at length before replying. "Do you have any comrades?" he finally asked for some reason.

Savinkov named Kalyaev, Moiseyenko, and a third person. He also gave Azef detailed biographies and characterizations of each. Azef listened in silence, and then rose to leave. He said nothing about the young men Savinkov had described.

In the next few days, Azef made several more similar visits to the boarding house and treated Moiseyenko in the same way as Savinkov. Each time, he said little himself but listened very carefully as he slowly and methodically made up his mind about the two young men and how they could fit into his plans.

Finally, after several weeks, the visit came when Azef announced what Savinkov and Moiseyenko had been longing to hear: "It's time to go to Russia," he said.

With that simple phrase, they learned that they were now members of the Combat Organization.

"But first," Azef added, "leave Geneva and spend a few weeks in a small town somewhere so you can check if you're being watched."

Azef had reason to fear that his game could be spoiled by some zealous Okhrana agent in Geneva who might stumble across these suspicious-looking young Russians and want to investigate them. He needed constantly to balance his activity on a razor's edge: if the police discovered his betrayal, they would arrest him and hang him; if the Socialist Revolutionaries did, they would try to kill him. Azef's police handlers in Paris and Saint Petersburg took great pains to keep his identity secret and to protect him from any interference, but he had to be constantly on the alert himself as well.

By 1903, Azef had also acquired an unassailable reputation among the Socialist Revolutionaries for his rare and wide-ranging administrative and practical skills: transporting and organizing the distribution of clandestine publications, devising and maintaining punctilious security protocols, managing finances, and, most importantly, mastering the chemistry of dynamite production, setting up clandestine laboratories, and carrying out tests of bombs.

Because Azef appeared to succeed brilliantly at anything he undertook, the SR leaders spoke of his "golden hands." Gershuni had bequeathed the Combat Organization to Azef even before his own arrest. Chernov considered Azef's lucid, "mathematical" mind simply irreplaceable. Gots always treated him with the greatest respect.

But their admiration did not stop there. The more the SR leadership got to know Azef, the more they also became convinced that beneath his unappealing appearance and taciturn manner there dwelt a very sensitive soul.

Gots was once deeply moved by the sight of Azef breaking into sobs after hearing a former prisoner describe a whipping he had received in Siberia. An old revolutionary recalled being moved by Azef's tenderness toward every little Jewish boy trying to sell him something on the streets of Vilnius and Warsaw.

The way Azef expressed his emotions could be as clumsy as his physical appearance, but even this was interpreted as an endearing trait. Party members remembered how he would walk up to someone with whom he had been arguing and give them an unexpected conciliatory kiss. As a result, the majority of his comrades treated him not only with respect, but with care, attention, and genuine affection.

There were some rare dissenting voices. Women seemed to notice something about Azef that put them off. Kalyaev also did not like him either the first time they met, explaining that there was something about him he did not understand.

There were occasional suspicions about Azef's duplicity. After a meeting with Azef in 1902, a member of the SR Party who worked closely with Gershuni told him he suspected that Azef was actually a police agent because he seemed to know things that he could have gotten only from the Okhrana. He resolved to follow his hunch and to secretly collect incriminating information about Azef. But his investigation got nowhere because he was arrested a few months later. Someone had apparently betrayed him to the police.

�------⟡

Despite Azef's vaunted expertise, Savinkov and Moiseyenko soon discovered that there would be no training in terrorism and that they would have to learn whatever they needed to know by doing it. No one explained to them the best ways to spot someone following you; no one described how to escape from pursuers.

Nevertheless, following Azef's instructions, the next day they left Geneva by train for Freiburg in southern Germany and settled into a modest pension. They watched for several days, but nothing happened. Savinkov and Moiseyenko were beginning to learn how much of a terrorist's life consisted of just tedious waiting.

Finally, after two weeks Azef arrived and for the first time revealed the target he was assigning them. It would indeed be Minister Plehve, the second most powerful man in the Russian Empire. Savinkov's and Moiseyenko's most ardent wish had come true.

Azef explained that Plehve knew that terrorists wanted to kill him and, as a result, spent most of the time in his apartment inside the Okhrana headquarters building itself at 16 Fontanka Embankment, on one of Saint Petersburg's main canals. He ventured out rarely, but he did make weekly reports to the tsar at his various residences, which changed depending on the season.

Because getting into the heavily guarded building would be extremely difficult, Azef had developed an ingenious new plan of attack. Members of the Combat Organization team would disguise themselves in ways that would make them inconspicuous in the streets—as newspaper sellers, cabbies, peddlers—and would track the minister's coming and goings until they knew all his routines and itineraries. After choosing the optimal place and time, they would blow up his carriage with a bomb that was designed to be thrown and to explode on impact.

Azef added that because the police had no experience with terrorists hiding in plain view like this, the plan had a good chance of success. He concluded with a tone of conviction that was unusual for him: "If there is no betrayal, Plehve will be killed."

Whatever negative impression Azef may have produced by his unfriendly manner and appearance during his first meetings with Savinkov was erased. Azef now seemed to him the embodiment of uncompromising revolutionary commitment and acumen.

First Steps

By the second half of October 1903, Azef put the plot against Plehve in motion. Moiseyenko left for Russia, intending to use the border crossing into Russian Poland at Alexandrovo and to smuggle in a supply of mercury fulminate, a strong but dangerously unstable explosive that would be used in the bombs' impact fuses. Savinkov did not have a passport, so he first had to travel to Krakow, a Polish city that was then part of Austria, to get a counterfeit before he could proceed to Russia. Azef stayed behind for a few days, claiming that he needed to carry out experiments with explosives in remote locations on the outskirts of Geneva.

Savinkov arrived in Saint Petersburg without incident in early November. Despite his total lack of experience, Azef had put him in charge of coordinating the attack on Plehve. But Azef also instructed him to wait until he arrived himself and promised this would be soon.

As before, days and then weeks passed, and Azef was nowhere to be seen. Savinkov's first steps as a terrorist on Russian soil were disorienting and frustrating. He felt paralyzed and was at Azef's mercy: he wanted to act, but did not know what to do.

In the meantime, Azef was warily pursuing his own devious agenda. During the preceding five weeks, between September 20 and October 29, 1903—when Savinkov was waiting in Geneva for his assignment and, later, after he left for Russia—Azef had sent seven letters in secret to Leonid Rataev, head of the Foreign Agency of the Okhrana. This subdivision of the imperial police was housed in two modest rooms on the ground floor of the Russian embassy in Paris, located within a walled compound on rue de Grenelle in the elegant 7th Arrondissement on the Left Bank.

The mandate of the Okhrana's Foreign Agency was to monitor all anti-tsarist activity by Russian revolutionaries living in France, Switzerland, and England, and it did so in time-honored ways: by employing Russian and French "tails" (called *fileurs*, from the French *filer* or "to shadow") who watched and followed suspects, by intercepting correspondence, by bribing the likes of concierges and chambermaids to eavesdrop and pass on any papers they could lay their hands on, and by cultivating informants in the revolutionary organizations themselves. To keep track of the mountains of data that accumulated, the Foreign Agency maintained an efficient, elaborately cross-referenced system of card catalogs, files, and photographs containing information about thousands of individuals. (In a remarkable twist of history, this material eventually made it to the United States and has been in an archive in California for many years.)

The letter Azef wrote on September 20 was typical—a routine report about the activities of the Socialist Revolutionaries, including such details as their recent congress abroad, a list of members who were supposed to leave for Moscow "with terrorist plans regarding" Grand Duke Sergey, the name of a new arrival from Russia (not Boris Savinkov), the membership of the SR central committee, and the promise to hand over personally a copy of a letter that Gots had received. Azef gave his code name and return address as "M-r Aristoff, rue École de Médecine" in Geneva.

During October, Azef sent additional letters to Rataev from Zurich, Baden, Bern, and Geneva, which he signed "Ivan." In them he discusses and touches on a wide range of topics, including the possible origins of "two bombs in Krakow," the absence of serious threats against the Russian emperor during his coming visit to Italy, a request for reimbursement of 450 rubles, the comings and goings of various Socialist Revolutionaries, the names of Party members in several Russian cities, advice about where to arrest one of them, the whereabouts of Babushka and others, an acknowledgment of receipt of money, the rumor that "Bronshtein (Trotsky)" may be coming to Geneva and the nature of his ideological differences with Lenin, the fact that one of Rataev's secret agents has clumsily blown his cover, a request for another reimbursement because "I now have very little money left," and a complaint that he has not gotten responses to several of his letters.

In none of these letters does Azef mention the plot that he was beginning to hatch against Plehve. By contrast, he had warned Rataev of a plot against the minister more than a year earlier, on June 4, 1902, and had also specified that the terrorists were planning to use a bomb. For personal reasons about which one can only speculate, Azef decided to reveal the first and conceal the second.

Part of what allowed him to succeed in his complex game was the structure of the Socialist Revolutionary Party. In its finances, choice of targets, and planning, the Combat Organization was largely autonomous from the party's governing body, the Central Committee, which, even though it authorized assassinations and celebrated successful ones, concerned itself with ideology, fundraising, and agitation. This separation was of course necessary to protect the Combat Organization's secrecy and security. But it also created a yawning divide between those who stayed in places like Geneva and Paris and talked about the need for terror, and those who plotted and carried out attacks on the streets of Russian cities.

Even against the background of Russia's often tragic history, which is filled with lurid events and outsize individuals, Azef is an unbelievable figure. Like the religious mountebank Rasputin, with his malignant influence on Nicholas II and Alexandra and through them on the entire country, Azef was both a symptom and an agent of the forces that were tearing Russia apart and preparing it for the unprecedented human disasters that defined the twentieth century.

CHAPTER TWO

THE MINISTER

The man Savinkov was assigned to kill in his first action was appointed as minister of the interior by Nicholas II on April 17, 1902, two days after his predecessor, Dmitry Sipyagin, was assassinated by Balmashov. Vyacheslav Konstantinovich von Plehve—the surname was German; his grandfather had emigrated—was a highly experienced bureaucrat with thirty-five years of ever-ascending appointments in the Russian imperial service. A lawyer by training, he was intelligent, skillful, hardworking, and adept at navigating court politics. He was also a true believer in autocracy, and all his efforts during the different stages of his career focused on strengthening the state's institutions of domination and control.

Plehve began to live up to his reputation for being tough as soon as he was appointed. Because Balmashov was one day short of his twenty-first birthday when he shot Sipyagin, he was technically still a minor, which, according to Russian law, meant that he could not have faced the death penalty in a civil court. But Plehve wanted to make an example of the young man and had him turned over to the military for trial, which handed down a death sentence.

Plehve's other policies were similarly brutal, but much more ambitious in scale.

Because he refused to differentiate between radical and moderate opposition, he treated as insubordination any signs of independence by the *zemstvos*, an important and widespread system of restricted local self-government in the provinces, thereby alienating and inflaming their often well-born and civic-minded members.

Plehve's known dislike for Jews—he once told the Russian minister of war that they needed to be "taught a lesson" because they were "conceited" and "in the forefront of the revolutionary movement"—together with the anti-Semitism endemic in the imperial bureaucracy encouraged the authorities in the Bessarabian city of Kishinyov to do nothing when a notorious pogrom broke out on Easter Sunday, April 6, 1903. The event caused outrage around the world and spawned additional pogroms in Kiev, Odessa, Baku, and Warsaw.

Plehve continued the forced "Russification" of Finland and Armenia begun by his predecessors. He ordered police to quell a strike by workers in Odessa and ordered troops to fire upon striking workers in Kiev, Kharkov, Tiflis, Baku, Batumi, and other cities. In the Poltava and Kharkov governments, peasant demonstrations were broken up by beatings and over 1,000 individuals were put on trial. Investigators later found that police and Cossacks had raped peasant women and girls.

However, Plehve had good reason to believe that decisive action could stamp out the Russian revolutionary movement that had sprung back to life in the last few years. Two decades earlier, as director of police, he had effectively destroyed the People's Will Party after they assassinated Alexander II. He did so by increasing the reach and powers of the national police, by participating in the investigations himself, and, most notably, by employing a double agent, a certain Sergey Degayev, who became a police informant while simultaneously holding a high position in the party. Degayev's revelations led to the arrests of many members of the People's Will, which never recovered from the blow.

When Plehve assumed his new exalted position, he fully expected to repeat the same tactics. Azef's astounding achievement in June 1903, when he became the leader of the Combat Organization, exceeded the Okhrana's wildest conspiratorial ambitions, and Plehve believed that his victory over the terrorists was now assured. In an interview with a French reporter, he announced that he expected terrorist activity to die down very soon because of new police measures. When the reporter remarked that it must have required courage to assume the post in which Sipyagin had been killed, Plehve boasted: "My security is impeccable. An assassination attempt against me may be accomplished only by accident."

Plehve's security was indeed designed to foresee every eventuality. In addition to living most of the time in the heavily guarded Okhrana headquarters building in the capital, he never ventured out unless extreme precautions had been taken. His carriage had armored window shades and was accompanied by detectives on bicycles. The country house where Plehve spent summers was so well protected that an official who once visited him there was surprised when he glimpsed body armor under Plehve's shirt.

"Do you suppose that I would simply decide to let you come to see me without having all the necessary safeguards in place?" Plehve asked. "What if you should suddenly thrust a dagger at me?"

Plehve did not know that for the Combat Organization, the days of daggers and revolvers were over.

Amateur Days

Everything in Savinkov's plot against Plehve went wrong at first, and it could easily have been the end of his career as a terrorist.

The same day he arrived in Saint Petersburg in November 1903, he went to look for one of two comrades, Ignaty Matseyevsky, who had come to the city earlier and who was supposed to disguise himself as a cigarette street vendor. The second man, Ignaty's brother, Iosif, was going to be a horse-drawn cab driver. Without any specific guidance from Azef, all three were planning to see what they could learn about Plehve's movements on their own. None had stalked a target before.

Ignaty's unshaven, pinched face and rough sheepskin coat changed his appearance so much that when they first met Savinkov did not recognize him. This was very encouraging. So was Ignaty's report on how he had deceived the police guards outside Okhrana headquarters, where he had spent time watching for Plehve. Pretending to be a country yokel and rattling off folksy expressions as he doffed his cap, Ignaty even got a guard to tell him who lived in the building. Iosif's disguise also worked well, and the police ignored him as he drove his cab around the Fontanka neighborhood where the Okhrana building was located.

But there were problems that the team did not know how to solve. It was very difficult for Ignaty to sell cigarettes on the street and watch for Plehve at the same time because as a peddler, he was required to keep moving. There was also a lot of competition from other street vendors who had staked out territories on sidewalks. Iosif had trouble watching too because passengers were constantly hailing his cab. He could not refuse them all without drawing suspicion to himself and had to keep leaving his observation post.

Savinkov had hoped to catch a glimpse of Plehve by chance, which would not be easy in the heavily trafficked streets. When December arrived, Azef was still nowhere in sight and the three members of the team had learned almost nothing about Plehve's routine. Whether Savinkov made occasional surreptitious visits to Vera and his children, who lived in the city, is not known, but seems probable.

Sankt-Peterburg

As Savinkov and his comrades also discovered, the imperial capital is an especially uncomfortable place to spend a lot of time outdoors in winter. The Baedeker guide describes its climate succinctly as "raw, damp, and very unsettled." Because it is located at a high northern latitude (like Juneau, Alaska), the sun appears for fewer than eight hours a day. The light is diminished even more by the city's location on the coast of the Baltic Sea. Clouds drift overhead on four days out of five; rain or snow falls on one out of two; fog rolls in regularly. Sometimes it is like a sheer curtain drawn across the cityscape; at others, it is so thick that you cannot see more than a few yards in front of you. Much of the city is only a few feet above sea level, prone to flooding, and interlaced by canals. The pervasive moisture makes the winter cold feel even more penetrating.

But all this also adds to the city's unusual and mysterious allure. The mists soften the stately rhythms of the city's buildings; the thin light mutes their pastel facades; vistas at a distance become less distinct and invite the play of imagination. During long winter nights, the city's third dimension seems to fade altogether. Palaces, streets, and bridges arching over glistening darkness drift and dissolve into patterns of black and gray, with only blurs of occasional streetlights breaking the gloom.

Saint Petersburg now appeared to Boris Savinkov in a very different aspect than during his days as a student. The routes he followed when stalking Plehve were all within the city's historical core, and the palaces, monuments, parks, and waterways he saw then are still there now. But to the knowing eyes of a revolutionary the city was a palimpsest where an often violent past glimmers through the stone, water, and air.

Just steps from the Okhrana building on the Fontanka is the Summer Garden, with its neatly trimmed hedges, gnarled trees, centuries-old Venetian marble statues—and memories of the birth of terrorism in Russia. A chapel near its entrance (torn down by the Bolsheviks in 1930) commemorated Alexander II's escape from the first assassination attempt on his life in 1866. Additional attempts were made in 1867, 1879 (twice), and 1880 (a massive explosion in the Winter Palace itself), before the People's Will finally succeeded in 1881 on the Griboyedov Canal Embankment in the center of the city. On that spot, less than a fifteen-minute walk from the tsar's Winter Palace in one direction and the Okhrana headquarters in the other, was erected a cathedral in Russian Revival style that was given the chilling name Savior on the Spilled Blood, and that became one of the city's most famous landmarks. Alexander II was also not the first Russian emperor to meet a violent death; two others were killed by courtiers in 1762 and 1801.

One of the places Savinkov would have expected to spot Plehve's carriage when it drove to the Winter Palace was along the Palace Embankment on the shore of the Neva. Visible from any location there across the river's broad expanse is the Peter and Paul Fortress, part of which was the notorious political prison in which Savinkov himself had spent ten weeks before his exile to Vologda. Another ten minutes' walk beyond the Winter Palace stands the symbol of Saint Petersburg—*The Bronze Horseman*, the larger-than-life equestrian statue of Emperor Peter the Great, the city's founder. The square by this statue was where Russia's first revolutionaries gathered in December 1825 to demand a constitution, basic freedoms, and the abolition of serfdom. Scores of them were killed, hundreds were imprisoned in the Peter and Paul Fortress, and the uprising's leaders were questioned in the Winter Palace by Emperor Nicholas I himself before being executed or exiled.

———

When Savinkov undertook his grim hunt for Plehve on the city's streets, he also strolled through verbal shadows from the past that fell on everything he saw. His mother and his schooling had made him a reader, and classical Russian literature was central to the creation of a disquieting and potent myth of Saint Petersburg. "The Bronze Horseman," a celebrated narrative poem by Alexander Pushkin, Russia's national writer, made the statue of Peter into a symbol of the irreconcilable opposition between the individual and the state. Nikolay Gogol's "Petersburg Tales," which are among the most valued treasures in Russia's literary gold reserve, conjure a metropolis filled with tragic conflicts between the weak and the strong and nightmarish transformations of reality. Dostoyevsky's *Crime and Punishment* is set in Saint Petersburg, and Raskolnikov's decision that an exceptional individual can give himself permission to kill so that he can do good directly prefigures the moral struggles that Savinkov and his closest comrades would experience when planning terrorist attacks. Savinkov's own novels reveal the extent to which he viewed existence through the lens of Russian literature.

Flee to Fight Another Day

Boris Savinkov had been stalking Plehve for over a month with nothing to show for it and without any news from Azef when an event occurred in mid-December 1903 that convinced him the police were on his tail. Unexpectedly one morning, a scruffy-looking, middle-aged man in a shabby frock coat appeared at the door of Savinkov's room in the Rossiya Hotel and addressed him by the name that was on Savinkov's counterfeit passport. He explained that he wanted to hire Savinkov to write for his commercial newspaper, but as he spoke, his eyes nervously scurried over everything in Savinkov's room.

The absurdity of the man's proposal, his behavior, and the fact that he knew about Savinkov's alias meant that he could only be a police spy, although not a very skillful one. Savinkov managed to bluff his way out, but then saw police spies on the street. After shaking them off, he abandoned everything in his hotel once again, as he had in Archangel, alerted his comrade, and boarded the evening train to Kiev. He had done nothing that could have tipped off the police to his presence in the city or allowed them to identify him. Savinkov could not explain the mystery at the time, but he also did not forget it. At least there was some comfort in discovering that he could see through police deception and evade pursuit.

Savinkov chose Kiev as a refuge because it was the only place where he knew members of the SR Party who could help him get out of the country without a passport, which he had left with his other things in the hotel. In a few weeks, his escape route was set. Together with another terrorist who had been hiding in the same safe house in Kiev, he made it to the town of Suvalki in the north-western corner of Russian Poland, where his new comrade knew a Jewish woman smuggler.

The smuggler had added both terrorists to a large party of Jews—men, women, and children—who were preparing to escape from Russia and begin the long trek to new lives in the United States. A bribed Russian border guard led them to the staging area near the German frontier. The night was freezing and a full moon was out. They all sat in the snow for a quarter of an hour as they waited for the signal to cross and warily watched the guards' fires glimmering in the distance to the left and right of the "window" that had been prepared in the border. When the faint, drawn-out whistle finally came, everyone leapt to their feet. Jostling one another and slipping on the ice, the Jewish fugitives rushed down the moonlit road leading to the border with East Prussia. Savinkov and his comrade followed. It was exhilarating to step across the invisible line that meant freedom and safety. Several days later, after a sequence of trains to Königsberg and Berlin, Savinkov was in Geneva at SR headquarters.

The Novice Speaks Up

Savinkov arrived wanting an explanation from the Party leaders why Azef had abandoned him and the others in Saint Petersburg for the past two months. To his satisfaction, he discovered that his willingness to "work" in terror had given him new stature in the leaders' eyes and that he no longer had to accept passively everything they said. When Victor Chernov was unable or unwilling to give him a satisfactory answer, Savinkov went to consult with Gots, who was resting in Nice. Gots initially attempted to soothe Savinkov by excusing Azef, and then tried to hurry Savinkov along, urging him to return to Russia and to seek out Azef person-ally. But Savinkov refused. He had learned enough in Saint Petersburg to know that without changes in people and resources, it would be pointless to risk going back.

Savinkov's arguments and self-assured manner impressed Gots. He relented and gave Savinkov everything he wanted: money, contacts, and the names, whereabouts, and specializations of the three members of the Combat Organi-zation who would be added to his team. Remembering his old friend Kalyaev, Savinkov asked that he be added as well. Gots agreed to this too. It was a notable gesture of confidence in someone who had no experience.

With new counterfeit passports in hand, Savinkov and Kalyaev left for Russia via Berlin. Kalyaev was ecstatic and talked excitedly the entire way about the easiest way to kill Plehve, laughing with delight when Savinkov told him that he might have to be disguised as a street peddler.

In the end of January 1904, Azef finally arrived in Moscow as well and immediately confronted Savinkov, questioning by what authority he had left Saint Petersburg. But Savinkov stood his ground. He answered that he had done so because he had not gotten any news for months and the police were closing in on him. He also bristled at the implication that he was somehow the guilty party.

Neither one would yield during their rancorous meeting. In the end, having aired their grievances if not erased them, they turned to the impending attack on Plehve.

What neither Chernov nor Gots nor anyone else in the Socialist Revolutionary Party knew is that Azef had left Savinkov adrift in Saint Petersburg because he had been busy with his own dark affairs. He had traveled widely and sent messages from Paris, Copenhagen, and Saint Petersburg to Rataev at the Okhrana office in Paris; he also met with Rataev on January 6. On no occasion did he say anything about the plot against Plehve. However, it is not known if he tipped off the police about Savinkov in Saint Petersburg in December.

Terror in Time of War

The resurrection of the plot against Plehve coincided with a momentous historical development that would do much to amplify the shock of an ambitious assassination. On the night of January 27/February 8, 1904, in what would prove to be a dress rehearsal for Pearl Harbor, the Imperial Japanese navy launched a devastating surprise attack on the Russian Pacific fleet lying at anchor in the outer harbor of Port Arthur at the tip of the Liaodong Peninsula in China. This was the culmination of a long series of aggressive political and military maneuvers by Russia, Japan, and several Western European powers to acquire spheres of influence in China and Korea. Russian and Japanese ambitions had collided head-on over the partition of Manchuria.

The debacle of Port Arthur would be only the first of the military disasters that giant Russia suffered at the hands of little Japan, whose military power Russia had grossly underestimated. As reports of new defeats on land and on sea shocked the nation, discontent with the imperial regime's improvidence and ineptitude grew. Within a year, on January 9/22, 1905, the war that began 4,000 miles to the east of Saint Petersburg would catalyze a revolution that would shake the Russian Empire from top to bottom, leaving cracks that would help to bring it crashing down a dozen years later.

The Socialist Revolutionary Party joined the widespread condemnation of the war. As a matter of principle, it advocated peaceful coexistence among peoples and replacing standing armies with popular militias. It also actively agitated against the war by distributing leaflets among workers and peasants that demanded the "immediate cessation of the war with Japan, which is onerous, wasteful, bloody, and unnecessary for working people!" But the Party also saw an opportunity that it could exploit. By striking a powerful blow against the Russian Empire when its manifest failings were multiplying, the revolutionary cause would gain unprecedented support—enough, perhaps, to overturn the regime.

To be able to execute a successful attack on Plehve, Savinkov first had to get to know the members of the Combat Organization that had been assigned to his team by Gots and Azef. Most of these young men would become legendary figures in the history of the Russian revolutionary movement.

The first was Alexey Pokotilov, a nobleman, the son of an army general, and a former student at Kiev University, who would be in charge of explosives and assembling the bombs. Savinkov invited him to the celebrated restaurant Yar, located near the northwestern edge of Moscow on the main road to Saint Petersburg. It is hard to imagine a more unlikely location for revolutionaries to meet. This was one of the finest restaurants in Russia, and "not cheap," as Baedeker's Guide put it with Anglo-Saxon understatement. It was also notorious for occasional displays of what Russians, and especially rich members of Moscow's merchant class, liked to call their "broad" nature—the ability to demonstrate dash or unbridled passion in a way that would make people notice and remember. Savinkov's choice reveals the streak of bravado that would become a hallmark of his revolutionary activity. It also reflects his personal style and taste for comfort, which he indulged when he could. SR headquarters had evidently supplied him with enough cash to satisfy his sybaritic tendencies.

When he first walked into Yar, Savinkov had difficulty recognizing Poko-tilov because of how completely he blended in with the restaurant's well-heeled clientele. However, Pokotilov's polished appearance belied his emotional state. He was so keyed up about the prospect of killing Plehve, and insisted so vehemently on his right to throw the first bomb during the attack, that the chronic eczema from which he suffered flared up and small drops of blood began to ooze out across his forehead. Savinkov's description of the encounter in his memoir inevitably makes one think of wounds from an invisible crown of thorns and all that implies.

By early February 1904, Savinkov had returned to Saint Petersburg to com-plete his round of meetings with new members of his team. He accepted Maxi-milian Shveytser, a short, clean-shaven, and elegantly dressed young man who looked like a foreigner and produced the impression of calm, contained strength. A former student at Moscow University and the son of a successful Jewish banker, he had been trained by Azef as a bomb maker in several European locations after he joined the Combat Organization.

A few days later Savinkov met Yegor Sazonov, the last new member of his team, who was supposed to assume the disguise of a cab driver, like Iosif Matseyevsky. Sazonov had joined the Combat Organization after escaping from Yakutsk in far eastern Siberia, where he had been exiled for belonging to a revolutionary organization. He had an unusual past for a revolutionary because he was from a family of religiously conservative peasants who became rich in the timber business. But like Shveytser, he had also been radicalized at Moscow University. Sazonov embraced his disguise as a cabbie with the zeal of a "method" actor, and before coming to Saint Petersburg had perfected his new role by practicing in the provincial city of Tver.

Savinkov met Sazonov on a quiet street in an outlying green area on Vasil-yevsky Island, where he was waiting in his ragged cab behind a sorry-looking nag. When Savinkov got in and they drove slowly across the island and talked, he felt himself being charmed by Sazonov's lighthearted stories about a cabbie's life and moved by his deep religiosity which, like Kalyaev's, was fused with his faith in the revolution. Sazonov responded to Savinkov in kind, and later char-acterized him as being like "some marvelous flower, carried in by a breeze from God knows where. Everything he did had a strangely personal character: he fought as if he had been *personally* insulted, as if his honor had been impugned. And he fought in a way that was an example to us all."

The powerful personal bond that arose between the two would become a hallmark of Savinkov's relationship with all members of his team. It was unlike friendship in civilian life because it was rooted in mortal danger: not only had you resolved to kill your enemy together, but everything you did also determined whether your team members lived or died.

The ties among these Russian revolutionary terrorists resembled nothing so much as the loyalty that soldiers through the ages have reported feeling for their comrades when they are on the front line—the ones they can literally feel with their elbows. Such personal connections were often far more important for those who had experienced them than all the lofty-sounding goals proclaimed by their commanders or by the kings and ministers far in the rear.

March 18, 1904

This time Azef had decided to guide the initial stages of the attack on Plehve himself. He also instituted strict rules of secrecy. Meetings had to take place rarely and only on the street or in public locations such as restaurants, bathhouses, or theaters. Members of the team were forbidden from having any contacts with family or friends, or even writing to them. And all were instructed to dress and behave in ways that made them blend in with life in the city.

By the first days of March 1904, all the preliminary arrangements had been made, and Savinkov was eager to get started. Kalyaev, Pokotilov, and Shveytser left Saint Petersburg and were lying low in provincial cities, ready to return on short notice. Savinkov, Sazonov, and Matseyevsky were tracking Plehve in the streets. A seventh member of the team, David Borishansky, a replacement for Matseyevsky's brother and already known to Savinkov, was expected to arrive soon from Geneva.

The team's surveillance had determined that Plehve went to the Winter Palace to report to the tsar every Thursday around noon, taking the route along the Fontanka River Embankment and the Palace Embankment that Savinkov had walked often. He returned via different routes, however, and the men tracking him had not been able to determine if there was a regular pattern. Nevertheless, Savinkov decided that there was one location where they could intercept Plehve's carriage without fail—right in front of Okhrana headquarters at 16 Fontanka.

The plan was not only bold but rash, and when Savinkov laid it out Azef objected vehemently. Savinkov insisted, however, and managed to persuade

Azef at least to ask Sazonov and Matseyevsky what they thought. After some hesitation, both agreed with Savinkov. Azef still tried to talk them out of it, arguing that a risky attempt like this could sink the entire campaign, although he said this slowly and reluctantly, in his usual, strangely phlegmatic manner. Savinkov disagreed even more harshly, and Azef finally relented. Why he did is unclear because the plan seemed suicidal. Shortly thereafter, Azef left Saint Petersburg, and Savinkov sent messages to gather the entire team. He set the attack for midday on Thursday, March 18.

As the team's leader, Savinkov assigned everyone specific tasks. Shveytser would assemble and distribute the bombs, after which he would stay out of sight. Three of the men would be bomb throwers—Pokotilov, who had insisted on his right to be the primary assassin, Sazonov, and Borishansky. Two others, Kalyaev and Matseyevsky, would be lookouts. Savinkov would observe.

<hr />

In an attempt to distract themselves, Savinkov and Pokotilov spent Wednesday night on the eve of the attack at the Variety theater on the Fontanka, just a thirty-minute walk from the Okhrana building, watching the lighthearted fare. Pokotilov was pale and nervous, the pupils of his eyes feverishly dilated. Savinkov saw small drops of blood ooze out on his forehead again. After the performance, as they walked, Pokotilov kept repeating the phrases of his simple credo, as if stacking and restacking bricks in a defensive wall: "I believe in terror. For me the whole revolution is terror. There are few of us now. But you'll see: there will be many. Tomorrow, perhaps, I'll be gone. But I'm happy because of this, I'm proud: tomorrow Plehve will be killed."

At 10 A.M. the following day, Shveytser, who had spent the night assembling five bombs in his room on Vasilyevsky Island—two each for Pokotilov and Borishansky, and a bigger one weighing seven pounds for Sazonov—was picked up by Sazonov in his cab. Following a prearranged route through the city, they distributed the bombs to the throwers. An hour later, each was at his position along the Fontanka on either side of the Okhrana building together with the watchers who were supposed to signal when they saw the minister's carriage approaching.

The disposition was very confusing and spelled disaster. Not only was the whole area teeming with police agents and guards, but because the watchers as well as the throwers were not sure of the direction from which Plehve's carriage would come, they had to keep looking in different directions to keep track of one another's signals and movements.

Savinkov's inexperience, impatience, and eagerness to prove himself had endangered all their lives. The risk that Kalyaev and Matseyevsky faced was especially unnecessary because they were unarmed lookouts and could not take part in the actual assassination. Savinkov would understand all this only later.

With noon approaching and all the men in their assigned places, Savinkov crossed to the other side of the Fontanka, entered the Summer Garden, and sat down on a bench to wait.

Half an hour passed. The cold was penetrating.

Suddenly, Savinkov heard what sounded like a distant explosion. He involuntarily rose to his feet and looked across the Fontanka. But everything on the other side was unchanged—there was no smoke, no shower of broken glass; no figures running in front of any of the buildings.

A second later Savinkov realized it was only the noonday gun—a regular, daily signal—that had been fired from the Peter and Paul Fortress across the Neva. Then he saw Pokotilov entering through the Summer Garden's gates. He was pale and walking quickly, the pockets of his fur coat bulging from the two bombs.

He collapsed onto the bench near Savinkov and said: "Nothing worked; Borishansky ran away."

Savinkov could not believe what he had just heard. When they walked out of the garden and reached the street, it was as if blinders suddenly dropped from Savinkov's eyes and he began to understand the debacle that was unfolding. He saw Kalyaev at his post on the Tsepnoy Bridge, and was struck by how obvious he was, with his unnaturally tense pose, like a gun dog pointing out the prey. Kalyaev had been there for an hour and it now seemed incomprehensible that the police agents stationed in the area had not paid him any attention.

Just then, as Savinkov and Pokotilov were hurriedly crossing the bridge, a grand carriage behind a pair of black horses with a liveried footman on the box appeared and thundered past them at a fast trot. Plehve's calm face—gray hair, fleshy jowls, walrus moustache—flashed by in a window. Pokotilov reached for one of his bombs but it was too late. The carriage was already too far away and approaching Sazonov. Savinkov and Pokotilov froze; they knew Sazonov was holding his heavy bomb on his lap under a rug. But as they watched helplessly, Plehve's carriage quickly swerved around Sazonov's cab, turned into the building's open gates, and disappeared inside.

Sazonov had been caught completely by surprise. He was facing the wrong way because he had been forced to turn his rig around to avoid suspicion—the other cabbies had ridiculed him for not lining up like them. As a result, he had not seen Matseyevsky's signal or the carriage's approach, and although he had reached for his bomb, he was not quick enough.

Bitterly frustrated and disoriented by their failure, the terrorists lingered in the area for another half hour, hoping for a second chance and again risking being spotted. But the ineptitude of the police continued to match their own and extended their luck. They all managed to get away.

The team had agreed earlier to gather in the North Pole restaurant on Sadovaya Street for a postmortem of the attack. On the way there, Savinkov ran into Borishansky and confronted him about why he had abandoned his post. A calm, stony-faced man, Borishansky replied that anyone would have done the same and denied he was a coward: he had been surrounded by so many plainclothes policemen that he expected to be arrested any minute.

Because Savinkov had seen them himself, he decided to drop the matter. By now he had also realized who was really at fault. This first failure had taught him and the others a great deal. As he put it, using a Russian saying that underscored the need to resist doing anything rashly, "measure seven times and cut once."

Azef's Designs

Azef had again moved his pieces strategically on the chessboard. While Savinkov was putting his team together in February 1904, Azef maintained regular contact with Rataev and provided him with descriptions of the terrorists. He concentrated especially on Kalyaev and Shveytser, although he lied that he did not know their real names. Rataev so valued Azef's reports, which he took at face value, that he once confessed to him: "More than anything in the world I am afraid of compromising you [in the eyes of the revolutionaries] and losing your services."

Azef did not stop there, however. Closer to March 18, he had informed Alexey Lopukhin, the director of the police department in Saint Petersburg, that the terrorists were planning an attack near the Okhrana headquarters on the Fontanka. But he also lied again—this time about the target, saying for some private reason that it would be Lopukhin himself and not Plehve. Nevertheless, the result was that Lopukhin deployed such a large number of police agents in the area that the usually imperturbable Borishansky felt threatened and fled. This helped disrupt the plot, although the police also blundered badly by failing to recognize or arrest a single member of Savinkov's team despite having Azef's descriptions of two of them.

For several more years, Azef would continue in the same vein—giving information to the police that was either correct, or only partially correct (and therefore misleading), or completely false. The one constant was that he withheld any information that might compromise him, and he always had alibis for doing so. But why he betrayed some revolutionaries and not others, why one plot and not the next, and why during one period and not another, remains a mystery to this day.

This mystery is compounded by another one: Azef sent revolutionaries to the gallows by betraying them, but he also participated in some thirty terrorist acts against leading figures of the Russian imperial regime, either by actively organizing the attacks or tacitly approving them.

Why did Azef do what he did? The one certain motivation is money. Azef liked comfort, living well, fine clothing, easy women, and good food and wine. He took money from both the police and the revolutionaries and accumulated a sizeable sum as a result. During the last years of his career, the police were paying him what amounted to an enormous salary by the standards of the day, 12,000 rubles a year plus bonuses up to the same amount (roughly $400,000 or more today). This exceeded the 10,000 rubles the Russian Empire's director of the police earned in 1907.

Power may have been a motivation for Azef as well—his ability to outwit dangerous revolutionaries and to control the behavior of imperial grandees. One of his old school friends believed that Azef found deep satisfaction in the idea that someone from his humble background "holds in his hands the fate of both warring camps and that, to a certain extent, the march of events in Russia and perhaps the entire world depends on him." And in fact, Azef's recommendations regarding issues of personal security directly influenced the behavior of ministers and the tsar himself. They would decide where they could or could not go based on the threats that Azef reported.

The ability to wield such power inevitably fed Azef's sense of self-worth. His wife, Lyubov (the name means "love" in Russian), remembered what a striking egotist he was and the contempt with which he spoke about peasants, workers, and Russians in general. Azef's sense of superiority even colored his attitude toward his admiring younger brother Vladimir, who also worked in the revolutionary movement but whom Azef mistreated and considered "a fool." During the peak years of his career Azef's self-esteem could only have been inflated even more by the adulation he received from the senior members of the SR Party, Gershuni, Gots, and Chernov. For Savinkov and other members of the Combat Organization, Azef became a revered figure.

Azef's origins in the Pale of Settlement must have played a role as well. As a Jew who experienced Russian anti-Semitism in his childhood and youth, Azef could have been moved by hatred for the regime that fostered such discrimination as well as by contempt for the people among whom it was widespread. There is evidence that this influenced his specific animus against Plehve. But Azef's willingness to betray revolutionaries who were Jews—and there were many in the SR Party, including the leadership—suggests that he was not fixated on Russian anti-Semitism alone.

Finally, fear and the inability to get out—the feeling of being trapped between two dangerous enemies—must also have been an ingredient in the poisonous brew of motivations that kept Azef maneuvering between the revolutionaries and the police. Every successful action that he undertook on behalf of one side required lying to, or at least withholding information from, the other. He could also not abandon one side and work only for the other because he would become an enemy of the one he had left and his life would be in danger.

Regrouping

After their attempt on Plehve failed, Shveytser disarmed the bombs and took them back to Libava on the Baltic coast. Matseyevsky and Sazonov continued their surveillance, and the others dispersed to different provincial cities. Savinkov and Pokotilov were supposed to meet with Azef in Dvinsk, a city in what is now Latvia, to consult about the failure and decide what to do next, but Azef was nowhere to be found; neither were there any telegrams or messages from him. His disappearance at such a crucial moment was so unexpected that Savinkov and Pokotilov could think of only one shocking explanation—he had been arrested.

With Azef apparently gone, Savinkov hesitated about taking over the entire operation because the failure of the March 18 plan had taken a toll on his self-confidence. But none of the others wanted to lead the team either, and rather than letting it disband, Savinkov decided to summon everyone to a meeting in Kiev so that they could consult.

There was no unanimity about a single course of action. The team agreed to go on without Azef, but then they blundered by deciding to split their forces and attack Plehve plus a new target—the reviled governor-general of Kiev, Nikolay Kleygels. Savinkov initially opposed this move because it would create two smaller and weaker teams, but Pokotilov insisted, saying that he was prepared to blow up the entire building at 16 Fontanka by himself if necessary. Savinkov did not feel he had the authority to override him and acquiesced.

Pokotilov and Borishansky left for Saint Petersburg, where Pokotilov, who now took over the role of the team's technician, holed up with his equipment and explosives in a hotel. Late in the morning on March 25, armed with two bombs each, Pokotilov and Borishansky went out to look for Plehve on the streets of Saint Petersburg. But they did not see his carriage where they thought it was supposed to pass and decided to try again in a week. It was another painful disappointment. Pokotilov collected all the bombs and defused them for safety.

Then, on the night of March 31, he started arming them once again in preparation for the new attack the following morning. This was always a delicate and dangerous procedure, and Pokotilov worked very carefully. But on this occasion, he appears to have accidentally broken one of the thin glass tubes filled with sulfuric acid that was part of the bomb's firing mechanism.

The explosion was devastating. It instantly tore Pokotilov to bits and destroyed the room, reducing even the main structural ceiling beams to splinters. Pokotilov's corpse was so mutilated and charred that at first the police thought it might have been a woman because of the diminutive size of a fragment of one foot. It was a miracle that the three remaining bombs in the room did not go off.

Savinkov and the other members of the team in Kiev learned what happened from the newspapers. This was a far heavier blow than the failure of March 18. Not only had a cherished comrade died tragically, but their entire plot had been disrupted. The team now had only enough dynamite for one bomb, and this meant that they could not make another attempt on Plehve.

Azef the Savior

It was in this moment of confusion and despair that Azef demonstrated his ingenuity and willpower in a way that impressed Savinkov deeply. Right after Pokotilov's death, Azef unexpectedly showed up at the apartment in Kiev where Savinkov was staying.

"What right did you have to change the decision of the central committee on your own authority?" Azef demanded, his face clouded with anger, and began to berate Savinkov for starting a campaign against Kleygels and for leaving Saint Petersburg.

Savinkov had no choice this time but to take the rebukes like an errant schoolboy. Azef brusquely dismissed the fact that he did not come to the meeting in Dvinsk, claiming that he had noticed police agents following him and had spent three weeks traveling around Russia to shake them off. This, of course, sounded entirely plausible.

Savinkov was also on the verge of announcing that he wanted to give up on Plehve. But seeing the sullen anger darkening Azef's face, he thought better of it and kept silent.

"People learn by doing," Azef admonished him sternly. "No one gets the right experience all at once."

Savinkov made a final attempt to argue, saying that because the Combat Organization was now too weak to mount an act of "central" terror, they should focus on a smaller-scale target, like Kleygels.

But Azef would have none of it. "What are you saying to me?" he objected: "What do you mean we don't have the forces to kill Plehve? Pokotilov's death? . . . If there aren't enough people, we'll have to find them. If there's no dynamite, we'll have to make it. But we can never abandon the plan. Plehve will be killed in any case."

Azef's tirade chastened Savinkov and also inspired him in a way that he never forgot. Savinkov felt that Azef had breathed new life into him, and even years later, after Azef's incredible deceptions were revealed, Savinkov acknowledged this with a mix of wonder and admiration:

> Azef's persistence, calm, and self-assurance lifted the [Combat] organization's spirits, and it began to seem strange to me that I could have decided to end the attempt on Plehve . . . It would not be an exaggeration to say that Azef resurrected the organization, and we set out to kill Plehve with faith, determination, and without regard to the cost.

Azef also did not just limit himself to a pep talk. He gave Savinkov specific instructions about which members of the team were to go where and what their tasks would be, he recruited new members, and he involved himself in all the technical and tactical details of the preparations. He also conducted long and kindly discussions with Sazonov to revive his revolutionary fervor, which had been shaken by the failures.

But in secret, Azef continued to pursue his own agenda. At the same time that he was inspiring Savinkov and his team, he was badmouthing him to the other members of the SR Party for having botched the Saint Petersburg operation. Azef even cunningly tried to undermine Savinkov's own self-confidence by telling him that another Party member refused to join the Combat Organization because "Pokotilov perished as a result of the fact that you, Savinkov, abandoned him to his fate in Saint Petersburg and left." This was a devastating thing to hear. However, it allowed Azef to cow Savinkov and to maintain his supremacy in the organization even as he was motivating Savinkov to prepare a new attack on Plehve.

Azef had a more sinister goal as well: he now actually wanted Plehve killed. Despite his paradoxical indifference to politics and to systemic Russian anti-Semitism, Azef had a score to settle with Plehve specifically because he blamed him for the notorious Kishinyov pogrom in April 1903. A senior police official who also had no love for Plehve once witnessed how Azef "shook with rage and spoke about Plehve with hatred" when the subject of the pogrom came up.

As a result, Azef began to lie regularly to Rataev about the Combat Organization's immediate intentions. At the end of April 1904, he wrote to Rataev in vague terms about the explosion in the Northern Hotel that killed Pokotilov and pretended that he was not even sure if he had ever met the man. He also feigned ignorance of what had actually happened and suggested that the revolutionaries would not use explosives any longer. In May, Azef also misled Rataev about Sazonov, saying that he may be involved in a plot but provided no details. In late June, he lied again when he said that the Combat Organization was delaying a new attack on Plehve because they did not have any bombs and that it would take a long time to prepare new ones.

However, Azef had in fact already solved the Combat Organization's dynamite problem by helping Shveytser get access to a provincial government laboratory where he could secretly manufacture a new load of explosives. After a close call when a chemical reaction began to accelerate out of control before he managed to neutralize it, as a result of which he suffered several bad burns, Shveytser succeeded in producing forty pounds of dynamite. By June, he had recovered from his wounds in a hospital and brought the explosives to Saint Petersburg.

New Female Recruit

Even though women had taken part in revolutionary terrorism in Russia from its beginnings in the 1870s (Vera Zasulich shot Fyodor Trepov, the governor-general of Saint Petersburg, in 1878), it was still largely a male affair in the early twentieth century. But when Savinkov began to rebuild his team, he decided for the first time to add a woman who had been recommended to him. His decision was in keeping with the Socialist Revolutionary Party's commitment to an equitable restructuring of Russian society, and both the Party and even its Combat Organization were open to women, although they never made up more than 20 percent of the membership.

Savinkov's new recruit was Dora Brilliant, the daughter of a prosperous Jewish merchant from Kherson, a port on the Black Sea. Her parents, in keeping with their cultural traditions, had strenuously opposed allowing her to get an education, but she rebelled and managed to attend high school and then become a midwife. (Because the upbringing of Jewish women in Russia was usually more sheltered than the rest of the population, they had an even more difficult time finding occupations outside the traditional ones of marriage and family.) After participating in a student demonstration and being exiled to Poltava, a provincial city in what is now eastern Ukraine, Dora met Grigory Gershuni, the head of the Combat Organization. He produced such a powerful impression on her that she joined the Socialist Revolutionaries. All who knew her were struck by her commitment on the one hand and her strange, unvarying sadness on the other. A comrade who met her in Poltava remembered "her deeply-set, dark eyes, which expressed some sort of inconsolable melancholy and grief. Someone aptly said that the age-old sorrow of the Jewish people was expressed in them."

Savinkov proceeded slowly and deliberately before accepting Dora, and in June made a special trip to Kiev, where she was working on Socialist Revolutionary propaganda. From the first, she struck Savinkov as "a person who was fanatically devoted to the revolution," one who wanted, more than anything, to sacrifice herself for the Russian people.

Savinkov would learn the actual depth of her commitment later, in Saint Petersburg, during a conversation that he never forgot. They were by the shore on one of the outlying islands and sitting under pine trees that sighed in the light breeze. It was a warm and sunny day. Snatches of cheerful tunes from an orchestra drifted in from a distance, couples in light summer attire strolled past. The contrast between the setting and her words could not have been more stark.

"You know, somebody has to go . . . ," she began. "It's necessary to kill. It's better that it be me. Oh, how much better . . . I want to die," she added. "You don't know how much I want to die. I can't live like this and I can't live any other way. I can't live every day and think about how to kill . . . What torture, what torture . . . Better right away . . . Let me die . . . Let me . . ."

Some moments pass as Dora traces designs in the sand with the tip of her parasol. "Just think," she continues, "we kill . . . It may be the enemy. But we still kill. Of course, we have to kill. Blood is necessary. Yes, it's necessary . . . But let me die too. Don't torture me—let me."

Savinkov understood that she would never be able to reconcile her conscience with the need to kill, but she was committed to spilling blood nonetheless. Terror was the burden that she yearned to bear, and her own death would be the atonement for her sin.

Although Savinkov let Brilliant join his team, he would never allow her to do what she wanted most. Despite his revolutionary political program, Savinkov still felt he had to "protect" Brilliant because she was a woman. It was a form of chivalry, and was of a piece with his propriety, his buttoned-up manner, and his belief in old-fashioned virtues such as honor and loyalty.

Azef's Theatrical Plot

In April 1904, Azef gathered everyone in Kharkov to go over plans for the attack on Plehve. He announced that there would be several new members on the team, including Yegor Dulebov, an experienced terrorist who had killed a provincial governor the previous year. He would join Matseyevsky and Kalyaev in stalking Plehve using the proven camouflage of cigarette peddlers and cabbies.

But the others would do something quite unprecedented. Azef's idea was to go beyond the individual disguises of people who tried to blend in on the streets and to stage an elaborate group charade that would still hide the participants in plain view. It was as if he wanted to involve the entire team in an elaborately theatricalized plot like the one he was living himself. Had he given a title to this new production, it could have been "The Rich Couple."

The idea was that Savinkov would play the role of a wealthy foreign businessman and rent an expensive apartment in the center of Saint Petersburg. Dora Brilliant would live with him as his mistress and assume the disguise of a former singer in the city's popular Bouffe theater, which was famous for its operettas, variety acts, and other light fare. It is hard to imagine a role less suited to her character.

Sazonov would be their lackey, and Praskovya Ivanovskaya, an older revolutionary whose career began in the 1880s, would be the cook. Initially, Azef wanted Savinkov to buy an automobile that would be used to make the attack on Plehve and to have Borishansky train as a chauffeur, but gave up the idea when Savinkov objected that this could draw the attention of the police. Automobiles were expensive as well as rare in Russia in 1904, even in Saint Petersburg, where horse-drawn transportation would dominate for years to come and anyone driving around in a private car would stand out.

Onstage

When they got to Saint Petersburg, Savinkov and the others settled into a grandly proportioned, high-ceilinged, and fully furnished but run-down apartment at 30 Zhukovsky Street, in which electric chandeliers, large mirrors, and oil paintings hung cheek by jowl with artificial flowers, dirty carpets, and stained wallpaper. It had just been vacated by two generals who left for the war in Manchuria and was only a fifteen-minute walk from Okhrana headquarters.

Once the terrorists had their stage, they entered into their roles with the same attention to realistic detail that had recently come into vogue at the celebrated Moscow Art Theater under Konstantin Stanislavsky and Vladimir Nemirovich-Danchenko. The duo's staging of Chekhov's plays in particular would revolutionize acting in the twentieth century throughout the world. And it is a bizarre coincidence that terrorism, which depended on spectacular public, "theatrical" effects to achieve its political aims, used some of the same techniques for creating verisimilitude as contemporary revolutionary theatrical practices.

Savinkov assumed the disguise of an Englishman, "George McCullough." It is a testament to his daring while "onstage"—if not his foolhardiness—that he chose to impersonate a citizen of a nation whose language he could not speak. Passing as a courtly Pole or Frenchman (his Polish was native and he spoke French fluently with an excellent accent) would have been easy for him. But he appeared to prefer the cachet of understated self-assurance that was associated with Great Britain in the popular mind and that might prove off-putting to the average curious official or policeman. It is also likely that this kind of persona appealed to his vanity.

The business Savinkov pretended to pursue was importing bicycles into Russia, and every morning he received catalogs in the mail from English, French, and German companies which he made a point of displaying in the apartment. He also "went to work" every morning, which entailed, as it did for the entire team, tracking Plehve's movements around the city.

Savinkov's disguise worked very well, judging by the fact that when Ivanovskaya, the team's "cook," first ran into him by accident, she did not think he looked Russian "at all." What she saw instead was an impeccably dressed and polished foreign gentleman who even spoke Russian with an accent. She did not find him attractive initially because of his narrow brown eyes, balding head, small moustache, and what she described as his "weak" chest. She also did not care for his expression of "aristocratic haughtiness." For his part, Savinkov was also completely taken in by Ivanovskaya's lower-class disguise during their first encounter.

But later, as Ivanovskaya got to know Savinkov, his charisma won her over. And when she managed to peer behind his public façade, she saw "in him, deep inside, some sort of fine-spun 'something' that elicited a great deal of interest, deep loyalty, and love for his gifted nature." Savinkov became for her a "new representative of the young generation" of revolutionaries, radically different from her own, and a new kind of person—someone who had "dismantled and overturned previous values and who put his individuality boldly and sharply in the foreground."

Although the differences in personality and character could not have been greater among Savinkov and his comrades, the nature of their work and the intensity of their ties would lead Sazonov to claim that "the word 'brother' does not express sufficiently strongly the essence of our relations." Savinkov agreed, finding that their bond eliminated the distinctions between veterans and novices, working-class and educated comrades. In a sense, it was a model of the future socialist state of which they all dreamed.

Savinkov also believed that this sense of connection inspired Brilliant's demanding performance as the plot developed, which required her to act a role that was completely alien to her—a rich man's kept woman. Elegantly dressed and wearing an extravagantly plumed hat, she went shopping accompanied by her "lackey" Sazonov, blending easily with the cosmopolitan crowds in the fancy stores on Nevsky Prospect and other major thoroughfares. At home, she fended off the pandering landlady's attempts to find her a more generous patron by explaining that she lived with "the Englishman" out of love.

In fact, however, the deep sorrow that struck Savinkov when they first met had not left her big, almond-shaped eyes, which transfixed interlocutors and made passersby stare. This added to her success in playing the part of an alluring object of desire, despite the irregularity of the features on her small, mobile, nervous face.

It was easier for Sazonov to play his part. Like Brilliant, he conceived terrorism as a personal exploit and a sacrifice; he was also convinced that Plehve's death was necessary for Russia, for the revolution, and for the triumph of socialism. Unlike Brilliant, however, he faced his future sacrifice calmly and happily. He was also tall and strong, with sparkling eyes and pink cheeks radiating health, and easily made friends with the doorman and custodians. His good looks allowed him to win the hearts of a number of chambermaids and thereby become privy to all the local gossip, which helped ensure the team's security.

In her role as cook, Ivanovskaya was also in a good position to learn if the team had raised any suspicions among the other tenants or the police. She established cordial relations with the building's senior custodian and his wife and began to treat him to coffee every morning in the apartment's kitchen so that they could chat. Ivanovskaya's life had been difficult, and she had spent much of it in prisons and exile. But despite her infirmities and advanced age (at fifty-two, she was old by the standards of the time), she managed to learn the intricacies of her new profession by imitating cooks from wealthy households when she saw them buying provisions in the better food shops. Her age also led her to assume a maternal role toward the other members of the team, who were mostly in their twenties. It was not in her nature to be very demonstrative—to speak kindly, to console, to approve, to speculate about the future—but Savinkov sensed that she held them all in deep affection.

If at First You Don't Succeed

Within a few weeks, Matseyevsky, Dulebov, and Kalyaev had successfully tracked Plehve and knew where he would be vulnerable. Kalyaev was especially diligent: he would hoist his peddler's tray onto his shoulders at eight in the morning and wander about the center of the city, watching, until late at night. He got so good at recognizing Plehve's carriage that he could pick it out of the thick stream of other carriages without fail from a hundred paces. He could even tell from the way police officers on duty were behaving at a particular location if Plehve's carriage had just passed or was shortly expected.

Even though Savinkov had known Kalyaev since childhood and they had already been through much together, as they were finalizing the attack against Plehve Savinkov was struck anew by how Kalyaev's revolutionary zeal seemed to be part of something bigger. Kalyaev's latest passion was the poetry of the then famous "symbolists" and "decadents," as they were called—Valery Bryusov, Konstantin Balmont, and Alexander Blok—who aestheticized life or strived to communicate the mysterious and mystical dimensions of existence. Poets such as these were hardly popular in radical political circles, where tastes generally ran to civic and revolutionary verse, but Kalyaev saw them as daring artistic rebels with whom he shared something important.

Savinkov also understood more fully the degree to which faith had come to define the core of Kalyaev's being: "his love for art and the revolution were illuminated by one and the same fire—his unconscious, humble, but deep and strong religious feeling." And terrorism for Kalyaev "was not just the best possible form of political struggle, but a moral, perhaps even a religious, sacrifice." Kalyaev tried to rationalize his commitment by openly invoking John 15:13: "No one has greater love than to give up one's life for one's friends." But like Dora Brilliant, Kalyaev could not overcome the sense of sinfulness that came from realizing that the difference between him and Christ was that Christ did not kill.

There was now enough information about Plehve's routine to set the date of the attack. At a series of meetings, Savinkov and other members of the team again went over the plan with Azef, who continued to be the calm voice of cold-blooded pragmatism, and chose Thursday, July 8, 1904. Since Dora Brilliant still insisted on participating, Savinkov also consulted about her role. Azef replied that he saw no principled reason why a woman, and especially a committed one like Brilliant, should not be allowed to throw a bomb. Sazonov and Shveytser agreed. But Savinkov objected vehemently, saying that he believed a woman should not be allowed to participate in a terrorist act unless the Combat Organization could not proceed without her. He also added that his mother would never forgive him if he agreed to let a woman do what was a man's duty. Either because Azef was not indifferent to such a sentimental argument, or because it would be easier to let Savinkov have his way as the director of the attack, Azef let him exclude Brilliant.

And then, shortly after the meeting and when everything seemed settled, Savinkov suddenly decided that he was short a pair of hands. Considering the amount of time he spent fine-tuning the plan with Azef and the size of his existing team, this seems very odd. Without counting Savinkov himself, there were six men and two women in Saint Petersburg, including three bomb throwers. Why one of the male watchers, or Savinkov for that matter, could not have assumed an expanded or additional role remains unclear. Savinkov was not only still making things up as he went along, but because of either inexperience or self-doubt, or both, he was not thinking very clearly.

Moreover, Savinkov's choice seems incomprehensible. Perhaps he believed that since revolutionary zeal had been enough for him to become a terrorist, it would be enough for anyone.

Shimel-Leyba Vulfovich Sikorsky was a twenty-year-old tanner from Bialystok, a small city with a majority Jewish population in what is now eastern Poland. Younger-looking than his age because he was beardless, Sikorsky arrived in Saint Petersburg on July 5, just three days before the scheduled attack. He was a member of the Socialist Revolutionary Party but had no relevant experience. He also spoke Russian badly and did not know his way around the city. However, he had long wanted to participate in an attack on Plehve, which he considered a great honor. Borishansky, a member of the team, vouched for him and took him under his wing, bought him a cloak so that he could conceal a bomb under it, gave him advice, and showed him exactly where he was to dispose of his bomb if the attack failed. Savinkov judged Sikorsky to be a stalwart and courageous young man and was touched by his naïveté.

A Stumble

How the attack actually unfolded resembles a comedy of errors or a farce, albeit with a dark bass note throbbing below the stumbles.

The location chosen for the attempt was near the Baltic Station in the southwestern quarter of Saint Petersburg. On July 8, as was his habit, Plehve would take the 10 A.M. train to Tsarskoye Selo, Nicholas II's magnificent summer palace an hour south of the city that had originally been built for Empress Catherine the Great in the eighteenth century.

Shveytser spent the entire night of July 7 arming four bombs in his room in the first-class Grand Hotel.

Earlier that same day, Azef sent Rataev a regular report from Vilnius, where he had arranged to meet with members of Savinkov's team after their attack. He described in detail the Socialist Revolutionary Party's plans for a conference in Moscow in August and the various organizational and policy matters that were on the agenda for discussion. He also asked for money. However, he did not breathe a word about the plot against Plehve.

On the morning of July 8, Dulebov used his horse-drawn cab to pick up Shveytser, who carried the bombs in a small suitcase. Dulebov drove him to the drop-off points near the Baltic Station, where the four throwers were supposed to be waiting.

But Kalyaev was the only member of the four-man team in his assigned place with a bomb, and he could not risk making the attack alone. The entire plan had disintegrated because of a series of misunderstandings and mistakes, as a result of which members of the team gave up when they could not see one another at the specified time and where they were supposed to be.

Despite some bitter recriminations among the members, Savinkov concluded that the plan was basically sound and that they would try again a week later.

First Blood

On Thursday morning, July 15, which was uncharacteristically bright and sunny, the team went into action again. On this occasion Shveytser distributed the four bombs successfully to the throwers; they were also on time and at their specified locations several streets north of the Baltic Station, near the Imperial Mariinsky Theater, famous for its ballet and opera.

Sazonov, the designated first thrower, was dressed in the brass-buttoned uniform of a railway worker and got the biggest bomb—twelve pounds, cylindrically shaped, wrapped in newsprint and tied with a cord. It looked like any other everyday package, and he carried it openly. Shveytser had made it twice as big as the others because the Russian chemicals he used when manufacturing the dynamite were not as refined as those from Western Europe, and, as a result, the power of the explosive was weaker.

Kalyaev, wearing a doorman's cap trimmed with gold braid, had a bomb wrapped in a kerchief and carried it in the open as well. Borishansky and Sikorsky wore regular street clothes and hid their bombs under their cloaks.

Timing their approach and keeping forty paces apart to reduce the risk that an accidental explosion of one bomb could set off the others, the four made their way to Izmailovsky Prospect, down which Plehve would approach the train station. They spread themselves out over a distance of several hundred yards, with Borishansky at the far northern end. Plehve's carriage would pass him first on the way toward the other throwers, who were closer to the station. Borishansky's assignment was to attack if they failed and Plehve tried to escape via the way he had come.

Savinkov followed the men at a distance. He was walking down the same stretch of Izmailovsky Prospect when he noticed a police officer on a corner pull himself together and snap to attention.

Further down the street Sazonov bobbed into view, his head raised high, holding the heavy bomb awkwardly in the crook of his right arm. The sidewalk around him was filled with people.

Then Savinkov heard a loud trotting noise coming from behind. A carriage pulled by a pair of black horses sped by with a detective seated on the rear box. Following close behind was a one-horse cab with two more detectives.

As the carriage passed him, Savinkov looked back toward Sazonov, but he was no longer visible because of the crowds. Savinkov guessed that by now he must be in front of the Warsaw Hotel on Izmailovsky Prospect.

Plehve's carriage disappeared in the traffic. Several interminably long seconds passed.

Suddenly, the regular clamor of the street was shattered by a strange noise like a massive clang, as if someone had struck a giant cast-iron plate with a sledgehammer. This was followed by the plaintive tinkling of broken window glass. Savinkov saw a narrow funnel of yellowish-gray smoke edged with black surge upward from the far end of the street. The smoke quickly rose as high as the fifth floor of the surrounding buildings and mushroomed over the entire area. After a few seconds it dissipated.

Savinkov had been expecting the explosion, but it still took his breath away. He ran down the street in a daze. When he got to the location in front of the Warsaw Hotel's entrance, all he could see was the wheeled chassis of the carriage. The enclosed cab was gone. The wounded horses were galloping away, and there was a smell of burning in the air.

Sazonov was lying in the street a few paces from the sidewalk with his left hand pressed into the cobblestones. His face was pale, his eyes were half closed, and there were streaks of blood on his forehead and cheeks. A large crimson pool had formed by his legs and there was a dark stain on his stomach.

Savinkov peered into Sazonov's face for several long moments without understanding. He heard someone's voice behind him ask, "What about the minister? They say that the minister got away."

Neither then nor for several hours afterward could Savinkov fully grasp what had happened. The shock was too great. He had never seen a bomb explode before; he had never seen the bleeding body of a comrade with whom he had spoken minutes earlier.

In his confusion, Savinkov got it all backward and concluded that Sazonov had been killed but Plehve had escaped. A police officer, his face pale, his jaw trembling, waved Savinkov away weakly with his white-gloved hands: "Leave . . . Mister, leave . . ."

Savinkov started to walk toward the train station. Crowds of stonemasons in dust-covered aprons and other people yelling something were running up the street and on the sidewalk.

Savinkov's mental eclipse prevented him from noticing Plehve's mutilated corpse and fragments of his coach several paces from where Sazonov was lying. He also did not realize that Sazonov was still alive.

For some time, Savinkov wandered the area until he came to Dulebov's cab parked a few streets away. He got into it and told Dulebov that Plehve was alive but that Sazonov had been killed. Dulebov dropped his gaze; his cheeks began to shake as if he was about to start sobbing.

And then, remarkably, Savinkov and Dulebov started making plans to renew the attack on Plehve that same day between three and four in the afternoon, when he was scheduled to return from Tsarskoye Selo. Savinkov decided that this time he and Dulebov would be throwers together with any other members of the team who were still alive.

⚬━┼━⚬

This decision says a great deal about Savinkov's tenacity and about the inertial force of the decision with which he had lived for weeks. But it also underscores the shock that extreme violence can cause to the neophyte perpetrator. For how could Savinkov have expected Plehve to follow an established routine and not take extraordinary new precautions if he escaped a terrorist attack earlier the same day? How could Savinkov have imagined that the police would not be swarming over the area where the bomb had detonated and looking for any traces of the perpetrators? How could he not have checked to see if Sazonov was still alive?

Savinkov's recollection of his mental state after the attempt also reveals his exceptional honesty. In his memoir about the event, he makes absolutely no excuses for his blindness and does not allow himself the slightest self-aggrandizement. In this regard, the memoir in which he describes the horrific event is also a grotesque lesson in humility.

⚬━┼━⚬

Still in his overwhelmed state and hoping that some of the other throwers had survived, Savinkov went to the gathering point in Yusupov Garden, an oasis of green in the middle of the noisy city, where the team had agreed to meet in case the attempt failed. But no one was there. As Savinkov would find out later, Kalyaev and Borishansky saw what happened to Plehve, realized that their bombs were no longer necessary, and, following protocol, got rid of them by dropping them into ponds in other parks they had scouted before, after which they promptly took trains out of the city.

The only thrower who failed to do this was the novice Sikorsky. He acted "as we might have expected," Savinkov commented ruefully later, thus also admitting his mistake about letting Sikorsky participate. Instead of disposing of his bomb surreptitiously where he had been instructed near the secluded Petrovsky Park, and where Borishansky had actually taken him to ensure that he would do it properly, Sikorsky did something absurd. He hired a rowboat on the Neva and, in full view of the boatman, dumped his bomb in the river. Making matters even worse was that he chose a location near a battleship that was under construction. When the incredulous boatman asked him what he was doing, Sikorsky silently offered him 10 rubles, in response to which the boatman immediately took him off to the local police station. Sikorsky was so bewildered that he neither resisted nor attempted to escape.

Savinkov remained in a state of shock until the afternoon, when he was finally jolted out of it. He had booked a private room in the luxurious Central Bath House to give himself a place to spend time unobserved and rest, and left it at 2 P.M. to find Shveytser and prepare for the new attack. But this too is evidence of Savinkov's confusion, because he had forgotten that the team had agreed to "drown" unused bombs after a failed attempt and that Shveytser did not have any left. Only when Savinkov mechanically bought a newspaper on the street, thinking that it had news about the war in Manchuria, did he see on the front page a photograph of Plehve surrounded by a black band and his obituary.

⚬═╋═⚬

In Sazonov's eyes, the attack went exactly as planned. He first saw Plehve's carriage approaching when it was a considerable distance away. Despite the large number of uniformed police officers stationed along Izmailovsky Prospect, as well as officers in plain clothes feigning nonchalance on the sidewalk, Sazonov was able to get within eight paces of the carriage. He noticed with relief that there were no pedestrians or cabs nearby.

The minister's fleshy face was clearly visible through the window. As Sazonov rapidly approached, Plehve noticed him and leaned forward, his eyes opened wide. Feeling a surge of elation because his dream was about to be fulfilled, Sazonov drew back his right arm smoothly and hurled the heavy bomb straight at the glass.

He did not remember the explosion itself. When he came to, he was lying in the street, and his first reaction was surprise that he was still alive. He tried to raise himself up on one arm, and although his vision was clouded, he could see a general's uniform coat and something else lying on the ground nearby; the carriage and the horses were gone. Sazonov realized that he had succeeded in killing Plehve and shouted, "Down with autocracy, long live the Combat Organization!"

Sazonov could feel that he was badly injured. Fearing that he might reveal secrets about the Combat Organization to the police, he tried to pull out the revolver he had in his pocket so that he could shoot himself, but he was too weak. Then the police ran up and began to beat him. More guards joined in and hauled him into the Warsaw Hotel. Some pummeled him while others spat in his eyes and face, demanding, "Where's the other bomb?"

Sazonov was operated on that same day in a hospital for workingmen with Minister of Justice Nikolay Muravyov in attendance. His eyesight was damaged and his eardrums had been ruptured by the blast; there was a nearly fatal wound on the right side of his abdomen; his left foot was shattered. For several days he was delirious. Police agents disguised as doctors kept trying to ferret information out of him, but he kept to the SR Party policy of denying the authorities anything they could find useful and refused even to reveal his own name at first. All he said was that he had carried out the Combat Organization's death sentence against Plehve for the crimes he had committed against the Russian people.

The police did not give up. To disorient Sazonov and to excite him so that he would lose self-control, they kept waking him up as soon as he fell asleep. They insisted that Sikorsky—"the little Jew," as they referred to him—had already told them everything. They also tried to rattle Sazonov by exploiting the bits of information he revealed in his delirium. Police scribes sat by his bed and produced a detailed transcript of everything he said; it includes his whispered recitation of the Lord's Prayer.

Especially tormenting for Sazonov was the police claim that there were other victims of his bomb, an old woman and her two-year-old granddaughter. Seeing how this upset Sazonov, the police brought him to utter despair by telling him that after his bomb had gone off and he had lost consciousness, one of his comrades accidentally dropped a bomb in a crowd and killed an additional thirty-nine innocent bystanders. The last claim was a lie, although Sazonov would not know it until later. According to one source, the only other victims in addition to Plehve were his coachman and a police captain who was slightly wounded;

according to another, several more people were hurt. Sazonov was prepared to die in the attack, and his reason for getting as close as possible to Plehve's carriage with no one else nearby was to minimize any chance of accidental victims.

⌘

Azef was in Warsaw with the old revolutionary Ivanovskaya on July 15, waiting anxiously for word from Saint Petersburg. Around 1 P.M., as they were strolling along one the city's grand main thoroughfares, they saw newsboys running and shouting something in their high-pitched voices about a bomb that had been thrown at a minister's carriage. A few moments later, another group of newsboys ran by with freshly printed sheets prominently displaying the words "Zamordowano Plewego." Neither Azef nor Ivanovskaya knew Polish well enough to be sure that "zamordowano" meant "killed" and not "wounded," so he went to a local newspaper office to find out.

"The matter was carried out cleanly," he told her when he came back.

It seemed to Ivanovskaya that the two Polish words were being repeated by people everywhere around them. People hurried through the city holding copies of the announcement, their faces shining with joy; shopkeepers stuck big sheets of paper in their windows with the two words in large black letters.

On Friday, July 16, Savinkov came to Warsaw, and Ivanovskaya went to meet him by herself. Azef had unexpectedly decided to leave the city the same day, claiming that he had noticed police spies following him (always his alibi when he was playing his Combat Organization role).

He had done everything he could to ensure Plehve's death, but the news that he actually succeeded still shocked him. He was also worried about explaining to his Okhrana paymasters how the assassination could have happened without his knowledge. But luck continued to favor Azef, and the Okhrana never even investigated him. In fact, in an ironic twist, the head of the Warsaw section of the Okhrana concluded that if Azef did not know about the plot against Plehve, it must have been because the terrorist conspiracy was too good to penetrate.

When Ivanovskaya first saw Savinkov, she was not sure that she recognized him because of how much he had changed in just a few days. His deathly pale face looked the same and yet different—"like a landscape after a flood," as she put it, and she thought she saw on it the "incompletely assimilated horror that filled his soul." It would be several more days before Savinkov learned that Sazonov had in fact survived.

The joy at Plehve's death that Azef and Ivanovskaya witnessed in Warsaw, where traditional anti-Russian feeling fueled the reaction, also spread through the rest of the empire. Predictably, the revolutionaries were ecstatic, whereas many figures in the imperial establishment were appalled. So were newspapers around the world, which published lead stories condemning the assassination the same day it occurred. But according to an eyewitness, some average passersby on Moscow's streets were seen congratulating each other on July 16 as if "news of a great victory in the war had arrived" (a bitterly ironic remark, given that the actual war with Japan was going very badly).

Even some prominent individuals who were far from radical circles expressed satisfaction and relief. In Saint Petersburg, members at a meeting of the liberal Constitutional Democratic Party broke into spontaneous applause when they heard the news. Count Sergey Witte, a senior government minister, could hardly conceal his pleasure and was reported to have said that the slain coachman deserved public sympathy more than Plehve. Alexey Lopukhin, the director of police who had been appointed by Plehve, complained that the minister had been "stifling everybody." Countess Sofia Sukhotin-Tolstoy, the oldest daughter of the world-famous writer who had become a leading pacifist in his later years, noted that "It is difficult not to be happy because of this." And when at the end of July Savinkov's mother made another one of her emergency trips to Saint Petersburg to intercede with Count Pavel Kutaysov, the governor-general of Irkutsk, because of a new complication in Alexander's sentence, she was shocked to hear him refer to Plehve as a "blackguard."

The Bomb's Echoes

Sazonov fully expected to be sentenced to death. However, on July 30, Empress Alexandra finally gave birth to a son after having four daughters, and in celebration of his new heir Nicholas II issued a manifesto banning the death penalty and corporal punishment. Widespread discontent with the disastrous war in the east had also tilted Nicholas away from the repression he normally preferred and toward conciliation.

In keeping with his new mood, Nicholas appointed Prince Pyotr Svyatopolk-Mirsky, a liberal and an opponent of Plehve's policies, as the new minister of the interior, with a mandate to make concessions to public opinion and to heal the divide between the imperial regime and society. Svyatopolk-Mirsky quickly went to work to win public support with a series of reforms affecting the judiciary, censorship, and religious minorities, including Jews. He succeeded to such an extent that initially some thought a new age was dawning in Russia. With Svyatopolk-Mirsky's approval, in November 1904 representatives of the grassroots *zemstvo* civic organizations met in Saint Petersburg and passed resolutions calling for a constitution and a parliament for the first time in modern Russian history.

Sazonov's bomb had in fact moved the empire and seemed to validate the key element of the Socialist Revolutionaries' tactics. Even colonel of the gendarmes Alexander Spiridovich, who had captured the first head of the Combat Organization, Grigory Gershuni, and who would later command the tsar's palace guard, admitted that the assassination proved that the terrorists' tactic worked.

<hr>

When Sazonov and Sikorsky were put on joint trial in November 1904, their defense attorney announced that Sazonov's bomb was "filled not with dynamite, but with the tears and sufferings of the entire Russian people." In the new, more liberal climate under Svyatopolk-Mirsky the court was receptive, and, as a result, Sazonov was sentenced to life at hard labor and Sikorsky to twenty years. The following year their sentences were reduced in connection with a manifesto that Nicholas II had been forced to issue in an attempt to quell what would become known as the 1905 Revolution.

In the letters Sazonov sent to his family from Siberia, he continued to profess his belief in God and his conviction that socialists, and not Christian churches, were the true followers of Christ's teaching. But even though he insisted that he would never have committed a terrorist act out of personal vengeance and that he killed Plehve for the good of the Russian people—that he acted selflessly, in imitation of Christ—he could never reconcile what he did with Christ's cardinal teaching about forgiving one's enemies. When speaking with Savinkov before the attack, he said that he expected to feel "pride and joy" after killing Plehve.

Later, in a letter from Siberia, he wrote that *"the consciousness of my sin never left me."* Savinkov would revere Sazonov to the end of his own life. He also acknowledged that he had learned the feeling of sinfulness from Sazonov, and that this surprised him because he had not expected it.

In 1910, Sazonov committed suicide in a Siberian prison camp as a protest against the administration's abusive treatment. He explained that he wanted to sacrifice himself in order to prevent other prisoners from doing the same. Sikorsky's fate after his sentencing is unknown.

On Leave

After Warsaw, Savinkov traveled to Socialist Revolutionary Party headquarters in Geneva, where the leadership greeted him with open arms in an atmosphere of joyful celebration. Gots's condition had deteriorated even more, but he listened with rapt attention, his eyes shining, as Savinkov described the details of the attack on Plehve. During this visit, Savinkov became closer to Gots than ever before, and began to think of him not just as a "comrade—he was a friend and a brother."

The SR Party felt newly empowered. It was skeptical that Svyatopolk-Mirsky's appointment would make much difference, but it was clear that killing Plehve had played "a major role" in "shaking" the regime and in making Russian society speak more boldly about change. Azef's and the Combat Organization's reputations soared, money poured in from donors, and volunteers clamored to join.

With Azef's approval, and after consultations with Shveytser and Kalyaev, Savinkov drafted the Combat Organization's code of regulations, which was adopted by the Party in August 1904. Its most important provision was the preservation of the Combat Organization's operational autonomy from the Party's "civilian" control, something that a number of Party members tried to introduce to curtail the terrorists' growing status as the organization's elite. Savinkov was also made Azef's second-in-command.

With these administrative matters settled, Savinkov and several others left for Paris, where Shveytser had set up a dynamite laboratory and workshop in a rented apartment. Helping him were Brilliant, who had now been trained in explosives by Azef, and his younger brother Vladimir, a chemist by profession who was kept ignorant of his brother's machinations.

Shveytser's respectable neighbors in the tony Grenelle quarter of the 15th Arrondissement just south of the Eiffel Tower and the Champ-de-Mars could never have imagined what the self-possessed young Russian and his two friends were up to, or why Savinkov, Kalyaev, Dulebov, Borishansky, and Moiseyenko kept coming and going from his apartment. The chemicals they used to make the explosives for their bombs had a strong, sharp smell resembling almonds. People reacted differently to this; in some cases, such as Savinkov's, the effect could be overwhelming and cause severe migraines and even vomiting if inhaled for a period of time. Technicians always had to keep windows open or use fireplace flues to let the fumes escape. One wonders what Shveytser and the others did to keep the smell from being noticed by their neighbors, or how they camouflaged or explained it.

The Warmth of Azef

The violent goals the terrorists pursued did not prevent them from enjoying Paris or one another's company. Some fifteen or twenty minutes away by cab from Shveytser's apartment was the apartment Azef shared with his wife on rue de la Glacière in the 13th Arrondissement. (The Russian Embassy at 79 rue de Grenelle in the 7th was also a short cab ride from the terrorists' apartment, which would have been convenient for Azef when he needed to meet Rataev.) Lyubov was a naïve and friendly woman who had married Azef when he was still a student, who believed totally in his importance as a revolutionary leader, and who had no idea about his duplicitous game. Together, the Azefs cultivated an atmosphere of warm and friendly domesticity with members of the Combat Organization, whom they treated like close friends, hosting convivial gatherings, showing favorite places in the city, and offering such practical help as finding lodgings.

The more Savinkov interacted and worked with Azef, the more he was drawn to him, not only as a wise tactician but as a close friend. Despite his clumsy manner, Azef was both cunning and skillful at playing on others' feelings. He was also able to exploit Savinkov's penchant for forging intense emotional bonds with his "frontline" comrades—those with whom he believed he had shared life-threatening danger.

As time went on and Savinkov's life became more entwined with the Combat Organization, these bonds began to include the terrorists' families. In a letter to Savinkov from early 1905 that deals with Party business, Azef adds a warm personal message to Savinkov's wife—"I kiss and greet Vera Glebovna"; he also passes on regards from his own wife. Later the same year, in a sign of increasing intimacy, Azef decides to switch from the polite plural to the familiar singular Russian form of address in a letter to Savinkov—from "vy" to "ty," like the French "vous" and "tu." Eventually, Savinkov and Vera start to write joint letters to Azef, revealing that even though she was not directly involved in her husband's terrorist activities, at some point she not only met but got to know Azef (perhaps during or after the campaign against Plehve in Saint Petersburg).

There is no doubt that Savinkov took these relations at face value. But is it possible that Azef also felt a genuine attachment to him? Perhaps at times and within very circumscribed limits. In light of what would eventually become known about Azef, it is hard to imagine anything that would have prevented him from sacrificing Savinkov or anyone else if he believed it would save him from the police or the revolutionaries, or if a profit and loss calculation demanded it.

Not everyone was so blinded, however, and during the period of Azef's ascendancy some in the Combat Organization had disquieting suspicions. Praskovya Ivanovskaya, the member of Savinkov's team who had masqueraded as his cook in Saint Petersburg and was also in Paris, once caught a revealing glimpse of Azef in a moment of indecision and fear.

She had come to his apartment on party business shortly after Plehve's assassination and accidentally looked into his bedroom. It was an unguarded moment, and at the time she did not understand what was happening to him: Azef was lying on a wide bed, half-dressed, his obese body "quivering like a vibrating bog," as she put it, his eyes jumping around the room, and his flaccid, sweating face contorted by an expression of fear, "like that of a dog that was being beaten." It turned out that he was terrified at the prospect of having to return to Russia on SR business in the near future. Ivanovskaya would subsequently also learn that just before she glimpsed him, he had implored his wife to abandon everything and flee with him to the United States to prevent his imminent unmasking and ruin. But the danger passed, Azef reverted to his old roles, and his star remained undimmed among the Party's leaders.

As far as Savinkov was concerned, the successful attack on Plehve allayed any doubts he had had about the strange changes in Azef's behavior during the past year with regard to the plot, when he shifted from being passive to aggressively active.

CHAPTER THREE

THE GRAND DUKE

In the fall of 1904, leaders of the Socialist Revolutionary Party began to hold meetings in Paris to plan their next steps. Emboldened by the attack on Plehve, and convinced that Russia was on the verge of a revolution and that more assassinations would help fuel the fire, they sentenced to death the governors general of the three most important cities—Saint Petersburg, Moscow, and Kiev. All three were judged to be deeply complicit in the regime's crimes against its subjects.

The Okhrana knew nothing about the plans, however. Azef concealed them from Rataev even though he continued to send him a steady flow of messages about the Party's activities and in October visited him a number of times in his Paris office. Instead, he invented that the Combat Organization was preparing an attack on Nicholas II during his forthcoming visit to Odessa, the major port on the Black Sea. "For me there is no doubt about this," he wrote, presumably to divert Rataev's gaze from the real plans and simultaneously to play into the Okhrana's worst fears. But to keep his police employers happy, Azef did betray several Party members, including Chernov's brother-in-law. In this and in similar instances, the SRs ascribed their losses to the competence of the police and, unfortunately, the high cost of waging war.

On September 1, in a letter from Geneva, Azef mentioned Boris Savinkov to Rataev for the first time, although he referred to him by one of his conspiratorial name-and-patronymic combinations—"Pavel Ivanovich." He explained that the man had recently arrived from Saint Petersburg but then added some smoke by saying that "It's difficult to figure out what his role is . . . in any event, he's a big shot." Later that month Azef actually went so far as to conceal Savinkov's identity by telling Rataev that "Pavel Ivanovich" does not have "quite the same physical characteristics" that police files showed for Boris Savinkov and asked for a photograph in order to determine if they are one and the same person.

Savinkov suspected nothing of this and continued to believe that he was a trusted second-in-command. He described his role in terms of positions on a warship, where Azef "held the post of ship's captain and I that of the first officer; it was I who communicated with all the comrades, had direct contacts with them, and was close friends with many. He . . . did not leave his cabin but gave orders through me, led the organization through me."

An Imperial Highness

Savinkov and his team—Ivan Kalyaev, Dora Brilliant, and Boris Moiseyenko—eagerly took on the assassination of Grand Duke Sergey Alexandrovich, who was both the tsar's uncle and his brother-in-law (they had married sisters), as well as the governor-general of Moscow. Azef participated in several planning sessions, provided members of the team with passports and money, and authorized Savinkov to add a fourth member, if necessary. After that he spent most of his time abroad.

By now Savinkov believed that he had sufficient experience to work out all the details of the plan by himself and in consultation with his team. Sergey was the most important target that the Combat Organization had ever chosen. He was protected by palace walls and scores of guards from the military and the police. But the success with Plehve made Savinkov and his team feel they had grown wings. They would use the same methods that had succeeded with Plehve.

⚬—✦—⚬

Grand Duke Sergey, a son of Emperor Alexander II, was one of the most influential members of the entire reactionary Romanov clan and thus, in the eyes of the Socialist Revolutionaries and other radicals, an embodiment of injustice. He had been appointed governor-general of Moscow in 1891 by his brother Alexander III and began his duties by brutally expelling the city's 20,000 Jews; moreover, he did so on Passover. He showed heartless indifference during the notorious Khodynka tragedy in 1896, when several thousand peasants and working-class Muscovites were trampled to death during the bungled coronation celebrations for Nicholas II.

He let police and Cossacks use bloody force to suppress dissent and to break up demonstrations in Moscow by protesting students and others. At the end of 1904, with the country in turmoil because of the disasters in the war with Japan and many groups demanding reform, Sergey urged his nephew Nicholas II to stand firm against change, leading the tsar to announce to his chief minister Witte: "I shall never, under any circumstances, agree to a representative form of government because I consider it harmful to the people whom God has entrusted to my care."

Not only revolutionaries but also liberals seethed at the mere mention of Sergey's name. He was even disliked by many members of his own family and by their numerous royal relations in Europe; indeed, one of the other Russian grand dukes summed him up as "a very poor officer . . . a complete ignoramus in administrative affairs . . . obstinate, arrogant, disagreeable." But Sergey's sense of his exalted rank immunized him from all criticism, and his appearance and manner were those of a martinet. Over six feet tall, very slim, handsome, with refined features, he imitated Prussian officers by wearing a corset to accentuate his figure and upright posture.

First Steps

In early November, Savinkov and the others set out from Paris, and using their counterfeit passports crossed the frontier into Russian Poland without any difficulty. They also successfully smuggled in a big load of dynamite—several dozen pounds hidden under their clothing—and an ample supply of money, despite the border guards who normally searched both luggage and passengers. The days of bomb-sniffing dogs were still in the future, but human error has always been around.

To preserve utmost secrecy, when they got off the Warsaw train at Moscow's Alexandrovsky Station, they did not contact any of the local Socialist Revolutionary Party members who could have provided information about the grand duke's routines and whereabouts. Savinkov decided that his team should not risk revealing its presence even to sympathizers who might be eager to help but who could also be under surveillance by the secret police.

When they first got to Moscow, Savinkov and his comrades did not know where Sergey lived. He had several palaces at his disposal, no home address was listed in the city directory, and with police spies everywhere, members of the team did not want to call attention to themselves by inquiring about him openly. The problem was solved by Moiseyenko.

Pretending to be a tourist, he went to the Kremlin, the famed giant fortress with crenelated walls and soaring towers that dominates the city center, and climbed to the top balcony of the sixteenth-century Ivan the Great Bell Tower. At over 300 feet, this was the second-tallest structure in Moscow and had unobstructed views over the entire low-lying city, in which most buildings at that time were only two or three stories high.

For a tip, the friendly tower guard agreed to show him the famous landmarks of what Russians called their country's "heart" and still honored as its "second capital," even two centuries after the nation's actual capital had been moved to Saint Petersburg. As Moiseyenko surveyed the vast cityscape before him, with its scores of golden church cupolas shimmering above an ocean of rooftops, the plumes of smoke from innumerable chimneys merging into a gray haze in the distance, and the curves of the Moscow River glinting like polished steel, he also casually inquired about the location of the governor-general's residence. The guard pointed to an imposing building on the city's main street and facing Tverskaya Square, less than a mile to the northwest. Sergey had taken up residence in the governor-general's palace itself.

Once the team knew where to start, they began to search for a place and time to carry out their attack. Using the Combat Organization's previous experience, Moiseyenko and Kalyaev decided to become cabbies, which would allow them to watch the grand duke's comings and goings freely in the streets.

Because heavy winter snowfall often made wheeled vehicles impractical, Moiseyenko and Kalyaev bought horse-drawn sleighs—the first, worn and shabby, with a nag to match; the second, more stylish, with a sturdy, well-groomed horse. Kalyaev was already a veteran of this game. Moiseyenko also picked up the skills quickly, so much so that he looked completely natural when he drove inside the Kremlin and parked near the giant Tsar Cannon, a famous historical relic and tourist attraction, without the police or guards paying him any attention. In those idyllic days, entry into the Kremlin was unrestricted.

Dora Brilliant, who had recently added bomb making to her repertoire of revolutionary skills, assumed the role of the team's chemist and technician. In

Moscow, she did not need the disguise of a vampish "kept woman" that she had used in Saint Petersburg and reverted to her actual appearance: she was small, demure, quiet, and insignificant-looking. But nothing had changed in her character, and her reticence and downcast gaze still concealed a fanatical devotion to the revolution and a martyr's yearning for self-sacrifice. As the stalking of the grand duke progressed, she stayed out of sight in a hotel near the Kremlin, withdrawing even more into herself, waiting patiently for the call to assemble the bombs.

Soon after the team began its surveillance, it became evident to Savinkov that two stalkers were not enough, and he decided to add a third person, as Azef had authorized. Savinkov's choice fell on Pyotr Kulikovsky, a former student at a teacher's college, who, although an SR Party member, had no previous experience in terrorism. Tall, with strikingly large and kindly eyes, he impressed Savinkov with his fervent desire to take part in a revolutionary assassination, even after Savinkov tried hard to talk him out of it.

One might have thought that Savinkov's sad experience with Shimel-Leyba Sikorsky during the campaign against Plehve just six months earlier would have made him wary of taking on a complete beginner once again. But either because he wanted to help train the next cohort of revolutionaries, or because he was always susceptible to the powerful emotional attachment that developed among those who stood shoulder to shoulder in the terrorist trenches, Savinkov decided to give him a chance. Kulikovsky took on the role of a vendor with a tray of sundries slung around his shoulders, which also allowed him to blend in on the streets and to walk about freely.

For himself, however, Savinkov took the opposite approach and hid in plain view, just as he had in Saint Petersburg. His papers, which had been donated by a sympathizer abroad, were genuine this time and again identified him as a rich Englishman, a certain "James Galley." Savinkov still had not learned English, but he moved about Moscow playing the role, relying on the rarity of English speakers and on his fluency in French.

Once again, Savinkov's appearance helped him pass. He now looked older than his years. He was pale, his brown hair was thinning in the front, and he sported a reddish-blond moustache. The somewhat Asian cast to his unsmiling eyes made him hard to place (the Okhrana described them as "Japanese, that is, almond-shaped"). To help keep the curious in check he deployed what he took to be an off-putting Anglo-Saxon mien—steely gaze, compressed lips, phlegmatic speech.

All this again came easily to Savinkov. His ability to transform himself into an unrecognizably "aloof Britisher" surprised a member of the SR Party who ran into him in Moscow by accident and who remembered him from previous encounters as a warm-hearted conversationalist capable of charming his companions when he wanted.

Another reason the role suited Savinkov was that he enjoyed living well. Donations to the Combat Organization increased after Plehve's assassination, and Savinkov spent money freely (thereby annoying some other members of the Socialist Revolutionary Party, who would call him to task about this before long). To ward off Moscow's freezing winter, and in keeping with the role of a rich foreigner who would naturally want to take advantage of Russia's world-famous luxury fur trade, Savinkov acquired an expensive fur coat with a magnificent beaver collar and matching hat.

Such behavior went beyond mere camouflage, however, and Savinkov appears to have reveled in his ability to perform a risky role with swagger. When he thought that a nobleman who was sympathetic to the Socialist Revolutionaries might provide information about the grand duke's schedule, Savinkov met him in Hermitage, one of Moscow's most fashionable restaurants. He was evidently gambling that his appearance and behavior would shield him from the Okhrana, despite their dossier on him, which included photographs. As additional insurance, he always carried a loaded revolver in his trouser pocket. And he appears to have kept in touch with Vera and possibly even risked visiting her and the children in Saint Petersburg, despite the restrictions that Azef had imposed.

The Most Russian of Cities

The difference between Moscow and Saint Petersburg was striking, and Baedeker's guide alerted visitors from abroad that Moscow—"the sacred city of the Russians" and "the heart of Russia"—was where "The characteristic life and tendencies of the people are seen in much greater purity . . . than in Saint Petersburg and are much less influenced by W. Europe, though even Moscow is rapidly becoming modernized of late years."

The difference is even reflected in the cities' geographies. Whereas Saint Petersburg's straight streets reflect how they were laid out by men with rulers and Enlightenment ideals starting in 1703, Moscow grew organically over eight centuries, like a tree adding rings. On a map it looks like a giant wheel with the Kremlin as its hub and the main boulevards radiating outward like spokes to a band of broad boulevards encircling the city's core. Moscow was Savinkov's favorite Russian city, and he embraced all its motley richness—its "Russian language, crooked side streets, ancient churches, squalor," and deep layers of history preserved in museums and other monuments.

The center of Moscow was a bustling place, and tracking Grand Duke Sergey's movements through the crowded and noisy streets required sharp-eyed attention. Steady streams of sleighs, carriages, wagons, and trams wended their way through the city, with an occasional automobile roaring past, leaving acrid exhaust and rearing, frightened horses in its wake. Warning shouts from coachmen blended with the tolling of bells from hundreds of churches to form Moscow's unique soundscape. Copious snowfall quickly turned into dun-colored mush because of the amounts of horse manure, and only the freezing temperatures dampened somewhat the city's barnyard smells, which mingled with whiffs of wood and charcoal smoke from countless stoves and samovars.

Because snow was piled up in high banks that narrowed the sidewalks, navigating through the crowds of pedestrians could be a slow process for a watcher like Kulikovsky. But the city's heterogeneous population made it easy for anyone to blend in. Many Muscovites wore European clothing, or what simple folk referred to as "German" dress, and were indistinguishable from Berliners or Londoners. Western European visitors were also common in the city, and many shops had signs in French and German. But side by side with them walked traditional Russian Moscow—bearded peasant men and kerchiefed women in rough gray sheepskins, patched caftans, and felt winter boots; long-haired Orthodox priests in dark robes sweeping the ground; old-fashioned merchants in fur hats, their wives adorned with strings of pearls, their stoutness a display of commercial success. Also much in evidence in the city was the multiethnic character of the Russian Empire—two-thirds of which lay in Asia—and its location as a crossroads between continents. On any given day one could encounter exotic types from various distant lands—Circassians, Tatars, Bukharians, Greeks, Persians.

⚬—⚬

After several weeks of watching, Savinkov's team began to understand the grand duke's routine as he drove from his home, to his offices, to the theaters, churches, and charitable institutions where he attended official functions. Moiseyenko and Kalyaev learned to recognize Sergey's roomy, old-fashioned carriage with its distinctive white reins and bright white acetylene lamps. They also noticed that the only other carriage in the city with lamps like these was used by Sergey's wife, which meant that their carriages could be easily confused, especially at night. To remedy this, Kalyaev and Moiseyenko memorized the faces and appearance of all the coachmen who drove each member of the couple.

But Kulikovsky's inexperience quickly became a problem. He proved unable to carry out the task of hawking his wares to passersby and watching for the grand duke at the same time. He also needed spectacles to see anything more than a short distance away, a serious handicap for a would-be assassin that Savinkov appears inexplicably to have missed. The result was that a few days after Kulikovsky began, he took up a stationary position monitoring the Kaluga Gates, a major thoroughfare on the city's southern edge. There he proved somewhat more useful, although later his ineptitude would come close to upending the entire plot.

The Moral Terrorist

The winter of 1904–1905 was a restive time in the Russian Empire. The war with Japan that the Russians had expected to win hands down—"we'll knock them down with our hats!"—was going from bad to worse in Manchuria and causing political and labor disturbances in Moscow and other cities. In response, Sergey moved his household from the governor-general's palace in the center to Neskuchny Palace on the outskirts. Then, suddenly, the situation deteriorated further.

On January 9/22, 1905, a day that would go down in history as Bloody Sunday, troops in Saint Petersburg shot hundreds of peaceful and patriotic demonstrators who were approaching the Winter Palace in an attempt to petition the tsar to improve labor conditions and end the unpopular war. Singing the imperial anthem "God Save the Tsar" and carrying religious banners and icons, they had been organized and led by a young, handsome, and charismatic Orthodox priest in a traditional Russian display of fealty and faith that the tsar would personally set everything right.

The carnage triggered outrage throughout the empire and around the world. Protest meetings took place in many cities; local and private organizations condemned the regime's brutality in the harshest terms; within days 400,000 workers went on strike in the largest action of its kind in Russian history. University students abandoned their classrooms. Especially violent disturbances broke out in the borderlands, and several hundred people were killed in Warsaw and Riga. Additional waves of unrest and violence would continue to roll across the country for months. By the spring and summer of 1905, peasant unrest had spread through nearly one eighth of Russia's entire vast territory. In mid-June sailors mutinied aboard the battleship *Potyomkin*, the star of Russia's Black Sea fleet. Bloody Sunday was the day, many said, when the people's faith in the tsar was killed.

On the day following the massacre, January 10, Sergey sought even greater safety and retreated to the Nicholas Palace inside the Kremlin's walls. Each of his moves interrupted the team's stalking for a while, but they soon picked up his trail again.

The growing revolutionary storm in the country also became an additional prod for Savinkov to act, and some members of the Socialist Revolutionary Party began to criticize him for not doing enough to capitalize on the situation. When Praskovya Ivanovskaya, his old "cook" from Saint Petersburg, saw him in Moscow, she was struck by how haggard and exhausted he looked. He seemed despondent and complained to her that he did not have the resources he needed and feared the attack would have to be delayed further.

⚬—✦—⚬

Finally, in late January 1905, Savinkov saw a chance. He read in Moscow's newspapers that a benefit concert for a military charity would take place on February 2 in the Bolshoy Theater. This was the city's premier house for grand opera, and Fyodor Chaliapin, the internationally celebrated basso, would be singing the title role, which he had made famous, in Mussorgsky's *Boris Godunov*. Sergey's wife, Grand Duchess Elizaveta, whose sister Alexandra was the empress of Russia, was the patroness of the charity, which she recently established to aid soldiers wounded in the war raging in the Far East. Savinkov concluded that the grand duke could not fail to attend the benefit and set the assassination for that day.

On Wednesday afternoon, February 2, as the thin winter light filtered through the window of her room in Slavyansky Bazaar, a hotel popular with well-to-do merchants located only a few streets from the Kremlin, Dora Brilliant assembled two bombs weighing several kilograms each. Savinkov met her in an alley nearby at 7 P.M. Handling the soldered tin boxes that she had wrapped in cloth very carefully, he transferred them to a briefcase.

The team's surveillance had determined that Sergey usually left the Kremlin through the Gothic-spired Nikolsky Tower Gate, which opened directly onto the northern end of Red Square. There were only two routes his carriage could take from there to the Bolshoy Theater half a mile away: it could pass either to the left or the right of the Imperial Russian Historical Museum, a large redbrick building in an ornate Russian style that sat on the edge of Red Square. Either route would bring Sergey past one of the men who would be waiting.

By 7:30 P.M., Savinkov finished delivering the bombs to the two throwers. He had given the first to Kalyaev. They said their farewells and then embraced.

Savinkov would remember the moment in detail. Several days earlier he had noticed a marked change in his old friend. Previously, Kalyaev had been his usual mix of religious, political, and aesthetic exaltation. Now, however, he looked gaunt and his normally radiant eyes were sunken. To Savinkov he also seemed to be brimming over with a new, nervous excitement because he sensed that his own life would end soon. And never before had Savinkov heard him speak of his love for the team and its mission with such ardor.

"And if I fail?" Kalyaev then added, struggling to express himself. "Do you know what? I think then, like the Japanese . . ." His voice trailed off.

Savinkov did not understand: "What—like the Japanese?"

"The Japanese don't surrender in battle," Kalyaev explained.

"So?"

"They commit hara-kiri."

⊷

At 8 P.M. Kalyaev took up his position in front of the redbrick Moscow City Hall building on the northern edge of Red Square. A hundred yards away, by the tall iron gates to Alexander Garden, which stretches along the Kremlin's western wall, stood Kulikovsky. Both men dressed inconspicuously as peasants in *poddyovki*—long, fitted coats with pleated backs—peaked caps, and tall boots. Each also carried a cotton bundle that sagged under the weight of the bomb inside. Moiseyenko had returned to his coachman's livery yard. Savinkov went into the depths of the garden to wait for the explosion.

A blizzard was beginning, and the cold was intense. The few streetlights in the area did little to lift the gloom of the heavy northern night, which seemed even darker because of the clouds hanging over the Kremlin's sharp towers. There was hardly any traffic on the nearby streets and squares. Passersby were few and difficult to make out through the layered shadows.

A few minutes after 8 P.M., Kalyaev saw the white acetylene lamps of the grand duke's carriage emerge from the passageway between the Kremlin and the Historical Museum 100 yards away from where he was standing. Despite the distance and the darkness, he thought that he also recognized Andrey Rudinkin, the grand duke's stout, bearded coachman sitting on the driver's box.

Kalyaev had anticipated this moment for months and did not hesitate. He raised his right hand with the bomb and began to run over the snow-covered ground, intending to cut the carriage off as it crossed Voskresenskaya Square in front of him. In seconds, he was close enough to see inside.

But what he glimpsed stunned him. Silhouetted against the padded white silk interior was Sergey, but on the seat next to him was a woman, the grand duchess, and in the seat opposite—two children.

Kalyaev stopped as abruptly as if he had run into a wall. He then let his arm drop and stood watching as the carriage rolled away toward the lights of Theatrical Square. There was no one around—no mounted guards, no escorting police vehicles—and neither the coachman nor anyone inside the carriage had noticed him.

⚬—✦—⚬

To Savinkov waiting in Alexander Garden, time had dragged so slowly that it seemed as if entire years had passed. He had seen the lights of the grand duke's carriage flash by and turn toward Kalyaev, but no explosion followed. All he could hear was the whistling of the wind in the garden's leafless trees. Then, as he peered into the freezing mist and gloom, he saw Kalyaev approaching, the snow on the path crunching under his feet. His expression was anxious, his eyes searching.

Savinkov stared at Kalyaev with bewilderment.

"You have to understand . . . ," Kalyaev began, trying to explain.

But he was so shaken that he had difficulty stringing words together: "I'm afraid. Wouldn't it have been a crime against us all? . . . But I couldn't do otherwise, you have to understand, I couldn't . . . My arm dropped by itself . . . There was a woman, children . . . Children . . ."

Only then did Savinkov understand what had happened.

Kalyaev looked exhausted and was visibly shivering. He clutched his bundle with frozen fingers, as if he was afraid to part with it.

"Tell me, was it the right thing to do?" he asked. "It was right, wasn't it? Let them live. Are they guilty? Or do you think that I'm afraid? No, you don't think that . . . I ran right up to the carriage."

The children Kalyaev had glimpsed were Sergey's and Elizaveta's nephew and niece, Grand Duke Dmitry and Grand Duchess Maria, ages twelve and thirteen. Sergey and his wife, who had no children of their own, formally adopted them two years earlier after their father, Sergey's younger brother Grand Duke Pavel, was banished from the Russian Empire by the tsar for marrying a divorced commoner. The children's mother, Pavel's first wife, had died just hours after her son's birth.

Despite Kalyaev's agitation and his own shock, Savinkov could see that his friend understood the enormous consequences of missing this unique chance to kill Sergey. By staying his hand, Kalyaev had risked arrest and death for himself and the entire team.

However, the moral imperative not to spill innocent blood eclipsed revolutionary justice. Savinkov replied to Kalyaev that not only did he not condemn him, but he fully approved what he did.

Savinkov's response buoyed up Kalyaev, although not enough to calm him completely. In an improbable display of Russian soul-searching at a moment like this, as if he was an overwrought character in a novel by Dostoyevsky and not a terrorist holding a bomb with a hair-trigger fuse in the middle of Moscow, Kalyaev proposed that he and Savinkov settle right then and there a question of principle that the Combat Organization had never discussed before: could killing someone like Sergey justify the collateral murder of innocents?

"You decide. I can't alone," Kalyaev continued. "If it's necessary for us, for the Party, for everyone—on the way back no one will survive. Neither him, nor her, nor the children."

But Savinkov's reply was again unequivocal. He said that a political assassination that also killed innocents was impermissible. It did not matter how many crimes against the Russian people Sergey had committed.

For a while, Kalyaev and Savinkov huddled close to each other in the freezing darkness as they talked, the trees groaning around them in the wind and snow eddies sweeping along the garden's paths. A few moments later, Kulikovsky appeared. He was much relieved when he saw Kalyaev. Although he had also seen the grand duke's carriage heading toward the City Hall, when he did not hear an explosion, he thought Kalyaev had been seized by the police.

It was then that Savinkov probably realized that they had been the beneficiaries of an incredible, an absurd stroke of luck. The grand duke's security was so criminally lax—despite the death threats he had received recently and the constant danger haunting the entire imperial family—that no one had been around to see a man running toward his carriage with an arm raised and holding something. No alerts had been sounded, no searches begun, no new precautions taken. The team might have another chance.

The extraordinary turn of events shook Savinkov and confused his thinking again. At first, he thought that Kalyaev might have been mistaken and not actually seen Sergey in the carriage. But when they went to check at the Bolshoy Theater, a ticket scalper by the entrance confirmed that the grand duke and his wife were inside.

Savinkov then decided that they still had to try to make another attempt that same night. He thought there was a chance that the grand duchess might decide to leave separately in another carriage with the children and that Sergey would return to the Kremlin alone in his. But after wandering around the area in the freezing temperature for several hours they returned to the theater only to see Sergey, his wife, and the children leaving together. For tonight, it was over.

At midnight Savinkov met Brilliant near her hotel and returned the bombs to her so that she could disarm them. She listened in silence as he described what had happened.

When he finished, he asked if she thought that Kalyaev had made the right decision.

Brilliant lowered her eyes. "The Poet acted as he had to," she replied.

Later that night the three men decided to try again the day after next, a Friday, when, following a routine they had observed many times, the grand duke could be expected to drive from the Kremlin to his office in the governor-general's palace on Tverskaya Street.

Death to the Tyrant

In the morning on Friday, February 4, Brilliant reinserted the firing mechanisms into the bombs and wrapped each in a cloth. She met Savinkov in a narrow alley near her hotel and handed them to him. Moiseyenko was again the driver and was going to take Savinkov to the locations where Kalyaev and Kulikovsky were supposed be waiting.

The sleigh's runners barely began to squeal on the dirty snow before Moiseyenko twisted around in his seat to tell Savinkov that there was a problem: things with Kulikovsky were "very bad." That morning he told Moiseyenko he had overestimated his own strength and now felt that he had to drop out of the attack on the grand duke.

This was a serious blow at such a crucial moment and put Savinkov in a quandary. Either he or Moiseyenko would have to take Kulikovsky's place, or Kalyaev would have to make the attempt alone. But even under such extraordinary circumstances, Savinkov would not even consider allowing Brilliant to throw one of her own bombs.

For several moments, Savinkov vacillated. There were problems with the different alternatives. If Moiseyenko were arrested, the police would discover how members of the Combat Organization stalked their targets disguised as cabbies or street vendors; this method needed to be kept secret because it was still unknown to the Okhrana, as far as Savinkov was aware. And if Savinkov himself were arrested, this would betray the Englishman who had made his passport available to the Russian revolutionaries. A solution might be to suspend the operation against Sergey so that Savinkov would have time to acquire a new identity, after which he could take part in an attack. But then Brilliant would once again have to risk her life disarming and later rearming the bombs. And if Kalyaev were the sole bomb thrower, he might fail to destroy his target.

As Savinkov drove to where Kalyaev was waiting in Yushkov Lane three blocks east of Red Square, he decided that the plan against Sergey should be put off and that he and Moiseyenko would assume new disguises.

But Kalyaev would not hear of it. When he got in the sleigh and Savinkov explained his reasoning to him, Kalyaev became very agitated and began to object: "Under no circumstances . . . We can't subject Dora to danger once again . . . I'll do it myself."

Savinkov tried to argue with him, but Kalyaev insisted: "Can it be that you don't believe me? I'll manage it on my own, I'm telling you."

Savinkov argued that if something went wrong and there was no backup, the plot would fail and the team could be arrested, but Kalyaev was adamant: "If the grand duke makes the trip, I'll kill him. Have no fear."

His self-assurance made Savinkov waver.

At this moment Moiseyenko turned toward them on his box: "Decide quickly. It's time."

Savinkov made up his mind. Kalyaev would attack alone.

They got out of the sleigh and walked the few blocks through the crowded Ilyinka Street business district toward Red Square. As they were passing between the ornately faceted, cream-colored stone façades of the Upper and Middle Rows shopping arcades, the clock on the Kremlin's Spasskaya Tower struck two. Kalyaev stopped. They said goodbye. Kalyaev then kissed Savinkov on the lips and turned right, walking along the east side of the square. He was planning to wait at a spot near the Iberian Chapel that he had reconnoitered before, where he had noticed a framed patriotic picture attached to the corner of a building. By standing with his back to the Kremlin he could see the Nikolsky Tower Gates reflected in the picture's glass, which would also allow him to watch for Sergey's carriage without calling attention to himself.

⌐━━⊸

Savinkov felt himself drawn irresistibly to where the attack was about to unfold. He crossed Red Square, passing Saint Basil's Cathedral with its fantastically colored cupolas twisting themselves into the sky, and entered the Kremlin through the Spasskaya Tower Gate. Once inside, he stopped by the giant monument to Alexander II. The bronze statue of the tsar on a red granite pedestal was over twenty feet tall and was surmounted by a canopy nearly 120 feet high held up by sixteen bronze columns with an imperial Russian eagle on top. History was about to repeat itself: Alexander II was Grand Duke Sergey's father.

The statue of Alexander II faced Nicholas Palace, the grand duke's residence, several hundred feet away. A carriage was waiting in front of the palace with the coachman Rudinkin on the box, a sign that Sergey was about to leave for his office. Savinkov walked past the carriage and the guards standing by the palace's entrance, down the length of Senate Square, and exited the Kremlin through the Nikolsky Tower Gate onto Red Square. He then headed up Tverskaya Street. He had made plans to meet Brilliant in Siu's French confectioner's shop a short walk away on Kuznetsky Most Street, home to the city's most elegant stores, and then to return with her to the Kremlin to witness the bomb's explosion.

At that time, Sergey and his wife, known as Ella in the family, were finishing lunch in the palace. Sergey was in an "especially happy" mood, Ella later recalled, because that morning he had received a gift from his nephew the tsar—a miniature portrait of his late brother, Alexander III, framed in a gold laurel wreath. Sergey's staff had tried to get him to change the timing and routes of his trips outside the Kremlin because of the threats he kept getting, but he refused and left the palace as usual around 2:30 P.M.

Ella was also preparing to go out for her daily visit to the wife of their chamberlain, Countess Mengden, who was recovering from a recent serious operation. Ella was an exceptionally kind person, and the countess was such a close friend that Ella had stayed with her and held her hand during the entire procedure, which had to be performed without an anesthetic because the patient's heart was too weak.

All that morning Ella had felt an "inexplicable anguish." But she was gratified that she had at least managed to persuade Sergey to cancel a trip to Saint Petersburg because of the possibility of an attack.

The denouement came just as Savinkov was approaching Siu's shop, and he was not ready for it.

One might have thought that all Savinkov's senses would be straining to the utmost in anticipation of Kalyaev's attack, even if by his reckoning the explosion was supposed to occur only some minutes later. That is not what happened.

The only thing Savinkov remembered hearing was a "distant, hollow sound," as if someone had "fired a revolver" in a side street. The noise was so "unlike the boom of an explosion," he recalled later, that he did not pay any attention to it and kept walking.

The growing tension and anxiety of the last several weeks, and especially of the last few minutes after he had left Kalyaev, had evidently taken such a toll on Savinkov that he could not fully grasp what was going on around him. Continuing with his plan like an automaton, he met Brilliant at the confectioner's and began to walk back toward the Kremlin with her.

When they were just a few dozen steps away from Red Square, a boy who had lost his hat in the excitement ran past them and yelled: "The grand duke's been killed, his head was torn off."

But even the boy's shout did not produce an impression on Savinkov at the time, or so he claimed later, although he remembered seeing people running toward the Kremlin. Savinkov continued to walk with Brilliant to the Nikolsky Tower Gate, where they saw a crowd so big that it was impossible to get through.

Suddenly, Savinkov heard someone address him: "Sir—here's a cab."

Turning around, he saw Moiseyenko, ashen-faced and beckoning them into his sleigh. They got in mechanically and as they slowly drove away from the Kremlin, Moiseyenko asked: "Did you hear?"

"No," was all Savinkov replied.

Moiseyenko explained: "I was waiting here and heard the explosion. The grand duke has been killed."

When Brilliant heard this, she leaned against Savinkov and began to sob, her whole body shaking. Savinkov tried to calm her, but she sobbed more loudly and kept repeating: "It was we who killed him . . . I killed him . . . I . . ."

"Who?" Savinkov asked in his dazed state, thinking that she was talking about Kalyaev, and still unable to understand what he had heard twice in the last few moments.

"The grand duke."

Finally, he understood.

According to eyewitnesses, the bomb went off at approximately 2:45 P.M. and was so powerful that it was heard even in distant parts of the city. Kalyaev had run right up to the grand duke's carriage sixty-five paces inside the Kremlin's walls, when it was still on Senate Square heading toward the Nikolsky Gates, and hurled the bomb from a distance of only a few feet. There were no guards close enough to intervene.

The explosion was devastating. Kalyaev felt himself sucked into its vortex and for a split second glimpsed the carriage disintegrating; then a blast of hot smoke and splinters hit him in the face and tore his hat off. A narrow column of dirty yellow and black smoke shot into the sky. Miraculously, Kalyaev remained on his feet.

When the smoke cleared, some five paces away he saw a low, shapeless mass consisting of fragments of wood from the carriage, shreds of the grand duke's clothing, and what was left of his body. The sight was horrific: the head was missing, and most of the torso was completely destroyed; mutilated parts of an arm and a leg could be made out amid the wreckage; the snow all around was splattered with blood. One of Sergey's fingers and other small bits of flesh were found on surrounding rooftops weeks later.

All the windows in the Senate and the Arsenal facing Senate Square had been knocked out by the blast. At first people working inside thought that their buildings were collapsing because of an earthquake or that one of the Kremlin towers had fallen. Rudinkin, the coachman, was badly burned and suffered more than 100 wounds in his back.

For a few seconds, Kalyaev stood alone facing the devastation, his clothing shredded and scorched, blood flowing freely down his face from numerous small cuts. He was surprised to be alive. He knew that he could not escape but started walking away anyway; then he heard cries from behind and felt people seize him. A police sleigh almost ran over him, and he remembered his disgust when he heard a panicked detective prattling with relief: "Check if he has a revolver. Ah, thank God—and how is it that I wasn't killed, we were right here, too." Kalyaev did not resist when he was bundled off in a cab to a local police station and from there to prison.

<hr>

Grand Duchess Maria, the girl spared by Kalyaev two days earlier, remembered what happened inside Nicholas Palace. For several minutes after her uncle departed everything had been calm and quiet; then "a horrible explosion resounded that made the window-panes jingle." A crushing silence followed. For several heart-beats, no one moved, looked at each other, or dared say anything. Ella realized immediately that something appalling had happened to her husband, ran down-stairs, and dashed out of the palace wearing only a loose cloak over her shoulders.

Some people had begun to gather around the gruesome mass in Senate Square. One or two tried to stop the grand duchess from approaching; she pushed past them. In shock, but showing exceptional self-control and enlisting others to help her, Ella knelt in the snow and started to gather what she could of her husband's bleeding remains. She pressed her face to what was left of his right hand and pulled off the rings. For some minutes, she kept rummaging in the snow, amid splinters from the carriage, picking up pieces of the body and bits of bone and cartilage. She placed these on an army stretcher that someone had brought from a workshop she had set up in the palace. Ella also found a length of gold chain and several medallions that Sergey had worn around his neck and clutched them tightly. Her cheek, both hands, and the sleeves of her dress were stained with blood, its sickening smell persisting through the freezing temperature.

Soldiers who ran over from the Kremlin's barracks located at the far end of Senate Square covered the small mass of Sergey's remains with a greatcoat and carried the stretcher to the palace. Through a private passage they entered the adjoining fourteenth-century church of Saint Alexey and set the stretcher down in front of the steps leading up to the altar. The first prayers for the dead were chanted over the remains at 4 P.M. Blood seeped through the stretcher and formed a small dark pool on the floor.

The residents of the Kremlin entered deep mourning. When members of the imperial family in Saint Petersburg got the news later that day, they were shocked and horrified, even if many had no personal affection for Sergey. They were also terrified about their own safety, just as the Socialist Revolutionaries had planned, and neither the tsar nor several other senior members of the family risked coming to Moscow for the funeral several days later. Because of the danger of appearing in public, they were even advised not to attend requiem services in Saint Petersburg's major cathedrals.

⊙━━⊙

Beyond these inner circles, however, the reaction was mostly indifference. The British consul in Moscow reported to his embassy in Saint Petersburg that there was much sympathy for the grand duchess because of the affection she had won through her efforts to help sick and wounded soldiers, but although newspapers condemned the assassination, he added, they said little "in favour of the late Grand Duke." The same proved true in the imperial capital, where the British ambassador received a report that "restaurants were crowded and bands playing notwithstanding the presence of officers in uniform who did not even suggest that the orchestras should stop." By contrast, in a central Moscow prison, when political prisoners heard the news, they began to sing "La Marseillaise," France's national anthem, which had also become the international hymn of revolution.

In the following two days, front-page headlines and lead stories shouted the news around the world. The assassination was shocking, but readers everywhere were getting used to the idea that Russia was in a perilous state.

The Grand Duchess and the Assassin

The disparity in public attitudes toward the grand duke on the one hand and his wife on the other was very striking, especially in light of Ella's foreign origins. She had been born in Germany as Princess Elisabeth of Hesse and by Rhine to Ludwig IV, grand duke of Hesse, and his British-born wife, Princess Alice, granddaughter of Britain's Queen Victoria. When Ella married Sergey in 1884, she followed tradition by adopting a Russian name and converting to Russian Orthodoxy. It was at this wedding that Nicholas, the future tsar, first met beautiful Ella's equally beautiful youngest sister, Princess Alix, who would become his wife Alexandra, empress of Russia.

Ella embraced her new faith with ardor, which was tested harshly at times by her husband's behavior. Sergey was a homosexual and had been involved in a notorious scandal with aristocratic young men from imperial guards' regiments and actors from the Alexandrinsky Theater in Saint Petersburg that had to be hushed up. It was also rumored that he had not consummated his marriage with Ella. But she never complained and remained loyal to Sergey. Ella even wrote to Queen Victoria, her great-grandmother, to defend her life with her husband against the "abominable lies" that circulated widely and continuously in the upper reaches of Russian society.

By contrast, Ella was able to find comfort in how affectionate Sergey was toward their adopted niece and nephew, even if the children feared him, and how conscientiously—in his own way—he tried to carry out his duties as governor-general. Sergey was known for working very hard, for paying great attention to myriad details in his vast vice regal domain, for fighting fraud and corruption, and for involving himself in matters that he could easily have left to subordinates. At times, he even traveled through Moscow incognito to see things for himself, and was much distressed by the widespread poverty he saw, which he tried to alleviate as best he could by fostering charities.

In the days that followed Sergey's death, despite her shock and grief, Ella showed striking courage and stoicism as well as her characteristic charity. Her kindness extended to her concern for the coachman Rudinkin, whom she visited in the hospital on the day of the assassination itself. To spare his feelings, she did not reveal the truth about her husband. Rudinkin died from his wounds soon after, still believing that his august master was unharmed. The day after the attack, Ella also visited Countess Mengden, the chamberlain's wife, and out of concern for her weak state again concealed the truth: she wore everyday clothing instead of mourning and behaved as if nothing unusual had happened.

<hr />

However, the greatest test—and proof—of Ella's faith and fortitude was her astonishing visit to Kalyaev. She made a request to the Moscow authorities to meet with him just three days after the assassination, and he was brought from the central prison where he was being held to a police station not far from the Kremlin. On Monday evening, February 7, Ella made the trip in greatest secrecy and saw Kalyaev alone. He had no idea why he had been moved and was not forewarned that the grand duchess was coming. When he saw a woman wearily entering his cell, dressed all in black and heavily veiled, he did not recognize her. Then Ella raised her veil. Her face with large, sad eyes under a pensive brow was drawn with suffering.

"I'm his wife," she whispered as she drew near.

Kalyaev was so shocked that he did not rise. He watched in amazement as she dropped helplessly into a chair next to his, then took his hand firmly in hers, and began to weep.

It was an amazing, surreal encounter of two people from irreconcilable worlds who managed briefly to share a common humanity in the face of one death and a second that was imminent.

Their meeting lasted about twenty-five minutes. Kalyaev later described it in letters to Savinkov, to other comrades, and in a moving poem.

He felt pity for the grand duchess. In his poem, he wrote that "I didn't reject her—I spared her / This slave from the tsar's camp." He also treated her respectfully, although he had difficulty remaining calm. At first, and incredibly, *he* even tried to console *her*.

"Your Highness," he began, "don't cry. It had to happen." And then, musing out loud, he added ruefully: "Why do they talk to me only after I have committed a murder."

Ella, in turn, and also incredibly, responded to him with compassion: "You must have suffered a lot, to make this decision."

But upon hearing this, Kalyaev jumped up and interrupted her, exclaiming loudly that his suffering was nothing compared to the suffering of millions of others who have no way of "protesting against the cruelties of the government, and against this most horrible war."

The grand duchess agreed: "Yes, it's a great pity that you did not come to see us, and that we did not know you earlier."

Several times after this, Kalyaev's agitation overwhelmed him and he interrupted the grand duchess when she tried to explain her and her husband's position. He stressed the horrors of Bloody Sunday, said that he would give his life "a thousand times, not just once," for Russia to be free, and rejected her conception of the "good" of the people.

When the grand duchess started to speak of her husband—explaining that he had been expecting death, that he had recently left the post of governor-general because of this, and that he was a good man—Kalyaev interrupted her once again.

But then, to spare her feelings, he stopped himself: "Let's not talk about the grand duke. I don't want to talk with you about him. I'll explain everything at the trial. You know that I carried this out completely consciously. The grand duke was a political figure and he knew what he wanted."

"Yes, I can't enter into political discussions with you," the grand duchess agreed, "I only wanted you to know that the grand duke forgives you, and that I will pray for you . . ."

For a long moment they looked at each other with something like a "mystical feeling," as Kalyaev later characterized it, "like two mortals who had remained alive. I—by accident, she—by the will of the organization, by my will, because the organization and I deliberately strived to avoid unnecessary bloodshed."

Ella held out her hand with something in it: "I ask you, accept this icon from me as a memento," she said. Then she added, "I will pray for you."

Kalyaev took the icon, but could not resist replying: "My conscience is clear."

When Ella got up to leave, Kalyaev rose too.

"Farewell," he said. "I repeat that it pains me greatly that I caused you grief, but I carried out my duty, and I'll carry it out to the end and will endure everything that awaits me. Farewell, for we'll not see each other again."

He then bowed his head, took her right hand in his, raised it to his lips, and kissed it.

Although Ella left Kalyaev unrepentant, she was comforted to hear from one of the prison warders that he had placed the icon next to his bed.

⊶

Kalyaev would later claim that he saw the grand duchess's gift of the icon as symbolizing that she acknowledged his victory, that she thanked fate for sparing her life, and that she repented for the grand duke's crimes.

But, of course, the icon meant nothing of the sort. Kalyaev misunderstood Ella because his revolutionary zeal blinded him. As a pious Christian, Ella cared about Kalyaev's immortal soul; as a true believer, she wanted to do what she could to reconcile a sinner with God. And as her late husband's loyal wife, she acted in accordance with what she knew to be Sergey's deep concern for the souls of sinners who died without repentance. It is not surprising, however, that Kalyaev, or anyone else for that matter, would have found this hard to believe.

Two Mortals

Their meeting was supposed to be secret, but word got out and newspapers picked up the sensational story, presenting what had happened in a way that Kalyaev found deeply offensive. On March 24, he wrote a harsh letter to Ella, accusing her of betraying their private encounter and what he claimed was his purely human expression of compassion for her grief. He said he rejected her attempt to implicate him in her own faith, which he characterized as "the religious superstition of slaves and their hypocritical masters." He added that he regretted that during her visit he had concealed his hatred for her and her ilk, and he accused her of being unworthy of his magnanimity.

On April 5, 1905, Kalyaev was tried by a special commission of the Imperial Governing Senate and sentenced to death. On April 27, he wrote to Savinkov for the last time. He asked forgiveness for anything that he may have done to wrong him, acknowledged his love for him, and asked him, if it became necessary, to defend his revolutionary honor. His last words were "Farewell, my dear, my only friend. Be happy! Be happy!"

He also wrote a poem before his execution, a profession of faith titled "At the Foot of the Cross," in which he appealed to Christ for guidance because of how much suffering there is in the world. However, Christ is silent and the poet asks despairingly if the only path to redemption is once again death on the Cross. The answer is yes: the poet will imitate Christ by sacrificing himself for those who suffer. But he will do so by murdering a tyrant, which is a sinful act, and redemption for it will be the deliverance that the poet-terrorist brings the people at the price of his own life.

Kalyaev was hanged at dawn on May 10, 1905, in Shlisselburg Fortress, an old political prison located on an island in the Neva twenty miles east of Saint Petersburg. He retained his composure until the end. But the executioner botched his job. The rope was too long, and Kalyaev's feet hit the ground when the block was kicked out from under him. He convulsed hideously until the executioner and his two assistants grabbed the rope and hauled on it to finish him.

⌦

Grand Duke Sergey's funeral was held on February 23, and his coffin was interred in a specially prepared vault beneath the Church of Saint Alexey in the Kremlin. Ella withdrew from the world after that and dedicated the rest of her life to her faith and to good works. In 1908, after selling her jewels to buy land in Moscow, she founded the Martha and Mary Convent of Mercy, which was dedicated to tending to the city's poor and sick. In 1910, she took the veil herself and became the convent's abbess.

After the Bolsheviks seized power in October 1917, they arrested Ella and her followers, as well as many other members of the imperial family. Unlike the Socialist Revolutionaries, the Bolsheviks had no compunctions about killing innocents. The following year, on July 17, their political police, the Cheka, executed Nicholas II and his family.

Later the same day, a detachment of the Cheka took Ella and several of her followers to an abandoned, water-filled mine shaft in the Urals and pushed them in alive. When the guards heard splashes and voices singing prayers, they threw in two hand grenades; when this did not stop the singing, the Cheka filled the shaft with brush and set it on fire. In 1984 the late grand duchess was canonized a martyr saint by the Russian Orthodox émigré church in New York City. Eight years later, after the dissolution of the Soviet Union, Ella's canonization was recognized by the Moscow Patriarchate.

Terror's Aftermath

Savinkov's disorientation following Kalyaev's attack on Sergey is a testament to how profoundly traumatic he found participating in a killing, even though he was not the actual assassin, even though he was convinced that it was justified, and even though he had gone through the same experience just seven months earlier with Plehve.

Under the circumstances, it is remarkable that in his *Memoirs of a Terrorist* Savinkov did nothing to embellish his behavior or his emotional response to Sergey's death, as he had not to Plehve's, despite the fact that both were defining events in his career as a terrorist and resounding thunderclaps in the revolutionary storm that was building in Russia. Savinkov's memoir is his frank acknowledgment of the enormous effort he had to expend, emotionally, physically, and psychologically—over the course of years—to become the nemesis of tyranny that he wanted to be. As such, his memoir is a sobering warning about the realities of revolutionary terrorist practice.

Savinkov and the remainder of his team left Moscow shortly after the assassination, on Friday evening, February 4. He went to Saint Petersburg, Brilliant went to Kharkov, and Moiseyenko, after selling his horse and sleigh, joined her there. Kulikovsky had had enough and resigned from the organization altogether, although he would later perish in an unrelated revolutionary action.

In Saint Petersburg Savinkov discovered that the plot against General Dmitry Trepov, the governor-general (his father had been targeted by Vera Zasulich in

1878), was going badly because several members had been arrested. After consulting with those who remained, Savinkov had them shift their focus to Grand Duke Vladimir, Sergey's brother. Savinkov also got a report that the hunt for General Kleygels, the Kiev region's governor-general and military commander, was going even worse than the one in the capital.

In light of these problems, Savinkov decided to go to Geneva to consult with Azef and other party leaders, including Father Gapon, the priest who had fled abroad after organizing the workers' demonstration that culminated in Bloody Sunday in Saint Petersburg on January 9, an event that had made him the new star of the Russian revolutionary movement. The setbacks in Saint Petersburg and Kiev seemed temporary and reparable. The assassination of Sergey was a spectacular success, and the Combat Organization's prestige was at an all-time high among different strata of Russian society. Azef's position, even though he had not been directly involved in the assassination, was at its zenith. The next logical targets for the terrorists would be other imperial grandees, and even Tsar Nicholas II himself.

⎯⎯

When Savinkov left Russia in mid-February, he did not know how lucky he was to get out unscathed. Shortly after Sergey's assassination, Azef had decided to give Savinkov up to the Okhrana and informed them where he would be crossing the Polish-German frontier. For some reason, however, Savinkov changed his plans and took the northern route through East Prussia, as a result of which he escaped.

Azef continued to play his other hands as he saw fit. Because he had been abroad for some time when Sergey was killed, he could use this as an alibi when explaining to the police why he did not inform them of the impending attack. At the end of February, he received a photograph of Kalyaev from Rataev and was asked to identify who the man was. Azef decided it would be too risky to reveal his familiarity with the assassin, whose name the police still did not know. He replied evasively: "I think I may have met this gentleman somewhere," and added that it may have been in Berlin or Paris several years ago. Knowing that Kalyaev would not escape execution and that his past would die with him, Azef could safely keep his connection with him secret.

CHAPTER FOUR

CATASTROPHES

An Accident

On Saturday, February 26, 1905, at 4 A.M., Maximilian Shveytser, whom Savinkov had appointed leader of the Combat Organization team in Saint Petersburg, and who was also the team's technician, began preparing bombs for the most ambitious attack that the Combat Organization had ever planned. On March 1, they would try to kill four men: Grand Duke Vladimir, brother of Sergey and the senior grand duke of the imperial family; Dmitry Trepov, the governor-general of Saint Petersburg, who was held responsible for the slaughter of innocent demonstrators on Bloody Sunday; Alexander Bulygin, the new minister of the interior; and his assistant, Vice Minister Pyotr Durnovo.

The previous day Shveytser had met with two members of his team to consult about his plan—the motherly old veteran Praskovya Ivanovskaya and Tatyana Leontyeva, a young, beautiful, blond noblewoman who had joined the Combat Organization recently. Leontyeva came from a rich and socially prominent family—her father was a provincial governor—as a result of which she was admitted to imperial court balls. Her status provided the Combat Organization with a potentially very valuable form of access to the regime's innermost circles.

Sitting in the empty and silent Summer Garden, as large, soft snowflakes covered everything around them with a thin white shroud, the two women tried to persuade Shveytser that the attack was premature and that more planning was necessary. But he insisted that the team absolutely had to act on March 1. He had gotten it from an unimpeachable source that all four grandees would be crossing the Troitsky Bridge on the Neva at the same time to attend a service in the Peter and Paul Cathedral in the Fortress. One coordinated attack could kill them all.

After getting up to leave, Shveytser hesitated. "I'll stay with you a bit longer," he said and sat back down.

He was normally reticent and self-controlled, but what was coming unnerved him. Some minutes passed in silence. When they finally parted, he took and held both women's hands with a tenderness that touched Ivanovskaya.

Shveytser had a room in the Bristol Hotel, across the square facing the massive, domed Saint Isaac's Cathedral—the largest church in the city. It was an expensive neighborhood filled with private mansions, palaces, government ministries, and foreign embassies. The Winter Palace was a short walk away.

Combat Organization technicians always tried to do their work when the hotel staff was not likely to come to a guest's room, so it was still dark outside when Shveytser got up that Saturday. Dressed only in his underclothes, he went to a table by the window and began to assemble a bomb when either a part slipped out of his hands or he spilled an ingredient.

The explosion was instantaneous. The walls, floor, and ceiling of Shveytser's room caved in and several adjoining rooms and a French restaurant were destroyed. Thirty-six windows on the building's façade were shattered, and the entire wall of his room facing the street ballooned outward. The sidewalk in front of the hotel and parts of the street were covered with a mass of lumber, plaster, pieces of furniture, and various objects that had been blown out of the rooms.

When the police arrived, they found a horribly disfigured corpse of a man lying on a pile of debris. Judging by the extensive bloodstains on the ceiling, the body had been thrown against its rear part by the force of the blast and then slipped down, landing on its back. Vladimir Nabokov, the future writer, whose family's mansion was nearby, remembered how "in one of the linden trees" in Saint Isaac's Square "an ear and a finger had been found one day—remnants of a terrorist whose hand had slipped while he was arranging a lethal parcel in his room on the other side of the square."

Reports of the explosion appeared in Geneva's newspapers later the same day, and Savinkov realized immediately that it was a repetition of Pokotilov's tragic fate. This was a grievous loss: Savinkov admired Shveytser's "practical mind and iron will" and thought of him as "one of the most valued members" of the Combat Organization. His death also imperiled the entire Saint Petersburg team.

Seeking out Azef, Savinkov told him that they had to go to Saint Petersburg to see what they could salvage of the operation. Azef agreed, but asked for a delay, claiming that he needed to finish some business in Europe.

While waiting, Savinkov used the occasion to visit the ailing Gots, who had moved to Nice on the French Riviera to escape the Swiss winter. The sentimental side trip inadvertently saved Savinkov, because another disaster was looming.

The Rout

After Shveytser's death, the team in Saint Petersburg tried to regroup, and the veteran Boris Moiseyenko, who had taken part in the attack on Grand Duke Sergey, took over the leadership. They were waiting for Savinkov and Azef to arrive when, before dawn on Thursday, March 17, 1905, the entire team was arrested. Several other related arrests took place in Moscow. Some seventeen people were seized in all.

Savinkov read the reports in a French newspaper and his heart sank. He realized that virtually the entire Combat Organization in Russia had been destroyed with one blow and that all hopes for inflaming the revolutionary turmoil sweeping the country were dashed. Any thought of returning to Russia was now also out of the question, especially because, to his surprise, Savinkov saw his own name listed among those who had been arrested. He would eventually find out that the police had mistaken his old comrade Moiseyenko for him, despite the photographs and physical descriptions they had in their files, and which they apparently failed to consult.

Guilt by Association

On the same night when the police made their arrests in Saint Petersburg and Moscow, and believing that they had caught Boris Savinkov, they also raided his parents' apartment in Warsaw.

In recent months, life had been very tense for them. Their oldest son, Alexander, was barely coping with his harsh exile in far northeastern Siberia. Their second son, Boris, was abroad, they believed, but Sofia did not know where. Victor Mikhailovich's health was deteriorating because of his anxieties, and he seemed to be visibly fading. The only joy he got any longer was from reading letters from his sons; when there were none, which was the case for long periods of time, Sofia continued to write fakes to try to calm him.

The blow fell shortly after Sofia had gone to sleep at 2 A.M. She felt someone grab her arm and woke up to see Victor, her youngest son, a nineteen-year-old gymnasium student, standing near her bed holding a lit candle.

"What is it?" she asked anxiously.

"It's a search, mama! Try not to be frightened. But the house is full of gendarmes. Papa is too worried. Go to him, mama!"

Trembling with apprehension, Sofia hurriedly got dressed. She could hear footsteps behind the door, the ringing of spurs, and her husband's loud, agitated voice. She rushed to his study. He was standing in the middle of the room, pale, his eyes filled with tears, clutching a photograph of Boris to his chest. A gendarme captain, a detective, and a police officer were facing him.

"I won't let you have my son! I won't let you have my son!" Victor Mikhailovich kept repeating.

The sight of the distraught, white-haired old man was so moving that the captain and his companions were not sure what to do next and paused, shifting awkwardly from foot to foot. Sofia intervened and asked them for permission to put her husband to bed. He resisted at first, but she managed to get him to agree by promising that he could keep the photograph of Boris with him.

Then she calmly offered the captain the keys to all the closets, cabinets, and chests in the apartment, and for the next eight hours watched him and the others search everything, their clumsy and indifferent hands once again riffling through possessions that were a storehouse of the family's intimate life and memories. She had no idea what they were looking for. The captain was polite and thorough but found nothing incriminating. When the three men left, they apologized for the inconvenience they had caused. A wave of relief washed over Sofia when she realized that the search had not been connected with her youngest son, Victor.

But the bad news was not over yet. Later that morning Sofia opened her usual Warsaw newspaper and started to read the urgent telegram about the arrests that had just been made in Saint Petersburg. When she saw Boris Savinkov's name, her eyes went dark, and the paper fell from her hands. Now she understood what the search had been about. She would have to rush to Saint Petersburg immediately to do what she could to save him. The newspaper account frightened her because of how damning its tone was about those who had been arrested. With disorder sweeping the country, the imperial regime had again harshened its policies and courts were handing down death sentences to revolutionaries.

Later the same day she took a train to Saint Petersburg, leaving Victor Mikhailovich in the care of friends.

By the following morning, she was at the gendarmes headquarters building in the capital. Little had changed there since her nightmarish visits during the past several years in connection with Alexander's arrests. At first, a polished, glib, heel-clicking colonel greeted her very politely and asked how he could be of service. When she explained that she had read about her son's arrest and wanted to see him, the colonel initially refused categorically, saying that the crime was too severe to allow visits. But after a while, he seemed to relent and asked Sofia to come back several hours later.

When she did, the colonel began by leading her down a series of corridors until he stopped at a closed door. Then, in dramatic fashion, he threw it open, and urged her: "Embrace your son!"

Sofia felt as if thunderstruck and peered into the face of the young man sitting in the room. She had never seen him before (it was Moiseyenko, but they had never met). For a moment, she felt so overwhelmed that she could not utter a word. Then she came to her senses. Everything that she had suffered during the past several days erupted in one continuous tirade as she berated the officials for their mistake.

The police were reluctant to believe her when she insisted that the young man was not her son. They even contrived to have her spend a few moments alone with Moiseyenko, expecting that she would stop her pretense and acknowledge Boris. When she was finally able to leave, Sofia at least knew that Boris was safe somewhere—abroad, she hoped.

But Sofia's travails were not over. When she got back to Warsaw, her youngest son was waiting for her on the platform with heartbreaking news: Victor Mikhailovich had suffered a nervous breakdown when he found out that "Savinkov" had been arrested. At home she found a copy of a newspaper on her husband's desk with the story circled.

"Gendarmes! A search! They're looking for my sons, my sons!" the old man kept whispering. At night Sofia would see him get out of bed, tiptoe to the front door, press his ear against it, and listen, sometimes for hours. Soon he had to be placed in a clinic, but none of the treatments helped and he descended ever deeper into his paranoia.

And just when Sofia decided that things could not get any worse, they did. Alexander's letters from Siberia had been getting darker and more despondent. It was late March when she got his last letter, and she calculated that his term would end in only four months, at the end of July 1905. Hoping to win an earlier release for him, Sofia again hurried to Saint Petersburg, but to no avail—there would be no clemency. When she got back to Warsaw, the news was waiting for her that Alexander had shot himself. Eight months later, on November 17, 1905, Victor Mikhailovich died. During the last weeks, all he could think about was that his sons would soon be restored to him.

Ties that Bind

Savinkov's ties to his parents, to Vera and the children, and to his brothers and sisters were loving. But the life path he chose did not allow him to manifest them the way he wanted. Looking back on his past shortly before his death, he wrote: "In essence, I defined my entire life not by family and personal happiness, but by what is called 'an idea.' Even if I took the wrong path with this 'idea,' no one can reproach me that I was trying to secure personal welfare." It was a classic, time-honored, and painful choice.

Vera's position was similar in the sense that she was also pulled both ways, but she tilted in the opposite direction. She was a loving mother and committed to the well-being of their two children. In order to provide them with a life that was as normal as possible, she had to live in Saint Petersburg, where she had a large network of relations and friends. But she was also emotionally and intellectually committed to her husband's career as a revolutionary, and she loved and believed in him passionately. It was a constant strain for her to have to live apart from him for long periods of time in between their surreptitious meetings, while simultaneously offering him moral support and trying to keep track of his secret and dangerous campaigns. The only hope for either was the revolutionary unrest in Russia and the change that it might bring.

In the meantime, he and Vera kept in touch as best they could. Vera also continued to act as liaison with his mother in Warsaw.

In a letter from April 27, 1905, the day after their daughter Tanya turned five (Vitya was three and a half), and in another from around the same time, she showers him with ardent endearments: "My dear, my own, my little boy . . . my joy . . . endless, big, big kisses . . . I send you hugs for myself and the children." She says that she cannot begin to tell him how important his letters are to her. No matter who is before her, she feels deeply alone; it's "like a worm gnawing inside me." She is doing her best to fight her unhappiness, however, and is sure she "will prevail."

Vera reports all family events, big and small. She describes touchingly their children's simple joys—Tanya's excitement about the "enormous doll" that she got as a birthday present and how thrilled Vitya is with the toy top he was given to help celebrate his sister's birthday, how he played with it all day and even took it to bed with him. "By night I'm very tired," Vera confides, "but during the day I don't have the slightest opportunity to write." There is a young woman living with them, a former teacher who spends a lot of time with the children and tells them stories, which is very helpful to a harried mother.

Savinkov turned to Vera for emotional support that he could not get elsewhere. After the attack on Sergey, he admitted that he felt so profoundly disoriented in the world of ceaseless revolutionary plotting and so overwhelmed by its consequences that he yearned for oblivion, for moments when he could simply stop registering what was around him. During the peak of the terror campaign in 1905, he wrote to her about his inability to reconcile his sense of guilt with the need for revolutionary violence.

"My soul aches for you and for your disappointments," Vera replies to one of his laments. But then, in order to pull him out of his depression, she tries to inspire him to even greater deeds. Her admiration for what he can still achieve knows no bounds; perhaps he will even be Russia's savior: "it sometimes seems to me that the fate of us all depends on you, not just our family . . . and you will be strong and great."

Rank Amateurs

Vera's heartfelt encouragement fell on ready ears. Despite his fatigue and bouts of despondency and soul-searching, Savinkov had no intention of stopping his terrorist campaigns and remained committed to the tactics he used before.

How to carry this out now was a problem, however. The Combat Organization's ranks were depleted, and it would take time to find new recruits capable of attacking such prominent and difficult targets as General Trepov and Grand Duke Vladimir. Savinkov lowered his sights to a lesser figure, General Nikolay Kleygels, the governor-general of Kiev, who should be easier to kill.

Savinkov's choice was also dictated by the fact that the only potential members of his new team were three Jews. Two were total novices who had just joined the Combat Organization, and the third was a party member who knew how to make explosives but had no "frontline" experience. Savinkov was the opposite of an anti-Semite, as his whole life demonstrates. However, he had reasoned that it would be "inappropriate" for Jews to assassinate a senior member of the regime in Saint Petersburg because their ethnicity might skew public perceptions of the event and make it look like a parochial act of vengeance rather than a revolutionary blow against the empire. An attack on a leading figure in Kiev, however, would appear justifiably motivated by the history of pogroms in Ukraine and would eliminate one of the regime's local pillars at the same time.

Perhaps Savinkov was too eager to get back into the revolutionary fray; perhaps he was again too generous in his evaluation of inexperienced recruits; perhaps he was too sure of his ability to lead. All three reasons appear to have contributed to his decision to accept the novices, which proved to be another mistake. The impression Savinkov produced on others at this time does suggest that self-confidence bordering on, or even crossing over into, hubris was not alien to him.

The new mistake was even worse than his earlier ones because now his entire team was inexperienced and untested. Were it not for the touching naïveté and deadly earnestness of the new members of Savinkov's team, the campaign against Kleygels that Savinkov initiated in the spring of 1905 would read like an absurd comedy.

The three new members were Lev Zilberberg, Maria (Manya) Shkolnik, and Aron Shpayzman. Savinkov had recently met Zilberberg in Villefranche-sur-Mer on the French Riviera, where Zilberberg was working in an SR dynamite laboratory that had been set up in a private villa. Like many other members of the Combat Organization, Zilberberg was a former student who had been arrested and radicalized in Siberian exile. Broad-shouldered and muscular, with a hard stare and a long nose above a thick, wide moustache, he resembled the late Shveytser in his restrained strength and pragmatism. Savinkov liked him very much and decided that he was too valuable as a potential leader and future replacement for himself to risk losing in an actual attack. He told Zilberberg that in Kiev he would play a background role in order to get experience running a terrorist operation. Subsequent events would show that Savinkov had read Zilberberg accurately, and both he and, especially, his beautiful sister Evgeniya would later play crucial roles in Savinkov's life.

Manya Shkolnik was born into a poor Jewish family in the Pale of Settlement and became involved in revolutionary activity at an early age. Arrested and tried in 1903, she was exiled to Siberia, but in March 1905, in part because of the shock of Bloody Sunday and in part out of empathy for the simple Russian folk she got to know in exile, she decided to join the Combat Organization and escaped to Geneva. The third member, Aron Shpayzman, had a similar background. A bookbinder by trade, he was a close friend of Shkolnik's and had been tried with her and also exiled to Siberia. He escaped several weeks before she did and made it to Geneva as well.

Because Shpayzman already knew members of the Combat Organization, he arranged for Shkolnik to meet with Azef and Savinkov. After prolonged scrutiny both were admitted. Savinkov gave them a brief orientation in Paris and then sent them off to Russia.

The first act of the tragicomedy came at the border crossing with Germany, when a Russian customs official discovered the dynamite and revolver that Shpayzman had concealed under his clothing. Incredibly, Shpayzman managed to talk his way out of arrest by claiming that the dynamite was actually medicinal camphor and that as a Jew he had the right to carry a gun to defend himself during pogroms. Once in Russia, however, Shpayzman failed to meet Savinkov in Vilnius, as they had agreed, and then, fearing he had been followed by police spies, got rid of the dynamite. More confusion ensued before Shpayzman and the others finally gathered in Kiev. However, although Kleygels was easy to spot on the streets, Shpayzman and Shkolnik kept coming up with excuses for not preparing an attack.

Savinkov began to doubt Shpayzman's commitment, but he decided that he had no choice and had to rely on him because the time was ripe to strike the regime, which had recently suffered another defeat in the East. In mid-May, the Russian Baltic Sea Fleet, which had sailed halfway around the world to the Straits of Tsushima between Korea and southern Japan, was largely destroyed by the Japanese navy. This disaster ended any hopes the Russian regime had of distracting the population and staving off reforms with a glorious military victory.

As a result, political tensions rose even higher in the country, which was already wracked with discontent. The municipal councils of Moscow and Saint Petersburg and other civic organizations increased their calls for political reforms. Even leading members of an association of Russian nobility expressed the fear that Russia was on the verge of anarchy because of its ineffective government and called on the tsar to seek the assistance of "elected representatives of the entire land"—an especially radical idea in the Russian context.

But Savinkov's gamble on Shpayzman was not justified, and in the end, there was no attack on Kleygels. The reason for the Kiev fiasco was all too simple and human: Aron Shpayzman had fallen in love with Manya Shkolnik and was trying to shield her from any personal danger. Ironically, he did not value his own life any more than she did hers: both were prepared to sacrifice themselves without a moment's hesitation in a terrorist attack. But their personal relations interfered with what they saw as their revolutionary duty. Aron was prepared to use force to stop Manya from risking her life, and she was too attached to him to act against his will.

After they left Savinkov's team, they did not end their commitment to terrorism, but their attitude toward their relationship changed. On January 1, 1906, they attacked Governor Alexey Khvostov of Chernigov, a provincial city to the north of Kiev. Aron's bomb failed to explode, but Manya's wounded the man. A military tribunal sentenced Aron to death, and he was hanged shortly thereafter. Manya got twenty years but did not finish her sentence. In 1910, she escaped from Siberia to China and then moved to Europe and the United States. She returned to Soviet Russia after the Bolshevik coup in 1917, managed to survive the Stalinist maelstrom that destroyed many old revolutionaries, and died there in 1955.

Betrayals

Savinkov finally learned a lesson from the failure of the Kiev operation and concluded that if all new recruits were vetted more rigorously, the Combat Organization could be reconstituted to its previous effectiveness. By late July 1905, the process seemed well on its way. In addition to himself and Azef, there were now six watchers—several of whom, like Zilberberg, already had experience working in the streets—and a three-person technical group, including the veteran Dora Brilliant.

But there were traitors in the organization.

In early August, the new Combat Organization gathered in Nizhny Novgorod, an important commercial center on the Volga River 250 miles east of Moscow, during its enormous annual trade fair, which brought visitors from all over Europe and Asia. Savinkov and his team were full of confidence and began to plan an attack on the governor, Baron Pavel Unterberger, who they believed would be a relatively easy target and good practice for General Trepov in Saint Petersburg.

However, when Azef arrived, his first words to Savinkov were "We are being watched."

Savinkov had not noticed anything and at first did not believe Azef. He also initially refused to abandon the attack on Unterberger because the failure of the Kleygels plot still rankled. But then he and Zilberberg became suspicious of how the servants in their hotel were behaving around them, and Savinkov thought he recognized an Okhrana agent he had not seen since his student days in Saint Petersburg.

That was enough. Savinkov hurriedly instructed the team to scatter. He and Azef arranged to meet in Saint Petersburg in three weeks; they would use the intervening time to cover their tracks. Zilberberg succeeded in getting out of Nizhny Novgorod without being seen and left for Saint Petersburg, where he would lie low. One new member of the team, an experienced old revolutionary, tried to escape but was arrested.

After consulting a train schedule, Savinkov left for Moscow and began a multiday, multicity, zigzagging trip of thousands of miles, with sudden changes of trains and cabs, and periods of hiding with friends, in an attempt to lose the *fileurs* he could see and those he suspected might be following him.

Only when he got to Finland, where one of Vera's brothers had a country house, did he feel safe. Finland was part of the Russian Empire, but it had a degree of autonomy, which meant Savinkov could not be arrested there. He was at a loss to explain how the police had been able to pursue him and the other members of the team.

By coincidence, on the day after Savinkov got to his brother-in-law's dacha, an SR from Saint Petersburg arrived with some shocking news. A member of the SR committee in the capital had received an anonymous letter claiming there were two Okhrana *agents-provocateurs* in the Party (the term in Russian is *provokator*). One was Nikolay Tatarov, an esteemed revolutionary who had recently been released from Siberian exile and given a senior position in the Party's Odessa branch. The other was Azef. The anonymous letter also listed what each had revealed to the police.

The recipient of the letter rejected its accusations categorically and immediately showed it to Azef himself, who managed to maintain his composure and only turned pale. In Savinkov's eyes, Azef's reputation was inviolate, and Tatarov, whom Savinkov had known well since Warsaw, was beyond suspicion. The only effect the letter had on Party members was to elicit sympathy for Azef, because he was seen as a victim of vile calumny. Savinkov was certain the police were behind it but did not understand why they would plant such patently false accusations. He decided that he urgently needed to consult with Gots and Azef himself. Enlisting the help of sympathetic Finnish revolutionaries, who got him across the border into Sweden via the simple expedient of renting a sailboat, Savinkov traveled to Geneva in early September 1905.

<hr />

Savinkov would not know it for some time, but luck had favored him once again, because he had been in the crossfire of two separate betrayals. The first was in fact Tatarov's. While in Siberian exile, he had made a deal with the governor-general, who was an old friend of his father's, to become an Okhrana informant against the Socialist Revolutionary Party in exchange for a shortened sentence. It was Tatarov's betrayal of the Combat Organization in Saint Petersburg that led to the mass arrests of March 17, 1905. Later, in August, he also informed the Okhrana of the reconstituted Combat Organization's presence in Nizhny Novgorod, which resulted in the disruption of the attack on Unterberger. For his work during this six-month period he was paid very handsomely—16,100 rubles, or approximately $250,000 in today's money.

The second betrayal was Azef's. He informed the police of Savinkov's whereabouts after he fled from Nizhny Novgorod, which explains the *fileurs'* uncanny ability to "follow" Savinkov wherever he went despite all his efforts to shake them off. This was also Azef's second attempt to sink Savinkov during the summer of 1905. On June 19 and July 15, Rataev reported to his superiors in Saint Petersburg on Savinkov's plans to visit the capital and its suburbs; moreover, he referred to Savinkov as the "leader of the Combat Organization." Such highly secret information could only have come from Azef, and he must have gotten it from

Savinkov himself. At the same time, Azef continued the charade of maintaining warm and "familial" relations with Savinkov and sent his regards and "kisses" to Vera when he wrote.

The Visible Traitor

When Savinkov arrived in Geneva in the first days of September 1905, the atmosphere was grim: many Party members had begun to suspect that there was indeed a *provokator* in their midst. Like Savinkov, Gots also thought that the anonymous letter about two traitors was police disinformation, but he was not prepared to accept Savinkov's assurance that Tatarov was trustworthy and insisted that he be thoroughly investigated. As for Azef, Savinkov expressed what everyone in the Party believed when he later wrote: "I considered . . . the spreading of disgraceful rumors about . . . the head of the Combat Organization to be an insult to the honor of the party, especially the honor of each member of the Combat Organization. Defending that honor was my Party duty."

The Socialist Revolutionary Party was a very principled organization and scrupulously careful and democratic in its procedures. It also strived to be as transparent about its activities as security would allow and always to occupy the highest moral ground. Accordingly, Gots asked the Party's Central Committee and other senior members to gather in Geneva in early September 1905 and opened the meeting with the proposal that they begin by considering all those present to be possible suspects because no one in the Party should be exempt from scrutiny.

Under the circumstances, it is highly ironic that Azef decided to get out of the way and moved to Italy for the entire period that the Party engaged in its soul searching. As he very likely anticipated, suspicion at the meeting quickly fell on Tatarov. Gots began by raising questions about where Tatarov had gotten a sizable sum of money that he used for a publication he had recently started. The resulting investigation was exemplary in its thoroughness, and in the end, Tatarov's guilt was proven unequivocally.

Savinkov was fully convinced and offered to organize Tatarov's execution for the Party's Central Committee. He admitted that the prospect depressed him deeply, more so than any of the assassinations he had planned, but he felt he had two compelling reasons: to punish Tatarov for the damage he had done to the

Combat Organization and the entire terrorist movement in Russia, and to avenge Azef's and his own besmirched honor as well as that of the other members of the Combat Organization. The Central Committee approved his request and issued the money necessary for the operation.

No Terror in Time of Reform

But then the historical ground in Russia shifted unexpectedly in a way that put the utility of terrorism in question. Shortly after the Tsushima naval debacle in May, an association of labor unions began to agitate for a nationwide strike to force the regime to make reforms. By June, discontent among all classes of the population became so widespread that the tsar assented to having some of his ministers begin discussions, in secret at first, about establishing a Duma, or representative parliamentary body (*duma* is an old Russian word meaning "thought"), that would give people a voice in their own rule. In August, a scheme for a consultative body was announced. But although it was too tepid to satisfy anyone, it established a crucial precedent and whetted oppositional appetites for more, because just eight months earlier the tsar had proclaimed that he would "never" accept any form of representative government.

On August 23, the Treaty of Portsmouth in New Hampshire, which President Theodore Roosevelt brokered, ended the war with Japan on terms that were surprisingly favorable to Russia. However, the regime's hope that this would have a calming effect on the country was not realized. Within days, radical university students allied with workers began to organize political gatherings on campuses. In September, strikes started to unroll. On October 6, Moscow's railroad workers went on strike and isolated the city. The railway strike quickly spread, and factory, telegraph, telephone, and white-collar workers also struck, leading to violent clashes with police and Cossacks. The situation throughout the empire had become so unstable that Count Sergey Witte, the chairman of the Council of Ministers and Russia's envoy at the Portsmouth Peace Conference, told the tsar he had only two choices: to appoint a military dictator who would restore order by brutal force, or to make major political concessions.

All of Nicholas II's instincts were against yielding, and he began by offering dictatorial powers to his cousin, Grand Duke Nikolay Nikolaevich, who had the military experience and who looked the part: he was a senior cavalry general and an imposing figure at over six feet tall. However, the grand duke rebuffed the idea and replied that there were not enough troops in the imperial capital to impose order. He is then reported to have drawn his revolver and threatened to shoot himself right then and there if the tsar did not sign a manifesto proclaiming major reforms. The tsar did so the following day, and wrote in his diary, "May the Lord help us save and pacify Russia."

∘—✦—∘

The Manifesto of October 17, 1905, as it became known, was unprecedented in Russian imperial history and encompassed three major points: the country's population was granted a bill of rights guaranteeing "the principles of genuine inviolability of person [and] freedoms of conscience, speech, assembly and association"; a state Duma was established that would be elected via universal male franchise; and the Duma would approve all the laws of the land and participate in supervising imperial appointees. On paper, it was an extraordinarily liberal reform of the government.

Initially, the proclamation of the October Manifesto set off jubilation across the empire: no one had expected such major dramatic concessions. In Moscow, a crowd of 50,000 people gathered in the square in front of the Bolshoy Theater. Thousands of singing and cheering people demonstrated in other cities. The general strike began to collapse in Saint Petersburg, Moscow, and elsewhere.

∘—✦—∘

In Geneva and throughout the Russian revolutionary diaspora, news of the October Manifesto produced enormous excitement. It was "greeted as the beginning of a new era," as Savinkov recalled, and prompted a wave of public meetings, with speakers extolling the significance of the reforms. Savinkov spoke at one himself about the significance of terrorism in the history of the Russian revolutionary movement.

Then telegrams began to arrive with more dramatic news: almost all the members of the Combat Organization arrested on March 17 had been amnestied and released; prisoners in the notorious Shlisselburg prison were freed as well. Even skeptics in the revolutionary emigration began to believe that the reforms were real.

For Savinkov, however, this became not so much a time for rejoicing as for renewed action. Because Tatarov had been exposed and was now living in isolation while awaiting his fate, Savinkov believed that the Okhrana no longer had any *provokators* in the Socialist Revolutionary Party. Moreover, he saw the October Manifesto as a sure sign of the imperial regime's unprecedented confusion. (And he was right: a senior officer in the Okhrana remembered that the entire organization fell into chaos and came to a standstill in the wake of the October Manifesto because no one knew what it meant for their work.) The moment was ripe, Savinkov thought, to resurrect the Combat Organization in all its previous vigor. And now was the time, he insisted to the SR Central Committee, to deliver the final blows to the imperial regime.

Most members of the Combat Organization agreed with Savinkov, including his old comrades Lev Zilberberg, Dora Brilliant, and Boris Moiseyenko, who had been in the group released from Shlisselburg. But to Savinkov's shock, the Central Committee and many of the Party's rank and file opposed the resumption of terror. Their position was that terrorism was allowable as a tactic only in countries that did not have constitutions or freedom of speech and the press. In Russia, however, the October Manifesto had in effect established a constitutional monarchy with guarantees of personal rights and mechanisms for legal change. As a result, terrorism was now inadmissible as a matter of principle.

Savinkov was incensed and argued vehemently that only a strong Combat Organization could guarantee the preservation of the rights that the Russian people had just won from the imperial regime. He demanded that the Combat Organization be given as many new members and as much money as possible so that it could renew its campaigns of central terror.

But he lost the argument. After some debate about keeping the Combat Organization in reserve for possible future use, Gots expressed his view that all terrorist activity should cease and that the Combat Organization should be disbanded immediately.

To Savinkov's great shock and disappointment, Azef, who was now living in Geneva and attended the meeting, agreed. For him the October Manifesto was the perfect opportunity to get out of the dangerous game he had been playing for years and to do so without losing face or arousing suspicions among the revolutionaries or the police. A member of the Party remembered the glee with which Azef spoke about the October Manifesto and his desire to retire from terrorism: "This is the finale of terror—period, the end," he kept repeating. During the debates about whether or not to keep the Combat Organization "under arms" or disband it, Azef readily admitted that he was "only a fellow-traveler of the Party" and that as soon as the constitution took effect, he would become a "legalist and evolutionist" with regard to the future course of Russian government.

⌘

Savinkov saw the Socialist Revolutionary Party's decision to disband the Combat Organization as a tragic mistake, because it was a failure to exploit a turning point in Russian history, one that was nothing less than the "single most favorable moment in the history of terror." Out of solidarity he would abide by the Party's decision. But it left him devastated, and not just because of the historical and political consequences.

Perhaps even more important for understanding Savinkov is that the dissolution of the Combat Organization left him personally traumatized. The salient characteristic of terrorism for him—one that became so psychologically compelling that it appears to have become addictive—was a total submission of the self to an overwhelming and deadly common task. In a situation like this, one's relations with comrades, and consequently one's sense of self, are entirely functions of prolonged, highly disciplined, and dangerous conspiracy. An experience like this intensifies and defines every moment of existence. To be suddenly deprived of it was disorienting, and a return to civilian life was very difficult. Savinkov wrote to his wife that he felt "as if I'm at the bottom of a deep well. In my soul there is darkness. I have no desires. Almost indifference to everything. Life has exhausted me." He was not alone in feeling this way. When he talked with Dora Brilliant about the dissolution of the Combat Organization, he could hear tears in her voice.

The Revolution of 1905

However, Russian history was moving too quickly and unpredictably for Savinkov to be sidelined very long. Events after the October Manifesto showed that the Socialist Revolutionary Party had been too high-minded when it decided to give the imperial regime the benefit of the doubt about its reformist intentions. The Party had also been too optimistic about the October Manifesto's transformative effects on the country.

As Nicholas II discovered to his great disappointment, the October Manifesto not only failed to pacify Russia but soon made disorders worse. On October 18, 1905, the day after its proclamation, there was not only jubilation; new forms of violence began to erupt across the empire as well. Monarchists in cities and towns, mostly from the lower classes, resented Russia's embarking on a path that broke with ancient traditions. Rumors spread that Jews and maybe students had taken the tsar hostage and forced him to sign the manifesto. The sight of triumphant processions of liberals and leftists carrying red flags in many cities exacerbated right-wing fears. Squads of Black Hundreds began carrying out murderous pogroms against Jews; beating high school and university students; and assaulting intellectuals, municipal council employees, and other members of the intelligentsia. In places, it became dangerous to wear eyeglasses on the street.

In the countryside, peasants did not understand the October Manifesto at all and took it as a license to expropriate the farmland they always coveted. Emboldened by the pogroms and unchecked violence sweeping the country, they began to attack landlords' estates, yielding to a vague, quasi-messianic belief that all land that was not already theirs would soon be redistributed to them.

The October Manifesto also had the effect of aggravating opposition by the most radical socialist parties, which did not view the reforms as sufficiently progressive and did not trust the regime to live up to its promises unless it was forced to do so. The failure of the regime during the fall of 1905 to stop right-wing violence—police often looked at it through their fingers—seemed to be evidence that it had not abandoned its reactionary path.

The imperial regime's counterreaction was predictable. On December 3, the police arrested several hundred members of the Saint Petersburg Soviet, a body of representatives from different socialist groups that had constituted itself in October to agitate for revolution. In response three days later, the Moscow Soviet, which was dominated by the more radical, Bolshevik branch of the Marxist Socialist Democratic Party, voted to begin an armed revolution to overthrow the tsarist regime and establish a democratic republic.

On December 7, Moscow was paralyzed by a general strike. Huge rallies and meetings broke out in the city. Several thousand armed revolutionaries—mostly workers and students—threw up barricades in the streets and engaged in pitched battles with troops and the police. At one point, the revolutionaries seized control of most of the train stations and much of the city, except for its core.

The American ambassador in Saint Petersburg sent a coded telegram to Washington: "Russian nation appears to have gone temporarily insane; government practically helpless to restore law and order." Because the Moscow garrison proved incapable of suppressing the rebellion, the imperial government brought in the elite Semyonovsky Lifeguard Regiment from Saint Petersburg. Using artillery against the revolutionaries' stronghold in the city's industrial Presnya district, on December 18 the guards finally crushed the rebellion, thus ending what would become known as the 1905, or "first," Russian Revolution. Several thousand revolutionaries and civilians had been killed and wounded, and entire districts of the ancient city were smoldering ruins.

Between the time when the Combat Organization was disbanded in October and the Moscow uprising broke out in December, Savinkov led a twilight existence in Saint Petersburg, marking his time. The amnesty that accompanied the October Manifesto allowed him to live quite openly and to collaborate with a Socialist Revolutionary newspaper.

When fighting started in Moscow, Savinkov took on new revolutionary duties even though his heart was not in it. After first refusing, he relented out of a sense of party loyalty and agreed to help Azef prepare a military mutiny and an armed uprising in Saint Petersburg. But the world of soldiers, sailors, and officers with their regimentation and hierarchy was unfamiliar to him (this would change markedly later in his life), and he did not believe that a military mutiny could ever succeed. Neither did he believe that there were enough revolutionary workers in the capital ready to stage another massive strike and to follow it with an armed uprising.

He made an attempt to help organize blowing up a bridge on the main line linking Moscow and Saint Petersburg to prevent troop reinforcements from getting to Moscow from the capital and to catalyze a strike by other railroads. But the plan went nowhere because all the participants were arrested as soon as they began their work. All his other plans—blowing up the Okhrana headquarters in Saint Petersburg; destroying electrical and telephone lines; kidnapping the new prime minister, Count Witte—ended in failure too, in part because security was so tight that it seemed to Savinkov as if the police were being systematically warned of the plans in advance. When, following Azef's instruction, Savinkov set up two dynamite laboratories in Saint Petersburg, both were raided by the police on the same night, and most of the people in them were arrested, including Dora Brilliant.

Only later and with the benefit of hindsight would it become clear to Savinkov that there was a second *provokator* in the Party. But, as he put in his memoir, against the background of the vast revolutionary storm raging in Russia at the time, "the circumstances of these arrests were forgotten . . . and they remained unexplained."

The arrest ended Brilliant's career. She was imprisoned in the Peter and Paul Fortress, where the harsh conditions aggravated her anguished melancholy, and went mad. She died in the prison in October 1907. Dora Brilliant had been one of Savinkov's oldest and most valued comrades, and he would eulogize her "as one of the most prominent women of terror."

To Revive Terror

Though the Moscow uprising was put down by the imperial regime, the fact that it happened showed that Russia was on the edge of a revolutionary cliff. The situation in the country was changing so rapidly that the Socialist Revolutionary Party decided it needed to reconsider its options and organized a general congress in Finland during the final days of December 1905 and the beginning of 1906. There it passed two major resolutions: it would not cooperate with the regime in any way and would consequently boycott the coming elections to the Duma, and the Combat Organization would be resurrected.

The argument in favor of renewing central terror had prevailed over arguments that the Party should concentrate on fomenting a broad-based popular uprising. It was decided that there was not yet sufficient support for the latter.

The first targets that the Party's Central Committee chose were Minister of the Interior Pyotr Durnovo, who was accused of supporting the violently anti-Semitic Black Hundreds monarchist bands, and the governor-general of Moscow, Vice Admiral Fyodor Dubasov, who was held responsible for the recent bloody "pacification" of Moscow.

In its punctilious fashion the Central Committee also stipulated that in order to demonstrate that the Party was not trying to sabotage the nascent process of reform itself, both assassinations had to be carried out before the opening of the first session of the Duma on April 27, 1906. Furthermore, all terrorist acts would be suspended for the duration of the Duma's session.

Savinkov's wish had been realized. Immediately after the congress ended, he joined Azef in what he thought would be an effort to rebuild the Combat Organization.

However, a return to terror was not what Azef expected or wanted, although he also did not want to lose his senior position in the Party or break with the Okhrana. Holding on to everything would require some tricky maneuvering.

He began by trying to shed just his role as the leader of the Combat Organization by appealing to his comrades' feelings. During a meeting in Helsinki with Savinkov and Moiseyenko, he suddenly told them that he needed to rest and wanted them to take over. He also added that he did not believe their former methods of stalking victims would work any longer.

As Azef surely knew they would, Savinkov and Moiseyenko objected vehemently, arguing that they were not strong enough to assume responsibility for central terror, that the Central Committee had appointed him head of the Combat Organization, and that it was not at all certain that the other members of the Party would accept their leadership.

For a while Azef sat in silence as he seemed to weigh his response. Then he raised his head and said, "All right, let it be as you wish. But in my opinion—nothing will come of our work."

This proved to be not so much an expression of Azef's opinion as his prediction. The challenge he faced now was how to simulate that he was directing real attacks while sabotaging them through mismanagement or betrayal and concealing his own true role. Fortunately for him, he had powerful allies in the persons of his potential dupes—Savinkov, Moiseyenko, and the other members of the Combat Organization—all of whom, as he had just witnessed, could not conceive of acting without him.

⚬━⚬

Azef was methodical in creating the illusion that he was reviving the Combat Organization. He reserved all recruiting decisions for himself, and by early spring of 1906, there were nearly thirty members. Savinkov argued that this was an impractically large number and that some of the recruits would have to be inactive as result, but Azef overruled him. Azef then devised a series of what appeared to be very ambitious plans for assassinations in Moscow, Saint Petersburg, and Sevastopol. But despite the facts that he had recently disparaged the street surveillance techniques used by the Combat Organization and that the March 17 arrests had revealed information about them to the police, he did nothing to modify the procedures. Azef also tried to assign a woman in an advanced state of pregnancy as Savinkov's bomb technician and initially dismissed his strenuous objections. Only when Savinkov threatened to resign from the Combat Organization did Azef yield and assign another female bomb maker.

⚬—╾—⚬

It did not make any difference that Savinkov had gotten his way. None of the attempts on Dubasov that he tried to coordinate in Moscow succeeded. On March 2, the bomb throwers failed to spot their target; they tried again the following day, with the same result. Regrouping two weeks later, they tried on four separate days but failed each time because they could not locate Dubasov or something interfered. The emotional and physical toll of the failures on the designated throwers and on Savinkov was very heavy. "If you haven't participated in terrorism," he wrote later, "it's hard to imagine the anxiety and strain that overwhelmed us after the series of failed attempts."

Things were going so badly that Savinkov went to Helsinki to consult with Azef. But he also made the mistake of revealing to him that the Moscow team would attack Dubasov when he went to one of the Kremlin cathedrals for a holiday service. The result was that shortly after Savinkov returned to Moscow, both he and the other members of his team began to notice that they were being followed by *fileurs* and barely escaped.

Still oblivious to what was happening, Savinkov made a second attempt to consult with Azef, who reacted to his report with insulting skepticism but agreed to some changes. Despite this, when an attack on Dubasov was finally carried out, he was only wounded, while his adjutant and the bomb thrower were killed. The attack on Durnovo in Saint Petersburg went no better. The members of the Combat Organization team noticed *fileurs* following them and began to scatter, but the police managed to arrest a number of them shortly thereafter.

Azef did not limit himself to betraying revolutionaries to the police so that they would be imprisoned or hanged. On at least one occasion, he imperiled a technician's life by instructing her to disarm a bomb that had been assembled by someone else. Because all bombs were handmade and could have peculiarities known only to their builder, Combat Organization safety protocols required that arming and disarming be done by the same person. But an order from the exalted head of the organization had to be followed.

Maria Benevskaya was a young, very pretty, blond, blue-eyed noblewoman from a military family who had studied science and medicine and joined the Combat Organization because of her deep religious convictions. As Azef once commented about her, the only problem she had in the organization was that everyone kept falling in love with her.

When she began to work on the bomb, she did not know about a defect in the glass tube that was part of its fuse, and it detonated, blowing off her entire left hand and several fingers on her right. It was sheer chance that the dynamite itself did not explode. With the assistance of a comrade, Benevskaya managed to stanch the extensive bleeding, then sent him off with the remainder of her incriminating materials. She left the room by herself after turning the key with her teeth and was able to get herself to a clinic. But she was arrested before her comrades could come to her assistance and was sentenced to ten years of hard labor in Eastern Siberia.

When looking back at this period in the Combat Organization's history, a member commented sadly that it seemed "as if some sort of evil fate was hanging over" it.

Azef's Close Calls

Azef constructed his plots very skillfully over the years, but even so, he had to manipulate too many people with too many different interests to be able to control the results completely.

The first genuinely close call he had was the anonymous letter naming him and Tatarov as *provokators*. However, no one believed the accusations against him while Tatarov's guilt was easy to establish. As a result, Tatarov became a lightning rod for all the Socialist Revolutionary Party's rage and vengeance. Savinkov orchestrated his execution concurrently with the campaigns against Dubasov and Durnovo, and on March 22, a member of the Combat Organization stabbed Tatarov to death in Warsaw during a grotesquely mishandled attack that also wounded his aged mother.

Azef had a second occasion to deflect attention from himself when he exploited the discovery of another traitor in the SR ranks—no less a figure than Father Georgy Gapon, the heroic leader of the demonstration that led to Bloody Sunday and triggered the Revolution of 1905. Although masses of workers revered Gapon and he played a significant role in planning the armed uprising in Saint Petersburg during the summer of 1905, the SRs discovered to their dismay that he had become a well-paid agent of the police.

Savinkov and other party leaders immediately proposed that Gapon be assassinated, and Azef naturally agreed. However, he added another cunning and self-serving twist to the plan by suggesting that Gapon be killed together with Pyotr Rachkovsky, vice director of the Department of Police in Saint Petersburg, who also happened to be Azef's own secret handler. Azef did not entirely trust Rachkovsky's discretion and was willing to sacrifice him to eliminate someone who knew a lot of compromising information. The SRs laid a trap for Rachkovsky, but he proved too wily to fall into it. However, Gapon was successfully lured to a remote dacha outside the capital and garroted by Pyotr Rutenberg, the same member of the Combat Organization who had helped him escape the carnage on Palace Square on Bloody Sunday.

Paradoxically, the most serious threat Azef faced up to this point in his career came from his employers in the imperial police, although in the end he handled them with the same virtuosity as he did the revolutionaries.

On April 10, 1906, Azef was in Saint Petersburg during the plot that was unfolding against Minister Durnovo. He intended to thwart it and had already informed the Okhrana about the three "cabbies" watching Durnovo's comings and goings in the streets. As a result, they were now being closely followed by agents who were biding their time before making arrests. Then chance intervened, and one of the more experienced *fileurs* noticed that the three "cabbies" met regularly with a fourth man—a round-faced, heavyset fellow in fashionable clothing who seemed to be their leader. And although the *fileur* did not know the man's real name, he recognized him as one of the Okhrana's secret agents whom he had seen in Moscow several years earlier.

As a result, Azef became a pawn in a territorial struggle between two senior officials in the imperial security establishment. Incredibly, Rachkovsky, Azef's police handler, had never informed the head of the Saint Petersburg Okhrana, General Alexander Gerasimov, that he had a mole in the Combat Organization. Rachkovsky withheld this information for security reasons (the fewer people who knew about Azef, the safer he would be) and because of interdepartmental rivalry, despite the fact that the Okhrana's job was to protect senior figures in the imperial regime.

When Gerasimov found out that the "fourth man" was supposed to be a secret agent, that he had never heard of him, and that he was involved with known terrorists, he began by quizzing Rachkovsky about him. But Rachkovsky had no difficulty in lying to a colleague and denied any knowledge of secret agents. (He was also well practiced in machinations. Some years earlier, when he had been stationed in Paris, he is believed to have played a role in fabricating the notorious anti-Semitic invective *The Protocols of the Elders of Zion*.)

Gerasimov had a strong sense of self-importance, which was reflected in his pugnacious appearance—a round head with narrow eyes and a thick, dramatically upturned moustache resembling a boar's tusks. He also outranked Rachkovsky, did not like him, and did not trust him. He ordered that Azef be arrested immediately, but in such a way that his "cabbie" comrades would not notice. Accordingly, several *fileurs* caught up with Azef on a quiet street, grabbed him under the arms, and, ignoring his loud protests, hustled him into a closed carriage waiting nearby. He was quickly delivered to Gerasimov's office.

Azef began by presenting his forged passport and denying any association with the police. But Gerasimov was experienced in dealing with "difficult" prisoners: to soften Azef up and give him a chance "to think," Gerasimov had him locked up in a solitary cell at Okhrana headquarters. Two days later Azef cracked and requested to meet with Gerasimov, stipulating that "my former boss" Rachkovsky be present as well.

The scene that played out in Gerasimov's office could have been a burlesque on one of the city's vaudeville stages. Gerasimov was delighted with the opportunity to humiliate Rachkovsky by catching him out in a bald lie while at the same time getting to the bottom of who Azef was and how he could be useful.

In a display of duplicity that it hard to believe, when Rachkovsky arrived he feigned that he had forgotten who Azef was and remembered him only now. Extending both hands, and the usual hangdog expression on his moustached and goateed face replaced with a sycophantic smile, he rushed to greet Azef like a long-lost friend, exclaiming, "Ah, my dear Evgeny Filippovich, it's been ages since we've seen each other. How are you?"

But Azef would have none of it. After the arrest and two days in a prison cell, he was in a towering rage and attacked Rachkovsky with an extraordinary tirade of the most vulgar curses (one of the riches of the Russian language). Even Gerasimov, with all his experience in dealing with Russia's criminal classes, was impressed by Azef's ingenious conglomerations of "choice swearing."

Azef accused Rachkovsky of ingratitude, inhumanity, and every other crime of which only the most unscrupulous person was capable. Referring to how a recent administrative reshuffling had affected him personally—in August 1905 his former immediate supervisor, Rataev in Paris, had been forced to retire and was replaced by Rachkovsky—Azef yelled, "You left me to my fate without instructions, without money, you didn't respond to my letters." And then, in what can only be described as the crowning moment of a brilliant performance that concealed his actual role in the Combat Organization, Azef shouted, "To earn money, I was forced to start working with the terrorists!"

The gullible Gerasimov was won over completely and listened to Azef's tirade with great sympathy. "Rachkovsky's unscrupulousness also outraged me," he later recalled, because "he had exposed one of his most important people to extreme danger . . . I felt pangs of conscience myself for Rachkovsky's actions."

In the end, Azef restored his standing with the imperial police agencies, and all participants agreed that henceforth he would report to General Gerasimov, who would be his main contact. The erstwhile pawn had become a king again.

<hr />

Gerasimov now saw Azef as opening new and very promising opportunities for combating terrorism—ones that he believed the unimaginative Rachkovsky was incapable of appreciating. He immediately agreed to Azef's demand to be paid 5,000 rubles for the wages he was owed, plus an additional sum for expenses (or a tidy total of some $100,000 in today's money). Azef then proceeded to consolidate his standing with Gerasimov even more by making several new revelations about the Combat Organization. He also gave the Okhrana information that allowed them to thwart assassination attempts on General Min and Colonel Riman, the commanders of the Semyonovsky Lifeguard Regiment that crushed the uprising in Moscow.

Gerasimov soon became convinced that Azef was completely trustworthy, and the two collaborated on developing a general tactic to stop terrorism: the police would not arrest all known members of the Combat Organization, because this would only result in others taking their place. Instead, the police would disrupt the terrorists' plans by using techniques such as overt surveillance to scare them off. There was actually a staff of special *fileurs*, called *mikhryutki*, or "sad sacks," whose role was to seem ineptly obvious when pursuing someone. Gerasimov expected that the terrorists would eventually give up trying to organize plots out of sheer frustration at being followed everywhere.

The final part of Gerasimov's plan for Azef could have been written by Azef himself. He was supposed to bring disorder into the Combat Organization's finances, which were in excellent shape with accumulations in the hundreds of thousands of rubles, by drawing generously on them as often as possible for his own needs and to put away as much as possible for a rainy day. "However, as I quickly learned," Gerasimov later noted wryly—and naïvely—in a memoir, "Azef did not need my advice. He'd been doing this before we met."

Savinkov Must Die

Despite Azef's and Gerasimov's decision not to liquidate the Combat Organization by arresting all its members, Savinkov was too important a figure in their eyes to be allowed simply to roam freely and only occasionally spooked by *fileurs*.

In late April Azef met with Savinkov in Saint Petersburg to assess the Combat Organization's losses during the last months and to consider what could be done. Savinkov again insisted on a leaner organization and argued that it was necessary to introduce "technological" innovations and not to rely as much on watching in the streets. This was an important shift in his thinking, and Azef pretended to go along. But he also resolved to deal with Savinkov once and for all: he proposed that he go to Sevastopol, home of the Russian Black Sea fleet, and assassinate its commander, Vice Admiral Grigory Chukhnin, for his brutal suppression of the naval mutiny of November 1905.

Savinkov readily agreed despite all the suspicious events that kept happening to him. Recently he had been stopped by the police at the Finland Station in Saint Petersburg, instructed to open his luggage for inspection, and then simply allowed to leave. The message was clear: we are watching you. But when Savinkov told Azef about the incident, Azef simply laughed, saying that this was probably just a coincidence. The event did not shake Savinkov's resolve. Just before leaving

Saint Petersburg, he ran into an old friend from his Vologda days, the writer Alexey Remizov, who was struck by the expression of "anger and mercilessness" on his face.

———

Savinkov arrived in Sevastopol on Friday, May 12, planning to start his surveillance with the other members of his team on Sunday, May 14, the anniversary of Nicholas II's coronation, when Admiral Chukhnin was expected to attend a service commemorating the event in the city's main church, the Cathedral of Saint Vladimir.

Around noon on Sunday, Savinkov was sitting in a park reading a newspaper and waiting to meet the technician Rachel Lurye, who was supposed to arrive with dynamite that day, when he heard the distant rumble of an explosion. He recognized the telltale sound but had no idea what was going on. Assuming that he was safe because he had not informed the local SR Party that he was in the city and had not noticed police following him, Savinkov returned to his hotel. However, no sooner had he begun to climb the stairs than he heard someone behind him shout: "Sir, you're under arrest!" and felt his arms being violently grabbed from behind. When he twisted around, he saw two soldiers holding him. More soldiers with rifles were pouring onto the stairway landing and quickly surrounded him with a ring of fixed bayonets. A pale-faced police officer stuck the muzzle of his revolver into Savinkov's chest while a detective shook his fist at him and cursed. "It's not worth bothering," a nervous-looking naval officer muttered angrily. "Let's just take him outside and shoot him."

Despite these threats, Savinkov was taken to the hotel's dining room and treated with unexpected civility while a preliminary report was written up. A junior officer asked him if there was anything he would like, and Savinkov asked for soda water and cigarettes. The water was brought to him. But when the senior officer in charge of the arrest took a cigarette out of his own case and contemptuously tossed it across the table, Savinkov lost his temper at the insult. Ignoring the armed men around him, he grabbed the cigarette and threw it in the officer's face, shouting: "You forget, sir, that I am no less a gentleman than you!"

However, after his outburst Savinkov felt a curious sense of relief. He had known for a long time that he would be captured someday. He was also very tired because of the life he had been leading. One of his first thoughts after being arrested, even though he knew he would face the death penalty, was, "Now I'll be able to rest."

The three other members of Savinkov's team were also seized the same day and locked up in prison cells in the Sevastopol Fortress. None of them had had anything to do with the explosion that occurred earlier, which they learned was an attack by members of the local SR branch on the commander of the fortress, Lieutenant General Neplyuev. Nevertheless, someone had implicated Savinkov's team and tipped off the police, who now assumed that he was the ringleader. (It was of course Azef, as Gerasimov would later reveal in his memoir.) That same evening Savinkov and all the others were charged with belonging to a secret organization, possessing explosives, and trying to kill Neplyuev. The commander of the local military district ordered that they be tried by a military tribunal following the procedures used in wartime. He set the trial for Thursday, May 18, 1906.

<hr />

Savinkov understood that the early date and the military jurisdiction meant there was a rush to sentence him to death. His appointed defender, an artillery captain named Ivanov who had no legal training, admitted as much, then added: "I won't conceal it from you. The sentence will be carried out on Friday the 19th."

Savinkov took the news stoically; he had long been prepared to die.

But it bothered him to die for something he did not do and would never have approved. One of the perpetrators of the attack on Neplyuev was a sixteen-year-old, Nikolay Makarov. From Savinkov's point of view, to involve someone that young in an assassination "contradicted my conscience as a terrorist." Even worse was that when Makarov's bomb failed to explode, his co-conspirator, a sailor in the navy, began to push through the crowd toward Neplyuev with a second bomb concealed under his clothing. The jostling set it off by accident, killing not only him but six others and wounding thirty-seven more. Savinkov thought this was criminal.

However, it was Makarov's youth that unexpectedly saved Savinkov from being quickly hanged. When the police found out Makarov's age, they felt obligated to start a legal process to determine if he could be tried as an adult; this delayed his and everyone else's trial. Savinkov's military defender also proved to be a very principled and decent man, despite his loyalty to the imperial regime and staunch opposition to revolution. He treated Savinkov with great courtesy, as if he were an honorable enemy captured on the field of battle. He also bent the rules and agreed to send telegrams on Savinkov's behalf to his mother, Sofia, and his wife, Vera, informing them of what happened.

To Save Savinkov

Sofia had not seen Boris since her visit to Vologda four years earlier and believed that he was safe in European exile. She was also not fully aware of the nature and extent of his terrorist exploits, which he and Vera concealed to spare her after the deaths of Alexander and her husband. When she opened the telegram at her home in Warsaw on the evening of May 16, she was thunderstruck: "Immediately take express Sevastopol son wants to see you—defender Ivanov."

Sofia felt the blood rush to her head and kept rereading what was on the slip of paper, trying to understand. From newspaper accounts she knew about the attempt on Neplyuev in Sevastopol, but Boris's name had not been included in the list of those arrested. Then panic seized her: the newspapers had mentioned there would be a military trial, and she knew what this implied. She wanted to rush to her son's side immediately, but because that evening's express to Moscow, where she would have to change trains, had already departed, she had to agonize until morning.

Other forces in Savinkov's camp also began to stir. Leaving the children at home in Saint Petersburg with her brother Alexander, Vera rushed off to Sevastopol accompanied by one of her other brothers, Boris. She also mobilized a team of four lawyers, including an old friend of her husband's from his gymnasium days, Alexander Zemel, who had given him refuge and helped him escape the police in Saint Petersburg the previous summer.

At the same time, but acting independently of Boris Savinkov's family, the efficient and tough-minded Lev Zilberberg, Boris's close comrade from several Combat Organization campaigns, also arrived in Sevastopol. When he first learned about the arrests, he immediately decided that he had to help Savinkov and the others escape from prison and went to Azef for money to carry out his plan. But this was not something Azef wanted to hear: for all he knew, Savinkov might have become suspicious about how the police were able to get on his trail in Sevastopol. Azef even tried to talk Zilberberg out of his intention for a long time, arguing that it would be impossible to engineer Savinkov's escape, much less the entire team's; that the Combat Organization could not sacrifice any of its members for such an obviously impossible scheme; and that he, Zilberberg, should just bide his time and wait for the resumption of terrorism once the Duma session was over. However, Zilberberg would not listen and turned to the SR Central Committee, which readily opened its coffers to him.

In Sevastopol, Vera became the liaison between her husband and Zilberberg. All three discovered that there were people inside and outside the prison who were eager to help. Their strength was not in their numbers, but in the strategic positions they occupied, in their selflessness, and in their ardent sympathy for Savinkov, the Combat Organization, and the entire Socialist Revolutionary Party program. Without them, Savinkov would surely have been hanged in the Sevastopol Fortress, someday just before dawn in the spring or summer of 1906.

Savinkov became aware of the kind of support he had inside Sevastopol Fortress as soon as he was locked up. The guards in the prison wing were drawn from several rotating regiments, and the first ones he met were from Bialystok, a city in Russian Poland with a majority Jewish population. Many of the soldiers had been radicalized during the Revolution of 1905 and identified with Socialist Revolutionaries, Marxist Social Democrats, and other revolutionary factions. A number of noncommissioned officers were active members of revolutionary organizations as well.

When ranking officers were not around, the guards routinely flouted regulations by leaving the cells unlocked and allowing the prisoners to congregate freely. Savinkov was touched by the guards' goodwill and spoke openly with them about the people's need for land, a constituent assembly, and a democratic government; about the burdens of their military service; and about the role of terror.

With each change in regiments, Savinkov discovered new soldiers who were eager to talk. Some were willing to go even further.

The first was Israel Cohen, a private from Brest who introduced Savinkov to other radicalized soldiers. One of these was a sentry outside his cell who agreed to help with an escape when he and his friends were next on duty. He did not want money or anything except help in fleeing abroad. Savinkov passed information about his contacts to Zilberberg, and they began to work together.

They dismissed any plan that might result in the death of any of the guards. This meant that the only way to escape would be with help from someone on the inside, even though this also meant that not all members of the team could escape at the same time.

After bribing one of the police gendarmes in charge of the prison to look the other way, Savinkov organized a meeting with his team to discuss what to do next. All immediately insisted that he had to be the one to escape. Savinkov tried to argue that the only fair way to proceed was to draw straws, but they would not hear of it. He then offered to yield his place to anyone who wanted it, but again they refused. Savinkov finally agreed because he assumed that he was the only one facing certain death.

And then seeming disaster struck when the court suddenly decided to schedule the trial for May 26, which was only days away and would not allow enough time to organize an escape. But one of Savinkov's lawyers argued for a postponement of the trial based on a technicality, and after long deliberations the court agreed with him. Boris's mother and wife were in attendance when the announcement was made and joined the rejoicing that broke out in the courtroom. Sofia was able to visit Boris in prison soon thereafter. The trial was now put off for several months, which gave the plotters plenty of time.

Escape

The key figure in Savinkov's network proved to be Vasily Sulyatitsky, a private in the Lithuanian regiment stationed in the fortress who was a "volunteer" soldier, not a conscript like most of the others, and who enjoyed certain privileges as a result. The son of a Russian Orthodox priest, he was a member of the SR committee in Simferopol, the Crimean capital, and was about to complete his term of service. At the end of June, Savinkov and Zilberberg were introduced to him by Israel Cohen and another Jewish soldier who was a member of the Bund—a secular Jewish socialist organization widespread in the Pale of Settlement. Very tall, fair-haired, and with what Savinkov described as "laughing" blue eyes, Sulyatitsky impressed Savinkov when he walked into his cell and announced in categorical terms that he would take charge of his escape personally and would not yield this task to anyone else.

The first attempt was set for July 3 and depended on Sulyatitsky's being in charge of a squad of prison guards. But the plan quickly fell through, as did another one to duplicate the key to the corridor where Savinkov's cell was located.

A day later, Sulyatitsky tried again. He had gotten a doctor affiliated with the SR Party to lace a cartridge bag full of candy with morphine and planned to feed it to all the guards and their officers. The doctor had assured him that the dose was not harmful but would make everyone who consumed the candy fall into a long and deep sleep, thus allowing all the prisoners to escape at the same time. It sounded far-fetched to Savinkov, but seemed worth a try.

That night Savinkov heard Sulyatitsky offering the candy to the guards; then the iron door at the end of the corridor slammed shut when he left. After a moment's silence, Savinkov heard the men talking:

"Ugh, this candy's really bitter!"

"Well, the gents gobble them . . ."

"Phooey!"

Savinkov stayed up all night, waiting, but not one of the guards fell asleep; none of them showed any lasting ill effects, either.

Four days later, Sulyatitsky tried once more to be put in charge of the prison guards for a night. On July 15, he succeeded and was back at his old post in Savinkov's corridor. He told Savinkov to be ready that same night during the third watch, between 1 and 3 A.M.

Three o'clock came and went, and Savinkov was about to give up and go to sleep when Sulyatitsky finally walked into his cell. Calm as usual, he sat down on Savinkov's cot, lit a cigarette, and asked, "So, we escape?" He then handed Savinkov a revolver. After a brief discussion, both agreed that if an officer tried to stop them, they would shoot him, but if it was a soldier and there was no escape, they would turn their guns on themselves.

Savinkov put on a pair of soldier's boots that Sulyatitsky had stolen for him from a neighboring cell, then tossed a towel over his shoulder and walked out of his cell with Sulyatitsky following, pretending that he was going to the washroom. The ruse worked, and they passed several guards without difficulty. While Savinkov was washing up Sulyatitsky got him a uniform blouse, a cartridge bag and belt, and a service cap, and helped him shave off his moustache. Now Savinkov looked like any other soldier. He followed Sulyatitsky down a series of corridors and past guard rooms where men were sleeping; in one a group of soldiers was listening to someone reading to them. A sentry saw them as they passed but then noticed their epaulettes and said nothing. In a minute, they were outside the fortress walls and rushing down the hill to the town below.

Their escape was discovered a mere five minutes after Savinkov walked out of his cell. Patrols were quickly sent out from the fortress to scour the city. Vera's apartment was also searched. But Savinkov and Sulyatitsky had managed to get to the apartment where Zilberberg was waiting for them and where they changed out of their uniforms and into civilian clothes.

The thrill of the successful escape went to their heads like wine. Savinkov and Sulyatitsky exulted, and Zilberberg abandoned his usual cool manner and embraced them. They were in such high spirits that the same night they wrote an announcement that was soon printed by the SR Party and distributed widely through their clandestine network:

> On the night of July 16, in accordance with the decree of the Combat Organization of the Socialist Revolutionary Party, and with the assistance of volunteer soldier V. M. Sulyatitsky of the 57th Lithuanian Regiment, Boris Viktorovich Savinkov, a member of the Socialist Revolutionary Party, was freed from the main Fortress guardhouse.
> Sevastopol, 16 July 1906.

At Night, across a Storm-Tossed Sea

Still ahead was having to escape abroad, which would not be as simple as Savinkov's previous illicit border crossings because now all of Sevastopol's police and gendarmes knew what he looked like and were searching for him on foot and on horseback. What struck and moved Savinkov, however, was how many strangers were willing to risk their lives to help him and the cause he embodied.

Savinkov, Sulyatitsky, and Zilberberg left Sevastopol the night after the prison break. A worker who had helped them hide in the city and a student from a local engineering institute acted as their guides as they made their way through the surrounding hills and steppeland to the farmstead of a German colonist, Karl Stahlberg, where a refuge had been prepared for them.

Stahlberg was a descendent of the German settlers who had been invited to the Crimea by the imperial regime in the early nineteenth century and worked his family's farm in a secluded valley about twenty-five miles outside the city. He was in his forties, with calloused hands and a tanned, weathered face that reflected his life of toil and hardship. He wanted to shelter Savinkov and the others because, as he explained to their surprise, he had decided to abandon his farm and family (who could manage without him, he said) and become a Socialist Revolutionary.

"You're going abroad," he told Savinkov, "so take me with you. I want to meet Babushka Breshkovskaya and Gots, and then I'll go to the Volga region to work with the peasants." Savinkov tried to talk Stahlberg out of it but failed and promised that he could come.

To minimize risk, the men slept away from Stahlberg's house under the open sky amid picturesque green hills that receded in waves toward the sea. Crimea is Russia's Riviera; its summer is especially warm and dry, and the scenery is luxuriantly Mediterranean. From a high point nearby they took turns watching the road to Sevastopol for any signs of police. The farmer's brood of small children understood what was going on and also took turns watching the road, trying to be helpful in any way they could. "We became friends with them," Savinkov recalled. They must have reminded him of his own son and daughter and of how little time he was able to spend with them. Being free and out of doors after two months in a malodorous, dimly lit cell was exhilarating. The ten days that he and the others spent on Stahlberg's farm became "one of the happiest memories in my entire life," Savinkov recalled later.

⊶

Zilberberg walked the long way to Sevastopol a number of times to explore possibilities for getting out of the country. Trains were impossible, as were scheduled passenger ships in the harbor, because of how well-known Savinkov had become. That left Romania, which was some 200 miles across the Black Sea.

On July 25 Zilberberg reported that he had found a small but sturdy one-masted sailboat that could manage the trip and that it had been leased for an ostensible pleasure trip by an SR sympathizer, an experienced former lieutenant in the Russian Navy. He had resigned his commission in protest after the suppression of the naval mutiny in Sevastopol the year before and was looking for an opportunity to join the Combat Organization.

At dawn on July 26, Savinkov and his comrades, including the farmer Stahlberg, began their voyage from a concealed location in a river mouth near Sevastopol. They had chosen the port of Constanța as their destination largely because of its rail connection to Bucharest, the capital, where the Socialist Revolutionary Party had influential friends.

But shortly after casting off, they had the first of a series of close calls that nearly ended the trip. As bad luck would have it, during the night an entire Russian naval squadron anchored nearby to conduct gunnery practice, and Savinkov and the others watched anxiously as an officer on the deck of a battleship examined them through binoculars. Fortunately, they managed to sail past without incident. Then, they spotted a mine sweeper that seemed to be heading for them until, to their relief, it turned away.

However, soon the weather turned against them. The wind began to quicken, and before long was gusting with gale force. By the night of the twenty-seventh they were in a full-fledged storm, and there were moments when it looked as if their boat would be swamped. Savinkov and his comrades knew nothing about sailing and watched helplessly as the lieutenant struggled with the helm. Soon he announced that he was unable to keep course for Constanța any longer and that they would have to head for Sulina, a smaller port at the mouth of the Danube that was closer. Late on the twenty-eighth they saw Sulina's lighthouses and finally reached the safety of its harbor.

One last obstacle had to be overcome. The lieutenant and his crew were allowed to sail back to Sevastopol. But Sulina's border and port officials would not allow Savinkov's group to stay in Romania without valid passports. Moreover, the Russian consul in Sulina had to be kept in the dark about the reason for their unorthodox arrival out of fear that he would telegraph Sevastopol to make inquiries.

The ingenious solution that Savinkov found was to ask to be allowed to travel from Sulina to Bucharest under police guard, and once there to go to the home of Zamfir Arbore-Ralli, a leading Romanian socialist who had been born and educated in the Russian Empire. He was now the Russian-language teacher of the heir to the Romanian throne and had considerable influence in the capital.

Arbore-Ralli responded very warmly to Savinkov's appeal and immediately sent a telegram to Sulina demanding that all his "nephews" be allowed to join him; if they were not, he threatened to complain to the king. The Romanian police promptly delivered Zilberberg, Sulyatitsky, and Stahlberg to Arbore-Ralli's home, where he, his wife, and children enveloped them with warm hospitality. "For the first time, we were completely out of any danger," Savinkov noted, "and my gratitude toward this family will always be preserved in my memory."

He sent his mother a postcard with one word on it: "Greetings." She saw the Romanian stamp, recognized his handwriting, and almost fainted from relief.

The farmer, Stahlberg, got his wish and traveled to SR headquarters in Geneva. Savinkov, Sulyatitsky, and Zilberberg went to consult with Gots, who was in Heidelberg. On the way, Savinkov sent a letter—remarkable both for its presumption and the nobility of its sentiments—to General Neplyuev in Sevastopol, in which he repeated that he and the members of his team, although proud members of the Socialist Revolutionary Party, had not been involved in the attempt on the general's life. Savinkov also added an ironic note to the letter by using the conventions of epistolary politesse and addressing it "His Excellency Lieutenant-General Neplyuev. Dear Sir!" and signing it "With my deepest respects."

The letter must have infuriated its recipient. But it may also have helped at the October trial of the men who had remained in prison while Savinkov escaped. They were spared the death penalty and sentenced to hard labor for between four and seven years. The teenaged Makarov, who had actually participated in the attempt on Neplyuev, was given a harsher sentence of twelve years in prison. But he could not endure it and escaped after a few months. Soon thereafter, he killed a senior prison warden in Saint Petersburg and was captured and hanged.

CHAPTER FIVE

CROSSROADS

The escape across the Black Sea and the pleasure of seeing Gots again initially buoyed Savinkov's spirits. Even though Gots's health had deteriorated during the past year and his face was more pale and hollow-cheeked than before, the same "live fire" that struck Savinkov when they first met still burned in his eyes. Savinkov also felt again the magnetic pull of his mentor's charisma, what he characterized as his "precious ability" to grasp what was most important in someone after meeting him just a few times and then to respond in a way that accorded perfectly with that person's nature. Gots "did this with such sensitivity and love, with such an extraordinary understanding of people," Savinkov recalled, "that personal relations with him provided enormous moral support."

This was Savinkov's last meeting with Gots. In early September, several weeks after he left Heidelberg, he would learn that Gots had died after undergoing an unsuccessful operation in Berlin. Savinkov took the loss very hard: "In my eyes," he wrote later, "Mikhail Gots was and remains the most important revolutionary of our generation . . . His death was an irreparable loss for the party." In light of Savinkov's future life, it is noteworthy—but not surprising—that he does not grant the mantle to the Bolshevik leader Vladimir Lenin.

Hopes Dashed

After escaping to Europe, Boris Savinkov entered a period in his life when it seemed as if the fates actually had turned against him and everything he valued. He discovered that even though Vera still shared his commitments, the long periods he spent away from her and the children had strained their relations badly. The Combat Organization to which he had dedicated his life was now paralyzed. And the movement for reform in Russia that began when the First Duma opened with great fanfare on April 27, 1906, had suddenly stalled.

Expectations about the Duma had initially been so high that many believed the country was on the verge of rebirth. However, because neither the elected deputies nor the imperial regime had any experience with democratic institutions, what ensued was bewildering contradiction and confusion. On the one hand, deputies who were carried away by a heady atmosphere of freedom made inflammatory speeches in favor of revolution, liberal and revolutionary publications flooded the country, and established newspapers savagely criticized the imperial regime. But on the other, the government, which had not expected such vitriol and was unsure about what to allow and what to forbid, continued to condemn, repress, hunt, and arrest revolutionaries.

The government's irresolution came to an end on July 8, when an increasingly exasperated Nicholas II, who had been assured by his advisers that liberalization would calm the country's discontent, peremptorily dissolved the Duma after it had been in session for only ten weeks. In protest, a large number of outraged deputies decamped to Finland to continue their meetings. They also called on the empire's subjects to stop paying taxes and providing army recruits.

The regime, inevitably, escalated in turn. Nicholas II reacted forcibly by appointing Pyotr Stolypin, his strong-willed minister of the interior, as the new prime minister, a position in which he would serve until his assassination in 1911.

Stolypin would prove in many ways to be the ablest statesman in the history of the Russian Empire. If anyone could have guided the ailing country to some form of viable constitutional monarchy, even against towering odds, it was he.

In addition to instituting a range of visionary reforms, especially his plan to transform peasants into independent, land-owning farmers, Stolypin would also attempt to restore order in the country. But the measures that he used to crush the revolutionary movement were so harsh—including his notorious military tribunals, which meted out several thousand death sentences and thousands more of hard labor—that he became one of the most reviled figures in the imperial regime not only among revolutionaries but liberals as well.

Given Russia's poisoned atmosphere, it was a foregone conclusion that revolution-aries would try to kill Stolypin. On Saturday, August 12, 1906, three members of the ultra-radical Union of Socialist Revolutionary Maximalists, which had broken off from the mainstream Socialist Revolutionary Party, attacked his villa in an outlying part of Saint Petersburg. Their bombs were so powerful that they destroyed the entire front part of the two-story building, killing the terrorists themselves as well as twenty-seven petitioners and guards, and wounding over thirty others, many seriously. Stolypin's three-year-old son and twelve-year-old daughter were also injured, but he escaped with only some bruises.

Savinkov had arrived in Heidelberg just as news of the sensational attack was being trumpeted all over Europe, its scale shocking even those who had gotten used to terrorist bombings in Russia. The attack galvanized the SR Party leaders as well, who were much concerned with their party's "good name" and with public opinion, which did not always distinguish among the different revolutionary factions. Savinkov and Gots rejected what the Maximalists had done because of the horrifying number of innocent victims, although they also took it as a clarion call to rethink their own paralyzed terrorist program. Even Azef got involved: continuing to play his role of the sober and principled Party leader, he composed a proclamation that disavowed the Maximalists and that was issued as an official statement by the SR Central Committee.

Soon after, another sensational attack—which would have seemed straight out of a farce if it had not been so bloody—made the need for the SRs to find a way out of their tactical impasse even more urgent. On August 20, 1906, at a resort in Switzerland, Tatyana Leontyeva, the beautiful young noblewoman who had been a member of Shveytser's team in Saint Petersburg in February 1905, shot and killed a rich, retired Parisian who was calmly eating his lunch in the restaurant. She had mistaken him for Pyotr Durnovo, the former Russian minister of the interior.

Leontyeva had been arrested for participating in Shveytser's plot, and after spending several months in the Peter and Paul Fortress became mentally unstable because of the harsh conditions there. When she was released, she initially appealed to Savinkov to let her rejoin the Combat Organization, but he saw the state she was in and put her off by saying that she needed time to recover. Instead, she approached the Maximalists, who lived up to their name and accepted her. The Okhrana erroneously believed that Boris Savinkov had directed her attack in Switzerland and added it to the official list of his sins in their files.

But simply condemning the Maximalists was not enough, and the SRs had to find a way to reestablish themselves as an effective and honorable revolutionary force. When the Duma was dissolved, the Party's Central Committee responded by mandating a new campaign of terror to force the regime to restore reforms. Stolypin would be the first target, and Azef and Savinkov would again be in charge. One can only imagine Azef's frustration with his subordinate's uncanny ability to survive every betrayal, and with the ineptitude of the police to whom he had repeatedly tried to hand him.

After the Maximalists' attack, Stolypin moved into the impregnable Winter Palace and traveled only by boat to Peterhof, the tsar's lavish summer palace on the Gulf of Finland, for his daily reports. His precautions worked, and after more than two months, from September to November, the Combat Organization team that was stalking him concluded that it would be impossible to get close enough to attack.

This failure became a turning point for Savinkov. He told Azef that it was pointless to continue campaigns using the old methods of surveillance and stalking, which the police had learned to detect and thwart, and that until some kind of innovations were introduced, he would withdraw from terror. Savinkov's suggestion played directly into Azef's plans. He had been continuing to look for an escape from terror and agreed. Several days later, Savinkov appeared before the Party's leadership and, speaking for himself and Azef, set out their case. At the end of the hearing, the Central Committee announced its decision to relieve both of their duties as leaders of the Combat Organization.

Out of the Action

The goal for which Savinkov had lived was now gone. He felt so uprooted that initially he did not know what to do and turned to Vera for help. The last time he had seen her was briefly in the courtroom during his trial in Sevastopol, and he yearned to be with her again. Savinkov wrote her an impassioned letter in late August 1906 that was a prolonged cry of pain and an avowal of love.

He has no money, he spends most of his time completely alone, and has "absolutely nothing to do." He feels that he has reached an absolute dead end: "I've lost everything, in effect, or almost everything that I had, and I'm thrashing about like a fish on dry land. I stagger from place to place . . . where will I wind up? I hardly know. Maybe I'll take the first ship to New York." There is also nothing to which he can return: "No matter how much I look around me, I clearly see only one thing: if I follow the old road I'll break my head, and there is no new road." His only hope for the future is to try to find new bearings with her help: "I need to catch my breath, spend at least a month without anxiety and with you."

Boris acknowledges that they have been apart too long, that they have grown distant, and that a life of caring for two small children with very little money has been extremely difficult for her. He says it pains him deeply when she tells him he should find a new companion who will be at his side: "Don't think about a 'friend,' don't talk about it. You repeat this so often that it sounds as if you want to be rid of me . . . I love you and want to be with you, specifically with you, and not with anyone else." He is hurt that he has to ask her to write and that he gets no letters for long periods of time. "If you could give me the hope that I would be able to see you, I would wait and try somehow to find a place to settle."

Savinkov also turned to his mother, whose love never wavered. Life had been very hard for her after her husband's and son's deaths. Although Savinkov's escape from the gallows in Sevastopol was an enormous relief, she now had new worries because he was a notorious fugitive. The well-being and future of her other four children were also very much on her mind because they all either sympathized with or worked for revolutionary organizations and were in constant danger of running afoul of the police.

"When I think of how hard it is for you, I feel my heart constrict until it hurts," Sofia wrote in response to Boris's lament in the fall of 1906. She tells him that she is not well off and that she is concerned that she will be unable to set anything aside for the other children's futures. But she does have a bit of money now and some more will be coming later, so she can spare 300 rubles and will send it soon in several installments by mail and telegraph.

Both Vera and Sofia responded to Boris's calls for help. Somehow, they managed to scrape together the funds to travel to see him in Paris. After a relatively short stay, Sofia went back to Russia (and was deeply outraged when the police detained her to find out whatever they could about her son), but Vera remained in France with Boris for several months.

The Terrorist in Repose

Boris's reunion with Vera in Paris was passionate, judging by their subsequent correspondence and what their acquaintances reported. They also got a respite from worrying about money, at least for the time being, because Boris was able to get enough for them to live comfortably, most likely by drawing on subsidies and loans from the SR Party as well as from its rich members, which was a widespread practice in Russian revolutionary circles.

Paris was like a second home to Boris Savinkov, but with the onset of cold weather he and Vera moved south to Beaulieu-sur-Mer, a town on the French Riviera between Nice and Monaco. The choice was not unusual. Russian revolutionaries living in exile in Europe often decamped to the Mediterranean shore during the colder months, typically choosing places between Cannes in the west and the Ligurian coast of Italy in the east. Small fishing villages near the French border and Genoa were special favorites because they were not only picturesque but often poor, which made life in them relatively cheap.

Even in winter Beaulieu-sur-Mer was paradisiacal, with mild temperatures, clusters of palm trees across the scenic landscape, and glorious vistas of the rocky shore descending to the azure of the Mediterranean. Boris rented a villa surrounded by gardens and lemon trees on the narrow, two-mile-long peninsula, Saint-Jean-Cap-Ferrat, that juts into the sea just south of Beaulieu-sur-Mer. The house was beautifully situated, high on a ridge and facing east, with views of the French coastline, Monaco, and Italy in the distance; behind it lay a bay sharing the same lilting name as another nearby town, Villefranche-sur-Mer. At night the view was especially enchanting—the sea shining like silver in the moonlight, the flickering lights of seaside villages, and the dark vault of the sky filled with myriad bright stars.

Even if only temporarily, life in Beaulieu-sur-Mer was a balm for Boris's and Vera's battered souls. They led a quiet, settled life (it seems that she left their children in the care of her relatives in Saint Petersburg), and they were able to indulge their fondness for hospitality, as they had during their Vologda exile, which was the last time they lived together for any length of time and which now seemed a lifetime ago. Boris was always very loyal toward veterans of the Combat Organization, no matter whether their roles had been big or small, and often hosted visitors.

The Russian Joan of Arc

Not long after Boris and Vera arrived on the Riviera, they learned that Vera Figner, a legendary member of the People's Will Party, was living in Alassio, an Italian seaside town some fifty miles to the east. The French writer and future Nobel laureate Anatole France had nicknamed her the "Joan of Arc" of the Russian Revolution, and Savinkov was eager to meet her. Vera also had an old family connection with Figner that she wanted to revive, so she took a train to invite her for a visit.

Figner had been released just a few months earlier from exile in provincial Russia after spending more than twenty years in the Schlisselburg Fortress prison for her role in plotting the assassination of Alexander II in 1881. Vera grew up hearing about Figner and this landmark event from her father, whose admiration for the People's Will was unbounded. He idolized her to such an extent that he is reported to have broken into sobs when he heard that she had been arrested. And when she was given a death sentence (which was later commuted), he had a note smuggled to her in prison that read "How I envy you!"

By nature, Vera was nervous and shy; meeting an old woman who had been a heroine in her father's eyes made her feel even more awkward (Figner was actually only fifty-four, but in 1906 that was a much more advanced age than it is today). The hard life Figner had endured during her long prison term had taken a heavy toll on her, and she looked worn-out, like a tired schoolmistress, with her long face, determined gaze, severely parted hair, and thin unsmiling lips. But she remembered Gleb Uspensky's loyalty and liked Vera as soon as she saw her. She was also curious about Savinkov and the current generation of Russian terrorists, about whom she had heard a great deal, and accepted the invitation to come to Beaulieu. Her visit a few weeks later went so well and Figner was so charmed by the Savinkovs' villa that she decided to settle only a few minutes' walk from them for a number of months. They became even closer after Vera and Boris invited her to take all her meals with them.

⚬———⚬

Figner saw Savinkov during a pivotal period in his life, when he was taking stock of his past and trying to find a new direction into the future. The impression he produced on her was very strong: she would write later that their meetings were "one of my most significant memories," and "of all the people I *ever met* he was the most brilliant." In light of her own dramatic life, this was an exceptional evaluation.

Savinkov and Figner spent hours sitting in his villa talking and looking out at the view. Together with Vera, they took long walks and carriage rides to the lighthouse at the end of Cap-Ferrat, where they watched the waves break on the craggy cliffs. After two decades in a prison cell, Figner did not think she could ever tire of the Riviera's beautiful vistas.

Figner did not like Savinkov's narrow face, with its angular profile, and found his usual cold expression alienating, despite the fact that he was very warm and solicitous toward her. But she was very taken with his polished manners and elegance, even though she thought that his well-tailored suits and fondness for the comforts of life were out of character for Russian revolutionaries, who typically paid little attention to their appearance (and thus lived up to their portrayal in European caricatures as bearded and wild-haired fanatics). Like others before her, Figner also thought Savinkov looked like a foreigner more than a Russian—an Englishman, perhaps.

In intimate settings Savinkov was a captivating speaker, and Figner was enthralled by his stories about the origins of the SR Party, the plots in which he had been involved, and the people he knew. She valued personal loyalty very much and admired the way he spoke about close comrades like Gots, Kalyaev, and Brilliant. She was especially moved by how emotional he became when he described the tragic accidents that Pokotilov and Shveytser had suffered.

But Savinkov continued to reserve his highest praise for Azef, who still hypnotized him, even after everything that had happened during the past year. Savinkov spoke with the deepest respect about his "great talent as an organizer" and his ability "to foresee all dangers and eliminate all obstacles." Figner felt swayed by Savinkov's loyalty, even though she had not been impressed by Azef when she met him in Alassio before she moved to Beaulieu.

<hr />

Savinkov enjoyed having Figner as an audience and read short pieces to her that would become parts of his *Memoirs*. He also read poems out loud by his favorite modernists and recited others from memory in the singsong, incantatory style that was fashionable at the time. At first Figner found Savinkov's "howling"—as she called it—comical, but soon she admitted that it had won her over.

Savinkov's ideas intrigued Figner, even though she found much of what he said unconvincing or contradictory. One of his oddest claims, in her view, was that his generation of revolutionaries had a "mystical" view of existence in contrast to her generation, who were strict materialists, rationalists, and Darwinians. As examples, Savinkov gave Kalyaev and himself, and explained that although he was not a Christian like his late friend, he nevertheless believed in "something" indefinite and otherworldly, a "divine spark," as he put it, one that existed outside human beings and nature. Figner remained skeptical that such views were widespread among SRs and concluded that Savinkov's claim was more about his own preoccupations and soul-searching at the time, which she ascribed to his unfortunate lack of a good scientific education.

But the most shocking thing Savinkov told Figner was that he no longer believed in good and evil. He said this one midnight, when they walked out into the garden to admire the distant views. Savinkov began to speak with an effort, as if he was uncertain of what he wanted to express, which was unusual for him.

"*There is no morality. There is only beauty*," he said, stressing the words. Then he continued:

> And beauty consists in the free development of the human personality, in the unhindered development of *everything* that is placed within it—placed in *the form of a divine spark* . . . as for morality— that is, all rules and prescriptions . . . these rules are imposed on a human being by upbringing, example, suggestion, and the endless influences of the surrounding environment . . . They are what weigh on a human being all his life long.

Figner was right to be confused by this because it is entirely unclear how Savinkov could reconcile what he said with his past career as a terrorist. During his campaigns, like all his closest comrades in the Combat Organization, he constantly worried about the morality of harming innocents. The nihilistic views Savinkov avowed were also inherently anathema for Figner, who believed that humanity as a whole made progress only as a result of the selfless ethical choices that individuals make.

But Savinkov bristled at the idea that only selflessness could be the path to virtue: "If someone tries to suppress something within himself *he will turn into a sack of dead bones*," he argued. He claimed that indulging even what others considered self-destructive tendencies was also justified if it led to personal fulfillment, and gave as an example the popular contemporary Polish writer Stanisław Przybyszewski, arguing that his alcoholism enabled him to write works of "genius." Going even further, Savinkov concluded that *"Ugliness is also beauty"* and insisted that they are merely different forms of the same thing.

Figner did not believe that Savinkov's ideas should be taken at face value, even if they could not be dismissed out of hand. She mentioned her impression to Vera, and Vera agreed, adding "He's better than his words."

Figner decided to test Savinkov's commitment to his outlandish ideas, and at one point an opportunity presented itself when they made an excursion to Monte Carlo, which is only a fifteen-minute train ride from Beaulieu.

While strolling through a park, they happened on a ring of leafless trees, their twisted branches and trunks as black as if they had been scorched by fire.

"What beauty!" Savinkov exclaimed and froze in admiration.

"What ugliness!" Figner replied.

After they had walked some distance, she asked Savinkov: "You have a son and a daughter. In what sense would you like your children to be beautiful—in the generally accepted, old one, or in your current understanding of beauty?"

Savinkov was quiet for a moment, and then, lowering his voice, admitted: "In the old . . ."

⚬──┼──⚬

What was Savinkov's goal when he floated his extreme ideas, which clearly have roots in the popularized versions of Friedrich Nietzsche's philosophy that were in vogue in Russia and Europe at the time? It appears to have been a thought experiment related to his writing plans, not his life. The idea of following one's inclinations wherever they may lead obviously had some attraction for him—and for whom does it not? But there is no evidence that Savinkov acted in this way. Throughout his life, he remained dedicated to fighting on behalf of what he saw as the interests of the Russian people, although, of course, in the way that satisfied him too. However, he would soon begin a novel that would bring him new fame, notoriety, and a place in Russian literature, in which a terrorist's nihilistic individualism would be the central theme.

The Bukhalo Flying Bomber

Even though he had announced his retirement from the Combat Organization the previous fall, Azef was not resting on his laurels. Early in January 1907, he came to visit Savinkov in Beaulieu and brought some exciting news about the very matter Savinkov had insisted was essential for resuming terror—technological innovation. In fact, the fit between Savinkov's ideas and Azef's news was so perfect that Azef may well have concocted his plan in direct response to Savinkov (and for his usual reasons—to maintain his reputation as a brilliant operative and to benefit financially).

To Savinkov's shock and delight, Azef announced that the Combat Organization was going to build its own airplane.

Heavier-than-air flying machines were a dazzling new development in the first years of the twentieth century, and experiments with them were progressing at an equally dizzying pace: the Wright brothers first flew in 1903, covering 852 feet in 59 seconds; in 1906, Alberto Santos-Dumont set the first world speed record by flying 700 feet in 22 seconds; just three years later Louis Blériot would make the first flight across the English Channel, 22 miles in 36 minutes. Every new achievement made news around the world and galvanized the public's imagination: the age of human flight had begun.

Azef told Savinkov that he had found an expatriate Russian engineer, Sergey Bukhalo, who lived near Munich and had drawn up plans for a powerful new machine with capabilities that exceeded anything anyone had built before. He claimed it could reach any altitude, descend as readily as rise (there was as yet no consensus among experimenters about the best way to control airplanes in flight), carry a heavy weight, and reach the speed of eighty-five miles per hour, which seemed incredible because the record for flight in 1906 was only twenty-five miles per hour. By conviction Bukhalo was an anarchist, but he was prepared to place his invention in the service of the Combat Organization to assassinate Nicholas II.

Azef assured Savinkov that he had personally checked Bukhalo's design and calculations, and concluded that, in theory, he had solved the task. It would take him only nine or ten months to build his machine. There was one practical problem, however: Bukhalo did not have the money for a workshop or the equipment and supplies he would need.

Savinkov listened to Azef with astonishment. Everything he said sounded like a fantasy come true. The speed of Bukhalo's machine would make it possible to start an attack on Saint Petersburg from several hundred miles away, in Sweden, Norway, even England; its lifting power was such that it could carry a bomb big enough to destroy an entire palace; and its ability to fly at any altitude would ensure the attackers' invulnerability.

Savinkov knew nothing about machines and engineering and took Azef's word that the project was feasible. He also agreed that it was worth risking the large sum required—20,000 rubles, or around $300,000 in today's money. The only stipulation Savinkov had was that it should come from private donors who knew what they were getting into and not from the SR Party's limited funds. Azef readily agreed. To him it made no difference what the source of the money was. He did not bother to tell Savinkov that he had already attempted, and failed, to get it from the Party by arguing that the investment was worth the risk and that Bukhalo's invention could win hundreds of thousands of rubles in aeronautical prizes and be sold for even more. Three rich Russian SR sympathizers were found who quickly donated the necessary sum. Bukhalo set up his workshop outside Munich, hired assistants, and set to work.

Savinkov was elated. "I will fly on this airplane," he told Figner, his voice ringing with pride and conviction. The Combat Organization would become invincible, and he would be at its center again.

<hr>

And so, it turns out that nearly a century before 9/11, and before practical flying machines *even existed*, the idea of an attack by air was already filling the febrile imaginations of terrorists. One wonders what precautions Savinkov believed he could take to spare the lives of innocents as his spindly craft with its giant bomb droned toward the sprawling imperial palaces at Tsarskoye Selo or Peterhof. And what sort of accuracy did he imagine he could achieve? Even when airplanes began to be used widely in 1914 during the Great War, aerial bombardment was highly inaccurate and remained a technological challenge. Of course, there was always the Combat Organization's history of suicide attacks, and perhaps a pilot would be moved to anticipate the kamikazes of World War II.

However, Savinkov's exultation that he had found a way to defeat the imperial regime's vigilance was not entirely justified. As soon as the first successful flights of airplanes were reported in the world's press, the Okhrana started to pay attention, realizing perfectly well the potential danger the new technology represented. In 1909, when airplanes emerged from inventors' workshops and actually went into serial production, the gendarmes were ordered to monitor all flights in the Russian Empire, as well as aviators, students learning to fly, and members of "aero-clubs," all of whom were required to register with the government.

⚬━━⚬

Savinkov waited impatiently for Bukhalo's airplane throughout that winter and into the spring of 1907. To see it for himself and to start his training as an "aviator," he traveled in August to the outskirts of Munich. But to his surprise and disappointment he discovered that nothing was finished. Still believing in the project, Savinkov decided that he would settle near the workshop and take charge of it himself. But when Azef found out about this, he became angry and agitated, and did all he could to persuade Savinkov to drop the idea. Control of the finances for the airplane's construction was especially important for Azef, and he did not want Savinkov to interfere.

In subsequent months, new problems with Bukhalo's project kept accumulating, and, in the end, all his efforts came to nothing. Whether or not Azef had foreseen this from the beginning, and whether or not he had siphoned off large sums from Bukhalo's budget for his own benefit—which seems very likely—he undoubtedly wasted a great deal of money that could have been used for other revolutionary purposes. Azef had also effectively sidelined Savinkov for over a year.

The Russian Sherlock Holmes

Simultaneously with acting as Savinkov's comrade and friend, Azef continued to use whatever opportunities arose to damage his reputation among Socialist Revolutionaries and to tip off the police so that they could arrest him.

In October 1907, knowing that Savinkov had just boarded a ship, the *Polaris*, from Finland to Copenhagen, Azef telegraphed the information to the Russian police so that they could intercept him. Only a stroke of luck saved Savinkov when a friend who was planning to meet him noticed agents of the Okhrana and a Danish detective examining his photograph and apparently waiting to arrest him. With his friend's help, Savinkov hid in the city and then got safely to Paris.

This close call proved pivotal because it convinced Savinkov that someone near the center of the SR Party must have informed the police in Denmark about his arrival. But the fantastically ironic consequence of his conclusion was that he went to share his suspicions with Azef.

As always, Azef listened carefully; he then coolly replied: "The fact that you were on the *Polaris* was known to only three people: Grigory [Gershuni, the venerable SR who had recently escaped from Siberia], Vera [Figner] and me. That means that one of us three is a *provokator*. Choose."

"I was lost in conjectures," Savinkov recalled later, "but I could not suspect any of my comrades."

⚬━⚬

Others did have suspicions, and over the years muted drumbeats of accusations against Azef kept reaching the SR Central Committee. However, no one in the leadership ever believed them, even when rank and file members expressed shock at how flagrant Azef could be in disregarding basic conspiratorial precautions and how exceptionally "lucky" he seemed to be because he was never detained by the police. Azef's authority remained unassailable, all accusations against him were dismissed as police deceptions, and all those who dared to bring them were cowed into silence or gave up. When the accusations reached Azef himself, he skillfully bluffed his way out.

The SR leaders were unable to judge Azef not only because of his reputation but also because of their own self-regard: as the apostles of a new, salvific creed they could not conceive that a Judas was seated among them. It would take an outsider to finally see through Azef and attempt to bring him to justice.

⚬━⚬

Vladimir Lvovich Burtsev was a historian and an investigative journalist by profession and not a member of the Socialist Revolutionary Party. However, he was close to many of its leaders, sympathized with the revolutionary movement, and had spent time in prison for his activities. A dignified, studious-looking man with a moustache, goatee, and wire-rimmed glasses, Burtsev was forthright, intelligent, diligent, and extremely tenacious, traits that would lead to his becoming known during the early decades of the twentieth century as the "Sherlock Holmes of the Russian Revolution."

Burtsev returned to Russia from European exile in late 1905, after the October Manifesto announced the formation of a Duma and other reforms. The new atmosphere of liberalization that was sweeping the country inspired him to start a journal, *The Past* (*Byloe*), that would publish documentary materials and essays in support of "the liberation movement" (including the memoirs by Savinkov's mother). Burtsev was good friends with Savinkov, and Savinkov's younger sister, Sofia, became a member of the journal's staff.

The new journal's incendiary content went far beyond anything that had been published openly in Russia before and attracted a lot of attention from the police as well as sympathizers who wanted even more revelations. In May 1906, a young man by the name of Mikhail Bakay walked into Burtsev's editorial office in Saint Petersburg and asked for a private meeting. He explained that he worked in the Okhrana but was an SR by conviction and wanted to help the revolutionary movement. He then astounded Burtsev by revealing a mass of details about the imperial regime's plans to crush the revolutionary ferment that was growing in the country. On later visits Bakay reported a great deal more, including that the Okhrana knew exactly what the SRs were doing at a Party congress in Finland that was supposed to have been highly secret.

At first Burtsev did not trust Bakay, but after checking concluded that he was telling the truth. Because Bakay was a relatively low-level employee of the Okhrana, his knowledge was largely limited to information that happened to cross his desk. Nevertheless, Burtsev realized that he had discovered a peephole in the wall surrounding some of the Okhrana's most closely guarded secrets. He began to persuade Bakay to follow his conscience and resign his position so that he could concentrate on writing up everything he knew about the inner workings of the Russian political police. By the end of 1906 Burtsev had succeeded, and this is when Bakay revealed that there was an important *provokator* among the SR Party's "influential members" and that his code name in the Okhrana was "Raskin."

The allegation stunned Burtsev, and he began immediately to try to figure out if it was true and who the person could be. As his discreet digging progressed and he discovered new tantalizing details, he began to slip into a state bordering on panic. Not only was the idea of a *provokator* explosive all by itself, but Burtsev was terrified of making a mistake and besmirching someone who may be innocent.

Bakay's claim also prompted Burtsev to search his own memory. Thinking back, he recalled that many terrorists had been arrested in the summer of 1906, including Savinkov and his comrades in Sevastopol, and that he had never been entirely persuaded that these were accidents or the result of unusual diligence by the police. Burtsev also remembered how he had recently seen Azef and his wife riding openly in a carriage on the English Embankment along the Neva. He did not know Azef personally, but he was well aware of his role in the SR Party and that he was the head of the Combat Organization. If he was able to recognize Azef so easily, Burtsev wondered, how is it that the police did not recognize and arrest him when he appeared on the central streets of the imperial capital?

The convoluted answer Burtsev came up with shows how difficult it was even for a skeptical outsider to believe in Azef's treachery. Burtsev surmised that the Okhrana may have placed a *provokator* in Azef's entourage, someone who was close enough to Azef to provide inside information about the Combat Organization's plans; thus, it was not in police interest to arrest Azef himself.

But no matter how hard Burtsev tried to sort through all the members of the Combat Organization to figure out who this "Raskin" could be, he was unable to settle on a single name. No one stood out because of their personal qualities, or their biographies, or where they happened to be during past terrorist attempts.

At a loss about how to proceed, Burtsev finally allowed himself to ask the one remaining question: could Azef himself be Raskin? His initial reaction was that the idea was "monstrously preposterous." But he could not get it out of his mind, and he soon had to start admitting to himself that the more he tried to dismiss suspicions against Azef, the more probable they became.

In the meantime, Azef did not relent, and the Okhrana's successes accelerated in early 1907, which fueled Burtsev's suspicions even more. In February Azef gave information to the police that resulted in the arrest of Lev Zilberberg and several others. Zilberberg was tried, imprisoned in the Peter and Paul Fortress, and, on July 16, 1907, hanged in its courtyard; he was twenty-seven and had not revealed his real name. Before dying, he managed to get a message to the SR Central Committee that he had been captured because of a hidden traitor in the Party, although he did not know who it was. Savinkov was still in Beaulieu when the news reached him. He had long admired Zilberberg, considered him and his entire family close friends, and in his memoir inscribed him in the pantheon of his most cherished comrades, together with Kalyaev and Sazonov. Azef, however, remained true to form—when news of Zilberberg's execution reached him, he made a great show of weeping over the news on the breast of Zilberberg's mother.

Azef was also a dangerous opponent and fought back when threatened. In March, he got wind of Burtsev's digging and turned the tables on him by tipping off the police that Burtsev was collecting information from a source in the Okhrana itself. Bakay soon began to notice police spies following him everywhere and was arrested on March 31. That same day Burtsev's editorial offices were searched, and he barely escaped arrest by hurriedly leaving for Western Europe for several weeks. When he returned to the relative safety of Finland, he discovered, with the help of Savinkov's sister, Sofia, more incontrovertible evidence of Azef's betrayals. He also realized that he would have to present his case to the Central Committee and other leaders of the Socialist Revolutionary Party. But he could never have imagined how ferocious a battle he would have to wage.

Zinaida and Two Dmitrys

As Boris Savinkov's involvement with the Socialist Revolutionaries waned, writing became an increasingly important pastime for him. His mother had tried to encourage him to write even when he was in the midst of his hair-raising terrorist campaigns (and judging by the highly detailed accounts he eventually composed, he must have made extensive notes while his impressions were still fresh). Before leaving for Paris, Savinkov admitted to comrades in Finland that "It's as essential for me to write as it is for a bird to sing. I can't not write, although I've never been able to give myself over to art completely." To Vera he explained that he needed to unburden himself: "I am full of impressions of the past, and I can't not write; what I've endured weighs on me and I'll be able to free myself of the sharp pain by writing everything down."

Savinkov's career as a writer received a major boost in the winter of 1907–1908 from the most famous "power couple" of early twentieth-century Russian letters,

Dmitry Merezhkovsky and his wife, Zinaida Gippius. Both were leading figures in the modern literary "symbolist" movement that intrigued Savinkov. Dmitry wrote poetry and plays and was especially famous for long historical novels about eternal spiritual truths that glimmer below the surface of human experience and that foreshadow the Apocalypse. Zinaida was best known for her intimate "prayer-like" poems about sensuality, narcissism, and the ties between the spirit and the flesh. Her explorations of the dark side of the human soul led some contemporaries to label her a "decadent Madonna."

"Couple" is actually something of a misnomer for the Merezhkovskys, because starting in 1906 they acquired an inseparable companion who also became an ally in all their artistic and ideological endeavors—the critic, publicist, and religious activist Dmitry Filosofov. Together they constituted a memorable "trio": Zinaida—attractive and wasp-waisted, with a mass of red-blond hair, emerald eyes, a lorgnette, and a penchant for cross-dressing; her husband, Dmitry—a small, introverted, scholarly looking man with a trim beard and big, wide-set, wary eyes; and the "second" Dmitry—a handsome, tall, and haughty-looking young aristocrat.

But contrary to what their triangular relationship seemed to imply, and what many contemporaries believed, theirs was not a classic ménage à trois: their relations, which were otherwise very intimate, did not include physical consummation. Over the years, the three had homosexual and heterosexual affairs and romantic entanglements with others, some of which were very intense. But they saw whatever sexual tensions that arose among themselves as evidence of a spiritual union they had formalized in a kind of ascetic spiritual marriage. Or, to put it differently, they sublimated their erotic feelings into what they believed was a profound metaphysical tie.

By 1903, their salon in Saint Petersburg had become the obligatory proving ground for Russian literary talent new and old, and each publication of a poetry collection by Zinaida was a major cultural event for Russian cognoscenti. Her husband, Dmitry, was famous not only in Russia but throughout Europe, and he would in fact be nominated for the Nobel Prize in literature some ten times in future years. (Sigmund Freud read his novel about Leonardo da Vinci and used it for a psychoanalytical study of the artist's childhood.)

The trio emigrated to Paris in the aftermath of Bloody Sunday and the Russian defeat in the war with Japan, both of which shook their worldview to the core. They lost all faith in the Orthodox Church and the brutal tsarist regime because of their mutual support for each other, and, instead, developed a fantastic system of belief centered on themselves.

The Merezhkovskys became convinced that their own triple union was a variation of the Christian Trinity and that it should form the core of a new church. Their mission would be to advocate a spiritual revolution to transform Russia by raising the Russian revolutionary movement from the social and political planes to the metaphysical one. As the founding prophets of a new religious consciousness, they would get other members of the intelligentsia to join them in bringing enlightenment to the Russian people and thus lead them away from the old forms of faith and life.

Given these views, it was natural that the Merezhkovskys would come to Paris because of the number of active revolutionaries in the large Russian émigré community—some 80,000 in 1907. Even though their own approach to revolution was openly mystical and apocalyptic, to say nothing of egotistical, and was anathema to the vast majority of revolutionaries, the Merezhkovskys believed there was much they could learn from the traditions of radical French revolutionary thought and from veterans of actual barricades and terrorist campaigns.

⚬╼⚬

For a novice writer like Savinkov, meeting the famous Merezhkovskys was a notable event (their ages made a difference as well: he was twenty-eight, Zinaida was thirty-eight, the older Dmitry was forty-two, and the younger Dmitry was thirty-five). But they were also very interested in him because of the name he had made for himself as a terrorist.

The Merezhkovskys first met Savinkov at the apartment of a mutual friend, Ilya Fondaminsky. The son of a rich Russian Jewish merchant, Fondaminsky was a brilliant orator, a religious thinker, and a leading figure in the SR Party. (A remarkably kind and generous man during his life, he would convert to Russian Orthodoxy in a Nazi concentration camp and be canonized a martyr saint by the patriarch of Constantinople.) They were immediately struck by Savinkov's elegant appearance and aesthetic interests, in contrast to the rough manners and style of most other revolutionaries they had met, which they found distasteful. They continued to interact with him socially when he returned from the Riviera to Paris in November 1907 and rented a small apartment a block away from theirs, which had a view of the Eiffel Tower, on rue Théophile Gautier.

In Paris, the Merezhkovskys reestablished their practice of hosting a salon in their home to discuss the issues that consumed them and to recruit people to their cause. They were thrilled to have Savinkov as a frequent visitor. It was one thing to know a terrorist by reputation and from a distance, but an entirely different matter to meet him in person.

Zinaida was always very quick to develop an intense interest in new acquaintances who seemed unusual or exceptional, although she was also quick to become disenchanted in those who did not live up to their promise. This did not happen with Savinkov. Her first impressions of him were that he was "sharp, daring, proud, stubborn, willful, and smart." Soon her admiration grew, and she decided that he was not only "very gifted" but "talented to a degree that was frightening."

Her husband, Dmitry, was the primary ideologue of their new "church," and after meeting some of the Socialist Revolutionaries who were in Paris, he decided that they could indeed become the revolutionary vanguard he wanted to create. The one problem was that these terrorists did not have a sufficiently developed religious sense. As a result, he, his wife, and their acolyte Dmitry would have to lead the *bombisty,* or "bombers" as they called them, to the light.

⚬—⚬

There is no evidence that the Merezhkovskys had any ironic distance on themselves or what they set out to do, which was really quite fantastical if not absurd—to try to merge their hothouse mix of apocalyptic mysticism and sublimated sexuality with the gritty, dangerous, and bloody business of blowing up imperial ministers on Russia's streets.

Nonetheless, long conversations ensued, with the Merezhkovskys pouring their ideas into Savinkov, while he revisited his own experiences over and over again. For a time, it seemed to them all that they might have found some common ground when talking about the essence of terrorism, and aspects of Savinkov's actual experiences appear to have seeped into the trio's drawing room fantasies.

According to Zinaida's recollections, Savinkov spoke darkly about how the blood of those he hunted still weighed on him. It even seemed to her that he might be hoping to hear a final judgment about this from her husband, Dmitry—either a justification of revolutionary terror or a condemnation of it. But although it is not surprising that Zinaida would seek to elevate her husband to the status of a moral arbiter, it is unlikely that talking with the Merezhkovskys in their well-cushioned living room while enjoying fragrant tea and cigarettes had much to do with Savinkov's reliving the moral quandary that had been central to the lives of his closest comrades—Kalyaev, Brilliant, Sazonov, Zilberberg.

More likely is that Savinkov's vivid recollections of the stalking, the pools of blood, and the shock that followed assassinations—descriptions of which he had already begun to set to paper—fed into the Merezhkovskys' attempts to formulate their program. On February 21, 1908, the senior Dmitry gave a public lecture titled "On Violence" in a Masonic hall in Paris to an audience of over 1,000 Russian emigres of various revolutionary persuasions—Marxists, anarchists, and SRs (the traditionally anticlerical stance of Freemasonry made the setting appropriate). The lecture caused a sensation because of the subject matter and the speaker's fame. Despite his bookish and distinctly nonviolent appearance, Dmitry spoke with mesmerizing pathos and concluded with the invocation: "Yes, yes, violence is not right, but it is justified! You must not spill blood, this is impossible! But for this impossibility to become a reality, it is essential!" There is evidence that his lecture was based on a piece Zinaida had written, which in turn was inspired by her meetings with Savinkov.

The trio influenced Savinkov as well, even if only for a while. He had already developed a sense or an intuition that human existence was connected to something otherworldly before he met the Merezhkovskys, as Figner had noticed with displeasure in Beaulieu. But under their influence he began to think and talk about historical Christianity, and this was a major change for him.

Central to the trio's teachings was that a true revolutionary needed to sacrifice him- or herself in imitation of Christ's self-sacrifice for humankind. Savinkov brought this up so often with his SR comrades in Paris that they became perplexed: they had not heard him speak this way before, even if it was an idea that motivated some of his closest comrades in the Combat Organization. However, rather than being evidence that Savinkov had discovered faith, it seems more likely that he repeated the Merezhkovskys' idea because he experienced "survivor's guilt" over having remained alive while his comrades were executed or condemned to hard labor for their actions. This was another of the "frontline" syndromes—together with fighting for the comrade whose elbow you can feel with yours—that revolutionaries had in common with soldiers.

Some of the SRs in Paris even began to look askance at Savinkov because of his "mysticism." "You can imagine what kind of nonsense this sounds like to those he has to deal with," one wrote to a mutual friend about Savinkov's new Christology; "they call him a renegade, if not worse."

Were it not for Savinkov's earlier achievements in the Combat Organization, the damage to his reputation would have been more severe.

⊙━━⊙

In the end, Boris Savinkov's individuality, self-regard, and sense of reality took the upper hand, and he backed away from the trio's esoteric urgings. However, he did not give up his intuition that life could not be explained by science and reason alone. As he wrote to Figner, who continued to criticize his "mysticism," he felt he had to be true to himself and to continue to struggle against all forms of "unfreedom" and conservative behavior that are ingrained in people who think they are free when in fact they are not. And for him this included the spirit of positivism, rationalism, and materialism that imbued the current generation of revolutionaries to the exclusion of everything else. He could not accept this any more than political or religious conservatism.

Savinkov admitted to a friend that because of the Merezhkovskys he had come to the purely intellectual conclusion that one must have religious faith, but with the crucial difference that he could not actually embrace faith himself. Nevertheless, the common ground that remained between Savinkov and the Merezhkovskys was substantial: mutual admiration, friendship (despite ups and downs), revolutionary politics, and literature. Before long they would also have a decisive influence on him when he began what would become his most famous work of fiction.

A New Love

But first a personal drama interfered. After Boris had prepared his apartment on rue La Fontaine, Vera came back to Paris in late November 1907, and this time brought their two children. This visit was not a happy one, however, because the crack in their marriage, which looked as if it had closed during their stay in Beaulieu, opened again.

The cause was the classic "other woman." Unlike the Merezhkovskys with their rationalization of sexual tension as spiritual reality, the love drama that enveloped Boris, Vera, and Evgeniya Zilberberg was decidedly more earthly and painful. To the Merezhkovskys' distaste, it also played out before their eyes (as well as that of the Okhrana agents who had penetrated Savinkov's cover and watched and reported his every move).

Evgeniya Zilberberg (Somova by a marriage of convenience) was the twenty-three-year-old sister of the late Lev Zilberberg, whose memory Savinkov cherished. Like other members of her family, she had participated in revolutionary plots, including smuggling dynamite. Savinkov's feelings for her developed when her brother was still alive, and Evgeniya seems to have reciprocated early on. The death of Evgeniya's brother probably brought them even closer because of their shared grief.

The Merezhkovskys not only knew Savinkov well, but they also felt they had a special attachment to Vera's family because of the senior Dmitry's great respect for her father, the writer Gleb Uspensky, whom he had once visited on a kind of pilgrimage. One day in mid-January 1908, their close mutual friend Ilya Fondaminsky—who worried about all the members of what he considered "his" SR Party and who was especially fond of Vera—arrived at the Merezhkovskys, looking distraught. He reported that Savinkov had run into Evgeniya Somova at some event in town a few days ago and had completely lost his head over her. Ilya had tried to implore Savinkov to forget Evgeniya and not destroy his family, and now wanted the Merezhkovskys to help patch up the marriage as well.

Zinaida and the younger Dmitry (the senior Dmitry was away) did not want to get involved: Savinkov's love life was no concern of theirs. But Ilya insisted.

When Savinkov arrived, he began to spill his soul, addressing himself primarily to Dmitry. This went on for a while, until Zinaida got rather tired of it all.

"Well, I see that you are a rather weak person," she interjected in an indifferent, matter-of-fact tone.

This so shocked Savinkov that he turned "pale as death." Dmitry became genuinely frightened by his reaction and quickly took him into another room, where he began to console him, assuring him that Zinaida has spoken accidentally and without thinking. When Savinkov left the apartment, Dmitry reproached her for being careless, for not understanding Savinkov's psychology.

But Zinaida would not back down. She found the entire matter rather "disgusting," as she put it, and thought that she had glimpsed an important feature of Savinkov's character that she had not noticed before—his tendency at times to be emotionally self-indulgent. For all her subtleties and esoteric tastes, Zinaida could be strikingly unsentimental. As she said of herself, she felt at times that she was a male psyche caught in a female form.

Zinaida's judgment of Boris Savinkov was both right and wrong. He did do a lot of soul searching because he was introspective by nature. But it is not at all certain that she had evaluated or understood this trait accurately. The fact that Savinkov turned pale when she commented that he was "a weak person" could have been the reaction of a proud man whose courage was being questioned. It could also have been his shock at having his intimate thoughts rudely belittled by someone he believed was an intimate friend.

Savinkov vacillated for several weeks, tormenting Vera, Evgeniya, and himself. A few days after Fondaminsky's imprecations and Zinaida's rebuke, he decided to give up Evgeniya and go back to Vera. But Vera had decided that enough was enough and told him bluntly, "I can no longer live with you, I understand it finally . . . There is no happiness . . . I am calm, am not suffering in the least, and, on the contrary, my soul is clean and clear." Savinkov implored her "by all that is holy" not to destroy their life together. Then he changed his mind and went off to Monte Carlo with Evgeniya for several days, and then changed his mind yet again. Evgeniya left the Riviera for Paris but wrote him an impassioned letter, predicting that he would not be able to break with her, insisting that although he may think he loves Vera, he does not—"it's a lie and you'll perish"—and that he is in fact exhausted by his past life. She reminds Savinkov of her "great past love for him," and wonders "why did fate bring us together again?" She says that she too is exhausted, and ends by sending greetings to him and to the Azure Coast's "sky and the sea and the lovely flowers."

The turmoil had a sadly predictable effect on Savinkov's family, whose life descended into chaos as Vera struggled to find her emotional bearings with two small children on her hands in an unfamiliar city. The situation was observed by their maid, who had been found for the Savinkovs by a friend of theirs, Sofia Petit, a Russian lady who lived in Paris with her politically well-connected French husband. At the very time when Savinkov's affair was spinning out of control, the maid wrote a nearly hysterical ten-page letter to Mme Petit complaining that "Mme Lechneff" (Vera used Boris's conspiratorial surname) was clueless about running a household, that the children cannot be left alone for a minute without breaking or dirtying something, that they are dressed like ragamuffins, that disorder reigns in the kitchen and at mealtimes, and that she, the maid, is treated with disdain. Even allowing for the possibility that Vera was not the ideal bourgeois housewife, what the maid evidently witnessed but did not understand was that Vera's life was falling apart.

Savinkov's indecision lasted until early February. But on the eighteenth the Okhrana agents who watched him in Paris, and who were well aware of his marital difficulties, reported to their superiors in Saint Petersburg that he has definitively separated from his wife "Vera Glebovna" and taken up with his mistress "Evgeniya Somova."

The *fileurs* also drew a detailed verbal portrait of Evgeniya that sounds frankly admiring and helps explain why Savinkov was smitten. She is very striking, with black hair, black eyebrows, and an olive complexion; but her eyes, which gaze at the world with frank composure, are an unexpected deep blue. Her features are generously proportioned—lips that are "large and ripe," a beauty mark on the upper right lip, and a prominent nose. Her hands are small and her fingers are covered with rings. She is slender, has taste, and dresses in fine clothes, favoring new fashions. The agent summarizes her "type" as "a beautiful Jewess."

⚬━♦━⚬

What did Savinkov's realignment of affections mean in the context of his speculations about good, evil, and individual freedom (a topic that would also be central to the novella that was gestating within him as his domestic drama was developing)? His inability to break with Vera easily, his changing his mind several times, and his agonizing about his decisions suggest he was moved by an all-too-common and familiar tension between passion and a sense of obligation or loyalty and not by nihilistic self-indulgence that presumed to be above conventional good and evil. (He would also remain deeply attached to Vera and their children, and actively concerned about their welfare, for years to come.) In this aspect of his life as in his revolutionary activities, Savinkov shared many of the same principles that were widespread among members of his class and had tried to act honorably (which, however, did not stop Vera Figner from breaking with him over what she saw as his guilt in the failure of his marriage).

Initially, Vera and Boris parted on reasonably amicable terms. They both realized that the distance and borders that had separated them for years had led to an emotional separation. Despite this, they wrote to each other regularly, and Vera's early letters—she sent the first just days after she left Paris—are filled with descriptions of her and the children's states of mind, with homely details about their trip and daily lives, and with heartfelt good wishes.

February 21, 1908 (approximately): "My dear, please do not telegraph and do not worry, we got back well, we were greeted warmly, children and I feel quite good." She is looking for a new apartment and finds that life in Saint Petersburg is expensive. Things big and small still bind them and she reminds Boris not to "forget to send me the wooden case that's in your room, it's especially valuable to me." She concludes with, "from my heart I wish you health and strength."

February 25: "Got the baggage several days ago, now life is completely set and children feel great, they go to school, which gives them a lot . . . I know your finances aren't very good so please don't send me money this month."

March 7 (approximately): "the children are well, they remember you, they will write themselves."

However, the money to which she referred would soon become a problem for them all.

Regicide

The leaders of the Socialist Revolutionary Party did not look favorably upon Savinkov's marital drama or his association with the Merezhkovskys. They were also well aware that he had turned to writing and spent the spring of 1908 on his memoir. But his past experience was too valuable to ignore, so when a new plot to assassinate Nicholas II was hatched in June, Mark Natanson, the chairman of the Party's Central Committee in Europe, set aside Savinkov's resignation from the Combat Organization and offered him one of the two leadership roles.

Azef was back in action as well and recently devised two ingenious plots against the emperor, although he was simultaneously playing an ambiguous game that is difficult to decipher. One involved crew members on the imperial yacht *Shtandart* (Standart) who were supposed to carry out the assassination.

Azef did not to breathe a word about the plan to the police even though he could have done so and not compromised himself with the revolutionaries. It remains unclear to this day why it was not carried out. Azef also came up with a plan to infiltrate members of the Combat Organization into the groups of peasants who worked as beaters during imperial hunts near Saint Petersburg and to kill Nicholas that way, but this too went nowhere. On the other hand, he continued to give up revolutionaries to the police, even the sainted Babushka (Ekaterina Breshko-Breshkovskaya), whom he betrayed in September 1907.

By early 1908 it became a question of time and who would succeed first—Azef as a regicide or Burtsev as the investigator who would expose him.

Azef's newest plan focused on an armored cruiser, the *Ryurik,* which was being built for the Russian Navy in Glasgow, Scotland, by Vickers, Sons & Maxim, a major shipbuilder and armaments manufacturer for the British Navy. One of the ship's Russian engineers was a member of the SR Party's military committee and had organized a successful propaganda campaign that radicalized many of the crew, including a handful of sailors who were willing to assassinate the tsar when he would come aboard at Kronstadt, the Russian naval base outside Saint Petersburg, to inspect the ship.

The daring and innovative nature of the plan and the importance of the target appealed to Savinkov greatly, and he immediately agreed to take part. He traveled to Glasgow with his partner in the plot, Pavel Karpovich, an old acquaintance from their student days in Berlin. Their initial intention was to conceal a stowaway aboard the ship with the help of crew members; when the ship arrived at Kronstadt and the tsar and his retinue came on board, the stowaway would emerge and attack them with a bomb. Savinkov offered to be the stowaway even though his chance of surviving the attack would be negligible.

But this plan had to be abandoned when he and the others realized that there was no place on board where anyone could survive for the many weeks it would take for the ship to be outfitted and then sail to Russia.

In the end of June, Azef arrived in Glasgow to check how things were going and agreed that secreting someone on board was impractical. Instead, he suggested that two sailors armed with revolvers could shoot the tsar. But to Savinkov it seemed that Azef was not really committed to the attack. He was also perplexed by his choice of men because neither of them was experienced or appeared psychologically ready.

Nevertheless, Savinkov again deferred to Azef and went back to Paris to wait for the telegram that he hoped would bring news of the tsar's death. Azef was there too, waiting with a prepared announcement containing the autobiography of one of the shooters, which the SRs planned to use as propaganda.

On September 24, 1908, the imperial inspection of the ship took place in Kronstadt. Despite the general threat of terrorism, it appears that no special security measures were taken, such as checking the crew members for unauthorized weapons or verifying their political reliability. Apparently, the imperial security services could not imagine that a sailor who had sworn allegiance to the "God-anointed" tsar could ever betray him.

At one moment, the designated shooters were two steps away from Nicholas II as he walked by the assembled line of sailors, both with loaded Browning automatic pistols in their pockets. They could have fired at point-blank range. But neither made a move. During another phase of the inspection, one of the armed sailors escorted the tsar through various parts of the ship and thus spent several long moments completely alone with him. But despite the commitment he made, he again did not act.

Why both sailors did nothing is unknown. It is possible that Azef had discerned a lack of resolve in them and counted on it to disrupt the assassination. However, it is also possible that Azef had done everything to prepare the assassination of the tsar and that it failed only because the sailors lost their nerve. Supporting this alternative is that Azef never informed General Gerasimov, his primary handler in the Saint Petersburg Okhrana, of the plot. Nicholas II would never know how close he had been to death that day. And no one outside the small circle of planners and participants learned of it either, until the Romanov dynasty fell in February 1917 and revolutionaries began to speak and write openly about their carefully guarded secrets.

Burtsev Strikes

Burtsev had spent more than a year gathering documents, verifying testimonies, and triangulating details of Azef's perfidy. His dedication to identifying police spies in revolutionary circles was legendary, and contemporaries likened him to a "mongoose"—the small, supremely nimble Indian mammal known for its ability to fight and kill big venomous snakes, particularly cobras. In May 1908, Burtsev decided he was ready and began his attack: he informed the Central Committee of the SR Party that Azef was a *provokator.*

Burtsev would need all his celebrated courage and tenacity during the coming months because his accusation was greeted with not just incredulity but outrage by the senior members of the Party, including Savinkov. In their eyes, Azef had been a pillar of the Party since its founding and had played a leading role in over two dozen successful and attempted assassinations, including several against the tsar. The plan connected with the *Ryurik* completely exonerated him of any suspicions, they argued, because a *provokator* could not possibly also be a regicide. As for the revolutionaries under Azef's command who had been arrested, hanged, and imprisoned, they were the inevitable and sad casualties of war. Burtsev's claim "did not instill even a shadow of a doubt about Azef's honesty," Savinkov remembered. "I did not know how to explain the rumors and accusations, but my love and respect for Azef were not shaken by them."

Initially, not only did Burtsev fail to convince anyone, but the Party leadership decided to bring him before a "court of honor" for spreading unproven and insulting allegations against an esteemed member and for actions that demeaned the Central Committee. In the summer of 1908, the judges were chosen. They were three revolutionaries whose careers began in the previous century: Vera Figner, German Lopatin, and Prince Pyotr Kropotkin.

All had impeccable credentials and were celebrated figures. Savinkov knew Figner personally, the others by reputation. Lopatin was a friend and collaborator of Karl Marx and Friedrich Engels, a veteran of the terror campaigns by the Russian People's Will Party, of several European revolutionary movements, and of twenty-two years' imprisonment in Schlisselburg Fortress. A handsome, patriarchal figure with a flowing beard that framed his high-browed face, he breathed life into everyone around him with a joyous energy, curiosity, and helpfulness that belied his age.

Prince Kropotkin was born into a Russian noble family that traced its genealogy back a thousand years to Ryurik, the semi-legendary Scandinavian founder of the proto-Russian state; as a result, Kropotkin's noble lineage was older than the reigning Romanovs'. By the 1870s Kropotkin had become one of Europe's leading theorists and advocates of anarchism and socialism and, after several periods of imprisonment for his revolutionary activity in both Russia and Europe, settled near London. Sixty-six years old in 1908, as bald as an egg, with a broad bushy beard and mischievous eyes, he was still very active in radical circles—speaking very rapidly, always hurrying, eager to share his encyclopedic knowledge of revolution, politics, and society with anyone around him.

Savinkov assumed an uncompromising stance and began by doing everything he could to prevent the court from even convening, arguing that doing so would be an "insult" not only to Azef's "honor" but to the Combat Organization's as well as his own. However, he was overruled by Victor Chernov and Mark Natanson, both members of the Central Committee, who persuaded him to join them on the court.

Savinkov kept detailed notes of the proceedings, which are filled with references to "dignity," "debasement," "insult," "contempt," and especially "honor," "honor," "honor." These words constitute the conceptual lens through which he viewed the entire long and sordid process. But paradoxically his own acute sense of honor also made him blind to honor's complete absence, as when he failed *even to imagine* that Azef could be a cynically self-serving traitor. In this, Savinkov strikingly confirmed what Vera Figner concluded about the Socialist Revolutionaries in general: "they are stupidly honest" (*glupo chestny*), in the sense that "An honest person sees honesty in everyone, whereas a rogue sees a fraud in everyone."

Events over the next decade would demonstrate that Figner's insight was the key to understanding both Savinkov's and the SR Party's fatal behavior.

The "court of honor" held its first meeting in late October 1908 in Paris in a Russian émigré library on the Left Bank near the Sorbonne. Then, for greater privacy and security, they moved to Savinkov's apartment on rue La Fontaine.

When Burtsev first arrived to start making his case, with his spectacles, shabby dress, and unassuming and quietly fussy manner, he looked more like a studious librarian than a *provokator*-slayer. The way he kept blinking his eyes as he peered at everyone through his lenses made him seem especially naïve. But the expression in his eyes was serious and probing.

He began by laying out what he knew and what he had inferred about the numerous arrests of members of the Combat Organization in recent years, and how everything pointed to Azef's betrayal. He also summarized what he had learned from Bakay, the former Okhrana agent who had given him a lot of information.

Almost immediately, things began to go badly for Burtsev. The SR Party members who were on the court—Savinkov, Chernov, and Natanson—argued that the attempt to discredit Azef was the result of a police plot to damage the Party by planting false information. Bakay, they insisted, was completely untrustworthy and had deceived Burtsev.

This was a powerful blanket argument of a kind that could be used to convert any "evidence" into lies and that would be exceedingly hard to disprove. Figner was struck by how Savinkov and Chernov defended Azef "like lions" and attacked Burtsev "like experienced prosecutors." By contrast, Burtsev failed to parry their critiques, replied unconvincingly, and behaved like a dazed child being backed into a corner.

Very quickly after the trial started, Burtsev's entire case seemed lost and the proceedings appeared to reach a critical point. Then, unexpectedly, Burtsev dropped the bomb that he had been holding in reserve. Nothing in his appearance or manner had indicated what was coming.

He looked around and quietly announced: "I have additional proof: the former director of the police department, Lopukhin, confirmed to me that Azef is a *provokator* and receives payments from the secret police."

The room filled with stunned silence. Keeping an imperturbable expression on his face, Burtsev proceeded to tell the story of how he had met Lopukhin on a train in Germany and had persuaded him to reveal the truth about Azef.

⸻

Alexey Lopukhin had been the imperial director of the police from 1902 until February 1905, when he was cashiered for not having done enough to prevent the assassination of Grand Duke Sergey. Embittered by his treatment and disgusted by what he saw as the imperial regime's underhanded practices in dealing with radical groups—stirring up animosity against them, using *provokators*, and sending bands of Black Hundred thugs to attack them—Lopukhin tried at first to fight such tactics through official channels. When this did not work, he turned to his own initiatives, which stemmed from his liberal convictions and from his connections with Russian Freemasonry, which, like all branches of this secretive movement, was motivated by an ethical and reformist zeal.

The story of how Burtsev, an avowed revolutionary sympathizer, "happened" to meet Lopukhin on a train between Cologne and Berlin in September 1908 is murky. But the meeting appears to have been cunningly orchestrated by Lopukhin himself because he knew of Burtsev's investigation and wanted to help him (Burtsev, however, would later present it all as a result of his own diligence). During their meeting Lopukhin was deeply shaken by what Burtsev revealed to him about Azef. As far as Lopukhin knew, the *provokator* employed by the Okhrana was known only by his code name, Raskin. It was then that Lopukhin concluded that the two were one and the same and provided Burtsev with new and incontrovertible evidence that Azef was employed by the police.

After their initial shock at Burtsev's revelation, Savinkov, Chernov, and Natanson collected their wits and began to object vociferously. Lopukhin!? The director of the police department! Is it possible to trust him? That's the same dirty source as Bakay, just a higher rank! The secret police are trying to besmirch a member of the Central Committee and to damage the Party, to discredit it!

But not everyone on the court was as credulous. Lopatin, who had not been mesmerized by years of contact with Azef and had never even met him, was shaken by what Burtsev reported: "Well, that's the kind of evidence that justifies killing someone," he said. Lopatin was also perceptive enough to suggest that Azef had played both sides of the fence and was not just a double agent.

Burtsev now had a thin lifeline for his case, even though the SR Party members on the court remained obtusely skeptical about him and protective of Azef. What ultimately saved Burtsev, however, was that the SRs were motivated by a fervent, almost religious commitment to fairness and due process. As a result, they felt obligated, in spite of their skepticism, to verify the evidence that Burtsev had presented, and in early November sent a trusted Party member, one Argunov, to Saint Petersburg to interview Lopukhin.

Lopukhin not only confirmed to Argunov what he told Burtsev, he also threw oil on the fire by describing how, just several days earlier, on November 11, Azef had unexpectedly arrived at his door and implored him not to reveal that he was on the police payroll. (By this point in his career, Azef was getting 14,000 rubles a year, more than $200,000 in today's money.)

This was a shocking and damning new revelation, although it also raised the question of how Azef had gotten wind of Lopukhin's secret information, which was supposed to be known only to the members of the court. It turns out that it was from Savinkov himself, whose "loyalty" continued to make him blind and gullible: he unwittingly revealed Burtsev's source to Azef when he kept in touch with him during the trial, even though he had committed to maintaining its confidentiality.

Lopukhin also made another incendiary revelation to Argunov—that General Gerasimov himself, the head of the Okhrana, had visited him following Azef. Gerasimov was convinced of Azef's personal loyalty and threatened Lopukhin with repercussions if he revealed anything about Azef's status to the revolutionaries. It emerged that Azef had visited Gerasimov as well, looking haggard and pale and weeping, to ask for help against Burtsev, and it was Gerasimov who told Azef to try to persuade Lopukhin to be quiet. When this did not work, Gerasimov gave Azef a number of excellent fake passports and several thousand rubles to help him escape the SRs.

One would have thought that when Argunov returned to Paris with Lopukhin's amazing testimony, members of the court would finally be persuaded of Azef's guilt. But that was not the case. Not only was a police source always inherently suspect, but Azef had an alibi that also needed to be checked, which was that he had traveled to Munich and Berlin in November (without, of course, ever mentioning his trip to Saint Petersburg to seek Lopukhin's and Gerasimov's help). Savinkov volunteered to go to Germany to verify Azef's story and, as he fully expected, to disprove Lopukhin's claims.

However, Munich was where the first crack in Savinkov's faith appeared. When Azef was quizzed about the details of his trip to Germany—Where did you stay? Whom did you see? What were the rooms like?—his descriptions did not jibe with what Savinkov discovered when he went to investigate.

If Azef had been only slightly cannier in his small lies about his stay in Munich, he probably would have gotten away with his betrayals once again, and Burtsev would have been found guilty of calumny.

Now, however, Lopukhin's words fell on more receptive ears. And when in December 1908, Lopukhin came to London from Saint Petersburg to repeat to Savinkov and Chernov everything he had told Burtsev about Azef, Savinkov and Chernov were finally convinced.

For want of a nail the shoe was lost. For want of a shoe the horse was lost. For want of a horse the battle was lost.

Azef Exposed

Boris Savinkov's first thought was immediate vengeance—he wanted to kill Azef personally and without any further discussions. But the SR Party remained committed to due process; moreover, its hierarchy was split, with only a small minority siding with Savinkov. The majority were concerned with procedural and political issues and questions of Party morale. Because of Azef's high standing, and because there had not been any public questioning or open trial of him, the rank and file would not accept his being executed without any explanation. A further complication was that if Azef were killed in France, the French government would likely arrest the entire foreign section of the Party's Central Committee and expel it from the country, thus effectively paralyzing the Party at the very moment when the Azef affair was throwing it into chaos. As a result, the Central Committee decided to stick to its democratic principles and invited a number of additional respected revolutionary figures to a meeting to decide the matter. Not unexpectedly, the result was an awkward compromise: to continue the investigation by subjecting Azef to formal questioning and simultaneously to prepare his execution in a secret location in Italy.

Savinkov objected to the delay because he feared that it would give Azef a chance to escape, but he was overruled. He then considered killing Azef without the Party's "permission" but rejected the idea because he could not allow himself to cause a split in the Party or to put it at risk before the French authorities.

In the end, he could not bring himself to act ruthlessly at a critical moment, and the result was exactly what he feared.

On the evening of December 23/January 5, 1909, Savinkov, Chernov, and another SR Party member rang the doorbell to Azef's apartment at 245 Boulevard Raspail, which was across the street from the Montparnasse Cemetery in central Paris. Azef opened the door himself; when he saw who it was he turned pale. The three visitors demonstratively refused to shake his hand when he greeted them. Azef had no choice but to invite them to his study. He took a seat behind his desk in the comfortably furnished room while Savinkov and the others positioned themselves so that they blocked the door.

A long and tense inquisition ensued during which Savinkov and the others cross-examined Azef about many things—a letter incriminating him as a *provokator*, his secret visit to Lopukhin in Saint Petersburg, and the details of various failed terrorist attempts. Still looking very pale, Azef tried to conceal his nervousness with bluster and took his time as he systematically denied the validity and even the significance of all the evidence against him. In Savinkov's nearly verbatim protocol of the inquisition, Azef's responses are peppered with replies such as "I don't know anything"; "What nonsense. I don't understand anything"; "I never had any contacts with the police, and don't have any now."

Chernov then tried a conciliatory approach by playing on Azef's feelings and promising that nothing would happen to his family if he confessed. Azef in turn made a pathetic appeal to Chernov: "Victor! We lived in perfect harmony for years. We worked together. You know me . . . How could you come to me with such . . . with such filthy suspicion!"

And then, incredibly, they let him get away. Chernov told Azef that they were going to give him until noon on the following day to confess, and if he did, they would spare his life. From himself, Savinkov added darkly that tomorrow at noon, they would feel free of all obligations toward him.

The three then left Azef's apartment without taking the elementary precaution of leaving someone to guard it; perhaps the shock was too great for them to be able to think clearly. Later they would try to justify their lapse with vague references to imagining that someone else would take care of posting a guard.

⊶━⊷

As Savinkov and the others subsequently learned from Azef's wife, Lyubov, she had been in another room in the apartment all the time, as her husband had instructed her. When Savinkov and the others left, she came to Azef's study and found him frenziedly destroying papers, packing a small suitcase, and mumbling about having to get away at once. Around 2:30 A.M. he asked her to accompany him to the train station. He was in such a hurry that he did not even bother to look in on his two sleeping children, although he did remember to take most of the cash that was in the apartment. On the way to the station, Azef could barely contain his fear, jumping at every shadow and anxiously skirting ill-lit corners.

At the station, Azef parted gruffly from Lyubov, pushing her away when she tried to kiss him goodbye—"the situation is such that we can skip this part," he said—and gave her a forwarding address in Vienna.

In fact, however, he went to Germany to meet a mistress he had acquired over a year earlier, a fleshy and gaudy German cabaret singer known to her many fans as "*la belle* Hedy de Hero." Lyubov would never see her husband again, but "the beautiful" Hedy would remain Azef's faithful companion for the rest of life.

Azef assumed the German name that was on one of the fake passports Gerasimov had given him, and at first traveled widely with Hedy, spending time in Italy, Greece, Egypt, and various seashore resorts. He had plenty of money and indulged his passion for gambling in casinos, invested in stocks, and bought Hedy expensive diamond and silver gifts. They eventually settled in Berlin, where he passed himself off as a businessman. Azef never took any special pains to disguise himself, saying that he "despised" the revolutionaries' abilities as conspirators.

Things changed with the outbreak of the Great War in the summer of 1914. Azef suffered a serious financial blow because he had kept most of his money in Russian bonds, and these became worthless in Germany. He managed to regain his footing for a while by beginning a ladies' corset manufacturing company (he anticipated correctly that smaller sizes would be needed because of food shortages), but then another blow struck: he was arrested and imprisoned as a dangerous revolutionary by the German imperial police. Azef spent the last two and a half years of his life in prison under harsh conditions and was released just before Christmas 1917. Surprisingly, he claimed to have discovered faith and wrote to Hedy that "after prayer I am usually happy and feel well and strong in spirit. At times even suffering strengthens me. Yes, there is happiness even in suffering—a closeness to God." But this did not mean that he had a change of heart or that his conscience bothered him. His view of his past was that "a misfortune struck me, the greatest misfortune that can strike an innocent man and that can be compared only with the misfortune of Dreyfus." Comparing himself to the Jewish officer in the French army who was the victim of anti-Semitism and prosecuted on trumped-up charges in the last years of the nineteenth century may have made Azef feel better emotionally for a while. But by the time he was freed, his health had seriously deteriorated, and he lived for only several more months, dying on April 24, 1918, at the age of forty-nine.

After their meeting with Azef in his apartment, neither Savinkov nor any of the other Socialist Revolutionaries ever saw him again, despite their considerable efforts to find him. (The one exception was the dogged Burtsev, who somehow managed to arrange a secret interview with him in Frankfurt in 1912 and quiz him about his past.) A few days after disappearing, Azef sent the SRs a letter full of self-righteous indignation and bombast, accusing them of betraying the principles of "revolutionary honor and ethics," insisting that he would restore his "honor" despite the "stench and filth" in which they are mired and into which they want to drag him, and swearing that he would never forget the insult. Figner called it the most "brazen letter of any ever written by a human hand."

Blast Waves

On January 7/20, 1909, the Central Committee of the SR Party published a flyer detailing Azef's betrayal with a promise that a photograph and his physical description would be made available in the near future.

On January 17/30, the Party announced that, in light of the proof that Azef was a *provokator*, all accusations against Burtsev had been dropped.

Shortly thereafter, the Azef scandal became a front-page sensation around the world. The lead article in the *New York Times* for February 7, 1909, was headlined "POLICE AND REDS BOTH HUNT AZEFF. Only Question Seems to be at Whose Hands He Will Die. While Streets of Russian Cities Ran with Blood He Lived in Comparative Luxury with Family in Paris." For months, Burtsev provided newspapers in Europe and the United States with florid interviews and stories about his success and the double-dealing of the imperial government.

In Russia, the news caused a governmental crisis. On January 20, 1909, several deputies of the Third Duma raised the "Azef affair" during a legislative session and read into the official record a long letter that Azef had written to Savinkov revealing his involvement in a series of terrorist acts at the same time that he was a paid agent of the imperial police. The deputies' explosive accusation was that the imperial regime was involved in the practice of provocation—of having one of its paid agents abet terrorist activity.

On February 11, Prime Minister Stolypin was compelled to respond to the charges and defend the imperial regime. The Tauride Palace where the Duma met was packed with deputies, journalists, dignitaries, members of the imperial family, and foreign diplomats, all eager to hear what he would say about the extraordinary accusations. A handsome man with a penetrating gaze, square jaw, and commanding presence, Stolypin spoke with proud self-assurance, knowing that his speech would be widely reported in Russia and around the world. He forcibly rejected the accusation that Azef had provoked acts of terrorism and painted him instead as a secret police informant, pure and simple, who had acted within the boundaries of police department regulations.

Everything Stolypin knew and said about Azef, and everything that he ultimately reported to Nicholas II about him, came from a single source—General Gerasimov, and Gerasimov was convinced that Azef was a loyal government spy in the revolutionary camp. Incredibly, Gerasimov would continue to believe in Azef's honesty for at least the next twenty-five years, even after all the mountains of evidence about his multiple betrayals had been published, including his involvement in the plot to assassinate Nicholas II on the *Ryurik*. Savinkov had described the plot in detail in his *Memoirs of a Terrorist*, which were published in full in 1917.

Stolypin's speech succeeded, and despite some dissenting voices, enough deputies accepted his explanation for the Duma to drop the matter. As a result of Gerasimov's witless credulity, Azef had been whitewashed in the eyes of the imperial regime, and all the assassinations that occurred while he was embedded in the terrorist camp were explained away as having succeeded *despite* his efforts.

Those whom the gods would destroy, they first make mad.

For many others, the fallout of the Azef affair was devastating. On January 18/31, Lopukhin was arrested after he returned to Saint Petersburg from London. Because Gerasimov and Stolypin knew that he had given evidence against Azef to the SRs, including Savinkov, who was a well-known fugitive terrorist, Lopukhin was put on trial for abetting a revolutionary organization, and at the end of April he was sentenced to five years of hard labor. Two months later, however, in light of his former distinguished service and deteriorating health, Nicholas II commuted Lopukhin's sentence to exile in Siberia for life with a forfeiture of all his property. Lopukhin was amnestied in 1913 when the Romanovs celebrated the 300th anniversary of their dynasty, and he died in obscurity in Berlin in 1944.

For the Socialist Revolutionaries, the cataclysmic nature of the Azef affair can hardly be overstated. Vladimir Zenzinov, a member of the Party and friend of Savinkov's, characterized it as a "sharp barrier" that cut in half the lives of anyone connected to the revolutionary movement and that forced everyone to reevaluate their attitude toward everything—"the world, people, life itself." Chernov admitted that anyone who had not lived through those days would find it hard even to imagine the sense of "confusion" and "moral catastrophe" that Party members experienced. A police informant reported that following Chernov's speech about Azef's betrayal at a secret meeting of Party leaders (not all spies in the Party had been exposed), the chairman Fondaminsky "and many among those present were crying; others sat silently, their heads bent low."

The entire Central Committee of the Party resigned and demanded to be tried by a revolutionary court for their failure to investigate earlier accusations against Azef. The Central Committee also announced the disbanding of the Combat Organization because it had been irredeemably tarnished by Azef's treachery.

Personal Losses

Savinkov's pain was especially acute, although he admitted this fully only in his private correspondence. In a public statement, he acknowledged the disaster but tried to sound stoic and defiant as he invoked the most notorious precedent of betrayal in all of European culture (and also left the door open for future action):

> Two thousand years ago, Judas Iscariot betrayed Christ. Christianity has not died to this day. Who dares to say that Judas's sin has desecrated the doctrine of love? . . . Has terrorism died? Has the revolution died? Has Azef's sin desecrated the doctrine of socialism? . . . It was not Azef who created terrorism, it was not Azef who breathed life into it. And Azef cannot destroy the temple that he did not build.

Savinkov's pain was aggravated by the deterioration of his relations with Vera during the past months, which coincided with the Azef disaster. Ever since their break, he had supported her and their children financially, but now money was becoming increasingly tight. In a letter from February 9, 1909, she is unable to conceal her irritation and brusquely dismisses his concerns in order to turn to what is now weighing on her: "all that you write is wise and good but the money hasn't arrived." She reminds Boris of the obvious—that the children are no longer infants and that they have needs that cost money: Tanya is preparing for her gymnasium exams and Vitya, who will soon turn eight, is enrolled in school.

Boris tries to be conciliatory in a letter he sent two days later, even as he acknowledges that his life has been upended by the Azef disaster: "You know everything from the newspapers and I have nothing to add . . . only that everything is worse than could have been expected, worse and nastier." He asks her to forgive him for writing infrequently and for the delay in sending her money. He wants her to give the children a "big, big kiss for him" and to tell them that he always remembers them and will write to them soon. But just now he is "very busy."

His honesty and best efforts were not enough. Vera also felt a growing emotional distance from him, in part because, as she explained in a letter from the summer of 1909, she had so many difficulties of her own that she could scarcely find time for his. To make matters even worse, the children kept falling seriously ill—diphtheria and typhus had made Vera fear for their lives, and her relations with Sofia, her mother-in-law, had become painfully strained.

Nevertheless, somehow, Boris managed to support Vera and their children for several more years, even though at times he had so little money himself that he had to borrow it from friends.

But there were also periods when things went better between them and Vera warmed toward him. At times, she helped him with his literary affairs by acting as his representative in Saint Petersburg; she also looked out for his younger brother, Victor, who maintained friendly relations with her. And once, in August 1909, when she managed to scrape the money together for the trip, she even visited him in Paris while in Europe with one of her sisters. Despite the fact that it was Boris who had chosen a new life for himself far away from his children and never saw them, Vera loyally did her best to raise them so that they would think well of their father.

The Pale Horse

As the Azef disaster shook the foundations of Savinkov's life, writing became his intellectual and emotional outlet. He had worked steadily on parts of his

Memoirs of a Terrorist while he was spending time with the Merezhkovskys. But he also wanted to write a novella about terrorism to explore the emotional and ideological aspects of the experience that did not belong in a factual account. When he started it in Paris, Zinaida became its "godmother," helping with all aspects of the work.

The title of the book, *Kon Bledny* (*The Pale Horse*), was her suggestion and came from Revelation 6:8: "And I looked, and behold a pale horse: and his name that sat on him was Death, and Hell followed with him. And power was given unto them over the fourth part of the earth, to kill with sword, and with hunger, and with death, and with the beasts of the earth."

Zinaida also invented Savinkov's pseudonym, V. Ropshin, which alludes to Ropsha, a town near Saint Petersburg where Emperor Peter III was murdered in 1762 in a palace coup that put his wife on the Russian throne as Catherine II. The pseudonym thus has associations with Savinkov's past exploits, and the novel's title puts these into the context of Christian eschatology.

The Pale Horse consists of passages a page or two long, with the day and month (but no year), and told in first person, which makes the work look like a diary. Together with such casually introduced statements as "Three kilos of dynamite are under the table. I brought it with me from abroad," which appears a dozen lines into the opening description of a shabby hotel room, the novel's form made many readers think that the author had written an account of his own experiences. But although there are obvious echoes of the attack on Grand Duke Sergey in 1905 and other episodes from Savinkov's life, such as his escape from prison in Sevastopol, all of which were more or less known to the public, the story he tells differs significantly as well. And, in fact, the differences are more important than the similarities.

The primary motivation of the first-person narrator, known only as "Zhorzh" (George), is satisfying his need for freedom on the most basic, personal level: he is driven exclusively by his appetites and passions and does not even want to think about the reasons for whatever he does. Zhorzh apparently became a terrorist only because he believes that the Russian imperial power structure oppresses him personally. The usual ideological motivations for revolution—a desire to free the people, to destroy despotism, to establish socialism—are completely unimportant to him. He is, as a result, completely amoral: "what would my life be without the joyful realization that the world's laws are not for me?" he asks.

Zhorzh's aimless egotism has no relation to anything that mattered most deeply to Savinkov personally—his reverence for terrorism and the revolution; his loyalty toward comrades in the Combat Organization, including the memory of those who died; his love for Vera, the children, and Evgeniya; his rage and despair over Azef's betrayal; his unwavering "correctness" in his dealings with others; his sense of honor. Especially striking in light of Savinkov's values is that Zhorzh does not care if innocent bystanders are hurt during terrorist attacks. The two other terrorists in the novella, who have recognizable prototypes in Boris Savinkov's life, have much more traditional revolutionary views and fight for the benefit of the downtrodden. But to Zhorzh their beliefs are irrelevant.

By giving his central character an anarchical and selfish stance in life, Savinkov may have been trying to do something original—to grab the reader's attention by attacking the knee-jerk idealism of the Russian revolutionary movement. But he was also leaving reality behind because there were no Russian revolutionaries who believed what Zhorzh did.

However, there were other fictional characters who did. Zhorzh's ideas recapitulate a theme from one of the best-known works in Russian and world literature, Fyodor Dostoyevsky's *The Brothers Karamazov*. In this novel, which had been published thirty years earlier, the characters Ivan and his minion Smerdyakov famously argue that if there is no God, then all is permitted—that the individual is free do whatever he wants because there is no universal moral authority (a similar theme appears in Dostoyevsky's *Crime and Punishment*, where Raskolnikov also begins by believing that "all is permitted" for superior individuals). The connection between *The Pale Horse* and Dostoyevsky is overt, and Zhorzh refers to Smerdyakov explicitly. But whereas in *Brothers Karamazov* Smerdyakov's and Ivan's amoral idea is ultimately defeated—or at least strongly opposed—by the ideal of charitable Christian love and faith that are embodied and articulated by other characters, especially Alyosha and the monk Zosima, Savinkov has Zhorzh side with Smerdyakov, as when he proclaims: "If I don't have God, then I am god myself . . . How is Smerdyakov worse than others? And why should anyone fear Smerdyakov?"

Dostoyevsky's Christian ideal does appear in *The Pale Horse* as well, where it is embodied in the secondary character Vanya, a member of Zhorzh's team who is modeled on Ivan Kalyaev and who rejects the "Smerdyakovian" world view as an illness of the times. However, Zhorzh is coldly indifferent to Vanya's key idea that a terrorist should sacrifice himself for the common good by imitating Christ (something that was also very dear to the Merezhkovskys). Savinkov even has Zhorzh simply forget Vanya's impassioned ideas, including his agonizing about the sin of murder, shortly after he hears them, which diminishes them even more.

The other plot strands in *The Pale Horse* are two contrasted love affairs, whose function is to show that Zhorzh has the same stance no matter the arena of activity. Out of jealousy, he even kills the husband of one of the women in a hurried duel, but then simply forgets the woman. The novella ends with the clear implication that Zhorzh will commit suicide because he is bored and has nothing to live for.

Savinkov's actions after the novella was published also underscore his distance from Zhorzh. Starting the same month as it appeared in January 1909, the SR Party's Central Committee authorized Savinkov to resurrect the Combat Organization; that he failed to do so on this occasion is less important than his eagerness to try. Similarly, one month later, Savinkov defended the ideal of terrorism in print and insisted that Azef's betrayal had not undermined its importance.

In the end, *The Pale Horse* can best be seen as personifying ideas that Savinkov entertained for several years and shared with Vera Figner on the French Riviera in early 1907—that there is no morality, only beauty, and that beauty is the unhindered development of the individual's personality and thus the same as ugliness. Figner rejected these ideas and did not believe that Savinkov actually took them seriously.

Why, then, did Savinkov make Zhorzh the hero of *The Pale Horse*? One possibility is that he was exorcising ideas that he had found tempting and rejected. Vladimir Nabokov once explained that some of his villainous characters "are outside my inner self like the mournful monsters of a cathedral facade—demons placed there merely to show that they have been booted out." Perhaps the Azef affair contributed to Savinkov's rejection of amoral egotism. And perhaps Savinkov was intrigued by the artistic challenge of creating a fictional character who was mostly unlike himself.

But there may have been more to it as well. In Zhorzh, Savinkov strove to create a unique and refined character who would fascinate the reader with his ruthlessness, bravery, nihilism, artistic sensibility, attractiveness to women, and outbursts of passion. Zhorzh writes about himself in a terse, unemotional style, but he also tries to capture the drama of close calls when he escapes from the police. Despite being a violent and unprincipled man, he is cultured and quotes verses by well-known Russian and French lyric poets (Tyutchev, Verlaine) that echo his moods or the settings in which he finds himself. Parts of Zhorzh's DNA are the self-regarding Romantic literary heroes such as those one finds in Lermontov, Pushkin, and especially Byron, including the latter's many imitators (and all of whom also lurk in the background of Dostoyevsky's novels), together with a whiff of Nietzsche. Such characteristics suggest that aspects of Savinkov's own vanity may have colored his fictional creation.

It also has to be said that although the novella is highly original thematically, and would become the most famous of Savinkov's works of fiction, it is clearly a product of his literary apprenticeship. It has clumsy moments and produces the impression that he struggled to achieve what he thought were impressive effects, but failed. At times, when Zhorzh tries to be portentous or mysterious, he sounds merely maudlin. Perhaps this is what Gippius meant when she wrote about her efforts while editing the novella: "Oh, did I have my work cut out with him!"

It does Savinkov credit that he had no illusions about his achievement. He explained to a friend that he wanted to show that someone like Zhorzh who believes "all is permitted" will inevitably have to kill himself (which is in fact what Dostoyevsky has Smerdyakov do in *The Brothers Karamazov*). The comments Savinkov's friend made showed that she had not understood his point in the novella, and for this he blames only himself: "I didn't manage to pull off this very complex task, the task of portraying the dynamics of a soul and not its static state: You didn't understand Zhorzh. That's *my* fault."

It was in the middle of this disorienting and deeply unhappy period that Savinkov at last got some good news for which he had been waiting—*The Pale Horse* was published in the January 1909 issue of the influential literary-political magazine *Russian Thought* (*Russkaya mysl*). It immediately caused a sensation. The censorship had cut out some of its more politically sensitive moments (such as references to the 1905 Moscow uprising), but readers were still intrigued and shocked by its subject matter and the belief that it was based on fact.

Russian Thought accepted the novella because Dmitry Merezhkovsky was a member of its editorial board and had interceded. Continuing the role that his wife, Zinaida, had played as a mentor to Savinkov, in 1909 Merezhkovsky also published a glowing review, proclaiming that "If they asked me now in Europe which book is the most Russian and allows one to foresee the future of Russia, after the great works of Tolstoy and Dostoyevsky, I would point to *The Pale Horse*." It embodied, Merezhkovsky claimed in a memorable phrase, the distinctive Russian style of the early twentieth century: "the smell of dynamite mixed with apocalyptic incense."

Other literary lights whom Savinkov admired also praised the work, including the important poet Valery Bryusov, who added that it was "ten times better" than anything by Leonid Andreyev, who had published Savinkov's literary debut. Even Leo Tolstoy himself felt compelled to read it and went so far as to make numerous marks and comments in the margins (contents unfortunately unknown), although it is hard to imagine that he was anything but repelled. For a debut novelist, this was a spectacular launch.

Revolutionaries, however, were outraged by *The Pale Horse*, although this too only brought it more attention. The Socialist Revolutionary Party was undergoing a period of soul-searching and reorientation after Azef and some of its new leaders began to insist that Savinkov be expelled from the Party because of how he portrayed terrorists. One SR labeled him as "worse than Azef." Babushka Breshko-Breshkovskaya said that the novel made her "feel nauseous."

By the beginning of 1909, Savinkov was already famous and notorious as a leading revolutionary terrorist. But when his authorship of *The Pale Horse* became known, his fame and notoriety increased even more, and he began to acquire the status of a legendary figure.

Call of Honor

If the ability to persevere in the face of a devastating failure is a sign of courage and faith, then Savinkov showed his mettle when, shortly after Azef's escape, he resolved that he must reestablish the Combat Organization. He had two reasons. The first was "the honor of terror," as he put it: he believed it was essential to prove that it was not Azef who had created "central terror," and that it was not the connivance of the police that allowed it to succeed. A renewal of terrorism would thus "wash the stain" off both the living and dead members of the Combat Organization. The second reason was that although Savinkov still believed that only technological innovations would raise terrorism to the highest level of effectiveness, he was also convinced that the Combat Organization's old methods could still work, in a "palliative" or temporary way, if they were properly applied and if there were no *provokators*. He presented his arguments to the SR Central Committee in January 1909, and despite some skepticism, the Committee agreed to appoint him head of a new "Combat Group," one that would be allowed to assume the old name of "Combat Organization" if it succeeded in carrying out its first planned assassination.

Savinkov began with an especially rigorous selection of members, so when twenty-eight people volunteered to join his team, he rejected sixteen for various reasons, including the suspicion that three may have been *provokators*. He also imposed a severe, military-style discipline; took extraordinary precautions to ensure secrecy and security; and reserved for himself the exclusive right to make all decisions. Not all the SRs Savinkov approached were willing to go along, because they resented his self-assurance and that he abandoned a horizontal, "comradely" structure of relations for a strictly hierarchical one in which he alone was at the pinnacle.

Nevertheless, things initially went quickly. By the spring of 1909, Savinkov had narrowed his targets to Nicholas II and Minister of Justice Ivan Shcheglovitov (a notorious reactionary and anti-Semite). Soon afterward, he established a dynamite laboratory on Jersey, a British island off the coast of Normandy in France. By November, a sufficient amount of dynamite had been manufactured, and six members of the team had successfully entered Russia. Disguised as cabbies, they began to stalk Nicholas II and quickly established his itineraries around Saint Petersburg. The time seemed ripe to schedule the attack and smuggle the prepared dynamite into the country.

Then suddenly, things started to go wrong. First, a party member decided to infiltrate the Okhrana on his own initiative and simulate being a double agent so that he could get close enough to General Gerasimov to kill him. His attempt failed, although he did blow up a police colonel in December 1909. The SRs, who were still reeling from the Azef disaster, were appalled that a *provokator* was again involved in an assassination. Following this, reports began to reach Savinkov in France that the six cabbies were being followed by police agents. He recalled them all to London, but it was too late.

It subsequently emerged that the Okhrana had known everything about the new combat group for the past year and a half, virtually from the time

Savinkov established it. In the wake of the Azef scandal, this revelation about yet another betrayal became the death blow to the Socialist Revolutionary Party's attempt to resurrect terrorism, which now seemed to be irreperably tainted by provocation. Savinkov would not give up, however, and even in the face of the new fiasco announced that he was prepared to regroup and to continue. But the Party leadership had turned resolutely against him personally, against the Combat Organization as an institution, and against terrorism as a tactic.

Many of the Party's leading figures explained Savinkov's failure by claiming that he was a poor leader. Some accused him of cowardice because he had stayed abroad. Others complained that he had besmirched the revolution in his novella, that his break with Vera and involvement with Evgeniya were ignoble, and that he was corrupted by his fondness for gambling (about which more later). Even after everything that had happened, some compared him unfavorably with Azef.

Savinkov felt deeply guilty about his failures as a leader and his gullibility about Azef, and he was perfectly willing to accept criticism on these grounds. But he was devastated by the SR Party's rejection of the Combat Organization and of terrorism because this was an attack on the central axis of his life. By late 1910, Savinkov saw there was no hope and wrote to a friend: "I'm being thrown out. I'm being asked politely, delicately. But I'm getting it in the neck."

Even worse was to come. In the official report about the Azef affair that the Party's leadership finally completed and published in April 1911, Savinkov and other members of the Combat Organization were made scapegoats, and he was attacked for what was characterized as his insultingly superior and disrespectful attitude toward the Party's institutions and leadership. Some members of the Party labeled him a snobbish "horse guardsman," a "revolutionary duelist" and a "swashbuckler." Savinkov tried to protest, and many of his comrades supported him, but to no avail. The report's authors were motivated by personal animosity toward him and other veterans of the Combat Organization as much as by ideology and would not back down.

For Savinkov, this was the end. To his old friend Ilya Fondaminsky, he wrote: "they have spat upon everything and everyone, alive and dead. And there's nothing to be done." Looking back at his life from early 1909 through the end of 1910, he admitted to another friend, "my conscience torments me . . . for all the misfortunes and failures. All the guilt is mine, of course . . . I shattered the ship on underwater rocks like a bad, negligent and shortsighted helmsman. Now fragments float on the water. I try to collect them and nail them together. But what's the use? I'm still the same helmsman."

Savinkov took the only course of action left to him: he officially resigned as head of the combat group and dismissed all its members.

CHAPTER SIX

BEHIND THE LINES

When 1911 dawned, for the first time since he had committed himself to revolution a decade earlier, Boris Savinkov was out of the fight. All his efforts and sacrifice had come to nothing. The loathsome imperial regime still stood, the heroic legacy of the Socialist Revolutionary Party was no more, and he had neither an occupation nor a home.

For the next half-dozen years, Savinkov would continue to live largely in France, shuttling between Paris and various towns on the French Riviera, with sojourns to the Ligurian coast of Italy and occasionally to places like Naples and Capri. As far as he was concerned, his conspiratorial life was finished.

But that is not how the Okhrana saw it. Although they knew that Savinkov had broken with the Socialist Revolutionary Party and disbanded his combat group, they could not be sure that he was completely inactive and continued to watch him as closely as if he were planning another mission.

<hr/>

The surveillance was carried by a changing array of some dozen and a half French agents, including several women, hired by the Paris office of the Okhrana, all of whom had previous experience in the French police. The agents were nothing if not diligent and watched Savinkov and whoever was with him, wherever he was, night and day. They then regularly mailed letters to Paris Okhrana headquarters, sometimes more than once a day. In turn, the Paris office sent summaries and other information gathered by the field agents to Okhrana headquarters in Saint Petersburg, from which it also received information as well as instructions. This procedure varied over the years only in terms of the extent of the surveillance and frequency of the reports, both of which dropped markedly, but did not cease, after August 1914, when the outbreak of the Great War gave the Okhrana bigger things to worry about.

"Watching" Savinkov is what the French agents literally did, by lurking outside the places he lived and the restaurants, post offices, pharmacies, barber shops, etc. he frequented. They followed him on trains, on trams, on the street, and in automobiles; they disguised themselves as railway workers or pretended to be tourists; and they tried to get close enough to be able to note his behavior and read his facial expressions. When it seemed useful, the agents supplemented their verbal descriptions with sketch maps of the places he was living and even of the building interiors in which he spent time. They also intercepted and copied the letters, pneumatic tube messages, and telegrams he sent and received, and with the help of bribed maids retrieved torn-up scraps of paper from his wastepaper baskets. On several occasions, Savinkov spotted the French *fileurs* and managed to escape their scrutiny for a while.

The police were also not above staging an elaborate charade that was like a parody of what he had done himself in Saint Petersburg seven years earlier while planning the attack on Plehve. When he moved into an apartment in a building in an outlying part of Paris near the Bois de Boulogne that was very little built up at the time and consequently difficult to surveil, the French agents rented an apartment in the building as well. Knowing that Savinkov would be wary of any new tenants, they also hired a retired actor who was reasonably well known on the Parisian stage and settled him in the apartment with three agents, two women and a man, who pretended to be his sister, a servant, and a relative. The actor's past could be verified easily, which would allay any suspicions Savinkov might have, and the three agents could take turns keeping an eye on him. The local commander even proposed to headquarters in Saint Petersburg that a car be bought for the agents to use in following Savinkov around the city, but at 20,000 francs (around $100,000 today) this was judged as far too exorbitant and was not approved.

Under the circumstances, Inspector Clouseau–like moments were inevitable as well, such as when Savinkov noticed that his automobile was being followed by another one with two men in it, causing him to try to confront them. Boris's mother, Sofia, had similar experiences when she came to visit him. She once even wrote to the director of the Okhrana in Saint Petersburg to say that she would be happy to tell police agents where she was going to save them the trouble of following her (as a result of which the police concluded they had to find more skillful *fileurs*).

In the end, the Okhrana learned largely about the externals of Savinkov's existence—where and how he spent most of his time and with whom he associated. Had the police been able to understand his inner life more fully, they could have saved a considerable amount of trouble and money by leaving him alone.

Writing as Self-Reflection

Starting in early 1911 and continuing until the outbreak of the Great War in the summer of 1914, a period when his life was dominated by a profound sense of disorientation, Boris Savinkov occupied himself largely with writing. He had been longing to write more ever since *The Pale Horse*. Even while the Azef disaster was still reverberating, he confided to a friend how much he envied her creative freedom—that she has "books, sun, paper, and a favorite pen," whereas all he has is "dust, automobiles, spies, talk, discussions and meetings."

When he was finally free to write, the project to which he would dedicate most of his energy was an ambitious novel about the 1905 Russian Revolution. However, he also allowed himself to digress by writing poetry, a genre that had long attracted him, even though it would never be as important a part of his life or legacy as prose fiction. In fact, only a few of the poems would see the light of day between 1911 and 1913, and only some dozen from this period would be published posthumously. Nonetheless, the poems and the novel are clearly Savinkov's attempts to give voice to his recent experiences and to get them out of the echo chamber of his own mind.

Savinkov's verses are conventional, and his achievement as a poet is modest but not ineffective. At times, as in *The Pale Horse*, he hits false notes of pretense and pathos. However, the value and interest of the poems lie less in their verbal artistry and more in what they reveal about their creator's state of mind at a difficult time in his life. Lyric poetry necessarily reflects an individual psyche more readily than narrative fiction, which typically relies on a multiplicity of characters and perspectives.

All dozen poems, even those that are largely about nature on the Azure Coast, express a poignant sense of loss and regret about the past combined with pessimism about the future. There are clear allusions to Savinkov's career as a revolutionary terrorist. He writes that he was once full of grand hopes, but now he "lies face downward, like a meek slave," and life is "a petty and bothersome deception, / The falsehood of desires that have been lost forever." He even doubts that he was ever truly "summoned" to do battle in the past and feels that he is "vanquished." His "lost soul" is "a wound that will not heal."

In his current fallen state, he casts about for guidance and asks "To whom should I pray? Who will instruct me?" In one poem from 1911, he first thinks of "Christ," who is "love," and of "Golgotha," which is "redemption," and he expresses his faith "that sinners" will receive "His forgiveness." But in another poem from the same year, he concludes that he cannot be forgiven: "A murderer will not enter the city of Christ / He will be trampled by the Pale Horse / And the king of kings will come to hate him." Savinkov's pessimism sinks even lower in a poem dated two years later, in which the lyric persona is visited by an obnoxious, small, and malevolent demon (perhaps an echo of the prideful devil who appeared in Savinkov's first published story in 1902, but who is now the messenger of despondency): "Little and green / He will kill me." In the end, there is nothing but despair: "All is false. All is insignificant. / All is unnecessary. All is dark. / And the spindle of boring days / Turns hopelessly."

Savinkov's new novel was a much more substantial achievement. *What Never Happened (Three Brothers)* (*To, chego ne bylo [Tri brata]*) was serialized in the new Saint Petersburg journal *Zavety* (*Testaments*) in 1912 and 1913 before being published in book form in Moscow in 1914. The journal, which included articles on politics as well as works of literature, was founded by Victor Chernov with 10,000 rubles provided by a supporter and was conceived as an official organ of the Socialist Revolutionary Party. Savinkov's membership gave him an important "in" that facilitated his novel's acceptance, despite his strained relations with most of the senior Party members. He also entered a very select company because the journal published many of the most prominent writers of the day who would go on to earn permanent places in the history of Russian literature, including Maxim Gorky, Leonid Andreyev, Ivan Bunin (a future

Nobel laureate), Fyodor Sologub, Alexander Blok, Alexey Remizov, Evgeny Zamyatin, and others.

The new novel, like *The Pale Horse*, was published under the pseudonym V. Ropshin, and at 300 pages is more than twice as long. It tells the stories of the three Bolotov brothers, Andrey, Mikhail, and Alexander, as well as their family and of several of their comrades, against the background of the failed 1905 Revolution. An important subplot involves the discovery and execution of a major *provokator* in the revolutionary party in the novel. None of the brothers or other characters can be assumed to stand for Savinkov, and it is always risky to make direct connections between a work of fiction and the author's own life. Nevertheless, as contextual evidence indicates, when taken collectively, the brothers and the other characters can be seen as reflecting Savinkov's own state of mind during this time, as well as how he saw the Socialist Revolutionary Party and the revolutionary movement in general.

Andrey Bolotov is a prominent and respected member of the Party who decides (like his creator) that the endless talk and organizational efforts of its leadership are futile and that he must put his life on the line for the revolution. He first joins the armed uprising in Moscow, and, after it is crushed, becomes a terrorist and organizes an attempt on the life of a hated imperial prosecutor. The assassination is successful, but Andrey is captured and hanged. The youngest brother, Mikhail, is an exalted schoolboy who idolizes Andrey and dreams of revolutionary heroism on Moscow's barricades. However, just seconds after he manages to climb onto one for the first time, he is killed with hardly anyone noticing or even knowing who he was. The third brother, Alexander, is a naval officer who witnesses the destruction of the Russian fleet by the Japanese at Tsushima and endures the humiliation of being a prisoner of war. When he returns to Russia, he decides to devote his life to fighting the imperial regime because its ineptitude during the war betrayed both the country's military and the people as a whole. He joins the Party, but soon learns that there is a second *provokator* in it, in addition to the senior figure exposed earlier. Alexander identifies and kills the traitor. However, the man had already given him up to the Okhrana, and when troops come to arrest him, Alexander commits suicide. The plotlines about several other revolutionaries are similarly tragic.

What Never Happened is a very unhappy book. It expresses Savinkov's conclusion that he has failed as a revolutionary and that the Russian revolutionary movement as a whole has been defeated. However, in terms of Savinkov's growth as a writer, the new novel is a significant artistic advance over *The Pale Horse*. Even with the mixed critical reaction that the new novel received, he could still take satisfaction in having completed not only a longer but more ambitious work—one with an array of well-drawn characters with rich inner lives who embody different facets of Russian society during a climactic period in the country's history.

Outside the context of Savinkov's own life, however, *What Never Happened* still does not rise above the level of the kind of competent, mainstream realistic narrative fiction that was being published by dozens of other writers at the beginning of the twentieth century (to say nothing of writers of the first rank). It is also conventional and derivative in a number of ways both stylistically and thematically, and there are occasional longueurs and lapses of tone and characterization in it. But reading *What Never Happened* does not make one wince the way *The Pale Horse* can. Moreover, in addition to the successful characters and compellingly rendered scenes set in urban settings and in the countryside, if one knows the facts of Savinkov's biography and Azef's role in it, one can appreciate the pleasure he must have gotten from having the major *provokator* in the novel, Dr. Berg, executed by a vengeful Party member.

⚯

The Pale Horse was inspired by a nihilistic and corrosive idea in Dostoyevsky's *The Brothers Karamazov* that goes against the grain of what the work advocates as a whole. By contrast, in *What Never Happened* Savinkov turns to Leo Tolstoy, the other towering figure in the history of the Russian novel, and embraces his argument in *War and Peace* about the relation between the individual and history.

The central event in *War and Peace* is Napoleon's invasion of Russia in 1812, which Tolstoy uses to examine the hypnotic effect that the French emperor's personality and career had on people around the world during the first two-thirds of the nineteenth century. But rather than celebrate Napoleon as an existential hero—as an extraordinary man who raised himself to the heights of power through sheer force of will, and who can thus serve as an inspiration to others, which is how he was usually seen—Tolstoy dismantles his reputation by arguing that all historical events occur as a result of myriad interdependent causes that ultimately derive from a transcendent realm whose aims remain inscrutable to human understanding. As a result, will, volition, and freedom are illusory; all human beings are the playthings of fate; and the "great man" theory of history is a delusion. Wisdom thus lies in enlightened passivity—that is, in not trying to have one's way but in consciously going along with whatever one can discern about the constant flow of events, both big and small. The characters Princess Marya, Prince Bagration, and especially Field Marshal Kutuzov and the peasant Platon Karataev are Tolstoy's exemplary heroes in this regard.

But as Tolstoy also argues in the novel, there is a paradox at the root of the human condition because a belief in personal freedom—even if such freedom does not actually exist—is an inescapable aspect of human consciousness. This is what leads Tolstoy to depict his characters acting at length *as if* they have volition and personal agency, even if at other times they have sensed that they are merely elements in an immeasurably vast causal totality. "Man proposes, God disposes," is the way Platon Karataev neatly formulates this doubled conception.

Tolstoy's worldview in *War and Peace* is counterintuitive and gave rise to a great deal of resistance as well as misunderstanding since its publication in 1869. It is therefore all the more striking that a variant of Tolstoy's fatalism is embraced by Andrey and Alexander Bolotov in *What Never Happened*.

Andrey Bolotov realizes early on that the leadership of the Party has no effect on the grand historical forces unfolding in Russia during the 1905 Revolution and that the members of its central committee are not its "masters, but its docile and weak servants," which is a very Tolstoyan way of putting it. Savinkov also has Andrey invoke Tolstoy's fatalism overtly by quoting the historical character General Pfuel in the novel, who is the embodiment of self-assured pedantry and entirely ignorant of his actual impotence in the face of occult historical forces. There is little doubt that Savinkov came to a similar conclusion as a result of all his failed efforts and the Party's paralysis during the past few years following the Azef disaster.

Nevertheless, in spite of his fatalism, Andrey does not give up. Like all Tolstoy's characters who have glimpsed the true nature of things but still cannot help slipping into the delusion of thinking they are masters of their own fate, Andrey decides to become a terrorist. In Tolstoy, this kind of oscillation between insight (a recognition of one's dependence) and blindness (belief in one's freedom) is an inescapable and paradoxical aspect of the human condition, and his main male characters experience it. Savinkov does the same when Andrey agonizes over the morality of killing (underscoring his seeming freedom to choose), and also feels that what "pushed him to kill" was "a higher, incomprehensible power, millions of causes, and the sweep of centuries," which recalls Tolstoy's enigmatic transcendent. But in Tolstoyan fashion, this "elevated" perspective does not last. When the time comes for Andrey to walk to the scaffold, he suddenly succumbs to a feeling of unspeakable horror. This change can be interpreted as the final swing of his oscillation from the elevated perspective to the all-too-human and limited one. Later, as we shall see, Savinkov would face his own death with equanimity.

Andrey's brother Alexander echoes most aspects of Andrey's experiences and thoughts. Savinkov also broadens his portrayal of the revolutionary movement by including true believers in the effectiveness of the SR Party, as well as others who choose the Maximalist path that Savinkov and the SRs rejected on ethical grounds. It says a great deal about Savinkov's view of which forces were important in the Russian revolutionary movement that he does not mention the Bolsheviks at all (although Marx is referred to in passing).

Despite his deep pessimism about the current state of the revolutionary movement as a whole, Savinkov still ends the novel with a surviving revolutionary's soaring paean to the future liberation of Russia: "he felt how at the bottom of his fatigued soul, faith again flared up like a pure flame, faith in the people, in the task of liberation, in a renewed world built on love. Faith in eternal truth."

Critics

As soon as Savinkov's novel began to appear serially, it was attacked by the Socialist Revolutionary Party establishment and others on the political left. It is not difficult to understand why. Savinkov had blasphemed against the most sacred of secular beliefs by portraying the Party's leaders as ineffectual talkers divorced from reality and the revolutionary movement as eviscerated and moribund. Moreover, he also gave some of his fictional characters unflattering traits that were easy to trace to their real prototypes. Mark Natanson, the new leader of the SR Party and an opponent of Savinkov and terrorism, was incensed when he recognized himself in the character Arseny Ivanovich, a chatty veteran populist who peppers his speech with cloying, folksy expressions that are supposed to show his intimate knowledge of the peasantry. The polemic that developed as a result became such a sensation that even Vladimir Lenin felt obligated to weigh in by ridiculing both Savinkov's novel as well as the free speech defense of it that some, like Victor Chernov, invoked.

However, there were critics on the right who responded favorably to what they saw as the novel's antirevolutionary stance. And Savinkov's literary "godmother,"

Zinaida Gippius, also provided some important moral support, writing to him that the novel was "unusual, good, and broad," that it was an advance over *The Pale Horse*, and that he had demonstrated that he was a real writer and not a dilettante.

Savinkov was thin-skinned when it came to criticism of his writing and was more pained by negative reactions to *What Never Happened* than buoyed by the praise it got. "I'm being attacked disgustingly," he wrote to Vera in late 1912, admitting that "it's hard for me" and that he has never felt his loneliness as strongly as he does now because even the publisher does not support him. Nonetheless, he will not give up: "I'm going to finish saying what I think, no matter whether people like my opinions or not," even though "it's hard to work and to think that my labor will bring me nothing but misery." When the final installment was about to appear in the spring of 1913, he admitted to Vera that he had lived for little else during the past two years. Now that it was finished he felt "orphaned."

Money

Savinkov may have written the novel in an attempt to soothe his psyche by making sense of where he now stood in the world, but he published it for money. The details of his financial arrangement with *Zavety* are not entirely clear, although he was supposed to be paid relatively generously for the serial rights by the magazine's standards—in any event, more than such celebrities as Gorky and Andreyev, perhaps because he was a Party member and they were not.

However, *Zavety* was always in a precarious financial position and either delayed payments or did not make them at all. By the end of 1913, Savinkov had not gotten all of what he was owed and had to borrow 1,000 francs ($5,000 today) from a friend because he could not get a personal loan in France. Several months later, he had to write to the same friend for yet another loan because *Zavety* had still not paid him the full amount, he had no credit, and his financial situation was "very bad."

The only "peacetime" skill Boris Savinkov had that allowed him to earn money was writing, and he continued to pursue it as assiduously as he could. Zinaida Gippius tried to help in various ways, including suggesting that he write a review essay that she would get published about Andrey Bely's classic novel *Petersburg*, the first two parts of which appeared in 1913 and caused a sensation in avant-garde Russian literary circles. (Vladimir Nabokov would later rank it with Joyce's *Ulysses*, Proust's *In Search of Lost Time*, and Kafka's *Metamorphosis* as the greatest works of twentieth-century literature.) This involved Savinkov in the highly unusual experience of reading a novel in which a major character is very loosely modeled on him, and the central plot is a conspiracy to assassinate a senior government figure that is set in motion by a nefarious double agent who is clearly modeled on Azef. In his brief comments to Gippius, Savinkov explained that although he had much to say about *Petersburg*, he could not proceed without reading the concluding part. (He also does not appear to have recognized himself in the character Alexander Dudkin, who actually bears very little resemblance to him.) His judgment is that the novel is "difficult," "complicated," and "very gifted," but at the same time "false," "deeply repulsive," and "some sort of lie." This reaction is not surprising in light of Bely's practice of distorting whatever he used in his work in accordance with his own occult worldview. Savinkov apparently never wrote the review, which is unfortunate.

Gippius was more successful in helping Savinkov with his other initiatives: getting *What Never Happened* published, negotiating on his behalf with publishers, helping him make connections with periodical publications, and trying to place his short pieces and poetry (even though this could earn very little). His brother Victor also helped by trying to arrange reprints of *The Pale Horse* and *What Never Happened* in Russia, and some money came in from the translations of the novels into German, French, English, and Danish.

But writing was never enough, and Savinkov often had to fall back on loans from friends or on splitting living expenses with them (he did have limits, however, and refused to accept anything from the SRs in 1911). Finally, when there was no other alternative, he pawned some of his valuables.

Gambling

A writer's outer life is mostly solitary and silent, and there were times when the agents watching Boris Savinkov reported that he was writing constantly and, except for meals, had not left his room for several days. But Savinkov also needed distractions, and two that he favored in the years 1910–1913 were gambling and racetracks.

In late 1910, he began to visit the Casino of Monte-Carlo, then the world's most famous temple to the goddesses Chance and Fortune. A grand, elegant, and richly decorated pile of cream-colored stone, the Casino stood on a large square occupying the hill that looked over the city-state of Monaco and attracted a moneyed, cosmopolitan clientele. Whenever he was in Paris during these years, Savinkov went to the Auteuil Racecourse on the western edge of the city and the Saint-Ouen Racecourse to the north for harness racing, a popular and fashionable pastime.

These were not the kind of places or activities that the puritanically minded leaders and members of the SR Party approved of, and Savinkov's fondness for gambling seriously damaged him in their eyes. Worse yet was that a number of Party members accused him of gambling with Party funds. There is some evidence that this may have happened on at least one occasion, although the accusation was exaggerated by the SRs' animosity toward him. For Boris Savinkov, gambling was just an occasional pastime, and there were other things that defined him in more important ways.

But Savinkov was indulgent with money at times in a way that seems irresponsible from a commonsensical point of view. He was quite capable of complaining about not having enough, borrowing some from a friend like Fondaminsky, ostensibly to live on, and then risking part of it on table games. Why? Surely one reason was that it provided a surrogate for some of the risk and excitement to which he had become addicted in the Combat Organization.

Savinkov may also have hoped to supplement his income, although the degree to which he succeeded at the tables is unclear. The teams of French *fileurs* regularly followed him and his entourage—usually Evgeniya, but also visiting friends—inside the Casino of Monte-Carlo (whose security cooperated with them). Because of how absorbed he was in playing roulette, the *fileurs* boasted to headquarters that they were able to pass within "25 centimeters" of him without his noticing. They did not get close enough to tell how Savinkov did every time, but they witnessed him staking large sums, and both winning handsomely (6,000 francs once, or around $30,000 today) and losing heavily. Sometimes Savinkov went back night after night, but over the course of two and a half years the *fileurs* reported a total of only several dozen gambling sessions in Monaco and elsewhere on the Riviera.

Others

Savinkov was not a loner by nature. He needed a life partner, and when he separated from Vera in 1908 he entered into what was likely a common-law marriage with Evgeniya, a relationship that was further cemented when she gave birth to their son, Lev, on August 15, 1912. Several of Evgeniya's relatives lived with her and Savinkov at times as well, including her mother and her sister-in-law with a young daughter, thereby increasing the family circle even more. All evidence indicates that Savinkov's new family life was harmonious and that he was a caring father. When Lev was seriously ill, he carried and nurtured him in his arms until he recovered.

To mitigate the effect of spending most of his time at the writing table, Savinkov went for walks, swam in the Mediterranean, "played on the beach" with friends (the *fileurs* did not specify the activity), took long bicycle rides, and even secured a set of dumbbells to exercise. As the New Year's holiday approached in 1913, he took the initiative to organize a party for all politically like-minded Russians on the Riviera, including finding a suitable restaurant and setting the price per person. At times, he ventured beyond his home area specifically to see friends, including on the Ligurian coast, where a congenial Russian émigré community of several dozen people, mostly Socialist Revolutionaries, gathered in the warm season.

During the years when he and Evgeniya lived on the Riviera and in Paris, they had frequent visitors or houseguests, some who stayed for long periods of time. One such stay was exceptional because it was a friend who was slowly dying, and Savinkov's behavior toward her reveals much about his character and values.

Maria Prokofyeva had been the fiancée of Yegor Sazonov, von Plehve's assassin and one of Savinkov's most cherished comrades. Her life story was widely known and admired in revolutionary circles, which, despite their violent agenda, were far from indifferent to human pathos, especially when it enhanced the nobility of their cause.

An exceptionally beautiful young woman whose father was a prosperous merchant, Maria had been close friends with Yegor since childhood. They met again in 1906 in the Akatuy penal colony in eastern Siberia, where he was imprisoned and where she had come to help organize what became Gershuni's legendary escape in a sauerkraut barrel. Afterward, she returned to European Russia, joined the Combat Organization, and participated in several plots, including an attempt on Nicholas II. She was arrested in 1907 and sentenced to prison but managed to escape abroad and settled in Paris. That is where she met Savinkov when he accepted her into his resurrected combat group in 1909. During all this time, Maria corresponded regularly with Yegor, and her letters, brimming with love and the faith that they would soon be together, did much to support him emotionally. But in December 1910, only six weeks before he was supposed to be released from prison to start life in Siberian exile and Maria could join him, he committed suicide.

The news hit her very hard. She had already developed symptoms of tuberculosis in the spring of that year, and her condition worsened. There was no effective treatment for the disease in the early twentieth century, although doctors knew it was highly contagious. Her condition continued to aggravate during the six months she spent at a sanatorium in Davos, Switzerland. This is when Savinkov and Evgeniya decided to take her in, despite the risk of infection to them and, in time, to their newborn son.

Maria lived with Savinkov's family for the next two years as her health slowly declined. The relocations that Savinkov's household made from Théoule in France to San Remo in Italy and elsewhere on the Mediterranean coast appear to have been dictated in part by their desire to make her as comfortable as possible. Throughout this time, Savinkov's attention to Maria was very close. The French *fileurs* reported that he spent long hours talking with "the sick woman" (they eventually learned her name). On one occasion, they managed to find out—probably from a bribed servant—that she had "vomited blood."

Maria's youth, beauty, tragic history, and calm resignation in the face of death—all the elements of a novel about a romantic heroine—had a magnetic effect on people. After a visit with her husband, Zinaida Gippius wrote to Savinkov that she was deeply impressed by her and that her "bright" face seemed "not of this world."

Maria died in the Villa Vera, which Savinkov was renting in San Remo, on July 13, 1916. He would remember her death for the rest of his life and would write in his diary about his daily visits to her coffin—which had a glass window in it that allowed him to see her face—only ten days before he died himself.

The Great War

For nearly four years, Savinkov lived on history's sidelines. But in the summer of 1914, a terrorist act much like the ones he had organized in the past, although in a country he had never seen, triggered a sequence of events that would engulf him and everything he knew.

On June 28, 1914, in Sarajevo, the capital of Bosnia, a small Balkan state that was part of the Austro-Hungarian Empire, a nineteen-year-old Serbian member of the Black Hand terrorist organization assassinated the heir to the Hapsburg throne, Archduke Franz Ferdinand, and his wife. Gavrilo Princip, whose biography and character are not dissimilar from those of the young Russians on Savinkov's teams, had a specific and limited goal: to strike a blow against Austrian domination of the South Slavic peoples. But because of a tangle of international alliances that pitted the Central Powers (Austria-Hungary and Germany) against the Triple Entente (France, Great Britain, and Russia), Princip's shots led to a war of heretofore unimaginable scope. On July 28, one month after the archduke's assassination, the Austro-Hungarian Empire declared war on Serbia, claiming that the Serbian response to a harsh ultimatum had been unsatisfactory. Russia automatically backed Serbia because of the belief that the two countries shared the same "blood and faith." Germany then declared war on Russia on August 1 and on France on August 3. On August 4, after Germany invaded Belgium, Britain declared war on Germany. On August 23, Japan entered the war on the side of the Entente, and on October 29, the Ottoman Empire attacked Russia. Italy joined the Entente in 1915, as did the United States in 1917. The Great War, as it was known until World War II broke out in 1939, would destroy four empires—the German, Austro-Hungarian, Turkish Ottoman, and Russian. Fifteen million lives would be lost and millions more irrevocably changed in a dozen countries, and the war's aftereffects would reverberate around the world for decades after it officially ended.

⚬━━⚬

As the end of July 1914 approached, two opposing moods took hold in France. It was the height of summer vacations, and all the usual popular destinations on the beaches, in the countryside, and in the mountains were full of people enjoying themselves. Gaily dressed crowds strolled, children splashed in the water, and bands played; everything was pleasant and calm. At the same time, French newspapers kept printing ominous warnings that war was now inevitable, and banks had even stopped issuing gold and silver coin. Such alarms had been raised so often before, however, that many stopped believing them.

And then on Saturday, August 1, everything changed. Headlines appeared screaming that Germany has declared war on Russia and that a full mobilization had been ordered in France. Men around the country dropped whatever they were doing to rush home and pack so that they could get to train stations to join their units. In a matter of hours, all anyone could think or talk about was the war and the cursed Germans who had started it. Patriotism soared, and tens of thousands of volunteers flocked to recruiting stations to enlist.

The Russian exiles and émigrés in France were as galvanized by the news as everyone else. But their subsequent reactions diverged sharply depending on their politics. Some of the socialists on the radical left, including the Bolsheviks and some members of the Socialist Revolutionary Party, quickly condemned the war as an expression of imperialist competition among capitalist nations that had nothing to do with the interests of the working class. This would eventually lead to the so-called Zimmerwald Movement and its Manifesto of 1915, in which socialist signatories from eleven countries rejected all national claims in the war and called for a continuation of the domestic revolutionary struggles that had been interrupted by it. Among the Russians who signed were Vladimir Lenin, the leader of the Bolsheviks, and Mark Natanson, Savinkov's nemesis and the leading figure in the Socialist Revolutionary Party.

Savinkov's reaction could not have been more different. News of the war reached him when he was living in Juan-les-Pins, a town between Cannes and Nice. On July 31, even before Germany had officially declared war on Russia, he decided that he must find a way to take part in whatever was coming. His decision was shared by most Russian émigrés and exiles in France. During the first four months after the war began, 4,000 volunteered for the French Army; eventually, there would be 6,000, the majority Jewish. They were moved by a combination of reasons: admiration for the French republic, which had been born of revolution and was founded on the principles of "liberty, equality, and fraternity"; gratitude to France for giving them political refuge; a surge in patriotism because their homeland was imperiled; and revulsion at German militarism.

Savinkov, however, was frustrated that he literally could not afford to enlist in the French army because a soldier's pay would not have been enough for him to support the number of people who depended on him financially. At a minimum, it was five: Evgeniya and Lev in France, and Vera, Tanya, and Vitya in Russia. At a maximum it was eight: Evgeniya's mother and her sister-in-law with a baby were also part of his household on occasion. Some of Savinkov's political enemies in France who had volunteered and did not know his reasons or did not care about them accused him of cowardice.

Nevertheless, he decided that he had to get as close to the fighting as possible and began to bombard Zinaida Gippius with letters and telegrams asking her to use her connections to help him become a war correspondent for Russian newspapers. He wrote to her that at a time when "Russia is truly in danger," he was "spiritually incapable" of remaining "an idle observer of what is coming." He agreed in advance to "any compensation" he could get and to working for almost any Russian newspaper. He would do anything to escape Juan-les-Pins and his feeling of "wretched impotence."

For all Boris Savinkov's opposition to the Russian imperial regime, he now saw the Central Powers, and especially Germany, as the more serious enemy and believed their victory would be a disaster for his homeland. As he wrote to a friend, "this war is first of all a struggle against *Prussian militarism* . . . we have to take an active part in it because it is not just our fatherland that is in danger, so is the French Republic. Participation has to be in accordance with each person's strengths and skills." He imagined that this could take various forms—medical assistance, volunteering for the army, helping soldiers' families, or bolstering patriotism by writing. Shortly after August 1, he published an open letter in a Russian newspaper calling for a cessation of all revolutionary activity for the duration of the war because a continuing revolutionary struggle could lead only to the military defeat of Russia. This was a spectacular change of direction from someone with his revolutionary credentials. He went even further in a letter to Victor Chernov, telling him that any attack on the imperial regime was an attack on Russia herself. Chernov and several other leading figures in the Party had already proclaimed themselves "internationalists," or opponents of the belligerents' narrow national interests, and broke with Savinkov for having betrayed socialist principles.

Because the Eastern front of the war stretched across the entire European land mass, from the Baltic to the Black Sea, communication between France and Russia via mail and telegraph became difficult and unreliable. Nevertheless, by the beginning of September 1914, Zinaida Gippius was able to arrange for Savinkov to be hired as a war correspondent by the Saint Petersburg newspaper

Den (*The Day*; he would continue to use his pseudonym V. Ropshin; he also published pieces in the illustrated magazine *Niva*), and he began the process of getting authorization from the French military to go to the Western Front.

This proved to be far more difficult than he had imagined. All the Allied militaries feared spies, viewed newspapermen with suspicion, and imposed strict censorship. The French Army resisted Savinkov's application, but after considerable effort he managed to become accredited, which had required securing permission from the country's minister of war himself and observing strict regulations regarding travel and what could be reported.

By the second week of September, Savinkov was at the Front. Evgeniya stayed in Nice and on September 12 wrote to his mother in Saint Petersburg (in a letter the Okhrana copied) that he had already driven along 800 kilometers of the front lines and had sent her "three very good articles" to forward to the Russian newspaper. Over the next two and a half years, until early 1916, Savinkov would compose just over 100 of these pieces, running in length from one to three or four pages, and would collect them for publication as a two-part book titled *In France during the War*. He was the only Russian correspondent on the Western Front, a fact in which he took considerable pride, and approached his job very seriously by traveling everywhere he could, trying to see and experience as much as possible, and to interview as many people—military and civilian—as would talk to him.

In France during the War

If anyone ever doubted Boris Savinkov's Russian patriotism, his love for France, and admiration for honor, bravery, and loyalty—especially when exhibited by the common man, whether peasant or worker—his war correspondence should lay any reservations to rest. His reports from the front were censored, as he knew they would be, but in the collections that he published in book form in 1916 and reprinted after the February Revolution of 1917 (when he could have restored whatever he wanted), his aim remains consistent and clear: to stir his readers to support the Russian and Allied war effort until total victory over the Central Powers was achieved. *In France during the War* is also the most revealing autobiographical work that Savinkov produced after his *Memoirs of a Terrorist*.

The most numerous and often the most striking of Savinkov's pieces are about what he saw himself, beginning with September 1914, when the Germans, who had invaded through neutral Belgium, got within thirty-five miles of Paris, and ending around February 1916, when the front was largely frozen in trenches some 100 miles to the east and northeast of the city. All the pieces strive to move, inform, and inspire, and all are competently written. Most end on an up note. There are occasional lapses into sentimentality, but this is hardly unexpected in an overtly propagandistic genre aimed at a general newspaper reader during a time of war.

Savinkov traveled the full length of the front, from Le Havre on the English Channel to the province of Lorraine on the border with Germany, and tried to get as close to the fighting as possible. There were occasions when he was so far forward he could hear French artillery shells flying overhead. After having visited scores of towns and cities that had been attacked and occupied by the Germans, he describes in detail the widespread destruction they inflicted on homes, churches, farms, and businesses. In a tone of bitter incredulity, he catalogs the savagery with which the Germans treated the civilian populations they encountered: after carrying out what became known as the Rape of Belgium, they continued their depredations in France, executing thousands of innocent men, women, and old people; raping; and pillaging. He repeatedly refers to the war in Apocalyptic terms.

Savinkov focuses primarily on the experiences of the enlisted men who did the fighting and suffered the most, but also includes some noncommissioned and lower-ranked officers. He has little to say about senior commanders or grand strategy. The simple French soldier is his hero because of his willingness to sacrifice himself for his country, his quiet lack of pretension, his endurance, his humanity, and his good cheer. Savinkov recounts the soldiers' everyday trials, which are often horrible enough, but also records their extraordinary experiences. One private who has been fighting for seven months tells him about incidents that he will remember forever. During the heat of battle, he bayoneted a German soldier who was so young that he was still beardless. But he could not pull the bayonet out of the youth's chest and looked on in horror as his enemy spun to the ground, the protruding rifle swinging through the air in a complete circle.

Savinkov wants to let his readers see and experience what he had: "You are walking along the soft edge of a field. It is hard to see much of anything. But then an unexpected light flashes and immediately, that very second, the earth shakes resoundingly." He is in a field when his feet begin to sink into soft ground, and when he looks down realizes that he has accidentally wandered onto a makeshift cemetery of shallow graves. The sickening smell of corruption will continue to haunt him for days and weeks afterward, even when he is far away in Paris.

The British are on the Western Front as well, and Savinkov's descriptions of them help explain why he chose the disguise of an Englishman a decade earlier, during his campaigns against Minister Plehve and Grand Duke Sergey. Savinkov admires the British soldiers' tough and stalwart appearance, their calm self-confidence and joviality, the superiority of their equipment and provisions. He is impressed that the British soldier remains unflappable and "plays football when he is at war, takes a bath and has five o'clock tea." Savinkov does not know more than a few phrases in English, but he is particularly fond of "All Right!" which he quotes in the original and takes to be a national expression of easy grace and certainty of success.

Inevitably, his own homeland is never far from Savinkov's thoughts, even though he says little about the war raging on the Eastern Front, where Russia would lose more men, and in a shorter period of time, than any other country in the Entente. French landscapes in the Champagne region and elsewhere remind him of areas in Russia. He is deeply moved when he encounters Russian volunteers in the French army, some of whom have become so acculturated that their Russian is full of amusing Gallicisms. He also meets a few Russian soldiers who had been captured on the Eastern Front, succeeded in escaping from prisoner-of-war camps in Germany, and, against all odds, got to the French lines in the west.

In the same way that Savinkov feels both European and Russian, he constantly stresses the commonalities shared by the nationalities fighting as allies in the west. He tells his readers that the French regiments "go to die for me, for you, for France, for Russia, for our customs, our families, our dignity, our freedom." He finds that the same "great power of the earth" exerts its pull on all peoples that plow the land, whether French, Russian, or Belgian, and he invokes the parable of the seed that must die in order for there to be new life

(John 12:24) when he says that the soldiers "are all stalks in a field of rye. They are the sowers and the grain."

Savinkov extends his sense of the universality of human nature to include the colonial troops that France and Great Britain brought to fight in the war. He meets a Sikh soldier from British India and says that even though the man has differently colored skin and they have no language in common, "I understand him without words." "Where did I see his smile?" Savinkov wonders, and then remembers his own homeland: "In the Ryazan Governorate . . . ? Or at a public gathering on Devichy Field in Moscow on Palm Sunday?" As a socialist, he surely understood that the colonial troops were exploited by their imperialist masters in a war that had nothing to do with their national interests, but because of military censorship he limited himself to expressing sympathy for their humanity.

Savinkov's view that there is an international brotherhood of men reappears in a related form when he celebrates democracy as a national political ideal. He sees this in the ties between French officers and soldiers, among Italians who came to fight in France, and even in the way British officers treat the enlisted ranks. That he omits any references to class distinctions, snobbishness, and racism in these countries (or in Russia), of which he was certainly aware, is ultimately less important than his advocacy of social equality as an admirable and achievable goal.

The War in Russia

Although Savinkov does not mention the Eastern Front very often in his pieces, it was of course not due to a lack of interest. Russian censorship restricted all transmission of news at the time, from the press to private correspondence, and, as always happens with warring countries, the regime's policy was to present everything in as rosy a light as possible. Nevertheless, events in the east were of such a magnitude that they could not be concealed, and much of the news was bad. A year after the war began, Savinkov wrote to a friend: "There is a stone mountain on my heart—the Russian defeats. At home, they won't let me enlist (especially Lev Borisovich [i.e., his son]), but I think that as soon as I manage to arrange my finances somewhat—I'll go." He also yearned for amnesty by the imperial regime, even though he did not believe he would ever receive it.

In Russia, the outbreak of war had been greeted with an outburst of patriotism and enthusiasm from all strata of society, including the Duma. But for many, this faded quickly. Evidence kept accumulating that the country was woefully unprepared for a war of this length and magnitude. One month after it began, at the end of August 1914 (NS), a major battle took place in East Prussia, named Tannenberg by the Germans, that ended with the destruction of two Russian armies and the suicide of one of the disgraced commanders. It was not much consolation that this battle helped to stop the Germans from taking Paris when they were just thirty-five miles from the city.

In contrast to the way the Western Front congealed into bloody trench warfare with relatively little movement, in the east the war was wide-ranging, mobile, and even bloodier. After Tannenberg, in early September 1914, Russian armies won a major victory in the Austro-Hungarian province of Galicia. Soon Russia's situation became more complicated because a second front opened in the south against the Ottoman Empire, and five months after their defeat in Galicia, Austro-Hungarian armies launched an offensive to retake their lost territory. It failed, and the Russians advanced to threaten Budapest and Vienna, the twin capitals of the Hapsburg Empire. But then from May to October 1915, the Germans intervened, and a combined German and Austro-Hungarian advance in Galicia pushed the Russians not only out the region they had seized but also out of what had been Russian Poland since the end of the eighteenth century. Warsaw, the city in which Savinkov grew up, fell to the Germans on August 1, 1915, one year after the war began.

⚯

By this time, Russia had a million men killed or wounded and another million captured. There were insufficient arms and armaments, and fuel and electricity shortages began to appear in the cities. The British attempt to support and resupply Russia by forcing the Turkish Straits and opening a passage to the Black Sea ended in disaster at Gallipoli.

The news from Petrograd was also increasingly alarming, and it was becoming clear that the empire's center was not holding. Blundering through historical events that he could neither understand nor control, in September 1915 Nicholas II assumed command of all the Russian forces, even though he had no military experience, and effectively removed himself from direct oversight of his government. The Duma could have mediated between his regime and an increasingly anxious public, but because Nicholas was unwilling to consider any form of cooperation, a dangerous power vacuum formed in the capital. It was partially filled by his wife, Tsaritsa Alexandra, who intervened in government affairs while being herself under the influence of Grigory Rasputin, imperial Russia's extraordinary evil genius. As a result, during the year and a half following Nicholas's departure from the capital, a process that came to be labeled "ministerial leapfrog" took place, with twenty-two changes in the most important ministries. A few of the men were competent; most were craven and inept.

In 1916, the Russians achieved a great military success against Austria-Hungary in Galicia—the Brusilov Offensive, which almost knocked the Austro-Hungarians entirely out of the war. The need to rush reinforcements to the Eastern Front stopped the Austro-Hungarian invasion of Italy and halted the German offensive at Verdun. But it was a classic Pyrrhic victory. The Russian army suffered such staggering casualties and desertions that it began to disintegrate. Russian popular support for the war was plummeting, and revolutionary agitation against the imperial regime was growing, especially by the Bolsheviks. Shortages of fuel and foodstuffs worsened. The high cost of living made workers go on strike, including those in such critical industries as munitions, naval shipyards, and coal mining. The authorities responded brutally by drafting the physically able and arresting and prosecuting the rest. Troops had to be dispatched to Turkestan and Central Asia to put down a rebellion by Muslims conscripted to work in military factories. By the end of the year, the Russian Empire seemed on the brink of collapse.

⚬——⚬

Savinkov could not write openly about the deteriorating situation in Russia or about the need for radical change. But he alludes to them between the lines in his later reports from the front. He argues that unlike the other Allied countries, in which there is a continuum between the government and the governed, in Russia the two are sharply divided. The simple soldier is willing to die for Russia and is "her loyal son." But "who has she been for him?" Savinkov asks. His bitter answer is a play on the word *rodina* (a feminine noun meaning "motherland"):

Russia has betrayed her proper role by acting like "an evil stepmother . . . and not a mother."

Savinkov pins all hopes for victory on Russian soldiers alone, the vast majority of whom are peasants and embody the essential aspect of the national character in a pure form. Savinkov is not sure what to call this trait—"submission" or "Christ's love"—but it is expressed in the belief of the common people that Christ endured and commanded them to do so as well. This faith, which distinguishes the Russians from their European comrades, is what gives Russian soldiers the "calm and firm strength" that defeated all Russia's enemies in the past and "that tomorrow will defeat the invincible German." In other words, and paradoxically, Russia will be victorious because her people have been tempered by their rulers' despotism. Rather than destroying their will, oppression has made them strong enough to overcome anything. In addition, the Russian soldier's new experiences in the Great War have taught him to overcome fear and to stand up for his "outraged freedom." Savinkov implies that after defeating their nation's enemies on the battlefields, the returning peasant soldiers will never submit to domestic tyranny again. And he was right: it is difficult to imagine the Russian Revolution happening without the Great War.

It was inevitable that Savinkov's experiences at the front would bring into sharp focus what was and what was not important for him after the collapse of his career as a terrorist. His conclusion is that "in the trenches death conquers death," by which he means that those who survive the horrors of war enter into a "renewed life." This "rebirth" allows the survivors to cast a cold eye on the "mouse-like scurrying" of mundane existence, to renounce "the insignificant" and "the transient," and to learn to live for the "soul."

Although Savinkov's vocabulary in these and other passages is spiritual—at times he even invokes parables from the New Testament—he is in fact not professing religious faith but only aligning himself with its values emotionally or intellectually. He wants to live for something bigger than himself—for Russia—and this automatically includes his willingness to sacrifice himself for the good of the people. What Savinkov saw and learned at the front returned him to the examples of his revered comrades who died for the revolutionary cause—Kalyaev, Sazonov, Brilliant, Zilberberg—although, of course, he could not mention them openly in his despatches.

At the same time, for all the pathos implied by this view, there is an element of elitism in Savinkov's reference to the "mouse-like scurrying" that fills most lives. What differentiates his elitism from mere snobbery, however, is his willingness to sacrifice himself for his beliefs.

La Rotonde

When Savinkov was not at the front, he spent time in Paris or on the Riviera with Evgeniya and their son. Dipping back into family life was a comfort after what he had seen, and watching Lev growing up was a pleasure he had often had to deny himself with Tanya and Vitya. But the public attitude toward the war that he witnessed in Paris and in the newspapers shocked and angered him.

The lies were the worst. Often, when soldiers at the front found out that Savinkov was a journalist, they urged him to "either tell only the truth or not say anything." In Paris, by contrast, Savinkov often heard the opposite sentiment—that "an intelligent lie elevates the martial spirit." This, and the dearth of actual war correspondents at the front, he explains, is why newspapers fill their pages with long-winded and fanciful clichés drawn from the movies, such as stirring drum rolls, glorious charges, and the clash of steel. "In Paris, they don't know what war is," Savinkov noted bitterly in a dispatch, even though there is hardly a family that does not have a son or father in the army and many are in deep mourning. The complacency of the many Parisians who did not have to fight or even change their daily routines makes the city look almost normal during the day. Only at night when the city goes dark and searchlights anxiously scan the sky does Paris begin to look like a city at war.

Savinkov was always drawn to like-minded souls who were interested in literature and the arts. He initially found some among the hospitable Russian Jewish émigrés who lived in Paris, the Fondaminskys, the Petits (Sofia, née Balakhovskaya, who had married a Frenchman), and the Tsetlins, who were either SRs or leaned left and had a wide circle of bohemian acquaintances.

Like Ilya Fondaminsky, Mikhail Tsetlin had been born into a rich family of tea merchants and was independently wealthy. After participating in the 1905 Revolution and coming under investigation by the police, he escaped abroad, settled in Paris (where he owned a townhouse; he also had a villa in Biarritz), and dedicated himself to writing poetry on revolutionary themes and funding cultural initiatives. He was also very generous to Russian and foreign-born writers and painters. Savinkov knew the Tsetlins from his SR days, and introductions from them led to his meeting members of a very unlikely coterie for a former terrorist—an international circle of avant-garde artists and writers among whom he could find a refuge from the petty bour-geois values he deplored.

In 1915, Savinkov became friends with Maximilian Voloshin, a poet and painter who has a permanent place in Russian culture. A short, stout, bearded man with a penetrating, intelligent gaze and a big head that looked even bigger because of thick masses of hair that stuck out on either side, Voloshin liked to wear a homespun robe in imitation of an ancient Greek chiton when he was at his house in Koktebel in Crimea. His interests in the mythic past and the arcana of symbolism did not prevent him from having extensive connections in con-temporary France, and he shuttled regularly between Russia and Paris, where he did much to foster contacts between expatriate Russian writers and painters and their French counterparts.

Voloshin admired Savinkov (he would write a laudatory poem about him: "In his hand—a dagger, and in his heart—a cross") and introduced him to Ilya Ehrenburg, an avant-garde poet and journalist originally from Kiev. Ehrenburg would become a major figure in the Soviet Union as a result of his knack for turning in the right direction whenever there was a shift in the country's schizo-phrenic political winds—first as a celebrated writer favored by Stalin; then, as a leader of cultural liberalization after Stalin's death, but one who simultaneously took care not to go too far. Ehrenburg spent much time abroad, was skillful at cultivating people, and, during his long and productive life, got to know a who's who of leading figures in history and culture: Lenin, Trotsky, Picasso, Apollinaire, Einstein, Diego Rivera, Cocteau, Modigliani, Chagall, Malraux, and Hemingway, among many, many others.

When Savinkov met Ehrenburg in 1915, the latter was an undistinguished-looking, carelessly dressed young man a dozen years his junior, with long, greasy hair, a narrow face, and hooded eyes, who had become a habitué of bohemian cafés in Montparnasse. But he was smart and well read, had an ironic and mordant wit, and was fascinated by Savinkov: "Never before had I met such an incomprehensible and frightening person," he recalled. "What struck one in his face were his Mongolian cheekbones and eyes—sad one moment, cruel the next; he often closed them, and his eyelids were heavy and ghoulish." Savinkov enjoyed arguing politics with Ehrenburg; they talked about art and culture. They drank together and read their poems to each other, and Ehrenburg even wrote one about Savinkov. In his celebrated memoir, he would later claim that Savinkov did not actually believe the patriotic articles he wrote about the front, but this is very likely an example of Ehrenburg's toeing the Bolshevik Party line, which systematically cast Savinkov as a notorious Socialist Revolutionary "villain."

Boris Savinkov became a regular at the café La Rotonde, which was a favorite of the circle to which Ehrenburg and Voloshin belonged, as well as a kind of club for many other artists and writers who flocked to Paris from around the world. Located on the Left Bank at the intersection of the boulevards Raspail and Montparnasse, it was in those days a simple, dark little place that had recently been taken over by a butcher, Victor Libion, whose shop was next door. (It still exists but was transformed into a comfortable, middle-class establishment long ago.)

La Rotonde became legendary in the history of modern art and culture because of its clientele—most of whom were impoverished and struggling to establish themselves at the time, but many of whom would become famous—and because of the owner's kindness toward them. Some of the young artists even called him Père Libion because of the fatherly advice he liked to dispense and because of his generosity: he granted credit readily and would let anyone nurse a coffee for hours. If someone could not pay him, he would gladly accept a sketch or a canvas. The collection of works he built up over time would now probably make a museum curator's head spin.

Ehrenburg's and Voloshin's friends found Savinkov intriguing. Among the closest were the Mexican artist Diego Rivera and the Italian Amedeo Modigliani, both of whom would become world famous, the first as a powerful muralist, the second as a painter and sculptor in an exquisitely minimalist mode. Rivera was a Marxist, his politics were revolutionary, and he enjoyed listening to Savinkov's stories about how he had hunted imperial ministers on the streets of Russian cities. Modigliani, by contrast, was apolitical but had a goal that also resonated with Savinkov's interests: to create beauty in a fallen world. The two artists' fates were as different as their styles. Modigliani, who was handsome, dark, and slender and had a haunted look in his eyes, became addicted to "cocaine, hashish, and the bottle," as an artist friend put it, and died at thirty-five before his genius was recognized (one of his paintings sold in 2015 for $170 million). The same artist described Rivera as "a real colossus" because of his corpulence, and as a "kindly cannibal" because of his exuberantly sensual manner. Recognized and celebrated during his lifetime, he fulfilled many monumental commissions at home and abroad and died when he was seventy.

At the center of their little group was a young Russian painter, Maria Bronislavovna Vorobyova-Stebelskaya, whose complicated name was collapsed by the writer Maxim Gorky into the handier Marevna, which had flattering associations with a lovely princess in Russian folklore, and which the young woman adopted. A petite, pretty, blue-eyed blonde, Marevna was outgoing, very young, and idealistic. She wore brightly colored outfits and painted pointillist and cubist still-lives and portraits. She could be difficult and moody and drank too much at times, but she charmed her male companions and her many admirers at La Rotonde by balancing her relations with them on the thin edge between friendship and eros. Voloshin called her "the spirit of La Rotonde."

One evening Voloshin walked up to her with Savinkov: "Marevna, I want to introduce a legendary hero to you," he began in his florid manner. "I know you have a zest for the extraordinary and for real supermen. This man is an exemplification of every beauty: you will be passionately fond of him."

However, Marevna's first impression of Savinkov was very negative (such reactions were not uncommon—Voloshin also disliked Savinkov "intensely" when they first met). Unlike her exuberant artist friends, he seemed to be "solitary, withdrawn, and proud." She knew that he was famous in Russia and that his renown had followed him to Paris, where he was introduced in drawing rooms as "the man who killed Grand Duke Sergey" and where society ladies pursued him. But this did not matter to her; she was interested only in the intellectual and artistic lives of people, and like the painter she was, she initially sized him up with aesthetic detachment:

> Boris Savinkov was of average height, upright and slender: his face was long and narrow and his head half bald. He had faint creases round his eyes, which sloped up towards his temples, like those of our Kazan Tatars. He had a straight nose and long, thin lips. When he talked his eyes creased up even more, leaving his searching, ironical gaze just room to find its way between his almost lashless eyelids. He twisted his mouth slightly when letting the words out, showing the yellowed teeth of a great smoker. He wore neither moustache nor beard, dressed very correctly and always wore a black bowler hat. At the Rotonde and everywhere else he was called "the man in the bowler." A big umbrella, another inseparable companion, was always to be seen hanging from his left arm.

But Savinkov could be very charming when he wanted. In 1916, he was thirty-seven to Marevna's twenty-four and was attracted to her because she was young, pretty, lively, talented, and had the courage to abandon a conventional life in Russia to fulfill her dream of becoming an artist in Paris. ("Real talent is like a Bermuda pearl," he commented about her to Voloshin.) After a while, he began to win her over with his polished manner, attentiveness, and skill as a storyteller. He often joined her table in La Rotonde, visited her studio several times—where he read to her from *The Pale Horse*—and had her over to his apartment; they also met at the home of mutual friends. The two could stay up together until 4 A.M. In one letter, she reports to Voloshin that she and Savinkov talked about poetry and he explained to her the similarities he saw between the melody of Voloshin's own verse and that of Mikhail Lermontov, a nineteenth-century Romantic, universally acknowledged as one of Russia's greatest poets.

Soon they became good friends, although not because of what was central to each one's life. Marevna had no interest in Savinkov's radical politics, and, although he acknowledged her talent, he did not like much of the modern art that her circle produced. On one occasion, she took him to visit the studio of Ossip Zadkine, a Russian-born artist who would become internationally famous for his contorted cubist sculptures. When they were leaving, Savinkov commented with annoyance: "He's a buffoon, your Zadkine. Why does he act the clown?" The artist's reaction was symmetrical because he did not "get" Savinkov either: "He's an interesting character," Zadkine later told Marevna, "but why does he make himself out so important today, when everything's finished for him in Russia."

On an even more memorable occasion, Marevna, Savinkov, Voloshin, and Ehrenburg and his wife went to visit Pablo Picasso's studio (Marevna knew him very well and they would paint each other's portraits). The great artist's behavior could only have reinforced Savinkov's skepticism. As Marevna recalled, Picasso greeted them at the door of his studio wearing a "blue-and-white striped bathing-dress and a bowler hat," and after showing them around his cluttered rooms stopped in front of a "big and mysterious" canvas:

> No one at first risked asking what it represented, for fear of blundering. There we stood, respectful, silent, stupefied and amazed in spite of ourselves by the power and imagination of it. Picasso, who had already astonished us with his striped bathing-dress, was continuing his efforts in the same line. It was Voloshin, finally, who could not restrain a poet's curiosity and asked:
> "What does the picture represent, *maître*?"
> "Oh, nothing much, you know," Picasso answered, smiling. "Between ourselves . . . it's some dung—good for idiots."
> "Thank you, thank you," said Voloshin and Ehrenburg.

Even Marevna was unsure if Picasso was being sincere or intentionally provocative.

○━♦━○

In the bohemian atmosphere of the artistic Left Bank, romantic entanglements wound and unwound often and easily. Savinkov found Marevna attractive as a woman: "I would like to see her in a black dress," he confided in a letter to

Voloshin. She was temperamental, and their relationship had its emotional ups and downs, but it remained platonic. Savinkov treated her the way a fond uncle indulges a favorite if somewhat wayward niece, and judging by his reaction when she became involved with Diego Rivera, he was not competing for her affections with others, as some believed.[*] Rivera had a Russian-born wife, Angelina Beloff, who was a member of their intimate little group and had just borne Rivera a son early in 1917 when Marevna began an affair with him. Savinkov's reaction was calm and supportive: he expressed the hope that Marevna would soon be "married, and wearing lovely, long frocks, and hats and jewels." "Would you like to have children?" he asked in addition, and then with mock solemnity adjured her to "Go on being good: always be good; be the delicious child that you are today. But stop whistling in the street."

Savinkov's friendship with Marevna extended to his wife, Evgeniya, who hosted Marevna and others from La Rotonde in Nice when they came for visits and played an "aunt-like" role in the younger woman's life as well. Unable to conceive a child after living with Rivera for several years, Marevna turned to Evgeniya for advice about doctors, and the specialist whom Evgeniya recommended was able to save Marevna from undergoing a risky and unnecessary operation. Years later, when Savinkov's and Marevna's paths recrossed in Paris after the war and she was very hard up, he helped by giving her a job. He proved

---

[*]   Several writers have made claims about Savinkov regarding his unfaithfulness to his wives and his general libertinage, which supposedly included not only Marevna (Spence, *Savinkov*, 88), but various other women he met, including members of the Combat Organization, as well as visits to bordellos in Paris and resulting problems with venereal disease (Spence, *Savinkov*, 24, 25, 44, 63, 66, 69, 78, 84, 86, 88, 98, etc.; Zhukov, 33, 38; Pares, 761). Similarly, a French *fileur* report to the Okhrana (January 16/29, 1908, Hoover, Index No. XVIIi, folder 2, no. 36) refers to Evgeniya Somova as "one" of Savinkov's mistresses. The problem with all these claims is not that they cast a shadow on Savinkov—a biographer cannot but be intrigued by all facets of his character—but that it has been impossible to verify any of them. The claims are either made without references, or the references, when checked as thoroughly as possible, do not lead to the supposed documentary evidence. The same is true of allegations regarding Savinkov's supposed addiction to morphine and other drugs (e.g., Spence, *Savinkov*, 47, 51, 53, 99, etc.; Lockhart, *Ace*, 100, 117). Savinkov is known to have been a heavy smoker, to like to drink (apparently without being a drunk), to gamble in casinos, and to go to horse races. He also had many enemies who were happy to impugn his character in any way possible, and some of those who did (Lebedev, Kerensky) mention nothing along the lines of libertinage or addiction. Similarly, there is nothing about addiction in *Savinkov na Lubianke* (*Savinkov in the Lubyanka*), a selection of documents from the KGB (now FSB) archives that deal with Savinkov's final months, provide details of his various needs and desires, and would presumably have included any evidence of his need for drugs, had it existed.

to be "a boss to dream of!" as she exclaims in her memoirs, and adds that "I shall never forget the interest that he and his wife took in me."

Dejection

For all their colorfulness and avant-garde eccentricity, Savinkov's friends at La Rotonde provided him only occasional respite from either the front lines or the difficulty of scraping a living together. In late 1915, he wrote to Voloshin that "my affairs are so bad that I will probably drown and will have to return to Nice—to drag things out until the end of the war." But once he got to the south, things did not improve: "My son is here, my family, the sun, the sea, and you can smell flowers when you open the shutters in the morning. But how hard it is to live here. Hunger and poverty are all around."

Money would continue to be a problem during the war. The Russian newspapers for which Savinkov wrote paid him very irregularly, and it was hard for him to support his two families. Earning "every franc with his pen," as he put it, and borrowing money at times led to painful humiliations.

But whatever he did was not enough. In letters Vera sent in the spring of 1915, she complained about money repeatedly and implied that she did not believe that he was as hard up as he claimed. This hurt Savinkov deeply: "Haven't the past 7 years proved to you that I always remember the children and that it's sinful to raise money issues with me," he asks, and then gives a detailed accounting of his finances to show his difficulties. Half a year later, his situation is still the same:

> Don't forget that I live abroad, that I have no credit at all since the beginning of the war, that it could happen at any moment that I will be temporarily without work, that to struggle to make a livelihood is very difficult for me and not only because I have many obligations but also because I am completely alone in this struggle and no one helps me.

As the war progressed, Savinkov's relations with Vera deteriorated further. He tried to get her to help him place translations of French articles in Russian newspapers to earn more money, but she began to resent the burden this put on her. In the fall of 1916, as the third year of the war began, Savinkov felt compelled to raise the issue of a formal divorce. Because casualties on the Western Front had reached levels beyond anything the French high command had ever imagined, the French parliament began to discuss drafting resident foreigners like Savinkov who had not been called up in their home countries. He was willing to go despite the financial hardship this would cause him, but he began to worry about the status of his and Evgeniya's son, Lev. The boy was officially "illegitimate" and could not take his father's surname because Savinkov was still legally married to Vera. If he were killed, Savinkov explained to Vera, Lev would remain "without name, kith or kin." But Vera refused to grant a divorce for reasons that she would not explain, and in the end, Savinkov would leave France before he could be drafted. Throughout the entire process, he never stopped sending as much money as he could.

For her part, and despite her difficult relations with her estranged husband, Vera loyally continued to raise their and son and daughter to think of him as their loving father. Over the years, her letters began to include messages from the children. When they were still little, these were touching, affectionate, dutifully phrased, and carefully written holiday greetings; later came descriptions of school, activities, and what they were reading. Expressions of regret about his absence were constant, and phrased as if the children had been raised to hope they would see him soon. By the time Tanya was seventeen, she sounds grown-up; moreover, she has become her mother's amanuensis. She tells her father that she has been reading an installment of his *Memoirs of a Terrorist*, describes the pneumonia from which she is slowly recovering, provides detailed information about how to transfer money to them, and ends with a gentle rebuke: "Please write, is it really possible that you don't have a spare minute to write a few words to your sick daughter. Be well. I give you a big, big kiss. Vitya too. Mama sends her regards. Yours, Tatyana Savinkova."

⚬━⚬

Money was not the only source of Savinkov's unhappiness. There was also his feeling of purposelessness: "I am possessed by one of the worst demons: the demon of boredom," he wrote to Voloshin in late 1915. "Maybe because there is a war and I am not in it, but everything I see around me arouses overwhelming boredom. La Rotonde is the only place where I could be myself a bit," Savinkov admits, but it was never enough to completely fill the void in his life. A few months later, after he had gone back to Nice to be with his wife and son, Savinkov wrote to Voloshin that he still feels as if his "wings are broken." He also admits that "I drink." How much is unclear, although his enemies would always be tempted to exaggerate.

Revolution in Russia

It is paradoxical that Savinkov would feel reborn and find a new purpose in life as a consequence of the destructive historical forces that were building in his homeland.

By the third year of the Great War, the Russian Empire was under mortal threat from within as well as without. The tsar, his ministers, and his generals focused largely on the external danger from the Central Powers and were committed to winning the war at all cost. However, they failed to recognize or to address the threat to the empire's entire social order from vast swaths of the disaffected population, including troops at the front, peasants, and workers. With every month, the economy deteriorated and the country hemorrhaged more men. Conditions were rapidly ripening for revolutionary groups to exploit the situation and to foment open rebellion.

It began on February 23 (OS) or March 8 (NS), 1917, in Petrograd. (The capital had been renamed when the war began because "Saint Petersburg," which was actually derived from the Dutch, sounded too "Germanic" to newly sensitized Russian ears.) Hundreds of thousands of workers who had been striking for months in the outlying factory districts to protest shortages of bread and fuel began to pour into the city center to demonstrate their anger directly to the authorities. The tsar was at military headquarters at the front and ordered the commander of the capital's garrison to disperse the demonstrators, but the troops refused to fire on the crowds. Soon, soldiers and some officers started to fraternize with the demonstrators and to join them; sailors of the Baltic fleet also mutinied. The insurgents began seizing control of sections of the city and attacking government buildings. Firing broke out between the police who attacked the crowds and the troops and Cossacks who sided with the demonstrators; hundreds were killed and wounded.

On February 26, as the rebellion spread to Moscow and other cities, Nicholas II ordered the Duma, which had been pressing him for reforms, to dissolve.

Most members refused, and on the following day took matters into their own hands and announced the creation of a Provisional Government, consisting largely of liberal and progressive members. More radical elements formed a rival center of power—the Petrograd Soviet (or Council) of Workers' and Soldiers' Deputies—a split that would have disastrous consequences as events developed because it established what Russians came to call *dvoyevlastiye*, or dual rule. The tsar made a halfhearted attempt to return to Petrograd, but after learning that both of the empire's capitals were in the hands of rebels and that he had no support from his generals, on Thursday, March 2/15, he abdicated for himself and his son, Alexey, in favor of his brother, Grand Duke Mikhail. The next day, the latter abdicated in favor of the Provisional Government. As a historian put it, the 300-year-old Russian Empire died "with hardly a whimper." In a hopeful gesture of support for the Russian war effort, within a few days after the Provisional Government was formed, first the United States and then the members of the Entente recognized it.

Throughout the country, news of the monarchy's collapse was greeted with elation. Sculptures and images of the two-headed eagle, the symbol of the monarchy, were torn down everywhere. Nicholas II's name and initials, the Romanov crests, photographs, paintings, and all other trappings of the imperial family were ruthlessly destroyed. There was even talk in Petrograd of melting down Falconet's famous statue of Peter the Great, *The Bronze Horseman*.

Moscow was spared the violence that convulsed the capital. If at first there were tense confrontations between troops and the rebellious crowds in front of the City Duma building near Red Square, soon the soldiers joined the insurgents and tied red ribbons to their bayonets. Masses of people in the city center carried red banners in support of the Revolution in Petrograd and sang "La Marseillaise." On Sunday, March 12, a giant "Liberty Parade" wound through the heart of Moscow. An American who saw it was much impressed by its orderliness despite the absence of police, the good cheer of the crowds that gathered, and the easy mixing of the social classes. In a sign of the hybrid times, the procession blended the new with the old—banners with revolutionary slogans such as "Land and the Will of the People" and prayers at the Chapel of the Iberian Mother of God at the entrance to Red Square. The crowds especially enjoyed a circus troupe with a camel and elephant covered with revolutionary placards that was in the procession and that gave it a carnival atmosphere.

The sense of liberty that the collapse of the monarchy had unloosed was unprecedented in modern Russian history. Countless meetings broke out in towns and cities on street corners, at workplaces, and in former government buildings, with speakers holding forth on anything they wanted to the rapt attention of their audiences. Newspapers that had been gagged by censorship began to publish joyfully vituperative articles. Incendiary pamphlets, posters, and proclamations appeared everywhere. Long-ingrained social relations were also suddenly upended as servants began to refuse tasks like shining shoes for patrons in hotels and demanded to be addressed as *tovarishch* ("comrade"). Smirking soldiers occupied seats in tram cars and restaurants while officers stood and waited. Workers demanded double pay and shorter working hours, and appointed themselves as members of committees in charge of offices and utilities.

The liberty that went to the people's heads also had a dark side—a crescendo of vigilantism and crime, which were aggravated by the dissolution of the imperial police forces and the arrest or murder of many of its officers. In Moscow, insurgents had disarmed and disbanded the police even before Nicholas abdicated. Upon assuming power, the Provisional Government announced broad civil liberties and granted an amnesty to all political prisoners, including terrorists. Some 2,000 thieves and murderers were released from prisons in Moscow as well, resulting in a crime wave, with robberies in the streets and attacks on homes and businesses. Students and some other volunteers formed a new city militia, but it was ineffective, and city residents had to organize their own associations for mutual protection. This was but foreshadowing of the greater anarchy to come.

On the days after March 15, the news of the Russian Revolution began to dominate headlines around the world. Savinkov was in Nice and had been following the growing turmoil with feverish attention. He called the tsar's abdication "the happiest day" in his life and immediately applied to the Provisional Government for a new passport. On March 22, his brother Victor in Moscow wrote to him that the Ministry of Foreign Affairs had arranged for it to be issued by the Russian consulate in Paris.

However, at the same time, like a parent suddenly struck by the fragility and vulnerability of a newborn child, Savinkov admitted that even though "I am happy . . . there is anxiety in my soul. I fear that with their agitation, Chernov, Lenin and others will ruin such a brilliantly managed affair and we will again be left no better off than before." Savinkov knew that Chernov wanted to limit Russia's war aims to something short of total defeat of the Central Powers and that Lenin was among the leaders of the movement in Russia to pull out of the war altogether. Savinkov's fear was that if Russia signed a separate peace with Germany and Austria-Hungary, they would win the war. Ehrenburg remembered hearing the same anxious question everywhere he went in France during the first weeks and months after March 15: "The Russians—what are the Russians going to do?"

Returning Home

Overnight, the Revolution had transformed Savinkov and thousands of other Russian exiles from political pariahs into long-lost sons and daughters of a motherland that yearned to welcome them home. "Everyone was shaking with fever: home, home!" Chernov recalled the excitement among revolutionaries in France. The new Provisional Government in Petrograd felt honor-bound to redress the wrongs of the tsarist regime and charged the Russian embassy in London with organizing the return home of "all Russians who desire to do so" from everywhere in Europe—Paris, Rome, Berne—and provided ample money for the purpose.

But to achieve this was not simple. Travel by land was impossible because of the two fronts that cut across the continent, and travel by water was dangerous because Germany had recently announced a policy of unrestricted submarine warfare against all Allied shipping, whether military or civilian. As a result, the British government devised a complicated itinerary from Great Britain across the North Sea to Scandinavia using troop carriers escorted by destroyers, and then trains to Petrograd. The limited number of ships available and the large numbers of passengers clamoring to get home necessitated instituting a strict quota system.

Savinkov, Chernov, and about a dozen other prominent Socialist Revolutionaries who were "in a desperate hurry" to get to Russia so that they could take part in formulating the new government's policies received priority places on one of the first ships. Less famous Russians who wanted to return had a harder time. (It helped Savinkov that his patriotic stance was known to the chargé d'affaires at the Russian Embassy—Constantine Nabokoff, uncle of the future writer—who organized the repatriation, who was also strongly pro-war, and who even attempted to delay the return of "defeatists" he did not like, such as Chernov.) However, because the situation in Petrograd was uncertain and the British Admiralty balked at letting women aboard its ships, Savinkov had to leave Evgeniya and Lev in France.

The reception given the group with which Savinkov had traveled home was ebullient, although it was not because of him. When their train reached Petrograd's Finland Station shortly before midnight on Saturday, April 8, they were greeted by an enormous, cheering crowd of some 10,000 people that had come for Chernov and several other prominent Socialist Revolutionaries who were seen as "martyrs of the Revolution" and expected to assume important roles in the new government. As the returnees descended from the train, they were embraced by old Party comrades who had come home earlier, and as they walked along the platform amid crimson banners inscribed with famous Socialist Revolutionary slogans in gold letters—"Land and Freedom," "Through Struggle You Will Attain Your Rights"—military units presented arms, a band struck up "La Marseillaise," and searchlights swept the platform and the sky, catching the light falling snow in their beams. There were speeches in the waiting room and speeches to the crowds outside from improvised platforms, from trucks, and even from an armored car. It was a dizzying experience for someone who had spent years abroad plotting revolution and dreaming of precisely this kind of moment. Chernov was deeply moved by the revolutionary euphoria of the crowd before him, and by what he saw as the people's almost religious faith that the transformations rolling across the country would never be abandoned and would lead to a total renewal of life in Russia.

However, Savinkov did not even wait for Chernov's speech to be over before he left. He had been met at the station by his friend Yury Annenkov, a well-known artist, and neither one was interested in Chernov's predictable rhetoric. With some difficulty, they got through the massive crowd flooding the square in front of the station until they reached a nearby street. It was nearly empty and there were no cabs, so they started off for Annenkov's apartment on foot, with

Savinkov carrying his single small suitcase by himself. He already knew what he wanted to do in Petrograd as soon as he could—to meet with the Provisional Government's minister of war.

Into Action

As Savinkov had feared, Chernov's path lay in the opposite direction. Shortly after arriving, he went to the Tauride Palace, which was the former seat of the Duma and which had been taken over by the Soviet of Soldiers' and Workers' Deputies. The chairman of the Soviet welcomed him warmly in a speech, Chernov replied in kind, and the deputies promptly elected Chernov vice chairman of both the Petrograd and All-Russian Soviets. Chernov had thus joined the radical power block in revolutionary Russia that opposed the Provisional Government at every turn. If the Provisional Government's aim was to contain and preserve the Revolution that had already occurred, the Soviet's was to deepen and expand it.

The first action the Soviet had carried out in this regard—and which was of primary concern to Savinkov—was the notorious "Order No. 1," issued on March 1/14, or the day before Nicholas II even formally abdicated. It proclaimed that the Soviet had the right to countermand any of the Provisional Government's orders regarding military matters, and that every unit down to the size of a company should elect soldiers' committees to decide how it would act in any given situation. The intent of this order was "democratic"—to abolish the imperial army's hierarchical command structure. But its consequences would be disastrous for two reasons: it undermined the army's ability to fight the Central Powers, and it also sounded the death knell for the army as a whole, which, although greatly weakened by early 1917, was still the only organization that might have been able to resist the centrifugal political forces that were beginning to tear the country apart.

The Germans, Lenin, and the Bolsheviks

What was bad for Russia was good for her enemies, however. It is no surprise that Germany would want to do whatever it could to foment revolutionary turmoil in

Russia: at the very least, the Russian army's effectiveness would be diminished; at the most, the army would collapse entirely, allowing the Central Powers to shift all their military might against the Entente in the west.

With this aim in mind, the Germans enacted one of the most effective and malevolent political actions in the history of modern European warfare by shipping the Bolshevik leader Vladimir Ilyich Lenin (original surname Ulyanov) into Russia. This tactic, and Lenin specifically, had been suggested to the Germans several years earlier by Alexander Parvus, born Israel Helphand in what is now Belarus, who became a leading Marxist theoretician, anti-tsarist revolutionary, and rich businessman. Lenin was living in exile in Switzerland, and to get him to Petrograd via Sweden and Finland, the Germans decided to send him and some of his followers directly through Germany rather than follow the roundabout Northern European sea route that Russians like Savinkov had used. As Winston Churchill characterized it using an apt medical metaphor: "Lenin was sent into Russia by the Germans in the same way that you might send a phial containing a culture of typhoid or cholera to be poured into the water supply of a great city, and it worked with amazing accuracy."

Lenin's commitment was to worldwide revolution, not just the one in his homeland, and this made him dangerous to his German handlers. In order to prevent him from infecting anyone in Germany with his radical ideas, he and his party were quarantined in railway cars and prevented from having any contact with locals. And because Lenin did not have much support in Russia and might not succeed on his own, the Germans provided him with a generous sum of money, 5 million marks, the equivalent of over $30 million today, to ensure that he could buy whatever he needed to achieve his goal of "treason from within." The Provisional Government was wary about letting Lenin into the country because it knew his stance against the war but, in the end, issued him a visa out of idealism. Lenin arrived at Petrograd's Finland station shortly before midnight on Monday, April 3/16. A short, balding man with a moustache, a goatee, and an Asian cast to his eyes, he spoke energetically with an incongruous upperclass burr, and the reception he got from his followers was as grand as Chernov's five days later.

Lenin would put the German money to good use, but not by initiating a political campaign to win over ideological opponents. He was a willful, smart, and unscrupulous ideologue and had no interest in coming to power democratically or in negotiating a role for himself and his followers with other factions—even with other Marxists, to say nothing of more moderate political parties. As soon as he read an article in a Zurich newspaper about the February Revolution and the formation of a Provisional Government, and even before he knew anything about the new government's policies or intentions, he began to plot a coup d'état against it. On March 6/19, or just three days after the Provisional Government assumed power, Lenin sent a telegram from Switzerland to his followers in Petrograd:

> Our tactics: complete mistrust, no support for the new government. We especially suspect Kerensky [a Socialist Revolutionary and minister of justice in the Provisional Government, later minister of war and prime minister]. The arming of the proletariat provides the only guarantee. Immediate elections to the Petrograd [Municipal] Duma. *No rapprochement with the other parties.*

This was also not an impulsive reaction to unexpected news: Lenin repeated variants of the same intransigent principles on the night after he arrived in Petrograd and again the following day in what became known as his "April Theses." He also quickly overcame the resistance he initially encountered from some of his followers, who thought his ideas were fantastic. As far as Lenin was concerned, the Bolshevik Party was an extension of himself, and although he referred to "elections," his only goal was his own success, without regard for the cost.

To Win the War

Savinkov also had one overriding goal when he returned to Petrograd—Russia and the Entente's total victory. This was the result of all he had seen during his tours of the Western Front and written about in his articles. To do whatever he could to achieve it, shortly after arriving he made his way to the Mariinsky Palace, the seat of the Provisional Government, near Saint Isaac's Square in the city center.

The war and the Revolution had changed the city greatly since Savinkov last saw it at the height of its peacetime prosperity and grandeur. It now looked shabby and dejected, with muddy streets and half-empty shops. There were scarcely any cabs, and whatever tram cars rattled by were overflowing with passengers. Forlorn-looking, burned-out buildings with soot streaks above the windows were visible reminders of the violence that had convulsed the city as the imperial regime collapsed. In the early days, mobs of workers, soldiers, and sailors roamed the city, storming and looting police stations and government ministries; civilians turned on police, disarming and killing them; soldiers murdered officers. A crowd stormed the Litovsky Castle prison and set all the prisoners free, without regard to whether they were political or criminal, after which the building and the records it contained were set on fire. The façades of buildings and shop signs bore scars where crowds destroyed imperial insignia and replaced them with banners bearing revolutionary slogans or red flags and bunting. Soldiers on the streets strode by with scraps of red tied to their bayonets, and civilians pinned crimson bows to their lapels as demonstrations of their loyalty to the Revolution.

The Mariinsky Palace, an imposing building with a columned facade that was the former home of the Imperial Council of Ministers, was the focal point of Savinkov's hopes for Russia's future. Savinkov came to see Alexander Guchkov, the minister of war, about what he could do to support the faltering Russian war effort. In 1917, the army's collapse had begun to accelerate: large-scale desertions were common; some units mutinied against their officers; others began to fraternize with the Germans and Austro-Hungarians across the front lines. However, the Provisional Government believed it had a debt of loyalty to the Entente. It also wanted the rewards that victory was supposed to bring, especially Russian control of Constantinople and the Dardanelles, which would give her ships untrammeled access to the Mediterranean and, from there, to the oceans of the world. As a result, the Provisional Government persisted in trying to whip up enthusiasm for the war. It seemed that if only the army could gather itself up and continue to press the enemy, victory would be certain.

Politically, Savinkov and Guchkov, who was a constitutional monarchist, would have been enemies during any earlier period, but now they were united in their commitment to military victory. Guchkov offered Savinkov the position of Commissar of the Seventh Army on the Southwestern Front, and Savinkov immediately accepted. Newly created by the Provisional Government in response to the imperative to democratize the military, commissars functioned as arbiters between soldiers and officers and as liaisons between the civilian government and the military—both the actual commanders of army and naval units and the soldiers' and sailors' committees that were formed everywhere after "Order No. 1." The commissar was the chief political officer in charge of ensuring the government's policies were being observed, resolving conflicts between the military and civilian branches, and mediating between troops and their commanders.

It was a responsible and very demanding position. The Seventh Army comprised something like 100,000 men in the spring of 1917 and was located in western Ukraine, near the border with Romania, where it faced both Austro-Hungarians and Germans. It was one of the four armies that during the previous year had distinguished itself in the Brusilov Offensive, although its combat worthiness had deteriorated seriously since then.

The Provisional Government's policies on many issues were in the process of development. Moreover, Savinkov was one of the first commissars appointed, before all the functions of the position were fully codified. The result was that after his initial consultation with Guchkov, Savinkov seems to have decided largely by himself that the greatest danger to the army's discipline and effectiveness was Bolshevik propaganda against the war and that he needed to "combat" it. This inevitably put him on a collision course with Lenin and his policies. It also put him into conflict with the Petrograd Soviet of Soldiers' and Workers' Deputies, who, as he would soon learn, were "displeased by his activities."

The Revolution had breathed new life into Savinkov, and he had taken a step toward center stage as a political activist squarely in public view. And whereas he had previously striven to destroy a social and political order, he was now committing himself to defending and saving the new order that the Revolution had created.

Never a man of half measures, he dedicated himself to the task with a zeal that tied his personal fate to that of his homeland. As he was leaving Petrograd for the front, he wrote to Zinaida Gippius: "I will write of course, but not now. Now there is only one thing—praying for Russia."

CHAPTER SEVEN

DEFENDING THE REVOLUTION

T he trip to the Southwestern Front from Petrograd via Moscow and Kiev was over 1,200 miles by train and took several days, giving Savinkov time to think about the duties he would face as soon as he reached the Seventh Army. He knew he would need to improvise much of the time because he did not have any previous military experience; he had also not been given any detailed instructions or specific mandate following his appointment other than to keep the army fighting. But his personal resources were hardly negligible. He had spent much of his life outside the regular patterns of civilian life, which meant that he knew how to adapt to novel circumstances. He knew how to discipline himself and others. He knew what it felt like to want to kill your enemies and to actually kill them. He had also faced enemies who wanted to kill him and nearly succeeded. He had spent enough time on the Western Front to see what modern war was like. And even if his duties as commissar were not the same as those of a frontline soldier, he would be fighting for something he believed in for the first time in years.

The Commissar

Shortly after taking up his duties in April 1917, Savinkov met Fyodor Stepun, an artillery lieutenant who was active in the local soldiers' councils that had sprung up in the Seventh Army, as they had everywhere else in response to "Order No. 1." Stepun would become a friend and collaborator and would pen a revealing memoir of Savinkov during this pivotal period in his life. What makes his recollections especially valuable is that he was a battle-hardened veteran who had been in the army since 1914, which put him in a good position to judge Savinkov on strictly military matters. Stepun was also a thoughtful and unusually well-educated man who had completed a doctorate in philosophy in Germany before the beginning of the Great War (where he would eventually be exiled and become a well-known professor).

"From the first moment," Stepun recalled, Savinkov "struck me with his absolute difference from all the people around him, including myself." Part of Stepun's excitement was about recognizing the famous terrorist and author of *The Pale Horse*. But what came to fascinate him even more was Savinkov's genius for dealing with professional soldiers.

When they met in early May at a major congress organized by the Provisional Government to raise the spirits of the armies on the Southwestern Front, the first thing Stepun noticed about Savinkov is that he did not look like anyone else. He was wearing his new commissar's uniform, which was modeled on an army officer's, but with differences that stood out: a service cap without the usual insignia and a gray-green military jacket with an unfamiliar-looking turnover collar. Nevertheless, it was close enough to army issue to make Savinkov look like he was part of the military and not a civilian. The uniform was well tailored, and Savinkov looked elegant in it; here as before, he had dressed with care.

There were many speakers at the congress, and Savinkov also behaved differently from the others when it was his turn to ascend the rostrum. He spoke forcefully, as the occasion required—"in short, energetic phrases, as if hammering nails into a wall," in Stepun's words—but he was much more controlled in his manner and eschewed the dramatic arm gestures that Russian orators habitually favored.

Even Savinkov's face seemed unusual to Stepun. He thought that its expression was strangely impassive under the circumstances, and that his features did not look Russian but Western European (impressions that others had noted often before). At times, Stepun's attempts to capture Savinkov's traits appear to have been colored by *The Pale Horse* (to this day, readers of the novella continue to make the mistake of equating Savinkov and his melodramatic character Zhorzh). He thought that Savinkov's "narrow, sad, and cruel eyes" did not "shine" so much as "burn" with a "gloomy fire." And he noted that his left cheek was marked by "a deep fold" that ran from his nose to his "predatory and bitter" mouth (a description that leaves out the possibility that this feature could have resulted simply from Savinkov's habitual squinting from cigarette smoke).

For all his fascination with Savinkov, Stepun did not think he was a very effective orator and characterized his voice as "quiet and somewhat hoarse." He was also not persuaded by the content of Savinkov's speech, which consisted of formulaic phrases about having to continue the fight (Savinkov rehearsed speeches and at times repeated them verbatim in different locations, with the same intonations and gestures). However, Stepun was prescient in discerning what lay beneath the surface of Savinkov's speech—his conviction that "the time for words was over and that the time for quick decisions and decisive actions had arrived." Soon Savinkov would in fact start calling for initiatives that would put him at odds with the most powerful forces at work in revolutionary Russia.

Initially, many of the other officers in the Seventh Army resented having to answer to Savinkov as the official representative of the Provisional Government and were put off by aspects of his past. Even for those who embraced the February Revolution and acknowledged Savinkov's struggle against the imperial regime, his career as a terrorist was incompatible with their sense of military honor, and his association with the notorious Azef compromised him. There were also conservative officers who could not forgive Boris Savinkov for having dared to raise his hand against the emperor himself.

Knowing these views, Stepun was greatly surprised by how quickly and easily Savinkov managed to overcome the officers' resistance and not only enter their circles but be thoroughly "assimilated" by them. Moreover, Savinkov achieved this without sycophancy and in a principled manner: he neither abandoned his Socialist Revolutionary slogans nor tried to ingratiate himself with the officers by taking their side in their disputes with the enlisted men.

Savinkov succeeded because of his demeanor, his trustworthiness, and his breeding. In Stepun's words, the officers quickly lost their initial sense of "organic enmity" toward Savinkov because everything about him was "stylistically" very close to them—his crisp military appearance, the disciplined way he gestured and even walked, and the concise, businesslike nature of his orders. Even Savinkov's preference for silk underwear and English soap contributed to the impression that he was a gentleman if not an actual officer.

But most decisive in Stepun's view was that during his years in the revolutionary underground, Savinkov had developed his inborn gift of command and ability to lead people, which was the most important skill that an officer could have. Savinkov's manner even won over the Seventh Army's commander, General Leonid Belkovich, who had arrived to assume his position in April, just before Savinkov. A forty-year veteran who had fought the Turks and the Japanese before the Great War, Belkovich did not approve of commissars on principle, because he saw them as undermining traditional military authority. But, as he freely admitted to several Belgian visitors who were making a tour of the front, Savinkov was a great help to him in reestablishing discipline in the army, and that "it was a pleasure, moreover, to have personal dealings with a man possessed of such good common sense."

⊙━━━◦

Savinkov's work often required him to spend time in advanced observation positions and in the trenches, which brought him under enemy fire. This was the first time in his life that he had experienced anything quite like this, and the general lack of fear that he felt during moments of greatest danger surprised even him. Writing to his old friend and literary adviser Zinaida Gippius, who had also returned to Russia and who took a keen interest in his fate, Savinkov recalled how

> When I was lying with my nose pressed into the grass for the first time and shrapnel was bursting two steps away, I felt happy and surprised. It wasn't frightening. It became frightening later, another time, when heavy shells were bursting, even though there was no danger because they were far away. And when I thought that I was going to die because I could tell from the shell's whistling that it was "mine," "for me," there was no time to be scared; and when I remained alive, I felt that that was how it has to be. I'm not afraid of the wounded or the dead. I'd like to say a prayer, but I don't know how.

Savinkov even flaunted his courage at times, and word of it began to spread as officers who had seen him in action moved to other parts of the front. On one occasion, when he was dealing with a mutinous reserve unit while being shelled by German artillery that had wounded several men near him, and was also being watched by a thousand soldiers eager to see any sign of cowardice or even nervousness on his part, Savinkov turned to his aide with a smile and coolly asked for a light because he did not have a match.

There was danger behind the lines as well from Bolshevik soldiers who did not hesitate to take potshots at Savinkov when he was exhorting rebellious units to return to their duties. But he remained calm and did not bother to duck. Stepun thought that Savinkov took a dark joy in experiencing mortal danger because it heightened his sense of being alive. But he also speculated that Savinkov risked death because he was fascinated with it, a notion that seems prompted more by what Stepun read in Savinkov's fictions and projected onto their author than by what actually motivated Savinkov's bravery. As we will see, the dominant feature of Savinkov's life from 1917 forward was an increasingly ambitious military and political agenda that had nothing to do with a morbid fixation on death.

Rebellions in the Ranks

Boris Savinkov's responsibility was to keep the army fighting and committed to winning the war, which required him to be constantly on watch for mutinous outbreaks and be ready to speed off in an automobile over horribly rutted roads and past destroyed villages and shell-pocked fields to try to cajole or coerce the men into resuming their duties. If the situation was particularly complicated, he would at times telegraph the Ministry of War to coordinate his actions. When words alone did not work with a particular rebellious unit—which could range in size from a squad to an entire division—Savinkov would have it disarmed, arrested, and escorted to the rear. Initially this method kept other units in check because they feared a similar punishment. But when word got out that nothing happened to the disarmed troops, which were simply kept idle in the rear, sterner methods had to be devised.

It soon became clear to Savinkov that the influence of the Bolshevik Party far exceeded the number of actual members it had among the troops. Many soldiers knew little about the party's ideology but supported those positions that affected them directly, such as refusing to carry out orders, agitating others to do the same, trying to fraternize with the enemy, and insisting on immediate peace with Germany. These Bolshevik-inspired arguments were especially effective among soldiers because of their natural reluctance to risk their lives by going into battle, their often poorly developed sense of patriotism, and the ineffectiveness of significant numbers of the army's commanders.

Shortly after the end of the army congress in early May, a large rebellion broke out that became a serious test for Savinkov when about two-thirds of the infantry in a division left their trenches. They demanded that they be taken immediately to Kiev and that special courses be organized for them so that they could discuss in detail whether or not the continuation of the war was detrimental to the progress of the Revolution. The rest of the division, including its artillery and other specialized units, comprising about half the men in total, opposed the rebels and decided to return to the front.

From the perspective of a military commissar, the demands of the mutinous soldiers were ludicrous and demonstrated not only their political naïveté but also the ease with which they could be swayed by ideologues. (Some memorably naïve and touching demands that soldiers' committees made at other times included that the Provisional Government should immediately undertake the liberation of South African Blacks from capitalist exploitation by the British.)

Savinkov and Stepun both addressed the massed troops and seemed on the verge of persuading them that their demands were unrealistic and that they should return to their positions when, unexpectedly, an excited rifleman ran up to the grandstand. Insolent, glib, and thoroughly radicalized, the man began to hurl provocative questions at Savinkov: where had he come from? Whose money had he lived on in Europe while the soldiers of the Seventh Army froze in the snows of Galicia and had to tear Austrian barbed wire with their bare hands?

Savinkov was not expecting this. He had not spoken about his revolutionary past publicly since he had arrived at the front. The soldier's insults enraged him and he shouted to the crowd:

> And where were you, comrades, where were you . . . when I, without
> sparing my life, together with a handful of brave companions,
> fought against your oppressors for your land and your freedom? Did
> you know . . . that condemned to death by the tsar's court and with
> a noose around my neck, I spent years hiding under a false name
> in Russia and abroad so that you could have the very freedom that
> I now call on you to defend? No, it is not for you to accuse me of

cowardice and a carefree life! I honor your struggle and your suffering. But you are suffering for the third year and because you have been ordered to, whereas I have been suffering and fighting for you for the past twenty years and of my own free will. Let us unite our efforts in one great triumphal push to defend Russia as well as our revolution, our land and our freedom! Comrades, I ask you for the last time—will you take your places in the trenches or will you give up your freedom and betray those who defend it?

It was a powerful and heartfelt argument, and the mutinous troops yielded. As Savinkov wrote to his mother about a similar event, he took pride in quelling a mutiny without having to resort to armed force.

But it was difficult to keep repeating the same arguments when soldiers, like the population in general, believed that the Revolution had granted them unbridled freedom in all things. Bolshevik agitators among the troops were especially effective when they railed for immediate peace instead of continuing a war that was rooted in imperialism and chauvinism and had nothing to do with the interests of the common people. German propaganda leaflets written in Russian and dropped from airplanes or hot-air balloons echoed Bolshevik arguments and aggravated the problems with the troops' morale.

A Polish Ally

Stronger and more radical action was necessary. Savinkov did not delay and began to develop his plans when he was invited to visit the neighboring Eighth Army by Karol Wędziagolski, a Russophilic Polish officer and a member of its Revolutionary Committee with whom he would become close friends.

Wędziagolski was a refined-looking man with a long, straight nose and calm gaze who was very proud of his noble Polish family's lineage, which went back to the thirteenth century. His ancestry and patriotism made him sympathize with the Socialist Revolutionaries because their aims included self-determination for all the subject nationalities of the Russian Empire, including Poles, but also Jews. In the revolutionary years 1904–1905, he broke the mold of Polish anti-Semitism by training members of the Jewish Self-Defense League in Vilnius in using firearms. He and Savinkov had met briefly in 1908 when Savinkov tried to recruit him into the Combat Organization (he had heard that Wędziagolski was a quick draw and crack shot with a handgun), but the young Pole thought it was ignoble to waylay imperial ministers in the streets.

When they met again nine years later, Wędziagolski discovered that Savinkov wanted to ask him and others in the Eighth Army's Revolutionary Committee to join an ambitious new plan he had developed to save the army from disintegration.

It was mid-May, and Savinkov was visibly buoyed up by his initiative. Spring had transformed the landscape all along the front. Chestnut and linden trees were beginning to bloom. Masses of lavender-colored flowers covered the lilacs and poured out their strong, sweet, heady aroma. To Savinkov it seemed as if nature herself was echoing his faith that the "Russian people's army," as he now liked to call it, would be renewed and would fulfill its duties "before the motherland, freedom, and Russian and European democracy."

Savinkov laid out his plan with calm intensity. If the Russian army collapsed entirely, "Austro-German bayonets" would overthrow the Russian Revolution and negate all its achievements. The only solution was to put "our army in the hands of rational, honest, and decisive commanders," even if this went against the policy of collective decision-making established by the February Revolution:

> Exceptional people are needed, people who are imbued with love of country and who understand the practical needs of the revolution. *Such people will not be swayed by those who oppose their truth and their faith. A time has arrived when we must impose our will and our truth upon others by force.* [Emphasis added]

Savinkov was arguing that a hierarchical command structure had to be reinstated in the army to protect the freedom and democracy that the Revolution had won; in other words, that the ideals of the Revolution had to be set aside now so that they could be saved and implemented in the future.

It was a daring position to take in the resolutely populist atmosphere that the February Revolution had created and put him in direct conflict with the Bolsheviks and "Order No. 1." But it was also dangerous because it embodied a classic paradox about means and ends: would dictatorship ever willingly cede power to democracy?

Savinkov and the General, Part 1

Savinkov wanted dictatorial leadership to be reinstated in the Eighth Army because of the leading role it had been chosen to play during a major summer offensive across the entire Russian front that was to be coordinated with the Entente's attack on the Western Front. The aim of the combined offensives was nothing less than total victory over the Central Powers.

In Savinkov's view, the success of the coming offensive on the Southwestern Front hinged on one man, General Lavr Georgievich Kornilov, and he began to urge Wędziagolski and the others to join him in a campaign to persuade the Provisional Government to have Kornilov put in command of the Eighth Army. Over the next several months, Savinkov's advocacy of Kornilov for a specific but limited task would grow into a commitment that would affect the history of the Russian Revolution.

⚬══⚬

Kornilov was a tough, experienced, and highly respected senior general who had recently become a legendary figure because of his daring escape from an Austro-Hungarian prison. Born into a modest Cossack family in Eastern Kazakhstan, with Central Asian blood in his veins, narrow, slanting eyes, and bronze-colored skin, he was slight of stature and had what contemporaries described as an impenetrable gaze. He made a brilliant career as he rose through the ranks, including a daring reconnaissance mission into British territory in Afghanistan, fighting heroically in the Russo-Japanese War, and winning dramatic and bloody victories in the early years of the Great War before being captured. Kornilov never lost his fondness for the peoples of his native Central Asia, to the extent of learning several Turkic dialects and having as his bodyguard Tekke Turkoman cavalrymen, whose uniforms included red robes and shaggy Astrakhan hats.

Especially important for Savinkov was that in addition to his military prowess and "iron will," Kornilov was "a true democrat who had nothing in common with the aristocratic military elite of the Tsarist regime nor with the court camarilla." He could be trusted, therefore, to remain loyal to the Provisional Government and the achievements of the February Revolution, and, as Savinkov argued, was Russia's best last hope: "If Kornilov, as the commander of your army and with your help, cannot regenerate the fighting qualities of the troops, that means that no one can do it. In that case we may consider our national and revolutionary cause irrevocably lost."

Savinkov's campaign on Kornilov's behalf was successful—almost all the soldiers' committees of the Eighth Army passed resolutions requesting his appointment and sent them by telegraph to the authorities in Petrograd. Their campaign was aided by Kornilov's own desire to return to the front. After he had escaped from Austrian captivity, he was given the prestigious command of the Petrograd Military District, but this entailed duties he found repugnant, such as having to arrest the imperial family and place it under protective custody, and fighting constantly and unsuccessfully against the corrosive influence of the Petrograd Soviet in the army. He took command of the Eighth Army in May.

By leaving Petrograd, Kornilov had demonstrated his purity of purpose—that he was a soldier's soldier whose domain was combat, not politics. However, by choosing to escape the ambiguous shades-of-gray struggles for power in the capital for the black-and-white simplicity of the front lines, he also revealed his unwillingness to engage the full range of forces that were pushing historical events in Russia. As time would show, political battles in Petrograd would play a far more important role in determining the country's future than fighting the Central Powers. Other than the Bolsheviks, few understood this before it was too late.

When Kornilov arrived at his new headquarters, he was greeted warmly by most of the soldiers and officers, who admired his personal heroism and military reputation. However, his harsh words about sparing "no efforts for the revital-ization of the battle readiness of the troops, in order to attack the enemy . . . to be victorious or die" made the more radicalized soldiers start to mutter about "counterrevolution." This accusation would follow him everywhere in the coming months and grow louder. But as Wędziagolski noted, everyone who got closer to Kornilov "felt a power exceeding the bounds of superficially worldly or official relations." Savinkov in particular would fall under his sway more powerfully and fatefully than anyone else.

The Minister of War as an Ally

In late April 1917, at Lenin's instigation, the Bolsheviks had made their first, half-baked attempt to seize power in Petrograd. The Provisional Government suppressed the armed demonstrators with the assistance of the Executive Committee of the Petrograd Soviet, many members of which opposed the coup, but a governmental crisis ensued and several ministers resigned their posts. To form a new cabinet, the Provisional Government created a coalition that included six socialists—a significant shift to the left in comparison to the first, "bourgeois" cabinet. Chernov, Savinkov's former comrade and frequent critic in the SR Party, achieved a lifelong dream by becoming minister of agriculture. And Alexander Kerensky, the former minister of justice, changed portfolios to become the all-important minister of war.

Kerensky had no military background—he was a lawyer by training and a moderate Socialist Revolutionary—but his unique standing in the Petrograd Soviet (where he was a vice chairman), his support for the war, and his impressive rhetorical gifts were all expected to appeal to the army as it was being prepared for the summer offensive. Together with Kornilov, Kerensky would play a defining role in Savinkov's life during the next several months, and the complex interactions among all three—a mixture of admiration, solidarity, disappointments, misunderstandings, disagreements, dishonesty, and recriminations—would determine the course of the Russian Revolution and what followed it.

Savinkov first got to know and began to admire Kerensky when he toured the Southwestern Front in May and saw how effective the new minister of war was at rallying the troops. Kerensky was only thirty-six, intense and youthful, but otherwise undistinguished-looking, with a narrow face dominated by a long, meaty nose and a weak, petulant mouth, and topped by short hair brushed up above his high forehead. But he became transformed when he spoke. Wearing a quasi-military jacket and jodhpurs, and moving so quickly that he seemed to run up to the rostrum, he riveted the attention of soldiers and officers alike with his extraordinarily passionate speeches about defending "Russia and the Revolution, the land and freedom." He punctuated his words with commanding gestures, such as letting his outspread arms drop down toward the crowd in front of him, as if trying to scoop up some of the energy from the agitated sea of people at his feet, and then thrusting them dramatically into the sky. As Kerensky's excitement grew, frenzied, high-pitched notes would appear in his voice when he demanded that he too be given a rifle so that he could lead the offensive and either conquer or die. On one occasion, Stepun saw a severely wounded lieutenant, his face and body twitching from agitation, limp up to Kerensky, pull the Saint George Cross for military valor off his chest and pin it onto the minister's jacket. After shaking the man's hand, Kerensky passed the medal to an aide as a contribution to a military charity, which promoted a stream of more medals. When Kerensky finished speaking, soldiers and officers clamored to shake his hand and be photographed with him, and waves of applause and patriotic shouts filled the air.

Kerensky's passage along the front was likened to that of a "cyclone" because of the agitation he left in his wake, which persuaded him and many others that he was succeeding in his aim. In Savinkov's view, he had become the embodiment of the people's will to defend their revolution with victory in war.

Kerensky soon singled Savinkov out as well, both for his activity at the front and his work in the Ministry of War in Petrograd, to which he was recalled and where he spent several weeks in May and June. While he was in Petrograd, Savinkov threw himself into his duties with the same energy as at the front, working sixteen hours a day and hardly sleeping. Even so, as he complained in a letter to his mother, he was unable to accomplish everything he wanted to. For his dedication and success, Kerensky promoted Savinkov to commissar for the entire Southwestern Front, a much bigger and more responsible position that came with a large staff and that again required him to spend most of his time visiting frontline positions.

The Kerensky Offensive

Finally, the day arrived that many believed would turn the war around on the Eastern Front. On June 16, 1917, Russian artillery began to bombard the Austro-Hungarian and German positions on the Southwestern Front, and on June 18, the ground offensive began. For the next two days, the Russian armies made good progress, advancing into enemy territory and capturing prisoners and equipment. Kornilov's Eighth Army especially distinguished itself when it attacked on June 23 and took two enemy cities after capturing thousands of prisoners and hundreds of pieces of artillery. Savinkov's expectations about Kornilov's abilities had been amply fulfilled. When the two men met face-to-face for the first time, Savinkov became convinced that Kornilov deserved an even bigger role in the army.

But then the offensive ground to a halt. The strongest and most motivated "shock troops" leading the attack suffered such heavy losses that they were knocked out of the fight, which left only regular units that had been ambivalent about the offensive from the beginning. Deciding they had done enough, most of the regular units announced they would attack no longer and began to "fraternize" with the enemy and to hold meetings. In the northern sections of the Russian front, things went even worse, and the offensive failed altogether when most units refused to advance. Within weeks, German counterattacks in the southwest had pushed the Russians back beyond their starting positions, transforming many of the Russian units into fleeing, unruly, and panicked mobs. This was the Russian Army's "last gasp" during the Great War and signaled its collapse as a national fighting organization.

The failure of the Kerensky Offensive, as it became known, was a catastrophe for Kerensky personally and politically because of all the effort, planning, and resources—men and materiel—he had committed to it. It was a blow for Savinkov as well, although his disappointment was mitigated by the greater success of the armies in which he had been active as a commissar. On June 18 and 19, he was in Petrograd at the Ministry of War with Kerensky and his staff. When the initial good news from the Southwestern Front arrived, Kerensky proclaimed excitedly in front of everyone: "Where Savinkov was in charge of the army we have victory; where it was the Army Chief we have failure." Savinkov thought this was "an enormous exaggeration," but his standing with Kerensky and other powerful figures in the Ministry of War had risen considerably. If it had not occurred to Savinkov before, this may have been the time when he began to develop the sense that he was also one of those exceptional, single-minded men the country needs during its time of troubles.

The Army as Touchstone

Savinkov's experience in the active army, especially his close contact with soldiers and officers on the front lines, became his touchstone for judging governmental and political life in the capital, and he found them wanting. Despite his duties, he managed to write a series of sketches that he united under the title *From the Active Army*, and in one he characterized Petrograd as a "city of fog": "Not only fog from the Neva River, but from words. For every ten people who do something, there are hundreds and thousands in Petrograd who talk . . . and because of it faith collapses and disappears." To Wędziagolski, Savinkov described the politicians as "sleepwalkers" who were engaged in "incoherent mumblings."

He did not see the culture of dialogue and discussion that the Revolution had unleashed as evidence of a new popular faith in democracy and the possibilities of reasoned discourse. Rather, when practiced by members of political factions jockeying for advantage, it was evidence of irresolution that easily leads to demagoguery: "How easy it is to inflame a crowd," he noted bitterly. "How easy it is to have success at a meeting."

In the army, by contrast, "it is easier to breathe. In the army, where people sacrifice their lives, die and kill, the word has another, heavier weight—like lead I would say. There to say means to do."

Savinkov found not only truth and honesty in the army, but also deep personal fulfillment of a sort he had not known for a long time, perhaps of a sort he had never known anywhere. Writing to his mother, Savinkov summarizes his state of mind after returning to the front during the last week in June: "I've gotten as dark as a boot-top from the sun, I sleep in hovels, eat the devil knows what, swallow dust in automobiles, but am healthy and happy."

A week later, he wrote even more frankly to Gippius:

> I am completely with Kerensky in spirit . . . If the war ends in defeat everything is finished. I don't think about anything. I live, i.e., I work as I've never worked in my life before . . . I love Russia and that is why I do what I do. I love the revolution and that is why I do what I do. In spirit I have become a soldier and nothing more. Everything that is not war is distant, almost alien. The home front infuriates me, Petrograd makes me nauseous from a distance.

The Peasant Soldiers of Russia

The purity and simplicity of purpose that Savinkov discovered at the front was due not only to the stark contrasts between life and death, victory and defeat, but also to his close contacts with the Russian peasant soldier. This is ironic, considering that he had spent his entire career as a terrorist fighting on behalf of the peasantry who were the SR Party's primary focus. However, what Savinkov knew of peasants in those days was largely secondhand. His terrorist plots had played out in major cities, and he never lived among peasants for any length of time, as other Party members did when they went into the countryside to do political work. In the army, by contrast, around 85 percent of the soldiers were of peasant origin. Even though they had been pulled out of their homes and thrust into the midst of war, most of them still preserved their age-old peasant character. For Savinkov it was a revelation to see them close up: they were "the long-suffering people who have pined for truth" to whom "each of us is tied by blood and for whom it is worth living."

He admired them for their simplicity, stoicism, faith, and courage, traits he captured in a series of sketches about the front that have literary antecedents and echo Leo Tolstoy's admiring portrayals of peasant soldiers in *The Sevastopol Tales* and *War and Peace*. (The cultural associations of the term "peasant," which ultimately derives from the Latin and means "person from the countryside," differ markedly from those of the Russian word *krestyanin*, which means "person of the cross.") In one sketch Savinkov describes a meeting in the trenches which he had called to spur the soldiers on:

> The men gather. They are all peasants, tillers of the soil—broad shoulders, sunburned faces, calloused hands. The laboring Russian people, dressed in a soldiers' uniform . . . They listen like only a peasant knows how to listen—greedily, fervently . . . We talk about land and freedom. About what the earth means and the meaning of long-wished-for freedom. And when they hear these new words their eyes, which had grown dim in the trenches, light up, and their tired lips whisper something . . . "We will die for land and freedom!"

Savinkov is so moved that when the men prepare to go into action at night, he hurries to embrace and kiss them when he says farewell. He feels beards, lips, the tears on their rough cheeks, hands reaching out to him from the darkness, and hears their voices growing louder as they exclaim: "For land and freedom! For freedom! For the motherland! For the people!"

A special, elite unit in which all the officers and men have sworn to succeed or die in battle—named the Assault Battalion of Death—kneels and prays before beginning their advance. Two female nurses stand silently before them, one holding an old silver-clad icon and the other a scrap of red-and-black cloth, the colors of revolution, life and death. The nurse with the icon breaks down and begins to sob. Then she speaks: "Comrades, we bless you. Not us—but your mothers, your wives, your sisters in Russia. Your path is hard. You have sworn to defend liberty or die. Keep your vow. Defend it. Protect it. Save it."

Savinkov hears the kneeling soldiers promise that they will before they again fall silent. He then turns to his reader with an invitation to try to understand what he just described:

> If you have ever prepared for death, if the decision to give your life freely, joyously ever ripened in your soul . . . if you have ever, even for a brief moment . . . comprehended your minuteness, your vanity, and said to yourself "Only death tramples death," then you will understand what I am writing about now, you will understand that unsullied spring of feelings out of which the soldiers' tears and the funereal sobs of the nurses spilled.

Such selfless units had appeared elsewhere in the army as well. There was even a Women's Death Battalion formed in Petrograd—the first of its kind anywhere in the world.

But such units were in the minority, and most of the peasant soldiers were neither selfless nor patriotic. Despite his boundless admiration and sympathy for frontline soldiers in general, Savinkov had no illusions about how exhausted and dispirited many of them were, how ill-supplied with everything from food to clothes to rifles, and how difficult it would be for them to gather the strength to fight until ultimate victory. By the summer of 1917, the soldiers' morale, which had been high when the war began, plummeted. Nearly half of all working-age peasant men (aged eighteen to sixty) had been mobilized, which decimated the agricultural labor pool and aggravated the economic conditions in the country as a whole. The increasing hardships in the villages disheartened many soldiers and made them receptive to radicalization and antiwar propaganda. In turn, their discouraging letters and the reports by those who were on leave, disabled, or had deserted steadily eroded support for the war at home.

Only at the front did Savinkov also realize, possibly for the first time in his life, how backward the peasantry was as a whole. Although many of the soldiers were ethnic Russians, others were conscripts from the empire's numerous non-Slavic and non-Christian populations, such as the Cheremis, Mordvins, and Bashkirs. However, despite the differences in their origins, their peacetime lives were largely the same, and they were all united in Savinkov's eyes by their overwhelming "impenetrable darkness." Most were illiterate; many were so ignorant of the world that they did not fully understand the meaning of the February Revolution even several months after it happened. Savinkov had difficulty explaining to them that "liberty is not freedom to do whatever one wants, that a republic is not the same as a meeting." He also had to struggle constantly against the inherently peaceable, submissive, and hidebound nature of the Russian peasants, who, like peasants everywhere, instinctively resisted change, including the violence they were forced to commit as soldiers.

Family in Time of Revolution

Savinkov's duties at the front—where he was busy "every single second," as he wrote to his mother—left him little time for personal relations, but during his occasional trips to the Ministry of War in Petrograd, he was able to reestablish ties with family members who lived in the city.

Of special importance for Savinkov was seeing his children. Tanya was now a young woman of seventeen and Vitya was fifteen. Both would grow into adulthood in the Russia that their father was trying to build. He visited them twice in May, but did not see Vera. By then, the parents had drifted too far apart.

Savinkov's mother was living in Petrograd as well. He tried to see her when he could, although she did not always make this easy. Once, when he managed to set aside several hours to visit her before going back to the front, she told him over the phone that she would be out at that time calling on friends. He was unable to reschedule, and she began to berate him, forcing him to protest his affections in the immemorial manner of a son trying to placate a miffed mother: "How can you doubt that I want to see you? It actually makes me laugh. You must know how much I love you . . . Dear Mama, don't be angry, know that you will always be my mother and do not doubt me."

Evgeniya and Lev remained in France during 1917, and it is unclear why they did not come to Russia to live with Savinkov—perhaps because he did not have a settled life or because of the worsening shortages in Petrograd. But Savinkov wrote to Evgeniya and arranged for money that he earned from his sketches about the front to be sent to Nice. He would not see her or Lev again until he returned to France in late 1918.

Savinkov's only contacts with any of his siblings about which anything is known were with his younger brother, Victor, who had followed in his uncle's footsteps and trained as a painter. They managed to see each other when Victor visited Savinkov and his family briefly in France in 1914. By 1916, Victor had become an artillery officer. It was in that capacity that he helped Savinkov with his paperwork to get a visa after the February Revolution. He also managed to get a short leave in early April to go to Petrograd when Savinkov returned to Russia. As Savinkov's standing in the Ministry of War rose, he was able to have Victor transferred to a section of the front closer to Petrograd so that they could meet at least occasionally. Their letters to each other were affectionate and familial.

The Bolshevik Coup of July 1917

One of the biggest advantages the Bolsheviks had over all the other factions in the great political scrum of 1917 was their relative indifference about Russia. For Lenin, the February Revolution was only a first step toward a radical, genuinely socialist revolution that still needed to happen in Russia, and it, in turn, would be only a springboard to something even bigger and more important—world revolution.

In keeping with this goal, the Bolshevik approach to Russia was to clear space for their new society by eradicating every aspect of the old "bourgeois" order wherever it existed. This gave the Bolsheviks a stark clarity of purpose the others lacked because it is far easier to negate and destroy everything that is "old" than to get involved in discriminating among aspects of a complex, rich, and varied culture like Russia's. Another advantage the Bolsheviks had was their simplicity of moral choice: whatever helps to advance the world revolution is good, and whatever does not is bad. Accordingly, when the June offensive stalled and the army's collapse accelerated, rather than trying to forestall a national disaster, the Bolsheviks renewed their efforts to aggravate the situation in Russia by undermining public support for the war.

In early July they decided to go beyond propaganda and made another attempt to seize power, this time by overthrowing not only the Provisional Government, which they saw as their enemy, but also the Petrograd Soviet, which, despite ideological divergences, was more their ally than anything else. These July Days, as they became known, would have a powerful effect on Savinkov. He realized that it would no longer be enough to combat low-level Bolshevik propagandists and sympathizers in the trenches or to support strong commanders on the front lines. History was accelerating, and the Bolsheviks had become such an obvious existential threat to Russia that he would need to move to Petrograd, the seat of power itself, to find a new way to defeat them.

○━━━○

The chain of events in July began when the Provisional Government, antici-pating a German counteroffensive, decided to send reinforcements to the front from the Petrograd garrison and chose the largest unit, the Machine Gun Regiment, which had nearly 12,000 men. Because it had been heavily radicalized by the Bolsheviks and was their main base of support, sending it to the front would also rid the capital of a dangerous armed force. How-ever, when the regiment learned of the government's plans, it mutinied and resolved to resist.

The Bolshevik leadership decided to take advantage of the regiment's rebellion, which was joined by other forces, and also orchestrated a takeover of the Petro-grad Soviet to give their actions the semblance of legitimacy. With everything in place, on July 4 thousands of armed men began to flood into the city center and to take up strategic positions. No troops loyal to the Provisional Govern-ment were available or willing to resist, and the stage seemed to be set for the Bolsheviks to seize power. But then, at a crucial moment, Lenin hesitated. His past connections with the Germans had caught up with him.

Two weeks earlier, the Provisional Government had received evidence from French Intelligence about Lenin's secret financial dealings with the Germans. Late on July 4, when the coup seemed to be just minutes away from succeeding, the Provisional Government's minister of justice, Pavel Pereverzev, decided to act. He summoned journalists and representatives of military units stationed in or near the city and laid out some of the evidence he had about Lenin's collaboration with the Germans.

The Bolsheviks tried to suppress the news but failed, and when it did get out, the effect on the army units was electrifying. Although most soldiers were indifferent about the form of civilian government in Petrograd, they cared very much about collusion with the enemy. Lenin's journey across Germany was well known and had made him deeply unpopular with the regular troops. As soon as Pereverzev's new evidence reached them, units from several guards' regiments and Cossacks marched on Tauride Palace, where Lenin and the others were meeting. The rebellious troops guarding the palace scattered without a fight. Lenin decided that all was lost and that the Bolshevik Party was finished; to save himself, he fled to Finland.

An Opportunity Missed

There were a number of moments in 1917 when Russian history seemed close to pivoting in an entirely different direction from where it appeared to be heading, and the July Days were one of these. Had the Provisional Government acted more forcefully, it might have survived and fulfilled what it considered its primary task—to oversee the country's transformation into a new and democratic state. However, it failed to act decisively or even consistently within its own legal mandate and took no lasting action against Lenin and his comrades.

A trial at which all the evidence of the Bolshevik Party's treasonous activity was made public could have destroyed it as a political force. But the Bolsheviks denied the accusations against them, and the Petrograd Soviet, despite having been targeted by their putsch, came to their defense. The majority of the deputies in the Soviet were socialists of different stripes and saw the Bolsheviks as ideological comrades who had merely strayed somewhat in response to the threat of counterrevolution; and from the perspective of the deputies, the real danger was counterrevolution, because it threatened not only the Soviet but the socialist movement as a whole. The Provisional Government also feared encouraging the counterrevolutionary right-wing forces by attacking the Bolsheviks and did not want to antagonize the Soviet, with which it maintained a shaky alliance.

The failed coup caused a governmental crisis, and a new cabinet was formed in which Kerensky became the central figure: he was named prime minister in addition to retaining the portfolios of war and navy. With so much power concentrated in his hands, Kerensky began increasingly to think of himself as Russia's unique savior. The relationship Savinkov had with him would become his own path to power.

Savinkov and the General, Part 2

While the Bolshevik putsch was unrolling in Petrograd, Savinkov was at the Southwestern Front continuing to struggle with the deteriorating discipline of the troops and with Bolshevik propaganda, which was becoming increasingly effective in most sectors. Soldiers routinely insulted and refused to salute officers or demanded that they be replaced. In some units, when ordered to advance, soldiers disobeyed and threatened to shoot their officers. There were numerous cases when they carried out their threats.

The one exception was Kornilov's Eighth Army, which demonstrated what a talented commander could achieve by enforcing iron discipline. His success also had a major effect on Savinkov personally, because he became convinced that both he and Kornilov had much bigger roles to play in the conduct of the war. On July 2, Savinkov began a campaign to have Kornilov appointed commander of the entire Southwestern Front. This was an exceptional initiative for someone who had been an indigent and irrelevant émigré just four months earlier.

Savinkov sent a series of telegrams about his proposal to Minister of War Kerensky, and copies to Commander-in-Chief Brusilov as well as General Alexey Gutor, the commander of the Southwestern Front whom Kornilov would replace. Initially, Kerensky and especially the hapless Gutor bristled at what they considered Savinkov's presumptuousness in trying to advise them about military matters that were outside his competence. However, Savinkov did not back down and in the end prevailed by enlisting the support of the Southwestern Army's soldiers' committees.

Kornilov was appointed on July 7 in what was also a triumph for Savinkov. He was summoned to the commander-in-chief's train to be told the news personally and to meet with Brusilov and Kornilov, which was a dramatic acknowledgement of his new standing. For some of the senior commanders in the army—and, even more importantly, for Kerensky—Savinkov's views on matters of national importance had acquired weight. Kornilov especially would come to value Savinkov as highly as Savinkov valued him. At one point he described Savinkov to Kerensky as "a major figure," one with "an enormous name as a revolutionary" and "real authority in broad democratic circles."

The Death Sentence

With every crisis, Savinkov's involvement in affairs of state kept increasing. During the July putsch in Petrograd, he was infuriated that the Provisional Government treated the Bolsheviks with "kid gloves," as he put it. When this was followed two days later by mass desertions of Russian troops in the face of a German counteroffensive in Galicia, Savinkov became convinced that only the most extreme methods could counter Bolshevik propaganda and restore the soldiers' willingness to fight. On July 8, he telegraphed the Ministry of War, urging that "revolutionary discipline" be introduced in the army "by any means necessary."

Savinkov knew this was a highly inflammatory proposal, because when the Provisional Government began to dismantle the worst aspects of tsarist rule, it started with the death penalty. Liberals and the left greeted the decision ecstatically as a sign that a new age had arrived in Russia. But army commanders opposed it, arguing that they were being deprived of an essential tool to enforce discipline at the front. On the eve of the great June offensive, the decision was even criticized by France, Russia's ally, which was anxious about the Russian Army's weakness and, like all the other powers in the Great War, relied on the threat of the death penalty in its own military (and executed over 600 during the course of the war). In this context, any talk of reimposing executions would be seen by the vast majority in Petrograd's governing circles as "counterrevolutionary."

For Savinkov, the Revolution's achievements remained sacrosanct as well, but he was also a pragmatist and willing to take another step along the authoritarian path that he believed was necessary to save Russia. His argument for reinstating the death penalty was that mutinies and desertions are initiated by small numbers of "cowards and traitors" who influence their units to refuse to fight, or to turn and run; this gives the enemy the advantage of being able to attack Russian positions at will, without fear of retaliation, which results in the tragic slaughter of numerous soldiers who could have been properly motivated. Executing the few who were guilty of poisoning the minds of their fellows would thus save the lives of many. If fully implemented, he believed it was a plan that could restore the army and save Russia.

On July 8, Kornilov drafted his own telegram as well and, in a sign of trust that was very gratifying for Savinkov, asked for his opinion before sending it. This simple act would prove to be a pivotal moment in the relations between the two men.

Savinkov approved Kornilov's call for the death penalty in the draft, but was completely taken aback by its conclusion, in which Kornilov made what sounded like a threat to impose a military dictatorship on the Southwestern Front, and perhaps even more broadly, in the event that his demand was not granted.

Savinkov objected immediately and in the strongest terms. He told Kornilov that any attempt to seize power by the military would destroy the country. He also warned him, with exquisite politeness but steely determination, that he would oppose such a move with force: "It is possible that a day may come, General, Sir, when you may feel the desire to execute me as a revolutionary, and I do not doubt that you would try to fulfil this desire. But I must warn you that on that same day I would want to execute you and I of course would make every effort to do so."

Means and Ends

It was inevitable that the subject of dictatorship would come up between Kornilov and Savinkov. With the army crumbling and power in Petrograd split between a vacillating Provisional Government and a Soviet trying to sabotage it at every turn, it was tantalizing to think that a strong-willed man could cut through all the contention and chart a straight course to salvation. For a senior professional soldier like Kornilov, this would have been an easy step to imagine. For Savinkov, taking matters into his own hands had been a habit since his days in the Combat Organization and had been reinforced by his successful advocacy of Kornilov's promotions on the front. Why, then, did he object to Kornilov's telegram?

As subsequent events would show, it was not out of an aversion to authoritarianism as such but because Kornilov threatened to proclaim a dictatorship unilaterally, without the sanction of the revolutionary government in Petrograd. For Savinkov, the rule of law was essential, as was the loyalty that a professional soldier owed the government he served. The only kind of dictator Savinkov would accept is one to whom the government ceded power willingly.

This was a highly paradoxical idea, based on beliefs that are difficult to imagine in the abstract, much less realize in fact. Savinkov was using his own character as a measure of what he thought was possible, and it was a recipe for conflict and misunderstanding. He would find that it was not easy to identify a middle ground between means and ends, between his belief that only authoritarian rule could save the army and Russia and his belief in revolution, freedom, and democracy. This was, in a different key, a recapitulation of the paradox inherent in terrorism—that violence could produce peaceful results.

○—■—○

Kornilov's agreeing to the revision of the telegram did not mean that he abandoned all his dictatorial inclinations. On the same day he sent the telegram, he ordered his unit commanders to use machine guns and artillery against any troops that deserted their positions. On the day after, without having received authorization from Petrograd yet, he ordered the execution of fourteen soldiers for participating in brutal attacks on local civilians. He then publicized what he had done to all the troops on the Southwestern Front and announced that henceforth deserters would be shot as well.

Savinkov's and Kornilov's efforts to change the government's policy succeeded. Kerensky vacillated at first in a way that was proving to be characteristic for him, but the pressure of the army's dissolution and the reality Kornilov had created on the ground were overwhelming and he had to relent. On July 12, 1917, the Provisional Government formally reintroduced the death penalty at the front.

○—■—○

It did not have the intended effect of saving the army. In some cases, and especially in the beginning, the threat of death chastened unruly troops and some mutinies were successfully put down when their instigators were executed. But the long period of the army's decay could not be reversed overnight. Desertions and disobedience not only continued but grew as the summer wore on. Many commissars, officers, and soldiers who were supposed to participate in military trials balked at condemning their rebellious comrades to death and tried to soften the sentences. There were repeated instances when confrontations between mutinous troops and those loyal to the government escalated into exchanges of gunfire, including artillery. Few could have imagined at the time that this was a harbinger of the horrific bloodshed that a civil war would bring in less than a year.

Minister Savinkov

Savinkov's success as a commissar, alliance with Kornilov, and loyalty to the Revolution and the Provisional Government kept him constantly in Kerensky's mind. On July 16 he summoned Savinkov to army headquarters in Mogilyov (a city now in eastern Belarus) for a high-level military conference that was attended by himself; the minister of foreign affairs, Mikhail Tereshchenko; the commander-in-chief, General Brusilov; and a number of other senior generals. Kornilov was unable to attend but communicated his views via telegraph. The conference was about the grave threat of invasion that the country was now facing and the radical methods that would be necessary to save it.

The conference was held in the white-marble, neoclassical governor's mansion, which stood on the steep, eastern bank of the Dnepr River and had served as supreme headquarters since 1915 and Nicholas II's residence while he was the titular head of the army. When Savinkov walked into it that afternoon, he must have felt considerable satisfaction that his importance was being recognized and in such an exceptional way: he was the only commissar Kerensky invited. But Savinkov's presence did not sit well with all the generals, a number of whom thought that commissars had done as much damage to the army as the soldiers' committees. Their high rank and criticism did not cow Savinkov, however, and although he was always stiffly correct in his manner, he expressed his views boldly, which brought him even more attention.

In his written communication, Kornilov made one new proposal that was even more blatantly "counterrevolutionary" than the reinstatement of the death penalty at the front: the introduction of executions and strict discipline in the rear as well, especially in reserve military units that were "breeding grounds for Bolshevism" and in civilian enterprises that impacted the military. This proposal went completely against the grain of the Provisional Government's commitment to republican and democratic principles, but the other generals supported it.

General Anton Denikin, the thoughtful, forty-five-year-old commander of the Russian Western Front, also used the occasion to launch a bitter attack on the Provisional Government, which he faulted for its weakness and for allowing the army to be politicized and undermined via soldiers' committees, commissars, liberal policies, and the like. As prime minister, Kerensky took the attack personally and could not help detecting threatening notes in it, but he decided to be diplomatic and concealed his feelings.

However, Savinkov did not hesitate to confront Denikin. It was an extraordinary scene in which the former terrorist and fugitive from the Okhrana presumed to lecture a general who had spent twenty-five years in the service of the tsar.

Savinkov told Denikin that his accusations were inaccurate because the Provisional Government had inherited serious flaws from the tsarist army, including weaknesses in the command structure—an implicit dig at those present—and problematic relations between soldiers and their officers; the latter, Savinkov stressed, commissars were now trying to repair. Savinkov also counterattacked Denikin, reminding him that the civilian government of the Russian Republic controlled the military, and warning him that commissars are "the eyes and ears of the Provisional Government." Perhaps most importantly from his own perspective, Savinkov told the generals, as he had already told Kornilov, that any reforms, such as instituting the death penalty in the rear, must be done only in cooperation with the civilian government. For Savinkov this remained an essential legal and moral condition for implementing radical changes that would temporarily roll back some of the freedoms the Revolution had won.

Savinkov's behavior at the conference and uncompromising response to Denikin persuaded Kerensky that he needed to have him by his side in the highest reaches of government. He began by taking Savinkov into his confidence. After the meeting ended, Kerensky told Savinkov that he did not think Brusilov should continue as commander-in-chief and asked him who his replacement should be. Without hesitation, Savinkov named Kornilov. Kerensky agreed and named him to the new post the following day.

Kerensky also asked Savinkov to accompany him to Petrograd instead of returning to the Southwestern Front. The prime minister had arrived in Mogilyov on a long and luxurious private train that had previously served Nicholas II; it was an ostentatious indulgence at a time when railroad transport was grinding to a halt throughout the country for lack of coal. As they started on their journey north, Kerensky revealed to Savinkov that there was a crisis in the Provisional Government because of the recent Bolshevik putsch and that a new cabinet had to be formed. Then, in an even greater sign of trust, Kerensky began to deliberate openly in front of Savinkov about who should constitute the new government, and continued to do so for the duration of the 400-mile journey.

It was enough to make one's head spin. At first, Kerensky considered keeping only the post of prime minister for himself and offering Savinkov the Ministry of War and the Navy. He said that he wanted a cabinet with a preponderance of politically right-wing members who would be in favor of decisive war measures. When the train got to Tsarskoye Selo outside Petrograd, Kerensky even went so far as to take Savinkov with him to call on Georgy Plekhanov, a veteran Menshevik who opposed the Bolsheviks and was in favor of continuing the war. On the spot, Kerensky offer him the Ministry of Trade and Commerce, and Plekhanov agreed.

Savinkov was elated. He believed that he was witnessing the beginning of Kerensky's and the Provisional Government's transformation. It seemed that the days of the prime minister's starry-eyed rhetoric and weak and ambivalent policies were over, and the difficult task of building a strong and viable Russian state had begun.

Savinkov's transformation was even more dramatic. In just four months, he had gone from being a rootless exile, impoverished writer, and irrelevant ex-terrorist to a position at the very center of power in his country. And although this power was gravely threatened by internal forces and by enemies massing at the borders, it was still possible for a team of forceful and well-meaning men to achieve a great deal and save the country.

But it was not meant to be. As Savinkov regretfully recalled later, the hopes for decisive change that Kerensky had kindled "to a considerable extent turned out to be false."

Upon returning to the capital, Kerensky began to consult about the composition of the new cabinet with various political figures, including the leadership of the Socialist Revolutionary, Menshevik, and Bolshevik parties. Under their sway his resolve faded and he decided to put together a coalition that would satisfy the greatest number of competing interests. This shifted the new cabinet even more to the left, and because of the Petrograd Soviet's influence on a number of members, it was not a body that could prosecute any focused or aggressive agenda. Chernov, as minister of agriculture, made it known that he would be completely opposed to any plan to militarize labor.

Kerensky did not end there. In a way that was typical of him, and would frustrate Savinkov more and more in the weeks ahead, he also changed his mind about several promises he had already made. He decided to continue as minister of war and navy himself, in addition to leading the government as prime minister. What he offered Savinkov instead was the position of director (or vice minister) of the Ministry of War, an important but secondary appointment that answered to the minister.

This was far less than Savinkov expected, and he hesitated; he was not sure that he would be able to accomplish anything in the kind of government that was taking shape. Initially, he even tried to return to the front, but Kerensky insisted that he stay in Petrograd. After a few days, Savinkov decided that he could still use the position to bring discipline to the rear and revitalize it. This would allow him to work in tandem with Kornilov, who, as the new commander-in-chief, would focus on resurrecting the army's combat readiness at the front. Savinkov accepted Kerensky's offer and began to attend cabinet meetings several days before his appointment became official on July 26. He would later also accept the post of vice minister of the navy.

In the Halls of Government

Boris Savinkov had been notorious in Russia for more than a decade, and news of his appointment brought him even more attention, not only at home but abroad. His terrorist past was not forgotten, but he began increasingly to be perceived as a figure of consequence on a governmental level.

In Russian civilian circles, reaction to him was mixed: his pro-war stance and open hostility to the Bolsheviks pleased the political right and alarmed the left. In the military, some frontline generals were willing to forget his past and welcomed his alliance with Kornilov, the new commander-in-chief, seeing them as a team that could turn Russia away from the dead end toward which she was heading. However, other leading senior commanders, some of whom had monarchist sympathies, did not think that a civilian, much less one who almost became a regicide, should be making decisions about the military. The fact that he was even involved, they felt, was evidence that the Provisional Government was incompetent and failing.

By contrast, the Entente's ambassadors to Russia, who watched events in the country very closely, were pleased. When Kerensky's new cabinet was announced, Great Britain's ambassador in Petrograd, Sir George Buchanan, singled Savinkov out in a report to the Foreign Office as one of the "good" men. But then he commented:

> We have come to a curious pass in this country, when one welcomes the appointment of a terrorist, who was one of the chief organizers of the murders of the Grand Duke Serge and Plehve, in the hope that his energy and strength of character may yet save the army. Savinkoff is an ardent advocate of stringent measures for both the restoration of discipline and for the repression of anarchy, and he is credited with having asked Kerensky's permission to go with a couple of regiments to the Tauride Palace to arrest the Soviet. Needless to say that this permission was not given.

The French ambassador, Joseph Noulens, was similarly impressed by Savinkov and described him as a "former terrorist who, since the beginning of the revolution showed himself to be an ardent patriot and statesman . . . His intelligence is keen, and his courage and composure unwavering." Moreover, in Noulens's view, Savinkov's decisiveness compared very favorably to Kerensky's well-known vacillation.

⚬━⚬

Savinkov threw himself into his work without reservation; "This man's supply of energy is enormous," an eyewitness noted. With Kerensky unable to give full attention to the Ministry of War, the scope of Savinkov's duties included everything from dealing with the collapsing front to the problems with discipline and military supplies in the rear. He also did not conceal his antipathy toward Bolshevism and named Stepun, his former comrade in the Seventh Army, as head of the ministry's political department with the task of assembling materials to prosecute Lenin and his comrades for treason. But events were brewing that would not allow time to finish this work.

Countless petitioners and officials deluged Savinkov as well, and he was unable to focus on everyone, no matter how urgent their need. The commanding general of the Kiev military district had to wait in an anteroom for a long time before being admitted. When his turn came, he was disappointed to learn that the acting director was unfamiliar with the situation in Kiev and did not even have time to listen to a full report about it. Then their conversation was interrupted by a telephone call summoning Savinkov to a meeting of the Provisional Government in the Winter Palace. The palace was not a refuge either, as Savinkov discovered when some woman who happened to be passing by on a staircase recognized him and, seizing him by the lapel, insisted that he explain why some "George is being kept in prison?"

The Dignity of the Office

In photographs taken during this time, Savinkov looks like his new prominence suited him very well. When gazing directly into the camera, his expressions range from impassive to dignified to skeptical. In a candid group photograph during a relaxed moment, he and Kornilov are standing side by side in the front row, like equals, looking at each other and smiling easily as they talk.

Savinkov wears the same uniform as when he was a commissar; it is also what his chief, Kerensky, wears. Even though there are still no insignia on it, it helps him blend in when he is with senior army officers, despite their epaulets, medals, saber belts, and resplendent aiguillettes. Uniforms are meant to suppress originality, but Savinkov's shows that he continued to care about his appearance and preserved his fondness for good tailoring. He manages to look more elegant than Kerensky, whose jacket seems made of rougher fabric and is somewhat rumpled. The regulation visored officer's cap that Savinkov adds when out of doors—without the standard cockade—sits sternly just above his narrow eyes. Together with his neat, straight moustache it completes his quasi-military appearance.

Always careful about how he behaved in front of others, and now with the dignity of a new office to uphold, Savinkov began to carry himself more formally in public. When he attended his first meeting of the Provisional Government, Vladimir Lebedev, a Socialist Revolutionary who did not like Savinkov's individualism and aloofness from the Party, noted the stately politeness with which he received greetings from other ministers and the gravity with which he spoke to journalists. It seemed to Lebedev that even the way Savinkov got into an automobile had something "ministerial" about it and that he had "a general's manner" in how he gave orders to his aides. The formality with which Savinkov organized the reception of visitors in the impressive, colonnaded Ministry of War building and his luxurious office decorated with paintings of battles also irritated the more populist and down-to-earth Lebedev.

Ehrenburg, Savinkov's old friend from La Rotonde, stopped by to visit him when he was in Petrograd and could scarcely recognize him. The man he remembered sitting at a table in a bowler and grinning despondently over his glass of cheap brandy was no more. Savinkov now spoke forcefully of the need for drastic measures, for dictatorship, for order. He had become disappointed with Kerensky and called him a "phrasemonger who delights in the sound of his own voice." He had nothing but contempt for the Provisional Government: "These people are out of their depth . . . ," he announced.

Savinkov always chafed when he was short of money and could not afford comforts and indulgences. But although the Russian economy was deteriorating badly during the summer of 1917, his new position provided some important, if still relative, material benefits. One was an official private car, still a rarity in Russia, where horses would dominate until the late 1920s. After the February Revolution, the Provisional Government took over two dozen automobiles from the tsar's garage, and Savinkov was assigned number 13, a luxurious, dark-green French Turcat-Méry limousine that styled itself "The Car of the Connoisseur."

Savinkov was also spared having to endure many of the hardships faced by the vast majority of Petrograd's population, for whom the sense of national crisis was aggravated by the breakdown of all aspects of daily life. Other than rare members of two competing militias, whose existence reflected the rancorous split between the Provisional Government and the Petrograd Soviet, there were few signs of police on the streets and traffic went unregulated. Bands of bored-looking soldiers wandered around the city, chewing sunflower seeds, spitting out the husks, and napping in parks. Ehrenburg saw two officers steal a bag of sugar from a woman and divide their booty in full view of passersby.

Basic foodstuffs were in short supply, and people stood in long lines for hours outside bread and other shops for their rations. The shortages were made more severe by the influx of soldiers and refugees into the city, whose population swelled from two to three million. Even when food was available, as in the luxurious Astoria Hotel on Saint Isaac's Square, the menu was very limited. One foreign visitor noted that the first course at lunch was "chopped meat and *kasha* [porridge] stuffed into cabbage leaves, and the second the same chopped meat and *kasha* inadequately hidden by the half of a cucumber." There were widespread fears that there would be famine during the coming winter. Shoes, warm clothing, and fuel were all either unavailable or in short supply, which made prices soar. The change from the prewar years seemed to be reflected even in the new currency—nicknamed Kerenki after Kerensky—that was issued by the Provisional Government to replace the old tsarist rubles.

Despite the forbidding array of tasks he faced in the Ministry of War, Savinkov did not entirely abandon his literary and artistic interests. He sought out his old friend Alexey Remizov, the writer with whom he had been in Vologda exile and had not seen for a decade. Physically, Savinkov looked the same, Remizov found, except that he was "even more stone-like" and his narrow eyes seemed even less visible. The years that passed did not make any difference and they talked easily about Savinkov's poetry and other famous poets of the day. Savinkov also regularly visited his old friends and literary mentors the Merezhkovskys, who had returned to their apartment in Petrograd and who were much impressed by his transformation into a willful governmental figure. He regaled them with the latest political developments of the day, which unfolded with kaleidoscopic unpredictability, but also spent time with Zinaida reciting his old poetry from memory and transcribing it, since he had left his papers with Evgeniya in Nice.

Another quasi-social, quasi-political indulgence he allowed himself was joining a Masonic lodge during the summer of 1917, the Great East of the Peoples of Russia. Rather than being concerned with esoteric knowledge, however, the lodge in Petrograd resembled a club for influential men interested in establishing a Russian democratic republic and transforming the Russian empire with its many subject peoples into a federated union of national republics. The members also opposed concluding a separate peace with Germany and were committed to remaining loyal to the Entente, especially France. Some dozen and a half Masons were either ministers or vice ministers in the various coalition cabinets of the Provisional Government, including Kerensky, and there is evidence that he chose candidates for different posts to a considerable extent based on whether or not they were Masons. Savinkov was apparently not an active member and did not take the movement seriously, except for its political stance.

The Kornilov Affair

Boris Savinkov's position as director of the Ministry of War gave him real power in the Provisional Government, and he did not wait long to use it. Just days after he was appointed, he initiated an extraordinary series of events that he believed would save Russia and eliminate the Bolsheviks as a political force. In his view, the first could not happen without the second.

When Savinkov and Kornilov assumed their new positions at the end of July, both saw very clearly that the situation at the front and behind the lines was so disastrous that this would be their last chance to change anything. On August 3, Kornilov came to Petrograd to report to the government and brought with him the draft of a proposal, which he and Savinkov had discussed earlier, for radical reforms in the army and on the home front. Before submitting it to Kerensky for discussion by the cabinet, he asked Savinkov's opinion.

Savinkov replied that the proposal had to be completely rewritten. First, it was focused too narrowly on military matters and needed to be broadened into an all-encompassing government policy. And second, it had to be brought into line with the legislative procedures of the Provisional Government, rather than being conceived as a strategy that could be imposed by fiat.

Kornilov again accepted Savinkov's judgment. He agreed to delay presenting the proposal to Kerensky for a week, until Savinkov's closest aide in the Ministry of War, Maximilian Filonenko, a junior officer who had also been Kornilov's commissar, finished revising it.

Savinkov needed Kornilov's revised proposal for a goal that was, in its own way, as audacious as what he had tried to achieve when he was a terrorist—to change not just the policies of the Russian government but its entire composition. He wanted to use an established governmental procedure to remove the current cabinet and replace it with one similar to what Kerensky had described after the military conference in Mogilyov, before he abandoned it under pressure from the left.

The key to Savinkov's plan was to get Kerensky to accept Kornilov's revised proposal. If he did, and if a majority of the cabinet also voted in favor of it, which was likely, a number of the more radical ministers whom Kerensky had appointed to placate the Soviet would inevitably vote against it and thus be forced to resign. As a result, the entire cabinet would have to be restructured, the Soviet's influence on the government would be greatly reduced, and the Bolsheviks, who were still in a weakened state, could be prosecuted for treason. If everything went according to plan, Savinkov would have engineered the goal he had from the beginning of his appointment as a commissar: a government that was solidly behind the war effort and that came to power through due process.

But that was not all. Savinkov also wanted expanded power for himself as a member of a triumvirate that would form the core of the new government. The other two members would be Kornilov, who was essential because of his reputation and authority among the military, and Kerensky, who would remain as prime minister and be the guardian of the ideals of the February Revolution. As Savinkov explained to Gippius, his close confidante while he was in the middle of his elaborate plotting,

> [Kornilov] loves freedom, I know this with complete certainty. But Russia for him comes first and freedom—second. As for Kerensky, freedom and the revolution come first and Russia—second. In my case . . . both of these unite into one. There is no first or second place. They are indivisible. That is the reason why I absolutely want to unite Kerensky and Kornilov now.

Savinkov believed he was uniquely capable of mediating between Kerensky and Kornilov. He also told Gippius what choice he would make if Kornilov were to fall under the influence of the reactionary "dark elements" in the army's headquarters in Mogilyov and try to seize power by himself:

Of course, I would not remain with Kornilov. I don't believe in him without Kerensky. I said this to Kornilov's face. And I said it bluntly: then we would be enemies . . . As a soldier, he understood me immediately and agreed. I see Kerensky now as the indispensable head of a possible Russian government. I serve Kerensky and not Kornilov. But I don't believe that Kerensky alone can save Russia and freedom . . . And I can't imagine how I can serve Kerensky if he decides that he wants to remain alone and to continue with the wavering policies that he is pursuing now.

If Savinkov's plan worked, he would become the key figure in the *troika* that would run the Russian government.

While he waited for his aide to finish revising Kornilov's proposal, Savinkov tried to prepare Kerensky for the four changes it would contain. The first and most radical would also require the most persuasion—the introduction of the death penalty on the home front for civilian and military personnel whose crimes had a bearing on issues of national defense and that would be handed down by new "military-revolutionary tribunals." This was a step toward declaring martial law to mobilize the entire country for the war effort and went openly against the spirit of the Revolution. The second and third provisions were extensions of the first—the introduction of military control over the railroads, which were falling ever deeper into chaos, and the militarization of war industries, whose production had declined catastrophically, by between 40 and 80 percent. The final provision concerned the notorious "Order No. 1" and returned command authority to officers while curtailing the function of military committees.

Between August 3 and 8, Savinkov tried on three separate occasions to bring the key point about introducing the death penalty to Kerensky's attention; he reasoned that if Kerensky accepted this one, the others would follow. The matter was also very urgent. Each day lost meant an advantage for the Germans, who were preparing to attack Riga, the biggest city of the Governorate of Livonia in the northwest of the country (now the capital of Latvia). In a few days, Kerensky was to leave for a major state conference that he had convened in Moscow to rally public support, and Savinkov wanted him to have the new policies in hand so that he could announce them at the momentous event.

But on August 8, after seeming to disregard Savinkov's earlier urgings, Kerensky suddenly announced that he would "never, under any circumstances" agree to a law that established military-revolutionary tribunals for civilians. He also unexpectedly declared that he did not trust Kornilov and was thinking of dismissing him and taking over as commander-in-chief himself, even though he had no military experience.

In one instant, all Savinkov's hopes collapsed. And because he had staked his appointment on a proposal that his direct superior rejected, he felt obligated to offer his immediate resignation from the ministry.

However, this would not be the end of Savinkov's career in the Provisional Government, although what followed was dictated less by his renewed efforts than by Kerensky's suspiciousness, duplicity, and growing emotional instability. Contrary to the impression Kerensky produced with his preoccupied manner during the last few days, he had paid attention to Savinkov's attempts to persuade him to accept Kornilov's revised program. But the paradoxical result was that he became fixated on the idea that Kornilov was complicit in plans for a right-wing coup. And because of the vast authority that happened to become concentrated in Kerensky's hands, he and not Boris Savinkov became the arbiter of Russia's fate.

The Kornilov Affair and Kerensky's Plot

Kerensky expected the state conference that opened in Moscow on August 14 to be an apotheosis of him and his government. Instead, when Kornilov arrived, crowds cheered and carried him aloft, and right-wing delegates responded to his speech, which Kerensky had originally tried to prevent altogether, with prolonged and rapturous applause. The sight shocked Kerensky, and he took it as a personal offense. It also confirmed his belief that a right-wing coup was underway and that Kornilov was involved.

In reality, nothing could have been further from the truth. As Kornilov had recently confided to his chief of staff, "I am not a counterrevolutionary . . . I despise the old regime, which badly mistreated my family." He knew that there could be no return to the past and wanted a strong government only so that it could end the war honorably and lead the country to free elections that would determine its future.

Filled with disquieting impressions of the Moscow conference and wracked by paranoia, Kerensky returned to Petrograd on August 17. He immediately launched a surreptitious campaign to thwart what he thought of as a "Bonapartist" coup against him (he later admitted that his political decisions in 1917 were heavily influenced by what he believed were the lessons of the French Revolution over a century earlier). The key tactic Kerensky chose was *provokatsiya*, or "provoking" Kornilov to carry out an action that would allow Kerensky to accuse him of treason. It was, in other words, a version of what Azef did when he organized terrorist actions and then gave up the participants to the police. Unbeknownst to Savinkov, his past was about to be repeated, except that this time he would be drawn into a deception that would determine the fate of his country.

Kerensky began by summoning Savinkov to the Winter Palace, where he now worked and lived, and informed him that he had changed his mind, agreed in principle with all aspects of Kornilov's program, and wanted Savinkov back in the government. To patch things up between them Kerensky also put on a self-abnegating performance and half-apologized to Savinkov for his insulting accusations of treason earlier. It worked. Savinkov was elated by the unexpected turn of events. He withdrew his resignation and returned to his duties "with a feeling of great satisfaction." All his hopes that had been dashed a week earlier were now resurrected and the path to the country's salvation seemed clear.

From Savinkov's perspective, Kerensky's change of heart also happened none too soon. On August 19, the Germans began their advance on Riga. The undisciplined and propagandized Russian troops retreated, with the result that the city fell to the Germans five days later. Petrograd, which was 300 miles to the northeast, was next.

Making the historical moment even more dangerous, in mid-August Savinkov received information from French intelligence that the Bolsheviks were planning another coup at the beginning of September. In addition, persistent reports kept arriving about a plot by army officers against the Provisional Government, although without Kornilov's participation. Kerensky did not believe that the Bolsheviks were a danger, but he saw the concatenation of threats as an opportunity to neutralize Kornilov, whom he now considered his archenemy.

On Sunday, August 20, Savinkov informed Kerensky that the statutes regarding new trials and the death penalty were ready. He also proposed that Petrograd and its environs be placed under martial law and that troops be brought into the city to suppress the Bolsheviks before they began their rising. To Savinkov's great satisfaction, Kerensky agreed, giving Savinkov the impression that he had "finally and irrevocably" accepted the program suggested by Kornilov. Most importantly for his own purpose, Kerensky authorized Savinkov to ask Kornilov to send a cavalry corps to the capital to enforce martial law and help defend the Provisional Government from the Bolsheviks. Although this seemed to be in support of Savinkov's plans, it was actually part of Kerensky's intended *provokatsiya*.

When Savinkov arrived in Kornilov's headquarters in Mogilyov on Monday, August 21, he found him in a very irritated state because of Kerensky's indecisiveness and equivocal politics. Kornilov bluntly announced that he could no longer serve a government with such a "weak-willed" prime minister or such "suspicious" members of the cabinet as Chernov, who was known to share state secrets with his friends in the Soviet who, in turn, leaked them to the Germans. But after Savinkov reported all the strong measures that Kerensky had just approved, the commander-in-chief admitted that he was reassured. Progress on the remaining matters was quick: Kornilov agreed to arrest any officers who were involved in the antigovernment conspiracy, worked out the borders of the Petrograd military district, and agreed to sending the Third Cavalry Corps to defend the government and give teeth to its decrees.

Everything seemed to be in place for a dramatic change in the Provisional Government's direction. Savinkov returned to Petrograd on Thursday, August 24, expecting that the new statutes had been authorized by Kerensky during his absence and accepted by the cabinet. But to his surprise, neither had happened yet. The following day, when he went to report to Kerensky and asked him to sign the proposal two times, Kerensky refused. Savinkov did so twice again a day later, on the morning of Saturday, August 26, with the same result.

Savinkov could not understand what was holding Kerensky back from fulfilling the promise he had made over a week earlier. He was also getting increasingly nervous that any further delay could in fact stoke a right-wing rebellion at military headquarters. When Kerensky refused to sign for the second time on Saturday, Savinkov asked for a private meeting. He did not mince words this time: the proposal Kerensky was rejecting had been prepared on his orders, his "indecisiveness was criminal," his "weakmindedness was destroying Russia," and if it were anyone else standing before him, Savinkov would be speaking with him "using entirely different language." The reprimands appeared to work, and Kerensky promised that he would sign the proposal that same day and also present it to the cabinet in the evening. Savinkov left the Winter Palace convinced that this time he had at last succeeded.

What Savinkov did not know was that Kerensky had lied to him again because of personal political calculations. The previous week, on August 18, a motion sponsored by the Bolsheviks in the Soviet to annul the death penalty for frontline troops was approved overwhelmingly by a vote of 850 to 4. In view of this, the chance that the Soviet would now accept the death penalty in the rear was nil, and Kerensky could not be seen as supporting any of Kornilov's harsh new proposals. The liberal and conservative factions reviled Kerensky, and his sole, even if shaky, political base was the more radical left; for his own survival he would do whatever he could to accommodate the Soviet.

When Savinkov returned to the Winter Palace on the evening of Saturday, August 26, he was exultant. He was looking forward to the discussion of the proposed statutes by the cabinet, as Kerensky had promised him that morning, and he fully expected them to be adopted with all the consequences for revamping the cabinet that would follow. He had also gotten word that the Third Cavalry Corps was scheduled to reach the capital in just a few days.

The Kornilov Affair as Hoax

The Provisional Government's cabinet meetings were held in what might seem to be an incongruous location for a populist and socialist government that had come into existence through revolution—the famous Malachite Hall of the Winter Palace. This was a large, ornate former living and reception space dating from the time of Nicholas I in the 1830s that got its name from the bright-green, veined, semiprecious stone used in a series of columns running along the walls as well as in two fireplace surrounds and several large vases. The contrast of the green with the abundant gold leaf on the elaborately worked plaster ceiling, the massive doors, the intricately inlaid wooden floors, and the raspberry colored drapes made for an especially rich decorative effect (which survives to this day).

Savinkov had been to important meetings in the hall before, but what happened on the evening of August 26 would mark it indelibly as the site of a catastrophe. As he and the ministers were gathering, he was informed that Kerensky wanted to see him in his private office, which was a few doors away, in what had been Nicholas II's library. This room was decorated in a heavy and gloomy Gothic style, which was a fitting setting for the grotesque scene that ensued.

When Savinkov walked into the library he saw Kerensky, pale and seemingly beside himself, hurrying toward him with a piece of paper in his hand. Shaking it as if it were the cause of his agitation, he proclaimed dramatically that "General Kornilov's conspiracy has been discovered" and that he would be removed immediately from his position as commander-in-chief because he was a "traitor."

Kerensky then silently handed the paper to Savinkov, who read what was scribbled on it. He could not believe his eyes. Signed by someone named "V. Lvov," it was a list of three "proposals" by Kornilov—that martial law be proclaimed in Petrograd, that all military and civil authority be placed in his hands, and that the entire Provisional Government resign until he forms a new cabinet.

Savinkov scarcely knew who this "V. Lvov" was and had no idea why he was involved in Kornilov's "proposals." He told Kerensky it was so absurdly unlikely that the "proposals" actually came from Kornilov that they must be "a hoax." He also insisted that Kornilov could not be involved in a plot and that there had been some terrible misunderstanding. But Kerensky rejected the idea, and claimed that he had verified the matter by contacting Kornilov himself.

The Kornilov Affair as Tragicomedy

Unaware of Kerensky's secret machinations, and believing that reason and goodwill could still prevail, Savinkov began to urge Kerensky to clarify matters with Kornilov and try to come to an agreement without making the rift between them public; otherwise, he added, the only beneficiaries would be the Germans. Kerensky categorically refused, saying that it was too late for any accommodation and that he had already sent a telegram to Kornilov relieving him of his post and ordering him to leave the army.

Nevertheless, Savinkov and a number of cabinet members and other prominent public figures tried to salvage the situation. That same night Savinkov went from the Winter Palace to the Ministry of War, where there was a Hughes telegraph, which printed regular characters on paper, so that he could communicate with Kornilov directly, but because of the slowness of the process and various interruptions their exchange did not end until well into Sunday the twenty-seventh.

In his initial communication Savinkov addressed Kornilov in the official manner of a member of the government who was facing a possible mutineer. Respectfully but firmly, he demanded that Kornilov submit to the Provisional Government, surrender his position, and leave the active army. Despite Savinkov's lofty tone and harsh demands, Kornilov kept his temper and explained in detail what had transpired among himself, Lvov, and Kerensky to produce the current crisis. As Savinkov and the others read Kornilov's long transmission, they concluded that the crisis was due to a misunderstanding: Kornilov had never actually demanded dictatorial powers or asked Lvov to act on his behalf. But because Kornilov felt grievously wronged by Kerensky, he concluded by writing that he would not step down as commander-in-chief. It was the height of irony that he thus formally became a mutineer after he had been falsely accused of being one and after he had convinced Savinkov that he was innocent.

Thinking that a way out of the crisis had been found, Savinkov hurried back to the Winter Palace to inform Kerensky. If Kerensky would now show the same restraint in dealing with the charge of treason against Kornilov as he had against Lenin after the July coup (where evidence of Lenin's guilt was incontrovertible), then the breach with Kornilov could be quickly healed.

<hr>

Sunday, August 27, was a bright and mild day, and although Savinkov had not slept the previous night, he entered the Winter Palace buoyant with hope that the information he was bringing would allow the conflict between Kerensky and Kornilov to be resolved. No word had yet reached the newspapers about Kornilov's "rebellion," and in an interview Savinkov even asserted that the general "had the full trust" of the government.

But Savinkov was wrong, and it was too late. He did not know that Kerensky had closed all avenues to reconciliation with Kornilov and even refused an offer from Allied ambassadors to mediate between them. He had also already sent an announcement that the commander-in-chief was a traitor to all the newspapers despite his promise that he would not act until Savinkov's communication with Kornilov was completed. Eyewitnesses reported that Kerensky had become hysterical, ranting and screaming about Kornilov's treason as he dashed about the sumptuously decorated halls of the palace and swearing that he would protect the Revolution. People tried to reason with him without success, to stop him for a minute to get his attention, but he seemed not even to hear what others were saying. His psychic state was aggravated by his dependency on morphine and drink, which he used to alleviate pain from stomach, lung, and kidney problems.

The situation had now become, in Savinkov's characterization, "irreparable."

There was another shock: Kerensky had assumed dictatorial powers while Savinkov had been on the telegraph with Kornilov. At a cabinet meeting that he called for midnight on Saturday, August 26, Kerensky announced that he needed "full authority" to deal with the military coup d'état. The ministers all agreed and resigned their posts, ceding their duties to Kerensky, which effectively ended the Provisional Government, although in a way that preserved the trappings of legitimacy.

In Mogilyov, Kornilov received Kerensky's telegram stripping him of his position and ordering him to Petrograd on the morning of Sunday, August 27. An eyewitness remembered that the impression it produced on everyone at headquarters was like "that of a bomb that had exploded." Kerensky's accusation against him turned Kornilov's despondency into rage because it impugned what he valued most—his lifelong patriotism. In response he sent his own message to all commanders at the front that branded Kerensky's announcement "a grand provocation" against him and claimed that the Provisional Government "under pressure from the Bolshevik majority in the Soviet, acts in full accord with the plans of the German General Staff, kills the army and shakes the country internally." He then carried out the formal break with the government of which he had been accused:

> My painful consciousness of the inescapable downfall of our
> country commands me during these fearsome moments to summon
> all Russian people to the salvation of their dying motherland . . .

I, General Kornilov, the son of a Cossack peasant, declare to each
and all that I personally desire nothing but to save Great Russia,
and I swear to lead the people through victory over the enemy to
the Constituent Assembly, where it will decide its own destiny and
choose the form of its new political life.

Savinkov eventually found out that the list of "proposals" that Kornilov supposedly made was the product of Kerensky's eagerness to sink the general. He
had taken advantage of the opportunity presented to him by his acquaintance
Vladimir Lvov, a former member of the Duma and Procurator of the Holy Synod
in the Provisional Government, who had decided on his own foolish initiative
to meddle in high affairs of state by trying to "mediate" between Kerensky
and Kornilov. The entire sorry affair was brought about by a perfect storm of
additional errors, deceptions, and misunderstandings: Kornilov's naïveté and
thoughtlessness in not verifying Lvov's identity when he presented himself
as Kerensky's emissary, Lvov's garbling Kornilov's responses to his questions,
Kerensky's lies to Kornilov during his crucial "verification" by telegraph, and,
as a subsequent investigation ascertained, Kerensky's cynical decision to twist
Lvov's absurd report to suit his own purposes. To this day, it is unclear what
exactly motivated Lvov, except for a desire to play a role in Russian history. And
he succeeded in a way that is without precedent in terms of the consequences.

Governor-General of Petrograd

To be a credible threat, a mutiny requires mutineers—an actual massing of men.
Kerensky was able to conjure them up by exploiting the fact that Kornilov's
troops were approaching Petrograd. Although they were coming as a result of
the request that he himself had authorized Savinkov to make to Kornilov, with the
express purpose of defending the Provisional Government from a Bolshevik
coup, now that the commander-in-chief had broken with the government and
been branded a traitor, the troops could be redefined as agents of his mutiny.

Kerensky also needed to mount a defense against the invented enemy that
was threatening the state. With a "heavy heart," as Stepun characterized it,

Savinkov offered his services as governor-general of Petrograd, and thus as the commander of all the forces that would be arrayed against Kornilov. Stepun explained that Savinkov had no choice, because if he sided with Kornilov after his rebellion against the democratic socialist Kerensky, it would have meant that Savinkov was renouncing his entire previous life. Even if Savinkov had resigned from Kerensky's government at a time like this, it would have been seen as tacit support for Kornilov.

Savinkov's offer surprised Kerensky, but he accepted it, and on Monday, August 28, appointed him the military governor-general of Petrograd. Savinkov's close collaboration with Kornilov did not disqualify him from the position in Kerensky's eyes, because he believed that Kornilov had begun his rebellion behind Savinkov's back.

⊶

Even in a life as filled with dramatic contradictions as Boris Savinkov's, this turn of events stands out for its paradoxicality, as he was himself well aware. He had been Kornilov's greatest advocate in the Provisional Government for months and admitted that he still "shared 'Kornilov's program' completely" after he accepted the new post. He felt personal "affection" for Kornilov and "believed deeply in his selflessness and whole-hearted love for the motherland." He also sympathized with him in simple human terms because of the insults and deception he had suffered at Kerensky's hands, and because of his grief over the fate of the army and his heartache for Russia.

Why, then, did Savinkov turn against him?

Because he considered himself to be a "military service member" who owed obedience to his commander, Kerensky. Even when a hysterical Kerensky delivered an unjustified verbal dressing down to him, Savinkov recalled that he took it "like a soldier," standing silently and at attention.

Savinkov also had a long-standing ideological commitment, a principle about which he had explicitly warned Kornilov on several occasions and which he could not surrender: "I became an enemy of General Kornilov in the same way that I would become the enemy of anyone who would try to establish a personal dictatorship because I had spent my entire life fighting for a republic." The instability in the army made Savinkov fear as well the possibility that reactionary right-wing elements in the army, including monarchists, might join Kornilov.

But no one rallied to Kornilov's side. During the three days after he broke with the Provisional Government and was anathematized by Kerensky, Kornilov tried to enlist support from the regular army and the Cossacks, and even ordered General Krymov, who was approaching Petrograd with the Third Corps, to occupy the city. However, all he got was moral support from the top generals, who also sent cables to Kerensky protesting how Kornilov was being treated. No military units joined him, and no conservative politicians did either.

⚬—⬥—⚬

Savinkov's first act when he assumed his new post was to issue a public proclamation condemning the man he admired. This can be seen as the classic tragic choice—duty over personal interest. But it could also be seen as a spectacular illustration of the "stupid honesty" that Savinkov's one-time friend Vera Figner said characterized the Socialist Revolutionaries in general. Indeed, years later, when thinking about this period in his life and his relations with Kerensky and Kornilov, Savinkov wrote something very similar: "I was absolutely honest with regard to both of them. Not even just honest but stubbornly and truthfully stupid."

Why "stupid"? Because Kornilov had rebelled against an inept regime whose only virtue was that it was born in revolution and whose greatest failing was that it was unable to defend that revolution's achievements. In light of Savinkov's acute sense of the dangers posed by the Bolsheviks to the principles that he valued above all else, it is unclear what he hoped to achieve by abandoning Kornilov, who was also dedicated to preserving the same revolutionary principles. If Savinkov had joined him and helped him gather support—and Kornilov had many sympathizers who could have been mobilized by a skilled agitator—together they could have changed history. Was adhering to the oath of loyalty that Savinkov took to Kerensky's government worth it?

This was also the second time in Savinkov's life that his determined pursuit of a goal resulted in the opposite of what he wanted. As in his involvement with Azef, he once again became the unwitting tool of someone else's machinations. And, as also with Azef, he succumbed because of his steadfast commitment to two principles that regrettably had little to do with the political realities surrounding him: loyalty and honor.

Once again, Boris Savinkov's character proved to be his destiny.

Arming the Bolsheviks

To stop the Third Corps from occupying Petrograd, Kerensky turned to the Executive Committee of the Soviet of Workers' and Soldiers' Deputies for armed help. The only force the committee could call upon was the Bolshevik Military Organization, which effectively made it the Soviet's fighting arm. To reinforce the troops loyal to the Provisional Government, Kerensky also distributed 40,000 rifles to the city's workers, most of whom became members of Bolshevik militias—the Red Guards—and would keep their guns after the Kornilov affair was over. Finally, Kerensky released almost all the Bolsheviks who were still in prison after the July coup as a sign that their sins were now forgiven.

It fell to Savinkov to coordinate the defense of the city. Waves of panic rolled through the Winter Palace. One of Kerensky's closest ministers resigned; others stopped sleeping at home out of fear that they would be arrested by Kornilov's followers. Kerensky's deputy urged that the Provisional Government cede all its power to the Soviet of Workers' and Soldiers' Deputies. The makeup of patrols by military cadets guarding the palace had to be changed several times a night because their loyalty to Kerensky was suspect. Radicalized sailors from the cruiser *Avrora* (soon to play a far more prominent role in Russian history) arrived to defend the palace and Kerensky.

The Soviet of Workers' and Soldiers' Deputies also became a hive of chaotic activity. Chernov rushed to Tsarskoye Selo to inspect personally preparations for the city's defense. Many in the Soviet did not trust Savinkov because of his former ties to Kornilov. Some deputies insisted that members of the Soviet's Executive Committee be present at Savinkov's military headquarters to control any orders he issued. Others spied on him and reported conversations they found suspicious to Kerensky, who either believed them or pretended that he did.

In the end, it was all for nothing. Savinkov's task proved chimerical, because there was never any real danger from the Third Corps. When some of the first units arrived, they came under light fire from the city's defenders on the outskirts of Petrograd. Workers from the city also dismantled railway tracks to prevent the troop trains from going any farther. But there was no bloodshed. On Tuesday, August 29, Kerensky sent a telegram to General Krymov, the commander of the Third Corps, telling him that all was quiet in the city and ordering him to stop his advance and prepare to move the corps to Narva, a city 100 miles to the west (in what is now Estonia). One after another, as the commanders of the divisions composing the corps realized that the city had not been seized by the Bolsheviks, they stopped and swore allegiance to the Provisional Government.

There were moments of tragicomedy and absurdity. Gippius, who feverishly gathered information from all sources including eyewitnesses, described the encounter between the main body of "Kornilov's" troops and soldiers from the city's garrison near Luga, some 100 miles south of the capital. The two forces stopped opposite each other, bewildered by what was happening. The "Kornilovites" were especially amazed: they were on their way "to defend the Provisional Government" and met the "enemy" who is also going "to defend the Provisional Government." So, they stood around for a while, thinking, but could not understand anything. Then, recalling the lessons of agitators at the front that "one should fraternize with the enemy," they began to fraternize avidly. What kind of "rebellion" was it, Gippius asked in her diary, when Kornilov, its ostensible instigator and commander, never even left his headquarters in Mogilyov? She also credited Savinkov with doing all he could to prevent any serious clashes between the corps and the Petrograd garrison.

<hr>

Despite the absence of any actual violence between the city's "defenders" and "attackers," the rhetoric coming out of the Winter Palace was triumphal: "Complete victory of the Petrograd garrison over Kornilov's troops." Kerensky had General Krymov of the Third Corps arrested and brought to the palace on Thursday, August 31. Although he was soon released, Krymov, feeling insulted and upset at how he had been treated, went to a friend's apartment and shot himself.

However, Savinkov understood perfectly well what had really happened: "It was not Kerensky, not the Executive Committee [of the Soviet], not the workers, not the sailors, not the regional military headquarters [where he was in charge], and not the Tsarskoye Selo infantry that repelled General Kornilov's action. Having reached Tsarskoye Selo, it weakened and fell apart by itself."

<hr>

How did Savinkov evaluate his own role in the Kornilov affair? In his recollections, he did not question his decision to defend the Provisional Government, despite his disdain for it. But he expressed regret in one of his memoirs for the price he paid for his principled stance: "In this way I became the enemy of a man whom I respected deeply, whom I viewed as irreproachable in all respects, and whose upright and fearless character instilled in me a feeling of affection."

Savinkov could also not have gotten much satisfaction from what happened to Kornilov after the affair. As the Third Corps's "advance" on the capital dissipated, Kornilov became convinced that he had been deliberately trapped by Kerensky and betrayed by Savinkov. He became so despondent that his wife feared he might commit suicide and persuaded him to give up his revolver. He did not resist when General Alexeyev arrived in Mogilyov on Friday, September 1, to arrest him and take over his command—it had taken Kerensky three days to find a replacement, and none of the other senior generals would take the post.

After being held briefly in Mogilyov, Kornilov and thirty other officers suspected of involvement in his attempted "coup" were moved thirty miles south to a prison in Bykhov Fortress. His loyal Tekke Turkoman bodyguards followed him to protect against attempts by revolutionary-minded soldiers to harm the "traitor." (The danger was real because the way the Provisional Government had propagandized the "Kornilov Rebellion" led to a sharp increase in attacks and murders of officers by enlisted men.) Two months later, after the Bolsheviks seized power, Kornilov and others escaped from Bykhov to the Cossack territories on the lower reaches of the Don River. There, with several other generals including Alexeyev, Kornilov founded the Volunteer, or "White" Army to fight the Bolsheviks. The official commission that was appointed to investigate the Kornilov affair completed its report in the middle of 1918, when the Bolsheviks were in power, and completely exonerated Kornilov; it also accused Kerensky of deliberately distorting the truth.

There were unexpected consequences of the affair for Savinkov as well. On Thursday, August 31, Kerensky telephoned him and dismissed him from his post as military governor-general of Petrograd. His appointment had lasted only three days. Savinkov understood where this was leading and that evening went to the Winter Palace to personally submit his resignation as director of the ministries of the army and the navy (the latter post had been added to his duties just eleven days earlier). Kerensky was in a frenzied state and delivered another theatrical performance, embracing Savinkov and assuring him that "he trusts him completely." Savinkov replied that "he, for one, can no longer trust him about anything at all." Kerensky did not offer to keep him in reserve for another position in the Provisional Government.

The abruptness with which Kerensky got rid of Savinkov was the result of a demand made by the Soviet of Workers' and Soldiers' Deputies, which was now under the increasing control of the Bolsheviks. Many of the more radical members of the Soviet did not believe that Savinkov's turn against Kornilov had been sincere. They also blamed Kerensky for opening the door to Kornilov's rebellion by appointing him as commander-in-chief and reinstating the death penalty at the front. To keep what little support he had, Kerensky strived to placate the Soviet in any way that he could.

Savinkov's comrades in the Socialist Revolutionary Party also began their own, parallel campaign against him. Chernov wanted Savinkov to be arrested for his complicity in counterrevolution: he accused him of attempts "to destroy democracy" and turn "the country into a barracks." As a result, the Party's Central Committee demanded that Savinkov appear before it to explain his role in the Kornilov affair. Savinkov replied that he was willing in principle but could not do so in the presence of individuals who had ties of any kind with the enemy, such as Mark Natanson, who, like Lenin, was transported into Russia by the Germans, had a "defeatist" stance toward the war, and supported the Bolsheviks. There had been friction between Savinkov and the Socialist Revolutionary hierarchy before, and he had not been active in the Party for years, but this was the end. The Central Committee expelled him in absentia. He had been a member for fifteen years.

A Civilian

Savinkov took the sudden change in his fortune philosophically, or perhaps fatalistically. The failure of grand plans was hardly a new experience for him after his years in the Combat Organization, which also helped him develop deep reserves of determination to regroup and fight on. Being demoted to civilian life left him with limited possibilities for action, but his intentions did not become peaceable.

Only a few days after he left the government and Kornilov had been taken to prison, Savinkov was invited by officers from the famous Native Division to a celebration in his honor. Stepun, who accompanied him, was perplexed that this would have been done by men from such an "especially reactionary" unit, one that was personally, in fact fiercely, loyal to Kornilov. Savinkov enjoyed himself thoroughly and Stepun concluded that the officers "felt that even after his victory over Kornilov, in his soul Savinkov remained a Kornilovite."

In a similarly unpredictable way, Savinkov also began to ally himself with Cossacks, who had also been among Kornilov's strongest supporters. Despite the fiasco of the Kornilov affair, the Third Cavalry Corps had shown that Cossacks preserved their sense of patriotism and duty more fully than the vast majority of regular army units. And although some Cossacks were affected by pro-Bolshevik agitators, most opposed the "Bolshevization" of the Soviet and the Revolution. Savinkov's formal association with Cossacks began in September 1917, when he started to explore the possibility of starting a newspaper that would advance their patriotic and militaristic views. He would turn to them for more important collaboration in October. This was another step on his path toward the right, which seems paradoxical only if one forgets that his motivation was the defense of the socialist February Revolution from what he saw as usurpers on the far left.

The British Agent

Savinkov's convictions that the Bolsheviks must be resisted actively and that Russia had to be kept in the war became well known not only at home but in Allied circles as well. His terrorist past and his novels, which had been translated into several languages, added to the resonance of his name. For these reasons, when Great Britain and the United States collaborated on sending a secret agent to Petrograd with the aim of doing whatever he could to keep Russia in the war, the man quickly found his way to Savinkov.

William, or "W.," Somerset Maugham was already a well-known English writer, with ten plays produced and ten novels published, when he took on this mission. He arrived in Petrograd at the end of August 1917, after crossing the United States, the Pacific, and Siberia under the cover of being a journalist. He admired Russian literature, had read Savinkov's novels, and was very curious to meet "the boldest and most determined of the terrorists during the last years of the Czarist regime."

Petrograd's appearance depressed Maugham. The city looked terribly dirty, with mud everywhere in the streets and splashed onto buildings as high as first-floor windows, missing pavement blocks, and grass growing between cobblestones of the formerly grand squares. Much of the population looked shabby, wizened, and hungry, and seemed to move about or wait in food lines with fatalistic resignation. But it was in Maugham's nature to observe and collect original personalities and he believed that walking on Nevsky Boulevard, the capital's main thoroughfare, had allowed him to see "the whole gallery of the characters of the great Russian novels so that you could put a name to one after the other."

For their first meeting Savinkov invited Maugham to dinner in a private room at the Bear, one of the most famous restaurants in the capital and just a few minutes' walk from Palace Square. Despite the shortages of food and fuel and continuing social upheavals, it was still trying to maintain its reputation for old Russian hospitality. Maugham had some Russian, but they spoke French, which was Maugham's first language.

Maugham was forty-three, shorter than average in height, and had an English face with a wide jaw and a determined, somewhat grim set to his thin-lipped mouth. He also stammered. Savinkov was thirty-eight but looked older, which lead Maugham to guess that he was between forty and fifty. He found Savinkov physically unappealing, concluding that he had "the prosperous, respectable look of a manager of a bank. There was nothing violent in his appearance," and he held himself in a way that was "quiet, reserved and modest."

But if Maugham was disappointed by the contrast between Savinkov's reputation and his placid mien, he found what he was looking for in the way Savinkov spoke. What first impressed him was Savinkov's command of French, which he thought was "excellent," despite—as Maugham noted pedantically in his reminiscences—the occasional mistakes he made in gender. He found Savinkov's voice to be "soft and pleasant" and appreciated that he spoke deliberately and clearly, choosing his words very precisely. In light of Maugham's own urbanity and extensive work on dialogue in his plays, the summary judgment he made of Savinkov is especially noteworthy: "I had never heard such a captivating talker. He was grave when the subject demanded gravity, humorous when there was occasion for humour, and . . . wonderfully persuasive."

The way Savinkov spoke also allowed Maugham to conclude that Savinkov deserved his reputation: "The deliberation of his speech, the impressive restraint of his manner, suggested a determined will which made his ruthlessness comprehensible. I have never come across anyone who filled me with a greater sense of confidence." Because Maugham wrote this evaluation some thirty years after he met Savinkov, it suggests the strength of the impression he carried away with him.

Savinkov's anglophilic streak would have predisposed him to Maugham, as, of course, would the famous writer's fascination with him and his novels. They became very friendly and met often as Savinkov regaled Maugham with stories of his past exploits. On one such occasion, Maugham commented that it must have taken great courage to carry out the two notorious assassinations. But Savinkov just shrugged his shoulders when he replied: "Not at all, believe me. It is a business like any other. One gets accustomed to it." When Savinkov told Maugham about his arrest in Sevastopol, Maugham asked if he had been frightened. "No," Savinkov answered, "after all, I knew that sooner or later I was bound to be caught, and when I was, strangely enough, I only felt relief." Savinkov admitted that the strenuous life he had led had exhausted him and he looked forward to being able to rest, even it meant his death.

Aiding their friendship was that their political goals and judgments were aligned. Savinkov welcomed Maugham's mission and appears to have awakened his interest in the Cossacks as a political and military force. They both had an equally low opinion of Kerensky. During September and October, Maugham observed the Provisional Government drift aimlessly and the country's future darken as the Bolsheviks gathered strength. When they seized power and he had to leave Russia, Savinkov's last words to him were: "Between me and Lenin it's war to the death. One of these days, perhaps next week, he will put me with my back to the wall and shoot me, or I shall put him with his back to another wall and shoot him. One thing I can tell you is that I shall never run away."

Maugham's final evaluation of his Russian friend was exceptional, considering all the celebrated people he knew during his long and active life. He said that Boris Savinkov was "the most extraordinary man I have ever met."

It was not only Savinkov's past that made Maugham say this but also what he believed his future could have been:

> [His name] might well have been as familiar to us all as that of Lenin, and if it had, Lenin's would have remained obscure. Boris Savinkov might easily have become a man of tremendous authority in Russia; I do not know whether he failed owing to some defect in his character or because the circumstances of the time were such that no man could have altered the course of events. There is no

more sometimes than the trembling of a leaf between success and failure.

October 1917

After Kerensky unexpectedly "rehabilitated" the Bolsheviks during the Kornilov affair, they began to plot in earnest to seize power. The Provisional Government had set November 12 as the date for elections to the Constituent Assembly, which would determine the country's future, but Lenin wanted to strike before then because he feared that the Bolsheviks would lose. He also managed to prevail against other party leaders who thought such an action would be premature and that he was too "impetuous."

On September 13, for the first time, the Bolsheviks actually won an election in the Workers' Section of the Petrograd Soviet. This was engineered by Lev Trotsky (born Leyba Davidovich Bronshtein), Lenin's goateed, curly-haired, pince-nez-wearing second-in-command. A former Menshevik, a learned and brilliant orator, and a ruthless tactician, he leveraged this success by starting to build a Bolshevik network of local Soviets in the country that paralleled and ignored an existing system dominated by other socialist parties, the Socialist Revolutionaries, and Mensheviks. Part of the Bolshevik scheme was to give their actions a veneer of legality by creating a "legislative" body packed with party members and allies who would legitimize the Bolsheviks' seizure of power when it occurred.

The Bolsheviks also wanted to try to provoke the Provisional Government so that they could launch their coup under the pretext of "defending" the Revolution. As usual, even though the other socialists understood that the Bolsheviks' nondemocratic maneuvers were illegal, they acquiesced to them. Stalin later bragged that the Bolshevik Party successfully "disguised its offensive actions behind a smoke screen of defenses in order to attract into its orbit uncertain, hesitating elements."

The Bolsheviks decided to use armed force differently as well. During their failed attempts to seize power in April and July, they learned that mass demonstrations and skirmishes in the streets were ineffective because of how difficult they were to control and because of the negative reactions they elicited from various quarters. They resolved that their new tactic would be for small bands of Red Guards, soldiers, and sailors to seize control of the city quietly while preventing the organization of a counterattack.

Kerensky's weakness helped the Bolsheviks immeasurably. As he had on other occasions, he underestimated their threat and fantasized that he would be able to crush any attempt they might make to seize power. He even announced, as Vladimir Nabokov *père* recalled, that he was ready "to offer prayers to produce the uprising" because he would then have the pretext to act against the Bolsheviks. But he failed to realize how his behavior during the Kornilov affair had fatally damaged him in the eyes of the military. And with Savinkov no longer a member of the Provisional Government, the strongest voice for aggressive preemptive action against the Bolsheviks was gone.

Savinkov followed the Bolsheviks' activities in September and October closely and consolidated his earlier relations with the Cossacks, becoming a member of the Soviet of the Union of Cossack Armies and being elected as their representative to a "Pre-Parliament" that Kerensky hoped would allow him to consolidate public consensus. Both were unlikely moves on his part, and Kerensky was one of many who marveled how Savinkov "had won the confidence of . . . an organization that was completely loyal to Kornilov," a man he had publicly called a "traitor."

Savinkov's reason for allying himself with the Cossacks was clear—they were a powerful and patriotic military force that largely opposed the Bolsheviks. He put very little stock in the Pre-Parliament or in other high-minded deliberative groups that continued to form. He agreed with Gippius that the time for talk was over, because the looming danger was too great.

Sometime between October 3 and 10 Lenin returned secretly to Petrograd from Finland, where he had been hiding, to take charge of the plans for the coup d'état, but for safety he wore a disguise and stayed out of sight in the city's outlying Vyborgsky District.

On Tuesday, October 24, it became clear to Savinkov that the Bolsheviks were on the verge of beginning their putsch. That same evening, at a meeting of the

Soviet of the Union of Cossack Armies, Savinkov and several other members tried to persuade three Don Cossack regiments to come to the Provisional Government's defense. But the Cossacks refused: they complained that Kerensky had insulted them by labeling them "counterrevolutionaries," that he had maligned Kornilov, and that he had deprived them of their freedom of conscience by canceling a grand religious procession and public prayer service they had planned in the city the previous Sunday. Savinkov admitted that their grievances were valid but nevertheless tried to persuade them to defend the Provisional Government in the name of saving Russia from the Bolsheviks. A delegation finally agreed to go see Kerensky later that evening; one of their conditions for agreeing to defend the government would be the release of Kornilov from prison. But Kerensky could not or would not grant the request, and the three regiments stayed in their barracks.

The Coup Begins

Under the cover of darkness on Tuesday night, October 24–25, groups of armed Bolshevik Red Guards, soldiers, and sailors took over railroad stations, post offices, telephone centers, newspapers, banks, and bridges throughout Petrograd. They met no resistance. When Kerensky learned what was happening, he contacted frontline commanders to ask for troops. However, General Vladimir Cheremisov, the commander of the Northern Front, reviled the Provisional Government, sympathized with the Bolsheviks, and replied that none were available. By the morning of Wednesday, October 25 (November 7, NS), 1917, a cold, overcast, and drizzly day, the Winter Palace was the only important building still in the hands of the Provisional Government. It was guarded by a motley assemblage of several hundred loyal troops—some Cossacks, military cadets, and a company from the Women's Death Battalion. At 9 A.M., Kerensky sneaked out of the Winter Palace in disguise and, using an automobile borrowed from the American embassy that was flying the American flag, left for the Northern Front to seek help. The other ministers remained in the Malachite Hall, where they were able to communicate with the outside world via two telephone lines that the Bolsheviks had failed to disconnect and waited for Kerensky to return with troops.

The first attempt by the Bolsheviks to take the Winter Palace took place the same morning, but their assault was half-hearted and easily beaten back by the defenders. This failure notwithstanding, at 10 A.M. Lenin sent declarations to the city's press that the Provisional Government "had been deposed." However, because the coup had not been authorized by anyone and was carried out quietly, the majority of the city's population did not take the announcement seriously. For many on this fateful day life went on as usual, with offices and shops open, factory workers going to their jobs, and entertainments operating.

A group of Americans visiting the city who intended to go to the celebrated Mariinsky Ballet that evening recalled that people strolling on Nevsky Boulevard, which showed no signs of the coup, seemed surprisingly relaxed. Lenin spent most of October 25 out of sight and disguised with bandages, a wig, and eyeglasses, waiting for the cabinet to be arrested and apparently unaware that Kerensky had escaped. He later said that starting a world revolution in Russia proved to be as easy "as picking up a feather."

It was beyond irony that when Kerensky was on his way to the headquarters of the Northern Front in Pskov, a city 200 miles to the southwest, he discovered that the only troops that could potentially move against the Bolsheviks in the capital were the Cossacks of the Third Cavalry Corps, the same ones he had accused of taking part in Kornilov's "treason." Most so despised him for his lies about Kornilov and for having pushed their commander, Krymov, to suicide that they would not listen to his pleas. But six squadrons of cavalry with a few light artillery pieces finally agreed, and under their commander, Major-General Pyotr Krasnov, began to advance on Petrograd via Luga.

At 6:30 P.M. on Wednesday, October 25, the Bolsheviks ordered the Provisional Government to surrender or be fired upon by the cruiser *Avrora* and the Peter and Paul Fortress, both of which were across the Neva from the Winter Palace. The ministers were still in the Malachite Hall, which had windows facing the river, but did not respond as they waited for Kerensky to arrive with troops.

Against the Bolshevik Coup

The only serious attempt to organize assistance for the Winter Palace and resist the Bolshevik coup was made by Boris Savinkov. Early on October 25, he began a frenzied search for any forces that could be enlisted in the fight. He had no official position in the government or the military, save for the tenuous one of being a member of the Cossack Soviet, and acted as a private person, albeit one with numerous contacts. He also found out that he was slated for arrest by the Bolsheviks and would have to take precautions, including leaving the friend's house where he had been living and finding another place to stay. Nevertheless, hoping to cobble together even a small group of fighters, he turned to associations of army officers, only to hear that they so despised Kerensky that not only would they not fight for him, they wanted him arrested.

Savinkov then returned to the Union of Cossacks and also approached General Alexeyev. Despite Savinkov's reputation for having "betrayed" Kornilov, he managed to get them to agree to help and by late evening on the 25th, Alexeyev and the Cossacks began to formulate a plan to defend the Winter Palace.

But it was too late. News came the same night that the palace had fallen.

At 9:40 P.M., the *Avrora* had fired a blank shell to signal the beginning of the attack on the Winter Palace, an event that was inflated to mythical dimensions in Soviet history of the October Revolution as the beginning of the "storming" of the Winter Palace.

But there was no storming of the palace. This was a Soviet fabrication with roots in two propagandistic works about the October Revolution from the 1920s—the first staged and filmed by the avant-garde playwright Nikolay Evreinov on the square in front of the palace, and the second filmed by the famous film director Sergey Eisenstein. Both "reenactments" included thousands of participants, far more than had actually been involved. After the *Avrora*'s signal shot, artillery in the Peter and Paul Fortress fired three dozen live rounds at the palace, which mostly missed; the few that hit did very little damage.

After the artillery fire ended, the Bolshevik forces around the palace stayed in place, and nothing happened for a while. As the night wore on and it became clear that no new troops would be arriving to support the Provisional Government, most of the units guarding the palace began to lose heart. The Cossacks left first, followed by the majority of the cadets. By midnight, all that remained was the company from the Women's Death Battalion, a few cadets, and a handful of army invalids. Only then did the Red Guards, soldiers, and sailors begin to enter the palace through the gates and doors that the defenders had failed to lock and to climb through open windows facing the Hermitage. Some gunfire was exchanged before the defenders surrendered. The ministers were arrested in the Malachite Hall at 2:10 A.M., after which they were taken to the prison in the Peter and Paul Fortress. On the way they barely escaped being lynched. The overall casualties were very light—five killed and several wounded—but members of the Women's Battalion were raped.

In the hours and days after the Winter Palace was taken, the attackers began to loot and vandalize the ornate rooms and halls: paintings were slashed, china cabinets emptied and their contents trodden underfoot, and silverware was stolen. The large tsarist wine cellars were also broken into, and so many bottles were smashed that, as Trotsky recalled, "wine ran down the channels into the Neva, saturating the snow, while drunkards lapped it up straight out of the canals."

The fall of the Winter Palace did not stop Savinkov. He acted quickly and organized a small, informal group of determined men who opposed the Bolsheviks and wanted to help him. On Thursday evening, October 26, from a friend's apartment where he took temporary refuge, Savinkov sent a Cossack and a cadet to reconnoiter south of Petrograd for any forces that would be willing to move against the Bolsheviks. They returned the following day and reported that there were Cossacks in Gatchina, a town only twenty miles from the capital. This was Krasnov and his six squadrons from the Third Cavalry Corps.

Savinkov still believed that the Bolsheviks in Petrograd could be defeated. Even though they had several tens of thousands of armed men, many were not regular soldiers, and the remainder would not be able to withstand an attack by disciplined and expertly led troops. With this in mind, he launched a furious, week-long effort to try to find units that would be willing to advance on the capital.

The same day Savinkov's scouts reported about the Cossack units south of the city, he set off to find them with several others from his group. He soon learned that Krasnov and his men were now near Tsarskoye Selo, only fifteen miles from Petrograd. However, to reach them, it would be necessary to pass through a strong Bolshevik cordon consisting of a company of soldiers and an armored car. After getting as far as he could by train, Savinkov borrowed an automobile and took only one of his men with him, Flegont Klepikov, an idealistic cadet from the Pavlovsk Military Academy in Petrograd who had become a loyal aide and a friend. Disguised as workers, they managed to get past the suspicious Bolshevik pickets when Klepikov browbeat their commander by claiming that he and Savinkov wanted to persuade Krasnov not to fight and threatening to complain to Trotsky himself.

⚊⚊

On Saturday, October 28, Krasnov scattered the Bolshevik forces in Tsarskoye Selo and occupied the town. The following day passed quietly as he waited for reinforcements from the front that Kerensky had promised. But none arrived and when, on Monday the thirtieth, Krasnov tried to advance on his own against the neighboring town of Pulkovo, he realized that he would have to fall back. Trotsky was in charge, and the force he sent against Krasnov was not only many times larger but also fought well.

Ironically, this setback proved to be the opening Savinkov had been looking for. He was committed to helping Krasnov in any way that he could but was unable do anything because he was a civilian. Krasnov remedied this by giving him an "official" position and sent him as an emissary to Kerensky's headquarters to find out about the reinforcements. Savinkov immediately initiated a series of rapid trips back and forth, attempting to move people and events in the direction he wanted. The result was a lot of frantic effort, confusion, anger, communication at cross purposes, and very little substance.

Kerensky did not know where the reinforcements were and announced that he would go to the front himself to get troops. Savinkov had to warn him not to because it would look as if he was abandoning Krasnov's Cossacks, who barely tolerated him anyway. He also accused Kerensky to his face of being responsible for the Bolshevik coup and Russia's ruin.

At one point, Savinkov even tried to persuade Krasnov to arrest Kerensky and to appoint a new head of government when they returned to Petrograd; he mentioned two distinguished socialists and himself as possible candidates. Krasnov replied that to his regret the Cossacks could not be relied upon to support such a move, in part because they resisted fratricidal fighting.

With no reinforcements in sight, at noon on Tuesday, October 31, Kerensky summoned a "military council" in which he included Savinkov, who had been elected commissar of Krasnov's tiny staff and confirmed in this position by Kerensky himself. Even with their world crumbling around them, with only an insignificant plot of territory under their control and a handful of troops, both still acted as if such actions meant something.

They met in Gatchina Palace, another of the imperial residences near Petrograd that dated from the eighteenth century. Kerensky was in a state of nervous exhaustion. He had recently appointed himself commander-in-chief, a completely illusory title under the circumstances, and kept changing his mind, issuing orders of little or no consequence, only to rescind them a moment later. The atmosphere around him was one of bewilderment and disorder. There was a growing conviction that the cause was lost, and people were beginning to panic.

Kerensky announced that in the present situation the only thing left was to enter into negotiations with the Bolsheviks. Savinkov and several others bristled at this idea. Refusing to give up hope, he argued they could buy time by what he called "honest treachery," or beginning discussions with the Bolsheviks and then breaking them off and attacking when reinforcements arrive. He was adamantly opposed to any genuine agreement with the Bolsheviks, which he described as a crime against "the motherland and freedom." But Kerensky disagreed and decided that talks should begin.

Savinkov called the decision a "disgrace" and refused to accept it. After the meeting broke up, he stayed to confront Kerensky and warned him that by beginning talks with the Bolsheviks he was assuming an "immeasurable responsibility." He then implored him to wait at least a few hours, until the hoped-for reinforcements arrived, and offered to go by automobile to look for them and hurry them along. He also suggested another alternative—he would drive to the Polish Corps' encampment near Petrograd and, in Kerensky's name, order it to advance on Gatchina. This large formation of some 20,000 men had been organized after the February Revolution from among the hundreds of thousands of Polish soldiers and officers who served in the Russian Imperial Army. The corps had struck a deal with the Provisional Government to support the creation of an independent Polish state and had preserved its discipline and fighting ability.

At first Kerensky resisted Savinkov's idea, claiming that "the reinforcements won't arrive. We're surrounded. You won't be able to get through anywhere. The Bolsheviks will kill you on the road." But Savinkov insisted and Kerensky finally agreed to issue him a pass to travel to the Polish Corps and an order to its commanding general.

Saving a Grand Duke

Before leaving Gatchina, Savinkov decided he had to take care of a confidential and very delicate matter, despite the urgency of his mission to the Polish Corps. One of the other residents of the sprawling Gatchina Palace was Grand Duke Mikhail Alexandrovich, a younger brother of Nicholas II, a general, and, for a brief period before the Provisional Government took power in February, the tsar's designated successor. Although Mikhail had opportunities to escape abroad or to the Crimea, he chose to remain and now was in danger of arrest by the Bolsheviks, or worse.

Savinkov summoned Klepikov and told him that he had a "top secret" task for him, explaining that "as long as I am alive it is not to be spoken of to anyone or under any circumstances." Klepikov was to go to the grand duke, describe the threat that was looming over him, and offer to take him somewhere safe. To his other confidante, Karol Wędziagolski, who was also involved in the plan, Savinkov explained: "We certainly cannot leave him here. The Bolsheviks will be here in a few hours." When Klepikov carried out the order, Mikhail listened carefully and thanked him, but "refused categorically" to leave Gatchina, saying that he never sought political power, would not become involved in political struggles, wanted to continue a simple life, and thought that the Bolsheviks were not a threat to him.

The grand duke was wrong. Several days later he was arrested by the Bolsheviks, taken to Petrograd, from there to Perm in the Urals, and killed in the summer of 1918. Savinkov's only reason to try to help a senior male member of a family whose role in Russia he deplored was common humanity, and he did not want his kindness toward a former enemy to become known.

Final Struggle

An hour later, together with his aides, Wędziagolski and Klepikov, Savinkov was on the highway to Luga sixty miles to the south. It was late autumn in northern Russia, and as night fell the temperature dropped and the road iced over. When they were crossing a forest near Luga it started to snow, further slowing their progress. Contrary to what Kerensky had feared, however, they encountered no Bolsheviks anywhere south of Gatchina. The area was sparsely populated, and as they passed through occasional villages, the peasants stopped them to ask what had happened in Petrograd and if it was true that Kerensky had been arrested.

They were incensed at the Bolsheviks, who, they said, had "forgotten God." Savinkov began to hope that the road would remain clear for him to return with reinforcements for Krasnov.

He would not know it for several more days, but on November 1, the morning after he left Gatchina, Bolsheviks who had come to an agreement with Krasnov's Cossacks arrived at the Gatchina Palace to arrest Kerensky. He barely managed to escape with the assistance of one of the palace's old wardens, who knew a secret passage to the outside.

⊶

Savinkov struggled to save the situation for another six days, more in his own name and the ideals of the February Revolution than of the overthrown Provisional Government. When he did not find the troops that he hoped could help Krasnov where he thought they would be, he drove farther, covering hundreds of miles as he zigzagged from north to south and back again. He hardly ate or slept. On the strength of nothing more than his being the "former director of the ministry of war," which is how he signed his telegrams and messages, he succeeded in getting senior military commanders to listen to his entreaties as well as to his threats regarding how they would be judged later for not defending the legitimate government once it was restored. He identified military formations that appeared to be willing "to fight the Bolsheviks," and he tried to persuade their commanders to act. All it would take, he insisted, were two or three divisions of infantry with some artillery and cavalry, and they could retake Petrograd.

But Kerensky was anathema to virtually everyone in the army, and the Bolshevik promise of "peace, land, and freedom" was too effective for most soldiers to withstand. There was also active opposition to Savinkov's attempt to have troops march on the capital from General Cheremisov, the senior commander who sympathized with the Bolsheviks, and who countermanded a subordinate's order that could have sent a force to Petrograd.

On Sunday, November 5, when he was in Pskov, a city 200 miles to the southwest of the capital, Savinkov finally concluded that he could do no more. He decided to return to return to Petrograd to consult with friends. Barely escaping arrest by Bolshevik guards who demanded to see his papers, and abandoning most of his belongings, Savinkov disguised himself as an infantry captain and together with his aides made his way through the chaotic streets to the train station. They managed to get on to a train packed to the limit with civilians and soldiers and by Monday evening were back in Petrograd.

October in Moscow

In Moscow, the coup went badly at first. The Bolsheviks there were less committed and not as well organized as their fellows in Petrograd, although on Thursday, October 26, they did manage to occupy the Kremlin. But by the following Saturday, the same day when Krasnov had taken Tsarskoye Selo in the north, cadets in Moscow attacked the Kremlin and drove the Bolsheviks out. Had Moscow's military and civilian authorities showed more resolve, they could have arrested the leading Bolsheviks and crushed their coup. Instead, they entered into negotiations, which allowed the Bolsheviks to bring in reinforcements, and on the night of October 30–31 they attacked. Thousands of men fought for both sides in the streets and house to house; many buildings were badly damaged, and the Kremlin was shelled. Several thousand were killed before the city's authorities told their troops to surrender on November 2. An American living in the city described the scene outside his apartment shortly after the fighting stopped:

> The house we are in is almost a wreck, and the boulevard in front
> is a most singular and distressing panorama of desolation. The roads
> are covered with glass and debris; trees, lampposts, telephone poles are
> shot off raggedly; dead horses and a few dead men lie in the parkway;
> the broken gas mains are still blazing; the black, austere, smoking
> hulks of the burning buildings stand like great barricades about the
> littered yards of the boulevard.

The Bolsheviks also took power by force in cities in other, central parts of the country. But the rural areas remained outside their control, as did most of the borderlands of the empire, a number of which declared independence. At first, despite the Bolshevik success, the vast majority of Russians had no idea what had actually happened because of the brilliance of Trotsky's ploy to disguise their coup as a transfer of power from the dual structure of government established in February to the Soviets alone.

However, the real nature of the new regime would soon become obvious to all.

CHAPTER EIGHT

THE WAR AGAINST THE
BOLSHEVIKS IN RUSSIA

When Boris Savinkov returned to Petrograd in early November 1917, the city was still reeling from what had happened and frightened of what was coming. The Bolsheviks continued to consolidate power and had recently suppressed a rebellion by cadets from several military academies, which left hundreds dead and buildings blackened and shattered by artillery fire. Many of the young men who were captured were cruelly tortured and executed. At night, rifle fire and grenade explosions resounded throughout the city as Red Guards celebrated their ascendancy. Active anti-Bolshevik resistance in the city had shrunk to nothing.

Savinkov knew most of the civic and political leaders in Petrograd and shortly after he arrived, he met Vladimir Nabokov Sr. in a secret attic apartment. Nabokov was the chairman of a group trying to organize resistance to the new regime and revealed to Savinkov that all hopes were now on the Don. Rumor had it that General Alexey Kaledin, who was recently elected *ataman*, or traditional commander, of the Don Cossacks, was forming an army to advance on Petrograd.

Savinkov resolved to join him. If Bolshevik ideology was taking root in the country's westernized capital, in Moscow, and in other major urban centers, the fight against it would begin far away on the periphery, in the rich soil of Russian agrarian communities, and would be led by the Cossack yeomanry of the Don.

Boris Savinkov was now again a wanted man. The Bolsheviks began to post announcements naming people they wanted to arrest, and one featured Savinkov's and Kornilov's names in giant letters with the label "Enemies of the Revolution and of Freedom." Savinkov's Polish aide, Wędziagolski, had friends in Petrograd who helped him and Savinkov get fake Polish passports and other documents that would allow them to pass through Bolshevik-controlled territory. Both men also acquired campaign caps with the white eagle insignia of an independent Poland to complete their disguise.

They left around November 12 for Novocherkassk, the capital of the Don Cossack lands, via Moscow and Kiev, a trip of 1,500 miles that would take well over a week. Trains were still running, but travel was difficult: cars were mobbed by passengers at stations, who packed compartments and corridors; schedules were unreliable; and the rolling stock constantly broke down because of poor maintenance during the years of war and revolution. When they got off the train in Moscow, they saw their names on a new list of "Dangerous Enemies of the People" who had escaped "Revolutionary Justice" in Pskov.

Savinkov sought shelter for himself and Wędziagolski with his old friends, the family of Samuil Tumarkin, a rich Jewish jeweler with close ties to the Socialist Revolutionary Party; the Tumarkins were also related to the Tsetlins, Savinkov's acquaintances in Paris. It was dangerous to harbor fugitives, but the Tumarkins greeted them warmly and hid them in their large, opulent mansion, trying to keep them out of sight of the radicalized servants as much as possible. Like many other members of the country's intelligentsia and other privileged elites at this time—who naïvely tended to project onto others the generous view of human nature they got from their own circles—the Tumarkins did not believe the Bolsheviks could possibly last very long because they were simply too radical and barbaric.

But what Savinkov saw in Moscow reinforced his conviction that the new regime would not collapse by itself and had to be defeated. There were signs everywhere that the Bolsheviks would not shrink from any brutality. When Savinkov and Wędziagolski were leaving from the Kursk Railway Station, they saw Bolshevik soldiers laughing as they threw a boyish-looking second lieutenant under a train because he refused to remove his shoulder boards, the cherished emblems of his junior rank.

On the train to Kiev, Savinkov and Wędziagolski had seats in what had been a first-class compartment for two passengers, but eight more men crammed themselves into it and spilled out into the corridor. Most of them were Bolshevik deserters who were suspicious of anyone using a handkerchief or having clean, uncalloused hands, which were signs of a "class enemy."

Muttering threats against the "filthy bourgeois," the ex-soldiers tried to quiz Savinkov and Wędziagolski about who they were. The two men succeeded in keeping them at bay by pretending that they were Poles who did not speak Russian, and they reached Kiev unharmed, although infested with lice.

In Kiev as in Moscow, the formerly grand, high-ceilinged train station was now ramshackle, with paint peeling from its walls, the floors filthy from the throngs of motley passengers, and the air thick with the smell of unwashed humanity.

Once again, the two went straight from the train station to another imposing mansion belonging to Savinkov's friends, the family of Daniil Balakhovsky, whose relative, Sofia Petit, lived in Paris with her well-connected French husband and had been very helpful to Savinkov when he was hard up.

The Balakhovskys welcomed them as if they were next of kin. In Kiev the political situation was relatively calm, and there was no danger from the Bolsheviks, who were, for the moment, unsuccessfully vying for power with the Ukrainian People's Republic, which had proclaimed its independence from Russia after October. But the passions at play in the city were still intense, and before leaving for the Don, Savinkov met with several local partisans of Ukrainian autonomy. In the kind of statesmanlike mode that would become increasingly important for him in the months and years ahead, he tried to persuade the Ukrainian nationalists that all forces need to overcome their parochial differences and unite against their great common enemy, the Bolsheviks.

The Don

Near the border of the Don Army Oblast, or province, in the south of Russia—the official name of the semiautonomous Don Cossack homeland northeast of the Black Sea and straddling the Don River—Savinkov and Wędziagolski came close to being shot by sailors from the Black Sea fleet, who had won an early reputation as especially zealous and violent Bolsheviks and who boarded their train. But they managed to bluff their way through with their false identity papers and reached Rostov-on-Don, the commercial center of the Don Army Oblast. On their way to Kaledin's base in Novocherkassk, they were almost shot again, except this time by suspicious Cossacks who thought that they were probably "Bolsheviks" or "spies." However, by luck one of the officers recognized Savinkov as a member of the Soviet of the Union of Cossack Armies. The two travelers were immediately transformed into friends and allies, feted that night at a celebratory dinner with much vodka and famous Don wines, and the next day were in Novocherkassk.

To Wędziagolski, Novocherkassk, the birthplace of the Volunteer Army, which would also soon become known as the White Army, in contrast to the Bolshevik Red Army, looked like an island of old Russia that had been largely spared the unrest of the Revolution. But there was no mistaking that it was a time of war, and uniformed Cossacks and army officers who had arrived from the north were everywhere. Savinkov's younger brother, Victor, who also came to join the Volunteer Army around this time, was much impressed by the proud bearing and smart appearance of the Cossacks, who showed none of the slovenliness that had become the norm for regular army soldiers among whom the revolutionary ethos had taken root.

However, despite their dedication and polish, too many of the Volunteers were officers or young cadets, and too few were the rank-and-file soldiers who had made up the vast majority of the old imperial army and who were now increasingly gravitating toward the Bolsheviks. From the start, there was a major class divide between the Reds and the Whites that the Whites would never overcome. Cossacks who returned home from the front also brought revolutionary ideas with them that went against their fathers' patriarchal beliefs. At the end of 1917, the Don was where an alternative to the Bolsheviks was being born, but the civil war would split it too.

No Place in the Ranks

Savinkov had traveled to the Don with great hopes, but it would take all his diplomatic skills to find a place for himself in the Volunteer movement because its commanders had not forgotten that he had been a terrorist or forgiven his role during the Kornilov affair. Soon after arriving, Savinkov and Wędziagolski started to make the rounds in Novocherkassk to find out how they could collaborate. In addition to Kaledin, the other prominent generals included two whom Savinkov knew well: Alexeyev, who was now in charge of the Don Civilian Soviet, the Volunteer Army's political arm, and Kornilov, who commanded the army itself.

The initial meetings did not go well. Kaledin first kept Savinkov and Wędziagolski waiting and then sent an aide to apologize that he was too busy to see them. Alexeyev was noncommittal. Kornilov agreed to meet them right away, although it appears to have been more out of a desire to vent his spleen than anything else. He accused Savinkov of being responsible for the "acts of the 'traitor' Kerensky and for Soviets, committees, and commissars"—in short, for all the things he loathed and had tried to oppose.

Ever respectful, Savinkov waited for Kornilov to end his tirade and then asked for permission to reply. Speaking calmly, he rejected all the accusations and then shifted to the present situation, which, he stressed, was perilous because the Volunteer Army was in danger of succumbing to the monarchists, capitalists, and other reactionaries who were trying to influence the movement's direction. This, he explained, would doom the entire enterprise by depriving it of crucial popular support. Kornilov was a pragmatist as well as genuinely committed to the republican and democratic ideals that had been proclaimed in February. Savinkov's arguments persuaded him again, as they had before; he calmed down and agreed that the composition of the Don Civilian Soviet needed to be changed.

Despite Kornilov's heartening response, any expectation Savinkov may have had about being given a prominent place in the Volunteer movement was soon ended. When he went to speak with General Ivan Romanovsky, Kornilov's chief of staff, Romanovsky told him frankly that any role he could have would be limited and advisory. In fact, he warned Savinkov that it would be better for him to "Go away at once. Tomorrow it may be too late. Help us from the outside. Here your enemies are stronger than your friends."

The warning was not idle or abstract. Over the course of the next several weeks, there were a number of unsuccessful attempts on his and Wędziagolski's lives by men dressed as civilians and as officers. On the last occasion, Savinkov confronted a heavily armed officer who asked to see him, after which the man lost his nerve and confessed his intention.

ABOVE: Boris Savinkov, ca. 1899 (GARF). BELOW: LOWER ROW: Vera Savinkova holding son Vitya, and Victor Mikhailovich Savinkov with Tanya. UPPER ROW: Vera's brother Boris, and Boris Savinkov. 1902 (GARF).

ABOVE LEFT: Ekaterina Breshko-Breshkovskaya, "Grandmother" of the Russian Revolution (*The Little Grandmother of the Russian Revolution*). ABOVE RIGHT: Mikhail Gots, leading Socialist Revolutionary (*Sotsialist-Revoliutsioner*). BELOW LEFT: Yegor Sazonov, assassin of Minister of the Interior von Plehve (*Sotsialist-Revoliutsioner*). BELOW RIGHT: Minister of the Interior Vyacheslav Konstantinovich von Plehve (Wikimedia).

ABOVE LEFT: Alexey Pokotilov, member of the SR Combat Organization (*Sotsialist-Revoliutsioner*). ABOVE RIGHT: Maximilian Shveytser, member of the SR Combat Organization (*Sotsialist-Revoliutsioner*). BELOW LEFT: Dora Brilliant, member of the SR Combat Organization (*Sotsialist-Revoliutsioner*). BELOW RIGHT: Ivan Kalyacv, shortly after his assassination of Grand Duke Sergey in 1905 (*Sotsialist-Revoliutsioner*).

ABOVE LEFT: Grand Duke Sergey Alexandrovich (Wikimedia). ABOVE RIGHT: Grand Duchess Elizaveta Fyodorovna, "Ella," as a nun after her husband's assassination (Wikimedia). BELOW: Remnants of Grand Duke Sergey's carriage after his assassination in the Moscow Kremlin (Wikimedia).

ABOVE LEFT: Zinaida Gippius, Dmitry Filosofov (center), Dmitry Merezhkovsky, c. 1920 (Wikimedia). RIGHT: Zinaida Gippius (Wikipedia). BELOW: Evno Azef (Wikimedia).

ABOVE LEFT: Vladimir Burtsev, early 1900s (Wikipedia). ABOVE RIGHT: Evgeniya Zilberberg (GARF). BELOW: Acting Minister of War Boris Savinkov (center) with Prime Minister Alexander Kerensky (2nd from right) and the Military Council, 1917 (Wikimedia).

ABOVE LEFT: Alexander Kerensky, Minister of Justice, Minister of War, Minister Chairman of the Provisional Government (Wikipedia). ABOVE RIGHT: Boris Savinkov (L) with General Lavr Kornilov, 1917 (Wikimedia). BELOW LEFT AND RIGHT: Baron Alexander Arkadyevich Dikgof-Derental (213, IISH) and Baroness Lyubov Efimovna Dikgof (GARF).

TOP LEFT: Boris Savinkov in Genoa, 1922 (Rome). TOP CENTER AND RIGHT: Police photographs of Gulenko, Savinkov's "double," in Genoa (Rome). MIDDLE LEFT: Artur Artuzov, head of GPU Counterintelligence (Wikimedia). MIDDLE CENTER: Felix Dzerzhinsky, head of the Cheka (Wikimedia). MIDDLE RIGHT: Boris Savinkov in Moscow after arrest, 1924 (Ogonyok Archive). BOTTOM: Boris Savinkov on trial, 1924 (standing upper L in suit) (Wikimedia).

Despite these failed attempts, there was the danger that another one would succeed. Nevertheless, Savinkov stayed in Novocherkassk for several more weeks to try to convince the generals to broaden the political representation of the Don Civilian Soviet in keeping with the principles of the February Revolution so that it would have the support of the Cossack masses. After extensive discussions, Savinkov succeeded in persuading Kaledin, Alexeyev, and Kornilov—who was the most amenable—to add four socialists, including himself and Wędziagolski. To publicize the change, the new soviet issued a declaration announcing its commitment to convening the Constituent Assembly and the principle that land should be owned by those who work it.

Strange Bedfellows

Becoming a member of the Don Civilian Soviet may have given Savinkov some small satisfaction, but he was disheartened by the deep problems he saw in the Volunteer Army and the political movement around it. Alexeyev and Kornilov did not get along personally, and Kaledin did not want to have the Volunteer Army based permanently on his territory, as a result of which the atmosphere in Novocherkassk was thick with rumors, intrigues, and plots. In response to Savinkov's insistence that it was necessary to win the support of the peasantry, the Cossack General Afrikan Bogayevsky proclaimed that "the time of democracy is over. We're counting on the bourgeoisie and the Cossacks."

There was no money. There was a shortage of weapons, ammunition, coats, and boots. Every volunteer had to find a way to cross Bolshevik lines to get to the Don, and the numbers arriving remained small. Savinkov complained in a letter to Gippius that too many of the officers and cadets in Alexeyev's faction were drunkards, carousers, and monarchists fond of singing the imperial anthem "God Save the Tsar"; he did allow, however, that they were at least willing to fight the Bolsheviks. Kornilov's men were more reliable, but there were not enough of them. The Cossacks were increasingly riven by dissent, and the numbers sympathizing with the Bolsheviks kept growing. The non-Cossack, Russian population of the region, especially the coal miners in the Donets Basin, or Donbas, as it was also known, were strongly in favor of the Bolsheviks because of their antiestablishment rhetoric and populist promises.

In view of the enormous task that lay ahead, and in light of what he had seen in Novocherkassk, Savinkov decided that he had to make a bold and pragmatic ideological compromise. He wrote to Gippius that henceforth he would work with anyone, of any political persuasion or economic class, who would provide material help or was willing to fight the common enemy: "I will personally continue to fight as long as I am still standing on my feet. To fight for Russia, 1st of all, for the Constituent Assembly, 2nd. Let the 'comrades' call me a 'traitor.'"

Creating a Mission

The generals in Novocherkassk had largely shunned Savinkov, but he was so determined to do anything to help the anti-Bolshevik cause that he accepted a mission designed to get rid of him. After a month and a half in the Don region, in early January 1918, he agreed to travel to Petrograd to recruit several influential members of the democratic, left-wing, anti-Bolshevik opposition to join the Don Civilian Soviet in order to broaden its political base and popular appeal. He suggested the names himself, in particular Plekhanov, the Menshevik he had hoped to see in Kerensky's government, and Nikolay Chaikovsky, a veteran moderate revolutionary socialist he respected greatly. Alexeyev gave Savinkov identification papers authorizing the mission, which he sewed into the lining of his sheepskin coat for safekeeping. For travel through Bolshevik-controlled territory he would again use a fake passport. Klepikov would go with him, and the Don Soviet delegated Wędziagolski as an emissary to Kiev. As a result, none of Savinkov's small team was left behind, which in retrospect would prove prudent.

Savinkov fully intended to return to Novocherkassk, because it was the only place in Russia at that time where there was any kind of organized resistance to the Bolsheviks. He was concerned about his family's welfare and before leaving wrote to his daughter, who had taken over the task of communicating with him, to suggest that she, her mother, and her brother might also want to move to the Don Army Oblast to escape the food and fuel shortages in Petrograd and the danger that the Germans would occupy the capital. (Tanya now used her mother's maiden name, Uspenskaya, probably because any association with

Savinkov was too dangerous under the Bolsheviks.) Savinkov had little money but continued to support them as best he could: "I'm sending you another 600 rubles. Will that be enough until March 1?" About himself he reports, "I am healthy and, most importantly, alive." His final words to Tanya are tender, as usual: "Christ be with you, my sweet little girl." He also asks her to pass on his "greetings to mama."

Savinkov was also able to help his second family in France, probably as a result of the high rank he had in Kerensky's government and the international connections he made. For a period of time in the spring of 1918, and possibly before and after as well, he arranged for the French Ministry of War to pay Evgeniya a monthly stipend of 1,000 francs (around $7,000 a month in today's money), which was generous under the circumstances. It was also unorthodox, as evidenced by the fact that the Ministry of War had to pay the money secretly.

<hr />

Savinkov's trip from Novocherkassk to Petrograd carried risks. The notorious Bolshevik political police, the All-Russian Extraordinary Commission for Combatting Counter-Revolution and Sabotage (*Vserossiískaya chrezvychaínaya komíssiya po borbé s kontrrevoliútsiey i sabotázhem*), or the Cheka, as it became known by its Russian abbreviation, had been established on December 7, 1917. Its inaugural director was Felix Dzerzhinsky, a Pole by birth and a fanatical and ascetic Bolshevik with the hollow-cheeked face and suspicious eyes of a Spanish grand inquisitor. Although still in its infancy, the Cheka was beginning the policy of state terror that would last the entire Soviet period of Russian history. On the eve of Savinkov's departure, the Volunteer Army's counterintelligence alerted him that the Cheka in Novocherkassk had found out about his mission and was planning to ambush him in Voronezh, a city at the midpoint between Novocherkassk and Moscow. But by relying on the skills he had honed when evading the imperial police, Savinkov made it to Petrograd, probably in early January 1918, without incident.

The Bolsheviks Choose Tyranny

Savinkov was in Petrograd during an especially ugly time, when the Bolsheviks cemented their rule via what was, in effect, a second coup d'état. After elections in the late fall—the first free and democratic nationwide elections in Russia's entire history—the long-awaited Constituent Assembly finally gathered in Petrograd on January 5. The Socialist Revolutionary Party had an absolute majority in the number of delegates, and their leader, Chernov, was elected chairman of the Assembly. But although all the political parties had waited for the Constituent Assembly for months and saw it as the one legitimate and clear-cut authority in the country (even the Bolsheviks had faulted the Provisional Government for being overly slow in organizing it), on the morning of January 6, Lenin had his troops disperse the delegates at gunpoint because his party did not have the votes to win legally. (Subsequently, the Bolsheviks would try to justify their action by claiming that the Assembly did not reflect the interests of the majority of the population—the workers and the poorest peasants). There were no repercussions from the Assembly, however, which had no armed force of its own.

The following day, the Bolsheviks announced that they would make peace with Germany and distribute gentry land to the peasants. Both were long-standing popular demands, which won them a great deal of initial support and helped divert attention from their ruthlessness. Shortly thereafter, all political parties, including those that had originally allied themselves with the Bolsheviks, were declared counterrevolutionary.

What happened in Petrograd was just a presage of the other radical policies the Bolsheviks soon began to impose throughout the country and reconfirmed Savinkov's determination to fight. His mission in the city had failed because Plekhanov was dying and he could not locate Chaikovsky. Nevertheless, he started back to Novocherkassk, but he got only as far as Moscow when everything suddenly changed.

On January 10, the Bolsheviks began a rising in the Don Oblast. It progressed with depressing speed: by February, the Red Guards had retaken Rostov-on-Don, and Novocherkassk had fallen. With most Cossacks now refusing to fight the Bolsheviks to defend their ancestral lands, Kaledin committed suicide in despair. Alexeyev's and Kornilov's small army was forced to begin a retreat through freezing weather and under enemy attacks to the Kuban steppes and the Northern Caucasus, an event in the history of the White movement that became known as the legendary Ice March.

Savinkov discovered that he was cut off from the Don Civilian Soviet. He did not even know if it still existed or if all its members had been shot.

Going It Alone

As a result, Savinkov decided to stay in Moscow and act on his own. This would allow him to escape the Volunteer Army generals' animosity as well as use his urban conspiratorial experience from his years in the Combat Organization.

Savinkov's decision was also timely, because now he would be in the new center of Bolshevik power. In early March, to escape the growing threat from the Germans, who had advanced to within 150 miles of Petrograd and even begun to bomb it from airplanes, Lenin and his regime moved to Moscow, thus restoring the ancient city to its status as the capital. Everyone else with a stake in Russia's future followed them, from representatives of foreign governments and their agents to international adventurers. The ground for covert action in the city would be very fertile.

So would the possibilities of exploiting the anger of large numbers of the city's population caused by the unimaginable policies the Bolsheviks began to implement immediately after seizing power.

In keeping with Marx's proclamation that a communist revolution signaled the dictatorship of the proletariat and the end of private property, the Bolsheviks systematically dismantled all the social and economic foundations of the Russian Empire. They eliminated former ranks and titles; they gave control of businesses and factories to committees of workers; they decreed that peasants should break up landowners' estates. Foreign trade was made into a national monopoly; banks and church property were nationalized; the old judicial system was replaced by revolutionary tribunals and "people's courts"; education and entertainment were placed under strict ideological controls. On January 31, 1918, the government marked a new era by adopting the New Style (NS) calendar.

Moscow was a cold, hungry, and dangerous place. Lenin's encouragement of the newly empowered peasants and urban proletariat to "rob the robbers," as he memorably phrased it—to seize what the communists claimed had been stolen from the working classes by the rich and powerful under the old regime—unleashed a wave of thefts, confiscations, and extortions that erased the boundary between state-sponsored expropriation and armed robbery. Private homes in Moscow were taken over as the new rulers saw fit and the inhabitants often thrown out into the streets. Bolshevik soldiers, members of the Cheka, or thieves masquerading as either—it made no practical difference to their victims—raided apartments under the pretext of searching for army officers or concealed foodstuffs, but often just to pillage. Venturing out at night became especially dangerous. Armed men stole fur coats and wallets from passersby or burst into restaurants and robbed the patrons of their money and jewelry. Even Lenin was the victim of an armed attack at the end of the year when a notorious Moscow thief and his band stopped the leader's Rolls-Royce, ignored his and the other passengers' protestations, robbed them, and took off in the car.

Nocturnal raids by armed bandits were not the sole method for "redistributing" wealth under the new regime. The Bolsheviks also began an official policy of confiscating bank assets. When the first wave of seizures failed to produce the $100 to $150 billion in today's currency that they wanted to consolidate power at home and project their revolution abroad, they turned to the contents of private safe-deposit boxes. By the middle of 1918 in Moscow alone, after cracking only a fraction of the total number of safes in the city, they had seized several thousand pounds of gold, silver, and platinum bullion; over a billion rubles in cash and bonds; and large sums of foreign currencies. The other safe-deposit boxes were cracked later.

Such expropriations of private wealth had a direct effect on Savinkov's plans. Organizing an anti-Bolshevik movement would require a lot of money, and many of the capitalists and other members of the haute-bourgeoisie on whom he was counting to form a strategic alliance and from whom he would have expected to receive financial support were suddenly left destitute (although some did manage to hide money and valuables, hoping to preserve them until the Bolshevik regime fell).

But paradoxically, a historical development that was devastating for Russia would also help Savinkov find money abroad. The Bolsheviks had made withdrawal from the Great War one of their principal aims when they seized power, and an armistice with the Central Powers had been in effect since the end of November 1917 (which did not prevent the Germans from continuing their advance deeper into Russian territory toward what would be the future border between the countries). However, the conditions Germans set for an actual peace treaty were so draconian that many of the Bolshevik leaders refused to accept them at first. Despite this, Lenin insisted on the treaty and was proven right, because had he not, the young Soviet regime would likely have been defeated and destroyed by the Germans. After several months of negotiations, a treaty was finally signed in the city of Brest-Litovsk in what is now Belarus on March 3, 1918 (NS).

Like many other patriots who were committed to victory, Savinkov found the treaty deeply humiliating. Among its provisions was the dismemberment of the former Russian Empire, with Ukraine, Poland, Finland, Estonia, Latvia, and Lithuania receiving nominal independence as German puppet states, and part of Transcaucasia ceded to Turkey. Overall, Russia lost over one-quarter of her population, her arable land, and her railway system; one-third of her crops and manufacturing industries; and three-quarters of her iron industries and coal fields. In addition, she was forced to pay a ruinous war indemnity. With German control of much of Russia's economy, she was suddenly transformed from being Germany's enemy to what was, in effect, an ally. For Savinkov and many others, memory of how the Germans transported Lenin to Russia in 1917 was also still fresh.

For the Allies, the treaty was a profound betrayal. When hostilities ceased, the Germans were able to transfer over half a million men from the Eastern Front to the Western Front. Even though Russian armies had been ineffective militarily for months, they had still helped tie down the Central Powers in the east. The American Expeditionary Forces, which started arriving in France in significant numbers around the time of the Brest-Litovsk Treaty, were initially only partial compensation. The Allies were also very alarmed by the Bolsheviks' announced intention to ignite a worldwide revolution against the so-called capitalist and imperialist states.

All this set the stage for France, Great Britain, the United States, and Japan to decide to intervene in Russian affairs and to try to destroy the Bolsheviks. And in this geopolitical atmosphere, any enemy of the Bolsheviks such as Boris Savinkov was now a friend of the Allies.

The Union for the Defense of the Motherland and Freedom

Savinkov had extensive connections in Moscow among various political factions. When he began to search for men with whom he could work, he discovered that there was a secret monarchist organization of some 800 former tsarist officers, primarily from elite guards and grenadier regiments, who were plotting an armed insurrection against the Bolsheviks. However, their politics were unacceptable, and he would not join anyone who did not support the program of the Don Civilian Soviet, whose four cornerstones were patriotism, the Allied cause, the Constituent Assembly, and land to the people. Savinkov realized that to implement this program, he would have to create a new underground organization himself.

His first and most important recruit was Colonel Alexander Perkhurov, a willful man with an intense, hawklike gaze, a high forehead, a prominent nose, and an aggressively pointed moustache. He was a veteran artillery officer who had fought with distinction in the Russo-Japanese War and the Great War.

In early March 1918, an acquaintance told him that Boris Savinkov was in the city and wanted to meet him in connection with some sort of new initiative. At first, Perkhurov refused: Savinkov's reputation as a Socialist Revolutionary, a terrorist, an army commissar, and a member of Kerensky's government were all unappealing to him. But after a few days he relented, and when they met, his attitude toward Savinkov changed dramatically: "He produced a most gratifying impression on me as a person who was to the highest degree intelligent, energetic and decisive, and who loved the Motherland."

They started to build the organization together, which Savinkov named the Union for the Defense of the Motherland and Freedom (*Soyúz Zashchíty Ródiny i Svobódy*), initially by finding former officers and cadets in Moscow who had also been cut off from the Volunteer Army in the south. Afterward, they broadened their recruitment to include anyone who agreed with the principles of the Don Civilian Soviet and who promised to fight the Bolsheviks. Each new member was asked to find four more men who were well known to him and completely trustworthy. And each new recruit had to swear an oath of loyalty to the organization's aims "and to act, wherever possible, with weapons in hand, or secretly, through cunning and deceit."

The individual's prior political orientation did not matter, and Savinkov took special pride in the ecumenical composition of the staff of the organization. Since he had broken with the Socialist Revolutionaries, he now characterized himself as an "independent socialist." A former lieutenant-general who became a member of the Union and commanded its military formations was a "constitutional monarchist," as was Perkhurov, who became the organization's chief of staff. The colonel in charge of the operations branch was a "republican," as was another colonel, a Latvian, who ran intelligence and counterintelligence. There were also two Social Democrats of the Plekhanov faction (i.e., moderate, anti-Bolshevik Marxists), two Mensheviks (also moderate Marxists), and two Socialist Revolutionaries. As Savinkov put it, "We were entirely justified in saying that we did not have rightists or leftists and had achieved a 'holy alliance' in the name of love for the fatherland." The organization's aims were "national" and were aimed at the "entire people." Boris Savinkov had created a small-scale version of a new Constituent Assembly that could serve as a model after the Bolsheviks were overthrown.

The Baron and the Baroness

One of the key members of the Union who deserves special mention because of the continuing role he would play in Boris Savinkov's life over the course of the next seven years is Baron Alexander Arkadyevich Dikgof-Derental (the second part of his surname was a pseudonym that stuck). His wife, Baroness Lyubov Efimovna Dikgof (it bears repeating that her first name means "love" in Russian), would be by their sides all this time as well.

Of Baltic German ancestry, Dikgof-Derental was six years younger than Savinkov and had been Perkhurov's trusted aide before becoming Savinkov's adjutant. Savinkov had first met both Dikgof-Derental and his wife in Paris before the war, where the baron had taken refuge in 1906 because of his involvement in the assassination of the priest-provocateur Father Gapon by the Socialist Revolutionaries. In exile, Dikgof-Derental worked as a writer, publishing fiction and reports on European political affairs in Russian periodicals. He enlisted in the French Army soon after the war began; served with distinction in Morocco, Albania, and France; was promoted to noncommissioned officer; and, following the February Revolution, in May 1917 transferred to the Russian Army and came home. Like Savinkov, he was an ardent Russian patriot and a socialist.

His wife, Lyubov, was born Emma in 1896 into a cosmopolitan Russian-Jewish and French family in Paris; her stepfather changed her name, and she took his patronymic (Efimovna). Strikingly pretty, graceful, and slender, with dreamy eyes and an elongated face like in a Modigliani portrait, she studied literature at the Sorbonne, then ballet, and tried her hand at performing on stage and in movies. She met Dikgof-Derental when she was only sixteen, and although his thoughtful and stolid-looking appearance did not make him an obvious match for her, they married soon after.

Boris Savinkov renewed his acquaintance with the couple in Petrograd and did so in pointed fashion. Shortly after Kerensky dismissed him from the Ministry of War, he sent his aide Klepikov to the Astoria Hotel, where the Dikgof-Derentals were staying, with an invitation to have dinner with him in the Neva, a well-known restaurant. The evening left an indelible impression on both him and Lyubov Efimovna. She is said to have remembered it down to the smallest details until the end of her life fifty-two years later, and Savinkov would claim that "the revolution itself brought us together that evening."

They renewed their relationship in Moscow, where Savinkov encountered the Dikgof-Derentals again in early 1918, when he sought refuge in their apartment while evading the Cheka after returning from the Don. Even though Savinkov's circumstances had changed markedly, Dikgof-Derental was struck by how he had remained true to himself, with "that same precise, succinct way of speaking of a man of action not words . . . the same steely gaze, the same immobile stone mask on his face. Death has passed him by too closely and too often not to have left signs of its cold breath on him." The baron would henceforth follow Savinkov in all his initiatives and peregrinations, while Lyubov Efimovna would develop into his secretary, become increasingly attached to him, and, as some believed, would play a fatal role in his life.

An Underground Army

The Union for the Defense of the Motherland and Freedom was organized according to military hierarchy and maintained secrecy through a system of cells. Discipline was strict, at least in principle, and punishment for betrayal was death. To conceal the Union's activities, one of Savinkov's closest collaborators, the medical doctor Nikolay Grigoryev, opened a clinic in mid-April in a quiet neighborhood southwest of the Kremlin. This seemed a perfect cover because members of the Union could come and go without standing out from the constant stream of real patients. To explain why so many of the clinic's patients were men, the rumor was spread that it specialized in "secret" illnesses.

In his typical fashion, Savinkov threw himself into building the organization tirelessly. Recruitment grew steadily through March and April, although not always smoothly. Significant numbers of professional officers who were monarchists were repelled by Savinkov's reputation and mistrusted him; a common judgment was "Lenin is scum and Savinkov is no better!"

But there were also many who did want to join, and by the end of May, the Union had 5,500 men in Moscow and thirty-four smaller cities who were organized into units of infantry, artillery, cavalry, and sappers. Some were already well armed, including with machine guns; others knew where Bolshevik armories were located and were prepared to equip themselves when the time came.

The Union also had counterintelligence agents who had penetrated the German embassy in Moscow as well as various branches of the Bolshevik government, even military headquarters and the Cheka. In Petrograd, members of the Union were prepared to sabotage naval ships if the Germans took the city. In Kiev, they organized guerilla bands behind German lines. Savinkov created a terrorist unit that was under his personal command and would try to assassinate Lenin and Trotsky as part of a series of armed risings.

Being a stickler for protocol and chain of command, Savinkov reported the creation of the Union to General Alexeyev of the Volunteer Army, which was re-forming in the south, and received his half-hearted approval. But there was no coordination with the Whites, and Savinkov continued to operate independently.

After considering seizing Moscow, Savinkov and Perkhurov decided not to attempt it. Despite the Union's numbers, there were still too many Bolshevik troops in the city, and they feared that a rebellion might cause the Germans to occupy it. Instead, they decided to move their headquarters and main operations to Kazan, a major city on the Volga River 600 miles due east. Perkhurov thought that Kazan would be easier to take, that it would be a better location from which to coordinate other risings, and that it was closer to the peasants on the upper Volga, who could be expected to support an anti-Bolshevik campaign. It was also where the Soviet regime had moved the imperial gold reserves it had inherited from the tsarist and Kerensky regimes to keep them safe from any armed threats in Moscow.

Foreign Money

The rapid early growth of the Union was made possible not only by opposition to the Bolshevik regime among different elements of Russian society but also because of significant support from abroad. After setting up the organization,

Savinkov left much of its regular activity to the headquarters staff and dedicated himself to seeking help from the Allies, both financial and practical.

The first infusion of money came from the Czechoslovaks under their nation-alist leader Tomáš Masaryk, who would go on to become the founder and first president of an independent Czechoslovakia in late 1918. The Czechs and Slovaks had gotten involved militarily in Russian affairs after the February Revolution because tens of thousands of them were among the hundreds of thousands of Austro-Hungarian prisoners that Russia captured during the war. Most of the Czechs and Slovaks were strongly anti-German and anti-Hungarian and were eager to turn their bayonets against their former overlords by fighting for the Allies on the Russian front. By 1918, there was a Czech Legion in Russia, an independent force of 40,000 well-armed men that was potentially strong enough to play a decisive role in the unfolding Russian Civil War, even though the Legion's primary aim was to move to the Western Front.

Masaryk was a Russophile, knew the language, had published a three-volume study of Russian culture, and had even read Savinkov's *The Pale Horse*. Like many other Europeans, he was fascinated by his career, and when he was offered the opportunity to meet Savinkov in Moscow, he accepted eagerly. They spoke twice in early March at the Hotel National, a luxurious establishment just across Manezhnaya Square from the Kremlin, which was where the Soviet government made its first home in Moscow (the Kremlin itself and buildings in it were still being repaired after the artillery damage they sustained in October). Considering the prominence of the hotel and the people who stayed there, it took nerve for Savinkov to be willing to enter it.

They discussed Savinkov's terrorist past and how relatively inexpensive his campaigns had been. Savinkov also described his new plan to overthrow the Bolsheviks and resume the war against the Central Powers. Masaryk agreed with the idea of abrogating the Brest-Litovsk Treaty and decided to give the Union 200,000 rubles, which is the equivalent of approximately $2 million today. As Savinkov recalled, Masaryk had no compunctions at the time about any of the money going to support the Union's planned terrorist campaigns (although later, when Masaryk became his country's head, he would find it necessary to lie about this).

This was a transformative sum that for the first time allowed Savinkov's orga-nization to pay its members monthly salaries. Previously, many had difficulty securing food and shelter, and some had to resign from the Union because they could not find enough work to feed themselves. Even Perkhurov had often slept in train stations.

The British Connection

There were also bigger and more ambitious foreign interests that wanted to keep Russia in the war by any means necessary.

The British initiative began in mid-January 1918, when Prime Minister David Lloyd George dispatched thirty-year-old Robert Hamilton Bruce Lockhart to Moscow to establish official contacts with the country's new Bolshevik leadership. A fun-loving Scot with a beefy face and wavy hair, Lockhart was an experienced "Russia hand" who knew the language and had been the British consul-general in Moscow before the October Revolution. He also had a strong adventurous streak and was more than willing to engage in clandestine work in Moscow in addition to his official diplomatic duties.

Although initially very much taken with the Bolsheviks, Lockhart's view of them plummeted in February and March as a result of their growing ties with Germany. Keeping this secret, he began to familiarize himself with the Bolsheviks' numerous opponents and soon became convinced that Savinkov, whom he had met in Petrograd after the February Revolution, stood the greatest chance of success and deserved British support. As a result, Lockhart began to collude closely with him, even reportedly allowing him to live secretly in the British consulate in Moscow—something that the British Foreign Office would not have approved—and thus helping to foil the Cheka's attempts to find and arrest him. Lockhart also began to provide Savinkov with money.

In May, Lockhart sent a top secret telegram to London about Savinkov's plans for a counterrevolution, which included the assassination of the Bolshevik leadership and establishing a military dictatorship under a well-known general. For himself Savinkov reserved the role of minister of the interior in the new government, an arrangement that resembles the one he had tried to realize with General Kornilov, except that now it was with General Alexeyev. The seemingly indomitable Kornilov had been killed by an artillery shell in April during a battle between the Volunteer Army and the Bolsheviks in the Kuban Region.

Lockhart also revealed to his superiors a surprising and highly confidential element in Savinkov's plan that was to be the key to its success: he was going to coordinate his uprising with "bountiful" help from the Allies. Savinkov told Lockhart that the French not only were providing the Union with money but also had promised him military support to overthrow the Bolsheviks. The French ambassador to Russia, Joseph Noulens, who had first met Savinkov when he was director of the Ministry of War and been impressed by him, even set the date for the French invasion, initially before the end of June, then revised to early July. There would be at least three divisions of troops landing in Archangel in the north of Russia, or between 45,000 and 60,000 men. The total amount of money the French gave Savinkov in May and June was 2 million rubles, with another 500,000 later, for the equivalent today of nearly $20 million. In exchange for their support, the French also insisted that Savinkov abandon his plans for moving the entire underground Union army to Kazan and focus instead on uprisings in a series of small cities between Moscow and Archangel to pave the way for Allied troops when they marched on the Bolshevik capital. Another condition the French set was that there should be evidence of significant popular support for the risings in the provincial cities before they committed troops to an intervention.

When Lockhart learned all this, he renewed urging the British government to support Savinkov's Union financially, and even offered to try to collect money for it locally on his own. He was also strongly in favor of British military intervention together with the French. But London did not share France's interest in getting involved in Russian affairs. The official in the Foreign Office who read Lockhart's report reacted to the dramatic news very calmly, with a "let's wait and see" attitude, if not outright skepticism.

Lockhart knew that the idea of Allied military intervention against the Bolsheviks was not as far-fetched as it might have sounded, because foreign troops had already begun to arrive on Russian soil. In early March, a few hundred British sailors and Czech soldiers came to Murmansk, a major port on the Kola Peninsula near Norway, initially and paradoxically at the invitation of the Bolsheviks to protect a large stockpile of military supplies from possible seizure by the Germans. These early attempts at cooperation between the Allies and the Bolsheviks did not last, however, and were soon replaced by more aggressive actions. A small Japanese contingent landed in Vladivostok in April, the vanguard of a larger force that foreshadowed Japanese territorial ambitions in Russia's Far East. At the beginning of June, 1,200 more English troops landed in Murmansk and 100 in Archangel, the port on the White Sea from which Savinkov had once escaped. In the months ahead, the number of foreign troops in the Russian North, Far East, and South in Odessa would reach tens of thousands, and even include 5,500 Americans in Murmansk.

The Ace of Spies

Lockhart was not the only British operative in Bolshevik Russia. On March 15, 1918, Mansfield George Smith-Cumming, the monocled, one-legged head of MI6 in London—whose agents called him "the Chief" or just "C" because his name was actually a closely guarded secret—invited a certain Sidney George Reilly for an interview. C was looking for someone he could send to Russia on a covert and dangerous mission to disrupt the Bolsheviks' fulfillment of the Brest-Litovsk treaty and to get Lenin and Trotsky to resume the war against Germany.

Reilly had been recommended to C because of his past exploits, his knowledge of languages, and his hatred of the Bolsheviks. But there were also enough doubts about him for C to have him investigated thoroughly and tailed over the course of several days in London. For one thing, Reilly's origins were uncertain because of the differing claims he had made about himself, such as that his father was an Irish sea captain, an Irish clergyman, a Russian nobleman, and a rich Polish landowner. In fact, Reilly was born Sigmund Georgievich Rosenblum in 1874 in Odessa, Russia, to a Jewish family that had converted to Catholicism, and he assumed his new name in 1899. He knew Russia intimately and had met Boris Savinkov, whom he admired, on a number of occasions.

Many of the stories that swirled around Reilly then and later are incredible and are likely his own inventions. But even though it is often hard to tell fact from fiction in his biography, there is also enough that sounds plausible to constitute an impressive resume for a spy. A selection includes his involvement in spiriting out plans of Russian naval fortifications in Port Arthur, Manchuria, to the Japanese before the Russo-Japanese War; inveigling the holder of concessions to Persian oil fields to sell them to Britain despite fierce competition from France; stealing German naval plans on the eve of the Great War and delivering them to London; and making a fortune as a shady arms dealer in New York during the war.

There was no doubt, however, about Reilly's chameleonlike ability to assume different personas, his facility with languages, or his ability to charm people, especially women. His spoke Russian, German, and English like a native; could pass as a national of any of these countries; and blended in easily with company that was high, middling, or low, as the occasion required. He was also an ambitious man. He had a long-term fascination with Napoleon and amassed a large and expensive collection of the French emperor's memorabilia. In fact, one of C's agents was struck by the way Reilly's hatred of the Bolsheviks merged with his "conviction that some day he was destined to bring Russia out of the slough and chaos of Communism" and that "he would do for Russia what Napoleon did for France." In this regard, there was more than a little resemblance between aspects of Boris Savinkov's and Sidney Reilly's personalities.

Reilly's physical appearance made him memorable as well. He had piercing brown eyes that seemed to protrude from under his thick eyebrows, a swarthy face with deep seams running from his large nose to a sensuous mouth, and black hair swept back, revealing a wide forehead. He was, as C's agent put it, "a man that impressed one with a good deal of power." (Over time, enough rumors and legends accumulated around Reilly for him to become known as the Ace of Spies and to serve Ian Fleming as an inspiration for James Bond.)

After meeting him, C decided that Reilly was exactly what he had been looking for. Several weeks later he was off to Russia, generously supplied with "£500 in notes and £750 in diamonds," or several tens of thousands of dollars in today's money. He arrived in Moscow on May 7 and quickly reestablished contact with Savinkov. It was Reilly who put Savinkov in touch with Lockhart in an attempt to help the Union find additional funding. Over the next few years, Reilly would become one of Savinkov's strongest and most loyal advocates and supporters.

Loose Lips

With an organization as large as the Union had become, security was an ever-increasing concern. Members took the standard precautions such as using false papers, communicating in code, and meeting only in "safe" apartments and other locations. But because the Bolsheviks had begun to fashion the first modern, twentieth-century police state, they became far more effective in rooting out opponents than the tsarist regime had ever been. As Savinkov described it, Bolsheviks penetrated all aspects of Russian society:

> under Nicholas II revolutionaries had only the police to fear.
> But under the Bolsheviks we were surrounded by volunteer spies.

> Whoever has white hands cannot conceal that he is a "bour-
> geois"; and every "bourgeois" is inherently suspicious . . . add to
> this the constant searches, the settling of Red Army "comrades"
> in private apartments, the police control of travel, the famine,
> the aggressive behavior on the streets of Latvian riflemen [espe-
> cially zealous partisans of the Bolsheviks] and sailors, and the
> total absence of any kind of guarantees regarding individual
> rights.

Despite these dangers, Savinkov did not suppress the theatrical side of his personality and even taunted the Bolsheviks at times. Although he used disguises, one of his acquaintances reported that he also walked around the city openly in an eye-catching black military tunic and yellow boots, with a cigarette in his teeth, insisting "that it is not very dangerous because any Bolshevik Chekist he happened to meet would be the first to try to disappear." He even revealed to the Bolsheviks that he was in Moscow by publishing a signed article in a newspaper on March 24, 1918 (the Bolsheviks were not yet in complete control of the press), in which he vented his spleen at them for "What they did to my Russia!" as well as at those who abetted them, such as his old nemeses in the SR Party Natanson and Chernov. Savinkov concluded his piece with an open call "to fight. To fight the Germans and to fight the Bolsheviks." He included the Germans because he was sure that their agents were working with the Cheka to destroy the Union and were funding the 200,000-ruble reward ($2 million today) that the Bolsheviks had announced for him dead or alive.

There were several thousand Union members in Moscow alone, and it was only a matter of time before the Cheka discovered the organization's existence, although it was not due to Savinkov's bravado.

In early May 1918, a young member of the Union was being treated in a medical clinic on the outskirts of Moscow and fell in love with his nurse. A week or so later, the young woman went to the headquarters of the Cheka (not yet the infamous building on Lubyanka Square) and told Yakov Peters, the Latvian who was second in command, that there was a secret anticommunist organization in Moscow planning to start an uprising very soon. Its first action would be to settle scores with the Latvian Rifles, a military formation that had become the Soviet regime's Praetorian guards, and the Chekists.

Why the nurse betrayed the young man and the plot in which he was involved is unknown. But Peters and Dzerzhinsky decided that the information deserved "the most serious attention," and by following this little thread they soon discovered the medical clinic where the Union was centered.

⊶

Thursday, May 30, 1918, was a lovely, sunny spring day. Savinkov was in his own "conspiratorial" apartment in another part of the city when his telephone rang. Speaking in code—"There's a typhus epidemic in the clinic"—Colonel Perkhurov informed him that everyone in the clinic had been arrested.

The Cheka raid was a major blow. By evening around 100 members of the organization were seized both there and in other locations around the city. The Cheka also found weapons, explosives, and information about the Union and its plan to shift operations to Kazan, including addresses of safe houses and passwords. Many of the arrested Union members were brutally questioned and tortured. The names they revealed led to more arrests, and many were shot soon thereafter.

But the Union's structure of isolated cells had prevented the Bolsheviks from discovering the full scope of the organization, and all the senior unit commanders and many members had escaped. (Later, the Cheka would actually compliment Savinkov and Perkhurov for creating an organization that ran with "clocklike precision.") Savinkov realized that despite their losses, they could continue.

On the day after the raids, the city newspapers published an official announcement trumpeting that the "hydra of counterrevolution" had been crushed. They included a detailed description of Boris Savinkov, intended to inspire members of the general population to help capture him.

It never came to that, even though on two occasions Savinkov ran into prominent members of the Soviet regime whom he knew personally on the city streets—Anatoly Lunacharsky, the commissar of education, who had been in Vologda exile, and Vyacheslav Menzhinsky, a senior figure in the Cheka, who had been a student in Saint Petersburg (and whom Savinkov would encounter again in a few years under vastly different circumstances). Savinkov noted with satisfaction that although both men recognized him, they hurried to leave rather than do anything or summon help. It was an advantage that his enemies feared him.

Two weeks after the Cheka raids, the Union for the Defense of the Motherland and Freedom had regrouped and was ready to proceed. In keeping with French plans for an intervention, Savinkov and his staff planned armed uprisings in a series of historic small cities arranged along a ninety-degree arc approximately 150 miles to the north and northeast of Moscow—Yaroslavl, Rybinsk, Murom, and several others. Taking them would secure an invasion route to Moscow for the Allied troops that would land in Archangel and also block a Soviet counterattack.

Simultaneously, as a second part of the overall plan, Savinkov was going to try to assassinate Lenin and Trotsky and had his terrorist team begin to stalk the two men as they moved around Moscow. In a bizarre twist, because of the way old revolutionaries from competing factions often knew one another, for a while Savinkov and Lenin actually communicated during this period through a person known to them both who passed on questions and answers from one to the other. As Savinkov recalled later, "Lenin quizzed this third person about the 'Union' and about me, and I answered him and asked him about his plans. I don't know if he was as careful in his replies as I was in mine."

The final element of the plan was to coordinate with the Czech Legion, which rebelled against the Bolsheviks at the end of May after Trotsky ordered its members to join the Red Army and arrested its civilian leadership in Moscow. The Czechs began by seizing large sections of the 5,000-mile-long Trans-Siberian Railroad and by June 8 had taken Samara, 500 miles southeast of Moscow, thus isolating the capital from rail and telegraph communication with most of Siberia. It looked like Kazan would be their next target. This was the first major military threat that the Bolsheviks had faced since the Brest-Litovsk Treaty.

The Uprisings on the Volga

If all three parts of Boris Savinkov's plan had succeeded, the Bolshevik regime could have been defeated. But too many components were ultimately not under his control, and the plan to assassinate Lenin and Trotsky did not get beyond stalking. When Savinkov looked back at that summer's events, he concluded bitterly: "As is often the case, what happened was the exact opposite of what we expected." He may well have been thinking of his efforts to reform and replace the Provisional Government during the Kornilov affair, which ended with the Bolshevik coup (or of Tolstoy's conception of individual volition in *War and Peace*, which he echoed in his novel *What Never Happened*).

The strategic key to the uprising in the cities between Moscow and Archangel was Rybinsk, a port on the upper Volga River that was connected to Moscow and Petrograd by rail. Rybinsk had the strongest organization of Union members of all the cities that Savinkov targeted, approximately 400 experienced officers, as well as the weakest Red Army garrison. Even more importantly, it was the home of a giant artillery depot with enough guns, shells, and other military materiel to "equip a White army occupying half of Russia," as a local Bolshevik leader subsequently characterized it. Savinkov was also convinced that many among the local population hated the Bolsheviks deeply and would join a rising against them; all they needed was a catalyst.

Savinkov and the Union's other senior leaders believed they could take Rybinsk readily. With the artillery they could seize there, they would be able to take Yaroslavl, the prosperous regional capital and manufacturing center sixty miles downstream, which had a population of over 100,000 and was another major transportation hub with rail links to both Moscow and Archangel; especially important was its railway bridge over the Volga. After defeating the Bolsheviks in Rybinsk and Yaroslavl, the Union would have to hold both cities for at least four days to give the Allied troops time to arrive by rail from Archangel via Vologda.

Savinkov put himself in overall charge of the rising in Rybinsk; Perkhurov was in Yaroslavl. And in a separate action to distract the Bolsheviks and spread the rebellion, Dr. Grigoryev was going to take Murom 300 miles to the southeast.

Savinkov divided his force in Rybinsk into a half-dozen units, each with its assigned strategic targets, and took command of one consisting of seventy men, including Dikgof-Derental and Klepikov. He had reconnoitered Rybinsk and Yaroslavl personally several days earlier and returned to Rybinsk from Moscow on the eve of the rising, staying with a merchant who owned a house on the riverbank that was close to the Soviet barracks and functioned as the Union's local headquarters. The rising would begin in early July, which was the time that Noulens, the French ambassador, had specified.

The plan for Rybinsk seemed foolproof. But shortly before it began, a seemingly minor contretemps occurred that Klepikov, who was the most personally devoted of Savinkov's aides, would never forget. In fact, he would later conclude that it was connected to how the entire Rybinsk operation played out.

The problem centered on Lyubov Efimovna, who had come to Rybinsk together with her husband. It was very unusual to have a woman at the site of a coming battle, especially one who was neither a trained nurse nor had any other military role. Even more unusual in Klepikov's view was that Savinkov allowed her to be present in the merchant's house when he discussed operational matters with his staff, as a result of which she became fully aware of all the units' plans. It is possible that Savinkov did this in keeping with the egalitarian traditions of the Combat Organization, in which women had an equal role in making plans even if not in executing them. Perhaps he had some other reason.

Whatever the case, Klepikov was a professional soldier and found Savinkov's permissive attitude toward Lyubov Efimovna highly improper. He worried about security leaks from someone who was not a member of the staff. He also began to feel stirrings of jealousy because he got the impression that Lyubov Efimovna was trying to distance him from Savinkov.

As a result, when Lyubov Efimovna started to make comments about tactical plans during a meeting just a few hours before the scheduled uprising, Klepikov exploded. He rebuked her "sharply and rudely" for interfering. Then, turning angrily toward Savinkov, he threw down an ultimatum—choose me or her—and stalked out, planning to return to Moscow.

This was the first time that anything like this had happened between Klepikov and his chief. In the dramatic scene that followed, Savinkov followed him up the creaking stairs that led to his room. He asked him not to leave. He also assured him that Lyubov Efimovna would not interfere in their plans again; the only request he made was that Klepikov not be "rude" to her.

Klepikov agreed to stay, and in the short term would even reconcile with Lyubov Efimovna. But several years later his suspicions about her would return and darken, and he would implore Savinkov, who seemed too trusting to him, never to forget the "monstrous Azef affair."

Savinkov waited in Rybinsk for word from Perkhurov that he had begun his attack and was ready for the artillery to be shipped to him. But the uprising in Yaroslavl did not begin smoothly or on time.

On the eve of his planned attack, Perkhurov had discovered that fewer men than he expected and needed showed up. Savinkov ordered more to be sent immediately from Moscow to Yaroslavl, but very few came. Nevertheless, Perkhurov decided to proceed.

Against all odds, he succeeded in taking and holding Yaroslavl for seventeen days, a remarkably long time under the circumstances. In addition to the element of surprise, his tactical skills, and the determination of his men, he also benefited from the ambivalence of some of the Bolshevik troops stationed in the city. At one early point during the rising, a unit of mounted police began an attack against Perkhurov's men but agreed to being disarmed rather than fight. There were also defections when instructors at a Red Army school decided to join the rebels and brought their machine guns and armored car with them.

Leaflets the Union had prepared and posted in the city made clear its political aims and its intention to overthrow the Bolshevik regime not only in Yaroslavl but throughout the country. Among the announcements was that "the Northern Army," as the Volga branch of the Union called itself, "is commanded by the old revolutionary Boris Savinkov." After the uprising started, the local population provided substantial help, both in men and materiel. Some civilians and former army officers in the city joined Perkhurov's force. Initially, so did significant numbers of peasants from surrounding villages, who even instituted their own conscription, although as the battle raged their reliability and effectiveness wavered. Women volunteered as nurses. The city's clergy and heads of monasteries and nunneries urged their parishioners to fight the "godless Bolsheviks" and provided shelter and aid to the wounded. During the course of the battle for the city Perkhurov's men overran all its strategic points and government buildings and began settling scores with the Bolsheviks. Members of the local Soviet administration were rounded up and arrested, with several score imprisoned in a barge on the Volga. There were reports that some were dragged out into the street and shot.

However, after an initial period of panic and chaos, which allowed Perkhurov's men to move quickly, the Bolsheviks rallied. Reinforcements began to stream into Yaroslavl from other areas, including units of foreigners—Germans, Hungarians, Latvians, and Chinese communists who supported the Bolsheviks. The forces opposing the Union soon became overwhelming, in terms of not only numbers of troops but also artillery. Perkhurov's men had two light field pieces with a very limited number of shells. The Reds were able to mass several dozen guns against them, including many of large caliber, and also used airplanes to bomb the city. Perkhurov's need for the artillery stored in the Rybinsk had reached the critical state.

Boris Savinkov did not learn until the following day, Sunday, July 7, that Perkhurov had begun his attack in Yaroslavl and that its initial phases were successful. However, because a local commander in Rybinsk said that he needed more time to gather his men, Savinkov gave the order to delay the uprising in Rybinsk until the following night, at 3 A.M. on Monday the eighth. This delay would prove fatal.

When Savinkov launched his attack, it initially went well, and his men seized a military barracks and an armory easily. They then started to advance toward the artillery depot that was their primary target when, suddenly, they were met with massive rifle and machine gun fire. Large numbers of Latvian Rifles and armed workers were blocking their way.

All the other units in Rybinsk also came under attack as soon as they began to move out from their mustering locations. The Reds clearly knew where they were. As soon as Savinkov learned what happened, he realized that the rising in Rybinsk had been betrayed.

But how the betrayal occurred was discovered only later by historians who studied Cheka reports in the local archives. It turns out that several weeks before the uprising, the Rybinsk branch of the Cheka had gone on alert because of continuing anti-Bolshevik disturbances by local residents. The Cheka also broadcast a public appeal for reports about any suspicious activity in the area. As an additional precaution, 500 more troops were dispatched to the city. Savinkov and the other members of the Union had heard nothing about these developments during their reconnaissance trips.

The betrayal happened just a few hours before the scheduled beginning of the rising at 3 A.M. on Monday: someone tipped off the Cheka that a number of men were lying low in the nearby village of Ivanovskoe. Had there not been the day-long delay in beginning, Savinkov's men could have succeeded.

Cheka agents rushed to arrest the suspects, who not only turned out to be armed but also carried documents that gave the time of the planned rising, the locations of the gathering points, and the targets in Rybinsk. Savinkov subsequently concluded that because of the extensive precautions he and others had taken, only someone connected to the Union could have been the traitor, although he never found out who it was.

When the Union members were arrested in Ivanovskoye, all the Red troops in Rybinsk were put on high alert by the Cheka and positioned so that they could intercept the rebels. Savinkov's unit was one of the few that made any headway before it was stopped by heavy fire. The rising that seemed assured of success had become a rout. Without control of Rybinsk and its arsenal, the rebels in Yaroslavl were in grave danger. The only hope was the French troops that were expected to arrive any day and begin their drive on Moscow. Savinkov sent an officer to Perkhurov to tell him to cancel his plans. But the officer never reached Yaroslavl, and by then it was too late to stop Perkhurov anyway.

By noon on Monday, July 8, the rebellion in Rybinsk was over and the city was quiet. Savinkov's unit had split up, and after walking for a dozen miles through mud and a constant cold rain, he and his aides managed to get to an outlying village, where a merchant sympathetic to their cause sheltered them. The following morning, Savinkov and his followers resolved to gather whatever remnants of the Rybinsk force they could find to start guerilla operations in the region in the hope that this could still help Perkhurov in Yaroslavl.

On the fourth day of the rising in Yaroslavl, as the Red artillery ringing the city pounded it to rubble and Perkhurov's casualties mounted, what seemed to be the promise of salvation from abroad finally appeared. Two officers from the French Air Force arrived at Perkhurov's headquarters and informed him that they were billeting officers attached to the army that was about to disembark in Archangel. Their job was to investigate where the thousands of French troops could be housed when they arrived.

As Perkhurov subsequently described the meeting, the two Frenchmen showed him several telegrams from Ambassador Noulens and General Jean Guillaume Lavergne, the chief of the French military mission in Russia, although these were vague and inconclusive about any specific actions. But orally the officers confirmed that the landing force would definitely disembark in Archangel, that its main units would arrive in Yaroslavl in a matter of days, and that the first trains would be loaded mostly with military equipment. They also expressed surprise that Perkhurov had not heard any of these details before.

After spending the night, the two Frenchmen asked Perkhurov for a pass to cross the railroad bridge over the Volga so that they could head north, toward Vologda, to hasten the arrival of the landing force.

Perkhurov's men continued to fight off the Red Army's onslaught day after day, pinning their hopes on lasting long enough until the French troops arrived. Yaroslavl was now completely cut off from Rybinsk, and Perkhurov did not know what had happened there; all attempts to communicate by radio failed, and the runners he sent did not return. When the third week began, the French had still not arrived. With the enemy pressing from all sides, mounting casualties, and shrinking supplies, Perkhurov decided that he had no choice but to try to escape from Yaroslavl with as many of his remaining men as he could. His destination would be Kazan, where other Union forces had moved from Moscow and which was close to the Czech Legion's area of activity. It would be a long and dangerous journey of 400 miles through forests and by water.

⚓

After they escaped from Rybinsk, Savinkov's men did succeed in blowing up a steamship carrying Bolshevik troops to Yaroslavl as well as a train with artillery shells. They also damaged the rail line connecting Yaroslavl to Petrograd, which made transporting reinforcements from the former capital more difficult. But they were unable to disrupt train transport on the Moscow line, and Trotsky, the head of the Red Army, was able to rush troops from the Moscow garrison to Yaroslavl. Soon the area around Rybinsk became too dangerous because of Bolshevik patrols. Savinkov resolved to move to Kazan as well, as did Dr. Grigoryev in Murom, who had also launched his uprising on July 8 but succeeded only in taking the local Bolshevik headquarters for a few hours before his men were forced to retreat.

The two French Air Force officers who came to Yaroslavl were the only "Allied troops" that anyone in the Union ever saw during the uprisings on the upper Volga. Savinkov and Perkhurov came to the incredible conclusion that the French had betrayed their promise to provide military assistance. This not only led to the needless deaths of many Union members but also nullified the Union's entire rationale for shifting its military efforts from Kazan to Rybinsk and Yaroslavl. Historians have subsequently debated whether or not the French actually planned to get involved in Boris Savinkov's Volga uprisings. But there is evidence that they did: a year after the events, when Dikgof-Derental was in Paris and happened to meet General Lavergne, the former chief of the French military mission to Russia admitted to him that "we are guilty before you. We betrayed you."

Bolshevik vengeance in Rybinsk was swift. On July 10 the local Soviet informed Moscow that the rising "was quickly crushed . . . The captured rebels are being shot." Next, the Soviets imposed an onerous "reparation" of 5 million rubles on the city's bourgeoisie (thus undermining their own claim that the Rybinsk rising did not have local support).

In Yaroslavl, on the day after Perkhurov and his small group of followers escaped, the Bolsheviks executed over 450 captives. This was the first mass execution that the Bolsheviks had carried out anywhere in Russia so far. Numerous smaller executions took place over the next several months. The losses to the city's cultural heritage caused by artillery were catastrophic—dozens of famous medieval churches and monasteries, twenty factories, and several score cultural institutions and government buildings, including some holding museum collections that had been evacuated from Petrograd. Nearly 30,000 residents were left homeless.

The campaign on the Volga was a bitter disappointment for Savinkov, but he still found something important to celebrate:

> For the first time . . . in Russia herself, almost in the vicinity of
> Moscow, Russian people, without anyone's help, rebelled against
> the Bolsheviks and proved that not all Russians acquiesce to the
> national disgrace of the Brest-Litovsk Peace Treaty and that not all
> Russians bow down before Bolshevik terror. Our honor was saved.
> Glory to those who fell in battle.

As he had many times before, Savinkov gathered himself up and rededicated himself to the fight against the Bolsheviks: "In my eyes the struggle was not over but had just begun," he wrote later.

By contrast, in an expression of the kind of infighting that would also characterize White military opposition to the Bolsheviks, the generals of the Volunteer Army condemned the risings on the Volga when they found out about them for being wasteful and completely ineffectual. The debate about what Boris Savinkov had accomplished continues in Russia to this day.

The Bolsheviks under Attack

The summer of 1918 was a perilous time for the young Bolshevik regime, which came within a hair's breadth of being ousted. Although Savinkov's venture on the Volga failed in military terms, his erstwhile comrades the Socialist Revolutionaries nearly succeeded with a plan in Moscow very much like the one he had abandoned when the French dangled the prospect of cooperation in front of him.

By early 1918, the SRs, who had disowned Savinkov the previous year, became convinced that the Bolsheviks had betrayed the Revolution by signing the Brest-Litovsk Treaty. On July 4, at a Congress of Soviets, the Left SR faction, which had allied itself with the Bolsheviks during their October coup and was rewarded with government positions, failed to have the treaty abrogated and to pass a motion of no confidence in the regime. As a result, they put into motion plans they had made for armed rebellion. The signal to begin was the assassination of Count Wilhelm von Mirbach, the German ambassador in Moscow, which the Left SRs expected would provoke a war between Germany and Soviet Russia.

It is a coincidence that the assassination was carried out on July 6, the same day that Perkhurov began his rising in Yaroslavl, although there was no coordination between the two events. Later that same day, armed units of Left SRs went into action throughout Moscow, arresting Bolshevik functionaries on the streets and even Dzerzhinsky in his own office. Left SRs also occupied the Central Post and Telegraph Office, from which they sent out an appeal to Russia and the "whole world" condemning the Bolsheviks and calling for "the masses" to rededicate themselves to revolutionary ideals.

As Savinkov had realized when originally planning his own Moscow uprising, the number of men necessary to seize power at this deeply unsettled time in Russian history was minuscule in comparison to the vastness of the prize that was at stake. The rebellion by the Left SRs confirmed this. They had only 2,000 troops, eight pieces of artillery, sixty-four machine guns, and several armored cars, but this would have been sufficient for them to seize the Kremlin and arrest the entire Bolshevik leadership, if they had wanted to. By the night of July 6, they were on the doorstep of the position that Savinkov had dreamed of when he created the Union for the Defense of the Motherland and Freedom.

But the Left SR leadership was strangely irresolute. Despite their formidable show of force, their aim was to stir up revolutionary fervor and not take power. Lenin and the rest of his government did not know this, however, and fell into a panic when the rebellion broke out. They remained paralyzed for hours, which further extended the time when the Left SRs could have acted. Only at 5 A.M. on the following day, July 7, did Latvian Rifle units loyal to the Bolsheviks begin their counterattack against the rebels. These were the only forces in Moscow that were willing to fight at the time and numbered 3,300 men, with fewer than 500 ethnic Russians.

The Left SRs fought fiercely, but by noon on July 7 they were defeated. That same and the following day the Bolsheviks liberated their comrades and arrested hundreds of Left SRs. However, rather than execute these rebels, as they would Perkhurov's men in Yaroslavl two weeks later, the Bolsheviks freed the majority of them. They could not afford to alienate the 60,000 members of the Left Socialist Revolutionary Party at the same time that conflagrations were breaking out around the country: uprisings in Yaroslavl, Rybinsk, and Murom; the Czech Legion seizing cities to the east and in Siberia; and a growing campaign by the Volunteer Army in the south.

This conciliatory stance during a period when the Bolshevik regime was weak did not extend to the former imperial family. In light of all the turmoil in the country, and fearing that the Romanovs, who had been brought from Petrograd to Yekaterinburg in the Urals, would be liberated by anti-Bolshevik forces, Lenin ordered their execution so that they could not become a "live banner" for the regime's enemies. Nicholas; his wife, Alexandra; their daughters, Olga, Tatyana, Maria, and Anastasiya (ranging in age from seventeen to twenty-three); their son, Alexey (fourteen); the family physician; and three servants were shot and bayoneted before dawn on July 17 by a group of eleven Chekists. Later that day Grand Duchess Elizaveta Fyodorovna, whose husband was killed by Kalyaev in 1905, and five other members of the Romanov clan were murdered 100 miles to the northeast.

⚬━━⚬

The assassination of Count Mirbach by the Left SRs did not lead to war between Germany and Soviet Russia, but the defeat of their uprising in July also did not end the broader Socialist Revolutionary Party's commitment to fighting the regime. Its branch in Petrograd had resurrected the Combat Organization in early 1918 and began to stalk several Bolshevik functionaries, resulting in the assassination on June 20 of Vladimir Volodarsky, a hated commissar for the press. After the Bolshevik government moved to Moscow, some of the members of the Combat Organization followed and chose Trotsky as their first target, whom they tracked around the city the same way they had tsarist ministers. But because he traveled a great deal and unpredictably, the stalkers shifted their attention to Lenin, only to discover that a fanatical member of the Party, Fanny Kaplan, was already making plans of her own. Her reasons for wanting to kill Lenin were the dissolution of the Constituent Assembly, the signing of the Brest-Litovsk Treaty, and, as she understood it, his betrayal of the idea of socialism. All were reasons with which Savinkov agreed. In effect, the SR Combat Organization in general and Kaplan in particular decided to pick up the kind of terror campaign that he had abandoned in Moscow.

Kaplan joined the Combat Organization and, like her pre-Revolutionary predecessors, affirmed that she was willing to die in her attempt. On Friday, August 30, after Lenin had finished giving a speech in a factory, she was able to get close to him and fired three times from a Browning automatic, wounding him severely in the neck. Kaplan was not an experienced assassin and had very poor eyesight; a better shot could easily have killed Lenin. Despite the severity of his wound,

Lenin recovered quite quickly and was back at work in the Kremlin six weeks later. Both the attack and his "miraculous" recovery led his closest associates to begin a policy of deifying him that would grow into a virtual cult after his death.

Kaplan refused to answer most of the Cheka's questions about her connections. This subsequently spawned conspiracy theories about who was ultimately responsible for her attempt, and even Savinkov once carelessly and hastily claimed some credit before he recanted. He may have seen her attempt as the wish fulfillment of a plan that he would have carried out if he had not been lured away to the Volga region. And had he or one of his men pulled the trigger, Russian history would have developed entirely differently.

Kaplan was not tried. On September 3, in an area near the Kremlin's Great Palace that was used as a parking lot, the Kremlin's commandant had the engines of several trucks started to drown out the noise and shot Kaplan in the back. Her corpse was then stuffed into a barrel near the Kremlin wall, doused with gasoline, and incinerated.

Kaplan's attempt on Lenin and, coincidentally, the assassination on the same day of Moisey Uritsky, the head of the Petrograd Cheka, catalyzed the Bolsheviks to respond forcibly, and several days later they implemented their notorious policy of "Red Terror." Even before it was officially announced, the newspaper of the Red Army started exhorting the country's population to take unprecedented vengeance: "Without mercy . . . we will kill our enemies by the scores of hundreds, let them be thousands, let them drown themselves in their own blood. For the blood of Lenin and Uritsky . . . let there be floods of blood of the bourgeoisie." Two weeks after the terror campaign was launched, Grigory Zinovyev, a high-ranking Bolshevik functionary, proclaimed that "We must carry along with us 90 million out of 100 million of Soviet Russia's inhabitants. As for the rest, we have nothing to say to them. They must be annihilated."

The Ambassadors' Plot

In addition to numerous domestic enemies, the Bolsheviks also had good cause to fear foreign powers in the summer of 1918. Shortly after the uprisings by

Savinkov's Union and the Left SRs, and while the Czechoslovaks were seizing cities in the east and in the Urals, the Cheka also discovered that representatives of the British, American, and French governments were plotting a coup d'état against the Soviet regime that was to be coordinated with Allied landings in northern ports. The Allies' aim in what became known, not entirely accurately, as the Ambassadors' Plot, or the Lockhart Plot, was to annul what they saw as the "obscene" Treaty of Brest-Litovsk and to reopen the Eastern Front against the Germans. Confirming the danger, in early August 8,500 British and American troops went ashore in Archangel; later, 11,000 mixed Allied troops arrived in Murmansk.

The threat from all the enemies was so serious that at a meeting in the Kremlin a despairing Lenin told his colleagues that their cause was "temporarily" lost and they would have to evacuate Moscow. The head of British intelligence in Petrograd noticed that Lenin and Trotsky began to spend more time in the former capital and reported the rumor to London that "Lenin is in Peterhof and a yacht under Swedish flag ready to take him away." Another British agent in Moscow informed the Foreign Office that "Many of the Commissars of the various departments were procuring passports and money and making general personal arrangements for safe departure."

Everything that Boris Savinkov had believed about the weakness of the Soviet regime was proving accurate. But even though he was hundreds of miles away and trying to regroup after the failures on the Volga, his friends and admirers among the coup plotters in Moscow had not forgotten him.

⊷

The Allied representatives in Moscow believed that the key to seizing power from the Bolsheviks was, paradoxically, the Latvian Rifles, their most loyal troops. Not all their rank and file were happy with the severity of Bolshevik rule or with the fact that the Bolshevik commissars had agreed to give the Germans control over the Baltic territories of the former Russian Empire, including their Latvian homeland. In July, some Latvian leaders working for the Bolsheviks entered into secret discussions with the Germans about coming over to their side if they were allowed to return home and guaranteed the return of their properties. This came to the attention of three men who began to conjure ways to exploit the Latvians' dissatisfactions: Captain Francis Cromie, the British naval attaché in

Petrograd and de facto head of British Intelligence in northern Russia; R. H. Bruce Lockhart, the British agent in Moscow who had helped Savinkov with funding for the Union and was looking to do more; and Sidney Reilly, the secret agent who had been dispatched to Russia by MI6 that spring.

However, the Cheka also got wind that some of their Latvians were having secret discussions with Germany. To draw out and neutralize these traitors the Cheka developed a brilliant *provokatsiya*: they established a fictitious organization consisting of Latvians who were supposedly ready to overthrow the Bolshevik regime if they got help from the Allies.

As Dzerzhinsky and Peters, his deputy, anticipated, this was the perfect bait for the British spies as well, and in fact all of them swallowed it. In turn, the duped British agents widened the number of foreigners who would be deceived by bringing in the French and the Americans, the latter represented by one Xenophon Kalamatiano. He was a naturalized citizen and businessman who has the distinction of being the first American spy in Soviet Russia, something he would live to regret.

Members of the Latvian organization set up by the Cheka persuaded the Allied conspirators that with enough money they could bribe the dissident Latvian troops and make them turn against the Bolsheviks. In the second half of August an unwitting Lockhart paid the Latvian commander of the units guarding the Kremlin, who was actually an agent of the Cheka, 1,200,000 rubles in several installments as a down payment. With the approval of the British government as well as the French and Americans, Lockhart also began to collect more money from rich businessmen and others in Moscow who had managed to hide cash and valuables for just such an occasion.

Then everything suddenly changed. The British plotters found out that although Allied troops had landed in the northern ports, they would not be marching on Moscow after all. But rather than abandon their plans, the British agents with Reilly at their center, decided on an even more ambitious plan—to seize power themselves and set up a three-man dictatorship. They would also create two armies, one to be commanded by Boris Savinkov.

It is unknown if the British plotters discussed this fantastical venture with Savinkov in advance, or if they simply assumed that he would be willing to take part. In any event, it was fortunate for him that he was not in Moscow at the time because it is very likely that he would have taken part in some capacity (he may have wanted something bigger), and then been arrested and executed, but without achieving anything.

Official Allied diplomatic representatives balked at Reilly's brazen plan, but he would not retreat and set the coup for September 6, to coincide with a meeting in the Bolshoy Theater of the entire Soviet leadership. However, the Red Terror was in effect, and the foreign plotters did not know about the Latvian false flag operation. Ignoring the principle of extraterritoriality, the Cheka raided the British embassy in Petrograd and killed Cromie, which caused a major diplomatic rift between the two countries. They also arrested Lockhart as well as hundreds of other citizens of Allied nations. The British government retaliated by detaining the Soviet ambassador in London and holding him until the Allied captives were released the following month.

The amateur American spy Kalamatiano was not so fortunate. He too was arrested and when questioned gave up the network of agents that he had created throughout Russia during the past year. The Supreme Revolutionary Tribunal condemned him to death before commuting the sentence to a long prison term. Only President Herbert Hoover's intercession secured Kalamatiano's release in 1921, but his health was ruined, and he died in the United States two years later.

The Supreme Revolutionary Tribunal also sentenced Reilly and Lockhart to death in absentia. Both verdicts were reconfirmed in 2005 and 2006 by the Supreme Court of the Russian Federation.

The irrepressible Sidney Reilley was the sole plotter to escape when he disappeared from Moscow several days before the arrests began. Using the passport of a Baltic German, he was able to get to Petrograd in a train compartment reserved for the German embassy, and from there, using several other false identities, traveled to London. He would resurface in Paris in 1919, where he and Boris Savinkov would start their close alliance and renew ambitious plotting.

Retreat to Fight Again

Savinkov's escape to Kazan after the Volga uprising was delayed by a bout of typhus fever, a disease spread by lice that was becoming increasingly common during Russia's civil war, both in cities and the countryside. In 1918 there was not much that could be done for someone who had it, except for sanitizing all the lice-infested clothing and trying to comfort the patient with cooling compresses. Lyubov Efimovna nursed Savinkov back to health under difficult circumstances because they were still in Bolshevik-controlled territory and under threat of capture. But her dedication even impressed Klepikov, as a result of which he (temporarily) softened his stance toward her.

Once Savinkov recovered and Dikgof-Derental returned from a side trip to Moscow, they all went to Petrograd to get new documents that would allow them to travel through Bolshevik-controlled territory. It was the end of July when they got there, and the Soviet regime was at the nadir of its power. The city had deteriorated even more since Savinkov's last visit at the beginning of the year and now looked to him as if it were "dying." As in Moscow, signs of economic and social collapse were everywhere. Cholera and typhus epidemics were breaking out; the streets were empty and filthy; the stores were shuttered; basic foodstuffs were in short supply. Groups of sailors in flat, cockily angled caps and with hand grenades hanging from their belts patrolled the formerly grand Nevsky Prospect. It was especially galling for Savinkov to see numerous German officers strolling along the storied boulevard with the arrogant air of victors.

The Petrograd branch of the Union for the Defense of the Motherland and Freedom prepared fake Bolshevik passports for them. Savinkov and Dikgof-Derental also changed into the kind of garb that had become a Bolshevik uniform—a long, loose shirt cinched in at the waist with a belt, tall boots, and a military campaign cap with the tsarist-era cockade removed. Camouflaged in this way, they left by train for Nizhny Novgorod, nearly 600 miles to the southeast and three-quarters of the way to their destination. The newspapers they bought at the station were full of reports about executions of captured Union rebels and sympathizers in Yaroslavl and Rybinsk.

Their fake papers worked smoothly most of the way, until the ship they took from Nizhny Novgorod had to stop well short of Kazan because of fighting farther downstream between the Bolsheviks and the Czechoslovaks, who had just taken the city. Savinkov and his group hired a wagon with horses and set off by land. At one point they had an encounter with suspicious Red soldiers, but Savinkov bluffed his way through by playing a man of some importance with a connection to Trotsky himself.

One hundred fifty miles still separated Savinkov's group from their destination, and rather than risk any more encounters with Red soldiers, they decided to travel along the northern, heavily forested side of the Volga, where there would be fewer patrols. Savinkov's encounters with local peasants, who became very helpful once they realized that his group was going to Kazan to fight the Bolsheviks, lead him to a conclusion about peasant opposition to the Bolsheviks that would play a defining role in his life: although he did not think that they could defeat the Soviet regime by themselves, neither did he believe that the regime could survive against them.

⚬━⚬

When his small caravan finally rolled out of the endless forest into cultivated fields, Savinkov realized that Kazan was not far ahead. Bolshevik troops were guarding approaches to the city, but the two wagons passed them by with panache and with the little bells attached to the horses' harnesses untied and ringing freely. It was an old Russian practice to have their merry tinkling announce a vehicle's passage and warn pedestrians. On this occasion, they would also signal that the passengers had nothing to hide.

Directly in front, across a vast expanse of undulating fields and low hills, gleamed the golden cupolas of Kazan's many churches. And in their midst, its pointed spire stabbing into the sky, rose the city's symbol—the famous leaning Tower of Syuyumbike, or "Tower of the Tatar Tsaritsa," as Savinkov called it, a seven-tiered brick structure within the Kazan Kremlin's walls that some believed dated to when the city was the capital of the Tatar Khanate, which Tsar Ivan IV ("The Formidable," aka "The Terrible") conquered in 1552.

When Savinkov's party got closer, they saw sentries on the road by the city aqueduct. They were Czechoslovaks.

Odd Man Out

Following the rebellion of the Czech Legion against the Bolsheviks, the Allies decided to use the numerous well-armed and experienced Czechoslovak troops as the core of a new army that would reopen the Eastern Front against the Germans. This required the Czechoslovaks to reorient their forces and move west, and in the end of May 1918, they began military action against Red strongholds in Siberia, taking a series of strategic cities including Omsk. By June 8, they had advanced into the European part of Russia and taken Samara. On July 21, they took Simbirsk (Lenin's birthplace, now Ulyanovsk). On August 7, together with White forces, they took Kazan.

This sudden liberation of important cities and large territories from Soviet control emboldened former delegates of the Constituent Assembly (who saw the Bolshevik dispersal of the Assembly in January 1918 as an egregious usurpation of power) to organize an anti-Bolshevik government in Samara. Calling itself the Committee of Members of the All-Russian Constituent Assembly (*Komitét chlénov vserossiískogo uchredítelnogo sobrániya*), whence its acronym Komuch, and headed by a group of five Socialist Revolutionaries, the new government announced in early June that it was abrogating the Brest-Litovsk Treaty, granting power to the Constituent Assembly, and reinstating democratic institutions and practices. Another, more localized anti-Bolshevik government that called itself the Provisional Government of Siberia was also formed by politicians in Omsk.

Kazan was a major commercial center and transportation hub with a population of 200,000 in 1918 and had long functioned as a gateway between the western and eastern parts of the vast Eurasian landmass that Russia straddled. Its size and location near the midpoint of the Volga gave anyone who controlled it sway over the entire river and even the approaches to Moscow. This was the primary reason why Savinkov's Union for the Defense of the Motherland and Freedom had chosen Kazan as its base after Moscow and started to move its members there before the French intervened with their plans. In turn, this is why Union members who survived the Rybinsk and Yaroslavl uprisings tried to get there as well, discovering to their surprise when they did that it had just become a Bolshevik-free oasis.

Savinkov arrived too late to realize his hope that members of the Union would be able to take Kazan on their own, although given what had recently happened there, it is likely that they could have. The only opposition the Czech Legion and the Whites encountered when they attacked the city was an undermanned Latvian regiment. A fabulous additional prize that the Czechoslovaks and Whites got in Kazan, and that could also have fallen into the Union's hands, was a cache of over 650 million rubles in gold from the former Russian Imperial Treasury that had been evacuated there for safety. This sum—which wound up being dispersed among various parties and was never fully accounted for in the chaos of the period—allowed the Czech Legion and several White armies in Siberia initially to conduct large-scale military operations against the Bolsheviks without having to rely on taxes or food confiscation. In principle, Savinkov's revived Union could also have done the same.

When Savinkov arrived in Kazan, he was initially encouraged by the large number of Union members there and the fact that his senior comrades, including Colonel Perkhurov, occupied prominent positions in its military. But the overall situation in the city was perilous. The Komuch government had tried to raise an army of its own from among urban volunteers as well as local peasants. However, the number of volunteers was small, and the peasants, despite being violently opposed to the Bolsheviks, believed that the Revolution had liberated them from ever having to serve any state again. As a result, they refused to fight, deserted, or even rebelled against their commanders.

For Savinkov, it was all a depressing case of déjà vu, and he blamed Komuch for repeating what he believed was Kerensky's cardinal mistake during the war—failing to grant officers disciplinary authority over the troops, such as instituting the death penalty at the front.

In the Red Army, the situation was different. While Komuch dithered and debated, Trotsky, as people's commissar of military and naval affairs, was rapidly building his forces in the east by conscripting hundreds of thousands of men, including former tsarist officers. He also did not hesitate to introduce the death penalty for desertion or cowardice in the face of the enemy, or to use it liberally. In the opinion of an experienced White officer, the discipline he instilled exceeded that of the old tsarist army.

Despite his disapproval of the Komuch government's ruinous policies, Savinkov decided that he could not oppose it, because "it was every Russian's duty to support a government that had taken upon itself the arduous effort of fighting the Bolsheviks." As a result, he formally dissolved the Union for the Defense of the Motherland and Freedom on the principle that a secret military organization may rightfully exist only in those parts of Russia that are occupied by Bolsheviks.

However, the attitude of Komuch toward Savinkov was not equally loyal or even conciliatory, and all his attempts to find a role for himself in Kazan were rebuffed. The situation was similar to how he had been treated in Novocherkassk when he arrived hoping to find a place in the Volunteer Army, except now opposition was from the left. From the point of view of the Socialist Revolutionaries who made up the government, Savinkov had committed many grave sins, foremost among them being his apostasy, his backing of Kornilov, and his willingness to admit monarchists to the Union. As Savinkov subsequently recalled, "The SRs surrounded me with spies and I walked the streets of Kazan as if during the time of the tsar. *Fileurs* followed me all the time." He had enemies on the opposite side of the political spectrum as well, and only a stern warning from their commander prevented a group of officers from trying to shoot Savinkov, whom they blamed for betraying Kornilov.

But Savinkov could not remain a bystander even if he was not going to be allowed to play a leading role in the fight. He initially asked to accompany Komuch troops as a war correspondent. After a few days of this, he decided that he was still too far away from the action, and on August 27 requested permission to join a cavalry squadron that was going to penetrate behind Bolshevik lines so that he could take part as a simple soldier. Its commanding officer, Lieutenant-Colonel Vladimir Kappel, who would soon achieve even greater prominence in the war against the Bolsheviks in the Russian East including Siberia, agreed and ordered that Savinkov be given a horse and a rifle. The squadron left the same evening. Despite Savinkov's inexperience in the saddle, he managed the sixty miles on horseback at night successfully and "did not complain," according to one of the officers. This was the first time in his often violent life that Savinkov would experience being a regular soldier.

The squadron consisted of 100 men, three quarters of them former officers, with two light artillery pieces. Its mission was to disrupt railroad and telegraph communications in the rear of Bolshevik headquarters in Sviyazhsk on the right bank of the Volga, twenty miles west of Kazan, as part of Kappel's plan to try to advance upriver. Trotsky had come to Sviyazhsk by train to direct military operations himself. When Kazan fell to the Whites and Czechs, the Soviet leadership became worried because they could easily imagine an attack on Nizhny Novgorod next and then a march on Moscow.

⸻

Fall came early in this part of eastern Russia, which lies at the latitude of southern Alaska, and by the end of August the nights were growing cold and the leaves of the birches and aspens in the forests were starting to turn yellow. Each day the squadron would rise in the chill of daybreak when everything was still shrouded in lilac-tinged mist, mount up, and begin to ride across the boundless fields that spread around the Volga. Over the course of a dozen days, they blew up railway tracks, chopped down telegraph poles, executed any individual Bolsheviks they came across, and skirmished with small enemy units. They did not encounter any large formations, but it was clear that the Red Army commanders had them in their sights. Local peasants warned the squadron that the Reds were planning an ambush. Several times Savinkov and the others heard the distant buzz of airplanes flying overhead. To avoid being seen, they would hide in forests and under stands of trees.

Several days after the squadron began its raid, a large Red force found it, and Savinkov witnessed and participated in the lopsided battle that ensued. He characterized its brutality as something that epitomized the Russian Civil War and that had never been seen before, even on the Western Front.

The squadron was in a village on a small hill from which they could see a ravine, train tracks, and beyond them a series of other hills. At noon smoke suddenly appeared on the horizon and two trains emerged into view, one of them armored. When both stopped, a large number of Red infantry spilled out of the cars, some 500 men, perhaps more. At the same time, the armored train began to fire its guns at the squadron's position. The Red commanders not only knew the squadron's location, they intended to liquidate it.

But then something very unusual happened. The firing from the train stopped, and instead of forming skirmish lines and attacking the squadron, all the Red soldiers went up to one of the hilltops and gathered in a crowd. The members of the squadron could not believe their eyes—the Bolshevik soldiers had decided to begin a meeting in full view of their enemy. Savinkov and the others could make out a speaker who was waving his arms and heard a muffled, approving "Hurrah." There was some sort of major disagreement between the soldiers and their commanders, and it seemed that the speaker was persuading the men not to go into battle.

And it was when the meeting reached a crescendo of enthusiasm, which, as far as anyone knew, could have led to some sort of peaceful resolution or withdrawal by the Red troops, that the squadron's machine gun opened up on the crowd. In a few minutes, the entire hill was covered with the bodies of soldiers. The survivors scrambled aboard the two trains, which began to back up hurriedly. As the armored train was drawing away, its guns started to shell the squadron, and the squadron's two field pieces replied. One of the cars caught fire; engulfed in flames and smoke, the train disappeared around a bend.

The squadron's captain ordered the men to mount, and they rode up to the hill where the meeting had just taken place. Savinkov did not have a greatcoat against the cold weather and was freezing. He was about to take one from a dead soldier lying on the ground, but when he saw that it was stained with blood he decided to leave it.

Savinkov may have been too fastidious to wear a bloodstained coat, but he was not squeamish about the kind of carnage in which he had just participated. Dealing with Bolsheviks brought out a cruel streak in him that was illustrated by another memorable incident during the squadron's traverse of the region. He was sitting with a staff captain, Vasily Vyrypaev, and several other men near a grocery shop in a village when some of the squadron's scouts appeared escorting a number of captured Red Army soldiers. Vyrypaev asked them his usual questions about what their unit was and where they came from, and they replied that they had been conscripted in Petrograd, which was nearly 1,000 miles away. The official policy of the Komuch Army in a case like this was to release any captured enlisted men after disarming them. More important prisoners, such as Bolshevik officials and commissars, were supposed to be sent to the rear for detailed questioning. In practice, however, the policy of "an eye for an eye" prevailed and prisoners were often executed, both at the front as well as in towns, although not as systematically as the Bolsheviks executed Whites and their sympathizers.

Vyrypaev let all the captured soldiers leave as soon as he was done with them, with one exception. The last captive was just a boy, no more than fifteen or sixteen years old, skinny and dirty, who was crying and shaking because of what he believed was awaiting him. His reaction elicited raucous laughter from the members of the squadron who were watching. This was when one of Vyrypaev's artillery men decided to teach the boy a lesson in an old-fashioned, paternalistic way.

"Allow me to give this stinker a good spanking on his bare butt," he asked Vyrypaev. "This so-and-so ran away from his mother and joined the Reds as a volunteer."

Vyrypaev readily agreed. The boy was ordered to drop his trousers and lie on a big boulder stomach down. The artillery man then proceeded to spank him, not very hard, while punctuating each slap with a repeated admonition: "Don't run away from your mother, don't join the Reds as a volunteer." Once the punishment was over, the artillery man instructed him: "Put your pants on, go back to your guys, and tell them that we don't shoot your lot."

After the grateful boy ran off, Savinkov, who had watched the entire scene, turned to Vyrypaev with a sigh:

Ekh, Vasily Osipovich, you're too kind and make too much of a fuss over them . . . Better if you had shot this scum, and that would have been the end of it. You know that if we had fallen into these guys' hands, they would tear our skin off in strips. I just escaped from them and saw what they do to prisoners.

⊶⊷

Kappel's attempt to take Sviyazhsk failed, and with it all hope ended that Komuch could grow and launch an attack on Nizhny Novgorod and Moscow. When Savinkov returned to Kazan in the first days of September, he discovered that the tide of the civil war on the entire Volga had turned against the Whites. Trotsky concentrated more than 30,000 troops and 150 guns near Kazan and began to shell it and its environs at will. Opposing them was an assemblage of Komuch forces that numbered fewer than 5,000 men with seventy guns that was further weakened by not being under a unified command. The situation in Kazan was also aggravated by Bolshevik agents, who propagandized factory workers and fomented a rebellion on September 3. Although troops loyal to Komuch put it down, the political price was high. Flegont Klepikov, who participated in the suppression, was seriously wounded, depriving Savinkov of his most valued aide.

On the evening of September 10, the Whites were forced to abandon Kazan. Simbirsk, Samara, Syzran, and all the other cities that the Czech Legion had taken fell to the Red Army shortly thereafter. The only path of escape for the civilian groups, military forces, and local governments that opposed the Bolsheviks was now farther east, out of European Russia toward the Urals and ultimately into Siberia. Savinkov, Dikgof-Derental, and Lyubov Efimovna evacuated together, traveling part of the way by horse-drawn wagon because regular rail transport was disrupted by fighting among the various armies.

Hope in the East

The disunity of the anti-Bolshevik movements had been a problem from the start, and with the collapse of the Volga front at Kazan the need for an alliance between Komuch and the Provisional Government of Siberia became desperately obvious. A conference was organized in Ufa, an important city with a population of 100,000 located approximately 300 miles east of Kazan near the Urals. Lasting from September 8 to 23, it was attended by over 200 representatives of a remarkable number and variety of organizations: established political parties like the SRs and Mensheviks; delegations from Komuch and the Provisional Governments of Siberia and the Urals; seven Cossack hosts located in southern Russia, the Urals, and Siberia; and leaders of several ethnic and geographic entities—Kazakh, Bashkir, a Muslim Turko-Tatar coalition, another from the Turkestan region, and even the Provisional Government of Estonia.

But for Savinkov, the conference confirmed his worst fears: "Many speeches were made . . . These speeches did not stop the Bolsheviks." On September 23 the conference elected five Socialist Revolutionaries who constituted the Provisional All-Russian Government, a collective ruling body that also became known as the Ufa Directory. It disavowed the legitimacy of the nearly year-old Soviet regime and proclaimed loyalty to the Constituent Assembly. Its announced aims were the defeat of the Bolsheviks, abrogation of the Brest-Litovsk Treaty, self-determination for the former Russian Empire's minorities, and renewed war against Germany and her allies. All were aims that Savinkov shared, but he did not believe the new government could achieve any of them.

Shortly after the conference, the Directory moved to a safer location 700 miles farther east, to Omsk in western Siberia. There were many practical reasons for leaving European Russia: Bolshevik rule over Siberia, which made up two-thirds of Russian territory, was spotty and relatively weak; Siberia was not suffering from the food shortages that plagued the western regions of the country; and the port city of Vladivostok on the Pacific coast, although over 3,000 miles to the east, was well supplied by the Allies and provided a means of further collabora-tion with them.

The chairman of the Omsk Directory (as it also became known after its move) was Nikolay Avksentyev, an eloquent and charismatic long-haired intel-lectual who had a German doctorate in philosophy, was a former member of the SR Party's Central Committee, and had been minister of the interior in Kerensky's Provisional Government when Savinkov was acting minister of war. Savinkov knew him (and the other members of the Directory) very well, but they were more ideological enemies than allies: Avksentyev had opposed terrorism by the Combat Organization and refused to confirm the arrest of most of the Bolsheviks that Savinkov had advocated after their attempted coup in Petrograd in July 1917. Nevertheless, Savinkov was too major a figure in the Russian anti-Bolshevik movement to be entirely left out of consideration by the new government.

There were several prominent voices in Omsk advocating his appointment to an important post. The chairman of the Council of Ministers of the Directory thought Savinkov should be minister of foreign affairs. So did the British Major-General Alfred Knox, who had been military attaché in Petrograd since 1911, knew Russia very well, and was an influential representative of an important Allied power. Later, Knox would provide Savinkov with letters of introduction to senior figures in the British Foreign Office and the United States government, characterizing him as "a very clever fellow and a man of action" who should be listened to because of his patriotic position and despite his terrorist past.

However, Savinkov's enemies prevailed. General Vasily Boldyrev, who was one of the five members of the Directory and supreme commander of its armed forces, gave Savinkov his due as "a very major figure" and "an important organizer." But he considered him to have been "poisoned too much by his underground work" and incapable of correctly grasping the current political situation. Avksentyev, the chairman of the Directory, and Vladimir Zenzinov, another member of the quintet whose former friendship with Savinkov had soured, also did not want to deal with him because of his reputation as a "troubling element" and because they had enough problems in their own governmental "cauldron" without him.

The Directory's solution was to get rid of Boris Savinkov by sending him into a kind of honorable exile as its representative in Paris; he would later say that he suggested this to Avksentyev himself. This resembled what the leaders of the Volunteer Army did when they dispatched Savinkov from the Don to Petrograd and Moscow to try to organize opposition there in the beginning of 1918.

Savinkov was appointed the head of what was officially called the Special Military Mission of the Provisional All-Russian Government in Omsk, which included several other people who made up his staff. Dikgof-Derental was his primary diplomatic assistant, and Lyubov Efimovna was the Mission's secretary. A major-general, Alexey Odintsov, was appointed the Mission's military attaché and Savinkov's assistant on technical military matters, and a lieutenant-colonel, Vladimir Ivanovsky, was his assistant on matters pertaining to artillery specifically. The Directory assigned the Mission the generous sum of 300,000 francs (close to $1 million in today's money) for expenses and arranged for additional funds to be made available in Paris via the Russian embassy, which had not recognized the Bolsheviks and continued to function in opposition to them and as it had under Kerensky.

At least for the time being, Savinkov was relieved of the money problems that often bedeviled his life. As head of the Mission, starting on October 13, he received 1,000 francs salary per month and 40 francs per day for expenses. Eight to nine thousand dollars a month is hardly an extravagant sum, and the others earned less, but at least the members of the Mission did not have to lead a hand-to-mouth existence, and their travel expenses were covered as well.

The Directory issued them all diplomatic passports on October 14. Before he left Omsk, Savinkov was also given written instructions regarding his duties that were labeled "Top Secret." Despite the cloud under which his appointment had been made, they were more ambitious and promising than might have been expected.

One task was to induce the Allies, as soon as possible, to live up to the promises they made to provide the Directory with military aid in its fight against the "Germano-Bolsheviks." A related aim was to publicize accurately the situation in Russia to European governments and the media and to keep the Directory informed of any initiatives by the Allies to begin peace talks with the Central Powers.

The second task of the Mission was to recruit expert French military instructors and to procure relevant equipment for a training program to be established in Russia that would allow the Directory's forces to learn the technical advances made during the Great War in the fields of artillery, demolition, illumination, aviation, armored and motorized vehicles, and combat engineering. In all his tasks Savinkov would have authority to act as he saw fit, although there were guidelines on how much money he could spend on recruitment, and he was expected to seek the cooperation of the Directory's diplomatic representatives in Europe as well as to keep in regular contact with General Boldyrev in Omsk, who was his direct superior.

It would not be an easy task, Savinkov realized, but his efforts in Europe could make the difference between winning or losing the civil war against the Bolsheviks.

By Ship to Europe

Savinkov's Mission left Omsk at the end of October, traveling across Siberia by train to Vladivostok, and then via Peking to Shanghai, which they reached in the first days of November. This was the busiest port in China, with connections to all parts of the world. Savinkov and his staff first thought of traveling via Yokohama in Japan, across the Pacific to San Francisco, by train to New York, and then again by ship to France, but learned that this would take too long because of delays in Japan and the United States. They chose instead to take the route via Southeast Asia to Marseille.

This turned out to be more comfortable than they probably expected, because Savinkov's chance encounter in Shanghai with a Belgian diplomat he had met in Omsk resulted in his Mission being offered passage on a French ship that was being used as a troop transport during the war. One of the newest and largest of the well-known French Messageries Maritimes line, the SS *Paul Lecat* was also the most luxurious on the Far East route. It normally carried around 500 passengers in three classes, including a sumptuous first class with public rooms decorated in Louis XVI style, an elevator, and a veranda café. Savinkov reserved three first-class cabins on the upper deck, one single for himself, a double for the baron and his wife, and a double for the two military men.

As final preparations for departure took place, momentous news reached Shanghai: an Armistice agreement had been signed between the victorious Allies and Germany on November 11 in the Forest of Compiègne north of Paris. The cessation of fighting meant that peace talks would start soon. For Savinkov it was essential to reach Paris in time to try to participate in them so that he could defend Russia's interests.

The SS *Paul Lecat* began its voyage on November 12 and would take approximately six weeks to reach Marseille. Savinkov was sufficiently well known in the West that his departure and mission were announced in newspaper articles, including one in the *New-York Tribune*.

Even though the SS *Paul Lecat* had lost some of her luster and the service onboard was not at prewar levels, Savinkov's team still traveled in a style and with a level of comfort that they found very welcome after the rigors of the last several months. There were stops in exotic locales, where Savinkov went on enjoyable shore excursions with Lyubov Efimovna, and he would remember some of the vivid impressions for the rest of his life: "the light blue hills of Hong Kong, Saigon with its blinding rays, Singapore in a downpour, Colombo's camphor trees and sugar cane, . . . and the radiant, shining, endless, bottomless Indian Ocean. Dolphins and flying fish. And Lyubov Efimovna." During a stop in Djibouti, at the entrance to the Red Sea, he was struck by the "white walls, a scorching sun, tiny donkeys like the one on which Christ rode, dust and bare rocks. And in the desert, to the side of the road, the carcass of a camel and vultures—long-necked, yellow, tearing at the bloody meat."

The trip was uneventful except for Savinkov's odd reaction at one point in Port Said. He was strolling on the deck with Dikgof-Derental, but when they walked up to the ship's railing, Savinkov suddenly grabbed his companion by the arm and pulled him away. He explained that he felt drawn to the empty space and that he feared for himself. Dikgof-Derental would never forget the incident, and it would come back to haunt him a half-dozen years later.

⊷

When Savinkov left France for Russia in April 1917, he was flying on the wings of elation about what the future held. Now, twenty months later, all he could do was hope that the disaster of October and its aftermath could still be reversed. The armistice in Europe, a joyous event, was also a blow to his plans because it meant that there was no longer a need to reopen the Eastern Front. This eliminated the most important argument he could have used to agitate for Allied help against the Bolsheviks.

But there was a second argument as well, and it was not negligible. The Bolsheviks made no secret of their aim to ignite a worldwide revolution and overthrow capitalism everywhere, which included the victorious Allied states. Consequently, it was still in the Allies' interests to help crush communism where it had been born, and it would be central to Savinkov's efforts to persuade them that the Bolsheviks were a continuing threat even after the defeat of the Germans.

CHAPTER NINE

THE WAR AGAINST THE BOLSHEVIKS FROM ABROAD

B oris Savinkov arrived in Marseille, the major French port on the Mediterranean, around Christmas Day, 1918. Eager to catch up on the news he had missed while on board the SS *Paul Lecat*, he was leafing through the last month's newspapers when he came across an article that shocked him: the Provisional Government in Omsk was no more. On November 18, it had been overthrown in a coup d'état by Admiral Alexander Vasilyevich Kolchak.

This was important news not only in Russia. It had been telegraphed to Vladivostok on November 19 and from there around the globe. Allied representatives and governments, including the United States, announced that they welcomed the event because of what it augured for the war against the Bolsheviks.

But for Savinkov the coup created a major quandary. The government, such as it was, that had authorized his mission no longer existed. He did not know Kolchak well personally—he had met him only once, shortly before leaving Omsk for Shanghai—although like many Russians, he knew him by reputation, as Kolchak knew him by his. However, Kolchak knew nothing about Savinkov's mission. A week after his coup he summoned General Boldyrev, a member of the overthrown government, to ask, very politely, "to whom and with what tasks" was Savinkov sent abroad? Boldyrev explained, but Kolchak delayed deciding what to do with Savinkov, whose past he found suspect for several reasons. When Savinkov read what had happened, he sent a telegram to Kolchak congratulating him on assuming power and offering to represent him before the Allies. There was no response. Savinkov was once again in the position of having to decide what to do by himself.

Kolchak

Kolchak first emerged into prominence at the turn of the century as an intrepid naval explorer of the Russian Arctic and then as a brilliant tactician during the Russo-Japanese War and the Great War. By 1916, he was vice admiral in command of the Russian Black Sea Fleet—at forty-two the youngest admiral commanding a fleet in any of the warring navies—and already one of the most famous and successful in Russian naval history.

By inclination Kolchak was a monarchist, and he never abandoned an imperial perspective on Russia and her place in the world. In February 1917, he reluctantly acquiesced to the establishment of the Provisional Government in Petrograd, but he resisted the revolutionary agitation and demands by the sailors under his command as long as he could. He rejected the Bolshevik coup, which caught him when he was on a mission abroad that included a two-month stay in the United States and meetings with President Woodrow Wilson and other high government officials regarding possible military cooperation. Not wanting to have anything to do with the new regime, he offered his services to the British, who were happy to accept him. But the outbreak of the Russian Civil War and the efforts of Kolchak's admirers, both Russian and Allied, made him change his mind and brought him to Siberia and Omsk.

The Socialist Revolutionaries who made up the Directory were wary of Kolchak politically, but his stature and expertise were such that they appointed him minister for the army and navy anyway. Two weeks later, after becoming convinced that the Directory was incapable of conducting an effective military campaign against the Bolsheviks, a group of Cossack officers overthrew it in a bloodless coup. The deposed government's Council of Ministers assumed power and then immediately and "temporarily" ceded it to Kolchak by electing him to the position of supreme ruler of the government and supreme commander of all its forces, thus making him dictator.

When he accepted the position, Kolchak announced that his aims were to create an effective army, defeat the Bolsheviks, and restore law and order "so that the people could freely choose the form of government that they desire and implement the great idea of freedom that has now been announced around the world." Kolchak's commitment to popular self-determination failed to mollify the left, and there was some opposition from partisans of the deposed government—Chernov in particular called for armed resistance against Kolchak—but it proved ineffective.

The way Kolchak came to power and the aims he announced made many see him as a Napoleonic figure. He also looked the part, and he appears to have believed that it was his role. Photographs show a face fixed in a taught expression of virile determination—hard eyes under straight brows, closely cropped hair, firmly set mouth above a prominent cleft chin, and a strikingly large, aquiline nose. Had his portrait bust been carved in marble, it would not have looked out of place in a gallery of Roman emperors or generals.

Family Matters

Boris Savinkov took the issue of his diplomatic "legitimacy" very seriously, as he did all questions of duty and subordination. Without Kolchak's reauthorization of his mission, he would be no more than a private person, which would make dealing with senior statesmen who had gathered in Paris for the Peace Conference very difficult.

But even with an uncertain political future, there was still the matter of Savinkov's personal affairs. His wife, Evgeniya, and their son, Lev, were living in Nice, which was only several hours from Marseille by train. He had not seen them in over a year and a half, Lev was now six years old, and much had happened to Savinkov while he was in Russia. From the scant evidence that is available, it seems that his relationship with Lyubov Efimovna remained platonic at this time and unobjectionable from her husband's point of view. And now that Savinkov was back in France, he wanted to reunite with his wife and son.

Evgeniya, too, was still committed to their marriage. As recently as September, she had begun an elaborate effort to enlist British help so that she could join her husband, even though all she knew was that he was somewhere in the vastness of Siberia, which was bigger than all of Europe. However, this proved unnecessary. Within a week of Savinkov's arrival in Marseille, Evgeniya and Lev were with him in Paris.

The City of Lights after the Great War

France had suffered terribly during the war. There were more than 1.3 million dead, 4.2 million wounded, and hundreds of thousands of widows and orphans. The fighting took place largely in the north and the heavily industrialized northeast of the country, which produced most of the country's coal and iron, and the region's factories, mines, railroads, towns, and villages lay in ruins.

But Paris itself had not seen the devastation of revolution and civil war the way Moscow and Petrograd had. There were some piles of rubble and boarded-up windows in the quarters where German bombs and shells had fallen, and a massive crater had torn up the Tuileries rose garden. A few chestnut trees on the Grands Boulevards had been cut down for firewood, and the magnificent stained-glass windows in the Cathedral of Notre Dame had been moved to safety and replaced by pale yellow panes. An incongruous sight were some German cannons displayed as trophies in the Place de la Concorde and on the Champs-Élysées.

Otherwise, the city was still very beautiful and looked the same as when Boris Savinkov last saw it in March 1917. The winter of 1919 was mild, and there was still some green grass in the parks and even a few flowers. It had rained for days before he arrived, and the waters in the Seine had risen. From a distance the lowering sky seemed to merge with the grays of the city's buildings, and the top of the Eiffel Tower dissolved in the clouds. Streetlights shimmered in the wet cobblestones. Flocks of pigeons wheeled across the sky. A poetically inclined Russian émigré noticed that when they "settled on the pearl-grey and black frieze of the Arc de Triomphe" and then flew off again it was like "stone melting into wing."

The most evident change in the city was the people. Flags celebrating victory adorned lampposts, windows, and buildings, giving the streets a festive appearance. But this lasted only until you noticed the men with missing arms and legs and demobilized soldiers in tattered uniforms begging for change on the corners. There were soldiers with horrific facial wounds, the victims of trench warfare, which protected bodies but left heads vulnerable to enemy fire, trying to hide their disfigurements under broad-brimmed hats and with scarves. It seemed that half of the women were dressed in mourning. Impoverished refugees from the devastated north filled the city, aggravating the hunger and cold suffered by many Parisians because of severe shortages of bread, milk, and coal. Strikes and protests rolled through one after the other that winter and into the spring, the left calling for revolution, the right for repression.

Despite all the sadness, however, Paris had also remained true to itself. There were still elegant women in shops and cafés, leading a Canadian delegate to the Peace Conference to write home that "Again and again one meets a figure which might have stepped out of *La Vie Parisienne*, or *Vogue* in its happier moments." Beautiful clothing and jewelry were still available, if you had the money. Fine restaurants served wonderful meals, when they could get provisions. Couples in nightclubs danced the latest steps to tangos and foxtrots. An electrifying new kind of music called jazz, which had been introduced by Black soldiers from the American Expeditionary Forces, was just becoming popular.

For Savinkov Paris was like a second home—since he became a revolutionary, he had lived there longer than anywhere else—and he reestablished himself in it very quickly. He may not have had an official appointment, but he had money because of what the Omsk government had issued him and settled in the chic 16th Arrondissement on the western edge of the city, near the Bois de Boulogne and the Auteuil Racecourse, which he had frequented before the war.

Savinkov also slipped easily into his urbane habits. He began to dress again like an "irreproachably elegant gentleman" and set up a very comfortable household with servants and a cook, according to his Polish friend and former aide Karol Wędziagolski, who visited him in Paris. Wędziagolski had never met Evgeniya before and found her to be "a very beautiful, elegant, and above all, sympathetic and unaffected lady"; he also thought that she and Savinkov seemed very well suited to each other. This period was a rare interlude of family harmony for Savinkov and Evgeniya. Their son, Lev, would recall that they went out often in the evening, both looking very debonair—a tuxedo for him and a long dress for her.

Savinkov began to look up some of his old acquaintances in the city and to reestablish social ties. In another expression of his habitual punctiliousness about matters of procedure, form, and etiquette, he also made a point of repaying debts to Sofia and Eugène Petit, the well-off French-Russian couple from whom he had borrowed money a decade earlier when he was especially hard up. That he did so barely a month after arriving in Paris—and that he remembered the sums so long after he incurred them—indicates their principled importance to him.

Representing "Russia"

Boris Savinkov understood that he could not succeed in influencing the Allies in Paris by acting alone, and even before landing in Marseille had contacted the Russian "ambassador" to France, Vasily Maklakov, to tell him that he was looking forward to working with him. Once in Paris, Savinkov needed him even more to give himself at least a veneer of quasi-diplomatic legitimacy.

But in fact, Maklakov's position was not much better than Savinkov's because the civil war in Russia had thrown him into a diplomatic limbo. He had been appointed by Kerensky's government, but when it was overthrown in October 1917, he stayed in the Russian embassy in Paris, prosecuting a resolutely anti-Bolshevik policy, playing an influential role in Russian émigré and White affairs, and mediating between them and the French and the other Allies. The French government acquiesced to Maklakov's indeterminate role because of its own opposition to the Bolsheviks (and would refuse to recognize their regime until 1924).

Maklakov was also not enough. Savinkov joined a group of nine prominent Russian political figures in Paris who had organized themselves as the Russian Political Committee to represent what they believed were Russia's national interests. Chaired by Prince Georgy Lvov, who had been the first prime minister of the Provisional Government, the Committee included Maklakov and several other ambassadors who also remained at their posts after the Provisional Government was overthrown, such as Boris Bakhmetev in the United States, as well as a number of socialists, including Nikolay Chaikovsky, known as the "Grandfather of the Russian Revolution," whom Savinkov had long admired and advocated for a government post to Kerensky.

The problem with the Russian Political Committee was that, like its individual members, it also had no official standing and was not recognized by any of the Allied governments, although the French did engage in some dealings with it. Moreover, the Committee consisted of people with such differing political orientations that coming to agreements would be extremely difficult.

This was further complicated in a way that especially irked Savinkov when General Denikin, the new head of the Volunteer Army in the south of Russia, sent Sergey Sazonov as his own representative to Paris. A polished man with a neatly trimmed beard and a calm and complacent expression in his eyes, Sazonov had been Russia's minister of foreign affairs from 1910 to 1916 and was an experienced diplomat. But he was also a reactionary. He remained a committed monarchist after the Russian Revolutions and continued to advance an imperial conception of Russia as "one and indivisible," thus going against the view prevailing in Europe after the war that formerly subject peoples everywhere should now be independent.

Sazonov's reputation was well known in Paris and cast a shadow on the White Russian cause in general. Georges Clemenceau, the French prime minister, would refuse to deal with him and warned off other diplomats as well "lest it be alleged the [Paris Peace] Conference was conspiring with tsarism." However, the Russian Political Committee, which was politically liberal overall, could not deny Sazonov membership because of his stature, although it tried to limit the damage he could do. Despite this, his behavior still frustrated Savinkov, who witnessed occasions when Sazonov spoke to foreigners "as if the tsar was sitting in a neighboring room and he was representing the tsar."

To Savinkov's additional disappointment, Sazonov's role in Paris was strengthened when Kolchak also confirmed him as his representative and "foreign minister" in Paris, which meant that Sazonov was now backed by the two most important anti-Bolshevik military movements in Russia. Kolchak went even further when he selected four members of the Russian Political Committee to be his government's official representatives at the Paris Peace Conference, which was scheduled to begin on January 18: Sazonov, Lvov, Maklakov, and Chaikovsky. This was a blow to Savinkov personally, because he had made repeated requests to Kolchak—and before that to the Directory—to be included in any group that would seek admission to the conference. Dealing with all these men would be a great test of Savinkov's diplomacy and patience, but he had no choice if he wanted to get anything accomplished.

The Propagandist

Savinkov also had no intention of limiting his efforts to collaborating with the ineffectual Russian Political Committee, and shortly after arriving in Paris he began an independent propaganda campaign to persuade Allied governments and popular opinion that it was essential to support the anti-Bolshevik movements in Russia. He gave interviews to the press and took every opportunity to give speeches as well.

The core points that he stressed and repeated many times were that it was essential to fight the Bolsheviks because they murdered the Russian people and plundered the nation's wealth, because they betrayed Russia and the Allies at Brest-Litovsk, because only a tiny minority of the population supported them, and because they relied on foreign communist troops to bolster their own forces.

Savinkov invariably also summarized the history of the heroic military struggles against the Bolsheviks, including his own Union for the Defense of the Motherland and Freedom. He defended Kolchak and claimed (with considerable exaggeration) that he had adopted a "radical" political program, and was supported by all of Russia's "democrats," "radicals," and "constitutional socialists." As for himself, Savinkov proclaimed that "I, a republican federalist and democrat applaud the Government of Admiral Kolchak. All my hope for Russia rests on this government." The specter of a newly empowered Germany, which although "beaten" did not admit to being "conquered," and which had long-term designs on Russia, was another element in Savinkov's repertoire of arguments. And he concluded with what he believed was the solution to the international evil the Bolsheviks represented—an Allied volunteer army of 200,000 to 250,000 men to help the White Russian forces fighting the Bolsheviks. It would consist largely of Slavic volunteers, such as Czechs and Yugoslavs, as well as former Russian POWs, with the Allied countries providing smaller contingents.

Like any experienced performer, whether a diplomat or an actor, Savinkov knew that how he presented himself would make a considerable difference in whether or not foreigners took him seriously, and to this end he regularly identified himself as the former "Acting Minister of War" in Kerensky's government, and at times as "General Savinkov." Even though he never formally received this (or any) military rank, his ministerial post justified it, according to old Russian bureaucratic norms. Moreover, the rank likely satisfied his sense of having played a historical role in Russia, which was also reflected in his courtly deportment at high-level social gatherings. In the captious world of émigré politics, however, there were those who did not seem to understand how the diplomatic game had to be played, and who saw Savinkov's self-presentation only as evidence of his fondness for empty posturing.

In addition to individual appearances, Savinkov also implemented the plan that he and the other members of his mission had formulated while still in China—to open a Russian propaganda office so that they could disseminate information about their anti-Bolshevik cause systematically. Within a few weeks of their arrival, an agency named Union (which incorporated the Russian Telegraph Agency and the Russian Press Bureau) opened just a few blocks west of the Jardin de Luxembourg.

The agency was a collaborative effort with Savinkov's old acquaintance, the investigative journalist Vladimir Burtsev, who also published his own newspaper and anti-Bolshevik literature at a nearby location. In short order, Savinkov's Union began to compose, compile, and reproduce scores of brochures, bulletins, telegrams, and articles about the anti-Bolshevik cause, and to send out tens of thousands of copies to the Allied publics, the press, and members of the French and other Allied governments.

A Seat at the Table

A major part of Savinkov's effort to influence the Allies against the Bolsheviks was the campaign that he and the other Russian "diplomatic" emissaries in Paris waged to have Russia participate directly in the Peace Conference. Members of the Russian Political Committee believed that because they represented the Whites, who saw themselves as the heirs of Russia's wartime commitments to the Allies, they had a moral right to take part in the deliberations and an obligation to defend Russia's postwar interests. The basis of the Committee's claim was the amount of blood that Russia had shed: in the first months of the war, by invading East Prussia at the cost of the annihilation of two entire armies, she saved Paris from being taken by the Germans, and then for three years she inflicted enormous damage on the Central Powers and absorbed even more herself. It is estimated that Russia suffered more casualties in the Great War than any other member of the Entente: approximately 2 million military deaths, 2.5 million wounded, and 5 million prisoners of war. To exclude Russia after her great contribution to the Allied victory, when the Allies were deciding the fate of Europe and much of the rest of the world, would be an egregious injustice.

But it was a futile effort. Not only did the Allies largely ignore the arguments of the Russian Political Committee, but they were also unable to develop a coherent or consistent policy with regard to Russia in general, in large measure because she was not a unified country at the time. On the one hand, the Bolsheviks controlled the two capitals and the central Russian territories. But the Allies were repelled by their ideology, resented their betrayal at Brest-Litovsk, and consequently refused to recognize the rump Soviet state. On the other hand, the Allies were also initially reluctant to recognize the small, regional White governments of Denikin (in the south of Russia) and Kolchak (in the east) as national governments, despite the fact that this is the status that the Whites, and especially Kolchak, claimed. Thus, from the Allied perspective there was no single legitimate Russian entity that deserved a seat at the Conference table. The most that any of the White representatives were allowed to do was present their views to the victorious powers in memoranda. However, these were seen as inconsequential.

Also preventing the Allies from developing a coherent stance toward the "Russian problem" were the conflicting views of the different countries and even of different ministers in the same country. Winston Churchill, a member of the British cabinet during the Peace Conference, grasped Bolshevism's violent nature and advocated Allied intervention. So did Marshal Ferdinand Foch, the top French commander and the Allied commander-in-chief. But David Lloyd George, the British prime minister, tried to dampen Churchill's zeal by raising the issue of the cost of intervention: "We cannot afford the burden." And President Woodrow Wilson said that he believed in letting the Russians "work out their own salvation."

The result was a series of half-hearted or confused initiatives, often carried out by individual countries without coordination, such as the landings by British, American, French, and Japanese troops on Russia's northern, eastern, and southern borders. As threatening as they may have seemed to the Bolsheviks and as encouraging to the Whites, none developed into the kind of intervention Savinkov hoped for. Even the most ambitious Allied military adventure, the French landing in December 1918 of a powerful and well-equipped international force of 70,000 troops in Odessa, the major Russian port on the Black Sea, ended in a "debacle" with a sudden and chaotic evacuation.

The one major effort the Allies did devise collectively was, in effect, an attempt to wash their hands of the entire Russian problem. They decided to convene a conference of all of Russia's warring factions at the end of January 1919 so that they could negotiate their differences face-to-face. They chose a location that would be relatively easy to reach—the island of Prinkipo (now Büyükada), located a dozen miles southeast of Constantinople (now Istanbul) in the Sea of Marmara.

The result was a fiasco. The Bolsheviks replied that they would come but did not agree to a cease-fire or address any of the high-minded principles in Woodrow Wilson's invitation. The Whites reacted to the proposal to meet with the Bolsheviks, whom they saw as illegitimate usurpers, with dismay and fury. Sazonov asked a British diplomat how the Allies could expect him to sit down with people who had murdered his family.

Savinkov's Union agency helped sink the Prinkipo proposal, and he took pride in what he saw as a notable achievement. In his view, the Allies had made the proposal largely to benefit their own interests rather than out of genuine concern for Russia. Despite their noble rhetoric, their primary motivation was to exploit Russia's vast natural resources, especially in the Caucasus and Caspian Sea areas: "I recognized the smell of oil" in their plans, he later recalled.

Persuading Kolchak

Struggling to sway the Allies and to get the Russian Political Committee to do something useful were not the only problems Savinkov faced in the spring of 1919. Kolchak became one too, and the difficulty with him was twofold. Despite regular, deferentially phrased reports in which Savinkov tried to demonstrate his value by summarizing his anti-Bolshevik activities, Kolchak had still not appointed him as his representative.

Savinkov also realized that Kolchak's authoritarianism was ruining any chance he had of receiving Allied support and that he would have to initiate a public relations campaign to help him. One part consisted of persuading Kolchak to change how he presented himself. The other would be to present Kolchak to the Allies in the best light possible. On March 9, in a telegram containing an especially pointed admonishment, Savinkov explained to Kolchak that the American government "would agree to a military intervention in Russia" only "if it receives a guarantee not only that a Constituent Assembly would be convened, but that a federated and republican form of government would be established, and that the peasants would be allowed to keep the landowners' lands that were transferred to them."

Savinkov understood that Kolchak's immediate concern was less the character of the future Russian state than mobilizing all his resources to fight the Bolsheviks so that a new state could be established. He also knew that Kolchak had publicly committed to a constitutional form of government as a matter of principle, once victory over the Bolsheviks was achieved. But because of Kolchak's reputation for conservative views, the way he came to power in a coup, and his vilification as a reactionary by some French socialists and émigrés such as Kerensky, whose opinions were still reported in the press and could do damage, Savinkov felt he had to do everything he could to change Kolchak's image. When trying to persuade the Allies that Kolchak deserved their help, Savinkov even used his personal support for him as evidence of Kolchak's rectitude, arguing that his own reputation as a revolutionary, republican, and democrat was a warrant of the admiral's commitment to liberal and representative government.

In fact, Savinkov was not being entirely honest, because he suspected that Kolchak's dedication to such principles as democracy and national self-determination was limited and conditional. However, by this stage in his life and in Russia's historical process, Savinkov was willing to compromise his principles even more than when he supported a (temporary) dictatorial role for Kornilov, who was by nature a democrat.

Finally, on May 26, Savinkov's and the Russian Political Committee's efforts seemed to be rewarded with what appeared at first to be a momentous Allied decision: the Council of Four, the leading nations at the Peace Conference—France, Great Britain, the United States, and Italy—announced that they were prepared to recognize Kolchak's government.

The actual timing of the council's decision was probably prompted more by Kolchak's recent military success in Siberia than anything that had been said in Paris. Beginning in March and into April, his armies began a rapid, broad, and deep advance to the west against the Bolsheviks that resulted in the seizure of vast territories and several important cities and that came within 100 miles of Kazan, which opened a direct line of attack toward Moscow. Lenin found the threat so serious that he named Kolchak the Soviet regime's greatest enemy and put a price of $7 million on his head (an enormous sum worth in excess of $100 million today).

Kolchak's status in the eyes of the Allies was further improved a few days later by the news that General Denikin, the commander of the Volunteer Army in the south of Russia, acknowledged Kolchak as the supreme ruler of the Russian government as well as supreme commander of the Russian Army. Denikin also capitalized on Kolchak's success in the east and began an aggressive advance toward Moscow. The unification of Kolchak's and Denikin's movements politically and militarily (although not geographically—their front lines were still separated by hundreds of miles of territory controlled by the Soviets) was a step toward the establishment of a legitimate White Russian state.

But for Savinkov the decision by the Council of Four was a disappointment. It failed to provide the two things he and his colleagues wanted most and that had been the primary aims of his original mission to Paris: foreign troops to help Kolchak, and Russian admission to the Peace Conference. Instead, the Allies announced that they would provide Kolchak with "expert military advisers and large quantities of arms and ammunition" and expressed the pious hope that he "will at last be able to bring order out of the chaos reigning in Russia."

Furthermore, the Allies set a series of conditions for their recognition, which paralleled what Savinkov had urged Kolchak to embrace in his telegram of March 9, and which implied that he still needed guidance because his own inclinations could not be fully trusted. (The conditions were not without hypocrisy, as Kolchak and others noticed, because although the Allies said nothing about giving up their own colonial empires, they insisted on national self-determination for the formerly subject nationalities of the Russian Empire.)

Kolchak had no choice. He agreed to all the Allied conditions, and on June 6 he handed his answer to the French representative in Omsk, who cabled it to Paris. The Council of Four reacted guardedly to Kolchak's response and found it "generally satisfactory." But the Allies also had no choice: if they wanted the Bolsheviks ousted, they had to back him, especially now that Denikin had joined him.

The sudden improvement in Kolchak's status among the Western powers and his pact with Denikin also breathed new life into Savinkov's efforts to be attached to the group of four members of the Russian Political Committee whom Kolchak had appointed. However, time was short. The Allied Council of Four had finished drafting the peace treaty and sent it to the printers on May 4; the Germans would get it on the seventh and have two weeks to submit their comments in writing; the signing ceremony would be in late June. At this stage, the chance for the Russians to influence the terms of the treaty had been reduced to almost nothing.

Nevertheless, Savinkov did not give up. Maklakov, one of the most respected figures in the Russian emigration, was willing to help him and sent a strong recommendation to Kolchak's prime minister, stressing that "Savinkov's politics here are impeccable and useful. His reputation as a revolutionary has repeatedly calmed the usual fears that [your] Government is reactionary . . . and he has created a very good position for himself in French political society." "It would be a shame not to use him fully," Maklakov adds, and cautions that "political circles here would not understand that a man like Savinkov could be kept out of important work."

Weeks passed, and there was no response. The military situation in Russia was not stable and neither was the Allied attitude toward the Whites. Being sidelined and unable to act was deeply frustrating. Savinkov sent another telegram to Kolchak in June. As he waited for a response, the last sliver of an opportunity for reviving the case for a Russian role in the Peace Conference disappeared.

⚬━┼━⚬

The peace treaty between the Allies and the Central Powers was finalized and signed in Versailles on June 28, 1919, the fifth anniversary of the assassinations in Sarajevo that had catalyzed the Great War. That night a great public celebration with singing and dancing broke out on the streets of Paris. Lights blazed in the buildings on the Grand Boulevards, and automobiles towed captured cannons behind them. The world government that had gathered in the city began to disperse as diplomats headed for home. Although the Peace Conference would formally continue to work on unfinished details in Paris until January 1920, the real decisions would henceforth be made by the national governments in London, Paris, Washington, and Rome.

Watching the jubilation of the victors must have been a bitter experience for Savinkov. He telegraphed Omsk again in July, again summarized what he had done in Paris, and offered once more to go anywhere to carry out "any kind of work"; all he wanted was to be useful to the Russia he believed in. He ended with praise for Dikgof-Derental and the other members of the original military mission, "who fulfilled their duty toward Russia and your government with devotion." Savinkov's last words are "Request response." None came. A few days later, Savinkov sent a pneumatic note to Maklakov, confessing that "I feel myself completely isolated and hounded."

⊶━━⊷

But Savinkov's dogged persistence finally prevailed. On August 19, he received the reply he had longed to hear for over eight months. Kolchak expressed his thanks to him and his colleagues for their "energetic and fruitful work" and acknowledged that it would be "very useful" if he were to stay on in Paris, where his connections and influence in political circles "are especially valuable." Kolchak then formally offered Savinkov a position as the fifth member of the Russian delegation.

The offer arrived too late for the Peace Treaty, and the position was less influential now than it would have been months earlier when matters in Paris were more fluid. Nevertheless, the invitation from Kolchak was seen as important enough to be announced in French newspapers under the rubric of "news from the embassies."

Changing Fortunes

Savinkov accepted Kolchak's invitation even though the relative political and military fortunes of the two White movements had changed so completely during the past four months that he feared his own reputation could be damaged by association with the admiral. By August Kolchak had lost the initiative, had been pushed back by the Red Army, and was on the defensive. At the same time, Denikin's advance "on Moscow," as he boldly characterized it, had succeeded spectacularly, and by late summer his troops had moved far north and into Ukraine. This reversal of fortunes changed the Allied view of the two movements, and not in Kolchak's favor, who now seemed to have been the wrong horse to back.

Moreover, Kolchak's reputation had recently deteriorated even further in Allied eyes when he showed his reactionary political colors and made what can only be called a major military and strategic blunder, one that especially upset Savinkov. General Carl Mannerheim, a former tsarist general who had become the regent and leader of an independent Finland, offered to attack Bolshevik-held Petrograd with a 100,000-man army in exchange for Kolchak's recognition of Finland's independence (already an accomplished fact) and some small territorial concessions. An intervention like this at a time when Denikin was successfully advancing from the south could have spelled the end of the Bolsheviks. But despite Kolchak's express desire for foreign help and his having agreed to the principle of national self-determination, which the Allies demanded as a condition for recognizing his government several weeks earlier, he refused Mannerheim, replying that he would never betray the idea of a great and indivisible Russia for any short-term gains. In response, one of his outraged ministers noted in his diary: "What horror and what idiocy!" The Bolsheviks, by contrast, had been willing to give up much more of the country at Brest-Litovsk to save their revolutionary government. In the end, Savinkov swallowed his disappointment, and rather than distance himself from Kolchak's failing venture, which would have accomplished nothing for the anti-Bolshevik cause, resolved to continue to advocate for him.

He also swallowed his pride when he and the other members of the Russian delegation tried and failed to persuade Kolchak to remove Sazonov as a member. Kolchak responded on October 8 that Sazonov had his unequivocal support. Savinkov's solution henceforth would be to sidestep Sazonov and take up much of what he was supposed to be doing.

Savinkov had to live with animosity from Denikin's camp as well. When one of his representatives, General Abram Dragomirov, came to Paris from the south of Russia in the summer of 1919 to seek Allied help, someone at a public gathering raised the subject of Savinkov with him. Dragomirov's reply was, "Let Savinkov come to us, we'll have him shot."

Savinkov would subsequently describe his constant struggle with the Whites as "the most difficult period in my life."

Winston Churchill

Savinkov spent a great deal of time trying to meet with all the government ministers who had gathered in Paris, and, overall, the experience left a very painful impression on him. It was demeaning to play the role of a mendicant and to endure endless slights and evasions: having to explain why he thought he deserved an audience with a busy minister when he did not have any real diplomatic credentials; listening to supercilious assistants of powerful men as they explained that "monsieur" would have to wait or return another time; smiling through a minister's condescension and polite suggestion that he might better address his concerns to someone else. "I cannot find the words to communicate the bitterness I felt," Savinkov admitted.

But he did have one notable success with Great Britain. He would later claim that his personal efforts "in particular" succeeded in getting "a great deal" of money and military materiel from the British for Denikin's army and lesser amounts for Kolchak.

Why did Savinkov succeed in this case? One might have thought that his past as a terrorist would put off staid British politicians. Instead, it appealed to a ruthless streak that several of them had and was what brought him to their attention in the first place. Prime Minister Lloyd George, a thoroughly establishment figure, admired what he believed was Savinkov's effectiveness as a revolutionary and commented (not altogether accurately) that "His assassinations had always been skillfully arranged and had been a complete success."

However, the crucial figure was Winston Churchill, who had read *The Pale Horse* and was impressed by it and by what he knew of the author's past. Churchill believed in using violence as a means to a political end, and what he liked about Savinkov was that he used radical methods to achieve down-to-earth goals. Churchill characterized him as "that extraordinary product—a Terrorist for moderate aims" and, in an especially pungent phrase, as "the essence of practicality and good sense expressed in terms of nitro-glycerine."

Savinkov first met Churchill through Sidney Reilly, whom Cummings, or C of MI6 in London, had sent to Paris in early February 1919 to keep an eye on the White Russians and the Bolsheviks who were there. Reilly fell under Churchill's spell as soon as he met him and realized that Savinkov would interest him as well. This gave Savinkov a high-level contact in the British government who was sympathetic to the Whites, open to using overt or covert force, and violently opposed to the Bolsheviks. Churchill would be the most important European statesman with whom Savinkov developed a relationship.

Churchill's animosity toward the Bolsheviks dates from when they took Russia out of the war in 1918. He had originally hoped that Britain would overthrow them by force, but after the Cabinet decided against it, he became willing to entertain any and all other methods, from subversion, sabotage, special operations, and underground conspiracies to proxy armies. In 1919 he went so far as to arm the small British expeditionary force in Archangel in northern Russia with shells and bombs containing a new and secret poison gas (the "M Device," which seriously debilitated but did not kill) that was used effectively against the Bolsheviks.

Many sources fed Churchill's abhorrence of the Bolsheviks before he met Savinkov, including reports by Englishmen from different walks of life who returned home after long stays in Russia and were interviewed by the Foreign Office. Summaries of their firsthand observations were printed and circulated widely in the British government and included detailed descriptions of privations, the Cheka's violence, the widespread disaffection of the population, and the weakness of the regime. In June 1919, Churchill had the prescience to brand the Bolsheviks not only a threat in distant Russia but a danger to humanity in general:

> Bolshevism means in every country a civil war of the most merciless
> kind between the discontented, the criminal, and mutinous classes
> on the one hand and the contented or law abiding on the other . . . it
> means . . . the slaughter of men, women, and children, the burning
> of homes, and the inviting in of tyranny, pestilence, and famine.

As a result, he was in favor of doing anything to "strangle bolshevism in the cradle."

Churchill was forty-five years old to Savinkov's forty and had already filled a long series of distinguished positions in the British government during the previous twenty years—member of Parliament, undersecretary of state for the colonies, president of the Board of Trade, home secretary, first lord of the Admiralty. In 1915, Churchill had to resign from government because he was blamed for the failure of the Allied campaign to take the Dardanelles and thus open a passage through the Turkish Straits to the south of Russia. But after serving as a battalion commander on the Western Front and a spell as minister of munitions, by 1919 he was again a senior figure—the secretary of state for war and air. He would achieve even greater heights during the Second World War, when he would consolidate his standing as one of the greatest statesmen in his country's long history.

When Savinkov met him, Churchill was a canny, willful, well-spoken, and handsome middle-aged man with a high brow, a round chin, and a noble gaze. He was still far from looking like the bulldog-jowled World War II leader with the half-smile, half-scowl in Yusuf Karsh's iconic 1941 photograph. Savinkov's French was fluent, Churchill's was functional, and they were able to communicate in the language.

Savinkov made repeated trips to London in 1919 to seek help for the Whites from Churchill, as well as from Lloyd George, Baron Birkenhead, the British lord chancellor, and other senior politicians. But whereas Lloyd George and the others showed no particular interest in the White Russian cause, Churchill was fully of one mind with Savinkov. In fact, Churchill's pronouncements at the time indicate that if he could have set British policy toward Russia entirely by himself, he would have implemented everything that Savinkov wanted, including a major military intervention.

This is not to say that Churchill's or his government's goals were entirely altruistic and concerned only with fighting a political evil. When meeting with different ministers in London, Savinkov noticed the insistence with which they kept returning to the desirability of forming an independent union of states in Transcaucasia, the area between the Black and Caspian Seas on the southern border of the former Russian Empire. These would include Azerbaijan, with its vast oil reserves, and Armenia and Georgia, which would have essential roles in transporting and shipping the oil. The obvious goal behind the "cock-and-bull stories about establishing such petroleum states," as Savinkov characterized them later, was British designs on oil deposits that would otherwise fall into Soviet hands.

Nevertheless, Churchill's sympathy for the cause Savinkov espoused was real, as was his fascination with the man himself. Churchill later recalled his impressions of Savinkov in a volume titled *Great Contemporaries*, which contained sketches of two dozen other famous and infamous men (ranging from Franklin Delano Roosevelt to Adolf Hitler to Charlie Chaplin):

> I had never seen a Russian Nihilist except on stage, and my first impression was that he was singularly well cast for the part. Small in stature; moving as little as possible, and that noiselessly and with

deliberation; remarkable gray-green eyes in a face of almost deathly pallor; speaking in a calm, low, even voice, almost a monotone; innumerable cigarettes.

"Nihilist"—"a person who believes that life is meaningless and rejects all religious and moral principles"—was the conventional but inaccurate term Europeans used at the time for revolutionaries of Savinkov's ilk, even when they had well-developed social and political programs, as the Socialist Revolutionaries clearly did. But in other regards, Churchill's portrait is one of the most compelling and suggestive that we have for this period in Savinkov's life, and does much to explain why he and Churchill hit it off:

> His manner was at once confidential and dignified; a ready and ceremonious address, with a frozen, but not a freezing composure; and through all the sense of an unusual personality, of veiled power in strong restraint. As one looked more closely into this countenance and watched its movement and expression, its force and attraction became evident. His features were agreeable.

At the same time, even when engaged in the present, Savinkov seemed shadowed by his past:

> though still only in the forties, his face was so lined and crow's footed that the skin looked in places—and particularly round the eyes—as if it were crinkled parchment. From these impenetrable eyes there flowed a steady regard. The quality of this regard was detached and impersonal, and it seemed to me laden with doom and fate. But then I knew who he was, and what his life had been.

Savinkov, Churchill, and the Whites

Savinkov's most important meetings with Churchill took place in late 1919, when Churchill became very concerned that all the White movements were faltering. In the end of September, General Nikolay Yudenich, who commanded the army of the anti-Bolshevik Northwestern Government that had recently been formed in Revel (now Talinn, Estonia), came within two miles of Petrograd and was on the verge of attacking the city. But he failed to cut a crucial railroad, and the Red Army reinforcements that Trotsky rushed to the front stopped his advance. Kolchak's forces had advanced briefly in September but were then pushed back, and by late October the Bolsheviks were threatening his capital, Omsk. Denikin's rapid drive toward Moscow had unexpectedly gotten bogged down in Ukraine.

Savinkov initiated the first meeting with Churchill in an attempt to help Yudenich, who wanted to resurrect General Mannerheim's offer of a Finnish army for an attack on Petrograd. Mannerheim was willing, but Sazonov objected to the plan because he did not take Denikin's setbacks seriously and was opposed to any Russian alliance with the Finns, claiming blithely that "We can do without them because Denikin will be in Moscow in two weeks." However, the rest of the Russian diplomatic delegation in Paris supported Savinkov, and he went to London with two of Mannerheim's aides to seek help with the enormous subsidy—100 million francs, worth perhaps seven times as much in today's dollars—that Mannerheim wanted.

Savinkov's appointment with Churchill was on Saturday, November 1, in the War Office Building, a massive, seven-story Baroque edifice, with domes and a busy façade of columns, arches, pediments, and sculptures, located on Horse Guards Avenue in central London, a five-minute walk from 10 Downing Street. Solicitous uniformed doormen tipped their top hats and ushered the visitors into a marble foyer and up a grand double staircase. It was the British analogue to the colonnaded Ministry of War building in Petrograd where Savinkov had presided in 1917. Despite the mauling that the British armed forces had suffered during the war (750,000 dead, 1.7 million wounded), Great Britain was still a globe-spanning empire, and the building was a visible reminder of its military might.

Churchill began by saying that he was in favor of Yudenich's alliance with Mannerheim and appreciated the need for immediate military action. However, he could offer no help because the very large sum required for a subsidy to Finland would have to be appropriated by Parliament, and the leftist political parties would surely block it.

Savinkov could not have been too surprised when he heard this—the amount of money was unrealistic in light of the damage suffered by the British economy during the Great War. But Savinkov did not have just Yudenich in mind and neither did Churchill.

After the two Finns left he asked to meet privately with Savinkov to talk about Denikin, whose Volunteer Army had recently experienced a dramatic change of fortune. Just a month earlier, it seemed unstoppable, as it took one important city after another, including Kiev, Voronezh, and Oryol, and was approaching Tula, which was only 100 miles south of Moscow. The army had grown to 150,000 men and controlled territories with a population of 42 million people. The advance had been so relentless that the Soviet leadership started making plans to evacuate Moscow for Vologda.

However, when the Volunteer Army entered Ukraine, it was confronted by strong nationalist aspirations that Denikin failed to understand or to exploit. He not only dismissed the very idea of a separate Ukrainian people, he rejected an anti-Bolshevik alliance with the Ukrainian irregular army under Simon Petlyura. (Petlyura would become notorious for his anti-Semitic pogroms in Ukraine and for "ethnic cleansing" of Russians, but these were not the primary reasons Denikin opposed him.) Even more shortsighted was that Denikin then attacked Petlyura, thus tying up a part of his army that could have been used against the Bolsheviks. Denikin was also unable to avoid a second local conflict with a peasant army led by the anarchist Nestor Makhno, known to history as "Batka" or Dad Makhno. In the end of September, Makhno's forces attacked the rear of the Volunteer Army, completely disorganizing it and disrupting Denikin's march on Moscow. It was a pivotal moment in the Russian Civil War, and Denikin would be unable to rebuild a stable front for months.

Savinkov's private discussion with Churchill showed him that he had found a genuine ally, one who, moreover, was very receptive to the arguments Savinkov made about Denikin's mistakes and what it would take to revive his chances. As a result of this meeting, Savinkov and Churchill appear to have agreed to coordinate their efforts, judging by the policies they would advocate to their constituencies in the days and weeks that followed. Churchill also asked Savinkov to act as his unofficial emissary and transmit a message to Denikin and the diplomatic delegation in Paris.

Savinkov met with his colleagues in Paris on Wednesday, November 5. He could have signed his own name under the message he passed on from Churchill: Denikin's domestic policies must change because they are insufficiently democratic, which alienates the peasant masses and many city dwellers and gives rise to movements like Makhno's; Sazonov does more harm than good because his old Russian regime attitudes make Allied Powers reluctant to have any dealings with him.

Savinkov knew that changing Denikin's domestic and foreign policies would be very difficult. But there was no choice because the Volunteer Army was now the only viable anti-Bolshevik force left in Russia. Kolchak had to evacuate Omsk on November 10, after which his troops kept retreating farther to the east. The same month, Yudenich's army fell back to the Estonian border, and after crossing it was disarmed and interned, thus ceasing to exist as a fighting force.

Meanwhile, in his parallel initiative across the English Channel, Churchill composed a document titled "M. Savinkov and Russian Policy," in which he summarized Savinkov's views and why he supported them. A printed copy was distributed to the members of the British Cabinet for discussion on November 27. It is a testament to how much Churchill had been impressed by Savinkov's ideas.

Churchill argues that the White campaigns failed because their leaders rejected the new ideas about national sovereignty that came into the world after the war, and that they need to involve all the peoples of the former Russian Empire in the fight against the Bolsheviks. Poland and Finland must have full independence. The other nationalities should have their own states, organized into a federated republic based on the model of the United States and in which they "enjoy the largest autonomy and all local liberties."

Churchill concludes with a concrete proposal. In order to persuade the Whites to change their policies, Great Britain should send someone to Denikin who represents the "principle Allied and Associate Powers" and has international standing and authority (Churchill may well have had himself in mind, an idea Savinkov supported). And because "Bolshevism is a world-wide danger," the only way finally "to solve the Russian problem in a resolute fashion" is for the

British government and the Allies to continue "their moral, material and financial assistance to anti-Bolshevik Russia."

The entire document reads like a stenographer's transcript of Savinkov's ideas, and Churchill puts the full weight of his support behind them, stating that "The principle of M. Savinkov's contention appears to be incontrovertible."

A Polish Connection

While Savinkov was in Paris struggling with Sazonov's and Denikin's reactionary views, an unexpected development occurred that promised to provide exactly what he and Churchill believed could save the White movement. Savinkov received a letter from his friend and former aide Karol Wędziagolski telling him that he was coming to Paris on a secret mission from the leader of newly independent Poland, Józef Piłsudski. The letter contained the mysterious but thrilling words "we will help you," and their effect on Savinkov, as Wędziagolski recalled, was "like the voice of the archangel's trumpet in the desert, calling pilgrims on the path to their goals."

When Wędziagolski arrived, he revealed that Piłsudski was proposing a military alliance between Poland and the Whites against the Bolsheviks, one that could also include several of the other smaller nationalities that had been part of the Russian Empire. The proposal corresponded to Savinkov's own convictions perfectly, and he embraced it without hesitation. The other members of the Russian delegation approved it as well, with the exception of Sazonov, who obstinately continued to oppose any accommodation with a formerly subject people. Because he also spoke for Denikin and Kolchak, the two military leaders with whom Piłsudski wanted an alliance, his opposition was meant to be decisive. But the matter was too important, and Savinkov and the other members of the delegation began to work around Sazonov by holding informal conferences in Paris with the Poles as well as with other nationalities open to the idea of a federation.

Savinkov also wanted to draw the British government into a plan to force Denikin and Kolchak to cooperate with the Polish initiative and to democratize their movements. To this end, he and his colleagues in Paris proposed organizing a conference in Warsaw between the Poles and the Russians that would include the Allies, who would use their influence to persuade the Whites that an alliance was necessary and mutually beneficial. Together with his colleague Chaikovsky, Savinkov went back to London at the end of November to persuade the British government and Churchill in particular to pressure Denikin to change his policies and to entrust their implementation to the Russian diplomatic delegation in Paris.

This was not just an ambitious but an audacious plan. In its attempt to change the very character of the White movements, it resembles Savinkov's efforts to change the nature of the Provisional Government. But, ironically, if in 1917 Savinkov was prepared temporarily to countenance dictatorship to save Russia, now he wanted to use Churchill's commitment to liberal pluralism to achieve the same end.

❦

After Churchill, there was only one person left whom Savinkov had to enlist—General Denikin himself. It could not have been easy to do, but Savinkov wrote to him in December as well.

He began by paying Denikin his due for his noble effort and for the patriotism, self-sacrifice, and bravery of his men. However, the point of the letter is a barely diplomatic appeal for major political change. Denikin has failed to defeat the Bolsheviks, and this is because he is too far from Europe to know how his movement is seen there in comparison to the Bolsheviks. "Almost all Jewry is with the Bolsheviks," Savinkov explains (he had earlier complained to Churchill that Denikin was not doing enough to fight the scourge of anti-Semitism among his men and in the territory he controlled). "Almost all socialists are with the Bolsheviks. Almost all the masses of people in England, France, Italy, Belgium, even Serbia—all dark, as they are everywhere—are confused by Bolshevik propaganda and do not know whom to choose, Lenin or you." Denikin needs to democratize his movement, and this will win him popular support in Europe. No one will be able to help you, Savinkov warns Denikin, if your government is believed to be reactionary, and without Allied help you cannot win. Savinkov recognizes the awesome responsibility that Denikin bears as a historic figure: "You will answer for Russia before God and history, for the heaviest burden of power lies on you." And although Savinkov's responsibility before history is far smaller, he still feels that he has the right and the duty to tell Denikin honestly and frankly: "the time has come when it is essential to make decisions of governmental importance."

The letter was a cry from the heart and a canny attempt at persuasion. But because of who it came from and the kind of critique it contained, Denikin must have read it with disgust. In any event, he does not appear to have responded. And in his memoir about the end of 1919, he does not even mention Savinkov or his role in securing material help for the Volunteer Army from the British.

This was unfair, because Savinkov's achievement was hardly negligible (even if he tended to exaggerate it for propaganda purposes). As he later estimated himself, during the period from November 1919 to January 1920, the overall assistance was worth 8 million pounds sterling (several hundred million dollars today) and included everything from weaponry to uniforms to food.

The task had also not been easy for Savinkov. Despite the rapport between him and Churchill, Savinkov found the experience of soliciting help humiliating. He also claimed later that he felt insulted by the proprietary attitude that Churchill developed toward the Volunteer Army. Once, when they were in his office, Churchill called him over to a spread-out map of southern Russia where the positions of Denikin's forces and those of the Red Army were marked by small flags. Pointing to Denikin's, Churchill commented, "And here is my army."

Savinkov recalled that he froze and felt as if his feet had stuck to the floor. He wanted to reply but said nothing. He thought of walking out and slamming the door behind him, but then it occurred to him that if he did the Russian volunteers on the distant front lines would be "left without boots." So, he clenched his teeth and "put his humiliation in his pocket."

Poland Beckons

As 1919 drew to a close, a war between newly independent Poland and Soviet Russia seemed ever more likely and Poland's need for allies was becoming increasingly urgent. Piłsudski did not give up on his earlier proposal to Savinkov. In January 1920, he sent Wędziagolski to Paris again, this time to invite

Savinkov to a meeting in Warsaw. The repeated offer was like a towline thrown to a man in a boat on a becalmed sea. But first Savinkov decided to try to prepare the ground in Paris by persuading influential Russian émigrés and representatives of the Allies to support a Polish–White Russian alliance.

The overall reaction was mixed at best. Many Russians saw Poland as too small and effete to resist the Bolsheviks or to make a good ally. Nevertheless, Savinkov still found enough support to begin forming a new Russian émigré organization dedicated to the alliance. Wędziagolski left for Warsaw to arrange for the visit by Savinkov and Chaikovsky, who was the one member of the Russian diplomatic delegation in Paris who fully shared Savinkov's views. Dikgof-Derental, as an essential aide, was included as well. But his wife, Lyubov Efimovna, stayed in Paris to work for the Union propaganda agency.

Wędziagolski had just met the baron and his wife and was surprised by his reaction to her. As he recalled in his memoirs, he claims he felt an "absolutely uncanny hostility" and "disgust" when he first saw her that he had difficulty explaining. He thought Lyubov Efimovna was "a lovely woman who attracted the eyes of all those present," but also that she was strangely vacuous and "immersed in inner contemplation of her truly uncommon but repellent beauty." He concluded that she was actually "false to the depths of her heart," although it is unclear if his judgment was prescient and based on something real or influenced by events that happened years later and that he did not fully understand.

Savinkov and his entourage arrived in Warsaw in mid-January 1920. The city had changed greatly since he last saw it before the war, when it was still the vibrant, busy, and sophisticated metropolis of his youth, famous for its dedication to high culture and the performing arts as well as a lively nightlife in numerous cafés and restaurants. Much of the carnage and destruction on the Eastern Front had taken place on Polish territory, and Warsaw suffered terribly when it came under German occupation a year after the war began. Hunger and disease were still rampant, including the notorious "Spanish" influenza epidemic that started in 1918 and decimated populations around the world. Crime was widespread; shortages of fuel and electricity made the city cold and dark. The formerly elegant and well-maintained buildings looked dirty and shabby, and the streets were filled with beggars and long lines of people waiting for rationed, barely edible bread made with flour surrogates.

But for Savinkov Warsaw represented the chance for rebirth. Piłsudski was offering him the opportunity to help rewrite the history and geography of Eastern Europe. Savinkov also had nowhere else to turn and consequently nothing to lose.

It helped their relations that Piłsudski had a background similar to Savinkov's. He too had been a socialist, a revolutionary, and a terrorist fighting the tsarist regime; he had also been arrested and exiled and spent time as an émigré in Western Europe. But when the Great War began, the two men had taken opposite sides, and Piłsudski, an ardent nationalist, raised and led Polish troops in support of the Central Powers against Russia in the hope that this would win freedom for his country. When Poland proclaimed her independence on November 11, 1918, or 123 years after the last partition among Russia, Austria, and Prussia, the country hardly existed in a geopolitical sense: it had no definite borders, no government, no regular army, no bureaucracy, and was surrounded by enemies. Piłsudski became chief of state, centralized all power in his hands, and set to work building a new Poland.

Sophisticated, well-educated, willful, and pragmatic, Piłsudski was also a forceful-looking man, with an intense blue-eyed gaze and a fierce, drooping moustache. During his first, three-hour-long meeting with Savinkov on the evening of January 16 in Piłsudski's residence in the Belweder Palace he charmed Savinkov with his unpretentious manner and allusions to their shared past. Most important was that they were in complete agreement about their common enemy.

Piłsudski not only proposed an alliance between Poland and the White Russians against the Bolsheviks, but also offered to help Denikin come to arrangements with the other new states that had emerged out of the former Russian Empire—Estonia, Latvia, Lithuania, and Ukraine, among others. He suggested that border disputes between Poland and formerly Russian territories be resolved via plebiscites conducted under the observation of Allied commissions once there is a "lawful Russian government in Moscow." Russia and Poland would reciprocate by giving up claims to specific territories, and Russia would allow Poland overland access to Baltic ports.

Piłsudski also made an unexpected proposal that especially caught Savinkov's attention. He offered to allow the formation of Russian military units under Russian commanders on Polish soil that would be used in the war against the Bolsheviks. Savinkov would be in overall charge of creating them, and Poland would pay the expenses, which was an extraordinarily generous offer from a country whose economy was ruined. These units and the Polish Army would coordinate their strategy with the Volunteer Army in the South of Russia.

Piłsudski's proposals correlated so closely with Savinkov's most fervent wishes that he could have composed them himself. He was being given the chance to take matters into his own hands militarily on a much larger scale than the Volga uprisings, and with assured state support.

Opening a new front against the Bolsheviks in the west was also timely because it would compensate for the collapse of Kolchak's movement in Siberia. After losing Omsk, his army retreated farther east and then dissipated. At the end of December 1919, Kolchak was arrested by the Czech Legion and shortly thereafter, through intermediaries, handed over to the Bolsheviks in Irkutsk. On Lenin's orders, he was executed on the night of February 6, 1920. The only White movement of any consequence that was left was Denikin's in the south of Russia, and it was still reeling from the collapse of its advance on Moscow.

Savinkov returned to Paris at the end of January 1920, and over the course of the next six months threw himself into trying to implement Piłsudski's broad range of proposals with the kind of single-minded dedication that typified the beginnings of all his initiatives.

He spoke with the Russian diplomatic delegation in Paris and with groups of émigrés in the hope of getting their support. He enlisted influential French friends to help sway the government of Prime Minister Millerand, then began a series of trips to London to meet with Churchill and Lloyd George. He sent Chaikovsky as an emissary to the south of Russia to meet with Denikin and persuade him to accept the Polish plan. Later he asked Chaikovsky to go to Belgrade to meet with Alexander I, the prince regent of the newly independent Kingdom of Serbs, Croats, and Slovenes (later renamed Yugoslavia), who was educated at the Imperial Corps of Pages in Saint Petersburg and was a Russophile. Savinkov's activities also became well-enough known to draw attention from unexpected directions. The Germans tried to have him ejected from Paris in an attempt to sabotage the alliance with Poland. The Japanese tried to persuade him that the fight against the Bolsheviks in the west was finished and should be resurrected in Siberia.

Churchill's reliance on Savinkov had grown to such an extent that, after getting Lloyd George's approval, he asked Savinkov to help him compose a strongly worded telegram to the British general who was attached to Denikin's army as an observer. As a result, the general was ordered to fully support Chaikovsky's mission, which, in addition to advocating the White-Polish alliance, included trying once again to persuade Denikin to democratize his movement. Savinkov even tried to force the issue and began a campaign to persuade Denikin to appoint Chaikovsky as the head of his civilian government, a move that would have done much to improve its international image.

But most of Savinkov's renewed efforts with the Russians failed: neither Denikin, nor half of the membership of the diplomatic delegation in Paris, nor the majority of the "Russian émigré public," as Savinkov described it, were willing to accept an alliance with Poland. For many, dreams of restoring the Russian Empire were not yet over, the Poles were seen as "ancient enemies" (because of their repeated uprisings during the years of partition), and Savinkov was trying to "sell out Russia." Whatever support Savinkov received was limited to a handful of individuals, such as Maklakov, Lvov, and some members of the moderate Cadet Party. There were even émigré attacks on the Union propaganda agency, which Russians on the left accused of being counterrevolutionary and those on the right of not doing anything, despite the reams of anti-Bolshevik materials it had disseminated across Europe during the past year.

The results of Savinkov's efforts with the Allies were also disappointing. Despite Churchill's advocacy, the British told him they would not help Poland during a war with Bolshevik Russia. In fact, Lloyd George wanted to reconcile with the Bolsheviks and urged the Poles to sign a peace treaty with them (on this Churchill disagreed). The French indicated that they would help the Poles to a limited extent with money, materiel, and military advisers (including a Major Charles de Gaulle), but were also perplexed by Savinkov's status. They knew that many émigré Russians did not support him and wondered if this was because they did not trust him. And whom did Savinkov actually represent, the French asked, if he was leading all negotiations between White Russians and Poland single-handedly?

All the disappointments and attacks on his efforts hurt Savinkov personally, more than many who did not know him well would have thought possible because of his sangfroid. In March, while Chaikovsky was still on his mission to Denikin, Savinkov confided to him that "without you it's very difficult for me. People are taking advantage of your absence and are trying to weaken me politically and to prevent me from bringing the Polish question to a conclusion." Not even those who sympathize with him are any help, and he has to do everything himself. Paris is nothing but "despondency, faintheartedness, readiness to make peace with the Bolsheviks, aligning with Avksentyev [the former chairman of the Directory government in Siberia] and Kerensky . . . in a word, an image of general weakness."

Under these circumstances, any moral and ideological support, or even simple human warmth, became especially important. Savinkov again turned to Chaikovsky, who had a reputation for being a fatherly figure to his comrades, with a heartfelt appeal:

> Don't leave me, Nikolay Vasilyevich, and remember that I, who believe hardly anyone, believe you absolutely and have come to love you very much. May God grant you health, success and happiness. I know that you will save Russia, I don't doubt this for a single moment. Forgive me this declaration of love—it isn't like me . . . I send you a heartfelt embrace.

Savinkov would never forget the bitterness of his dealings with Denikin and especially with the émigrés in Paris—their inability to escape their partisan views, their preoccupation with empty sloganeering, their inaction. After six months of effort his patience ran out and he decided to act alone.

But he had waited too long, and historical events outpaced him. The war between Poland and Soviet Russia, which had already produced a number of preliminary clashes, broke out in earnest on April 24, 1920, when Piłsudski, in alliance with Semyon Petlyura's nationalist Ukrainian Army, began a drive to Kiev. Piłsudski's aim was to win back territory taken by the Soviets and to help Petlyura establish an independent Ukraine.

This was a purely pragmatic aim for both sides. Piłsudski had no love for the Ukrainian nationalists but needed their troops because the Whites had refused his offer of an alliance. Many Ukrainians reciprocated by being as anti-Polish as they were also anti-Bolshevik. The advance succeeded initially, and on May 7 the combined Polish-Ukrainian armies entered a lightly defended Kiev. But several weeks later the Soviets counterattacked in force and began to drive the Poles back. It was only then, during the summer of 1920, a time of great Polish national peril, that Savinkov finally started implementing the plan Piłsudski had suggested to him at the beginning of January.

In Poland

The situation in which Savinkov found himself was extraordinary and possibly without precedent in recent European history. He was still just a private person, but on June 23, 1920, he signed an agreement with Piłsudski—who had recently been elevated to the rank of "marshal" of Poland—that was "secret, military and based on personal trust." As they had discussed before, it authorized Savinkov to create a Russian army with Russian commanders on Polish soil that would be strategically subordinated to the Polish high command. Its express purpose was defined as waging war "not against Russia but against the Bolsheviks, and not with the aim of conquest but of liberation." Savinkov insisted on this formulation, and Piłsudski agreed to it and issued it as a general order to the Polish Army.

Like Savinkov, Piłsudski had also given up on an alliance with the Whites, despite the changes that happened in their movement in recent months. On April 4, 1920, Denikin, who lost the confidence of other senior commanders after the failure of his drive toward Moscow, was replaced as commander-in-chief by General Baron Pyotr Nikolayevich Wrangel. A more able and charismatic leader than Denikin, Wrangel initially succeeded in expanding the territory that the Volunteer Army controlled in the south of Russia and began a series of reforms focused on agrarian, political, economic, and nationality issues that were promising steps in the direction that Savinkov would have approved.

But it was too little, too late, and Piłsudski did not want to try to reach an accommodation with Wrangel, who, in his view, was neither sufficiently authoritative nor democratic. The only benefit that would accrue to the Whites from Poland in the coming months was inadvertent: large numbers of Red Army troops were tied up in the Polish-Soviet War, which allowed Wrangel's movement to survive until the fall of 1920.

Without the Whites, a Polish-Russian alliance would include only whatever army Savinkov could create from nothing. This was an entirely different scheme from Piłsudski's original proposal, which would have entailed strategic coordination with Wrangel's army in the south of Russia. Although not entirely without historical antecedents, the new army would still be an anomaly that did not fit any familiar categories. It would not be a mercenary army, because the Russian soldiers would not be fighting for money but for the political aim of liberating their homeland. It would not be Savinkov's private army, because it would be part of the larger Polish campaign. Strictly speaking, it would also not be a Polish army, because its aim was not to advance Polish national interests but Russian ones.

What is striking about the rare examples of soldiers from a particular country joining that country's enemies during a war is that there were no successful outcomes. In the early nineteenth century, Polish troops joined Napoleon's invasion of the Russian Empire, mistakenly thinking this could lead to their country's independence. Several analogous movements existed under the Germans during the Second World War, with some Ukrainians seeking independence from the Soviet Union, and some Russians hoping for regime change at home. Closer to our own time and to American experience was Brigade 2506, the CIA-sponsored group of Cuban exiles that failed to overthrow the communist government of Fidel Castro during the disastrous Bay of Pigs Invasion in 1961.

The Russian Army in Poland

After signing his accord with Piłsudski, Savinkov established a civilian body in Warsaw, the Russian Political Committee, that would help him oversee the formation of the Russian army and activities related to it. He became its president and invited Dmitry Filosofov—the junior member of the Merezhkovsky-Gippius triangle, a committed anti-Bolshevik and a zealous supporter of the Russian-Polish alliance—to be the vice president. Merezhkovsky also joined—his standing as an internationally celebrated author, it was thought, would enhance the Committee's prestige—as did other Russian émigrés in Poland, including Dikgof-Derental.

Piłsudski assigned Savinkov and his team living quarters and offices in what had been a first-class establishment before the war, the Grand-Hotel Brühl near the Saxonian Garden in the city center. Their rooms were actually very humble. Savinkov's was so cramped that scarcely four people could fit in it, and it was furnished with a bed that took up half the space and a couch with a table above which hung an inscribed photograph of Piłsudski. Nevertheless, this is where he worked from morning until late at night and received countless visitors, from representatives of foreign governments to army privates who wanted to volunteer.

Piłsudski also granted the Committee a generous initial budget of 300 million Polish marks (the currency that the Germans introduced during their occupation, equivalent to perhaps $130 million today), in addition to the cost of all supplies and equipment. The total sum was conceived as a loan to be repaid by a future, "legitimate" Russian government.

Within days of signing the agreement with Piłsudski, Savinkov began to form an army near Kalisz, a historic city 130 miles west of Warsaw, where it could be kept out of sight. He had agreed to carry out the process in secret because radical Polish political factions opposed Piłsudski's plans; the army's existence would be revealed only when it was ready to go into action. Savinkov also had to work as quickly as possible because the war was going badly for Poland and the Red Army was heading toward Warsaw. At the same time, Savinkov founded a Russian-language newspaper in Warsaw, *Freedom* (*Svoboda*; later, *Za Svobodu!* or *For Freedom!*), to publicize his Committee's views about the Bolsheviks and the future of Russia, in which he published articles himself.

By the end of June, Savinkov announced that he had identified nearly 10,000 men who were ready to join his new force, including survivors of Yudenich's Northwestern Army, former Red Army soldiers who had come over to the Polish side, Russian ex-POWs from Poland, Germany, and Czechoslovakia, and remnants of White units that retreated from the south of Russia and had been interned in Polish camps. Savinkov further estimated that he would soon be able to increase the overall size of the army to 24,000 men, and that it would include infantry, artillery, cavalry, and engineering troops. With Wrangel's approval—which Savinkov sought in his typical attempt to act "legitimately," despite his distaste for Wrangel personally—the army's commander became

General Pyotr Glazenap, an experienced veteran who had fought in all the major White Russian campaigns—Denikin's, Kolchak's, and Yudenich's.

⚬——⚬

All this sounded very promising in terms of scope and speed. However, it is evident that Savinkov inflated his projections for propaganda purposes (the degree to which he did so depended on whom he was addressing and how much he needed to impress them) and the actual situation was more precarious from the start. Savinkov's initial problem was that he was not dealing with a normal process of recruiting men in a stable society that had shifted to a wartime footing; instead, he had to take whoever happened to wash up on Polish shores and was willing to join him. Another was that he had to rely on the largess of the Poles for all material support, from boots to rifles to bread, and they were struggling to supply their own troops. The third was that his reputation with veterans of the White movement was very mixed, and many of those in the higher ranks did not trust him and were loyal to Wrangel.

There was also the matter of Savinkov's actual relations with the Polish head of state. Savinkov clearly realized that his alliance with Poland would last only as long as Piłsudski found it useful. This is the reason he included a provision in his agreement with Piłsudski that the Russian troops he raised would not be interned if Poland signed an accord with the Soviets, but would be free to act on their own.

Bulak-Balakhovich

The postrevolutionary chaos in the territories of the former Russian Empire spawned a motley assemblage of small and large armed bands, some of which were explicitly military with political goals, while others were simply criminal. They roamed where they could, pursuing their own individual agendas, and at times functioned as wild cards in the main conflict between the Reds and the Whites (as when Makhno disrupted Denikin's advance on Moscow). When Savinkov accepted Piłsudski's invitation, he could never have expected that one of these military formations would become a major factor in the evolution of his war against the Bolsheviks and would show him an entirely different way to fight them.

Stanislav Bulak-Balakhovich was of Polish-Belorussian origin and humble background, and had served as a captain in the Russian Imperial Army during the Great War and then briefly with the Bolsheviks before switching to Yudenich's White Northwestern Army, where he was promoted to colonel and general. When Yudenich's army collapsed, Bulak-Balakhovich fought on behalf of anti-Bolshevik Estonian and Latvian movements. In March 1920, he changed direction again and brought his 640-man cavalry unit to Poland, offering to help fight the Bolsheviks.

Bulak-Balakhovich was a daring commander who specialized in raids behind enemy lines. He was also a highly controversial figure in the eyes of contemporaries because of his iconoclasm and his ambivalent stance with regard to anti-Semitism. Independent and willful to the point of unruliness, he cultivated the appearance of a swashbuckler, wearing at times a Cossack-styled black karakul hat with a death's head insignia on it that complemented the somber gaze of his blue-gray eyes, sunken cheeks, and severe triangular moustache.

⚬⚬⚬

Bulak-Balakhovich was willing to join Savinkov's movement but set a condition. He would ally himself with the Committee's political program only if he could retain complete freedom of action in all military matters, even though his cavalry unit, like the rest of the Russian army, was officially under Polish command. To reflect the aggressively populist stance he advocated that focused on the peasantry, he also named his formation the Russian People's Volunteer Army.

Allowing a smaller military detachment to act independently of the core army would be an obvious tactical mistake, but Bulak-Balakhovich could not be denied because Poland needed all the troops it could find. In July, it fell to Savinkov as the Russian Political Committee's president to try to adjudicate the matter, and he quickly found himself in the kind of administrative maelstrom he loathed—personal rivalries, political bickering, interference from outsiders, and factional plotting behind the scenes. Even Glazenap began criticizing Savinkov and promised, once the Bolsheviks were defeated, to hang him "the moment they set foot on Russian soil." Savinkov had to force Glazenap's resignation and replaced him with a more liberal commander, General Boris Permikin, a veteran of Yudenich's army. It all recalled what Savinkov had gone through when he was de facto minister of war under Kerensky.

The French also interfered. They were supporting Piłsudski as well as Wrangel and wanted Savinkov to acknowledge Wrangel as the overall leader of the anti-Bolshevik forces. Savinkov agreed out of political expediency, but it was a pure formality. There were never any practical consequences, and he did nothing to conceal his disapproval of the White Army's politics. When Savinkov wrote to Wrangel, he did so in the exquisitely respectful terms he always used and made a point of giving the general his due as the "only bearer of the Russian national flag." But he also added an acid-tinged line that Wrangel could not have failed to find insulting: "officially I cannot recognize you as long as your political program is unknown to me."

Throughout the summer and fall of 1920, these organizational and jurisdictional complications were compounded by a ceaseless cascade of other problems: delays in recruiting troops; delays in their being supplied with arms, clothing, and other equipment; obstruction by White officers who wanted to join Wrangel; and the appearance of additional military units under commanders who also wanted to act independently and initially resisted inclusion in Bulak-Balakhovich's army. The initiative in Poland seemed to be spinning out of Savinkov's control.

The Price of Loneliness

Negotiating with the various factions in Poland and abroad while dealing with the logistics of building an army required enormous effort, concentration, and patience. Savinkov was used to working long hours under pressure and had the physical stamina to endure it; heavy cigarette smoking also helped. However, it took an emotional toll on him, not only because he was making plans that would affect the lives of tens of thousands of men and the fate of his homeland, but also because he felt alone. He had colleagues and collaborators who were important for him, but he needed deeper emotional connections as well. This was not something that most of his admirers or detractors would have guessed about him, given the kind of self-possessed persona he projected in public.

Warsaw appears to be the place where Savinkov's relationship with Lyubov Efimovna began to develop into a deeper attachment. As was the case with him earlier in his life, the change was catalyzed by the deterioration of his relationship with another woman, although, surprisingly, this time it was not his wife. Evgeniya had remained in Paris with their son, and Savinkov does not seem

to have made any effort to bring them to live with him in Warsaw. This may
have been because life in Poland was difficult and uncertain, but it was also
because his feelings toward her had clearly cooled. Savinkov's break was with
his close friend Zinaida Gippius, who had become increasingly important for
him during the summer of 1920.

⚬━━⚬

Gippius, Merezhkovsky, and Filosofov had come to Warsaw because they placed
great hopes on Piłsudski and on his planned alliance with Savinkov against
the Bolsheviks. Unlike her two male partners, Gippius did not have a role in
Savinkov's organization when it was established (there was some talk of her
helping with propaganda that did not lead anywhere), but she nevertheless took
an intense interest in his plans, supported them fully at first, and observed his
dedication with a mixture of admiration and concern. Savinkov was touched by
her attention.

Then, one hot and sunny day in June, Savinkov's relationship with Gippius
suddenly darkened. He decided that he needed a break from his negotiations with
Piłsudski and sent Dikgof-Derental to Gippius's apartment with a note asking
her to come to see him straightaway. Their relations had become so familiar
that she was not surprised. Without any hesitation, she left the guests who happened to be visiting and walked over. She lived just across the Saxonian Garden
from the Brühl Hotel, where Savinkov's headquarters were located. Gippius's
recollections about what happened during this and subsequent encounters are
perceptive, multilayered, and elliptical. And they provide unique insight into her
relations with Savinkov and the fine-grained features of his character during a
trying period in his life.

Savinkov's room in the Brühl Hotel was simply furnished, long and narrow,
and faced the Saxonian Garden from a high floor, which he could not have
enjoyed because he did not like heights. Gippius had been there a number of
times before when he invited her and her partners to dinner. Savinkov put great
stock in being a good host, and she recalled how on one occasion he made a
touching effort to find a tablecloth. But such niceties were in short supply in
postwar Warsaw, and he had to settle for something that looked like a bedsheet.

When she arrived, Gippius and Savinkov sat down close to each other on
a small couch, and he began to unburden himself about the struggles he was

facing. He also confided openly to her about how isolated he felt. They were so comfortable with each other that it did not feel awkward when they fell into periods of silence.

Gippius thought that Savinkov was the most fascinatingly complex and contradictory person she had ever met. But she also believed that she understood "this willful, lonely man," and, as she tried to think of something she could do to help him, she put her arm around him in a half-humorous gesture, and then kissed him tenderly. Such intimacy had become habitual for them, she later recalled: "We kissed often and always, especially when we were saying goodbye. Each time we parted it was as if 'forever.'"

Savinkov was reserved by nature, and his willingness to engage in such gestures shows how important Gippius's friendship was for him and how well he understood her unconventional sexuality. However, on this occasion, and to her surprise, she sensed that Savinkov was yearning for something more and different in kind from the feelings they had shared previously. The kisses they exchanged suddenly no longer meant the same thing to them. Gippius struggled to express what she thought Savinkov wanted, and characterized it as "that intuitive tenderness, that spiritual sign, that women have in great abundance. This is what he was unconsciously straining toward." In other words, she sensed that what Savinkov needed now was a woman's conventional love.

The moment Gippius thought she recognized this in Savinkov, she recoiled from him. She knew from past experience that his "total 'masculinity' basically kills anything sexual in her." Gippius tried to conceal her reaction, but Savinkov noticed that a shadow had passed between them; memory of it would linger.

Gippius was incapable of a sexual relationship with a heterosexual man and could offer Savinkov only emotional closeness. However, he needed both. When he and Gippius tried to make sense of their feelings by talking about them, awkwardly, Savinkov explained that what he felt was not just physical desire: "I am not at all coarse in that sense . . . People don't know me . . . and I'm not a 'coupler.'" But at the same time, he admitted that "I don't understand spiritual closeness all by itself." He also suggested that their kisses had destabilized their friendship. Gippius answered that "I don't see things this way. I can't," to which Savinkov replied, "Then you shouldn't kiss on the mouth."

The gap that opened between Savinkov and Gippius was widened by her jealousy over Filosofov's growing involvement in the Russian Political Committee at the expense of his commitment to her and her husband. In her view, Savinkov was directly to blame because he "separated us from Dima by putting him completely under his influence." Even worse was to come. When Gippius and her husband decided to move to Paris, Filosofov broke with them altogether so that he could remain in Warsaw and continue his work for Savinkov's Committee. Gippius's view of Savinkov changed after this, and she soon decided that she had been wrong about him all along: "Savinkov is emptiness. And I threw Dima into this deceptive emptiness with my own hands." The psychosexual contretemps between Gippius and Savinkov also signaled Savinkov's openness to a new love.

This was the unhappy situation into which Lyubov Efimovna blithely stepped in her high-heeled Parisian shoes when she got off the train in Warsaw during the summer of 1920. Her husband had asked Savinkov (as head of the Russian Political Committee, which depended on Polish hospitality) permission to bring her from Paris. At first, Savinkov replied that it was Dikgof-Derental's personal affair and therefore up to him. But then Savinkov realized that Lyubov Efimovna could be useful in Warsaw because her French was native and she could help with composing telegrams to Paris, where she had recently done related work for the Union propaganda agency. Savinkov also probably welcomed her company because he was attracted to her.

When Gippius met Lyubov Efimovna, she scrutinized her with a mixture of curiosity, fastidious distaste, and prickly female rivalry. But she could also see the appeal of Lyubov Efimovna's frank and exotic sexuality, even if she admitted it grudgingly and with an anti-Semitic squint: "She's not bad, a kind of handsome Jewess, flamboyant, with painted lips; there's something of the courtesan about her, she's made for undressing; she rolls her 'r's at the back of her throat in the French manner. She has black hair and, for someone with crude taste, is beautiful."

In the context of Gippius's multilayered description of how she fell out with Savinkov, Lyubov Efimovna emerges as the clear victor. Gippius also suggests the effect that her presence in Warsaw will have on Savinkov by quoting Dikgof-Derental's gleeful remark to Filosofov: "My wife knows how to deal with Boris Viktorovich very well. If something's not right—go straight to her."

Missing the Historical Moment

The Soviet advance into Poland continued unabated throughout the summer, and by August the country was in grave danger. Five armies were approaching Warsaw under Mikhail Tukhachevsky, the *komfront* who had already distinguished himself against Kolchak and Denikin (the Bolsheviks eliminated traditional tsarist military ranks at the time and his title was an abbreviation for "commander of the front"). The ambitious goal the Bolsheviks had was expressed by Tukhachevsky's notorious—and oxymoronic—appeal to his troops: "Over the corpse of White Poland lies the road to worldwide conflagration. On our bayonets we will carry happiness and peace to laboring humankind. To the West!"

The Poles tried to recruit every able-bodied man they could find to defend the capital. It is beyond irony that the part of the Russian army under Permykin's command was still so underequipped and undermanned that it could not go to the front. Only Bulak-Balakhovich's unit joined the Poles during the momentous days in the middle of August when their country was on the verge of total defeat.

Poland was, and still is, a devoutly Catholic country, and it seemed to many that only divine intervention could save Warsaw from falling to the Bolsheviks. But it was Piłsudski who did. He took personal command of the capital's defense and devised a counterattack that seemed so risky the Soviets concluded it must be a deception when they captured a Polish soldier with a copy of the plan. The key was a cavalry assault on the rear of Tukhachevsky's forces that was launched on August 12 and lasted two weeks. Although at one point the Soviets approached within ten miles of Warsaw, Piłsudski's counterattack succeeded brilliantly and became known as the Miracle on the Vistula. The rout of the Soviets was so complete that Lenin had no choice but to sue for peace to minimize his losses. Polish-Soviet talks began at the end of September, an armistice took effect in October, and the Treaty of Riga sealing the peace was signed early the following year.

The Miracle on the Vistula not only saved Poland's independence, it also ended Soviet plans to spread communism to Europe, at least for the next several decades. But the peace that followed also shifted the ground under the Russian army that Savinkov was building. Five weeks earlier in Moscow, at a meeting of the Sovnarkom (Council of People's Commissars), the state's highest governing body, Trotsky proclaimed that Savinkov and Bulak-Balakhovich had become so dangerous because of their recent activities that one of the conditions of the armistice had to be an end to Polish support for Savinkov's military formations on its territory. On October 23, five days after the armistice took effect, the Polish minister of war, General Kazimierz Sosnkowski, announced that all Russian units had to leave Polish territory by November 2. He gave the Russians two choices: they could evacuate to the south of Russia with their arms and join Wrangel's army, or they could open a western front against the Bolsheviks in Belarus and fight there alone.

Even though Savinkov's agreement with Piłsudski anticipated exactly such a possibility, Sosnkowski's ultimatum was a major setback because of its timing. The Russian army was being abandoned by Poland before it even had a chance to justify its existence in battle. There is no evidence, however, that Savinkov took this turn of events in any other way than as a move on a geopolitical chessboard. He understood that Poland had her own interests that differed from Russia's, and he would always be grateful for the help the Poles had given his cause.

Savinkov put Sosnkowski's offer to a vote by the men in Permykin's and Bulak-Balakhovich's armies. Predictably, Permykin and most of his officers and men chose to join Wrangel. But Bulak-Balakhovich's Russian People's Volunteer Army voted to attack the Bolsheviks in Belarus, and Savinkov decided to join them. He was feeling the pressure of historical time and wrote to Gippius, with whom he had not yet broken: "It isn't right to wait. To wait is to deceive oneself and to miss what won't be repeated. I hope that things will sort themselves. And if not, it's necessary to throw oneself into the cold water."

⚬─┼─⚬

By this point in his life, Savinkov had again lost all patience with the political and jurisdictional squabbles in which he had become embroiled, and this may have clouded his judgment. His brother Victor, who had recently escaped from the Bolsheviks in Novorossiisk and came to Warsaw to work with him, recalled that Boris saw himself as facing a stark choice—either "engage in 'muttering' together with the émigrés"—that is, waste time talking—"or together with Balakhovich actively try to bring down the Bolsheviks." Considering the alternatives, Savinkov did not care about the questionable reputation that Bulak-Balakhovich and his army had. When someone told him that they were "rogues," he replied: "Maybe. But what am I supposed to do if honorable people don't want to fight and sit in Parisian cafes abusing those who are fighting while babbling about high-minded themes?"

By early November the Russian People's Volunteer Army had grown to an impressive size—four divisions totaling approximately 20,000 men. Savinkov was eager to take part in the campaign, as he had in the Rybinsk uprising and in the cavalry raid behind Bolshevik lines near Kazan. Together with his brother, he joined the First Division's First Cavalry Regiment, commanded by Colonel Sergey Pavlovsky. This choice was significant because it brought Savinkov into contact with men of a kind he had never known closely before. And although he could not have anticipated this, their commander would play an increasingly important—and ultimately a tragic—role in his life before very long.

Another surprising participant in the campaign was Savinkov's old friend and co-conspirator, the British agent Sidney Reilly, who had come to Warsaw under cover at Churchill's behest to get a sense of the anti-Bolshevik movement and to participate in the Anti-Bolshevik Congress that Savinkov organized. What he would see of the Russian People's Volunteer Army and the Political Evacuation Committee's clandestine activities would increase his admiration for Savinkov enormously and his desire to help.

A New Kind of War

The men in the First Division were the most experienced guerrilla fighters in Bulak-Balakhovich's army and had earned the name Division of Death. Victor Savinkov was fascinated by their dispassionate ruthlessness, noting that they "were completely indifferent to their lives and the lives of others . . . they were warriors who had reached the limit of martial practice; war had burned out and eaten away anything that was inside them and anything spiritual."

Savinkov's involvement with these troops and participation in Bulak-Balakhovich's invasion of Soviet territory caused a major reorientation in his approach to fighting the Bolsheviks and in his politics. While riding through the Belarusian hinterland, everything he saw forcibly reminded him that nothing had changed in Russia's demographics and that the vast majority of the population were still peasants. He watched how the Belarusian villagers interacted with the troops, he talked repeatedly with soldiers and peasants about their views, and he worked closely with Bulak-Balakhovich on policies they announced together. He realized that he had to refocus his attention on the peasants and make their needs the bedrock of his ideology for Russia's future. As a result, he abandoned much of what he had advocated since 1917 and returned to his Socialist Revolutionary roots, but in a way that was even more thoroughgoing and radical.

To distinguish his new views, he started to refer to his movement as Green in contrast to the binary of Red and White. He also began to argue that Russia needed a "third way" into the future, one that rejected the hierarchy of the old aristocratic order as well as the tyranny of the Bolshevik Party—"neither tsar nor commissar," as he put it. The articles he wrote for his Warsaw newspaper became the vehicle for publicizing his new views on military and political matters.

Savinkov also realized that he had to abandon his former plans for fighting the Bolsheviks. For three years, he had tried to persuade influential statesmen in London, Paris, and other capitals to intervene militarily in Russia's Civil War. But now he decided that the Bolsheviks could be defeated by the Russians themselves and in cooperation with the nationalities that had been subjects of the old empire (the kind of alliance he had advocated ever since the Finns offered to help Kolchak).

An even more radical change was that Savinkov revised the concept of regular armies and fronts, and decided that the fight against the Bolsheviks should be conducted by peasant militias waging guerilla warfare, in which armies like Bulak-Balakhovich's would function as nuclei around which the militias could organize. He argued that henceforth there should be no forced conscription of men, which is how the Whites and the Reds filled their ranks. Instead, militias would consist only of volunteers from the regions where the fighting was actually going on, and once the local danger had passed, the men would be free to return to their villages. Moreover, the militias would be subject to iron discipline only while in action, but outside the military, complete social equality for all would be the rule. Intertwined with the military plans was an exceptionally liberal and democratic political program he developed with Bulak-Balakhovich that included individual ownership of land by peasant-farmers, an absolute right to self-determination by all nationalities, and grassroots organization of local governments leading to a new constituent assembly.

But a war conducted in this way would still need experienced soldiers to supplement and help organize the peasant militias. Where would they come from? Savinkov's original and rather fantastical idea was from the Red Army itself. He believed that disaffection among its soldiers was already so widespread that they could be persuaded to defect and join an anti-Bolshevik peasant army. What was needed to achieve this was effective propaganda so that they would understand who their true friends and enemies were. If this practice were followed, Savinkov believed, the Russian Civil War would be transformed into a new revolution against the Bolshevik betrayers of February 1917. Examples of such defections had already occurred, such as in the spring of 1919, when several Red Army units rebelled and joined an anti-Bolshevik Ukrainian army. Savinkov knew about this event because the units renamed themselves in his honor as "The Boris Savinkov Russian Brigade."

The Invasion of Belarus

On November 4, 1920, Savinkov and Bulak-Balakhovich received a telegram from a new entity, the Belarusian Political Committee, with an appeal to help free Belarus from the "Bolshevik invaders." On November 6 they answered the call, and despite being poorly provisioned and equipped, the Russian People's Volunteer Army set out from the towns of Mikashevichi and Turov, which were then near the eastern edge of the territory that Poland had won in its war with Soviet Russia and are now in Belarus.

From a tactical point of view, it was an opportune time to begin the campaign. Bolshevik forces in Belarus were still in disarray following their catastrophic defeat by the Poles, and although the vast, low-lying Polesye region through which the army would pass was covered with thick forests and numerous swamps, Savinkov expected to proceed rapidly. He was counting on Bolshevik troops panicking at the sight of new forces and defecting to Bulak-Balakhovich's side, and on getting food and other support from discontented peasants.

Savinkov's and Bulak-Balakhovich's ultimate plan went far beyond liberating Belarus. After replenishing their army with provisions, communication equipment, and ammunition they would be in a position to cross into Russian territory and begin a drive toward Moscow, 400 miles to the northeast. The hope was that defections from the Red Army would fuel the Russian People's Volunteer

Army's growth. As Savinkov saw it, the beginning of the campaign in Belarus promised to be the beginning of the end of the Bolshevik regime.

Although from a historical distance Savinkov's optimism looks delusional, or like an expression of his need for action that was so strong it eclipsed the voice of prudence, there were others at the time who thought he had a chance. Maklakov, the anti-Bolshevik Russian "ambassador" in Paris, in a letter to his counterpart Bakhmetev, the Russian "ambassador" in Washington, DC, wrote, "I quite allow that Red Army soldiers will not want to fight" a peasant army like Balakhovich's and that "Savinkov may wind up in Moscow before Wrangel."

Relying on the element of surprise, the Russian People's Volunteer Army quickly advanced seventy miles to the east, and in a major operation on November 10 took Mozyr, an important town that is now in southeastern Belarus. Six days later, Savinkov and Bulak-Balakhovich signed an agreement on behalf of the Russian Political Committee with the newly proclaimed Belarusian People's Republic recognizing its independence. It appeared to be the beginning of a new anti-Bolshevik coalition. When, in addition, 300 Red Army prisoners volunteered to form an infantry battalion in Bulak-Balakhovich's army, Savinkov took this as "proof" that the plan for defeating the Bolsheviks through defections could be realized. To encourage more of the enemy to defect, he made proclamations that Bulak-Balakhovich's army was not waging war against the Red Army's soldiers but only their Bolshevik overlords, and in accordance with the new principle of voluntarism, no troops were forcibly conscripted in the occupied territory.

However, in comparison to the Red Army's total forces in Belarus, 300 defectors were a minuscule number, and it soon became apparent that there would be few others. There was also an unexpected blow when the fortunes of Wrangel's White Army plummeted. Savinkov and Bulak-Balakhovich wanted to act independently of him, but the fate of his forces affected their campaign because they were fighting the same enemy.

Two months earlier, in August 1920, Wrangel had made his farthest advance to the north, which helped the Poles greatly during their war because of the numbers of Red troops that were fighting him. But after the Polish-Soviet armistice, and despite continuing French political and material support, Wrangel began to suffer defeats and had to retreat. By early November his army was in the Crimean Peninsula with the Black Sea at its back. The only choice was to surrender or evacuate, and between November 12 and 15 Wrangel succeeded in boarding approximately 150,000 people—the remnants of his army and many civilians—onto more than 120 ships. Their destination was Constantinople, which the Allies had occupied at the end of the Great War and made into a safe haven. Wrangel's intention was to preserve his army in exile and then return to continue the fight, but his evacuation proved to be the death knell of the White movement in European Russia.

After Wrangel's defeat, tens of thousands of Red troops were rushed to Belarus and quickly put the Russian People's Volunteer Army on the run. It suffered serious losses of several thousand dead and captured, and most of its surviving troops were forced to retreat across the Polish border. Only a few small units remained behind enemy lines to continue guerilla warfare.

Looked at objectively and from a military standpoint, the results of the November campaign were disastrous. Bulak-Balakhovich's army was also tarnished morally. The region through which it passed was in the Pale of Settlement and had a large Jewish population. Everywhere Bulak-Balakhovich's troops went they carried out pogroms, and the local peasants, seeing an opportunity to rob and steal, joined in. One eyewitness was stunned that in some areas there was not a single village in which a single Jewish house had survived: "Such a hatred toward the Jewish population is simply inexplicable," he exclaimed. Another reported that the town of Mozyr "is an awful sight. There isn't a single house that hasn't been robbed . . . What soldiers didn't need was destroyed with fire."

The mayhem, murders, and robberies continued despite Bulak-Balakhovich's repeated orders that they cease. Some observers did not find his attempts to stop the pogroms convincing since they were made "when there was nothing left to destroy."

In an attempt to limit the damage to the army's international reputation, Savinkov's brother Victor initially tried to deny that the pogroms ever happened (although privately he described them in detail). But Savinkov acknowledged the pogroms publicly and fully from the start in a series of publications. In 1920, just weeks after the ill-fated campaign, he published a brochure in Warsaw titled "The Russian People's Volunteer Army in the Field" in which he condemned the pogroms and confessed that they made him feel personally ashamed. However, he also tried to explain—but not excuse—their origin and concluded that "the peasant, the Red Army soldier and the follower of Balakhovich perceives the

Jew as an enemy, as a true ally of the Reds. From this comes the hatred—that blind, unreasoning, spontaneous anti-Semitism that falls like a black spot on Balakhovich's glory."

In the brochure, Savinkov stresses that he personally did what he could to make Bulak-Balakhovich stop the pogroms when they broke out. He also insists that Bulak-Balakhovich deserves some credit for trying to do so because he ordered that perpetrators be shot on the spot, which is something that neither Denikin, nor Kolchak, nor Petlyura did when their troops carried out pogroms. Savinkov ends his report about this sorry episode in the army's history by insisting that it is the duty of every honest man to defend the Jews, who as a people are as innocent of being communists as the Russians are of being Bolsheviks.

Despite the military and moral defeats that the army suffered, Savinkov remained undaunted. After he returned to Warsaw, he was still convinced that the peasants and Red Army soldiers he talked with in Belarus had expressed genuine sympathy for the Russian People's Volunteer Army and its political goals. What was necessary now, he insisted, was to fan these flames into a major conflagration. Although the battle in Belarus was temporarily lost, the peasant-led fight against the Bolsheviks would go on.

Regrouping

Savinkov felt personally responsible for the welfare of the tattered remnants of Bulak-Balakhovich's army after they crossed back into Poland and were disarmed and interned in accordance with the terms of the Soviet-Polish peace treaty. (He also included Permykin's forces in his purview after they returned from Ukraine, where they had fought the Bolsheviks with Petlyura and planned to join Wrangel before he evacuated.) As a result, according to Savinkov's estimate, by early December 1920 there were 20,000 Russian soldiers back on Polish soil, all in need of food, shelter, clothing, and medical attention. It was winter, and typhus was breaking out in the camps in which the Poles confined the Russian troops. The Russian Political Committee had exhausted its funds, and the Polish government informed Savinkov that it could not afford to support more than 5,000 of the men.

Savinkov immediately began an energetic campaign to get money from the French, Wrangel, and others; he knew that the British would refuse.

But everyone refused. To make matters worse, Savinkov's political standing in Poland deteriorated when his patron Piłsudski came under attack because the presence of Russian forces on Polish soil jeopardized the peace treaty with the Soviets. Savinkov decided it would be wise to assume a lower profile, and on December 13 changed the name of the Russian Political Committee to the more conciliatory Russian Evacuation Committee.

This was merely a subterfuge, however. Savinkov had no intention of evacuating the Russian troops anywhere or stopping his anti-Bolshevik activity. He still had Piłsudski's tacit support and during the coming months managed to eke out a living for the interned soldiers in various ways, although conditions in the camps were hard and morale suffered. Some of the men asked to be transferred to the Polish Army; others wanted to join the French Foreign Legion. Still others were reported to be engaged in criminal activity. Savinkov also did what he could to soften conditions for those who remained by organizing cooperative canteens and workshops, providing newspapers and books, creating elementary courses in reading and writing (in one camp nearly 10 percent of the soldiers were illiterate) as well as general education courses, and conducting classes in foreign languages and propaganda.

Political problems continued and grew in severity, especially from Permykin's men. Many of them remained loyal to Wrangel, even though he was in exile, and were openly resentful of Savinkov's leadership. By the end of December 1920, things had deteriorated to the point that a French major reported to his superiors that Permykin's officers told him they would kill Savinkov if he visited their army. But with the Polish military's help, he reaffirmed his authority by dismissing the rebellious and reactionary officers and ensuring that they left the country.

A New Popular Revolution

While keeping a low profile in Poland, over the course of the next ten months, until the fall of 1921, Savinkov worked on developing a multipronged attack on the Soviet state that was more ambitious in its conception than any he had attempted before. He did not see his past failures as having any bearing on his new plans because he was now going to build on what he believed he had learned from the mistakes of the invasion of Belarus.

Sidney Reilly, his old comrade, was on a covert British mission in Warsaw at this time and talked with him at length about his new plans. He was struck by Savinkov's "extraordinary faith in his cause and in himself" and concluded that what made it possible for him to "set about the task of forging a new political weapon out of the debris around him" was the "superhuman doggedness which is his strongest characteristic."

Savinkov had concluded that the hatred of the Soviet regime he had seen among Belarusian peasants was part of a growing, nationwide wave of popular opposition. And he was right. Large numbers of peasants were in fact taking up arms to defend their traditional village life from Bolshevik attempts to impose a communist social, political, and economic order on the country. In January 1921 in Western Siberia, over 50,000 peasants rebelled against the regime's policy of *prodrazvyorstka*, or confiscation of grain and other food products. The Antonov peasant rebellion (named after its leader), which started in August 1920 in Tambov and other central provinces to the southeast of Moscow, grew to over 40,000 fighters by early 1921; it also included workers who sympathized with the peasants. In Ukraine, "Dad" Makhno fought the Bolsheviks on behalf of the peasantry from late 1920 until the summer of 1921, at one point fielding an army of 40,000 men. Numerous other smaller outbreaks occurred throughout the country. The Cheka reported that there were 118 peasant rebellions in progress during February 1921 in Ukraine alone.

The way Savinkov saw it, during the past three years the Soviet state had repeatedly hung by a thread, and several attempts to overthrow it had come close to succeeding. Now the country was even more ripe for revolution because of widespread opposition to the brutal policies of "War Communism" that the Soviet regime had instituted in 1918. In addition to stripping peasants of agricultural supplies below subsistence levels, it included state control of industry and trade, banning of private enterprise, oppressive labor laws and prohibition of strikes by workers, food rationing in cities, mass executions of "class enemies," and an expansion of the political police. The Bolshevik regime may have won the war against the Whites, but it now faced a war with large sections of its own population. In the spring of 1921, peasants in the western part of Russia actually wrote to Savinkov asking him to lead them in their struggle against the Bolsheviks. Little wonder that he believed that this time he could succeed.

For the Soviet regime, the peasant uprisings were aggravated by desertions and rebellions in the Red Army. In some areas, 20 percent of draftees failed to report; in others it was as high as 90 percent. Up to 250,000 men are estimated to have deserted from the Red Army in Tambov Province shortly after Antonov's rebellion began because they did not want to fight their own kind (the majority of soldiers were still peasants).

The most dramatic military rebellion of 1921 started in early March in the Kronstadt naval fortress guarding the approach to Petrograd, when thousands of sailors from the Baltic fleet—celebrated as "the flower and pride of the Russian Revolution" because of the central role they played in helping the Bolsheviks seize power in October 1917 and then in maintaining it—rose against the dictatorial regime and the policies of War Communism. Tens of thousands of loyal Red Army troops would be needed to crush the rebellion, which Lenin characterized as "undoubtedly more dangerous than Denikin, Yudenich and Kolchak combined." The overall situation for the Bolsheviks was so grim that in mid-March 1921 the Soviet leader privately confided, once again, that "we are barely holding on."

⚓

Realizing it was essential to move quickly to take advantage of a historic opportunity, in January 1921 Savinkov and his brother inaugurated an "Information Bureau" as part of the Russian Evacuation Committee. Its purpose was to disseminate anti-Bolshevik propaganda and to gather intelligence in all regions of Russia. It also established contacts with partisans, such as Bulak-Balakhovich's men who had remained in Belarus; oppositional groups in cities and in the Red Army; peasant groups; railway workers; some Socialist Revolutionaries (among whom Savinkov still had allies); and members of other parties. By September of that year, the Bureau had sent 500 organizers into Soviet Russia and established a network of 700 intelligence agents who assisted in the dissemination of more than 3 million copies of agitational publications that targeted peasants and soldiers. Savinkov believed that the new revolution could start in the spring.

He began military and paramilitary preparations as well. He had succeeded in preserving remnants of Bulak-Balakhovich's and Permykin's armies, which still numbered around 15,000 men, and in culling undesirable elements from it (including dismissing both of its commanders). He organized a terrorist cell in Moscow that could strike at the Soviet leadership and important command points. The Russian Evacuation Committee's agents infiltrated military units in the big cities and also targeted the famous First Cavalry Army of *komandarm* Semyon Budyonny, a hero of the civil war.

The plan was to orchestrate risings by the numerous irregular forces scattered throughout the European part of the country. Savinkov expected that this could be achieved through local organizations in the villages, which would collaborate to create regional networks, which, in turn, would coordinate with the Russian Evacuation Committee in Warsaw. In connection with this, Savinkov resurrected his old military organization from the days of the Volga uprising, the Union for the Defense of the Motherland and Freedom, and added "National" to its name to show its greater reach. Should local groups not have the necessary military expertise, the Committee would send officers to lead groups of guerillas. Also included in the overall plan was collaboration with the Don and Kuban Cossacks and with anti-Soviet movements in Finland and the Baltic countries.

There were chronic shortages of weapons, money, supplies, food, and clothing for the troops in Poland, about whose welfare Savinkov cared deeply, but he believed that these could be overcome and appealed ceaselessly to everyone he could think of for help. He also hoped that he could overcome the mistrust that his failed invasion in Belarus had awakened among anti-Bolshevik Russians, and the open animosity of Wrangel, Permykin, and their agents, who worked actively to sabotage his initiatives, including, as he believed, leaking information to the Bolsheviks.

New Blows

The Soviet leadership was well aware of the growing danger Savinkov represented and sought ways to fight back. In the spring of 1921, an opening appeared when a senior member of the National Union for the Defense of the Motherland and Freedom, Alexander Opperput-Staunits, whom Savinkov trusted fully, was arrested by Soviet border guards and became an informant for the Cheka. In the months that followed the Cheka arrested over 350 of Savinkov's agents throughout the country, including some who had infiltrated government agencies in Moscow and assumed important posts. The official Soviet government newspaper *Izvestiya* trumpeted the news and named Savinkov as the leader in its issue of July 24, 1921. These arrests did not destroy Savinkov's network, but they hurt it badly.

There were additional blows that Savinkov could not have foreseen. In March the Soviets suppressed the Kronstadt rebellion, thus eliminating one of the major focal points around which Savinkov was planning to build his uprising. In May Tukhachevsky's army defeated the Antonov peasant rebellion by using all the means of modern warfare, including airplanes and poison gas, and then carried out savage reprisals against the remaining local population.

Savinkov decided to delay his uprising until the fall harvest, when the Soviet regime would start requisitioning new crops, which he expected would reawaken the peasantry's animosity.

It could not have helped Savinkov's state of mind in the spring of 1921, when all his military plans were collapsing, that he also had to deal with a family problem.

In early March he received a heart-wrenching letter from Evgeniya in Paris. There are several spots on it where the ink had run, which could well have been her teardrops. Savinkov had stopped writing to her, either because he was overwhelmed with work or because of Lyubov Efimovna, or both. She asks him why, and assures him "No matter what happens, my soul is always filled with you . . . I can't live without you." She tells him that she has recovered from a serious illness, but that her physical suffering was nothing in comparison to her emotional pain: "I am like a tree with roots that have been cut. I don't have a home. I live only with thoughts of you."

Will he come to Paris, as he promised, Evgeniya asks. She wishes that he could return to her and find the moments of peace, love, and happiness that he does not have. She reports that her mother is ill and needs costly treatment, and writes a few lines about their son, using the affectionate diminutive "Lyovochka," who is now eight years old: he is "a wonderful little boy. He is very smart and talented. He understands a great deal. He misses and often speaks of you."

Savinkov also missed his son deeply. A friend noticed how lovingly he talked about him and the great feeling with which he showed his photograph. But Savinkov's life was elsewhere, and there was nothing he could do to repair the broken tie to Evgeniya. He did receive some comfort from being unexpectedly reunited with his oldest sister, Vera, who came to Poland with her family in late 1920 without knowing that he was there, and whom he was able to help.

History Waits for No Man

The Soviet regime's success in defending itself against multiple threats had been at an enormous cost to the country. An official estimate is that during the period 1918–1920 there were 9 million excess deaths due to war, executions, disease, and hunger (not counting those who perished during the Great War). The country's economy had largely collapsed. By the summer of 1921, agriculture was in such disarray that famine was beginning in the Volga basin and other areas.

To preserve power, Lenin had to do something to placate the country's rebellious peasantry, and what he chose was typically (and cynically) pragmatic. At the Tenth Bolshevik Party Congress in March 1921 he announced the New Economic Policy (NEP), which was a strategic retreat from the regime's attempt to impose socialism in the country and represented a partial return to capitalism. From the point of view of the party's membership, however, it was a shocking betrayal of the October Revolution and an admission of failure. Rancorous debates among the Party's leadership ensued, but in the end, as usual, Lenin prevailed.

Under the new policy all political power remained in Bolshevik hands, and the regime continued to control the nation's finances, heavy and medium industry, transportation, foreign trade, and wholesale commerce. The significant changes were on the grassroots level. The hated forced requisitioning of foodstuffs from the peasants was replaced by a tax and at a much lower rate; moreover, plans for collective farms were set aside and peasants were allowed to keep their land allotments. Because the peasants were now free to sell whatever they had left after taxes, they acquired a powerful incentive to increase production. Soon thereafter, the regime concluded that it had to expand commerce as well by allowing private enterprise in small industry and in retail trade.

NEP would eventually become a great success and would transform the country, until Stalin ended it abruptly in 1928. However, the program was begun too late to prevent a famine in 1921–1922, during which 5 million people died. The situation became so catastrophic that Lenin's regime had to solicit aid from its capitalist enemies, and Herbert Hoover, the future president of the United States, organized an extensive relief effort that fed millions.

For Savinkov, however, NEP was again a case of history outpacing his plans, and it was both a setback and a new opportunity. On the one hand, by restoring the peasants' livelihood, NEP undermined the need for a nationwide peasant uprising. On the other, NEP was also the Soviet regime's frank acknowledgement of disastrous economic weakness and loss of popular support. Both were reasons to continue the war against the Bolsheviks.

Moreover, not only were all the major forms of state tyranny still in place, but controls were being tightened. When NEP was introduced, thousands of members of other parties—Mensheviks, SRs, Cadets—were arrested, tried, or deported, thus effectively ending any organized political opposition in the country. In 1922, Lenin also used the famine as an opportunity to start destroying the Orthodox Church by seizing its property and killing clergy. Russian peasants were traditionally very devout, but when violent opposition from the local population broke out in a town in central Russia, Lenin's response was "The more representatives of the reactionary clergy and reactionary bourgeoisie we manage to shoot on this occasion, the better." Within the Bolshevik Party itself Lenin further consolidated his power by using conspiratorial methods to eliminate factions that had developed in it.

It is unlikely Savinkov believed Lenin's claim that the changes NEP introduced were "in earnest and for long," although there were those who did, both at home and abroad. Lenin's public pronouncements were designed to encourage Western help in the form of business investments. Internally, however, he confided that it is "the greatest mistake to believe that NEP has put an end to terror. *We will still return to terror*, and to terror that is economic." Whatever gesture Lenin may have made to the peasantry, he still believed in the dictatorship of the proletariat, which for him meant "power not limited by anything, not constrained by any laws, and based on force."

Last Man Standing

Even though Savinkov was unable to foment a peasant rebellion and some of his operations were disrupted by the Cheka arrests, he remained a thorn in the side of the Bolsheviks. Throughout 1921, his men, who surreptitiously continued to use Poland as a base, conducted guerilla warfare in the western Soviet provinces, attacking Red Army units, wrecking trains, and sabotaging and looting supplies. This was in direct contravention of the Riga Peace Treaty, which required Poland to withdraw its support for Savinkov. But because the Soviets were also infringing on the treaty by funding communist organizations in Poland, trying to orchestrate a coup d'état in the country, and flooding it with spies and agents, the Polish General Staff did not actively try to restrict Savinkov's activities. The Soviets protested repeatedly, but to no avail.

However, by the beginning of October 1921, they had had enough and decided to fight back more energetically. The Riga treaty stipulated that Soviet Russia had to pay Poland an indemnity of 30 million rubles in gold (around $200 million today). Knowing that the Polish government was worried about not being paid at all, the Soviets offered a deal: "Expel Savinkov and five of his principal agents and we will pay you immediately 10 million roubles in gold (about £1,000,000) on account of the 30 millions which we owe you in accordance with the treaty." The sum gives an idea of how much Savinkov was worth to the Soviets.

The offer was too good to pass up for some members of Poland's government who were at odds with Piłsudski and wanted the money for their economically troubled country. As Sidney Reilly would characterize it, this was the price for which Poland was willing to sell Savinkov's and his friends' right to asylum.

There ensued a month-long, increasingly complicated period of haggling, protesting, and outraged negotiations between the Poles and Savinkov's group. It included orders for everyone to leave on short notice; changes in those orders; Savinkov's surreptitious return to Poland by air from Prague, where he had sought sanctuary; debates in Polish government circles; Savinkov's friendly, four-hour long, but ineffectual meeting with Piłsudski; and expressions of support by his admirers. It all finally ended with everyone being escorted by police and gendarmes to the border with Czechoslovakia and expelled in two stages: Victor Savinkov, Dikgof-Derental, Miagkov, and several others on October 28, and Boris Savinkov on the thirtieth. Despite these last-minute maneuvers, Savinkov retained a lifelong gratitude to Piłsudski for the support and shelter he had given his movement.

Savinkov's expulsion from Poland was not just another twist in his roller-coaster life but can also be seen as the effective end of the civil war in Russia. The army he had organized in 1920 was the last sizeable force arrayed against the Bolsheviks that stood any chance of defeating them. What remained in the European part of the country in late 1921 were groups of partisans and terrorists who operated on a small scale. In the Far East, large armed bands continued to fight the Bolsheviks for several years longer, but they never represented a serious threat to the regime.

In the end, the Red Army won the Russian Civil War for several reasons. The Soviet regime controlled the core of the country with its two capitals, most of the population and industry, the inner lines of communication, and large quantities of military supplies remaining after the Great War. Their opponents were outnumbered and underequipped in comparison, and Allied help was too sporadic to compensate. The Red Army had a unified command, and its campaigns were coordinated, whereas their opponents, whether the Whites or Savinkov's forces, typically acted independently of each other. A major weakness of the Whites was their inability to accept the independence movements of national minorities; another was their inability to win over the masses of the population, especially the peasants. Savinkov tried to persuade the White leaders that such policies were folly, but they did not listen.

CHAPTER TEN

END GAME

After leaving Poland at the end of October 1921, Savinkov moved to Prague with the hope of renewing his relationship with Tomáš Masaryk, who had supported him financially in Moscow in 1918 and was now Czechoslovakia's president. The country had become very hospitable to Russian émigrés when it proclaimed its independence, and Savinkov imagined that he would be able to continue the work he had begun in Poland and even expand it. His goal remained a Green peasant uprising in Russia.

However, Masaryk's response was not what Savinkov expected, because shortly after arriving in Prague, he was asked to leave the country. The reason for this is not entirely clear, although it is likely that the Czechoslovak government wanted to limit the anti-Soviet activity that it would allow to be organized on its territory. But once Savinkov was in Paris at the end of November 1921, Masaryk renewed his covert support and even granted him a personal stipend.

Churchill's Adviser on Russia

Whatever anger and frustration Savinkov may have experienced after being forced out of two countries in one month was likely mitigated when he learned that Churchill wanted to meet with him in London about a pressing matter. Churchill had a different portfolio now than when they had last seen each other, but he was still an influential figure in the British government as secretary of state for the colonies. He was contemplating a complex gambit involving Russia and needed Savinkov's help. When he wrote about his plans to the prime minister,

Lloyd George, he added a note in red ink about Savinkov as "the only man who counts" when dealing with the Soviets.

Soviet Russia had started trying to emerge from her political and economic isolation by signing a trade agreement with Great Britain in March 1921, and by the end of the year Britain and France had begun to lean toward recognizing the country diplomatically. However, Churchill was resolutely against any accommodation with the Soviets unless they made fundamental changes in their draconian regime, and he concluded that the economic disasters that had led to NEP presented a historic opportunity to either force them to do so or isolate them further.

Churchill decided that Savinkov should be the person to send this message to the Soviets. The perfect occasion presented itself when Leonid Krasin, a senior Soviet political and trade representative (*polpred* and *torgpred* in Sovietspeak), came to England on the eve of an Anglo-French economic conference to seek a very large sum of money for rebuilding the shattered Russian economy. In a surprising and curious twist, in December 1921 Krasin also asked for a private meeting with Savinkov, with whom he had cooperated briefly on an SR campaign before the war.

In Churchill's scheme, Savinkov would inform the Soviets of the conditions they would have to meet in order to receive any Western aid. If they agreed, a major problem for Europe would be eliminated. If they did not, which was far more likely, the next part of Churchill's plan was to have Savinkov present the case for withholding aid from them to Lloyd George himself. In Churchill's view, there were instructive historical parallels between the Russian and French Revolutions. If the current economic chaos in Russia presaged the end of Bolshevism, then the time was ripe for a Russian Napoleon, and Savinkov would be an ideal candidate for the role.

But first Churchill had to get Savinkov to London, which took some doing. The British Foreign Office had decided that Savinkov was unreliable or even dishonest and turned him down when he applied for an English visa in Paris; C, the head of MI6, decided he would not help. Churchill's solution was to go behind their backs by using his personal contacts in British intelligence to have a visa issued to Savinkov anyway.

Savinkov arrived in London on Thursday, December 8. On Saturday he went to a private house in London—he never revealed the host's name—for the secret meeting with Krasin. It began with dinner, after which the host withdrew, leaving the two Russians to talk until 2 A.M.

Considering where the men stood on the political spectrum, it was an extraordinary meeting. Krasin was a highly placed member of the Soviet leadership and was close to Lenin. But he was very unlike his colleagues in his manner and appearance and eschewed their militant proletarianism, always dressing with great care in color-coordinated suits, shirts, and ties.

We know what the men talked about because Savinkov sent Piłsudski a detailed, top secret report at the end of the month. After Krasin made some formulaic remarks about the superiority of Marxism and the necessity of the Cheka, which Savinkov appears to have interrupted out of impatience, Krasin admitted that Soviet Russia was in a "catastrophic economic situation" and needed a loan of 50 million pounds sterling from the great powers (equivalent to perhaps $5 billion today). Without this money, which he claimed would allow the Bolsheviks to rebuild the country on capitalist principles, Soviet Russia would be dismembered by foreign interests. Then Krasin got to his main reason for the meeting: he offered Savinkov a position in the Soviet government, saying that his collaboration would be useful no matter which fate Russia faced.

Savinkov chose to summarize the meeting in a matter-of-fact style, and we can only imagine his amazement and cold fury at Krasin's offer. But he appears to have contained himself and his reply to Krasin was simple and straightforward: the members of the Bolshevik Party's "right wing"—those who were ready to accept the three principles of private property, free elections, and the elimination of the Cheka—should join with the Greens and destroy "Trotsky, Dzerzhinsky and Co." Savinkov added that if this collaboration did not occur, the peasants would destroy all the communists sooner or later anyway, without making any distinctions between those on the "left" and "right," including Krasin, Lenin, and all the others.

With a rebuff like this, Krasin gave the only reply he could: it was a mistake to think there is dissent among the Bolsheviks; Lenin, Trotsky, and Dzerzhinsky are as one; in ten years Europe will inevitably be communist; and the Greens are no threat.

There was nothing else to discuss, although Krasin tried to put a good face on the meeting, telling Savinkov he had learned much that was "new" and "unexpected" from him (the latter perplexed Savinkov), and that he would report their "very interesting" conversation to his comrades in Moscow.

Churchill was so eager to find out what happened during the meeting that he sent an aide to Savinkov's hotel that same night to find out. During the next two days, Savinkov met with Churchill several times, including at his home so that he could report his conclusions to Baron Birkenhead, the British lord chancellor. All three agreed that the Soviets could be recognized only if they accepted the three principles that Savinkov had formulated.

The denouement of Churchill's plot came on Sunday, December 18, when he sent a car to pick up Savinkov at his hotel and take them both to lunch with Lloyd George, who was staying at Chequers, which had just become the serving prime minister's country estate. It was in a quietly picturesque area of hills, forests, and farms thirty miles northwest of London. After the bustle and noise of the city, the drive there must have been very pleasant for Savinkov, especially in light of what the meeting with the prime minister augured. The weather that day was abnormally mild for December, with temperatures in the fifties and light winds. But it was still England, and the sky was largely overcast.

To Churchill's and Savinkov's surprise, Lloyd George was also being visited by a group of ministers of the Free Church of Scotland and a choir of Welsh singers, who proceeded to regale the Welsh-born prime minister and his guests with a performance of hymns lasting several hours. Churchill later recalled that they sang beautifully but added in a wry understatement that the "scene upon arrival must have been a novel experience for Savinkov." Finally, during lunch and afterward Savinkov was able to lay out what he had told Krasin; when Lloyd George responded, Savinkov was gratified to hear that he saw things in the same way as Churchill and Birkenhead: "*Lloyd George completely agrees with me,*" he emphasized in his letter to Piłsudski.

In fact, however, Lloyd George was not as committed as Savinkov believed. Privately, he was of two minds about the former terrorist and vice minister of war, although he kept this to himself. And at the meeting he restricted himself to suggesting that rather than trying to destroy the Bolsheviks, normalizing relations with them might be the best way to achieve peace and economic prosperity in Europe.

However, neither Churchill nor Savinkov thought that Lloyd George's reservations were very serious, and Churchill immediately began to make plans based on what he understood everyone had agreed to. He suggested that the British and the French should hold a conference with the Bolsheviks in Cannes in the near future, where they could be presented with Savinkov's three-point ultimatum. Churchill also invited Savinkov to attend the conference as an unofficial adviser. Before Savinkov left Chequers that afternoon, the secretary of state for war, Sir

Worthington Laming Worthington-Evans, also asked to meet with him and then told him that he "completely agreed" with his ideas.

As Savinkov drove back to London with Churchill that afternoon, he must have believed that he had reached the peak of his influence on the British government's policy toward the Bolsheviks. Never before had as many important ministers told him that they agreed with his ideas. And never before had he been invited to a major international conference and expected to function as an adviser to the British government.

There was more good news. Several days after the meeting in Chequers, Savinkov learned that Lloyd George had met with Aristide Briand, the French prime minister, and Louis Loucheur, the minister for liberated regions, and that both agreed with Savinkov's viewpoint. Churchill advised Savinkov to meet with Loucheur when he was back in Paris. The most encouraging news of all reached Savinkov just before he left England. In a meeting with Churchill's aide, Krasin said, "it will probably be necessary to come to an agreement with the Greens."

But once again, as if a malevolent fate was always waiting to thwart whatever Savinkov wanted most, nothing of what seemed to be within his grasp in England came to pass. In the first week of January 1922, an international conference was duly organized in Cannes with the aim of creating economic agreements that would "set Europe on her legs again," and Savinkov did attend it. However, Lloyd George went back on his agreement with him and abandoned the plan to present an ultimatum to the Bolsheviks. Churchill had lost his tug of war with the prime minister, and the other senior members of government acquiesced. The new British policy toward the Bolsheviks shifted from confrontation to recovering money that had been loaned to the Russian imperial government and insuring political stability at home.

Family Matters

By the end of 1921, Savinkov's marriage to Evgeniya was effectively over, and when he came to Paris he stayed in a hotel rather than with her. She knew about

Lyubov Efimovna and understood that it was not just geographical distance when he was in Poland that had kept them apart. However, the relations between them remained amicable. Evgeniya's tone in a letter she sent him in London is resigned and affectionate as she reports the family's news: she will fulfill his request and buy Lyovochka an album for collecting postage stamps as he recovers after an operation; he and her mother will spend two weeks in a small town in the country north of Paris, where it is very peaceful and the air is wonderfully clean; Savinkov's mother, Sofia, has recovered completely from her illness and feels well. Evgeniya admits that she is "very sad to be alone during the holidays," but realizes "there is nothing to be done." Whenever Savinkov was in Paris, he continued to play a role in his son's life by taking him on outings and even giving him lessons. And despite the change in their personal relations, Evgeniya would always remain loyal to Savinkov's life mission. In late January 1922 she admitted that she still feels "joy and pride for you—you, who used to be the closest person to me—because in your arduous boldness I now recognize the person I used to know in the Combat Organization . . . my entire soul is with you . . . May God help you and give you strength."

News about Savinkov's scattered siblings occasionally reached him as well, and it was mostly unhappy. At the end of March 1922, he got a letter from his brother Victor in Prague with the tragic news that their widowed sister Nadezhda had been shot in 1920 by the Cheka in Taganrog, a city on the Sea of Azov, leaving three children, one of whom subsequently also died of typhus. What "crime" Nadezhda committed other than being a "class enemy" is not known. Her late husband was Baron Roman von Maidel, the only officer who refused to order his soldiers to fire on the workers approaching the Winter Palace on Bloody Sunday in 1905, which did not prevent the Bolsheviks from executing him shortly after their coup. Savinkov's blood-soaked list of personal grievances against the Bolsheviks never stopped growing.

Mussolini

As Europe struggled to recover after the Great War, its political landscape began to change, and early in 1922, Savinkov turned his attention to Italy, where a prominent new figure and movement had recently emerged: Benito Mussolini and Fascism.

Very much a product of the feeling of injured Italian patriotism that appeared during the war, Fascism would metastasize after it ended—most notoriously to Germany, but also Spain, Hungary, and Romania. During the 1920s and 1930s, fascist movements attracted followers even in such bastions of democracy as Great Britain, France, and the United States. Together with Bolshevism, Fascism—especially its German variant—would become the most destructive force in twentieth-century history.

In comparison to Marxism, Mussolini's Fascism was ideologically relatively inchoate, but as the movement developed, several dominant characteristics emerged: ultranationalism; a revolutionary rejection of old credos, dogmas, organizations, and bureaucracies; subordination of class differences to the needs of the nation; regimentation of the economy; denigration of democracy; a cult of authority; a bellicose foreign policy; and animosity toward Bolshevism. In its early days during the 1920s, racial theories and anti-Semitism played no role in Italian Fascism, and Mussolini proclaimed that "the Jewish problem does not exist in Italy."

Fascism's novelty as a political party was its military organization, with members forming armed and black-shirted squads that preached and practiced violence against left-wing politicians and other opponents. By the end of 1921 the Fascists controlled much of Italy, had strong support among different strata of society, and Mussolini was talking openly about the need for a dictatorship.

⚬──⊹──⚬

Part of the reason for Mussolini's success was his effectiveness as a speaker. A short man with a large head, powerful jaw, and dark, piercing eyes, he had a knack for histrionics and demagoguery. During public appearances and photo ops, his trademark gesture became a pugnacious, uptilted chin thrust, followed by a scowl and a petulant pout of his lower lip. Many found his manner puerile and ridiculous. But in October 1922, 40,000 of Mussolini's Black Shirts carried out their spectacular and notorious March on Rome, which forced King Victor Emmanuel III to name the Fascist leader prime minister.

After taking power, Mussolini launched ambitious public works projects and industrial and agrarian initiatives to repair the Italian economy and fight unemployment. These further consolidated his support at home. They also impressed many political leaders abroad, including those who did not have a penchant for authoritarianism. Even after Mussolini assumed full dictatorial powers in 1925, he continued to be seen favorably for years by leaders of liberal democracies. In the United States Presidents Herbert Hoover and Franklin D. Roosevelt expressed approval of his regime, and Wall Street eagerly pursued economic deals with it. Ze'ev Jabotinsky, the Zionist leader, showed early interest in Mussolini's Fascism that lasted into the 1930s and claimed that it was a true ally of the Jewish people. Only after Mussolini's invasion of Ethiopia in 1935 and his alliance with Hitler in 1936 would any of this change. The first anti-Semitic racial laws and restrictions were introduced in 1938 as a result of Italy's growing dependence on Nazi Germany.

Savinkov had a lot of company when he was drawn to Mussolini, but what attracted him specifically? First and foremost, it was his hope that the Fascist leader would help him financially and militarily because of their shared opposition to Bolshevism, belief in nationalism, and readiness to use force to achieve their goals. Savinkov was also under the impression that Fascism was a genuinely populist movement that was supported by Italy's peasants and workers (a view that the Fascists spread but that was not entirely true either in the beginning or later). Finally, as he showed via his alliance with Kornilov before the October Revolution and with Piłsudski in Poland, Savinkov believed that authoritarian rule was necessary during times of national crisis.

In 1924, Savinkov summarized his idealized, if not paradoxical and naïve, view of the movement as follows:

> Fascism saved Italy from the commune. Fascism attempted to soften class warfare. It relies on the peasantry, it acknowledges and defends freedom and the property of every individual; the so-called imperialism of the Italian fascists is an accidental phenomenon that can be explained by an excess population in the country and the absence of good colonies, the preservation of the monarchy is the same kind of accidental phenomenon.

At the same time that Savinkov found excuses for Italy's aggressive imperialism, he remained loyal to the principle of self-determination for the peoples of Eastern Europe. He also remained a libertarian with regard to agricultural, economic, and social policies, all of which put him at odds with Fascism's collective and hierarchical emphasis.

◦━━━◦

In early March 1922, Savinkov arranged to meet with Mussolini in Lugano, a city in the mountainous, Italian-speaking border region of Switzerland. They must have spoken in French, which Mussolini knew well.

Their discussion was subsequently described as having been "sincere" and "comradely," although little of substance came of it. Mussolini did not offer Savinkov any financial support. He also rejected Savinkov's suggestion that they form a "Nationalist International" to oppose the Soviet Comintern or Communist International, saying that he was concerned only with the danger of communism spreading within Italy and not outside its borders. Instead, Mussolini proposed that Savinkov join him in fighting communists in Italy and in countries where Italy's interests were affected directly, such as neighboring Yugoslavia. This was not what Savinkov came for, but he agreed.

Mussolini then switched to a specific practical concern, one of considerable interest to Savinkov, which was the imminent arrival of a Soviet delegation to an international conference in Genoa. Mussolini feared that Italian workers and peasants would show their support for the Russian communists via meetings and mass demonstrations. To disrupt this, Savinkov agreed on a joint plan of action in which the Fascists would organize counterdemonstrations while he and his people would spy on the Soviet delegation (as they had already arranged to do for the French). Because Mussolini knew Savinkov's past, he also asked him to renounce any plans he might have to conduct terrorist operations against the Soviets while they were on Italian territory. Savinkov of course assured him that nothing of the sort would be attempted by the National Union for the Defense of the Motherland and Freedom.

The Secret Exposed

The meeting between Mussolini and Savinkov was supposed to have been secret, but only days after it took place a complete description of what they discussed appeared on the front page of the official Soviet government newspaper *Izvestiya* (*News*) in Moscow. How this could have happened remained unclear until 2001, when a report was found in the archives of the FSB that had been filed by the Foreign Section of the State Political Directorate (Gosudárstvennoye politícheskoye upravléniye, or GPU, one of the successors of the Cheka) and dated March 7, 1922. In other words, GPU agents in Europe were keeping such close track of Savinkov that they managed to infiltrate, or eavesdrop on, his meeting with the Fascist leader. The GPU then planted the report in the Moscow newspaper, which was a mouthpiece for the regime. It was the first round in a major new Soviet campaign against Savinkov and a continuation of one against Mussolini.

American and European newspapers picked up the story shortly after it appeared in Russian. Knowing Savinkov's reputation, they assumed that his intentions were violent and ran breathless headlines such as "Anti-Soviet Plot Alleged: Moscow Paper Reports Plan to Attack Genoa Delegates." A week later, to whip up the scandalous story even more, Georgy Chicherin, the Soviet Commissar of Foreign Affairs, who would head the Soviet delegation to Genoa, complained openly to the Western press about the risks he and his comrades would face from Savinkov in Genoa.

The GPU's "leak" to *Izvestiya*'s editors was a propaganda move that cunningly exploited the foreign press. As a result, Savinkov was publicly accused of something that he told Mussolini he would not attempt, which would damage the trust that had been established between them. Any element of surprise that Savinkov may have counted on when the Soviet delegation arrived in Europe was now gone. Western security services would be on alert to stop him, and their governments risked serious embarrassment if any attack took place. Overall, the GPU had successfully turned the tables on the West, where the Bolsheviks, who were seen as brutal oppressors, suddenly emerged as potential victims who needed protection.

Terror Reborn

Savinkov had in fact lied to Mussolini, and the accusations against him by Western newspapers were accurate. After the meeting in Lugano, he traveled to Berlin with Dikgof-Derental and another accomplice, Georgy Elvengren, a former tsarist officer who had been a member of the National Union in Poland.

They knew from newspaper reports that the Soviet delegation to Genoa would stop in Berlin before going on to Italy. Since his plans in Genoa had been exposed, Savinkov decided that he would stand a better chance of mounting an attack earlier and somewhere he was not expected.

For the time being he had the money he needed. His subsidy from Masaryk was supplemented by the Poles and the French, and he recently received a sizable sum from rich Russian émigré businessmen in Paris who had formed an organization called Torgprom (Russian Trade-Commerce and Financial Union). Opposed to any rapprochement between the Soviets and the West, and hoping that the Soviet regime would fail or be defeated so that they could reclaim their nationalized property in Russia, they were willing secretly to finance a terrorist attack on top-ranking Soviets who came to Europe; if it was successful, they told Savinkov, he would have a lot more money.

After arriving in Berlin, Savinkov and his team went to the apartment of Vladimir Orlov, an old schoolmate, friend, and co-conspirator who had organized a private anti-Soviet information center in the city and worked with the German police as well as White Russian and Western European intelligence organizations. He also collaborated closely with Sidney Reilly, who had instructed him to assist Savinkov.

Orlov had large collections of photographs and other documents about various leading Soviet functionaries and a small arsenal of explosives, jars of poisons, and other tools of sabotage and spy craft, all of which he willingly made available to Savinkov's team. He offered to get them weapons, passports if they needed them, and the addresses where the members of the Soviet delegation would be staying in the city. Savinkov asked for five revolvers and photographs of and information about four senior members of the delegation—Krasin (whom he had met in London), Chicherin (the delegation's leader), Karl Radek (a leading figure in the Comintern), and Nikolay Bukharin (a member of the Bolshevik Central Committee and candidate member of the Politburo).

The Soviet delegation, including officials, assistants, secretaries, and armed guards, arrived by train from Riga on Saturday evening, April 1, 1922. Savinkov had summoned several additional men from Warsaw and Helsingfors to augment his small team, and they began to track the Soviet delegates around Berlin the same way he had followed targets in Moscow and Saint Petersburg years earlier. There were no bombs this time. Each man was armed with a Mauser revolver on which Orlov had obliterated the serial number so it could not be traced. He also provided members of the team with walking sticks containing poison-filled hypodermic needles concealed in their tips that could be used to stab a victim.

However, security around the Soviets was so tight that getting close to them on foot proved impossible. The cars they used belonged to the German Ministry of Foreign Affairs and were free to ignore normal traffic speeds and rules of the road, as a result of which the terrorists' cars could not keep up.

Soviet security was also one step ahead of Savinkov and leaked information about him to the press, leading a reporter for the *New-York Tribune* to file a sensational story with the headline "Berlin Takes Elaborate Measures to Guard Reds. Savinkov, Who Plotted Death of Lenine, in City; Delegates To Be Lavishly Entertained."

In the end, the attack in Berlin had to be called off, most likely because there was not enough time to plan it thoroughly. The Soviet delegation left for Genoa on the evening of Wednesday, April 5, just four days after it arrived. Savinkov resolved to try again even though the fact he was on the hunt for the Soviets had been trumpeted all over Europe. He equipped himself with another Russian's papers (with dramatic consequences he could not have anticipated) and followed them.

Genoa

The Genoa Economic and Financial Conference had been proposed by Lloyd George at the end of the ineffectual conference in Cannes and was scheduled to be held in the historic city on the Ligurian coast of Italy from April 10 to May 19, 1922. Representatives of over thirty countries were invited to discuss the economic reconstruction of Germany and Central and Eastern Europe, as well as how to improve economic relations between communist Russia and the capitalist West.

Lloyd George's inclusion of Russia was a contentious decision in the view of France and some other countries because it implied de facto recognition of the Bolshevik regime at a time when none of the major European powers had yet recognized it. (Similarly, the French had been reluctant to include Germany, which they still saw as a pariah.) However, the Soviets were eager to participate, and the conference was crucially important for them, because it would mark the end of their international isolation.

Savinkov's aim was nothing less than to defeat the purpose of the conference by killing Chicherin so that negotiations could not even begin. The outrage this would cause in Moscow would be a major setback for both the Soviets and for Lloyd George's hopes of integrating Russia into the life of Europe.

To prepare the ground for the international scandal he wanted to cause, on Friday, April 7, the day after the Soviet delegation arrived in Genoa, Savinkov published an open letter to Lloyd George in the London *Times* in which he berated him for wanting to negotiate with the Soviet leaders rather than treating them like the criminals they were. He also made a thinly veiled threat and in effect threw down the gauntlet to the Soviets and the Western security services guarding their delegation, by referring to the "compliment" the Soviets paid him by "regarding me as one of their most implacable enemies." To people like Lloyd George and C at MI6, who knew Savinkov's past, the implications of his remark were clear, and precautions had to be taken to stop him.

The British government's administrative wheels began to turn in response. On the same day that Savinkov's letter appeared in the *Times,* London telegraphed its Passport Control Office in Rome and requested that the Italian National Police be informed that Savinkov appears to have summoned several known anti-Bolshevik terrorists from Prague to Genoa "to commit terroristic acts against delegates of the Soviet government." The telegram included the name of the man heading the group and described his physical traits. But there was nothing specific in it about Savinkov himself.

One against All

By the beginning of 1922, the GPU began to watch Savinkov with increasing attention and growing alarm. The Soviet security forces had accumulated an enormous amount of material (still preserved in FSB archives) showing that he was one of the most active anti-Soviet leaders in the emigration, and that fighting him would require great effort and resources.

It would also require great imagination. For Genoa, Savinkov developed the most ingenious terrorist plot up to this point in his life. He intended to hide in plain sight and gain access to the Soviet delegation through their own back door.

The primary burden of safeguarding the international delegations in Genoa necessarily fell on the Italian government, which took extraordinary precautions. An American newspaper reported that before the conference began the police even cleared out the city, raiding various "night haunts" and arresting 1,400 men and women who they thought might "molest or annoy" the visitors—criminals, fugitives from other cities, suspicious foreigners without papers, and beggars.

Tensions around the Soviet delegation were especially high. For security reasons and because of their delegation's size, the Soviets were not housed in Genoa itself but in Santa Margherita Ligure, a resort town on the coast fifteen miles to the east, near Rapallo (which would give its name to the important treaty that Soviet Russia and Germany signed on April 16, 1922, that surprised and outraged the Allies because it renounced all claims from the Brest-Litovsk Treaty). As the *New York Times* proclaimed, "Never even in the great days of Nihilism were the movements of the Czar of all the Russias so hedged about with precautions and secrecy as are those of his successors—Tchitcherin, Joffe and Litvinoff." When the delegation arrived by special train on the morning of Thursday, April 6, the 400 yards between their station and the hotel were lined with Italian troops. The grounds of the Imperial Palace Hotel, where they stayed (the Italian Communist Party did not fail to comment on the irony), were surrounded by a high wall and guarded by agents of the GPU and Italian carabinieri. Because the distance between Santa Margherita Ligure and Genoa seemed to create an opening for a terrorist attack, the Italian government arranged for the Soviet delegation to shuttle back and forth to the conference in a luxurious saloon car attached to a special train, one that would approach the conference site, the Royal Palace, on a private line that did not pass through city streets. And as a final precaution, the Italian authorities removed over 200 Russian émigrés who lived in the small town of Nervi on the coastline between Rapallo and Genoa (where Savinkov and Piłsudski, among other revolutionaries, had visited before the Revolution when they were in exile).

Savinkov's Double

Of all the cunning plots Savinkov hatched during his life, his attempt to assassinate Chicherin in Genoa is the second-most enigmatic (his final plot is the most mysterious) because a large number of relevant documents in the FSB archive in Moscow are not accessible to researchers now. All that is known about them is a very brief summary published by several historians who received permission to peruse them not long after the Soviet Union collapsed. There are also several dozen documents in the Central State Archive in Rome, but although they are open to researchers, they bear on Savinkov's actions obliquely. Nevertheless, when taken together, and despite the uncertainties and lacunae that remain, the Russian and Italian sources sketch a fantastic plot.

Genoa was in a state of feverish excitement during the conference, and the streets in the center were crowded with more kinds of security personnel than anyone had ever seen before—police in frock coats, gendarmes in operatic tricornes, guardsmen, soldiers in full military gear, and even airplanes flying overhead. In order to evade all the security agents who were looking for him and defending his Soviet targets, Savinkov decided to assume the identity of another Russian who had also come (or been summoned) to Genoa—one, moreover, of similar build and whose face looked very much like his own, at least from certain angles. This important fact—that Savinkov found an actual physical "double"—is not mentioned in the short summary of FSB documents about Genoa, which simply refers to his assuming a fake, paper identity (and which he had done routinely for years during his earlier plots). From the available evidence it also appears that the FSB archive has neither copies, nor any other knowledge, of the Italian archival documents about the confusion that the physical resemblance between Savinkov and the Russian would cause the Italian police.

The man Savinkov chose as his double was an émigré from Constantinople (where several hundred thousand Russians, including remnants of the White Army, had sought refuge from the Bolsheviks during and after the Russian Civil War). He arrived in the Italian port of Brindisi in early February and traveled to Rome before coming to Genoa. In Italian sources his name is Elia Golensko Gvosdovo (or Gvozdavo-Golenko, in addition to other spellings), while in Russian sources his surname is simply "Gulenko." (The Russian variant of his first name would probably have been Ilya, and the first part of his hyphenated surname was probably Gvozdyov.) Gulenko came to Italy as a journalist with an interest in religion. He presented himself as a former member of the Orthodox Church who had converted to Catholicism and written a book urging conversion, and who had ties to an Apostolic delegation and the Vatican. There is some evidence that he may have had a connection to Generals Denikin and Wrangel, both of whom were still involved with Russian émigré military organizations hoping to resume the fight against the Bolsheviks, as well as to General Anatoly Nosovich, who was a notorious White agent in the Red Army during the Russian Civil War. Very little else about Gulenko is known.

Why Savinkov decided to assume Gulenko's identity is clear enough because of the physical resemblance between them, but how he did so is not. It is possible that Savinkov acted without Gulenko's knowledge or cooperation, although in the past he had taken pains not to compromise the owners of the papers he borrowed as part of his disguise. Using a man's papers and identity can also cause obvious problems when both are in the same place. But it is also possible that Gulenko was in some way connected with Savinkov's plot and was an accomplice or a decoy.

Whatever the case, by pretending to be the Russian journalist Gulenko, Savinkov was able to establish contact with no less a personage than the GPU's station chief in Italy. To win the man's confidence, Savinkov passed himself off as a Bolshevik sympathizer, gave him a number of confidential documents of mostly historical significance that he probably got from his own archive, and in a crowning gesture of bravado offered his services to the GPU. The station chief fell for it and agreed to meet with Savinkov on several occasions. Savinkov's charade progressed so incredibly well that he was almost included in the team of Soviet guards assigned to protect Chicherin and the rest of the delegation.

Had Savinkov succeeded in killing Chicherin, it would have been the most significant assassination of his life in terms of the actual consequences. But then something happened and the plot was spoiled. On or shortly after Tuesday, April 18, Savinkov was arrested by the Italian police as he tried to force his way into the Imperial Palace Hotel, where the Soviet delegation was staying. He presented papers showing that he was Gulenko, and since he had established a relationship with the GPU by using this identity, he must have thought that they would lead to his release.

However, chance and the GPU's alertness spoiled his plot. With the help of a local German police officer, agents of the GPU in Berlin managed to get a copy of the temporary identification papers that Gulenko had been issued by the Italian consul in Constantinople and that Savinkov had used to return to

Italy from Berlin. The document included a photograph, although it is unclear of whom. The two Russian historians who summarized what they read in the FSB archives say it was a photograph of Savinkov. But this is very doubtful because the GPU was unaware that Savinkov had a "double" in Genoa and consequently had no reason to try to distinguish the two men physically. Supporting this conclusion is that the man in a photograph the historians did include in their volume of selected FSB documents (which focus on Savinkov's death) is misidentified as "Savinkov . . . photographed in prison in Genoa." It is in fact clear that the man is Gulenko.

In any event, the photograph the Soviet agents obtained in Berlin was sent to the GPU station in Italy and, not surprisingly, initiated a period of great confusion on the part of both the GPU and the Italian authorities as they tried to figure out if the detained man presenting himself as Gulenko was actually Savinkov.

This confusion was compounded by the arrest in Genoa around the same time, Tuesday, April 18, of the real Gulenko on suspicion of being the notorious terrorist Savinkov. He naturally insisted on his innocence, leaving the police with the quandary of figuring out who was who. They took the new prisoner's fingerprints, but this could not resolve the matter because Savinkov's were not immediately available for comparison. The police were left with relying on photographs and on people who thought they knew what Savinkov looked like. Because the one photograph of Savinkov they had showed his face at a three-quarter angle, they photographed Gulenko from the same angle for comparison. In these photographs the two men resemble each other to a considerable extent, so that only someone who knows either one well could tell them apart (among other features, their ears, earlobes and nostrils are noticeably different). In full-face photographs, their resemblance is not as close.

Gulenko's photograph was shown to several Russians in Italy, including the Soviet ambassador in Rome and members of the Soviet delegation in Genoa. All of them confirmed that the man in the photograph was actually Savinkov. However, Italian experts on photographic identification were not convinced and sent Gulenko's photograph to Edvard Beneš, the prime minister of Czechoslovakia, because he knew Savinkov personally, and to the French Foreign Ministry, because it was known that Savinkov had lived in France. Both denied that it was Savinkov.

It took several days, but by Saturday, April 22, the Italian investigators had figured out the truth with the GPU's help. Savinkov was already in their custody, and the following day they arrested four of his confederates, who were found to have a plan of the Imperial Palace Hotel in their possession. As for Gulenko, the GPU apparently remained ignorant of his presence in the city.

The Soviet regime was delighted that Savinkov had been arrested and tried to have him extradited to Russia as a major terrorist and criminal. They reasoned that putting him on a show trial in Moscow would generate useful propaganda and be far more "civilized" than having him killed abroad, which would harm the regime's reputation. However, the attempted extradition failed, and by the end of April Savinkov was back in Paris. It is likely that someone—perhaps Mussolini—had pulled strings on his behalf. In June, the Italians allowed the real Gulenko to take a ship from Naples back to Constantinople, despite their lingering suspicions about him.

Perhaps more details will emerge someday from closed Soviet-era archives that will resolve the mysteries associated with this episode in Savinkov's life. Another curious feature of Savinkov's decision to take on Gulenko's identity is that it reads like life imitating art because it recapitulates the key plot detail of an early novel by one of Savinkov's favorite authors—Dostoyevsky's *The Double* (1846). In it, a bland and timid clerk discovers to his dismay that his life is being usurped by someone who looks exactly like him but is much more aggressive and successful. Did the parallel occur to Savinkov when he took on the Russian religious reporter's identity as he plotted to change the course of European history?

The GPU Declares War

In the spring of 1922, the GPU decided that Savinkov had become an intolerable threat. He had come dangerously close to assassinating Chicherin and could strike another target anywhere and at any time. The only solution was to destroy him.

From May 6 to 8, the GPU Directorate met in the Lubyanka headquarters building in Moscow and established a new branch named Kontrrazvédyvatelny otdél (Counterintelligence Section), or KRO for short. Its task would be to combat foreign espionage, White émigré movements (the GPU's catchall designation for all Russian oppositional groups abroad, including the Greens), and underground organizations operating on Russian territory. Savinkov was involved in all three.

Appointed as the first director of the KRO was Artur Artuzov, who would develop into a worthy opponent of his regime's many enemies. With the impeccable bloodline of a proletarian (his father was a Swiss immigrant cheesemaker) and educated as an engineer, Artuzov joined the Bolsheviks in 1917 when he was twenty-six and took part in combating the Allied landings in Murmansk and Archangel the following year. He then joined the Cheka and began to specialize in counterintelligence.

Artuzov's appointment to the KRO was a reward for his unrelenting diligence and loyalty to the Bolshevik Party, and confirmed that he was a rising "star" in Soviet security. He looked the part: broad face, prominent chin, serious mouth, a steady gaze, and a small moustache with a pointed Mephistophelian goatee. He was smart, learned, cunning, and a very "decent" man according to his coworkers (which requires an expansion of the word's traditional meaning to include a willingness to be part of an organization that shed a great deal of innocent blood to protect the small political elite that ran the country in the belief that this would help establish a peasants' and workers' paradise).

The campaign against Savinkov was formally launched on May 12, or just four days after the KRO was founded. In an internal memorandum titled "On Savinkov's Organization" signed by Artuzov and Genrikh Yagoda (the deputy director of the Covert-Operational Section of the GPU), he was officially proclaimed one of the main enemies of the Soviet state. All sections of the GPU were requested to search their archives for old cases against him and his followers, and to account for every known member of his organization.

In keeping with recent GPU practice, the operation against Savinkov was given a special code name—Sindikát-2 (Syndicate-2). It would become famous in the history of the Soviet secret police and recognized as exemplary by counterintelligence agencies around the world.

The key idea of Sindikat-2 was formulated during a meeting between Felix Dzerzhinsky and Vyacheslav Menzhinsky, his second-in-command, during which Dzerzhinsky proposed that any operation against Savinkov should hinge on his ambition and egotism—on his belief that he was a unique and irreplaceable leader.

As subsequent events would show, this was an astute inference about Savinkov. The details of how to exploit it were worked out by Artuzov under Menzhinsky's direction, and they decided that Sindikat-2 should be the kind of operation known in the GPU as *legendírovaniye*, or "creating a legend." This meant that it would entail inventing a fictitious group of conspirators in Soviet Russia who were ostensibly plotting against the regime and who wanted to collaborate with like-minded émigrés abroad.

This was a time-tested method and had been used successfully by the Cheka to thwart the Ambassadors' Plot concocted by Lockhart and Reilly in 1918. Artuzov already had a similar, ongoing operation that could serve as a model for the one against Savinkov. Named Trest (or the Trust), it was launched in 1921 against Russian monarchists and former members of the White Army living in the Balkans and Western Europe who had established a military organization that was still hoping to resume the civil war; in the meantime, they carried out sabotage and terrorist attacks on Russian territory. The GPU responded by recruiting several individuals in Russia, including a former "genuine" monarchist, who could deceive the émigrés into believing that they had joined an underground monarchist movement (which did not actually exist). Over time, the "pretend monarchists" managed to persuade the émigrés—including the seemingly indomitable General Alexander Kutepov, a hero of the White struggle—that terrorism was counterproductive because it would lead the GPU to destroy the underground monarchist movement in Russia. The ploy worked and White terror abated for the half-dozen years the operation lasted.

Keeping the success of the Trust in mind, Artuzov began to study the records of dozens of Savinkov's agents, including those who had recently been arrested in Russia and others whom the GPU still had under observation. He understood that the only way to get to Savinkov, who had a great deal of conspiratorial and clandestine experience, would be through somebody he knew or would trust. Artuzov soon settled on a promising individual, one Leonid Sheshenya, a Cossack officer who was Savinkov's adjutant and had just been arrested.

The Bolsheviks Are Still the Enemy

The failure of Savinkov's operation in Genoa did nothing to diminish his commitment to fighting the Bolsheviks. All the news coming out of Soviet Russia indicated that the country was in a disastrous state because of the regime's brutal policies and that disaffection among the population was widespread. By the spring of 1922, the much-touted NEP reforms had been in place for a year but had not succeeded in stopping the famine that began in 1921. Lenin decided to take advantage of the famine under the pretext of raising money to help the hungry, and in the spring of 1922 launched a major campaign of confiscating valuables from the Orthodox Church. As he explained in a top secret letter to the Politburo on March 19, 1922: "Precisely now and only now, when there is cannibalism in famine-struck areas, and hundreds if not thousands of corpses line the roads, we can (and therefore must) carry out the confiscation of church valuables with the most frenzied and merciless energy, not stopping before the suppression of any resistance." The reason for the timing was to take advantage of the despair that the famine engendered in the masses, which will make them look upon the regime's actions in a favorable light or at least with indifference. This is also the time to initiate a broader antireligious campaign against the clergy, Lenin argued, and "to crush its resistance with such cruelty that they will not forget it for several decades."

Religious faith was deeply engrained in the Russian people, and many protested. The GPU's own records in Moscow for only one day, April 5, 1922, show that there were three instances when members of expropriation commissions could do their "work" only under the protection of armed soldiers. The biggest disturbance was around a church where a crowd of 5,000 gathered and kept growing. People threw rocks at Red Army troops and stopped passing cars; several communists and soldiers were beaten, and a student was killed. The commission and the soldiers guarding it were driven inside the church, and cavalry reinforcements had to be called in to protect them.

Even factory workers who reacted to the antireligious campaign with relative calm protested against the government's policy, arguing that gold should be confiscated first from the communists, their wives, and merchants, and only then from churches. General discontent with the regime among factory workers was widespread as well, and nearly 200,000 took part in numerous strikes across the country in 1922. In Moscow alone that year, the GPU recorded over 900 labor-related conflicts and over 100 strikes.

The regime also continued its policy of systematically suppressing all political opposition, including staging a large public trial of thirty-four Socialist Revolutionaries accused of "counterrevolutionary" and terrorist activity. Savinkov knew many of them and saw through the regime's charade of justice, which included orchestrated "people's" demonstrations demanding the death penalty and widespread propaganda to mobilize public opinion.

A Smaller But Dirtier War

After Genoa, Savinkov lost the financial backing of the rich Russians in Paris who created Torgprom and suffered cutbacks from other sources as well. He turned everywhere he could for support, even purportedly meeting with Henry Ford in the south of France about a large sum, 40 million francs. But nothing came of this, and he had to rely on whatever he could generate himself through the National Union for the Defense of the Motherland and Freedom.

The dramatic character of Savinkov's ejection from Poland at the end of 1921 was in part a smoke screen designed to deceive the Soviets, and his organization continued to operate in Warsaw under the unofficial protection of the Polish General Staff and with the collusion of the French Military Mission. Savinkov directed it from Paris, where he spent most of the time.

Because the organization was much smaller now and could no longer mount large-scale military campaigns, it shifted to terrorism, expropriation, guerilla warfare, and spying on Soviet territory. Savinkov still had a network of undercover agents in many cities who compiled information about the Red Army and the degree of popular discontent with the regime. The National Union sold this intelligence to the Poles and the French, and for a time it was the main source of his income.

⚬━✦━⚬

The men who carried out the National Union's raids on Soviet territory all had regular military experience—some had fought almost continuously on one front or another since 1914—and were recruited from among the interned Russian troops in Polish camps. But after they joined the National Union they passed into a world of dark operations that the Soviets found especially alarming because of how destructive they were.

The recruits collaborated closely with Polish Intelligence, which issued them weapons, money, fake documents, and passes to cross the border at prearranged "windows." Once they were across, they typically moved several tens of miles into the interior before they began their depredations to maintain the illusion that they originated locally. Their targets were typically members of the Bolshevik Party and other functionaries, institutions of Soviet state control, and units of the Red Army. No method was off-limits, at least in theory, and at one point the GPU claimed that captured members of the National Union were found to have large quantities of potassium cyanide that they were planning to use to poison the most loyal Red Army units. Savinkov's sense of what consituted a "legitimate" target had broadened since his days in the Combat Organization.

⚬━━⚬

There were many adventurers with blood on their hands in the National Union's guerilla forces in Poland, but one man stands out because of his exceptionally daring raids and his fateful relationship to Savinkov. Although he began as one of Savinkov's most fanatical loyalists, the role he would play in Sindikat-2 and thus in Savinkov's life would be more profound than even Azef's.

Colonel Sergey Pavlovsky was the National Union's military chief-of-staff in Warsaw. Powerfully built, blond, handsome, and young—he was only in his mid-thirties—he had earned a reputation for unusual bravery and for extreme cruelty toward Bolsheviks. His intense, unblinking stare and the cold-blooded expression on his face unnerved even experienced intelligence agents. It was he who commanded the cavalry unit during the ill-fated invasion of Belarus that Savinkov had joined.

Among the raids Pavlovsky carried out, one in particular stands out because of its duration and violence. Following Savinkov's orders, on May 22, 1922, he crossed the border into Belarus with five other members of the National Union and headed toward the Pskov region in Russia, 300 miles to the northeast. Their aim was to reconnoiter, try to organize groups of rebels, and cause as much mayhem as possible.

The raid would last nearly five months, and Pavlovsky's summary of it reads like a picaresque novel about brigands from an earlier age. During the first few weeks they searched (unsuccessfully) for buried gold, robbed the offices of the local Bolshevik administration in a small town, ordered the town's administration to issue the peasants receipts for taxes they had not actually paid, exchanged fire with pursuers, joined with some other "partisans" to take another town and rob its treasury despite the presence of a Red Army garrison, and released prisoners from the local jail.

The rest of the raid was a mix of similarly violent action alternating with periods of quiescence when they hid in forest camps. One member of Pavlovsky's band traveled to Moscow, Voronezh, and Petrograd, where he tried (unsuccessfully) to contact members of the underground. The GPU later claimed that Pavlovsky's band committed a total of eighteen armed attacks and robberies during the raid, killed over sixty people, and carried out bloody outrages against Bolshevik Party members, including torture. Finally, around mid-October, Pavlovsky and his men returned to Poland.

What is especially striking about this raid, however, is not so much its brutality as its ineffectiveness from the point of view of a revolutionary struggle against Soviet rule. Pavlovsky did not inspire rebellious groups in any of the towns he attacked, and although he wreaked havoc with some Bolshevik institutions, killed some Party members, and stole money, he did not shake the foundations of Soviet rule in the areas where he operated. Subsequent raids by him were similar, even when they involved attempts to unite small separate bands of "partisans" or "bandits" to fight the regime.

The one practical consequence of his raids is that he provided the National Union with some additional income, because the hundreds of millions of highly inflated Soviet rubles he amassed were convertible into other currencies, albeit in much smaller sums.

The GPU's Opening Gambit

Artuzov's plot began to take concrete shape in early August 1922, around the time of the XII All-Russian Conference of the Bolshevik Party in Moscow. One of the major problems raised at the conference was the increase in anti-Soviet activity by various "bourgeois" groups in the country that had been emboldened by NEP, the famine, and the regime's abrasive relations with the West. This fed into Artuzov's idea of inventing a secret organization that would be the bait to capture Savinkov. And knowing what would appeal to him, he named it the Liberal Democrats.

Artuzov also knew that Savinkov would be very suspicious of any overtures from inside Russia and that it would be necessary to move carefully to bring the nonexistent organization to his attention by someone he knew. Artuzov and his colleagues began by "turning" Sheshenya, Savinkov's adjutant whom they had arrested, using the time-tested method of a "stick" and a "carrot"—the first being the threat of execution, the second the argument that it is pointless to fight the Soviets and that he should join them. Sheshenya was a simple man and not particularly committed to the National Union's political program; he capitulated and divulged everything he knew. This allowed the GPU to arrest Savinkov's entire network on Soviet territory. But to keep him in the dark, the arrests were kept secret.

Artuzov also needed to create a "membership" for his fictitious Liberal Democrats and recruited two more men. The first was Mikhail Zekunov, one of the agents Sheshenya betrayed. Artuzov discovered that Zekunov not only had lost any interest in spying for Savinkov and was living quietly as a railroad guard, but that he actually sympathized with the Soviet regime and was willing to work for the GPU.

The second was an agent of the GPU itself, Andrey Pavlovich Fyodorov, who, in addition to coordinating the operation, would have the challenging task of impersonating a leader of the Liberal Democrats. Well educated, fluent in several foreign languages, a veteran of both the Russian Imperial and Red Armies, Fyodorov acquired clandestine experience when he worked behind enemy lines during the Civil War and successfully impersonated a White officer. With his forthright peasant face, Fyodorov also looked like a man of the people, which Artuzov knew would appeal to Savinkov. To protect Fyodorov's identity and the secrecy of Sindikat-2 from any agents that Savinkov might send into Russia without the GPU's knowledge, Fyodorov was assigned the fictitious surname Mukhin but kept his own name and patronymic.

With the key actors in place, Artuzov got Dzerzhinsky's approval to begin. Working closely with Sheshenya, who required constant guidance, Artuzov began to feed disinformation to Savinkov, including the intriguing news that there were new forces in the country that looked as if they were capable of rising against the Bolsheviks. Soon after, Sheshenya sent his chief a list of terrorist attacks and acts of sabotage that had supposedly been carried out by Zekunov, the National Union's agent in Moscow. These were actually entirely fictitious and consisted of various everyday accidents that had been reported in newspapers—train wrecks, fires, bridge collapses, and the like. However, Savinkov would not know the difference, and the stories that he would read in Soviet newspapers would "confirm" his agent's successful actions.

After whetting Savinkov's appetite, Artuzov had Sheshenya bait the hook. He reported that Zekunov had met a certain Andrey Pavlovich Mukhin, a former White Army officer who seemed reliable and who revealed that he was one of the leaders of an underground organization called the Liberal Democrats, which was dedicated to overthrowing the Bolshevik regime. Mukhin also told Zekunov that the organization was in some difficulty because it was divided about how to proceed. One faction, the so-called "activists," wanted to initiate a reign of sabotage and terror now; the others, the "accumulators," argued that it was necessary to wait for the right moment and, in the meantime, keep gathering strength. What the Liberal Democrats needed was an experienced leader who could bring the two sides together.

Artuzov's brilliant plot twist was that Savinkov's "own" agent Zekunov had "discovered" Mukhin and the Liberal Democrats. As a result, the initiative to establish contact with them did not appear to come from a group within Soviet Russia, which would have seemed deeply suspicious to Savinkov.

After planting the seed in Savinkov's mind and letting it germinate for a while, Artuzov dictated Sheshenya's next letter. He had him report that increasing numbers of influential members of the Liberal Democrats were leaning toward the idea that Savinkov was the one person who could unify their movement.

This message was like an echo of Savinkov's most cherished hopes. To verify the accuracy of the information Zekunov was providing Savinkov ordered him to come out of Soviet Russia and to meet with representatives of the National Union in Warsaw.

Artuzov realized that he would have to agree to what Savinkov wanted, despite the risk for Sindikat-2. Thus far, the deception involving Zekunov, Sheshenya, and Mukhin existed only on paper and was completely under Artuzov's control. But once Zekunov was abroad and alone, a single false word or other mistake could mean his end and the collapse of the entire operation. Artuzov had faith that Zekunov would not become a turncoat a second time and betray the GPU, but he was not at all sure that he could pass a close examination by Savinkov's agents or, should it come to that, by Savinkov himself.

The Black Horse

For Savinkov in Paris there was a lot of waiting in between the messages from Russia with their information about dizzying new developments. To occupy his time and because he still felt the compulsion, Savinkov returned to writing at the end of 1922. As he admitted to a friend, he had not lost "the writer's itch: the time comes when I absolutely have to get it out of me." In addition to being a compelling distraction, writing could also help boost his income. Selling intelligence gathered by the National Union had become less lucrative, and Savinkov was relying increasingly on personal subsidies from various sources.

He still lived in the stylish 16th Arrondissement in Paris that he preferred and tried to keep up appearances despite his straitened circumstances. His neighbors would have been greatly surprised if they learned about his violent occupation, but nothing in his behavior or appearance suggested it, and the volunteer bodyguards who are reported to have watched him and his apartment were apparently discreet. Savinkov continued to dress with conservative good taste, like a businessman or a lawyer, although one who had seen better times: his dark suits were inexpensive but well pressed; his shoes were worn but polished. The only indulgence in his sparsely furnished apartment was an overflowing bookshelf.

Savinkov worked on his new novella, *The Black Horse* (*Kon voronoy*), slowly and deliberately for nearly a year, until late 1923, and claimed in a letter to a friend that he "rewrote and corrected every page . . . no fewer than 15 times." The 100-page narrative that resulted is based very loosely on three periods in the National Union's recent history: the invasion of Belarus in late 1921, Pavlovsky's raids into Soviet territory in 1922, and the sabotage and terrorism carried out by Savinkov's agents in Soviet cities. Little of it is autobiographical (although, as usual, that is not how most readers eventually saw it), but it may suggest something about Savinkov's mindset at the time he wrote it.

The Black Horse resembles *The Pale Horse* in a number of obvious ways. It is again written under the pseudonym V. Ropshin and begins with two biblical epigraphs: the first from Revelation 6:5, "And I beheld, and lo a black horse; and he that sat on him had a pair of balances in his hand," and the second from 1 John 2:11, "But he that hateth his brother is in darkness, and walketh in darkness, and knoweth not whither he goeth, because that darkness hath blinded his eyes." Taken together, the two epigraphs suggest something of the novella's ambivalence about the nature of, and justification for, the murderous internecine violence that fills its pages.

Like *The Pale Horse*, the new novella resembles a diary and consists of short, dated episodes narrated by Yury Nikolaevich, a colonel who is also called Zhorzh by a woman with whom he had an affair (variants of Russian names allow the equivalence). This establishes a link to the protagonist in *The Pale Horse*, as do a number of direct quotations from the earlier work and several plot parallels, including two love stories. There are also numerous allusions to other, classic Russian novels and poems that showcase the narrator's (and Savinkov's) literary education and resonate with his themes. However, in the new novella Savinkov mostly overcomes the stylistic naïveté of *The Pale Horse*, especially its unconvincing attempts at portentousness. He is also more skillful in depicting human character during dramatic and violent action against the background of, and in counterpoint to, the beauties of nature. The elliptical narrative style, consisting of short sentences like brushstrokes, is generally effective in capturing scenes and moods.

To underscore that *The Black Horse* is a work of fiction and not a veiled memoir, Savinkov gives his main protagonist traits and attitudes that neither he, nor Bulak-Balakhovich, nor Colonel Pavlovsky, nor any of his other comrades actually had. Immediately after the Belarusian invasion came to an end, Savinkov characterized it as an unequivocally noble and heroic campaign, one that vindicated the entire Russian émigré fight against the Bolsheviks. But in *The Black Horse* Savinkov portrays Yury Nikolacvich as despondent about the civil war in which he is involved: his men often do not know what they are fighting for, much of the time neither he nor the peasants he encounters can see the difference between his side and the Bolsheviks in moral terms, and the guerilla raids he conducts on Russian territory fail to incite uprisings against the Bolsheviks. And whereas Savinkov and Bulak-Balakhovich saw the Whites more as ideological opponents than allies and acted independently of them, in the novella Savinkov makes Yury Nikolaevich into their reluctant agent. His commanders at "headquarters" have prerevolutionary titles ("His Excellency," "Baron," "Lord Chamberlain"), their military and political aim is the restoration of a "little tsar" (*tsaryok*) or a "caricaturish Napoleon," and he is himself a "White Guardist" (*belogvardeyets*). None of this has anything to do with Savinkov's

Green movement, his politics, or the Russian army he raised in Poland. But it does reflect the monarchist sympathies of some officers from whom he had systematically distanced himself.

Nevertheless, it is possible that the pessimistic view of the civil war in the novella, which Savinkov depicts in all its cruelty and violent detail, reflects how his attitude toward the kind of anti-Bolshevik struggle he was still leading had darkened as a result of his failures in Berlin and Genoa, and the GPU's success in liquidating his agents in Russia. But in light of Savinkov's willingness to continue his fight against the Soviet regime in alliance with the Liberal Democrats, there is no justification in assuming that Yury Nikolaevich speaks for him. In this regard, the relation between Savinkov and Yury Nikolaevich recalls that between Savinkov and Zhorzh in *The Pale Horse*—the characters are fictional embodiments of stances he may have entertained but rejected. The one trait the narrator in *The Black Horse* shares with his creator is a visceral love for Russia and hatred for the Bolsheviks, even when he sees little difference between their cruelties and his own.

Savinkov initially had difficulty finding a publisher for *The Black Horse*. Some rejected or even refused to consider it because they thought he was an amateur, others because of his politics. But after being partially serialized in the Warsaw newspaper that was edited by his old friend and colleague Filosofov, it was finally picked up by an émigré press in Paris in December 1923.

Savinkov's reputation and the novel's provocative politics resulted in a notable but largely very negative reception. As he characterized it, critics "cursed" and "trashed" *The Black Horse*. Zinaida Gippius accused the new work of being "antiartistic" and branded its author a "masochist." Inevitably, a reviewer accused Savinkov of having written a "confession" about the closed circle of his own life.

There were exceptions, but they were based on personal connections. Alexander Amfiteatrov, a well-known, second-tier writer, praised *The Black Horse* as a "book of the future" and explained that the attacks on it were prompted by the political fame of its author. When he wrote this, however, Amfiteatrov was colluding with Savinkov about various matters, including some very ambitious plans with the Italian Fascists. Similarly, Filosofov praised the novella on the pages of the newspaper *For Freedom!* Be that as it may, all the brouhaha resulted in enough sales to warrant a second printing the following year as well as a translation into English. By then, however, Savinkov's attention was absorbed by something more important.

Wolves in Wolves' Clothing

While Savinkov was struggling with his muse in Paris, Artuzov initiated the next phase of Sindikat-2. The GPU coached Zekunov about what he should say when he met Savinkov's representatives in Warsaw and then sent him across the Polish border on December 30, 1922. He first traveled to Vilnius, where he met Ivan Fomichyov, Savinkov's station chief, who oversaw his network of agents in Russia. A careless man who did his work without sufficient forethought, Fomichyov was tolerated by Savinkov because of his devotion to the National Union's cause. It was a decision he would come to regret. Fomichyov and Zekunov then traveled to Warsaw so that Zekunov could "report" to the local National Union leadership what he had learned about the underground organization in Moscow.

The committee that quizzed Zekunov was wary of a possible GPU deception and laid numerous traps to test him. But he managed to avoid them all without showing that he had caught on to what they were doing. He also succeeded in learning the names of several agents that Savinkov had sent into Russia about whom the GPU did not know. Satisfied by his responses, the National Union leaders instructed Zekunov to maintain his connection with the Liberal Democrats. And most importantly, they told him to invite Mukhin, his contact and one of the "leaders" of the organization, to come to Warsaw himself.

This is what Artuzov had been waiting for, and he took extra pains to prepare Mukhin for his mission. Unlike Zekunov, who had been a member of the National Union and knew it from the inside, Mukhin had no firsthand experience with Savinkov's people in Warsaw. Artuzov stressed that his mission would be to persuade them that the Liberal Democrats were a serious organization and that they respected Savinkov greatly. On March 21, 1923, Zekunov and Mukhin crossed into Poland through a special "window" in the border that the GPU had set up. Polish intelligence, which was in league with Savinkov's organization, provided them with safe passage to Warsaw.

Mukhin played his role very skillfully when he appeared before the National Union's steering committee. He revealed that the leadership of the Liberal

Democrats consisted of former tsarist and White officers who now held responsible positions in a wide range of military and civilian institutions in Moscow.
They were all committed to fighting the Bolsheviks and a number of them
were interested in collaborating with the National Union. To increase his cred-
ibility, Mukhin even withheld some details about the organization's intentions,
explaining coyly that he was not at liberty to say more.

The impression Mukhin produced in Warsaw was electrifying and everything
Artuzov could have wanted. When Savinkov got the report, he was greatly
encouraged. He had recently described the National Union to his brother as
having become so weak that it was not much more than a "fiction." Collaborating
with the Liberal Democrats was a chance for rebirth.

He decided it was time to pursue the connection. Savinkov ordered Fomichyov
to Russia to investigate matters personally, and in mid-April he crossed the Polish
border at what he believed was a "secret" location maintained by a member of
the Liberal Democrats who worked in the Soviet border guards.

Artuzov played Fomichyov like a master during his visit to Moscow. On
April 28, he had him introduced to a "plenipotentiary representative" of the
Liberal Democrats, one Vladimir Ostrovsky (a disguised member of the GPU,
of course), who began by throwing cold water on the idea of collaboration with
Savinkov, saying that "he does not see enough real strength" in the National
Union. Fomichyov was shocked and initially tried to defend the idea of uniting
the two organizations. Then he raised the ante and offered to arrange a meeting
between a representative of the Liberal Democrats and Boris Savinkov himself.

This was what Ostrovsky, Artuzov, and the rest of the KRO had been waiting
for. The proposal for a meeting in Paris had come not from Moscow but from
Savinkov's own representative. Ostrovsky "relented" and agreed to send Mukhin.
He also agreed to form a "provisional committee" consisting of representatives
of the National Union and the Liberal Democrats to explore the possibility of
cooperation between them.

The KRO's charade also did not end with the meeting between Ostrovsky
and Fomichyov. To pull the wool further over his eyes, disguised agents showed
him a series of anti-Soviet flyers and proclamations that had supposedly been
distributed by the Liberal Democrats in Moscow and other Russia cities. He

was even consulted about the content of a flyer being planned for May 1, International Workers' Day, and how it should be distributed. As a final sweetener, Fomichyov's new friends handed him a packet of "intelligence" that he could give the Poles (all of which had been invented by the GPU).

New Opportunities?

The news that an important member of the Liberal Democrats would be coming to Paris reached Savinkov soon after two new developments unexpectedly aroused his optimism about combatting the Bolsheviks.

The first was a major change in the Soviet leadership. Lenin's health had been declining since April 1922, when he had surgery to remove a bullet that had been lodged in his neck ever since the assassination attempt by Fanny Kaplan four years earlier. A month later he suffered a stroke. The Soviet regime initially tried to conceal the news and announced that he had a stomach ailment, but word soon leaked out that his condition was much more serious, prompting feverish speculation around the world about who would succeed him and what it could mean for the country if he should die. However, Lenin slowly recovered and managed to return to the country's helm. Then, in December 1922, he suffered a series of additional strokes, and on the night of March 9–10, 1923, a massive one that resulted in loss of speech, cognitive impairment, and partial paralysis.

Lenin's condition sent shock waves through the highly centralized Soviet regime. The Politburo feared that news of his incapacity would trigger antigovernment disturbances and even weighed introducing martial law. Dzerzhinsky was concerned that Russian émigrés would try to foment military interventions by Poland and France. Rumors circulated that Lenin had designated Trotsky as his successor, and several powerful members of the Politburo began to form a faction to oppose him.

News about what was happening in Moscow soon reached the West. Savinkov paid close attention and even wrote an analytical piece about the events for the Russian newspaper in Warsaw. His view was that the instability and factionalism in the Bolshevik regime seemed like an opportunity that could and should be exploited.

The same thought must have occurred to Mussolini or someone close to him. In March 1923, Savinkov received an amazing letter from an old acquaintance, the writer Alexander Amfiteatrov, who lived in Italy and sympathized with Fascism. He also had a connection to the regime in the person of his son, Daniil, who joined the Fascist Party in 1922 and even became a member of the Moschet-tieri del Duce (Leader's Musketeers), a special military unit that functioned as Mussolini's personal bodyguard and honor guard.

Amfiteatrov explained that he had recently been approached in great confi-dence by a highly placed person (whom he did not name) with the request that he compose nothing less than a "memorandum on the matter of an armed attack on Petrograd." Since Amfiteatrov had no military experience he decided to pass the request on to Savinkov, adding that he did so out of respect for his knowledge of tactics, strategy, and counterrevolution.

The originator of the request wanted answers to specific questions: Would the fall of Petrograd be a death blow to the Bolsheviks? From what direction would it be best to attack the city? How many men would be necessary and would 20,000 be enough? Would military assistance from Finland, Latvia, and Estonia be necessary? Could a foreign dictatorship unrelated to Russian political parties succeed in the city initially? What foodstuffs and supplies would the occupiers need to have? What kind of resistance could the Bolsheviks muster on land and on sea against a fast and decisive blow? If armed, would the city's population support the foreign invaders?

It does not say much about the military acumen of the person or persons who originated these questions that they posed them to someone like Amfiteatrov. However, it is also possible that Amfiteatrov was merely a trusted intermediary, if not an instigator of the inquiry, and that the intended addressee was Savinkov all along.

In any event, the political climate in Italy, as well as the instability in the Soviet leadership, help explain why the idea of a military blow against the Bolsheviks had occurred to someone in power. Early in 1923, relations between Italy and Russia were strained. The Soviets complained that their economic delegation in Rome was not being adequately protected from attacks by Fascists. And Mussolini accused the Comintern, Moscow's agency of world revolution, of engaging in subversion in Italy, which he fought with massive arrests of Italian communists.

Amfiteatrov's Italian contacts were not pleased with Savinkov's response, which was a repetition of what he had argued when he organized the invasion of Belarus: only a popular uprising inside Russia can overthrow the Bolsheviks, and any foreign intervention is doomed to fail because the people would oppose it. For a while, elements in the Fascist regime remained fixated on a dramatic military crusade against Bolshevism that would march across all of Europe. But in the end, nothing came of this fantastical idea, although it was a reminder to Savinkov that Mussolini might still become an ally.

The Man from Moscow

On the night of June 18, 1923, Mukhin began his epochal trip to Paris to meet with Savinkov. He crossed the border into Poland in the usual "clandestine" fashion and arrived in Vilnius around midday. Fomichyov greeted him with open arms. Waiting as well was a Polish captain from military intelligence who was looking forward to receiving the next batch of intelligence reports from Russia, for which he paid Mukhin in cash, and who arranged for Mukhin and Fomichyov to be issued Polish passports.

Mukhin's and Fomichyov's arrival in Paris late on July 14 was marked by a miscalculation that gave the beginning of Mukhin's dark mission an absurd twist. It was Bastille Day, the national holiday celebrating the French Revolution. All Paris was in the streets, dancing and reveling, and there were no rooms left in any of the hotels near the train station. After their seventy-two-hour journey from Warsaw and five connections, the two Russians had no choice but to join the merrymaking Parisians and stroll around the city until dawn.

When they finally arrived at Savinkov's door on the following day, he greeted Mukhin enthusiastically, shaking his hand long and hard as he peered searchingly into his face. Mukhin noticed Savinkov's worn but neat clothing and how sparsely the apartment was furnished. By contrast, Mukhin himself was wearing a good suit, and the little beard he had grown for the occasion added to his solid appearance. Savinkov began to quiz Mukhin, but in a way that seemed haphazard, jumping from question to question—about Moscow, the economic life of the country, new works of literature, what Soviet newspapers were reporting. Surprised by this, Fomichyov naïvely began to explain why the senior member of the Liberal Democrats had come all the way to Paris, but Savinkov interrupted him and said that they would talk more when they met again that evening.

When Fomichyov and Mukhin returned at 6 P.M. they were greeted by Lyubov Efimovna. Mukhin knew that she was Dikgof-Derental's wife and was struck by the intimate familiarity with which Savinkov treated her. The conversation again seemed to be haphazard because Savinkov was continuing to size up Mukhin. By contrast, Lyubov Efimovna took to Mukhin right away and noted that he "spoke intelligently, his stories don't sound at all like what keeps being chewed over in émigré newspapers. He insists that Russia is being reborn . . . cites numbers, facts. He seemed to us to be a man of a new generation." The visit ended around eleven that evening, and Savinkov invited Mukhin to meet again tomorrow in the late afternoon.

This time, it was a very different Savinkov. He was tough and tenacious as he darted around the room, showering both Mukhin and Fomichyov with specific questions about the Liberal Democrats that showed how thoroughly he had absorbed everything he had been told about them. Occasionally he also asked questions that were intentionally misleading and that could have trapped Mukhin if he had been less alert. Mukhin would later report in Moscow that during this meeting Fomichyov had done 90 percent of the work in trying to persuade Savinkov.

Over the course of the following week, Savinkov met with Mukhin a number of additional times, and on one occasion secretly, without Fomichyov, so that his enthusiasm would not cloud the discussion. To vary the atmosphere, some meetings took place over dinners in restaurants; Lyubov Efimovna and her husband attended one of them and, together with Savinkov, spoke at length and admiringly of Mussolini. When Mukhin met privately with Savinkov, he was careful to cite the same data and statistics about the political, economic, social, and military situation in Soviet Russia that the GPU had prepared for him and that he had already used in Warsaw and during Fomichyov's visit to Moscow. As a result, the picture he painted was consistent with what Savinkov and his men had heard before, which made it all seem truthful and persuasive. Savinkov was still not convinced by Mukhin, although he found him impressive and oddly opaque as well; he was a new "type," he decided, one that had appeared in Russia only after the Bolsheviks seized power.

On Sunday, July 22, 1923, Savinkov organized a farewell dinner for Mukhin in an especially good restaurant to which he also invited his most trusted associates, Pavlovsky, the Dikgof-Derentals, and Sidney Reilly, so that they could help assess the Russian visitor. Like all members of the KRO, Mukhin knew Reilly by his notorious reputation and that a Bolshevik tribunal had sentenced him to death in absentia. When Savinkov introduced the exotic-looking, polished, and dandyish Englishman as his very close friend, Mukhin realized that the dinner would be full of new dangers. The way Pavlovsky fixed his unblinking gaze on him reinforced the impression.

However, the dinner went well, and Mukhin managed his performance without any blunders, although he did not convince everyone. Pavlovsky replied that he trusted Mukhin when Savinkov asked him, but Reilly was skeptical, and Savinkov also had doubts.

Two weeks after the dinner, Mukhin was back in Moscow. Artuzov was very pleased with his report and told him that the information he brought back was of inestimable value. The KRO had learned a great deal about the state of the National Union and about Savinkov's ties to anti-Soviet organizations abroad as well as to important foreigners. There was now an opportunity to capture the elusive Pavlovsky. And there was even a chance that Savinkov would be willing to come to Russia himself.

The Only Option Left

After Mukhin left Paris, Savinkov was uncertain what to make of him. As he wrote to his sister Vera, he "suspected" that Mukhin had "aims unknown to me" and because of this Savinkov could "not put very much faith" in what he said. The Liberal Democrats sounded too powerful to be real, and Mukhin seemed too enthusiastic when describing the improving economy in Russia. Savinkov also valued the judgment of Reilly, who did not believe that there was an underground organization in Moscow and thought Mukhin was a GPU spy. But the possibility that the Liberal Democrats existed in some form, even if a weaker one than Mukhin had described, intrigued and energized Savinkov.

A rebellion in Russia was now also the only hope Savinkov had left. In June Amfiteatrov wrote that Italian interest in a military intervention in Russia had ended. However tenuous that possibility had been, the news was still disappointing. More bad news followed when Reilly informed Savinkov that he would be unable to support him financially any longer because of his own difficulties, although he did help with the translation of *The Black Horse* into English. The previous year Reilly had gone so far in his efforts to raise money for Savinkov that he auctioned off in New York his extensive collection of Napoleon Bonaparte memorabilia, which he had been collecting for over twenty-five years.

Pavlovsky's Mission

Shortly after Mukhin left Paris, Savinkov decided it was time to investigate the Liberal Democrats on their home ground. Because he trusted Pavlovsky completely and valued his exceptional toughness, he charged him with the task. In early August 1923, using a fake American passport, Pavlovsky went to Warsaw, and with the help of agents from Polish Intelligence—who presented him with a Colt revolver and a hand grenade as tokens of their admiration—crossed the border into Russia. He brought a bodyguard with him, and before heading for Moscow the two carried out a series of robberies, including a provincial post office and a passenger train, during which they killed several Bolsheviks.

In the meantime, Fomichyov, who maintained close contact with Polish Intelligence and was very excited by Pavlovsky's mission, felt it his duty to inform Mukhin that Savinkov's agent was on Russian territory. The KRO was immediately put on special alert. However, finding and stopping Pavlovsky required little effort, because on September 16, he showed up unannounced at the home of Sheshenya, whom he still believed to be Savinkov's operative.

Artuzov knew that Pavlovsky was dangerous—physically strong, skilled with weapons, audacious to the point of recklessness—and took special precautions when planning his arrest. With Sheshenya's collusion, Artuzov arranged for Pavlovsky to come to a "conspiratorial apartment" so that he could meet several members of the underground organization, including Brigade Commander Novitsky, ostensibly the military director of the Liberal Democrats but in fact Artuzov's assistant, Sergey Puzitsky. Pavlovsky was invited to join him and two other men at a table set with food and drink (two additional KRO agents were hidden in a neighboring room). After a while Pavlovsky let his guard down, made a few toasts and launched into a detailed description of the mission that Savinkov had given him. When he was winding down, Brigade Commander Novitsky raised his glass. It was a prearranged signal: all four KRO agents rushed Pavlovsky, knocked him down, and disarmed him, although not without difficulty, because he resisted violently. His bodyguard had been killed earlier that evening when trying to escape.

For several days after being locked up in a cell in the Lubyanka, Pavlovsky refused to talk. This lasted until his jailers showed him a long list of the crimes he had committed against the Soviet regime. Any one of them, he was told, was enough to warrant a death sentence. Pavlovsky first appeared to change his mind and started answering questions, then suddenly offered to help the GPU by taking part in their operations.

However, such reversals were all too familiar to the secret police. Artuzov understood that Pavlovsky hoped he would be able to earn the GPU's trust and then try to escape. In a cunning move, he decided to exploit Pavlovsky's hopes and to put him to use, while at the same time taking great care not to reveal that he had been captured and was securely locked up.

Under Artuzov's dictation—and close scrutiny to ensure he did not sneak in hidden messages—Pavlovsky began to write letters to Savinkov about his highly successful work with the Liberal Democrats: how the organization was "pulsing with life," how he had been drawn into its military wing and given a senior position, and how he now understood the enormous difference between ineffectual émigré efforts and the energetic organization in Russia. He also wrote reports about his supposedly successful acts of sabotage, evidence of which were stories in newspapers about fires, train wrecks, and the like, all of which had been composed by the GPU. Finally, he wrote about the two factions in the Liberal Democrats, helping to plant in Savinkov's mind the idea that he had to come to Russia to heal the rift.

⚬

The "legend" of Sindikat-2 was growing in size, complexity, and detail. In late October 1923, Mukhin informed Savinkov that he had been elected chairman of the Provisional Central Committee of the two newly unified organizations, the National Union for the Defense of the Motherland and Freedom based in Poland and the Liberal Democrats in Russia. Mukhin made nine additional trips to Poland and Paris for meetings with Savinkov's representatives and with Savinkov himself. During one visit he gave Savinkov $100 as compensation for his role as the chairman of the Provisional Central Committee in Moscow. This was a not insignificant sum, worth around $5,000 today, and an especially guileful move in light of Savinkov's chronic money problems. The GPU would both give and promise him much larger sums later, explaining that these were from Pavlovsky's successful "expropriations" on Russian territory.

Savinkov was very pleased with all the developments as well as the money, believing that there would be enough not only to organize large-scale activities in Russia but even establish an anti-Bolshevik newspaper in Paris. When Lenin died on January 21, 1924, Savinkov and other émigrés decided that the time had come when it might be possible to play factions in the Politburo off against each other.

To Moscow! To Moscow!

On April 30, 1924, Savinkov finally uttered the words that Artuzov and his KRO team had been waiting to hear for two years. Mukhin was in Paris again, and Savinkov told him that he thought the best way to strengthen the Liberal Democrats would be for him to go to Moscow. He also explained that he still believed in the efficacy of terrorism and had a number of targets in mind—two Soviet diplomats abroad and three senior figures in Russia: Mikhail Kalinin, the country's titular head of state; Grigory Zinovyev, a member of the Politburo and one of the pretenders to Lenin's mantle; and Joseph Stalin, also a member of the Politburo and beginning his successful climb to power. To carry out assassinations like this, Savinkov added, he would need a resolute fighter like Pavlovsky.

Savinkov had been troubled by Pavlovsky's long absence despite his very encouraging letters and wanted him by his side in Paris, especially now. He had just returned from a trip to Italy where he had tried unsuccessfully to meet with Mussolini again. This failure probably determined the timing of Savinkov's decision to go to Russia because he had run out of all other options. On May 5, he wrote to Pavlovsky (whose correspondence naturally passed through the hands of the KRO) that "all my financial hopes have fallen through." He insisted that Pavlovsky return to Paris because of a very important matter, adding that Mukhin would be able to tell him what it is "in part."

Sindikat-2 had reached a crucial juncture. When Artuzov learned that Savinkov was clamoring for Pavlovsky, he realized that he would have to come up with a way to explain why the colonel could not leave Russia that would not raise Savinkov's suspicions. Artuzov's decision was ingenious and entailed staging several elaborate deceptions for an audience of one—the hapless Fomichyov, who was still Savinkov's primary "fact-gatherer" and continued to make "clandestine" trips into Russia. Thus it was that on one occasion Fomichyov was invited to attend a "secret" high-level meeting of the Liberal Democrats at which Pavlovsky was "present" and "delivered" some weighty remarks. In preparation for the event, the colonel had been cleaned up, dressed appropriately, and thoroughly coached; all the other men around him were agents of the GPU and he did not risk stepping out of character even for a second. Fomichyov was so dazzled by Pavlovsky's performance that he shook his hand at length and repeatedly clapped him on the back. He also dutifully reported to Savinkov that Pavlovsky was too busy with important people and matters to return to Paris at this time. On a later occasion, Fomichyov was taken to see Pavlovsky lying in a bed after he had been "wounded" during one of his "daring raids" and was "convalescing" in a "safe house" under the care of a "doctor." Pavlovsky's condition, about which Fomichyov also reported to Savinkov in detail, explained once again why he could not return to Paris. After each performance, Pavlovsky was returned to his prison cell.

Final Preparations

By early May 1924, Savinkov's plans began to take concrete shape, and he told Mukhin he had decided to bring Lyubov Efimovna and Dikgof-Derental with him to Moscow. He requested three sets of "flawless" documents and that all of them be provided with money for the journey.

Savinkov was preparing to make a radical break with his past and wanted to leave everything in as much order as possible. He made a farewell visit to Zinaida Gippius and Merezhkovsky, and he left her his poetry. To settle what he saw as a personal debt, he made a request to Mukhin that must have seemed very odd, even absurd, but that testifies, yet again, to the importance of such concepts as honor, duty, and giving one's word in Savinkov's world: he asked him to arrange to repay Torgprom, the Russian émigré organization that had given him money for the attempt on Chicherin in Berlin and Genoa. There were other personal debts as well.

Because Savinkov's mother, Sofia, the senior member of his family, had died in Nice in March 1923, he summoned his older sister, Vera, from Prague and entrusted to her his voluminous personal archive and his will (which had a provision for Lyubov Efimovna as well as family members and friends). He then instructed her that if he did not come back, she should sell his papers in the United States and use the money to pay for the education of his son, Lev.

Savinkov also did what he could to regulate his relations with his wife, Evgeniya. They had been estranged for some time, and he disapproved of what he saw as her lack of attention to their son. He asked Mukhin to take over supporting her and the boy financially after he left for Russia. He also made a farewell visit to them in the village on the heights above Cannes, where they were spending the summer.

Despite his long absences, Savinkov tried to maintain paternal relations with Lev, and Evgeniya did not interfere. The boy was twelve years old when his father came to Mougins, and he remembered their meeting fondly:

> He had on his usual formal and somber but worn suit, a white collar, a black tie. He held my hand; we walked along a path between pines buzzing with cicadas. He asked me if I worked hard in school and what I wanted to be. Like all children, I replied that I wanted to be an explorer . . . a sailor . . . or an aviator. He said to me: "All that is good, Lyova. Just remember one thing: never get involved in politics." He did not say anything to me about his trip. After years of separation I was happy that he had come back . . . I had been told that he spent his time in all the capitals with the masters of Europe and that perhaps one day he would be the great man of Russia. When he left, that is what he believed—not that he would become the "master" but that he would overthrow those who had plunged the motherland into misery. He would, all alone, in his worn black suit.

Savinkov also felt that he could not leave for Russia before consulting with Reilly and wrote to him in New York, asking him to come to Paris "on a matter of grave importance." Reilly had gone to the United States to pursue a big lawsuit; it was going badly, and he was still very hard up, but he did not hesitate to make the long trip on short notice. He also brought his wife with him, a diminutive and pretty former chorus girl and actress who camouflaged her Anglo-German origin under a lilting stage name, Pepita Ferdinanda Bobadilla.

Reilly was skeptical about Savinkov's planned trip from the start and had tried to dissuade him repeatedly, but now he decided that any additional arguments would be pointless. He understood that Savinkov needed to go for political and personal reasons that were important to him and concluded that the trip would be a major event in the fight against Bolshevism even if Savinkov returned without achieving very much; he did not seem to imagine that his friend might not return. However, in the memoir Reilly's wife wrote years later with the benefit of hindsight, she claimed that after meeting Fomichyov and Mukhin in Paris she became so convinced "that the whole thing was a trap that I begged Dehrental to arrange for Savinkoff to have a small accident, which would prevent his going." "It was not to be," she concluded regretfully.

The Confession

Savinkov was still uncertain to what extent he was being deceived and decided to seek Vladimir Burtsev's advice as well. They had collaborated a number of times since Burtsev exposed Azef, most recently during the Paris Peace Conference, and Savinkov's affection and respect for him had only deepened. In recent years Burtsev had also used his acute intelligence and deep experience with clandestine operations to penetrate the tangles of Soviet espionage and provocation in Europe. In late July Savinkov went to his apartment twice. Burtsev was now sixty-two to Savinkov's forty-five and still looked professorial, with his gray goatee and glinting spectacles. "I am going to Russia and came to you to confess as if to a priest," Savinkov began. "I ask only one thing: hear me out to the end." There is no reason to doubt Burtsev's recollections of Savinkov's "confession."

What Burtsev heard both moved and distressed him, and when Savinkov finished laying out his plans, Burtsev immediately replied that the very idea of a vast secret organization in Soviet Russia was completely fantastical and that the trip would be suicidal. He went on to argue that although Savinkov had succeeded with major terrorist acts against the imperial regime and had shown that he was capable of inspiring others and leading them in military campaigns, he had always failed to carry out any kind of intricate revolutionary plot. He insisted that the only thing awaiting Savinkov in Russia was a colossal failure and that he had no doubt whatsoever that the "clandestine" organization had been thoroughly penetrated by the OGPU (the GPU had been renamed at the end of 1923 as Obyedinyónnoye gosudárstvennoye politícheskoye upravléniye, or Joint State Political Directorate). The only reason the organization had not been liquidated yet, Burtsev concluded, was that the OGPU had other plans for it.

Savinkov turned pale at Burtsev's words and could scarcely conceal his agitation. What he just heard echoed not only his own doubts but what others had told him. He once guessed that there might be only a "20%" chance that Mukhin and the others were not deceiving him; another time he decided that only failure awaited him. But Savinkov's emotional pendulum swung in the opposite direction too, such as when he concluded that his chance of arrest was only "20%." Nevertheless, even with all the uncertainty, he felt he had to go to Russia to help the peasants and workers fight the Bolsheviks.

Savinkov then decided to reveal the secret scheme he had in reserve. He told Burtsev that he knew Russia was not ripe yet for a general uprising. He had therefore decided to persuade whoever would follow him to abandon the plan to seize power and to join him in a terrorist campaign instead. For him it would be enough to focus on assassinating just one leading Bolshevik. There were people in Russia ready to help, and he knew how to get dynamite from abroad.

And even if he failed, Savinkov added excitedly, his death would still be a resounding statement: "I'm going to Russia to die fighting the Bolsheviks. I know that if I'm arrested, I'll be shot. But I'll show those who live here in the emigration how one should die for Russia. My trial and my death will be my protest against the Bolsheviks. Everyone will hear it."

Savinkov's words affected Burtsev deeply. He agreed that if Savinkov stayed true to himself, then his trip to Russia, his trial, and his death "would have enormous significance in the history of the struggle against Bolshevism."

During the course of their meetings, Burtsev began to understand that Savinkov's political goals had become intertwined with his need to resolve his tangled family affairs and finances. There was also nothing left for him in Europe because he had reached the limit of his endurance with the inaction and empty word-spinning that characterized the Russian anti-Bolshevik emigration.

When they parted, Burtsev doubted that he would ever see his friend again and thought that only chance could save him from being arrested and executed. But Savinkov's dedication had impressed him profoundly. Years later, when recalling their last meetings, Burtsev fixed his impression of Savinkov in the following words:

> Before me was a revolutionary who insisted above all else on a revolutionary struggle against the Bolsheviks—a democrat, a republican, an anticommunist, an ardent anti-monarchist; an angry man, one who had evidently suffered a great deal, who had enormous ambition, an unbounded sense of his own importance, who staunchly believed in his own star, and who had enormous plans for the future.

To the Border

On Saturday, August 9, 1924, Dikgof-Derental moved Savinkov's, his own, and Lyubov Efimovna's remaining belongings from their two apartments into storage at her family's home outside Paris. That same evening, together with the Reillys and Mukhin, they had a farewell dinner in a restaurant in town. Reilly was planning to head back to the United States soon. Fomichyov had already been sent ahead to Poland to prepare for the arrival of Savinkov's group.

The following morning, they left Paris on an express train to Warsaw, with Savinkov and Lyubov Efimovna sharing one compartment, and the baron and Mukhin in another. They arrived in Warsaw early on Tuesday, August 12. Savinkov was impatient to make the next leg of the journey that same night. He spent the day in a flurry of meetings with Filosofov and other members of the National Union, after which there was a brief farewell dinner at seven in the evening.

One of the people Savinkov wanted to see in Warsaw was the well-known writer Mikhail Artsybashev. They had never met before but had become friendly via correspondence. Artsybashev viewed Savinkov with great sympathy, and their meeting allowed him to draw a vivid sketch of Savinkov and his team at a pivotal moment in his life (although it was also likely colored by what Artsybashev learned about Savinkov's subsequent fate).

Before their meeting, Artsybashev had to wait outside Savinkov's room for a few minutes. When the door opened partially, what he saw first was

> a pale mask with a strange slant to its eyes and a bald skull. It looks at me for several seconds, as if observing and studying me, then the door opens slowly and a man quietly enters, not tall, slight, with the shaved face of either an actor or a Jesuit. This is Savinkov . . . I stand to greet him and feel the prolonged clasp of a small but firm hand. Savinkov is smiling, and this smile animates his face: it becomes tender, delicate and attractive.

They spoke briefly because Savinkov's time was short. However, Artsybashev was eager to tell him what he thought of Mukhin, whom he had met before and described as a "short, thickset little man, with a shaved and ugly face, protruding ears and tiny but sharp and restless eyes." Artsybashev said that Mukhin had produced a "most abominable" impression from the moment he had first laid eyes on him and that he was convinced that Mukhin was a *provokator*. But Savinkov refused to take the warning seriously: "I'm an old revolutionary rat," he replied, with either pride or bitterness, Artsybashev could not tell which. "I probed Andrey Pavlovich from all sides. He is simply a new type that came into being under the Bolsheviks and that is still unknown to you."

At the dinner that evening Artsybashev saw Savinkov's companions, or "the condemned," as he also referred to them, for the first time. He thought that initially the entire group behaved "like genuine heroes" and "did not show the slightest nervousness. Except perhaps for being slightly excited." Artsybashev enjoyed the lively table talk: "Savinkov described his last visit to Mussolini vividly and graphically, while the slender, blond Derental—a kind of Frenchified Russian boulevardier—was telling jokes."

However, the atmosphere became less festive as the dinner wore on, and people began to feel ill at ease. Artsybashev noticed that Derental "kept knocking back vodka like a man who was in no hurry to go anywhere," which was odd under the circumstances. Savinkov's cheerfulness became strained as he recalled his bitterness at Mussolini. Artsybashev was still anxious about Mukhin and Savinkov's dismissal of the warning he had made. Turning to Dikgof-Derental, he quietly asked him to watch Mukhin during the trip and to stop at nothing if he made the slightest suspicious move. Derental promised to "keep his eyes fixed on him."

Only one person at the table did not take part in the general conversation:

> The tall, dark and thin Madame Derental, who was dressed
> inexpensively but with Parisian chic, sat silently, her sharp elbows
> resting on the table, her slim arms bedecked with too many large
> bracelets. It seemed that she watched all of us attentively and warily
> with her somber, black Jewish eyes, but especially—Savinkov. One
> could imagine that she was afraid of some sort of indiscretion on
> his part.

Artsybashev tried to engage Lyubov Efimovna by asking if she was afraid to go to Russia. She replied, in a tone that seemed positively hostile to him, "I am used to everything!"

When it was time to leave, Savinkov and Dikgof-Derental exchanged kisses with everyone, as did Mukhin. Lyubov Efimovna, "with the air of a society lady who was leaving an unpleasant rendezvous, wrapped herself up in her shining silk cloak." Savinkov gallantly raised his Parisian bowler, and a moment later everyone was gone.

Savinkov, Mukhin, Lyubov Efimovna, and the baron left on a train for Vilnius that night, a distance of 250 miles as the crow flies (the city had been taken over recently by Poland), and arrived on the morning of Wednesday, August 13. Fomichyov met them and took them to his apartment. Mukhin spent the day making arrangements for the crossing with Polish Intelligence and the following morning left for the border to make final preparations. Fomichyov had agreed to bring Savinkov and the others to the "window" in the border at midnight on Friday, August 15, 1924.

⚬—⚬

In the meantime, an operational group of disguised OGPU agents under the command of Artuzov's assistant Puzitsky, who had taken part in Pavlovsky's capture eleven months earlier, arrived in Minsk. Roman Pilyar, Artuzov's direct deputy, arrived separately. The crossing point on the Polish-Belarusian border that had been selected was some twenty miles away in an area without any villages. In Minsk the operational group chose the apartment of the local OGPU representative as its base, and by Thursday, August 14, everyone was in position.

CHAPTER ELEVEN

THE GAMBLER'S LAST THROW

At noon on Friday, August 15, 1924, Savinkov, Dikgof-Derental, Lyubov Efimovna, and Fomichyov, in the role of eager guide, left Vilnius and headed for Radoszkowice, a town near the border with the Soviet Russian part of Belarus eighty miles away. Shortly before midnight, armed with revolvers and fake passports (Savinkov's in the name of Victor Ivanovich Stepanov), and assisted by two Polish intelligence officers who guided them past the border guards, the group reached the staging area near the "window" in the frontier that had been opened for them. From there they proceeded in single file, following a wagon with their luggage that was driven by a nervous local peasant who did not fully realize what he had gotten himself into.

⊷

The group's progress is slowed somewhat by the baron, who walks with difficulty because he is feeling ill. But turning back or delaying is out of the question.

The night is cold and strangely quiet, even though there is a village nearby. A full moon bathes the landscape of fields and trees with light so bright that everyone feels as exposed as if it is the middle of the day. No one speaks or smokes. The only sounds are the slight creaking of the wagon and feet brushing softly through the dew-soaked grass.

Lyubov Efimovna tries to remember everything, because she is planning to write a detailed account of their crossing. She notices that they have all begun to breathe more deeply, as if trying to drink in the fresh air of their homeland, which is somewhere just ahead. The wagon reaches a thick growth of bushes by the edge of a meadow, and the driver stops. He unloads the luggage, wishes them luck, and hurries back into Poland. Beyond the moonlit expanse, in a dark mass of trees, is Russia.

Standing in the shadows on the other side, near a post marking the frontier, are three men, Mukhin and two other OGPU agents—Puzitsky, who will use the surname Vasilyev, and Ivan Krikman, who will be known as Andrey Petrovich. They have been waiting patiently for several hours, until finally they see a light flashing on the Polish side. A moment later, a small figure starts to cross the bright field toward them, and as it draws nearer, they recognize Fomichyov.

When he reaches the men, he greets them happily and shakes their hands. A minute later he is heading back across the meadow, now accompanied by Mukhin.

Savinkov squints nearsightedly at the two figures coming from the Russian side until he recognizes Mukhin's short, thick, broad-shouldered figure— "Andrey Pavlovich?" he asks, then clasps his hand warmly. They had last seen each other the day before in Vilnius, before Mukhin had left for the border to make final arrangements for the crossing.

Mukhin turns around and goes first, followed by Savinkov and his companions, all carrying their own suitcases. They cross the meadow in single file, step over the invisible border, and approach the two men who are waiting in the shadows. For Savinkov and the Dikgof-Derentals, it has been nearly five years since they were last on Russian soil.

One of the OGPU agents, wearing the uniform of an officer in the Soviet border guard, comes forward, his spurs ringing slightly, and gives Savinkov a crisp military salute.

"Andrey Petrovich," Mukhin introduces him.

The third member of the OGPU team, a young man also in uniform and with a wedge-shaped, reddish beard, bows politely from a distance.

"Vasilyev," Mukhin says, and then adds casually, "a friend of Sergey's." The reference is to Pavlovsky. Mukhin knows that Savinkov is unaware that his man was captured and has been cooperating with the KRO.

The OGPU agents stay in character after the introductions. It is important to lull Savinkov and his group into feeling secure so that they can be lured deeper into Soviet territory. This will make it easier to prevent them from attempting to escape. The three "guests" also still have guns.

Andrey Petrovich invites all of them to follow and sets off. He knows the area well but intentionally chooses a winding path through bushes and undergrowth to make it seem as if crossing the border is no simple matter.

His ruse works. Savinkov and Fomichyov keep checking their surroundings, leaving the path at times to stop and listen for any signs of danger. The group walks this way in silence for nearly an hour, through alternating fields and stands of trees. Lyubov Efimovna, who is not used to being in the countryside after dark, and who half expects to hear a shot from a border guard's rifle at any moment, is startled several times by rustling noises; but these are only birds disturbed by the group's passing. In fact, there are no border guards nearby. The OGPU team instructed the commander in charge of this section of the frontier to remove all his troops in preparation for Savinkov's crossing.

The charade enters its next phase. Andrey Petrovich leads everyone to a gully screened by trees, where two wagons with sturdy farm horses in the harnesses are concealed and a soldier is standing guard. Mukhin and Vasilyev get military overcoats and hats from the wagons and give them to Savinkov and the two other men to put on. Andrey Petrovich explains that since they are still in a border zone, locals might get suspicious if they see a group of men wearing civilian garb.

These precautions seem thoughtful and reassuring, and the mood of Savinkov's team lightens. Lyubov Efimovna is even amused by the men's disguises. She is unaware that the hats with their pointed tops, red stars, and earflaps are standard Red Army issue; she thinks they resemble the spiked helmets Germans wore during the Great War and jokes to Savinkov that "he looks like Kaiser Wilhelm II."

After splitting up in the wagons they head out for Minsk, some twenty miles away. Savinkov and Lyubov Efimovna are together and two of the OGPU agents accompany them—Vasilyev sits next to them, and Mukhin, with a holstered revolver on his belt, takes the driver's seat. Lyubov Efimovna is feeling more and more cheerful, even a bit giddy from excitement and fatigue. She laughs out loud because she thinks that Mukhin's round face with its several days' worth of stubble and his overly long coat make him look like an old-fashioned coachman.

They pass a sleeping village with barking dogs, then fields, then some stands of trees, more fields, another village. The fresh night air is intoxicating, and

Savinkov and the baroness can think of only one thing: the fields are Russia, the forests are Russia, the villages are Russia. They are happy. They are home.

At sunrise on Saturday, August 16, as the last stars fade in the sky, the wagons stop in a field so everyone can rest. Andrey Petrovich tells Savinkov and the other men that they can take off their military disguises now: they are far enough away from the border that it is no longer risky to be seen wearing civilian clothes. The men spread their greatcoats on the grass, and Fomichyov pulls a bottle of vodka and some sausage out of a valise. He announces in a jaunty tone that "the buffet is open, lady and gentlemen!" He enjoys playing the host, and fusses about as if all danger is behind them.

The others relax as well and rib him because he forgot to buy bread. Fomichyov pours vodka into glasses and passes them around. But the OGPU agents decline.

"You're tired from the journey," Vasilyev says to Savinkov and his companions. "You need a drink more than we do."

The baroness thinks she may have glimpsed a strange, mocking expression on Andrey Petrovich's face, but is not sure.

Around seven in the morning, the two wagons reach the outskirts of Minsk and stop. From here they will split up into groups to be less conspicuous. Two will go by horse-drawn cab and on foot via separate routes to the apartment at 33 Zakharevsky Street in a quiet section of the city that has been prepared for them. The third will head for a hotel in the city, where Savinkov's former agent, the turncoat Sheshenya, is waiting.

They will all lie low until evening and then leave on the night train to Moscow to meet the leadership of the National Union. Savinkov, Fomichyov, and the baron do not think they need their revolvers any longer and give them to Andrey Petrovich.

The agents of the OGPU want to draw Savinkov a bit deeper into their trap and so have to continue their deception for an hour or so longer. They also relish the chance to toy with him after all the effort they put in.

But Fomichyov is a minor figure and can be treated unceremoniously, even though his naïve enthusiasm helped the OGPU's operation a great deal. Andrey Petrovich tells him that he will be going to a hotel instead of the apartment and that he will wait there until nightfall. They set off together, but as soon as they reach the hotel, Fomichyov is arrested and bundled off to the railway station, where he is locked up under guard in a special train car that the OGPU prepared for all the "guests." A month later, the OGPU Collegium will sentence him to be shot.

When Savinkov and the Dikgof-Derentals get to 33 Zakharevsky Street, they are tired after having been awake for twenty-four hours. The apartment is up a flight of stairs, and as they are climbing them, Lyubov Efimovna inquires innocently, "Do some members of our organization live in this apartment?"

"Yes," Vasilyev answers with a reassuring smile.

They ring the doorbell. A young man in a white shirt opens the door. The expression on his pale, small-featured face is severe, and his eyes are narrow and cold. He seems to be in a bad mood. The "guests" assume that he is unhappy about being awakened so early. The baroness feels a twinge of uncertainty—she thinks the young man looks exactly like how foreigners picture Bolshevik commissars.

The young man ushers them into a large dining room with faded wallpaper and the remains of last night's meal still on the table, then goes to announce their arrival. The baroness sits down to wait while Savinkov and her husband go to the kitchen to clean up. Her vague unease is growing.

A moment later a giant of a man in a military uniform appears on the threshold. She thinks that he appears surprised to see the "guests," but the expression on his big, moonlike face is pleasant. *This must be the apartment's owner*, the baroness thinks, and feeling somewhat reassured by his friendly mien offers him her hand.

The big man is very hospitable and invites the visitors to have some breakfast. But the baron will not eat anything—he is still feeling ill and goes to lie down on a couch in the room. The baroness tries several times to get the host to join them at the table; he politely declines every time: "I wasn't expecting a lady to visit. Please, I would like to serve you myself."

She turns to Mukhin and asks why Fomichyov is not with them. He should have arrived at the apartment by now.

"He's at a hotel with Sheshenya," Mukhin explains. "He'll come to the train station this evening." Sheshenya already bought all their train tickets for tonight, he adds, then gets them out and shows them to the baroness.

This all sounds reassuring. Savinkov is very satisfied with how things have gone thus far. He turns to the two men who live in the apartment and starts describing the crossing and his upcoming plans. They watch him with curiosity as he holds forth. The big man's last name is, appropriately, Medved—"bear" in Russian—and he is the ranking officer of the OGPU for the entire western part of the Soviet Union; the one in the white shirt is a senior member of its counterintelligence branch. They do not find this archenemy to be very impressive physically. He is a slender and rather plain-looking middle-aged man with a high forehead, thinning hair, and a receding chin. But his narrow, close-set eyes, which are sharp and intelligent, and his heavy gaze, reveal an exceptional personality. They know his past and that he can be dangerous.

Savinkov speaks his fill and pauses.

It is time, Mukhin decides. He pours a shot of vodka, raises it, and proclaims: "To your health!" He then says that he has to go into town and leaves.

Suddenly, there is a noise in the foyer: the double doors are thrown open and several men rush in, pointing handguns and rifles at the "guests."

"Don't move! You're under arrest!" one of them shouts.

Leading them is a man in a military uniform with a black beard, shining black eyes, and a big Mauser in each fist. To the baroness this is all so unreal that she can scarcely make sense of it: her first thought is that he looks like a "Corsican bandit," or something out of an old opera or novel.

A second later, she is shocked to recognize Andrey Petrovich among the armed men—he is supposed to be a member of the Liberal Democrats! Vasilyev is also an ally, so why is he continuing to sit calmly next to her with an impassive expression on his face?

More men crowd into the room from the kitchen and freeze, their weapons at the ready. The baroness's mind is still reeling: the men are so still that they look like wax figures in a museum.

But Savinkov understands. Not a single muscle moves on his face. For a few heartbeats, he takes in the scene. Then, in a calm and somewhat hollow voice, he says, "Neatly done! Would you allow me to finish breakfast?"

The leader of the men who burst into the apartment is Pilyar, second in command of the KRO. Savinkov's self-control is impressive, and Pilyar courteously allows him to continue. The armed men line up along the walls of the room with their weapons and watch Savinkov closely. But Pilyar cannot contain himself any longer: he drops down on the couch next to Dikgof-Derental and starts laughing. Pilyar is short with a blond beard, and his upturned nose, round spectacles, and arched eyebrows give his pale face a quizzical expression. He laughs so hard that his whole body shakes and he lifts his knees off the ground.

"Yes, neatly done . . . neatly done . . . ," he keeps repeating in between guffaws. "It's hardly surprising: we worked on it for a year and a half!"

Another agent sits down at the table. Savinkov glances at his clean-shaven face: "It's a pity that I didn't have time to shave," he says affably.

"It's nothing, you'll shave in Moscow, Boris Viktorovich," the man reassures him smoothly.

"You know my name and patronymic?" Savinkov asks, surprised.

"Good gracious! Who doesn't know them?" the agent exclaims.

Pilyar finally stops laughing and moves to the table next to the baroness. She thinks he looks intelligent; his expression is animated, and he is clearly enjoying himself.

The baroness no longer knows whom to trust. "There were five of us," she says to Pilyar, "now there are only three. We're missing Mukhin and Fomichyov . . . Does that mean all of them betrayed us?"

"Of course," Pilyar replies. Fomichyov was a dupe, but he does not bother to correct her.

"So, all of them," the baroness marvels, "and Sergey? Sergey Pavlovsky has probably already been shot," she concludes.

Hearing this, her husband unexpectedly speaks up: "Will they be paid a lot?" he inquires with acid politeness, implying that they were all betrayed for money.

But Pilyar scoffs at the idea. Mukhin is a loyal comrade and a committed communist. "As for the others," he continues, "each of them has his sins . . . Well, and each will receive remission of his sins."

He does not say what the price for the remission of their sins will be, but it is not hard to guess.

Pilyar continues to savor his success and turns to Savinkov. He wants to show off that the OGPU knows everything about him.

"I believe you recently wrote the novella *The Black Horse*," he says pleasantly, "and before that *The Pale Horse*?" he adds.

"It's a whole stable, isn't it?" Savinkov jokes.

"And now you'll write one more tale—*The Last Horse*," Pilyar answers, picking up the quip, and starts laughing again.

Savinkov's tone changes: "Personally, I don't care," he replies indifferently, "but I feel sorry for . . . them," he adds, glancing at the Dikgof-Derentals.

The baron starts to object, but Pilyar interrupts. "Let's not talk about such things . . . ," he says almost gently and lowers his eyes.

He is tactful toward Savinkov and the Dikgof-Derentals. Perhaps their manner reminds him of something in his own past and the noble Baltic German ancestry he rejected when he became a Bolshevik.

The baroness is still trying to make sense of what happened: "Why did you arrest us right away," she asks Pilyar, "without letting us see Moscow? We were in your hands."

"You people are too dangerous," he replies.

⎯⎯⎯

Before going to the train station, the captives are taken to separate rooms to be searched. A young blond woman is assigned to the baroness and seems embarrassed by her task. Noticing her discomfort, the baroness tries to put her at ease by describing what the current fashions are in Paris. She has no idea how bizarre this is to an employee of the OGPU from a Soviet backwater.

The baroness wants to give the young woman a small ivory necklace as a gift because she is sure that she will no longer need any of her belongings. Politely but firmly, the young woman refuses. When she comes back with the baroness's clothing after searching it, she returns everything, including the twelve American dollars that had been sewn into the hem of her dress.

Savinkov and his companions continue to be treated with surprising courtesy on the night train to Moscow. They are under heavy guard but are assigned two comfortable sleeping compartments—one for him, another for them—and are provided with cigarettes as well as a variety of food and drink. The guards allow the Dikgof-Derentals to visit Savinkov, although the three remain silent most of the time because the young commander of the guards sits with them and is very talkative. He is incredulous that Savinkov could have believed that he had any support among the peasantry in the Soviet Union.

On Sunday, August 17, at 5 A.M., the train arrives in Moscow's Belorussky Station, and two cars take the captives and their OGPU escort into the center. The windows of Savinkov's car are curtained and he cannot see out, but the Dikgof-Derentals can. They had last been in the city in 1918.

Soon the cars reach the Kremlin and turn left toward Theatrical Square, a vast space at one end of which stands the Bolshoy Theater; at the opposite is a giant portrait of Lenin made, incongruously, of flowers. The streets are surprisingly clean in comparison to the disorder and damage of the civil war years. They pass the imposing and elegant Hotel Metropol on the right. A few more streets and they pull into the courtyard of a large, five-story, yellow-brick building decorated in Neo-Baroque style. This is the notorious Lubyanka, headquarters of the OGPU, with an internal prison (before the Revolution, it had been the home of the All-Russia Insurance Company).

The three are taken down a long staircase to the basement, and after being searched again, each is locked in a solitary cell. Then the questioning begins as the OGPU seeks to verify what it already knows about Savinkov's activities, to fill in a few blanks, and to compile the final evidence against him. Everything moves very quickly, and he is not treated harshly. The Dikgof-Derentals are questioned too; they are also treated with consideration, although the OGPU attitude toward them is different. There is obviously some sort of planning that is going on behind the scenes.

A Deal with Satan?

At the end of Lyubov Efimovna's first week in prison, during which she was told nothing about the fate of her companions and felt buffeted by alternating waves of panic, tedium, and rage, Puzitsky unexpectedly walked into the room where she was being interrogated for the third time and announced, "Boris Viktorovich asked for a meeting with you." He explained the meeting would take place in his office later the same day, Sunday, August 24.

Lyubov Efimovna could scarcely believe it and spent the intervening time in her cell, pacing back and forth. The guard who took her to the meeting led her through endless hallways, walking slowly, dragging his feet. When she entered Puzitsky's office she saw several seated men and had difficulty recognizing the one who rose to greet her. He was wearing a rumpled, government-issued suit that was too big for him and a collarless shirt whose buttons had been removed for some reason. Lyubov Efimovna shook Savinkov's hand and peered into his face. It had grown thinner, but he looked completely calm. She thought she understood everything even before he uttered a word.

"Are you brave enough?" he asked.

"Yes," she whispered.

"I'll be tried by the Military Collegium in a day or two," he said, referring to the branch of the Soviet Supreme Court that had been established for the higher ranks of the Red Army and Navy. "You and Alexander Arkadyevich will be tried separately. I'm happy: I've been assured," Savinkov paused, then turned his head to glance at someone in the room for confirmation, "that neither you nor he is under danger of the death penalty."

Lyubov Efimovna covered her face with her hands.

"But you said that you were brave enough," Savinkov rebuked her gently.

Lyubov Efimovna could not tell him how much he had frightened her. Alone in her cell and believing they all faced the same fate, she could be strong. But the difference in their sentences unnerved her. She now had to imagine living after he died.

Savinkov tried to distract her with humor: "You've lost a lot of weight," he told her. "You must be pleased. In Paris you did heaven knows what to lose weight . . ."

But he also tried to get her to prepare for the future: "Is it very hard for you in prison?" he asked. "The spyhole in the door? The loneliness?"

"No, it's not too bad."

"So much the better. You'll probably have to stay in prison a long time . . . And you don't have anyone in Russia. Neither family, nor friends. I can't forgive myself that I agreed to your requests and allowed both of you to come with me . . ."

Savinkov turned to Puzitsky: "Lyubov Efimovna and Alexander Arkadyevich will be allowed to correspond when I'm gone?"

"Of course."

When the meeting was over, Savinkov took Lyubov Efimovna's hand and kissed it. He was so calm that it made her want to scream.

Lyubov Efimovna hardly slept that night. At one point she heard two shots somewhere in the prison. She spent most of the following day, Monday, August 25, in a stupor on the cot in her cell, and when a guard came for her in the evening she followed him "without thinking, like an automaton." He brought her to a closed door. When it opened she was amazed to see Savinkov standing in front of her. She thought that the shots she heard at night meant that he had already been executed. They talked for several hours about what happened since the crossing and also about Pavlovsky. Savinkov could not forget the colonel's former loyalty to him and said, "I'm less afraid of finding out that he betrayed us than that he has been shot."

⚊⊷

But something new also appeared in Savinkov's manner and in what he was saying. As Lyubov Efimovna characterized it in her diary, on that day he did "not so much talk with me as think out loud." Savinkov began by recalling how eighteen years ago, when he was facing execution in the Sevastopol prison and simple soldiers helped him escape, he felt as if all Russia was on his side. But now, he continued sadly, when he recently met with Dzerzhinsky in the Lubyanka, the head of the OGPU told him that "100,000 workers" would eagerly demand his death sentence as "an enemy of the people."

They were allowed to meet again on Tuesday the twenty-sixth. Savinkov told Lyubov Efimovna he had just learned that his trial was scheduled to begin the following day, at 10 A.M. And he again returned to his doubts about his past activity, except that now he added that he started having them as early as 1923.

Moreover—if Lyubov Efimovna's diary can be believed—this time Savinkov also began to say things that were the complete opposite of anything that anyone had ever heard from him before: he expressed admiration for the OGPU operatives who captured him, for Dzerzhinsky and Menzhinsky, for the humanity of Soviet sentencing policies, and for the economic rebirth of the country. He also told Lyubov Efimovna he believed it was necessary to face death with courage to expiate one's error, and his was that he had "gone against the people, that is against the workers and peasants."

⚬⚬⚬

This change in Savinkov's attitude is the single most enigmatic event in his entire life. It is so improbable that it could be compared to the pope of Rome suddenly professing admiration for Satan.

The enigmatic event is also reflected in the FSB archival records pertaining to it—or, rather, in the glaring absence of certain records, according to those who were given permission to see them. And this in turn points to the ultimate mystery that lies behind what happened to Savinkov.

The first lacuna is in Lyubov Efimovna's diary. Although she quotes Savinkov's shocking new "thoughts" during the two days prior to his trial, she does not express surprise, approval, or disapproval. This stands out because her previous entries in the diary are filled with emotional reactions to everything she describes and experiences. The implication is that someone intervened in the text of her diary that has come down to us.

It could have been Savinkov himself, because it is known that that he translated her French text into Russian with the hope that it might be published abroad. However, the fact that the diary was written in prison under the OGPU's watchful eyes and then preserved in the secret police archive for over seventy years suggests that it had important propagandistic value for the Soviet regime. And this implies that neither Savinkov nor Lyubov Efimovna was free to write whatever they wanted and that his "thoughts" may not have originated with him, either partially or fully.

A bigger gap in the FSB archive pertaining to Savinkov was identified by the Russian historians who were allowed to study it and publish their findings in 2001. All documents from the period prior to August 15, 1924, the day before Savinkov's arrest in Minsk, consistently portray him as "a principled fighter against the Bolsheviks." However, all documents after August 21, 1924, the date of Savinkov's first interrogation in the Lubyanka, show that he became a supporter of the Soviet regime. As the historians put it, they did not have at "their disposal" any documents from the five-day period during which Savinkov's change of heart took place. Whether such documents do not exist or were not shown to the historians by the FSB archivists is equally noteworthy. In light of their discovery, the historians conclude that the question why Savinkov underwent such a rapid and decisive change "remains open."

They also note that the remarks Savinkov made about the Soviet regime immediately after the five-day gap prefigure everything that he would say at his trial and later in his letters to family and friends, as well as in newspaper articles and essays. Savinkov's "thoughts" in Lyubov Efimovna's diary fit this pattern as well. And all this evidence suggests that Savinkov followed a "script," although the key question is, did he write it himself or in agreement with, or under the dictation of, someone else?

A partial answer can be found in a letter that Savinkov wrote to Dzerzhinsky months later in which he refers to the crucial period between or around August 15–21, 1924. The letter implies that Savinkov had struck a deal with the OGPU shortly after his arrest: in exchange for denouncing his anti-Bolshevik activities and proclaiming that he now "understands and appreciates the Reds," he would be "pardoned" and "given the opportunity to work." The letter also shows that Savinkov initially resisted Dzerzhinsky's demand to acknowledge the Bolsheviks. However, Savinkov ultimately agreed because he must have been told that this was his only chance to save his life. Whether or not he was being honest is another matter.

The Whole Truth and Nothing but the Truth?

Savinkov's trial was one of the first and biggest "show trials" in Soviet history and prefigured the notorious show trials under Stalin a dozen years later. Like them, it also had nothing to do with normal juridical procedures.

In contrast to a trial whose purpose is to ascertain a person's guilt or innocence, a show trial is a theatrical event staged by an oppressive regime with the aim of publicizing the crimes of a defendant who has already been found guilty and deserving of the severest punishment. It is not a matter of justice but of vengeance. It is also a form of propaganda and a display of the regime's power and infallibility.

Savinkov's trial departed from this pattern only in its timing: it was widely publicized after it was concluded rather than as it happened. Perhaps the Soviet authorities were uncertain about what Savinkov might do during the event and did not want surprises; perhaps they were still refining their methods.

The location chosen for the trial was the House of Unions, a historic eighteenth-century building in the center of Moscow that was originally home to the city's Assembly of the Nobility and that had been taken over by the Soviet regime to serve as the headquarters for professional unions and for major governmental events. Lenin gave some fifty speeches there, and when he died his body lay in state in its Hall of Columns (Stalin's would as well in 1953, to be followed by many other Soviet leaders). The same hall, the largest in the building, was chosen for Savinkov's trial. It was the perfect setting for political high drama, although it was necessary to mute its sumptuous old regime appearance with crimson flags and banners bearing appropriate Bolshevik slogans.

Presiding over Savinkov's trial was Vasily Ulrikh, who began his career in the Cheka and would come into his prime as the senior judge during the biggest show trials of Stalin's Great Terror from 1936 to 1938. His zeal extended not only to handing down scores of predetermined death sentences but also to attending and carrying out some of the executions himself. Ulrikh, two assistant judges, and a secretary, all wearing Red Army–styled uniform jackets with elaborate button flaps across the chest, sat at a long, fabric-covered table at the head of the Hall of Columns.

The "audience," which had received confidential invitations to the event, consisted of some 200 of the most important members of the Soviet regime who were then in Moscow. Walter Duranty, the Moscow bureau chief for the *New York Times* (and not yet the racist apologist for Stalin he would become later), received a coveted invitation and reported that "It was the keenest first-night audience that Moscow could offer. Every man and woman was agog with expectation, intensely conscious of the unrivalled treat before them and prepared to enjoy its piquancy to the utmost. Nor were they disappointed."

During the proceedings Savinkov stood near or sat on a bench to the side of the judges while armed guards loomed close by. He was dressed in what Duranty described as a "cheap double-breasted gray sack suit with a starched white collar and shirt and a thin black tie." Although physically slight and unprepossessing at first glance, Duranty thought Savinkov's "face suggested the pictures of young Napoleon, but was cadaverous and drawn, with deep shadows under the eyes. Savinkoff was quite unafraid, and glanced around with the curiosity of a man taking his last look at human beings and their funny little life."

The trial began with the reading of Savinkov's formal indictment, which was a detailed but not altogether accurate summary of what he had done, first in opposing and then fighting the Bolsheviks over the span of seven years. It was a long and damning list.

However, what probably shocked the spectators even more than all Savinkov's misdeeds was his response to the charges. "General Savinkoff," as Duranty referred to him, "arose from the wooden bench and turned his eyes on the spectators, lazily surveying them." After a pause, and "just as the tension became almost unbearable, he began to speak in a low, weak voice but one which was quite audible."

Savinkov admitted that he was guilty of all the charges. He did not once contradict Ulrikh or attempt to absolve himself of anything. The only correction he made was to the final date of his anti-Bolshevik activity, which he said was 1923 and not 1924. Although he surely knew better, Ulrikh accepted this without comment, which indicates that he did not want to make an issue of the fact that Savinkov had begun to spin what was at best a half-truth.

The entire trial lasted two long days, with sessions running late into the night, and ended on Thursday, August 28. There were no witnesses and no new evidence was introduced because the case was open and shut. Ulrikh quizzed Savinkov in detail about nearly all his activities—but also largely ignored several important events (details below)—and dwelled especially on his ties to foreign governments, one of the regime's biggest bugbears at the time. In keeping with the Bolsheviks' recent campaigns to destroy all other political parties in the country, Ulrikh also pressed Savinkov on any involvement he might have had with Socialist Revolutionaries and Mensheviks. To all the questions Savinkov replied at length and with seeming frankness, repeating that he made the wrong choices in the past, confessing that he began to have serious doubts about his activities in 1923, and admitting that he fully realizes his errors now. Key among these was, as he put it, his mistaken belief that the peasants and workers were opposed to the Soviet regime. Savinkov also lied on several occasions (as will also be detailed below) but, once again, Ulrikh did not call him out.

Then, in the morning session on the second day, Savinkov identified the source of all his errors: "my main mistake was that I went against you in October." This confession must have been the first part of what Ulrikh was waiting to hear. To punctuate the drama of the moment and allow the audience time to absorb it he immediately announced a fifteen-minute recess.

But Savinkov had prepared an even more dramatic admission, the necessary corollary to the first. At the end of his closing speech during the final session on Thursday, he announced (the italics are in the official published transcript): *"I acknowledge without reservations the Soviet regime and no other . . . If you are Russian, if you love your motherland, if you love your people, then bow to the workers' and peasants' rule and acknowledge it without reservations."* This was the denouement for which Ulrikh, Dzerzhinsky, Artuzov, and the entire regime had been waiting.

Savinkov concluded with a dramatic appeal to the court for understanding that is also surprisingly ambiguous and may contain a concealed message: "Let your revolutionary conscience remind you that in order for me . . . to say to you here what I have said—that I unconditionally recognize the Soviet regime, for this it was necessary for me . . . to live through incomparably more than what you can condemn me to." In other words, Savinkov announced that it was more difficult for him to acknowledge his acceptance of the Soviet regime than it is to face death. This can be understood as either that he forced himself to recognize the Soviet regime, or that he felt coerced to say that he has. The difference is between coming to a difficult but genuine change of heart and simulating the change. If the latter, there may be a connection with his lies during his testimony.

Savinkov uttered his final words in the same quiet, low voice as his earlier replies. It was a remarkable litany, a rhetorically charged attempt to exculpate himself while pretending not to. When he finished, he sat down, opened a cardboard box of cheap cigarettes, asked a guard for a light, and began to smoke. Ulrikh again announced a fifteen-minute break. Duranty's impression was that "nine-tenths of the audience believed in Savinkoff's sincerity," and that when he left the hall "it seemed that there was something triumphant in his exit—he had played his part in the manner expected of him."

The judges adjourned to consider their verdict. During the hours they were gone, the spectators buzzed with discussions of what they had heard. Duranty saw Karl Radek, a leading figure in the Comintern, circulating through the hall, talking with various groups. "It's a perfect melodrama," he said.

> Cesare Borgia in the role of Hamlet. What an amazing scoundrel
> is this Savinkoff, drenched in blood, yet compelling us to believe in
> his sincerity, making us understand and even share his soul's agony!
> For me I would shoot him out of hand. He is so utterly the plotter,
> so profoundly devoted to murder and destruction as to be incapable
> of anything else. And yet the man has elements of greatness.

It was already after midnight and early on Friday, August 29, when the judges returned to the hall. Savinkov rose to his feet. Ulrikh read the expected verdict: Boris Savinkov is condemned on all counts, he is sentenced to be shot, and all his possessions are to be confiscated. The spectators listened in silence; the impassive expression on Savinkov's face did not change.

But then Ulrikh did something completely unexpected. He announced that in view of Savinkov's rejection of all his previous anti-Soviet activities and recognition of the Bolshevik state, the court will appeal the death sentence before the Presidium of the Central Executive Committee of the USSR. When Duranty heard this he thought that Savinkov's "dark eyes blazed for a moment" because "he knew that, in reality, he had won the bitterest and most daring stake of all his desperate life."

The Presidium of the Central Executive Committee acted with surprising speed and later the same day commuted Savinkov's death sentence to ten years' imprisonment, explaining that it did so because of his contrition and because "motives of vengeance cannot guide the sense of justice of the proletarian masses." Ulrikh did not delay informing Savinkov and personally handed him a copy of the presidium's resolution at 6 P.M. that evening.

What Actually Happened

The speed with which all these steps occurred produces the impression of a process that was prearranged rather than contingent. Moreover, when seen together with the change of heart Savinkov underwent in the undocumented five-day period following his capture, his lies and half-truths during the trial, and what he subsequently wrote to Dzerzhinsky, there can be no doubt that he negotiated some kind of a deal with the OGPU or someone else in the Soviet power structures.

This is in fact what was repeatedly suggested, with varying degrees of plausibility, by different people since the 1920s. All the hypothetical scenarios overlap to some extent because they all proceed by inferring what Savinkov may have done on the basis of what is known to have happened and what was published about him, as well as by guessing about which Soviet leaders may have wanted to use Savinkov for their own purposes.

The most probable scenario of Savinkov's secret deal was devised by Vladimir Burtsev, the investigator who had exposed Azef, but it is persuasive only in its general outline and not its specifics because he also got carried away with absurd flights of fancy (such as that the OGPU's leaders wanted to enlist Savinkov in a struggle against Trotsky and Zinovyev to prevent right-wing reactionaries from seizing the country). Burtsev's greatest advantage over the others who speculated about Savinkov's fate was that he had actually been close to his subject and was an experienced and informed investigator. However, because he was in Paris, he had no way of learning with any certainty what went on in the OGPU's headquarters or anywhere else in Moscow. As a result, and as Burtsev himself admitted, the bulk of his "reconstruction" of what happened to Savinkov after he crossed the Russian border is based on "fragmentary accounts of more or less reliable witnesses and guess-work by various people."

Burtsev had heard Savinkov's important "confession" in Paris and knew that he wanted to carry out a terrorist attack against a senior member of the regime. To this Burtsev added the plausible inference that Savinkov wanted to exploit the power struggle that had begun among members of the Politburo after Lenin's death, especially between Trotsky and the others. Burtsev also knew that Savinkov hoped the assassination might foment a rebellion against the Bolsheviks and that he was prepared to die in the attempt. From all this it followed that Savinkov needed to be released from captivity, and the only way he could achieve this was by feigning collusion with the OGPU and proclaiming at his trial that he accepted the Bolshevik state. Once he was free, Savinkov could pursue his own double game.

Although Burtsev does not refer to Azef in his scenario, it is inconceivable that he would have forgotten about him in light of the two new deceptions he had just discovered—the one that lured Savinkov into Russia and the one Savinkov wanted to carry out in return.

To win this complex game in Moscow, Savinkov would have to out-Azef Azef.

Lies and Collusion

Evidence for Savinkov's collusion with his captors, on the one hand, and his lying to them, on the other, takes several forms. Burtsev points out that Dikgof-Derental, who was Savinkov's right-hand man for years and took part in all his recent "crimes" against the Soviets, was never mentioned in Savinkov's indictment or his trial; neither was Lyubov Efimovna, although she was implicated in Savinkov's activities as well. Burtsev's inference is that Savinkov struck a deal on behalf of the couple as part of his collusion. This was in fact confirmed by documentary evidence that emerged only long after Burtsev was dead. The FSB archives contain a transcript of an interview that the KGB conducted with Lyubov Efimovna in 1959 in which she claimed that after Savinkov's death sentence was commuted, Dzerzhinsky told him: "It's of no interest for us to keep you in prison. You should either be shot or given an opportunity to work with us. You'll spend a few months in prison under very good conditions and then will be pardoned by the Central Executive Committee. The Derental case will be dismissed and they can be freed right away." In addition to implying a deal, the fact that the couple was freed also inevitably raised suspicions that they were somehow complicit in Savinkov's capture.

Even more striking evidence of Savinkov's collusion with the OGPU is the difference between what he said during his interrogation on August 21 and what he admitted at the trial a week later. The minutes of the interrogation, which were published fully only in 2001, capture Savinkov's defiant pride in fighting for what he believes in "until the end, until that final minute when I either perish or become completely convinced of my mistake." During the interrogation he also hinted that he still had terrorist plans as recently as when he crossed the border a few days earlier.

All this differs markedly from Savinkov's testimony at the trial. When describing his activities and state of mind since 1923, he did not refer to his plan to lead a clandestine organization dedicated to overthrowing the regime and claimed instead that he crossed the border for a reason that might be characterized as ideological tourism: "in general I wanted to see what is going on in Russia, what the communists are doing." This was a lie, and because neither Ulrikh nor the other judges called Savinkov on it, it is evidence that by then both sides had come to an agreement.

The most important difference between the interrogation and the trial is that Savinkov initially refused to accept the Soviet regime (which is also confirmed by the letter he wrote to Dzerzhinsky). Instead, he admitted that since he had fought the Bolsheviks and lost, "it means that the Russian people were not with us but with the Russian Communist Party. And . . . whether the Russian people are bad or good, whether they are deluding themselves or not, I, a Russian, submit to them." In other words, Savinkov was willing to acquiesce to the Russian people's choice even if they were wrong to follow the Bolsheviks. This is far from what he would say at the trial and after it.

It is of course clear why the OGPU and the Soviet leaders would want to orchestrate Savinkov's performance at the trial. If he appeared before the court merely as a combatant who had reluctantly acknowledged defeat it would muddy the message he had to deliver—that he not only lost faith in his struggle but also saw the truth of Bolshevism.

Historians who had access to the FSB archives concluded that the transcript of the trial was not redacted before publication. Thus, the other major discrepancies between Savinkov's testimony and his actual activities—which the OGPU knew in detail but which Ulrikh also ignored—must be seen as part of his agreement with the regime as well.

The most egregious examples have to do with Italy, Fascism, and Mussolini.

When Ulrikh asked Savinkov about his activities following his expulsion from Poland, Savinkov admitted, among other things, that he tried and failed to organize a terrorist attack on the Soviet delegation to the Genoa Conference when it stopped in Berlin. But when Ulrikh asked about Genoa specifically, he omitted mentioning Savinkov's elaborate plot against Chicherin there, or his arrest, or the attempt the Soviets made to extradite him. Savinkov's reply was even more surprising: "I was absolutely never in Genoa. It's a mistake that I was supposedly there."

Why would the court want to conceal Savinkov's terrorist plot in Genoa, which the GPU had uncovered and which was even reported in newspapers? Perhaps because of the rapprochement that had recently taken place between Italy and the Soviet Union, which included an important trade treaty and Italy's recognition of the Bolshevik state, the first by a Western power. If this is the case, it shows that Savinkov was willing to misrepresent his past to accommodate current Soviet foreign policy, possibly hoping to gain additional credit with his compliance. By claiming that he had never even been in Genoa, Savinkov was bolstering the fiction that he had renounced his former life and joined the Bolsheviks. Or, to put it in the terms of his plot in Genoa, he was trying to create a compliant "double" of himself to conceal his true nature and commitment to striking one last blow against the tyrannical regime.

The same explanation may lie behind Savinkov's efforts during the trial to underplay his admiration for Fascism and Mussolini. He acknowledged that he met with Mussolini in 1922 and that nothing came of it. However, he did not mention his second attempt to meet with him in the spring of 1924, although he did refer to it during his pretrial interrogation.

But it went even farther than that. Anyone who attended the trial would not have had any idea how often—and how close to the time when he crossed the Russian border—Savinkov praised Fascism (and condemned communism) to different people. He did so to the writers Amfiteatrov in 1923, and Artsybashev in March, April, and May 1924, when he wrote that "Fascism is close to me psychologically and ideologically. Psychologically—because it stands for action and total effort in comparison to the lack of will and the starry-eyed idealism of parliamentary democracy; ideologically—because it stands on a national platform and at the same time is deeply democratic because it relies on the peasantry." On July 10, or just five weeks before he crossed the Soviet border, Savinkov again wrote to Amfiteatrov to insist that the Russian newspaper in Warsaw should "definitely follow a fascist line."

Savinkov also spoke openly about his Fascist sympathies to Mukhin in Paris and in letters he sent to the leaders of the "underground" organization in Moscow (not realizing that they were members of the secret police). Nonetheless, the OGPU found it expedient not to parade Savinkov's pro-Fascist stance during the trial.

But did they believe he had really abandoned it?

There is additional evidence suggesting—even if not definitively proving—that Savinkov lied about having gone over to the Bolshevik side. During his pretrial interrogation he tried to avert the OGPU's gaze from his greatest secret, which was his plan to assassinate a member of the Politburo. The task was especially difficult because it required him to backpedal. Not long before crossing the border, Savinkov had told Mukhin about his plans as well as about the new explosive he was developing, and even discussed with him how it could be smuggled into Russia. Nevertheless, during the interrogation Savinkov denied that he had any terrorist intentions or wanted to bring the new explosive to Moscow, saying, "It's all nonsense." Ulrikh did not raise the matter during the trial itself, perhaps to preserve Savinkov's image as someone who had given up in 1923. But did the OGPU really believe his denial?

The News Is Released

On Friday, August 29, 1924, the same day that Savinkov was sentenced, the secrecy around his case was lifted and the first notices about it appeared on the front pages of *Izvestiya* (*News*) and *Pravda* (*Truth*), Russia's two most important newspapers (by this time there was no independent press). The notices were identical, laconic, and vague. But they also featured the sensational revelation that Savinkov had publicly renounced his past errors, "exposed the activity of international interventionists," and called for all who "love the Russian people to unconditionally recognize the Soviet regime and to submit to it." The following day *Pravda* carried extensive additional information and also announced that Savinkov's sentence had been commuted. The full transcript of the trial was rushed into print before the end of the year by two different publishers.

Savinkov's activities had been newsworthy for years, and his arrest, trial, and embrace of the Bolsheviks caused an international sensation. Wire agencies worked quickly in 1924 and the first report appeared in the United States on the same day as it did in Moscow. Numerous other descriptions and analyses—all characterizing the events as "remarkable," "dramatic," "spectacular," "thrilling," or "extraordinary"—appeared soon after, everywhere from Europe to Asia.

The Russian émigré community reacted with even more excitement. Savinkov was, after all, one of the most notorious and famous members of the large Russian diaspora that formed abroad during the Russian Civil War (estimated at between 1.5 and 3 million people). The most common response to his embrace of Bolshevism, a system that many had risked their lives to escape, was of course outrage, although some also suspected that there was more to the story.

The Cadet newspaper *Rul* (*The Rudder*) in Berlin condemned Savinkov as a physically and morally spent force, as an adventurer who tried to resurrect his career on the Soviet stage, and as a traitor. But it also read between the lines and concluded that Savinkov became a propagandist for the Bolsheviks because he had made a deal with them, possibly because he had a secret plan of his own.

The influential émigré newspaper *Posledniye novosti* (*Latest News*) in Paris was more measured, though it still denigrated Savinkov in a lead article on September 5. It claimed that Savinkov's surfacing in Russia was yet another example of his adventurous nature and had more to do with his egotism than with any concrete or realistic political plans. However, the author also assumed that Savinkov's trip to Russia might have been his attempt to try his gambler's luck one last time by risking everything. It was possible, he concluded, that Savinkov was not finished and that "we may perhaps yet hear about him."

⚬—⚬

As part of his arrangement with the OGPU, after the trial Savinkov began to write propaganda for the Bolsheviks. It took two forms. The first was a five-page essay titled "Why I Recognized the Soviet Regime" that was published in *Pravda* and translated into all the European languages for reprinting abroad. In it Savinkov recapitulates much of what he said during his trial: there is no longer any reason to fight the Soviet regime; the country is coming back to life economically; the workers and peasants support the government; any collaboration with foreigners is a betrayal of one's people. The OGPU considered the essay so important that copies were sent to six members of the Politburo, including Stalin and his allies Lev Kamenev (still trusted then) and Vyacheslav Molotov.

In keeping with the essay's purpose Savinkov portrays Soviet reality in a very rosy light and cites economic data to persuade his readers abroad that the regime is successfully reviving the country's economy. Savinkov realized, of course, that this was the result of NEP, the New Economic Policy that Lenin announced in 1921 as a temporary measure. He could not have failed to understand that this meant full state controls would be reimposed on the economy once it had improved, but he makes no mention of it.

Savinkov also largely elides the issue of political freedom under the Soviets. He deals with it by asking: would not the Whites have imposed a dictatorship on the country if they had won? And his reply is that he prefers the dictatorship of the laboring class to the dictatorship of the generals, because workers have a blood tie to the peasantry and they all support their regime. It is hard to believe that Savinkov gave much credence to his own argument.

⁰━━┼━━°

In reality, Soviet Russia was far from being a homogeneous state, as the regime would have it believed. It was no secret abroad that NEP spawned numerous small businessmen and speculators, quickly branded "Nepmen," who became notorious for flaunting their new wealth in ways that angered impoverished and unemployed workers in cities. Peasants were hardly any happier. They had never been enthusiastic about the Soviet regime, and even though they were able to achieve striking improvements in food production when some of the restrictions on working the land were lifted under NEP, they resented the privileges that they saw Bolshevik Party members granting themselves. "You ought to know that the peasants curse you usurpers in their morning prayers," a peasant shouted at a Bolshevik agitator in 1924, according to a police report. "Where is truth? Where is justice? Why do you fool us with words such as freedom, land, peace, and equality?" Party members and the OGPU replied in kind, usually viewing both the entire NEP phenomenon and the peasantry—especially "kulaks," or those who were successful—with antipathy.

The relative calm of NEP, or what has been characterized as "a pause in the confrontation between society and the new regime" in Russia, lasted for less than five years, from the beginning of 1923 to late 1927. Its end was marked by a series of developments that anticipated the monstrous police state that was coming and that would last for decades: Stalin's success in outmaneuvering all his enemies in the Politburo and having them expelled and arrested; OGPU campaigns against kulaks and purges of Communist organizations; a harvest crisis that became the pretext for a return to requisitioning and repressions; the purge of "bourgeois specialists" and other remnants of prerevolutionary society. All this would pale before the state-induced Great Famine of the early 1930s, which cost 6 million lives, and Stalin's Great Terror later in the decade, with nearly 1.5 million imprisonments and executions. Savinkov would not live to see any of these horrors, but he was well aware of their earlier prefigurations.

In addition to his essay meant for wide dissemination in the West, Savinkov also wrote personal letters to his friends Filosofov, Reilly, and Burtsev. But despite his close and long ties to them, he largely repeated the same propagandistic arguments he had in the essay. The letters can thus be seen as part of Savinkov's "titanic efforts"—as characterized by historians who studied part of the secret police archive—to live up to the "compromise" he made with the OGPU by projecting a consistent image of himself as a loyal Bolshevik collaborator.

There is one curious exception in his letter to Burtsev, however, which may indicate that he tried to outwit his OGPU handlers at least once. Though Savinkov indicated that Burtsev could publish his letter if he wanted to, it starts with a reference to something enigmatic that only Burtsev could have understood:

> Before my departure for Russia, I visited you in Paris. I consulted with you about certain organizational questions. There was of course no discussion between us of recognizing the Soviet regime. And you are probably asking yourself if I concealed my true aims from you. Perhaps I went to Moscow to "stage" the trial.
>
> No. I was always frank with you and will be frank now.

The way Savinkov refers to the subject of their highly secret conversation— "certain organizational questions"—is very deceptive, given that during his visit he said he had come "to confess" to Burtsev "as if to a priest" and talked about his terrorist and revolutionary plans. Moreover, it is not clear why Savinkov would even mention this in a public letter that the OGPU would also read. Thus, perhaps the reference was for Burtsev's benefit alone and a signal that despite everything Savinkov said at his trial and the formulaic pro-Soviet content of the rest of the letter, he had not forgotten his plans for violent action in Moscow. From this point of view, the "propagandistic" remainder of Savinkov's letter is mere camouflage.

However, this hypothesis inevitably raises two questions. Did Burtsev see an encoded message in the letter? And how could he have acknowledged it if he had? There was obviously no way for the two men to communicate privately. The only public response from Burtsev that could have preserved Savinkov's secret was, paradoxically, outrage at his having joined the Bolsheviks, which was Savinkov's cover story. But how can genuine outrage expressed in a letter be differentiated from outrage that is feigned?

These ambiguities are not resolved by anything that passed between Burtsev and Savinkov. Burtsev accused Savinkov in print of "betrayal" and "apostasy" and called him a "renegade" and a "bolshevist slave." There is not a hint in any of Savinkov's other letters to Burtsev that a secret understanding had been established between them. Savinkov also sounds genuinely indignant at the way Burtsev attacks him and, in turn, accuses him of slander and of lacking the courage to verify his beliefs about the Soviet regime. But although Burtsev's final judgment was that Savinkov committed an unforgivable crime when he recognized the Bolsheviks, he later claimed in print that Savinkov did so as part of his plan to strike a blow against them.

Savinkov's falling out with Filosofov was even more acrimonious. Filosofov wrote an article titled "Traitors" that insulted Savinkov deeply because it accused him (and Dikgof-Derental and his wife) of striking a deal with the Bolsheviks when he was still in Paris and thus deceiving his friends and comrades before he went to Russia. Worse yet was an article by Artsybashev that Filosofov published that accused the Dikgof-Derentals of betraying Savinkov to the OGPU. Savinkov responded with cold fury and threatened Filosofov with physical retribution: "Sooner or later Alexander Arkadyevich and I will settle our account with you. You have been warned."

⚬——⚬

Reilly characterized the period between the first brief notices in Soviet newspapers about Savinkov's capture and the detailed reports about the trial that appeared later as "three weeks of hopeless nightmares." He initially refused to believe the announcements and even wrote letters of protest to an English newspaper. Knowing the value that Churchill placed on Savinkov, and hoping that Churchill would still be able to persuade the British government to support a counter-revolution in Russia, Reilly wrote to him as well. However, Churchill remained unpersuaded by Reilly's attempts to dismiss or re-explain the news from Moscow, although he invited Reilly to keep him informed about "anything further you may know on the subject, as I always thought Savinkoff was a great man and a great Russian patriot, in spite of the terrible methods with which he has been associated."

Reilly finally gave up attempts to find alternative explanations for what happened only when photographs of Savinkov's trial and his statements were published. He took the betrayal deeply personally and branded Savinkov "a renegade, the likes of which world history has not known since the time of Judas." He "was our ideological and political leader," Reilly lamented, and "hundreds of Union members proudly went to their deaths with his name on their lips." Savinkov had handed a "triumph of inestimable magnitude to the Bolsheviks," one that is "much greater than the victory over Kolchak, Denikin and others." And even if he had a secret plan to outwit the Bolsheviks, he can never be forgiven.

The Golden Cage

Because Savinkov fulfilled his commitment to propagandize his support for the Soviet regime, the OGPU held up its end of the bargain as well, or at least part of it, judging by the conditions in which he was kept in the Lubyanka. These were unlike anything anyone had ever seen in that notorious prison before or since.

William Reswick, a Russian-born American newspaperman, was one of two dozen foreign correspondents who were given a glimpse of the prison's interior and of Savinkov during the first visit that journalists from abroad were able to make the building. Reswick was initially anxious about entering what he thought of as a "human slaughterhouse," but was surprised by the clean and well-maintained prison corridor they saw and the adequately furnished and heated cells that were opened for them. However, the reactions of the prisoners, who had not been forewarned of the visits, were another matter.

When the first cell door was unlocked unexpectedly the prisoner inside assumed that he had been sentenced to death and was about to be taken to be shot. The handsome thirty-year-old man "was the living image of fright . . . he backed up against the wall, stretched out his arms, and, trembling from head to foot, stood before us like a crucifixion . . . '*Továrishchi!*' (Comrades!)," he cried. Most of the other prisoners reacted the same way. But Savinkov's cell, which the journalists visited last, "was the biggest surprise of the day. It was a beautifully furnished room with thick carpets on the floor, a large mahogany desk, a blue-silk-upholstered divan, and pictures on the walls." Savinkov himself, whom Reswick had long admired as a "valiant leader" and a "brilliant writer," was "clean-shaven and smelled of perfume as though the barber had just left him. Most astonishing of all was his state of mind. He behaved like a wealthy and gracious host receiving visitors." Reswick wondered to himself if this was "mere bravado . . . or absolute courage"?

The journalists had been instructed by a senior member of the OGPU not to speak to any of the prisoners expect for Savinkov, and they took the opportunity to shower him with questions. He replied in French and Russian with equal ease, his answers "quick, tactful, brilliant." When asked what made him return to Russia, Savinkov stepped to a window and pointed to the Kremlin: "I would rather see these towers from a prison cell than walk freely in the streets of Paris."

But the easy atmosphere changed very quickly. The correspondents had initially avoided asking Savinkov any questions that might embarrass him in front of his OGPU jailers. However, a Frenchman could not resist: "Are the GPU horror stories true or false?"

"Speaking for myself they are obviously untrue," Savinkov replied.

The senior OGPU officer's "black eyes flashed with anger" at this; after a few more moments he put an end to the visit with one curt word: "*Porá!* (It's time!)."

Reswick noticed that "the effect of the word was instantaneous. Savinkov turned pale and stopped talking. He still smiled as he saw us to the door, but it was a forced smile."

This visit did not exhaust what the foreigners learned about the OGPU's prize catch, however. Genrikh Yagoda, the deputy chief of the OGPU (whose career would soar even higher under Stalin, when, as director of the NKVD, he would be directly involved in the executions and imprisonments of millions), asked to meet with Reswick because he wanted to reveal some intriguing information to him. "In a burst of professional pride," Reswick recalled, Yagoda "informed us that Savinkov had been lured to Russia by a beautiful GPU 'operator,' who had gone to Paris for the purpose."

"Right now," Yagoda added, "we are having trouble with the lady. She is in love with him. Lately things reached a stage where we simply had to grant her permission to stay nights in his cell."

Yagoda did not name the woman and neither did Reswick, but it is obviously Lyubov Efimovna. Yagoda knew that his sensational "revelation" would be included by Reswick and the other journalists in their stories about visiting the Lubyanka. However, his reference to "the lady" as someone "who had gone to Paris for the purpose" of luring Savinkov shows that he did not actually know Lyubov Efimovna's biography or her long history with him (or intentionally misrepresented them).

This raises the question of why Yagoda would have bothered to "reveal" the supposedly confidential information that Lyubov Efimovna was an OGPU "operator"? The tangled hedgerows of the OGPU's secrets make it difficult to tell fact from fiction, especially without access to the relevant documentation kept in closed archives. Nevertheless, there are some likely possibilities. By implicating Lyubov Efimovna in Savinkov's capture Yagoda was throwing fuel onto the firestorm in the emigration, and in the West more generally, surrounding Savinkov's betrayal, and from the OGPU's perspective, it was always good to increase dissent and confusion in the enemy camp. Yagoda's remark could also have been an attempt to undermine Artuzov, the head of the KRO. There were struggles between rival factions in the OGPU, and Artuzov's agents belittled Yagoda's people for their ignorance of counterintelligence practices. Thus, if it was claimed that Savinkov ended up in OGPU hands because of Lyubov Efimovna's allure, the amazing achievement of Sindikat-2, Artuzov's brainchild, was diminished, if not negated. An additional "bonus" of the sadistic Yagoda's "revelation" was the pain it would cause Savinkov, Lyubov Efimovna, and her husband.

But could there have been any truth to Yagoda's claim about Lyubov Efimovna? When Filosofov published Artsybashev's allegation about her, Savinkov and Dikgof-Derental were enraged, and Dikgof-Derental went even further than Savinkov in threatening Filosofov physically for what he considered vile slander: "If fate ever brings me together with D. V.," he wrote to Savinkov's sister Vera, "I warn him in advance—I will beat him in a way that is completely uncultured, unsophisticated and indecent."

However, suspicions about Lyubov Efimovna's complicity would never end because of how the OGPU treated her. Yagoda was not lying when he told Reswick that she was allowed to spend nights in Savinkov's luxurious cell; this incredible arrangement had been authorized by Dzerzhinsky himself. Moreover, she and her husband would be released from prison early in 1925. How can such benevolence by the OGPU be explained without at least raising suspicions that it was payment for some kind of services?

Conjugal visits with his mistress in Moscow's main political prison was not the only unheard-of boon that Savinkov was granted. Soon Lyubov Efimovna would be allowed to live with him in his cell. As he noted in his diary, which he was allowed to keep, and fully appreciating the irony, this was the first time they ever lived together anywhere.

There were more privileges. Not long after the trial, Savinkov sent a list of requests to Puzitsky of a sort that no one familiar with Soviet prisons could ever have thought possible: a walk; regular baths, shaves, and haircuts; a return of his own linen that had been taken from him when he was arrested; two lunch servings a day (presumably to share with a visitor); two sets of silverware; cigarettes and matches; a chess set; books on various topics (the Soviet Constitution; the Revolution; Soviet literature; fiction; manuals on astronomy, geology, and chess; magazines; and newspapers); beer; a small mirror; paper, a pencil, pens, and ink; a clock; having the electricity turned off at night and a curtain removed—the list goes on and on. He was also in a position to help Lyubov Efimovna and her husband. On Dikgof-Derental's behalf he requested a shave and a bath, the use of scissors for five minutes, linen, and fiction. For her—visits with her husband "without witnesses," as he underscored in his written request.

At times, the conditions under which Savinkov was confined resembled "house arrest." OGPU agents took him on excursions to see theatrical performances and eat in restaurants. He went as a guest to the private apartments of two of his police minders. He met writers and friends. He was taken by car to a park on the city's outskirts so that he could enjoy the fresh air. After Lyubov Efimovna was freed but still living in Savinkov's Lubyanka cell with him, they were both occasionally taken on trips to the theater by OGPU guards.

Savinkov was also allowed to write fiction. Incredibly, three of his short stories (portraying émigrés and anti-Soviet fighters in a very unflattering light) were published in Soviet journals while he was in prison (albeit after "inappropriate" parts and plot twists were censored). He was paid for these, as he was for Soviet reprints of most of his major works: *The Pale Horse*, *What Never Happened*, *The Black Horse*, and *Memoirs of a Terrorist*. A Moscow film studio even requested permission to ask Savinkov to write a screenplay based on *The Black Horse* because of the "enormous agitational meaning a film like this would have not only in our Soviet Union but also among workers in other countries." The money he got from his writings was deposited into accounts that the OGPU and the State Publishing House kept for him and from which he could draw as he saw fit. "I am rich now," he wrote to his sister Vera in late November 1924, after she had sent him three British pounds (or approximately $300 in today's money, which was a difficult sum for her to raise), because she thought that he was suffering in prison.

Savinkov exaggerated his wealth, but in another one of the surreal twists that characterized his imprisonment, he earned enough to start sending money to support family members abroad—Vera in Prague; and in France, his son Lev and his mother-in-law, who took care of the boy (but not Evgeniya, who appears to have had a job, and whom he had also excluded from his will). And even though the OGPU provided Savinkov with everything he needed, including warm clothing, he also used some of his money to buy himself a fur coat, a suit, and boots, and a fur coat for Lyubov Efimovna.

Family members were allowed to visit Savinkov in prison. He reestablished contacts with his first wife, Vera, and their children, who lived in Leningrad (Petrograd's new name after Lenin's death) and whom he had not seen since 1917. His son Victor was twenty-three and had taken his mother's maiden name, Uspensky, probably to avoid the notoriety of his father's surname. Despite having grown up largely without knowing his father, he was drawn to him and came to Moscow a number of times. When they were apart, Savinkov kept up a correspondence with him about Russian writers, his own literary affairs, and his son's writing. Their relations in person and in their letters were warm and loving.

Savinkov also discovered that he was a grandfather. His daughter, Tanechka, as he called her fondly, was now twenty-four, married, and had an infant son, Alyosha. Because she was nursing him, she was unable to come to Moscow, but she wrote to her father, who responded with melting tenderness, asking her to "give Alyoshenka a big kiss from me" and for a photograph of them together.

When he received it, he wrote back to thank her and mused about the wonderful changes that were coming—how in just a few months Alyoshenka would start walking and talking, and how, twenty-three years ago, when she was the same age as her son is now, "I was locked up. And now it's the same." Then he added: "But don't tell Alyoshenka anything about the prison, just kiss his little eyes and whisper in his little ear that his crusty old grandpa loves him very much and wants him to grow up bigger than big, smarter than smart, and stronger than strong."

Savinkov's former wife, Vera, did make the trip to the Lubyanka, but their reunion was not a success. He was struck by how she had aged and especially by how all she wanted to talk about was money. The logistics of sending Vitya and Tanechka money from inside the Lubyanka were complicated, but Savinkov added them to the list of people he tried to support, thus returning full circle to the early period in his life when he was in exile. "They all sympathize with the Communists. Life is hard for them," was the unhappy summary Savinkov sent his sister Vera in Prague.

Savinkov's sister Vera became his most important correspondent while he was in prison, and he was immensely grateful to her (and her husband) for her frequent letters and for the concern for his welfare and affection she showed him when almost everyone else treated him as an outcast. "Only two people (I'm not speaking of Lyubov Efimovna and Alexander Arkadyevich) truly love me, of course—you and my son Vitya," he wrote to her in the end of November 1924. By contrast, his younger brother and sister, Victor and Sofia, denounced him in print for going over to the Bolsheviks and joined Filosofov in attacking Lyubov Efimovna, which especially upset Savinkov.

Vera also mediated on Savinkov's behalf with his son in France but did not involve Evgeniya, who by then appears to have started an independent life for herself. In addition to sending money for Lev's support, Savinkov was very eager to find out whatever he could about his life and to guide it as much as possible. He wrote to him as if the distance between them did not matter:

4 November 1924

My sweet Lyovochka,

    If you are going to a Russian high school, you might as well keep going, although I'd prefer a French one. You'd have to memorize more there, that's true, but having finished you'd really know something, while in a Russian one, I fear that you'd start being lazy. But, my boy, look out—if you really start getting lazy, then excuse me, sir. No swimming, target shooting, or anything else but quite the opposite. When you're in Paris sort the postage stamps and keep them in order. The stamps, my boy, are good ones and I collected them for you for a long time. Say hello to Hector. He's a fine fellow and I like him. Be well. Write, although not with a chicken scrawl but like a human being.

I give you a big kiss. Be well, my sweet.

Your papa.

Not all of Savinkov's letters were in this mock-gruff, affectionate tone that avoided mention of the conditions under which he was writing. When he sent Lev New Year's greetings, he also admitted "It's a pity I can't spend the holidays with you, my boy, because we would have gone to the movies, and then to drink hot chocolate. Yes sir." Even copies of letters like this were preserved in the OGPU files.

So was a copy of an eighteen-page diary that Savinkov kept for only a month, from April 9 to May 6, both notable days in his life. It is filled with reflections about his past and people who are dear to him, especially Lyubov Efimovna and Lev, comments about literature, and occasional remarks that would have pleased (and may have been written for?) his captors, such as admiration for Lenin's and Dzerzhinsky's selflessness in comparison to émigrés, and regret over the mistake he made in opposing the Bolsheviks. With time for reflection on his hands and the "privacy" of a prison diary, Savinkov wrote about himself in a way that he had previously reserved for personal correspondence. He is nostalgic, tender, sentimental. On April 20 he wrote "And still, after all is said and done, what is most valuable in life is love."

A Prisoner of the Times

The unique conditions of Savinkov's imprisonment gave him every reason to believe, at least initially, that the regime was going to keep its side of their agreement and release him.

The country's rulers were in fact keeping a close eye on him. Because of the importance of his case, Dzerzhinsky's and Menzhinsky's reports about his compliant behavior were discussed at Politburo meetings on September 11, 15, and 25, 1924. The Politburo also considered the question that was key for Savinkov—if or when he should be given his ultimate reward and released from the Lubyanka.

Their decision was—never. However, to ensure Savinkov's continuing cooperation this had to be kept from him, which required another deception. On September 18, 1924, or less than a month after the show trial, Dzerzhinsky handed down a decree from the Politburo to the Press Department, the government agency that oversaw newspapers and other means of mass information throughout the Soviet Union. Titled "On Savinkov," it instructed the editors to make certain that any articles that appeared in the country's newspapers did not "demean Savinkov personally and did not deprive him of the hope that he may yet make his way in life" (a curious euphemism for "the hope that he may yet be released"). The newspapers were also told to influence Savinkov to make additional disclosures about his past by not allowing him to think the regime doubted his sincerity (which indicates that the Politburo did not in fact trust him). Woven into Savinkov's "golden" cage were bars of disinformation whose purpose was to keep his hopes alive. By using a national press that it controlled to misrepresent its actual attitude toward Savinkov, the Soviet regime expected to squeeze more value out of him for use both at home and abroad.

Hope Abandoned

As the autumn of 1924 gave way to the hard Moscow winter, Savinkov began to feel the walls of his cell pressing in on him. Based on what Menzhinsky, Artuzov, and Pilyar had told him after he was arrested in August, he thought that his imprisonment would be brief and that he would be released in October or November. But December passed and the New Year came, and on January 12, 1925, he sent a petition for a pardon to Artuzov so that it could be presented to the Central Executive Committee of the Soviet Union. There was no response. Savinkov then shifted his hopes to being freed in February, and after that in March, and then in April. As he noted in his diary, "Time in prison does not flow the way it does outside. Every day is long in prison, but if you look back—how quickly a month, three months, half a year passed! Before you know it, it will be June, but to make it to the evening it's ten years."

The conditions under which he was kept in the Lubyanka were still exceptional, but small frustrations kept accumulating, depressing Savinkov's spirits even more: some letters and manuscripts he asked to be mailed did not reach their addressees; requests for meetings with Artuzov and other senior members of the OGPU got no response. Dealing with money issues and the outside world was a constant complication, because everything had to go through a chain of hands.

By March, Dikgof-Derental was released and living in the city. Lyubov Efimovna could have left the Lubyanka too but delayed to stay with Savinkov. Living with her husband was no longer feasible. Moreover, she had no other place to go. There was a severe housing shortage in Moscow, with entire families crowding into single rooms in "communal apartments," and she knew nothing about the practicalities of life in Soviet Russia. Because her health had been weakened by prison, the OGPU offered her a place in an outlying sanatorium, but she and Savinkov declined because it would be hard for her to visit him. When Dikgof-Derental and an OGPU agent finally found Lyubov Efimovna a room of her own, Savinkov had to rely on the assistance of his minder Puzitsky to arrange and pay for her move; it was all so complicated that he felt he had to apologize to him.

Lyubov Efimovna left the prison on April 9. "I'm alone," Savinkov wrote in his diary. "My cell has become deserted and sad." The visits she was allowed to make, sometimes with her husband, comforted Savinkov but also made him feel even more unfree. Lyubov Efimovna talked about how shaken she was by being released, by how bleak her room is, by the strangers she lived with, by her independence, by there not being a guard at the door.

With the arrival of spring Savinkov intensified his anxious petitioning. He wrote to Artuzov that "Imprisonment, or forced inactivity, is worse for me than being shot." As the weather warmed, he began to clamor for a trip to the countryside, although he added the unusual request that it be with fewer than the five guards who usually went everywhere with him. He explained that he did not have any plans to try to flee because "I was and am waiting to be freed. If I had wanted to escape, I could have done so more than once." He especially missed seeing and feeling the arrival of spring. A fiery sunset he glimpses through the grate on his window reminds him of the distant skies and landscapes he saw during his voyage from Shanghai to Marseille.

When May arrived and the days lengthened, Savinkov's mood darkened further. He was losing faith in the possibility that he would ever be freed. On Tuesday, May 5, he confided to his diary, "My eyes hurt and there is soot in my head. I write grinding my teeth and nothing comes out. I'll spend another year in prison, grow completely stupid and come out an old man." He spoke frankly about his despair with one of his jailers, Valentin Speransky, telling him "I can't and won't stay in prison. Either I'll smash my head against a wall, or you might as well shoot me." Speransky thought Savinkov was joking: "Your cell, Boris Viktorovich, is so small that you can't get a running start, and without it you can't smash your head against a wall." Savinkov responded grimly: "You keep joking, Valentin Ivanovich, but at my age I'm in dead earnest."

Savinkov's need to get out of his cell was also growing more desperate, and he added an unusual new request to the others he had made: "I'd like to move to another room, one without grates on the windows. This is on the fourth floor and I wouldn't be able to escape through the window anyway."

The following day, Wednesday, May 6, when Speransky walked into his cell, the first thing Savinkov asked him was when would he be taken out of the city "to smell the fresh earth and leaves." Speransky thought that Savinkov looked "very depressed and upset." "You understand," Savinkov told him, "I'm an old man, and I've aged a lot here, and it's not even years of imprisonment, just months—bits of the remnants of my life . . ." He paused, and then, as if as an afterthought, asked "By the way, you haven't forgotten to pass on my request . . . about moving me to a cell without grates on the window?"

The Abyss

On Thursday, May 7, Savinkov was finally granted his wish for a trip to the country. Before leaving the Lubyanka, however, he sat down to finish writing a letter to Dzerzhinsky in the hope that he still might be able to influence his own fate. Savinkov explained to Dzerzhinsky that when he was arrested, he thought there could be only two outcomes: the first and most likely was that he would be "put up against a wall"; the second was that he would be believed and given a job; a prison sentence seemed to be excluded. But more than six months have passed and now he fears that he is going to be kept in prison indefinitely, despite assurances from senior members of the OGPU that they believed him and that he would be pardoned. Savinkov admits to Dzerzhinsky that he has learned a great deal in prison, including how to "understand and appreciate the Reds," as Dzerzhinsky had told him he had to, and, in light of this, appeals to him to either release him or to tell him exactly what his future is going to be. After composing the appeal, Savinkov gave it to Speransky so that he could transmit it to Puzitsky and further up the chain of command.

The trip began at eight in the evening, as had become customary with Savinkov's excursions, either because it suited the schedule of his jailers or reduced the chance that he would be spotted by someone on the outside. Savinkov was brought from his cell to the fifth-floor office of the KRO and then proceeded downstairs to the waiting car. He had also gotten his wish for a smaller convoy and on this occasion was accompanied only by Speransky, Puzitsky, and a third agent, Grigory Syroezhkin, who was also a veteran of Sindikat-2. Their destination was Tsaritsyno, a large popular park surrounding an eighteenth-century palace built under Catherine II that was located on the city's outskirts, a dozen miles south of the Lubyanka.

Savinkov sat in the rear seat, between Speransky and Puzitsky. He seemed very jittery and kept lighting one cigarette after another, only to throw them down unfinished, which prompted Puzitsky to ask why he was so nervous. In reply, Savinkov asked what his opinion was of the appeal he had sent to Dzerzhinsky earlier that day. Puzitsky's response was chilling. Not only was he skeptical that it would have any positive result, but he thought that even raising the question of Savinkov's freedom at this time was completely premature. In fact, he added, it was not out of the question that Savinkov could be transferred from Moscow to Chelyabinsk, a city over 1,000 miles to the east, on the Siberian side of the Urals, or to some other remote prison. Puzitsky's blunt assessment dashed the last of Savinkov's hopes. Prison in Chelyabinsk would be a much harsher sentence than Savinkov's exile to Vologda in 1902 under the tsarist regime.

The men reached their destination after a thirty-minute drive. It was a warm night, and the air smelled of spring. When they got out of the car to walk to the park's entrance, Savinkov hooked his arm through Speransky's, as if trying to draw closer to him. This surprised Speransky because it had never happened before, but he explained it to himself as the consequence of Savinkov's nervousness that evening and the "comradely" relations Savinkov said he believed existed between them (which Speransky did not actually share, although he concealed this). The four men spent approximately an hour strolling through the park before starting back to the city at 10:30.

They reached the Lubyanka by 11 P.M. and went up to the KRO office to wait for the guards who would take Savinkov back to his cell in the prison section of the building. Speransky had developed a bad headache during the outing and stretched out on a couch opposite the office's window. Syroezhkin was standing by a desk located near the window. Puzitsky just came back after leaving briefly to get some water.

All this time Savinkov kept moving restlessly—first he sat down next to Speransky and said something about his exile in Vologda that Speransky did not quite catch, then he got up and walked around the room, periodically approaching the large window, which was wide open because of the warm weather, inhaling deeply and repeating how pleasant it was to breathe air that did not smell of a prison cell.

As Speransky later recalled, he had glanced at his watch to check the time—it was 11:20—when he heard a noise near the window. Something flashed in it, and as Speransky rose up from the couch he heard a sound like a gunshot from the courtyard below. Everything happened so quickly that he was unable to understand. He caught a glimpse of Puzitsky's pale face and of Syroezhkin, looking bewildered.

Then Puzitsky shouted "He's thrown himself out the window . . . quickly, sound the alarm!" before running out of the office with Syroezhkin following him, leaving Speransky in the office.

Syroezhkin later reported that when he saw what Savinkov was doing he made a dash to the window, but it was too late. Puzitsky claimed he saw a bit more: Savinkov first leaped onto the low windowsill and then into the darkness. But Puzitsky was also too bewildered to act.

When Syroezhkin and Puzitsky ran into the building's courtyard, they saw Savinkov's body lying on the asphalt. He was dead.

A commission consisting of the head of the OGPU's medical unit, a doctor from the Lubyanka prison, and an OGPU prosecutor carried out an official examination. They found minor contusions on the upper back and more serious ones on the left side of the chest and stomach. The rear of the skull was completely shattered, as were part of the crown and the temporal bones. They concluded that Savinkov had died instantly. In his report Puzitsky indicated that a search of the prisoner's clothing did not turn up any notes explaining his reason for committing suicide.

When the news reached Dzerzhinsky, he ordered an inquest. Yagoda was eager to find someone to blame for allowing Savinkov to kill himself, but the investigator, Vladimir Feldman, concluded that Savinkov had acted in accordance with what he had often said were his only choices: freedom or death. Feldman did not fault any of the OGPU operatives who accompanied Savinkov on the night of the seventh and recommended that the investigation be closed.

What was done with Savinkov's remains is not known, and there is no grave. The few possessions that he had willed to his son Victor—a gold wedding ring, a gold ring with a gemstone, a gold watch and chain, fourteen letters—were delivered to him by the OGPU later the same month.

Savinkov's importance for the Soviet regime had decreased over the preceding months, but his suicide was still a blow to its propaganda campaign. Dzerzhinsky kept the news secret for five days and only on May 12 told Artuzov to compose an announcement for the press. When it was done, Dzerzhinsky edited it himself and sent it for approval to Stalin in his capacity as general secretary of the Central Committee. The announcement was published in *Pravda* on May 13 but was not featured too prominently: a brief mention on the first page, and the note itself on page 4, laying out the bare facts and that Savinkov had been told he was not likely to be amnestied. However, Dzerzhinsky decided to mitigate the bad impression that Savinkov's suicide was bound to produce—a man who embraces the Bolsheviks does not kill himself—and also published the letter Savinkov wrote to him on the day of his death. At least it made Savinkov sound loyal. Dzerzhinsky reported to the Politburo about how he was handling the matter on May 15.

Skepticism about the official story appeared immediately. When Lyubov Efimovna was summoned to the Lubyanka and informed of Savinkov's suicide, she reputedly cried out in French, "It's not true! It can't be! You killed him!" She may have known what Savinkov once said to his son Victor during a visit: "if you hear that I've laid hands on myself—don't believe it." She could also have been trying to push away the pain.

Foreign newspapers initially repeated what *Pravda* had published. But very soon doubts about the official story began to appear in the West as well. Evgeniya refused to believe that her husband committed suicide and wrote to the French League of the Rights of Man, asking them to investigate. Evgeniya also wrote to Vera, Boris Savinkov's sister, about the suicide claim, and Vera responded that his death could not have been a suicide, given where his body was reported to have been found. Neither knew that he had been in an OGPU office without a grate on the window and not in his prison cell. Eventually, this too was reported widely.

The bloody reputation of the OGPU and the Bolsheviks inevitably led to rumors that Savinkov had not committed suicide but had been killed—in one version, while trying to escape, in another by being thrown out of the window after being poisoned. The rumors persisted for decades and were amplified by two famous Russian writers who survived the black depths of the Stalinist Gulag and brought back stories of deathbed confessions by old Bolsheviks. The Nobel Laureate Alexander Solzhenitsyn reported hearing that a dying Chekist admitted to participating in throwing Savinkov out of the prison window. Varlam Shalamov, the powerful chronicler of the concentration camps, heard a "camp 'goner,' a former Latvian Rifleman" say that Savinkov was thrown down a staircase.

Also predictably, because of Savinkov's fame and notoriety, rumors arose that he had not died at all. The writer Alexey Remizov, his old friend from Vologda, heard that Savinkov—or possibly his unquiet spirit—had been spotted twice in Moscow after his fall from the fifth-floor window. Once it was by someone who had known him well and saw him walking on Tverskoy Boulevard, but when accosted, Savinkov's double responded, "You're mistaken!" The second time was by two friends who recognized Savinkov in a restaurant for VIPs. When their eyes met, Savinkov addressed one of them by name and then walked away. The man was not timid, but he was so shaken by the uncanny encounter that his hands began to tremble and he could not reply. His friend saw Savinkov leaving too and froze, not believing his eyes.

The publication of the volume *Savinkov na Lubianke* (*Savinkov in the Lubyanka*) in 2001, containing over 500 pages of documents from the secret police archives in Moscow, including many pertaining to Savinkov's death, make it hard to argue that he did not commit suicide. Even if one assumes that misinformation and secrecy are the hallmarks of the secret police, and that collections of documents may include forgeries or be seriously incomplete, it would have been against the OGPU's own interests to kill Savinkov or to allow him to kill himself. As a Russian writer said about the OGPU and Savinkov, they "needed not his dead body, but his captive soul."

EPILOGUE

The Soviet Union was not kind to those who had been close to Boris Savinkov. After being released from the Lubyanka, Alexander Dikgof-Derental got a job in Moscow with the All-Union Society for Cultural Relations with Foreign Countries, in which he made use of his knowledge of French and other languages while accompanying foreigners on trips around the country. He also wrote plays for the small stage and translated operettas. However, in May 1937, at the beginning of the Great Terror, his anti-Bolshevik past was remembered. He was identified as a "socially dangerous element" and sentenced to five years in a concentration camp in Kolyma in northeastern Siberia. On March 2, 1939, his case was reviewed; he was sentenced to death and executed the same day.

Lyubov Efimovna was amnestied. When she left the Lubyanka and was given new papers she chose a variant of her maiden name, Emma (Aimée) Efimovna Storé. For a dozen years she worked in the French section of Vneshtorgizdat, a Moscow publisher of touristic and technical materials in Russian and foreign languages. In 1936, she was arrested as a "socially dangerous element" and, like her ex-husband, sentenced in May 1937 to five years in a concentration camp in Kolyma. However, she was freed after completing her term and allowed to live in Magadan, a subarctic port in the northeast of Siberia. In 1958 she applied to be "rehabilitated"—the term used after Stalin's death for vacating unjustified arrest and prosecution—but was denied. In 1960, she was permitted to move to European Russia and eventually settled in Mariupol in eastern Ukraine, where she lived in obscurity until her death in 1969. She remained loyal to the memory of Boris Savinkov but resisted talking to anyone about her past. A friend succeeded in having her rehabilitated posthumously in 1997 together with her late ex-husband.

Vera, Boris Savinkov's first wife, and their son, Victor, led lives marked by poverty, sickness, and tragedy; initially Tatyana shared their fate. Victor developed tuberculosis and a psychological illness that worsened over time. In 1934 he lost his job and his wife abandoned him, forcing him to ask his mother to take in his two-year-old daughter. Seen as a "socially foreign element" by the regime because of his past, Victor was arrested during a purge following the Kirov murder—an internecine struggle among leading Bolsheviks—and executed in December 1934.

Vera eked out a living on a minuscule pension and made repeated attempts to have it supplemented with money from Boris Savinkov's publications and the estate of her late father, the famous writer. In 1935, because of her class background, she was expelled from Leningrad to a provincial town. Her daughter, Tatyana, faced the same fate, as well as separation from her family, but Vera managed to save her by appealing to the wife of Maxim Gorky, who had become the leading official writer in the Soviet Union. In 1940, Vera was allowed to return to Leningrad. She died in 1942 during the German blockade of the city. Tatyana's husband, an engineer, had been arrested in 1937 on charges of terrorism and sabotage and sentenced to five years in a concentration camp in northeastern Siberia. When the war began in 1941, Tatyana and her three children were evacuated from Leningrad. After her husband was released in 1942 and given permission to live and work in Norilsk in northern Siberia, Tatyana and their children joined him there. In 1960, the family moved back to Leningrad.

Savinkov's brother Victor and sister Vera lived and died in Prague. The archive that Savinkov entrusted to Vera was seized by the Red Army and taken to the Soviet Union after World War II.

The indefatigable plotter Sidney Reilly could not leave well enough alone and stay in the West. After Savinkov's death, he fell prey to "the Trust," the OGPU's second great *legendirovaniye* operation, which it had launched even before Sindikat-2, against Russian monarchists and former members of the White Army who still hoped to resume the fight against the Bolsheviks. In September 1925, Reilly crossed the Finnish-Russian frontier—illegally, he believed—and was escorted by disguised OGPU agents to Moscow, where he was arrested and taken to the Lubyanka. Some of the same agents who had dealt with Savinkov were part of the operation against Reilly. After being subjected to a "mock execution" to break his resistance, he was thoroughly interrogated and then executed on November 5, 1925. Stalin especially had insisted on it.

Evgeniya, Savinkov's second wife, and their son, Lev, remained in France, where, although their lives were difficult, they were at least out of the OGPU's reach. Initially, she found work as a sketcher in a shop in the Louvre and then as a private decorator. While Evgeniya was still married to her famous husband, friends sometimes jokingly referred to her as "Princess" Savinkova. In an ironic twist, she actually acquired the title when she remarried. Her new husband, Prince Yury Shirinsky-Shikhmatov, was a member of an old noble family, a former cavalry guards' officer, and military pilot. In Paris he worked as a taxi driver. His open disdain for the Nazis during their occupation of France and refusal to cooperate with them led to his arrest and deportation to Auschwitz, where he died, apparently in 1942. Evgeniya died of cancer in 1940.

Lev worked as a journalist and a truck driver in Paris in addition to writing poetry in Russian and stories in French. When the Spanish Civil War broke out in 1936—and became a proxy war between Stalin on one side and Hitler and Mussolini on the other—Lev enlisted in the anti-Fascist International Brigade, which was composed of communists, socialists, and anarchists from many countries, where he rose to the rank of captain.

He also had several encounters with his father's past while in Spain. The commander of his unit was Grigory Syroezhkin, one of his father's OGPU minders and a witness to his suicide. A Soviet colonel in the International Brigade tried to "repatriate" Lev forcibly, despite the fact that he had been born in France and never set foot on Russian soil, but Lev escaped after pulling his revolver. Lev also met Ilya Ehrenburg, his father's old friend from their days in La Rotonde, who was in Spain as a war correspondent.

Lev returned to France after one and a half years, seriously wounded and ill with tuberculosis. Nevertheless, he continued to live up to his father's reputation for action in the cause of his beliefs. When the Second World War began in 1939, he volunteered for the French Army. Later he participated in the Resistance, helping Russian prisoners who had escaped from German camps. He died in 1987 and was buried in the Russian Orthodox cemetery outside Paris, Sainte-Geneviève-des-Bois.

Nemesis

For approximately a decade after Savinkov's death, almost all the agents involved in Sindikat-2 enjoyed distinguished careers in the secret police, which was renamed the NKVD in 1934. But when Stalin unleashed the Great Terror, they all became victims of the organization they created and had loyally served. It was like the punishments meted out in ancient Greek myth.

Puzitsky was arrested in April 1937 and accused of belonging to an anti-Soviet plot within the NKVD. He was executed in June 1937 and rehabilitated in 1956.

Pilyar was accused of being a Polish spy in May 1937 and executed in September. Rehabilitated in 1957.

Sheshenya was arrested in May 1937 for being a "traitor to the Motherland" and executed in August 1937. Rehabilitated in 1997.

Fyodorov ("Mukhin") was accused of being a Polish spy in August 1937 and executed in September. Rehabilitated in 1956.

When Syroezhkin returned from fighting in the Spanish Civil War, he received three major awards: the Order of Lenin, the Red Banner, and Honorary Chekist. He was arrested as a Polish spy in June 1938 and executed in February 1939. Rehabilitated in 1958.

Dzerzhinsky died in 1926 from natural causes, but Menzhinsky, who replaced him, died in 1934 from a suspicious illness. Later, Yagoda would be implicated in his death.

Yagoda was arrested in 1937 for a broad range of antigovernment plots and shot in 1938.

Artuzov, the mastermind of Savinkov's capture, received a number of awards and promotions for his distinguished career in counterintelligence. In May 1937 he was arrested and accused of being a spy for Poland, Germany, France, and Great Britain. While in prison, he used his own blood to write an appeal on a scrap of paper in which he countered the accusations against him. He was shot in August 1937 and rehabilitated in 1956. In 2001, the FSB instituted an award named in his honor for studies of the history of the country's secret police.

Suicide

Why did Savinkov throw himself out of the fifth-floor window of the Lubyanka?

If one believes, as I do, that he intended to deceive the Soviet regime when he decided to cross the border, and that his absolute commitment to personal and political freedom had not wavered, it is inconceivable that he could have acquiesced to indefinite imprisonment, especially with the burden of his notorious endorsement hanging over him. What he said to his jailers in the days preceding May 7 implies that he had been contemplating suicide for some time and that it was not an act of momentary desperation. It follows that if he came to Russia with the sole purpose of continuing to fight the regime any way he could, then his suicide was the only blow he could make against it after he concluded that he had lost his gamble and would never be freed. He had no other way to undercut his tactical endorsement of the Bolsheviks. Nothing else he could have said or done or written would ever have gotten outside the walls of the Lubyanka.

And even if one believes that Savinkov voluntarily embraced the Soviet regime—whether completely or partially—his suicide still undercuts his endorsement because it shows there was an unbridgeable gap between what he demanded for his loyalty and what the regime was willing to grant.

There is also the matter of Savinkov's sense of honor. It was a touchstone throughout his life—the source both of his strength as a freedom fighter and of his ineffectuality or blindness when facing unprincipled opponents. Could it also have played a role in his decision to kill himself?

When he proclaimed to his friends and comrades-in-arms that he accepted the Soviet regime and urged them to do the same, one could argue that he acted dishonorably, no matter whether he was telling the truth or not. Why? Because if he was being honest, he betrayed his comrades and his own long-held beliefs. And if he lied to them, they could not see through his conspiratorial reason for doing so (with the possible exception of Burtsev). As a result, everyone's reaction to his proclamation was the only one possible: outrage that he had abandoned the principles by which he had lived and with which he had inspired them. When Savinkov realized he would never be released from prison, never carry out an attack on a member of the regime, and never reveal his deception to the world, all he had left was the sense that he had failed in the biggest plot of his life and dishonored himself. From this perspective, his suicide can be seen as a gesture at redemption, one that would lighten the stain on his honor, atone partially for the injury he had done others, and allow him to take a step back toward his true self.

Savinkov's Legacy

That history is written by the victors is a truism Soviet Russia raised to the level of state policy. Boris Savinkov lost his war against the Bolsheviks, and even though he pretended (or tried) to make amends during his show trial, it was not enough: he could not expunge his original sin of taking up arms against them and their Marxist ideology. Aggravating this failure in their eyes were his contradictory personality and tempestuous life, which also did not fit the required ideological-biographical Bolshevik mold. As a result, Savinkov's fate was to be personally maligned and his deeds misrepresented, belittled, and obscured. Anatoly Lunacharsky, the first Soviet commissar for education, tried to reduce Savinkov's historical role as a revolutionary by characterizing him as an "artist of adventure." Karl Radek, the early leader of the Comintern, labeled Savinkov a criminal, not a political figure, and a mere "sportsman of revolution." Except for a handful of admiring Socialist Revolutionaries in the far-flung diaspora (many others had denounced him long before for not toeing *their* party line), Savinkov was written off as a failure by most Russian émigrés as well.

Such judgments are profoundly unfair because they are the result of ideological bias, not historical or psychological understanding. Savinkov dedicated his entire life to fighting to make Russia into a free, democratic republic. He used various tactics, relied on different allies, and adapted as the circumstances changed. Even though some of his plots may seem unrealistic in retrospect, at the time he hatched them historical processes were still fluid and could have swerved in the direction he wanted. Somerset Maugham's elegant observation about how little can separate success from failure, which I use as one of the epigraphs for this book, is particularly relevant for Savinkov's efforts. Even if we consider just Savinkov's final plot to assassinate a senior member of the Politburo, it is hard to overestimate the impact this could have had on the Soviet state and therefore the world. And what if his target had been Stalin?

But despite the efforts of Soviet historians to diminish Savinkov's historical standing, he remained a source of fascination in his homeland long after his death because of his dramatic and violent legacy, conflicted personality, and indomitable character. Even when seen as a profoundly flawed figure, he was still a daunting opponent, which made his defeat by the Bolsheviks all the more significant. As a result, Savinkov lived on in popular memory and culture, under his own name, or as a prototype, in a half-dozen novels and some dozen films and TV series, the most recent in 2017. Interest in him surged following the collapse of the Soviet Union, when the relative liberalization of historiography, the partial opening of archives, and, especially, the growth of the internet made possible the discovery and much freer dissemination of information. Entering

Savinkov's name and "Russian revolutionary" in Cyrillic in the Russian search engine Yandex yields millions of hits. His books are reprinted and readily available online, and numerous bloggers and writers, with widely differing degrees of expertise and sympathy or antipathy toward him, have posted and reposted countless pieces about him.

There is also a notable change occurring in professional Russian scholarship about Savinkov and his milieu. Several historians have been mining archives and publishing collections of documents and studies of Savinkov that eschew the biases of their Soviet-era predecessors and present him not only as a fascinatingly complex personality but as a major political figure. There are aspects of Savinkov's violent legacy that will, and should, remain frozen in the past as part of the historical record. But perhaps over time he will come to receive his due for his conception of a free Russia and for his remarkable struggle to bring it to life.

PERSONAE

Alexeyev, General Mikhail—senior Russian Army general, co-organizer of the Volunteer White Army

Amfiteatrov, Alexander—Russian writer

Arbore-Ralli, Zamfir—Romanian socialist

Artsybashev, Mikhail—Russian writer

Artuzov, Artur—first director of the counterintelligence section of the State Political Directorate, or GPU, the Soviet secret political police and successor to the Cheka

Avksentyev, Nikolay—leading Socialist Revolutionary and chairman of the Directory government in Siberia

Azef, Evno Fishelevich (Evgeny Filippovich)—head of the Combat Organization and police informant

Azef, Lyubov—Azef's wife

Benevskaya, Maria—member of the Combat Organization

Borishansky, David—member of Savinkov's Combat Organization

Breshko-Breshkovskaya, Ekaterina (Babushka [Grandmother])—old Russian revolutionary

Brilliant, Dora—member of Savinkov's Combat Organization, bomb maker

Bruce Lockhart, Robert Hamilton—British diplomat and secret agent

Brusilov, General Alexey—senior general, commander-in-chief of Russian Army

Buchanan, Sir George—British ambassador in Petrograd

Bukhalo, Sergey—airplane engineer

Bulak-Balakhovich, Stanislav—Savinkov's ally, cavalry commander in Polish Army

Bunakov-Fondaminsky, Ilya—religious thinker and leading figure in the Socialist Revolutionary Party

Burtsev, Vladimir Lvovich—investigator, journalist, historian

Chaikovsky, Nikolay—revolutionary socialist, "Grandfather of the Russian Revolution"

Chernov, Victor Mikhailovich—Socialist Revolutionary Party theorist and leader

Chicherin, Georgy—leading Soviet politician, minister for foreign affairs

Churchill, Winston—leading British politician and government minister

Denikin, General Anton—senior Russian general, leader of the anti-Bolshevik White Army

Dikgof, Baroness Lyubov Efimovna—Dikgof-Derental's wife, Savinkov's mistress

Dikgof-Derental, Baron Alexander Arkadyevich (Derental was a pseudonym that stuck)—Savinkov's close associate

Dubasov, Vice Admiral Fyodor—governor-general of Moscow

Duranty, Walter—Moscow bureau chief for the *New York Times*

Durnovo, Pyotr—Russian minister of the interior

Dzerzhinsky, Felix—Polish-born first director of the Cheka, the Bolshevik political police

Ehrenburg, Ilya—Russian and Soviet writer

Elizaveta Fyodorovna (Ella), Grand Duchess—wife of Grand Duke Sergey

Figner, Vera—old revolutionary

Filonenko, Maximilian—junior army officer, Savinkov's aide

Filosofov, Dmitry—publicist, religious activist, member of Merezhkovsky's and Gippius's household

Fomichyov, Ivan—Savinkov's station chief in Vilnius who oversaw his network of agents in Russia

Fyodorov, Andrey Pavlovich (Mukhin)—agent of GPU who impersonated an anti-Bolshevik activist to ensnare Savinkov

Gapon, Father Georgy—Orthodox priest, labor organizer, revolutionary, police agent

Gerasimov, General Alexander—head of the Saint Petersburg Okhrana

Gershuni, Grigory—leading Socialist Revolutionary

Gippius, Zinaida—writer, married to Dmitry Merezhkovsky

Gorky, Maxim—Russian and Soviet writer

Gots, Mikhail—leading Socialist Revolutionary

Grigoryev, Dr. Nikolay—member of Savinkov's Union for the Defense of the Motherland and Freedom

Gvozdyov-Gulenko, Ilya (Elia Golensko Gvosdovo, Gvozdavo-Golenko)—Russian émigré in Genoa whose identity Savinkov assumed

Ivanovskaya, Praskovya—old revolutionary, Savinkov's comrade in the Combat Organization

Kalamatiano, Xenophon—first American spy in Soviet Russia

Kalyaev, Ivan—Savinkov's close friend, member of the Combat Organization, assassin of Grand Duke Sergey

Kaplan, Fanny—Socialist Revolutionary who attempted to assassinate Lenin

Kappel, Lieutenant-Colonel Vladimir—anti-Bolshevik commander whose unit Savinkov joined

Kerensky, Alexander—leading minister in, and head of, the Russian Provisional Government

Klepikov, Flegont—military cadet, Savinkov's aide

Kleygels, General Nikolay—governor-general of Kiev

Kolchak, Admiral Alexander—head of anti-Bolshevik government in Siberia

Kornilov, General Lavr—senior military commander with whom Savinkov tried to ally himself, cofounder of the Volunteer White Army

Krasin, Leonid—senior Soviet politician and trade representative

Krasnov, Major-General Pyotr—first army commander to fight Bolsheviks in October 1917

Kulikovsky, Pyotr—member of Savinkov's Combat Organization

Lebedev, Vladimir—Socialist Revolutionary, opponent of Savinkov

Lenin, Vladimir—Bolshevik revolutionary leader

Leontyeva, Tatyana—sometime member of Savinkov's Combat Organization

Lloyd George, David—British prime minister

Lopukhin, Alexey—former Russian imperial director of police

Lunacharsky, Anatoly—first Soviet commissar of education

Lvov, Vladimir—former member of the Duma and Procurator of the Holy Synod in the Provisional Government

Makhno, Nestor—Ukrainian nationalist and anarchist leader

Maklakov, Vasily—Russian Provisional Government's ambassador to France

Mannerheim, General Carl—former tsarist general, regent of independent Finland

Masaryk, Tomáš—founder and first president of an independent Czechoslovakia

McCullough, George—English pseudonym used by Savinkov

Menzhinsky, Vyacheslav—senior figure in the Cheka

Merezhkovsky, Dmitry—writer, married to Zinaida Gippius

Modigliani, Amedeo—Italian artist

Moiseyenko, Boris—member of Savinkov's Combat Organization

Mukhin, Andrey Pavlovich (real surname Fyodorov)—agent of GPU who impersonated an anti-Bolshevik activist to ensnare Savinkov

Mussolini, Benito—Fascist prime minister of Italy

Natanson, Mark—Socialist Revolutionary Party leader

Nicholas II—last Romanov tsar

Noulens, Joseph—French ambassador to Petrograd

Orlov, Vladimir—Russian émigré anti-Soviet activist

Pavlovsky, Colonel Sergey—cavalry commander, Savinkov's agent who betrayed him to the Soviets

Perkhurov, Colonel Alexander—leading member of Savinkov's Union for the Defense of the Motherland and Freedom

Permykin, General Boris—Russian commander in Polish service

Petit (née Balakhovskaya), Sofia—Savinkov's friend, married to prominent Frenchman in Paris

Petlyura, Simon—Ukrainian nationalist leader

Piłsudski, Józef—leader of newly independent Poland

Pilyar, Roman—agent of GPU, Artuzov's second in command

Plekhanov, Georgy—Menshevik, Savinkov's ally

Pokotilov, Alexey—member of Savinkov's Combat Organization, bomb maker

Prokofyeva, Maria—revolutionary, fiancée of Yegor Sazonov

Puzitsky, Sergey—Artuzov's assistant in the counterintelligence section of the GPU

Rachkovsky, Pyotr—vice director of the Department of Police in Saint Petersburg

Radek, Karl—leading figure in the Bolshevik Comintern

Rataev, Leonid—head of the Foreign Agency of the Okhrana, the Russian imperial political police

Reilly, Sidney George—British secret agent and adventurer

Remizov, Alexey—Russian writer

Reswick, William—Russian-born American newspaperman in Moscow

Rivera, Diego—Mexican artist

Ropshin, V.—Savinkov's literary pseudonym

Savinkov, Alexander—Savinkov's older brother

Savinkov, Lev (Lyovochka)—Savinkov's son by Evgeniya Zilberberg

Savinkov, Tatyana (Tanya, Tanechka)—Savinkov's daughter by Vera Uspenskaya

Savinkov, Vera—Savinkov's older sister

Savinkov, Victor—Savinkov's younger brother

Savinkov, Victor Mikhailovich—Savinkov's father

Savinkov, Victor (Vitya)—Savinkov's son by Vera Uspenskaya

Savinkova, Sofia Alexandrovna—Savinkov's mother

Sazonov, Sergey—Russian minister of foreign affairs, White representative at Paris Peace Conference

Sazonov, Yegor—member of Savinkov's Combat Organization, assassin of Minister von Plehve

Sergey Alexandrovich, Grand Duke—governor-general of Moscow, assassinated by Kalyaev

Sheshenya, Leonid—Savinkov's adjutant who betrayed him to the Soviets

Shkolnik, Maria (Manya)—member of Savinkov's Combat Organization

Shpayzman, Aron—member of Savinkov's Combat Organization

Shveytser, Maximilian—member of Savinkov's Combat Organization, bomb maker

Sikorsky, Shimel-Leyba—member of Savinkov's Combat Organization

Smith-Cumming, Mansfield George ("C")—head of British Intelligence (MI6)

Speransky, Valentin—one of Savinkov's jailers in the Lubyanka Prison

Stahlberg, Karl—German colonist who helped Savinkov escape from Crimea

Stepun, Fyodor—military officer and Savinkov's ally

Stolypin, Pyotr—Russian minister of the interior and prime minister

Sulyatitsky, Vasily—Russian soldier who helped Savinkov escape from prison

Svyatopolk-Mirsky, Prince Pyotr—Russian minister of the interior

Syroezhkin, Grigory—veteran GPU agent

Tatarov, Nikolay—Socialist Revolutionary who became a police informant

Trotsky, Lev—leading Bolshevik

Ulrikh, Vasily—senior judge during the biggest Soviet show trials

Uspenskaya, Vera—Savinkov's first wife, daughter of writer Gleb Uspensky

Voloshin, Maximilian— Russian poet and painter

Von Mirbach, Count Wilhelm—German Ambassador in Moscow

Von Plehve, Vyacheslav—Russian minister of the interior

Vorobyova-Stebelskaya, Maria (Marevna)—Russian artist

Wędziagolski, Karol—Russophilic Polish officer in Russian Army, Savinkov's close associate

Wrangel, General Baron Pyotr—White Army leader in the south of Russia

Yagoda, Genrikh—deputy chief of the OGPU

Yaroshenko, Nikolay—artist, Savinkov's uncle

Yudenich, General Nikolay—White Army leader in the north of Russia

Zekunov, Mikhail—Savinkov's agent in Russia who went over to the Soviet side

Zenzinov, Vladimir—leading Socialist Revolutionary

Zilberberg, Lev—member of Savinkov's Combat Organization

Zilberberg (Somova), Evgeniya—Lev Zilberberg's sister, Savinkov's common-law wife

ACKNOWLEDGMENTS

It is a pleasure to acknowledge my gratitude to my friend and colleague Paul Bushkovitch, the Reuben Post Halleck Professor of History at Yale, who read and commented on the entire manuscript. I am also indebted to Dr. Constantine Muravnik, a friend and colleague in Yale's Slavic Department, for securing a copy of a rare early publication by Savinkov from the Russian National Library in Saint Petersburg. Leonid Vaintraub was very helpful with archival research in Moscow, as was Caterina Mancinelli in Rome, and I am grateful to them both.

A month-long stay at the Bogliasco Foundation's Study Center on the Ligurian coast east of Genoa, with unforgettable views and sounds of the Mediterranean, provided me with perfect conditions to rework a pivotal chapter. The setting was not only paradisaical but also inspirational because Savinkov very likely visited the area more than once during his tempestuous and peripatetic life.

My literary agent Michael V. Carlisle of InkWell Management played a crucial role in this book—first through his invaluable moral support and belief in it, and then by finding a secure and welcoming harbor for it in a publishing world buffeted by the COVID-19 pandemic. I am deeply grateful to him and to his able assistant Michael Mungiello.

I would like to express my heartfelt gratitude to Jessica Case, my editor at Pegasus, for her enthusiastic embrace of the book, and for her efficiency, attention to detail, and flexibility in bringing the manuscript to publication. I am also very thankful to Roger Labrie for his critical and editorial acumen.

My greatest thanks are to my beloved wife, Sybil, who has been both my lodestar and my mainstay in this as in everything.

SOURCES

ARCHIVAL AND UNPUBLISHED

AN   Archives nationales, "Fonds de Moscou," Paris, France. [French Sûreté archive seized by the Germans when they occupied Paris in 1940 and then by the Red Army when it took Berlin in 1945 before being returned to France after the collapse of the USSR. None of the detailed dossiers about Savinkov were included. Now contains only index cards and a few reports.]

BDIC   Bibliothèque de documentation internationale contemporaine [now "La contemporaine"], Paris, France.

GARF   Gosudarstvennyi Arkhiv Rossiiskoi Federatsii, Moscow, Russia.
F. 5831, op. 1, d. 177 Pis'ma Savinkova Viktora Viktorovicha (brat B. V. Savinkova) Savinkovu B. V.
F. 5831, op. 1, d. 178 Pis'ma Savinkovoi, Very Glebovny (urozh. Uspenskoi, 1-aia zhena i detei Savinkova, B. V.) Savinkovu, B. V. [Many of Vera Savinkova's letters do not have dates and some appear to be out of order, but it is possible to date quite a few of them through internal evidence. Some of the letters in her file were written by another person, probably Savinkov's mother.]
F. 5831, op. 2, d. 2, 3, 8, 58 Fotografii 1902–1940.

Hoover   Okhrana Records. Hoover Institution Library, Stanford University, Palo Alto, California, USA.
Boris Viktorovich Savinkov Papers.
Nicolas A. de Basily Papers.

IISH   International Institute of Social History, Amsterdam, Holland. "Boris Viktorovič Savinkov Papers" <http://search.socialhistory.org/Record/ARCH01237/ArchiveContentList>.
"Autobiography of Boris Savinkov, sent to the Russkij èvakuacionnyj Komitet" [Biografiia predsedatelia R. E. K. B. V. Savinkova], January 1921, doc. 126.
Aleksandr Dikgof-Derental'. "Vospominaniia chlena Soiuza Zashchity Rodiny i Svobody. Bor'ba s predateliami Rossii," doc. 250.
Anonymous memoir [Viktor Savinkov], doc. 271.

NAK   National Archives, Kew, Richmond, Surrey, England.

NARA II   National Archives and Records Administration II, College Park, Maryland, USA.

Rome   Archivio Centrale dello Stato, Rome, Italy.

"Spisok lits"   "Spisok lits pol'zuiushchikhsia postoiannymi avtomobiliami, prindalezhashchikh Avtomobil'noi Baze Vremennogo Pravitel'stva." Document. Ground Floor, Historical Museum, Moscow, Russia. Photographed December 17, 2016.

"Vu Du Front"   "Vu Du Front," Document. Exposition, Le Musée de L'Armée, L'Hôtel National des Invalides, Paris, France. Photographed November 9, 2014.

PUBLISHED SOURCES

Agafonov, V. K. *Parizhskie tainy tsarskoi okhrany*. 1941. Rpt. Moscow: Rus', 2004.

"Airplane. History." Wikipedia. Accessed May 20, 2019 <https://en.wikipedia.org/wiki/Airplane#History>.

"Akt ob obrazovanii vserossiiskoi verkhovnoi vlasti, priniatyi na gosudarstvennom soveshchanii, imevshem mesto v gorode Ufe s 8 po 23 sentiabria 1918 g." *Skepsis*, June 17, 2019 <http://scepsis.net/library/id_2898 .html>.

Aldanov, Mark. *Azef*, chap. 1. E-LIBRA elektronnaia biblioteka. Accessed September 9, 2020 <https://e-libra.ru /read/165070-azef.html>.

Alekseev, Denis Iu. "Boevye deistviia russkoi narodnoi dobrovol'cheskoi armii v noiabre 1920 g." *Voennaia istoriia Rossii XIX-XX vekov. Materialy V Mezhdunarodnoi voenno-istoricheskoi konferentsii*. Saint Petersburg: SPGUTD, 2012, 253–279.

Alexandrov, Vladimir. *The Black Russian*. New York: Atlantic Monthly Press, 2013.

Amfiteatrov, Aleksandr. "Russkii ugol v Ligurii." 1932. Rpt. *Zhizn' cheloveka, neudobnogo dlia sebia i dlia mnogikh, Tom 2*. Ed. A. I. Reitblat. Moscow: NLO, 2004, 164–170.

"Amfiteatrov i Savinkov: Perepiska 1923–1924." Ed. E. Garetto et al. Pp. 73–158 in *Minuvshee: Istoricheskii al'manakh* 13. Moscow-Saint Petersburg: Atheneum-Feniks, 1993.

Andreev, Catherine, and Ivan Savický. *Russia Abroad: Prague and the Russian Diaspora, 1918–1938*. New Haven, CT: Yale University Press, 2004.

Annenkov, Iurii. *Dnevnik moikh vstrech. Tsikl tragedii. Tom vtoroi*. Moscow: Khudozhestvennaia literatura, 1991.

Ardamatskii, Vasilii. *Vozmezdie*. Enlarged edition. Kishinev: Lumina, 1987. [In a series of appendices, this novel about Savinkov includes quotations from documents held in what are now the FSB archives.]

Argunov, A. A. "Azef—Sotsialist-Revoliutsioner." Pp. 13–133 in *Provokator: Vospominaniia i dokumenty razoblachenii Azefa*. Ed. P. E. Shchegolev, 1929. Leningrad: SPRU Fond vozrozhdeniia Leningrada, 1991.

Averbakh, Iurii. Chapter "Verkhovnyi glavnokomanduiushchii." *O chem molchat figury*. RIPOL-Klassik: Moscow 2007. Accessed September 6, 2020 <https://e-libra.me/read/437923-o-chem-molchat-figury.html>.

Baedeker, Karl. *Russia with Teheran, Port Arthur, and Peking*. Leipzig: Karl Baedeker, 1914. Rpt. New York: Arno Press, Random House, 1971.

———. *Switzerland*. Leipzic: Karl Baedeker, 1903. Accessed September 6, 2020 <https://archive.org/stream /01738549.5440.emory.edu/01738549_5440#page/n397/mode/2up>.

Bazhanov, Boris. *Vospominaniia byvshego sekretaria Stalina*. Pp. 7–234 in *Tainy istorii*. Moscow: Terra, 1997.

Bedford, C. Harold. *The Seeker: D. S. Merezhkovsky*. Lawrence: University Press of Kansas, 1975.

Besedovskii, Grigorii. *Na putiakh k termidoru*. 1930. Rpt. Moscow: Sovremennik, 1997.

Bilstein, Roger E., et al. "History of Flight." *Encyclopedia Britannica*. Accessed May 20, 2019 <https://www .britannica.com/technology/history-of-flight>.

"Blériot XI." Wikipedia. Accessed May 20, 2019 <https://en.wikipedia.org/wiki/Blériot_XI>.

Blobaum, Robert. *A Minor Apocalypse: Warsaw during the First World War*. Ithaca, NY: Cornell University Press, 2017.

Boldyrev, V. G. *Direktoriia. Kolchak. Interventy. Vospominaniia (Iz tsikla "Shest' let" 1917–1922 gg.)*. Ed. V. D. Vegman. Novonikolaevsk: Sibkraiizdat, 1925. Accessed September 6, 2020 <https://www.prlib.ru/item/407577>.

Bonsal, Stephen. *Suitors and Suppliants: The Little Nations at Versailles*. New York: Prentice Hall, 1946.

Boris Savinkov na Lubianke. Dokumenty. Ed. A. L. Litvin. Moscow: Rosspen, 2001.

Boris Savinkov pered voennoi kollegiei verkhovnogo suda S. S. S. R. Polnyi otchet po stennogramme suda. Ed. I. Shubin. Moscow: Litizdat NKID, 1924.

"Boris Viktorovich Savinkov" [photograph and note]. *Niva*, no. 17 (1917): 253.

Borisov, A. V. "Avksent'ev, Nikolai Dmitrievich." *Bol'shaia rossiiskaia entsiklopediia*. Accessed June 17, 2019 <https://bigenc.ru/domestic_history/text/1430047>.

Borisova, L. V. *Trudovye otnosheniia v sovetskoi Rossii (1918–1924 gg.)*. Moscow: Sobranie, 2006.

Broido, Eva. *Memoirs of a Revolutionary*. Trans., ed. Vera Broido. London: Oxford University Press, 1967.

Bromberger, Laurent. "Libion, premier 'prototype' du patron de brasserie Parisienne." Accessed February 23, 2015 <https://www.paris-bistro.com/univers/cafes-et-histoire/libion-patron-de-brasserie-parisienne>.

"Brusilovskii proryv." Wikipedia. Accessed December 15, 2017 <https://ru.wikipedia.org/wiki /Брусиловский_прорыв>.

B. S-t. [Boris Savinkov]. "V sumerkakh. Eskiz." *Revoliutsionnaia Rossiia* 35 (November 1903): 6–9.

Bunin, Ivan. *Novye materialy, Vypusk III, ". . . Kogda perepisyvaiutsia blizkie liudi" Pis'ma I. A. Bunina, et al.* Moscow: Russkii put', 2014.

Burtsev, Vladimir. "Azef i Gen. Gerasimov." *Novyi zhurnal* 63 (March 1961): 204–221.

———. "Kak ia razoblachil Azefa. Iz vospominanii." Pp. 173–285 in *Provokator: Vospominaniia i dokumenty o razoblachenii Azefa.* Ed. P. E. Shchegolev, 1929. Rpt. Leningrad: SPRU Fond vozrozhdeniia Leningrada, 1991.

———. "Nyneshnim zashchitnikam Savinkova." *Tri brata (To, chto bylo).* Ed., preface, notes by K. N. Morozov and A. Iu. Morozova. Moscow: Novyi khronograph, 2019, 934–935.

———. "Pechal'nyi konets B. V. Savinkova." *Byloe II* (Novaia seriia), kniga 47 (1933): 40–55.

"Burtsev, Vladimir L'vovich." Accessed May 21, 2019 <https://ru.wikipedia.org/w/index.php?title =Бурцев,_Владимир_Львович&stable=1>.

Bushkovitch, Paul. *A Concise History of Russia.* New York: Cambridge University Press, 2012.

Bushnell, John. "Russian Peasants and Soldiers during World War I: Home and Front Interacting." *Russian Studies in History* 56, no. 2 (2017): 65–72. Accessed May 20, 2020 <http://www.tandfonline.com/doi/full/10.1 080/10611983.2017.1372983>.

B-v. [Boris Savinkov]. "Peterburgskoe dvizhenie i prakticheskie zadachi sotsialdemokratov." *Rabochee delo,* no. 6 (April 1900): 28–42.

"Chaikovskii, Nikolai Vasil'evich." Wikipedia. Accessed October 14, 2018 <https://ru.wikipedia.org/wiki /Чайковский,_Николай_Васильевич>.

Chaikovskii, Nikolai. "Sofia Aleksandrovna Savinkova (Vmesto nekrologa)." *Posledniia novosti/ Dernières nouvelles,* no. 906 (April 4, 1923).

Chernov, Viktor M. *Pered burei.* 1953. Rpt. Moscow: Mezhdunarodnoe otnoshenie, 1993.

Chuikina, Sofia. Editor. "Interv'iu s Lidiei Aleksandrovnoi Uspenskoi (1906 g. r. urozhdennoi Miagkovoi)." *Ab Imperio,* no. 1 (2004): 309–356.

Churchill, Winston S. *Churchill by Himself: In His Own Words.* Ed. Richard M. Longworth. E-version, RosettaBooks, 2013.

———. *Great Contemporaries.* New York: Putnam's, 1937.

Combs, Jerald A. *The History of American Foreign Policy from 1895, Volume 2,* 3rd ed. New York: Routledge, 2017.

Conquest, Robert. *The Harvest of Sorrow: Soviet Collectivization and the Terror-Famine.* New York: Oxford University Press, 1986.

Cook, Andrew. *Ace of Spies: The True Story of Sidney Reilly.* Stroud, Gloucestershire: History Press, 2002.

Dabrowski, Patrice M. *Poland: The First Thousand Years.* DeKalb: Northern Illinois University Press, 2014.

Dan, Lydia. "Lydia Dan." Pp. 46–213 in *The Making of Three Russian Revolutionaries: Voices from the Menshevik Past.* Ed. Leopold Haimson et al. Cambridge: Cambridge University Press and Paris: Éditions de la maison des sciences de l'homme, 1987.

"Daniil Aleksandrovič Amfiteatrov." *Russi in Italia: Dizionario.* Accessed February 11, 2019 <http://www .russinitalia.it/dettaglio.php?id=189>.

Davydov, Iurii. "Savinkov Boris Viktorovich, on zhe V. Ropshin. Beglye zametki vmesto akademicheskogo predisloviia." Pp. 3–18 in Boris Savinkov, *Izbrannoe.* Leningrad: Khudozestvennaia literatura, 1990.

Delo Borisa Savinkova, So stat'ei B. Savinkova "Pochemu ia priznal sovetskuiu vlast'." Moscow: Gosudarstvennoe izdatel'stvo, 1924.

Denikin, Anton. *Ocherki russkoi smuty.* Five volumes, 1921–1926. Rpt. Moscow: Nauka, 1991.

———. "Soveshchanie v Stavke 16 iulia ministrov i glavnokomanduiushchikh." Vol. 1, chap. 33. Accessed September 5, 2020 <http://militera.lib.ru/memo/russian/denikin_ai2/1_33.html>.

———. "Vystuplenie generala Kornilova [. . .]." Vol. 2, chap. 6. Accessed September 5, 2020 <http://militera.lib.ru /memo/russian/denikin_ai2/2_06.html>.

———. "'Moskovskii tsentr' [. . .]." Vol. 2, chap. 16. Accessed September 5, 2020 <http://militera.lib.ru/h/denikin _ai2/2_16.html>.

———. "Smert' Generala Kornilova." Vol. 2, chap. 26. Accessed September 5, 2020 <http://militera.lib.ru/h/denikin _ai2/2_26.html>.

————. "Vneshniaia politika pravitel'stva Iuga. Parizhskoe voennoe i politicheskoe predstavitel'stvo. 'Russkii vopros.'" Vol. 4, chap. 25. Accessed September 5, 2020 <http://rushist.com/index.php/denikin -4/843-osoboe-soveshchanie-denikina-vneshnyaya-politika>.

————. "Nastuplenie VSIuR letom i osen'iu 1919 goda [. . .]." Vol. 5, chap. 4. Accessed September 5, 2020 <http ://militera.lib.ru/memo/russian/denikin_ai2/5_04.html>.

Department of the Army. *U.S. Army Combat Stress Control Handbook.* Rpt. Guilford, CT: Lyons Press, 2003.

"Dikgof, Liubov' Efimovna." Wikipedia. Accessed June 16, 2018 <https://ru.wikipedia.org/wiki/Дикгоф ,_Любовь_Ефимовна>.

"Dikgof-Derental', Aleksandr Arkad'evich." Wikipedia. Accessed June 16, 2018 <https://ru.wikipedia.org/wiki /Дикгоф-Дереталь,_Александр_Аркадьевич>.

Dikgof-Derental', L. E. "Dnevnik L. E. Dikgof-Derental'. Predislovie B. Savinkova." Pp. 197–219 in *Boris Savinkov na Lubianke. Dokumenty.* Ed. A. L. Litvin. Moscow: Rosspen, 2001.

"Dmitrii Merezhkovskii. Biografiia," *Merezhkovskii, Dmitrii Sergeevich.* Accessed September 10, 2020 <https ://merezhkovsky.ru/biography>.

"Dmitry Merezhkovsky." Wikipedia. Accessed September 10, 2020 <https://en.wikipedia.org/wiki/Dmitry _Merezhkovsky>.

"Doklad A. P. Fedorova o 8-i komandirovke za rubezh." Pp. 362–377 in *Boris Savinkov na Lubianke. Dokumenty.* Ed. A. L. Litvin. Moscow: Rosspen, 2001.

"Doklad A. P. Fedorova o desiatoi komandirovke za rubezh Moskva—Varshava—Parizh." Pp. 378–384 in *Boris Savinkov na Lubianke. Dokumenty.* Ed. A. L. Litvin. Moscow: Rosspen, 2001.

Dolgopolov, Leonid. *Na rubezhe vekov: O russkoi literature kontsa XIX—nachala XX veka.* Leningrad: Sovetskii pisatel', 1977.

"Dom Soiuzov." Accessed March 5, 2019 <http://domsojuzov.ru>.

Dopros Kolchaka [Stenogrammy]. "Zasedaniia chrezvychainoi sledstvennoi komissii," 30-go ianvaria 1920 g.; 6-go fevralia 1920 g. Leningrad: Gosudarstvennoe izdatel'stvo, 1925. Accessed September 6, 2020 <http://militera.lib.ru/db/kolchak/index.html>.

Duranty, Walter. "Death Penalty for Savinkoff." *Los Angeles Times*, August 30, 1924, 4.

————. "Soviet Spares Life of Gen. Savinkoff." *New York Times*, August 30, 1924, 1–2.

Eberle, Christopher J. *Justice and the Just War Tradition: Human Worth, Moral Formation, and Armed Conflict.* New York: Routledge, 2016.

Engelstein, Laura. *Russia in Flames: War, Revolution, Civil War, 1914–1921.* New York: Oxford University Press, 2018.

Erenburg [Ehrenburg], Il'ia. *Liudi, gody, zhizn'. Vospominaniia v trekh tomakh. Izdanie ispravlennoe i dopolnennoe.* Vol. 1. Moscow: Sovetskii pisatel', 1990.

"Erenburg, Il'ia Grigor'evich." Wikipedia. Accessed May 27, 2019 <https://ru.wikipedia.org/wiki/Эренбург ,_Илья_Григорьевич>.

Ermolin, Evgenii. "Iaroslavskoe vosstanie predlozhilo al'ternativu." *Regnum.* July 6, 2018. Accessed June 14, 2019 <https://regnum.ru/news/innovatio/2444058.html>.

Erofeev, N. D. "Predislovie." *Partiia sotsialistov-revoliutsionerov. Dokumenty i materialy. Tom 1, 1900–1907.* Ed. O. V. Volobuev et al. Moscow: Rosspen, 1996.

Fediuk, Vladimir P. "Boris Savinkov v vologodskoi ssylke." Pp. 125–133 in *Demidovskii vremennik.* Iaroslav': IarGU, 2013. Accessed February 12, 2019 <http://www.docme.ru/doc/1138698/1421.demidovskij-vremennik>.

Fifield, William. *Modigliani.* New York: William Morrow, 1976.

Figner, Vera. *Izbrannye proizvedeniia v trekh tomakh. Zapechatlennyi trud. Tom tretii.* Moscow: Izdatel'stvo vsesoiuznogo obshchestva politkatorzhan i ssyl'no-poselentsev, 1933.

Fischer, Ben B. *Okhrana: The Paris Operations of the Russian Imperial Police.* Langley, VA: Central Intelligence Agency, 1997.

Fitzpatrick, Sheila. *The Russian Revolution.* 2nd ed. New York: Oxford University Press, 1994.

Fleishman, Lazar'. *V tiskakh provokatsii: Operatsiia "trest" i russkaia zarubezhnaia pechat'.* Moscow: NLO, 2003.

"Flight Airspeed Record." Wikipedia. Accessed September 10, 2020 <https://en.wikipedia.org/wiki/Flight _airspeed_record>.

"Fondaminskii, Il'ia Isidorovich." Wikipedia. Accessed March 20, 2019 <https://ru.wikipedia.org/wiki /Фондаминский,_Илья_Исидорович>.

Frezenskii, Boris. *Nash zhestokii XX vek. Stranitsy istorii i kul'tury*. Moscow: AGRAF, 2016.

"Fyodor Stepun." Wikipedia. Accessed May 29, 2019 <https://en.wikipedia.org/wiki/Fyodor_Stepun>.

Gal, Reuven. *A Portrait of the Israeli Soldier*. New York: Greenwood, 1986.

Geifman, Anna. *Entangled in Terror. The Azef Affair and the Russian Revolution*. Wilmington, DE: SR Books, 2000.

———. *Thou Shalt Kill: Revolutionary Terrorism in Russia, 1894–1917*. Princeton, NJ: Princeton University Press, 1993.

"Genoa Conference (1922)." Wikipedia. Accessed September 28, 2020 <https://en.wikipedia.org/wiki/Genoa _Conference_(1922)>.

Gerasimov, A. V. *Na lezvii s terroristami*. [Originally published in French and German in 1934; Russian translation first published in 1985]. Rpt.: *"Okhranka": Vospominaniia rukovoditelei politicheskogo syska*, Vol. 1. Ed. Z. I Peregudova. Moscow: NLO, 2004, 141–342.

"Geules cassées." Wikipedia. Accessed September 14, 2020 <https://en.wikipedia.org/wiki/Gueules_casséees>.

Gippius, Zinaida. *Dmitrii Merezhkovskii*. Part 2, chapter 6. Paris: YMCA, 1951. Accessed September 6, 2020 <http://www.e-reading.by/chapter.php/96817/90/zhizn-i-tvorchestvo-dmitriya-merezhkovskogo.html>.

———. *Dnevniki*. Two vol. Moscow: Intelvak, 1999.

———. "Savinkov." Pp. 83–92 in *Laskovaia kobra. Svoia i bozh'ia*. Moscow: AST, 2015. Accessed September 7, 2020 <https://www.litres.ru/zinaida-gippius/laskovaya-kobra-svoya-i-bozhya>.

Gladkov, Teodor. *Artuzov*. Moscow: Molodaia gvardiia, 2008.

Goldovskii, O. "Evrei v Moskve." *Byloe*, September 1907, 153–168.

Golinkov, David. *Tainye operatsii VChK*. Algoritm-Kniga: Moskva, 2008.

Goncharova, E. I. "Revoliutsionnoe khristovstvo." Pp. 5–88 in *Revoliutsionnoe khristovstvo. Pis'ma Merezhkovskikh k Borisu Savinkovu*. Ed., intro., commentary, E. I. Goncharova. Saint Petersburg: Pushkinskii dom, 2009.

Gopper, K. "Iz vospominanii Tveritskogo uchastka oborony Iaroslavlia generala K. Goppera 'Chetyre katastrofy'." Iaroslavskoe vosstanie, 1918, Belye o Iaroslavskom vosstanii, doc. 2. *Fond Aleksandra N. Yakovleva*. Accessed August 29, 2020 <https://www.alexanderyakovlev.org/fond/1ssues-doc/64701>.

Gorbunov, Mark. "Savinkov, kak memuarist." *Katorga i ssylka*, part 1, no. 40 (1928): 168–185; part 2, no. 41 (1928): 163–172; part 3, no. 42 (1928): 168–180.

Gorodnitskii, R. A. *Boevaia organizatsiia partii sotsialistov-revoliutsionerov v 1910–1911 gg*. Moscow: Rosspen, 1998.

———. "B. V. Savinkov i sudebno-sledstvennaia komissiia po delu Azefa." Pp. 198–242 in *Minuvshee: Istoricheskii al'manakh* 18. Moscow-Saint Petersburg: Atheneum-Feniks, 1995.

———. "Tri stila rukovodstva organizatsiei partii sotsialistov-revoliutsionerov: Gershuni, Azef, Savinkov." Pp. 52–64 in *Individual'nyi politicheskii terror v Rossii, XIX—nachalo XX v*. Ed. B. Iu. Ivanova et al. Moscow: Memorial, 1996.

"Gots, Mikhail." *Elektronnaia evreiskaia entsiklopediia*. Accessed October 19, 2015 <http://www.eleven.co.il /article/11291>.

Gourko, General Basil. *War and Revolution in Russia 1914–1917*. New York: Macmillan, 1919.

Gul', Roman. Chapter 15, "Terror na terror." *Dzerzhinskii*. 2nd edition. 1974. Accessed July 27, 2020 <https://e-libra.me/read/320526-dzerzhinskiy-nachalo-terrora.html>.

Gusev, Kirill V. *Rytsari terrora*. Moscow: Luch, 1992.

Heller, Michel. "Krasin-Savinkov: Une rencontre secrète." *Cahiers du Monde russe et soviétique* 26, no. 1 (1985): 63–67.

Hidden Springs of the Russian Revolution: Personal Memoirs of Katerina Breshkovskaia. Ed. Lincoln Hutchinson. Stanford, CA: Stanford University Press, 1931.

Hingley, Ronald. *The Russian Secret Police. Muscovite, Imperial Russian, and Soviet Political Security Operations, 1565–1970*. London: Hutchinson, 1970.

Hosking, Geoffrey. *Rulers and Victims: The Russians in the Soviet Union*. Cambridge, MA: Harvard University Press, 2006.

Hughes, Michael. "Lockhart, Sir Robert Hamilton Bruce." *Oxford Dictionary of National Biography.* Accessed
    June 10, 2019 <https://doi.org/10.1093/ref:odnb/34578>.
Ianovskii, Vasilii S. *Polia eliseiskie. Kniga pamiati.* Saint Petersburg: Pushkinskii fond, 1993.
"Iaroslavskoe vosstanie. Material'nyi ushcherb." Wikipedia. Accessed June 13, 2019 <https://ru.wikipedia.org
    /wiki/Ярославское_восстание#Материальный_ущерб>.
Iarutskii, Lev. "Vdova Borisa Savinkova zhila i umerla v Mariupole," parts 1–4, December 19 and 22, 2011. *Staryi
    Mariupol.* Accessed June 20, 2018 <http://old-mariupol.com.ua/vdova-borisa-savinkova-zhila-i-umerla
    -v-mariupole-1>, <http://old-mariupol.com.ua/vdova-borisa-savinkova-zhila-i-umerla-v-mariupole-2>,
    <http://old-mariupol.com.ua/vdova-borisa-savinkova-zhila-i-umerla-v-mariupole-6>, <http://old
    -mariupol.com.ua/vdova-borisa-savinkova-zhila-i-umerla-v-mariupole-7>.
Il'in, Pavel, and Mikaella Kagan. "Moskva na perelome stoletii." Pp. 19–63 in Pavel Il'in and Bler Rubl, Eds.
    Moskva rubezha XIX i XX stoletii. Vzgliad v proshloe iz daleka. Moscow: Rosspen, 2014.
"Ilya Ehrenburg." Wikipedia. Accessed May 29, 2019 <https://en.wikipedia.org/wiki/Ilya_Ehrenburg>.
Iskhakova, O. A. "Delo Azefa," *Entsiklopediia "Petr Arkad'evich Stolypin."* Fond izucheniia naslediia
    P. A. Stolypina. Accessed May 22, 2019 <http://www.stolypin.ru/proekty-fonda/entsiklopediya-petr
    -arkadevich-stolypin/?ELEMENT_ID=304>.
Istoriia vologodskogo kraia XX nachalo XXI veka. Ed. M. A. Beznin. Vologda: GOU VPO, 2006.
"Iudenich, Nikolai Nikolaevich." Wikipedia. Accessed September 14, 2020 <https://ru.wikipedia.org/wiki
    /Юденич,_Николай_Николаевич>.
"Iurii Alekseevich Shirinskii-Shikhmatov." *Traditsiia, Russkaia entsiklopediia.* Accessed April 26, 2019
    <https://traditio.wiki/Юрий_Алексеевич_Ширинский-Шихматов>.
Ivanovskaia, Praskov'ia. *V boevoi organizatsii.* 1928. Rpt. *Zhenshchiny-terroristki v Rossii.* Ed. O. V. Budnitskii.
    Rostov-na-Donu: Feniks, 1996, 29–173.
"Iz pokazanii polkovnika S. Pavlovskogo." Pp. 283–299 in *Boris Savinkov na Lubianke. Dokumenty.* Moscow:
    Rosspen, 2001.
"Iz pokazanii S. N. Sletova (Zemliakova) Sudebno-Sledstvennoi Komissii pri TsK PSR po delu Azefa." Pp.
    138–149 in *Partiia Sotsialistov-Revoliutsionerov. Dokumenty i materialy. Tom 1, 1900–1907 gg.* Ed. N. D.
    Erofeev. Moscow: Rosspen, 1996.
"Iz politicheskogo obzora VGZhU za 1904 g. ssylnykh v Vologodskoi gubernii—svedeniia o prebyvanii,"
    dokument no. 286. "Vologodskaia politicheskaia ssylka." *Staraia Vologda.* Vologodskii gosudarstvennyi
    istoriko-arkhitekturnyi i khudozhestvennyi muzei-zapovednik. Accessed October 11, 2015
    <https://www.booksite.ru/fulltext/sta/raya/vol/ogda/13.htm#322>.
"Iz sekretnykh dokumentov. Po delu Sazonova." *Sotsialist-Revoliutsioner,* no. 1 (1910): 51–68.
"Iz zhurnala zasedaniia Vremennogo pravitel'stva No. 132 ob uchrezhdenii dolzhnostei voennykh komissarov pri
    glavnokomanduiushchikh armiiami fronta i ikh funktsiiakh 13.07.1917." *Al'manakh "Rossiia. XX vek."*
    Doc. no. 11. Accessed December 13, 2017 <https://www.alexanderyakovlev.org/almanah/inside
    /almanah-doc/75995>.
"Iz zhurnala zasedaniia Vremennogo pravitel'stva No. 139 ob obrashchenii k naseleniiu Rossii, 23.07.1917."
    Al'manakh "Rossiia. XX vek." Doc. no. 17. Accessed September 12, 2020 <https://www
    .alexanderyakovlev.org/almanah/inside/almanah-doc/76011>.
Jeffreys-Jones, Rhodri. "W. Somerset Maugham: Anglo-American Agent in Revolutionary Russia." *American
    Quarterly* 28, no. 1 (1976): 90–106.
Jones, Simon. "The Right Medicine for the Bolshevist: British Air-Dropped Chemical Weapons in North Russia,
    1919." *Imperial War Museum Review,* no. 12 (1999): 78–88.
Judge, Edward H. *Plehve. Repression and Reform in Imperial Russia, 1902–1904.* Syracuse, NY: Syracuse University
    Press, 1983.
Kaliaev, Ivan. "U podnozhiia Kresta." P. 74 n. 102 in *Nasledie Ariadny Vladimirovny Tyrkovoi. Dnevniki. Pis'ma.*
    Ed. N. I Kanishchev. Moscow, 2012. Accessed July 26, 2015 <http://doc20vek.ru/node/2688>.
Kanin, V. [Boris Savinkov]. "Noch'." *Kur'ier,* no. 245 (September 5, 1902).
Kaplan, Eran. *The Jewish Radical Right: Revisionist Zionism and Its Ideological Legacy.* Madison: University of
    Wisconsin Press, 2005.

Kara-Murza, Sergei. *Sovetskaia tsivilizatsiia*. Vol. 1. Chap. 4, "Sozdanie sovetskogo gosudarstva v pervyi period posle Oktiabr'skoi Revoliutsii." Accessed September 6, 2020 <http://www.patriotica.ru/books/sov_civ1 /s1-04.html>.

Kassow, Samuel D. *Students, Professors, and the State in Tsarist Russia*. Berkeley: University of California Press, 1989.

Kelly, Catriona. *Children's World: Growing up in Russia, 1890–1991*. New Haven, CT: Yale University Press, 2007.

Kenez, Peter. *Civil War in South Russia, 1918*. Berkeley: University of California Press, 1971.

———. *Civil War in South Russia, 1919–1920*. Berkeley: University of California Press, 1977.

Kennan, George. *Soviet-American Relations, 1917–1920. Vol. II. The Decision to Intervene*. Princeton, NJ: Princeton University Press, 1958.

Kerenskii, Aleksandr. *Delo Kornilova*. Moscow: Zadruga, 1918.

———. "Gatchina." *Izdaleka*. Paris, 1922. Accessed September 12, 2020 <http://gatchina3000.ru/literatura /kerenski_a_f/kerenski_gatchina3.htm>.

Kerensky, Alexander. *Russia and History's Turning Point*. New York: Duell, Sloan, and Pearce, 1965.

Kettle, Michael. *Sidney Reilly: The True Story of the World's Greatest Spy*. New York: St. Martin's Press, 1983.

Khairetdinov, Kharis. "Pervaia otsedka: Pol'skaia kar'era Borisa Savinkova." *Rodina*, no. 12 (1994): 112–113.

Khandorin, Vladimir. *Admiral Kolchak: Pravda i mify*. Tomsk, Russia: Tomskii gosudarstvennyi universitet, 2007. Accessed September 6, 2020 <http://kolchak.sitecity.ru/stext_1811043519.phtml>.

Kichkasov, N. *Belogvardeiskii terror protiv SSSR*. Moscow: Litizdata Narodnogo Komissariata po Inostrannym Delam, 1928.

Kidiarov, Aleksei E. "Iaroslavskii miatezh 1918 g. i pravoslavnaia tserkov'." *II Romanovskie chteniia. Tsentr i provintsiia v sisteme rossiiskoi gosudarstvennosti. Kostroma, 26–27 marta 2009 goda*. Ed. A. M. Belov and A. V. Novikov. Kostroma, Russia: KGU im. N. A. Nekrasova, 2009. Accessed September 6, 2020 <http://www.hrono.ru/proekty/romanov/2rc27.php>.

———. "Rybinskoe vosstanie 1918 g." *Vestnik kostromskogo gosudarstvennogo universiteta*, no. 5 (2015): 29–32.

Klement'ev, Vasilii. *V bolshevitskoi Moskve: (1918–1920)*. Moscow: Russkii put', 1998. Accessed September 6, 2020 <https://www.sakharov-center.ru/asfcd/auth/?t=page&num=5779>.

Knight, Amy. "Female Terrorists in the Russian Socialist Revolutionary Party." *Russian Review* 38, no. 2 (1979): 139–159.

Knox, Major-General Sir Alfred. *With the Russian Army 1914–1917. Being Chiefly Extracts from the Diary of a Military Attache*. Vol. II. London: Hutchinson, 1921.

Kotkin, Stephen. *Stalin: Volume I, Paradoxes of Power, 1878–1928*. New York: Penguin, 2014.

"Ko vsem grazhdanam tsivilizovannogo mira," Letuchii listok "Revoliutsionnoi Rossii," no. 4, July 28, 1904. Pp. 155-157 in *Partiia Sotsialistov-Revoliutsionerov. Dokumenty i materialy. Tom 1, 1900–1907 gg*. Moscow: Rosspen, 1996.

"Ko vsemu russkomu krest'ianstvu," Letuchii listok "Revoliutsionnoi Rossii," no. 4, July 28, 1904. Pp. 153-155 in *Partiia Sotsialistov-Revoliutsionerov. Dokumenty i materialy. Tom 1, 1900–1907 gg*. Moscow: Rosspen, 1996.

Lancaster, James R. "Churchill's French." International Churchill Society. Accessed September 28, 2018 <https ://winstonchurchill.org/publications/finest-hour/finest-hour-138/churchills-french>.

Lebedev, Vladimir. *Iz riadov frantsuzskoi armii. Russkie volontery vo Frantsii. Ocherki frantsuzskogo fronta i tyla. V Makedonii*. Moscow: Sabashnikov, 1916. Accessed April 10, 2019 <http://elib.shpl.ru/ru/nodes/32191#page /1/mode/grid/zoom/1>.

———. "Konets Savinkova." *Volia Rossii* [Prague], September 14–15, 1924: 164–189.

Levitskii, V. [V. Tsederbaum]. *Za chetvert' veka. Revoliutsionnye vospominaniia 1892–1917 gg. Tom 1. Chast' vtoraia*. Moscow: Gosudarstvennoe izdatel'stvo, 1927.

Levitskii, V. O. "A. D. Pokotilov." *Katorga i ssylka* 2 (1922): 157–172.

Liberman, Semen. *Dela i liudi (Na sovetskoi stroike)*. Chap. 10, "Narodnyi komissar Krasin." Biblioteka elektronnoi literatury. Accessed September 6, 2020 <http://litresp.ru/chitat/ru/%D0%9B/liberman-semen/dela -i-lyudina-sovestkoj-strojke>.

A Lifelong Passion: Nicholas and Alexandra: Their Own Story. Ed. Andrey Maylunas and Sergey Mironenko. London: Weidenfeld and Nicolson, 1996.

The Little Grandmother of the Russian Revolution: Reminiscences and Letters of Catherine Breshkovsky. Ed. Alice Stone Blackwell. Boston: Little, Brown, 1917.

Litvin, A. L., and Mogil'ner, M. "Boris Savinkov v istoricheskoi literature i dokumentakh." Pp. 33–52 in *Boris Savinkov na Lubianke. Dokumenty*. Ed. A. L. Litvin. Moscow: Rosspen, 2001.

Lockhart, Robin Bruce. *Ace of Spies*. New York: Stein and Day, 1968.

Lockhart, R. H. Bruce. *Memoirs of a British Agent*. 1932. Rpt. London: Macmillan, 1974.

"Lopukhin, Aleksei Aleksandrovich." Wikipedia. Accessed May 22, 2019 <https://ru.wikipedia.org/wiki /Лопухин,_Алексей_Александрович_(1864)>.

Lunacharskii, Anatolii. "Artist avantiury." Pp. 138–145 in *Delo Borisa Savinkova, So stat'ei B. Savinkova "Pochemu ia priznal sovetskuiu vlast'."* Moscow: Gosudarstvennoe izdatel'stvo, 1924.

———. *Byvshie liudi: Ocherk istorii partii es-erov*. Moscow: Gosudarstvennoe izdatel'stvo, 1922.

Lur'e, Feliks. *Khraniteli proshlogo. Zhurnal "Byloe": Istoriia, redaktory, izdateli*. Leningrad: Lenizdat, 1990.

Lyttelton, Adrian. *The Seizure of Power: Fascism in Italy, 1919–1929*. 3rd ed. New York: Routledge, 2004.

MacMillan, Margaret. *Paris 1919: Six Months That Changed the World*. New York: Random House, 2001.

———. *The War that Ended Peace: The Road to 1914*. New York: Random House, 2013.

Marnham, Patrick. *Dreaming with His Eyes Open: A Life of Diego Rivera*. New York: Knopf, 1998.

Martynov, A. P. *Moia sluzhba v Otdel'nom korpuse zhandarmov*. 1972. Rpt. *"Okhranka": Vospominaniia rukovoditelei politicheskogo syska*. Vol. 1. Moscow: NLO, 2004, 27–408.

Masaryk, Thomas G. *The Making of a State: Memories and Observations, 1914–1918*. Trans. Henry W. Steed. New York: Frederick A. Stokes, 1927.

Matich, Olga. *Erotic Utopia: The Decadent Imagination in Russia's Fin-de-siècle*. Madison: University of Wisconsin Press, 2005.

Maugham, W. Somerset. *A Traveler in Romance. Uncollected Writings 1901–1964*. Ed. John Whitehead. London: Anthony Blond, 1984.

———. *A Writer's Notebook*. New York: Doubleday, 1949.

Meilunas, Andrei, and Sergei Mironenko. *Nikolai i Aleksandra: Liubov' i zhizn'*. Trans. S. Zhitomirskii. Moscow: Progress, 1998.

Merriman, John. *A History of Modern Europe*. Vol. II. 2nd ed. New York: Norton, 2004.

Meyers, Jeffrey. *Somerset Maugham: A Life*. New York: Knopf, 2004.

Miliukov, Pavel N. *Istoriia vtoroi russkoi revoliutsii*. Saint Petersburg: Piter, 2014 [e-scan, no pagination]. Accessed March 21, 2018 <http://litresp.ru/chitat/ru/%D0%9C/milyukov-pavel-nikolaevich/istoriya-vtoroj -russkoj-revolyucii>.

Milton, Giles. *Russian Roulette: A Deadly Game: How British Spies Thwarted Lenin's Global Plot*. London: Sceptre, 2013.

Mogil'ner, Marina. *Mifologiia "Podpol'nogo cheloveka": Radikal'nyi mikrokosm v Rossii nachala XX veka kak predmet semioticheskogo analiza*. Moscow: NLO, 1999.

"'Moi trud ne prineset mne nichego, krome goria.' Iz perepiski B. V. Savinkova.'" Ed. Valerii Savin. Photographs ed. Lidiia Petrusheva. *Istochnik, Dokumenty russkoi istorii*, no. 4 (1995): 4–32.

Morozov, Konstantin N. "B. V. Savinkov i Boevaia organizatsiia PSR v 1909–1911." Pp. 243–414 in *Minuvshee: Istoricheskii al'manakh* 18. Moscow-Saint Petersburg: Atheneum-Feniks, 1995.

———. *Partiia sotsialistov-revoliutsionerov v 1907–1914 gg*. Moscow: Rosspen, 1998.

———. "Poiski otvetov na 'prokliatye voprosy' etiki i bogoiskatel'stva v eserovskoi srede v mezhrevoliutsionnyi period (iiun' 1907g.—fevral' 1917g.)." *Internet-zhurnal "Makhaon,"* no. 2 (March–April 1999): [no pagination]. Accessed May 22, 2019 <http://krotov.info/history/20/1900/1907moro.html>.

Morozov, Konstantin N., and Alla Iu. Morozova, ed. intro., commentary. *Tri brata (To, chto bylo). Sbornik dokumentov*. Moscow: Novyi khronograf, 2019.

Morrissey, Susan K. *Heralds of Revolution: Russian Students and the Mythologies of Radicalism*. Oxford: Oxford University Press, 1998.

Mozokhin, Oleg, and Teodor Gladkov. *Menzhinskii. Intelligent s Lubianki*. Moscow: Iauza, Eksmo, 2005.

"M. P. Artsybashev, Pis'ma Borisu Savinkovu." Ed. D. I. Zubarev. *de visu*, 4, no. 5 (1993): 49–69.

"Mussolini, Benito." *Shoa Resource Center*. Accessed January 2, 2019 <https://www.yadvashem.org/odot_pdf /Microsoft%20Word%20-%206478.pdf>.

Nabokoff, Constantine. *The Ordeal of a Diplomat*. London: Duckworth, 1921.

Nabokov, Vladimir. *The Real Life of Sebastian Knight*. New York: New Directions, 1959.

———. *Speak, Memory*. New York: Vintage, 1989.

———. *Strong Opinions*. New York: McGraw-Hill, 1973.

Newall, Peter. *Ocean Liners*. Barnsley, England: Seaforth, 2018.

Nicholas, Herbert G. "Winston Churchill. Prime Minister of United Kingdom." *Encyclopedia Britannica*. Accessed June 24, 2019 <https://www.britannica.com/biography/Winston-Churchill#ref60589>.

Nicolaievsky, Boris. *Aseff, The Russian Judas*. Trans. George Reavey. London: Hurst & Blackett, 1934.

"Nikolai Yaroshenko." *Tovarishchestvo peredvizhnykh khudozhestvennykh vystavok*. Accessed May 1, 2019 <http://www.tphv-history.ru/persons/Nikolai-Yaroshenko.html>.

N. N. [Boris Savinkov]. "Pompadur bor'by." *Osvobozhdenie*, no. 15 (1903): 260–261.

Noulens, Joseph. *Mon ambassade en Russie soviétique, 1917–1919. Tome seconde*. Paris: Plon, 1933.

Oberuchev, K. M. *Vospominaniia v dvukh chastiakh*. New York: Izdanie Gruppy Pochitatelei Pamiati K. M. Oberucheva, 1930.

"Obvinitel'noe zakliuchenie po delu B. Savinkova." Pp. 79–91 in *Boris Savinkov na Lubianke. Dokumenty*. Ed. A. L. Litvin. Moscow: Rosspen, 2001.

Occleshaw, Michael. *Dances in Deep Shadows. Britain's Clandestine War in Russia, 1917–20*. London: Constable, 2006.

"The Old War Office Building: A History." Accessed September 25, 2019 <https://assets.publishing.service.gov .uk/government/uploads/system/uploads/attachment_data/file/49055/old_war_office_build.pdf>.

Orlov, Vladimir. *Dvoinoi agent: Zapiski russkogo kontrrazvedchika*. Moscow: Sovremennik, 1998.

"O vyiasnenii sviazei I. P. Kaliaeva. 4 aprelia 1905 g." Tsirkuliar departamenta politsii nachal'nikam gubernskikh zhandarmskikh i okhrannykh otdeleneii o vyiasnenii sviazei I. P. Kaliaeva. Dokumenty XX veka. Accessed September 9, 2020 <http://doc20vek.ru/node/217>.

Pamiati Viacheslava Konstantinovicha Pleve. Saint Petersburg: Tip. Ministerstva vnutrennikh del, 1904. Rossiiskaia gosudarstvennaia biblioteka. Accessed September 10, 2020 <http://dlib.rsl.ru/viewer /01003723464#?page=53>.

Pares, Sir Bernard. Review of *Delo Borisa Savinkova*. *The Slavonic Review* 4, no. 12 (March 1926): 760-769.

"Le Paul Lecat." *L'Encyclopédie des Messageries Maritimes*. Accessed August 16, 2018 <http://www.messageries -maritimes.org/paulecat.htm>.

Pavlov, D. B. "Predislovie." Pp. 3–12 in *Pis'ma Azefa: 1893–1917*. Ed. D. B. Pavlov and Z. I. Peregudova. Moscow: Terra, 1994.

Penson, John Hubert. "The Polish Mark in 1921: A Study in External and Internal Values." *Economic Journal* 32, no. 126 (1922): 163–170.

Perkhurov, Aleksandr. *Ispoved' prigovorennogo*. Rybinsk, Russia: Rybinskoe podvor'e, 1990.

"Pilliar, Roman Aleksandrovich." Wikipedia. Accessed September 16, 2020 <https://ru.wikipedia.org/wiki /Пилляр,_Роман_Александрович>.

Pipes, Richard. *Russia under the Old Regime*. New York: Scribner's, 1974.

———. *The Russian Revolution*. New York: Knopf, 1990.

Pis'ma Azefa. 1893–1917. Ed. D. B. Pavlov et al. Moscow: Terra, 1994.

"Pis'mo B. V. Savinkova V. N. Figner," July 3, 1907. Pub. R. A. Gorodnitskii and G. S. Kan. Pp. 195–197 in *Minuvshee: Istoricheskii al'manakh* 18. Moscow-Saint Petersburg: Atheneum-Feniks, 1995.

"Pogoda istoricheskikh dat. Kak klimat vliial na razvitie znakovykh sobytii." *Argumenty i fakty*, May 7, 2015. Accessed August 15, 2019 <http://www.spb.aif.ru/society/people/pogoda_istoricheskih_dat_kak _klimat_vliyal_na_razvitie_znakovyh_sobytiy>.

"Pokazaniia A. A. Dikgof-Derentalia." Pp. 385–396 in *Boris Savinkov na Lubianke. Dokumenty*. Ed. A. L. Litvin. Moscow: Rosspen, 2001.

Polian, Pavel. "Emigratsiia: kto i kogda v XX veke pokidal Rossiiu." Pp. 493–519 in *Rossiia i ee regiony v XX veke: Territoriia—rasselenie—migratsiia*. Ed. O. Glezer and P. Polian. Moscow: OGI, 2005. Accessed September 6, 2020 <http://www.demoscope.ru/weekly/2006/0251/analit01.php>.

Politbiuro TsK RKP (b)–VKP (b) Povestki dnia zasedanii. 1919–1952. Katalog v trekh tomakh. Tom 1. 1919–1929. Ed. G. M. Adibekov et al. Moscow: Rosspen, 2000.

Popova, Valentina. "Dinamitnye masterskie 1906–1907 g. g. i provokator Azef." *Katorga i ssylka*, part 1, no. 33, 1927, 53–67; part 2, no. 34, 1927, 47–64; part 3, no. 35, 1927, 54–67.

"Poslednii den' Kaliaeva." By N. N. *Byloe*, no. 5 (May 1906): 186–190.

"Postanovlenie Politburo TsK RPP (b) 'O Savinkove'." September 18, 1924. F. E. Dzerzhinskii—Predsedatel' VChK—OGPU. 1917–1926. Fond Aleksandra N. Yakovleva. Doc. no. 965. Accessed April 12, 2019 <https://www.alexanderyakovlev.org/fond/issues-doc/1019982>.

"Predsedatel' Pravleniia Proletkino—TsK RKP (b) s pros'boi razreshit' Savinkovu napisat' stsenarii fil'ma." May 6, 1925. Fond Aleksandra N. Yakovleva. Doc. no. 87. Accessed April 9, 2019 <https://www.alexanderyakovlev.org/fond/issues-doc/1014383>.

"Prizrak Stavki na staroi ploshchadi." Mogilevskii oblastnoi ispolnitel'nyi Komitet. Accessed February 15, 2018 <http://mogilev-region.gov.by/news/prizrak-stavki-na-staroy-ploshchadi>.

"Prokof'eva, Mariia Alekseevna." Russkaia Italiia. Sait istorika Mikhaila Talaleia. Accessed September 14, 2017 <http://www.italy-russia.com/2014_07/prokofeva-Maria-alekseevna>.

"Protokol doprosa [Borisa Savinkova]." Pp. 64–75 in *Boris Savinkov na Lubianke. Dokumenty*. Ed. A. L. Litvin. Moscow: Rosspen, 2001.

"Protokol doprosa Pavlovskogo Sergeia Eduardovicha." Pp. 328–342 in *Boris Savinkov na Lubianke. Dokumenty*. Ed. A. L. Litvin. Moscow: Rosspen, 2001.

"Protokoly sionskikh mudretsov." *Elektronnaia evreiskaia entsiklopediia*. Accessed July 27, 2016 <http://www.eleven.co.il/article/13337>.

Prutskov, Nikita I. *Gleb Uspensky*. New York: Twayne, 1972.

Pushkarev, Sergei G. *Obzor russkoi istorii*, 1953. Rpt. London, Canada: Zaria, 1987.

"Quelle Mémoire pour les fusillés de 1914–1918? Un point de vue historien." La Mission du Centenaire. Accessed February 8, 2018 <http://centenaire.org/sites/default/files/references-files/rapport_fusilles.pdf>.

Radek, Karl. "To, chto bylo." Pp. 105–108 in *Delo Borisa Savinkova, So stat'ei B. Savinkova "Pochemu ia priznal sovetskuiu vlast'."* Moscow: Gosudarstvennoe izdatel'stvo, 1924.

Radzinskii, Edvard. *Stalin*. Moscow: Vagrius, 1997.

Raeff, Marc. *Russia Abroad: A Cultural History of the Russian Emigration, 1919–1939*. New York: Oxford University Press, 1990.

"Raport V. I. Speranskogo S. V. Puzitskomu ob informatsii, poluchennoi ot A. A. Dikgof-Derentalia." P. 171 in *Boris Savinkov na Lubianke. Dokumenty*. Ed. A. L. Litvin. Moscow: Rosspen, 2001.

Rappaport, Helen. *Caught in the Revolution: Petrograd 1917*. London: Hutchinson, 2016.

Rataev, L. A. "Istoriia predatel'stva Evno Azefa." Pp. 135–172 in *Provokator: Vospominaniia i dokumenty o razoblachenii Azefa*. Ed. P. E. Shchegolev. 1929. Rpt. Leningrad: SPRU Fond vozrozhdeniia Leningrada, 1991.

Ratkovskii, Il'ia S. *Khronika belogo terrora v Rossii. Repressii i samosudy (1917–1920 gg.)*. Moscow: TD Algoritm, 2016.

———. "Vosstanovlenie v Rossii smertnoi kazni na fronte letom 1917 g." *Noveishaia istoriia Rossii/ Modern History of Russia*, no. 12 (2015): 48–58.

Reilly, Sidney [with Pepita Bobadilla]. *Britain's Master Spy*. 1932. *The Adventures of Sidney Reilly*. New York: Carroll and Graf, 1986.

Remizov, Aleksei. *Iveren': Zagoguleny moei pamiati. Sobranie sochinenii, tom vos'moi*. Moscow: Russkaia kniga, 2000. Accessed September 5, 2020 <http://rvb.ru/remizov/ss10/01text/vol_8/02iveren/699.htm>.

———. *Vzvikhrennaia Rus'*. Moscow: Sovetskii pisatel', 1991.

Reswick, William. *I Dreamt Revolution*. Chicago: Henry Regnery, 1952.

Revoliutsionnoe dvizhenie v russkoi armii. 27 fevralia–24 oktiabria 1917 goda. Sbornik dokumentov. Ed. L. S. Gaponenko. Moscow: Nauka, 1968.

Revoliutsionnoe khristovstvo. Pis'ma Merezhkovskikh k Borisu Savinkovu. Ed., intro., commentary E. I. Goncharova. Saint Petersburg: Pushkinksii dom, 2009.

Riasanovsky, Nicholas V. *A History of Russia*. New York: Oxford University Press, 1977.

Riazantsev, Nikolai. "Iaroslavskii miatezh ne byl narodnym vosstaniem." *Regnum*. Accessed July 6, 2018 <https://regnum.ru/news/society/2443610.html>.

Rolland, Jacques-Francis. *L'Homme qui défia Lénine. Boris Savinkov*. Paris: Bernard Grasset, 1989.

Ropshin, V. [Boris Savinkov]. "Iz deistvuiushchei armii (Leto 1917)." Pp. 189–239 in Fedor Stepun, *Iz pisem proporshchika-artillerista*. Moscow: Zadruga, 1918.

———. *Kniga stikhov: Posmertnoe izdanie*. Ed. and intro. Zinaida Gippius. Paris: Rodnik/La source, 1931.

———. *Kon' blednyi*, 1909. Rpt. B. Savinkov. *Kon' blednyi. Kon' voronoi*. Saint Petersburg: Lenizdat, 2013.

———. *Kon' voronoi*, 1923. Rpt. B. Savinkov. *Kon' blednyi. Kon' voronoi*. Saint Petersburg: Lenizdat, 2013.

———. *To, chego ne bylo (Tri brata)*. 1914. Rpt. Boris Savinkov (V. Ropshin). *To, chego ne bylo: Roman, povesti, rasskazy, ocherki, stikhotvoreniia*. Moscow: Sovremennik, 1992.

Russkaia literatura kontsa XIX–nachala XX v. 1908–1917. Ed. B. A. Bialik et al. Moscow: Nauka, 1972.

Russkaia voennaia emigratsiia 20–40kh godov XX veka. Dokumenty i materialy. Tom 1, Tak nachinalos' izgnanie, 1920–1922 gg. Kniga vtoraia, Na chuzhbine. Ed. V. A. Zolotarev et al. Moscow: Geia, 1998.

Ruud, Charles A., and Sergey A. Stepanov. *Fontanka 16. The Tsars' Secret Police*. Montreal: McGill-Queen's University Press, 1999.

Safonov, V. N. "Glavnyi protivnik Bol'shevikov, ili istoriia o tom, kak chekisty poimali Borisa Savinkova." Lib.ru: "Klassika." Accessed September 6, 2020 <http://az.lib.ru/s/sawinkow_b_w/text_0100.shtml>.

"S. Pavlovskii rasskazyvaet." Pp. 299–324 in *Boris Savinkov na Lubianke. Dokumenty*. Ed. A. L. Litvin. Moscow: Rosspen, 2001.

Saul, Norman E. *War and Revolution: The United States and Russia, 1914–1921*. Lawrence: University of Kansas Press, 2001.

Savinkova, Sofia. "Gody skorbi (Vospominaniia materi)." *Byloe*, no. 7 (1906): 215–254.

———. "Na volos ot kazni (Vospominaniia materi)." *Byloe*, no. 1/13 (1907): 247–271.

[Savinkov, Boris]. Anonymous reviews in *Russkoe bogatstvo*: 1902, no. 4, N. Engel'gardt, 71–75, E. Bobrov, 75–77; 1902, no. 6, A. Belyi, 60–61, V. Lebedev, 62, A. Tarasenkov, 63–64; no. 12, P. N. Polevoi, 66–67; 1904, no. 9, V. Il'ich-Svitych, 96–97, V. Rozov-Tsvetkov, 97–98.

———. "Pis'mo B. V. Savinkova V. N. Figner." July 3, 1907. Pub. R. A. Gorodnitskii and G. S. Kan. Pp. 195–197 in *Minuvshee, Istoricheskii al'manakh* 18. Moscow-Saint Petersburg: Atheneum-Feniks, 1995.

Savinkov, Boris. *Bor'ba s bol'shevikami*. Warsaw, 1920. Rpt. *Literatura russkogo zarubezh'ia, Tom Pervyi, kniga vtoraia*. Moscow: Kniga, 1990, 151–175.

———. "Dnevnik Borisa Savinkova." Pp. 179–197 in *Savinkov na Lubianke. Dokumenty*. Ed. A. L. Litvin. Moscow: Rosspen, 2001.

———. "General Kornilov." Pp. 191-210 in *Miatezh Kornilova: Iz belykh memuarov*. Leningrad: Krasnaia gazeta, 1928.

———. "Iz vospominanii ob Ivane Kaliaeve," 1906. Rpt. Boris Savinkov (V. Ropshin), *To, chego ne bylo: Roman, povesti, rasskazy, ocherki, stikhotvoreniia*. Moscow: Sovremennik, 1992, 120–129.

———. *K delu Kornilova*. Paris: Union, 1919. Accessed September 6, 2020 <https://aldebaran.ru/author/ropshin_v/kniga_k_delu_kornilova>.

———. *Kon' blednyi. Kon' voronoi*. Rpt. Saint Petersburg: Lenizdat, 2013.

———. "K vystupleniiu bol'shevikov." *Russkie vedomosti*, November 21, 1917, 2–3. Accessed September 7, 2020 <http://elib.shpl.ru/ru/nodes/40261-255-21-noya#mode/inspect/page/2/zoom/9>.

———. "Nedorazumenie," 1925. Rpt. *To, chego ne bylo*. Ed. D. A. Zhukov. Moscow: Sovremennik, 1992, 630–647.

———. "O 'Soglashateliakh.'" Pp. 43–45 in *Za Rodinu i Svobodu. Na puti k 'tret'ei' Rossii. (Sbornik statei B. V. Savinkova)*. Warsaw: Russkii politicheksii Komitet, 1920.

———. "Poslednie pomeshchiki," 1925. Rpt. *To, chego ne bylo*. Ed. D. A. Zhukov. Moscow: Sovremennik, 1992, 612–629.

———. "Revoliutsionnye siluety. Dora Brilliant." *Znamia truda*, no. 8 (December 1907): 10–11.

———. "Rossiia i Pol'sha." Pp. 29-30 in *Za Rodinu i Svobodu. Na puti k 'tret'ei' Rossii. (Sbornik statei B. V. Savinkova)*. Warsaw: Russkii politicheksii Komitet, 1920.

———. "Russkaia narodnaia dobrovol'cheskaia armiia v pokhode." 1920. Rpt. *Boris Savinkov, Vospominaniia terrorista*. Moscow: Vagrius, 2006, 427–52.

———. "S dorogi!" *Russkie vedomosti*, no. 44 (March 24, 1918). Rpt. Live Journal, Sergei Tsvetkov. Accessed September 7, 2020 <https://www.livejournal.com/media/150419.html>.

———. "Shkol'nye vospominaniia. Iz posmertnykh rukopisei Borisa Savinkova." *Illiustrirovannaia Rossiia/La Russie illustrée* (Paris), part 1, no. 35 (120), August 27, 1927, 1–4; part 2, no. 36 (121), September 3, 1927, 4, 6, 8; part 3, no. 37 (122), September 10, 1927, 8, 10.

———. "Terror i delo Azefa." *Znamia truda*, no. 15 (February 1909): 11–12.

———. [V. Ropshin]. *To, chego ne bylo: Roman, povesti, passkazy, ocherki, stikhotvoreniia.* Ed. D. A. Zhukov. Moscow: Sovremennik, 1992.

———. *Vo Frantsii vo vremia voiny: sentiabr' 1914—iiun' 1915.* 1917–1918. Rpt. Moscow: Gosudarstvennaia publichnaia istoricheskaia biblioteka Rossii, 2008.

———. *Vospominaniia terrorista.* 1905–1909, 1917. Rpt. Moscow: Zebra E, Ast, 2009.

———. "V tiur'me," 1925. Rpt. *To, chego ne bylo.* Ed. D. A. Zhukov. Moscow: Sovremennik, 1992, 648–660.

Savinkov, Sergei. "Da, moi otets byl nastoiashchim russkim . . ." Pp. 185-189 in *Tri brata (To, chto bylo).* Ed., preface, notes by K. N. Morozov and A. Iu. Morozova. Moscow: Novyi khronograph, 2019.

Sazonov, Egor. *Materialy dlia biografii: Vospominaniia, pis'ma, dokumenty, portrety.* Moscow: Golos minuvshego, 1919.

Sergeev, Evgenii. "'Zagovor poslov' protiv Sovetskoi Rossii v 1918 godu: novaia interpretatsiia 'britanskogo sleda.'" *Mezhdunarodnaia zhizn',* [e-journal without pagination] no. 10 (2017). Accessed June 12, 2018 <https://interaffairs.ru/jauthor/material/1927>.

Shapovalova, Alena. "Iashka Koshelek—vor, kotoyi chut' ne ubil Lenina." *Life,* March 28, 2017. Accessed May 14, 2018 <https://life.ru/p/990029>.

Shchegolev, P. E. "Istoricheskii Azef." Pp. 5-12 in *Provokator: Vospominaniia i dokumenty o razoblachenii Azefa.* Ed. P. E. Shchegolev, 1929. Leningrad: SPRU Fond vozrozhdeniia Leningrada, 1991.

Shentalinskii, Vitalii. "Svoi sredi svoikh: Savinkov na Lubianke" [part 1]. *Novyi mir,* no. 7 (1996). Accessed September 5, 2020 <https://magazines.gorky.media/novyi_mi/1996/7/svoj-sredi-svoih.html>.

———. "Svoi sredi svoikh: Savinkov na Lubianke" [part 2]. *Novyi mir,* no. 8 (1996). Accessed September 5, 2020 <https://magazines.gorky.media/novyi_mi/1996/8/svoj-sredi-svoih-2.html>.

Shkol'nik, Mariia. "A Female Socialist Revolutionary Terrorist: The Memoirs of Mariia (Mania) Shkol'nik." Pp. 570–592 in *Everyday Jewish Life in Imperial Russia. Selected Documents [1772–1914].* Ed. ChaeRan Y. Freeze and Jay M. Harris. Waltham, MA: Brandeis University Press, 2013.

"Sidney Reilly: Russian Spy." *Encyclopaedia Britannica.* Accessed June 14, 2018 <https://www.britannica.com /biography/Sidney-George-Reilly>.

Simkin, John. "Alfred Knox." Spartacus Educational. Accessed August 13, 2018 <https://spartacus-educational .com/RUSknox.htm>.

Smirnov, Vice Admiral M. I. *Aleksandr Vasil'evich Kolchak (kratkii biograficheskii ocherk).* 1930. Rpt. *Okrest Kolchaka: dokumenty i materialy.* Ed. Andrey V. Kvakin. Moscow: AGRAF, 2007. Accessed September 7, 2020 <http://1914ww.ru/sobyt/1900sob/19181118kolchak.php>.

Spence, Richard. *Boris Savinkov. Renegade on the Left.* New York: Eastern European Monographs, 1991.

———. "The Tragic Fate of Kalamatiano: America's Man in Moscow." *International Journal of Intelligence and CounterIntelligence* 12, no. 3 (1999): 346–374.

———. *Trust No One: The Secret World of Sidney Reilly.* Los Angeles: Feral House, 2002.

Spiridonova, M. *Iz zhizni na nerchinskoi katorge,* 1925. Rpt. *Zhenshchiny-terroristki v Rossii.* Ed. O. V. Budnitskii. Rostov-na-Donu: Feniks, 1996, 427–499.

Spiridovich, A. I. *Zapiski zhandarma,* 1930. Rpt. Moscow: Proletarii, 1991.

Stafford, David. *Churchill and the Secret Service.* London: John Murray, 1997.

Stankevich, V. B. *Vospominaniia. 1914–1919.* Berlin: Ladyzhnikov, 1920.

Staraia Vologda. XII nachalo XX veka. Sbornik dokumentov i materialov. Gosudarstvennyi arkhiv Vologdskoi oblasti. Accessed September 7, 2020 <https://www.booksite.ru/fulltext/sta/raya/vol/ogda/index.htm>.

Startsev, Vitalii. *Tainy russkikh masonov.* Saint Petersburg: DARK, 2004.

"Stenograficheskii otchet o protsesse nad rukovoditelem Iaroslavskogo vosstaniia polkovnikom A. P. Perkhurovym." July 15, 16, 17, 18, and 19, 1922. Iaroslavskoe vosstanie. 1918. Sudebnye protsessy organizatorov i uchastnikov vosstaniia. Materialy sudebnykh protsessov. *Fond Aleksandra N. Yakovleva.* Accessed September 7, 2020 <http://www.alexanderyakovlev.org/fond/issues-doc/64351>.

Stepun, Fedor. *Byvshee i nesbyvsheesia.* 1956. Rpt. Moscow and Saint Petersburg: Progress-Litera & Aleteiia, 1995.

Szumiło, Mirosław. "Battle of Warsaw, 1920" [Russian text]. *Institute of National Rememberance.* Accessed March 10, 2021 <https://ipn.gov.pl/en/digital-resources/articles/4397,Battle-of-Warsaw-1920.html>.

Tashlykov, S. L. "Petrogradskie operatsii severo-zapadnoi armii 1919." *Bol'shaia rossiiskaia entsiklodeiia.* Accessed June 24, 2019 <https://bigenc.ru/military_science/text/3136608>.

"Tatarov, Nikolai Iur'evich." *Akademik.* Accessed July 11, 2016 <http://dic.academic.ru/dic.nsf/ruwiki/1838967>.

Tolstoy, Leo. *War and Peace.* Trans. R. Pevear and L. Volokhonsky. New York: Vintage 2007.

Tooze, Adam. "When We Loved Mussolini." Review of *The United States and Fascist Italy: The Rise of American Finance in Europe,* by Gian Giacomo Migone. *New York Review of Books,* August 18, 2016. Accessed July 19, 2019 <https://www.nybooks.com/articles/2016/08/18/when-we-loved-mussolini>.

Tri brata (To, chto bylo). Ed., preface, notes by K. N. Morozov, and A. Iu. Morozova. Moscow: Novyi khronograph, 2019.

"'Tri nedeli besprosvetnogo koshmara . . .' Pis'ma S. Reilli." Pp. 275–310 in *Minuvshee: Istoricheskii al'manakh* 14. Ed. D. Zubarev. Moscow and Saint Petersburg: Atheneum-Feniks, 1993.

Trotskii, Lev. *Moia zhizn'. Opyt biografii.* Accessed August 8, 2018 <http://magister.msk.ru/library/trotsky/trotl026.htm#st26>.

"Tsetlin, Mikhail." *Elektronnaia evreiskaia entsiklopdeiia.* Accessed October 27, 2017 <http://www.eleven.co.il/article/14614>.

Tsvetkov, V. Zh. "Ufimskaia direktoriia." *Bol'shaia rossiiskaia entsiklopediia.* Accessed June 17, 2019 <https://bigenc.ru/domestic_history/text/4703712>.

Uspenskaia, V. G., et al. to Peshkova, E. P. *Uslysh' ikh golosa. Zakleimennye vlast'iu. Po dokumentam fondov Gosudarstvennogo Arkhiva Rossiiskoi Federatsii, Memorial.* Accessed September 7, 2020 <http://pkk.memo.ru/letters_pdf/000169.pdf>.

"Uspenskii, Gleb Ivanovich." *Bol'shaia biograficheskaia entsiklopediia.* Accessed October 17, 2018 <https://dic.academic.ru/dic.nsf/enc_biography/126152/Успенский>.

Valentinov [Vol'skii], Nikolai. "Vstrecha s B. Savinkovym." *Novyi zhurnal,* no. 85 (December 1966): 266–270.

Van Der Kiste, John. *The Romanovs 1818–1959, Alexander II of Russia and His Family.* Thrupp, Stroud, Gloucestershire: Sutton, 1998.

Vandervelde, Emile. *Three Aspects of the Russian Revolution.* Trans. Jean E. H. Findlay. London: George Allen & Unwin, 1918.

"Vedomost' VGZhU o rozyske skryvshegosia iz ssylki B. V. Savinkova," document 285, July 14, 1903. "Vologodskaia politicheskaia ssylka." *Staraia Vologda.* Vologodksii gosudarstvennyi istoriko-arkhitekturnyi i khudozhestvennyi muzei-zapovednik. Accessed October 11, 2015 <https://www.booksite.ru/fulltext/sta/raya/vol/ogda/13.htm#321>; notes to document 285: <https://www.booksite.ru/fulltext/sta/raya/vol/ogda/23.htm>.

Vendziagol'skii [Wędziagolski], Karol. "Savinkov." Part 1, *Novyi zhurnal,* no. 68 (1962): 190–214; part 2, no. 70 (1962): 142–183; part 3, no. 71 (1963): 133–155; part 4, no. 72 (1963): 168–197.

Vinogradov, V., and V. Safonov. "Boris Savinkov—protivnik bol'shevikov." Pp. 3–32 in *Savinkov na Lubianke. Dokumenty.* Ed. A. L. Litvin. Moscow: Rosspen, 2001.

Vitte [Witte], Sergei. *Vospominaniia.* Vol. 2. "Glava 22: Naznachenie Sviatopolk-Mirskogo ministrom vnutrennikh del. Ukaz 12 dekabria 1904." E-LIBRA Elektronnaia biblioteka. Accessed September 10, 2020 <https://e-libra.ru/read/255525-vospominaniya-tom-2.html>.

"Vologda." *Entsiklopedicheskii slovar' Brokgauza i Efrona.* Vol. 7, 59–60. Accessed September 8, 2020 <https://ru.wikisource.org/w/index.php?title=Файл:Encyclopedicheskii_slovar_tom_7.djvu&page=63>.

"Vologodskaia ssylka." Vologodksii gosudarstvennyi istoriko-arkhitekturnyi i khudozhestvennyi muzei-zapovednik. Accessed April 16, 2018 <http://www.vologdamuseum.ru/content?id=51>.

"Voloshin [Maksimilian Aleksandrovich]." E. A. Takho-Godi. *Bol'shaia rossiiskaia entsiklopediia.* Accessed September 24, 2019 <https://bigenc.ru/literature/text/1927497>.

Voloshin, Maksimilian. *Izbrannoe. Stikhotvoreniia. Vospominaniia, Perepiska.* Ed., intro. Zakhar Davydov and Vladimir Kupchenko. Minsk: Mastatskaia litaratura, 1993.

"Vozzvanie k zhiteliam goroda Iaroslavlia o sverzhenii vlasti bol'shevikov i svoei programme." July 6, 1918. Iaroslavskoe vosstanie 1918, Listovki Shtaba severnoi dobrovol'cheskoi armii. *Fond Aleksandra N. Yakovleva.* Accessed September 7, 2020 <http://www.alexanderyakovlev.org/fond/issues-doc/63960>.

Vorobëv, Marevna. *Life in Two Worlds*. Trans. Benet Nash, pref. Ossip Zadkine. New York: Abelard-Schuman, 1962.

Vyrypaev, Vasilii O. "Kappelevtsy." Chap. 5, "Na Kazan'!" *Kappel' i kappelevtsy*. Part 2. Ed. S. S. Balmasov. Moscow: Posev, 2001. Electronic edition NETDA, 2003. Accessed September 6, 2020 <https://rusk.ru /vst.php?idar=321722>.

———. "Kappelevtsy." Chap. 6, "Na Moskvu!" *Kappel' i kappelevtsy*. Part 2. Ed. S. S. Balmasov. Moscow: Posev, 2001. Electronic edition NETDA, 2003. Accessed September 6, 2020 <https://rusk.ru/vst .php?idar=321722#s13>.

Warwick, Christopher. *Ella: Princess, Saint, and Martyr*. Chichester, West Sussex, England: Wiley, 2006.

Wedziagolski, Karol. *Boris Savinkov: Portrait of a Terrorist*. Trans. Margaret Patoski, ed. Tadeusz Swietochowski. Clifton, NJ: Kingston Press, 1988.

Weeks, Theodore R. "Monuments and Memory: Immortalizing Count M. N. Muraviev in Vilna, 1898." *Nationalities Papers* 27, no. 4 (1999): 551–564.

Weidhorn, Manfred. "A Contrarian's Approach to Peace." Pp. 24–53 in *Churchill as Peacemaker*. Ed. James W. Muller. Cambridge: Cambridge University Press, 2002.

Werth, Nicolas. "Part I. A State against Its People: Violence, Repression, and Terror in the Soviet Union." Pp. 33–268 in *The Black Book of Communism: Crimes, Terror, Repression*. Ed. Stéphane Courtois et al. Cambridge, MA: Harvard University Press, 1999.

"World War I Casualties." Wikipedia. Accessed September 12, 2018 <https://en.wikipedia.org/wiki /World_War_I_casualties>.

Woytinsky, Wladimir S. *Stormy Passage: A Personal History through Two Russian Revolutions to Democracy and Freedom*. New York: Vanguard, 1961.

"Zapis' vospominanii V. A. Davatsa i F. P. F." Iaroslavskoe vosstanie. 1918. Belye o Iaroslavskom vosstanii, document no. 7, *Fond Aleksandra N. Yakovleva*. Accessed September 5, 2020 <http://www.alexander yakovlev.org/fond/issues-doc/64706>.

Zavarzin, P. P. *Rabota tainoi politsii*. Pp. 411–493 in *"Okhranka": Vospominaniia rukovoditelei politicheskogo syska*, Vol. 1. Intro., ed., commentary Z. I. Peregudova. Moscow: Novoe Literaturnoe Obozrenie, 2004.

"Zaveshchanie B. V. Savinkova." Pp. 55–57 in *Boris Savinkov na Lubianke. Dokumenty*. Ed. A. L. Litvin. Moscow, Rosspen, 2001.

"Zavety (zhurnal)." Wikipedia. Accessed August 22, 2017 <https://ru.wikipedia.org/wiki/ Заветы_(журнал)>.

Zenzinov, Vladimir. *Perezhitoe*. New York: Chekhov, 1953.

Zhukov, Dmitrii. "B. Savinkov i V. Ropshin, Terrorist i Pisatel'." Pp. 3–119 in Boris Savinkov (V. Ropshin), *To, chego ne bylo: Roman, povesti, rasskazy, ocherki, stikhotvoreniia*. Moscow: Sovremennik, 1992.

"Zimmerwald Conference." Wikipedia. Accessed May 26, 2019 <https://en.wikipedia.org/wiki/Zimmerwald _Conference#Signatories_of_the_Zimmerwald_Manifesto>.

Zlunitsyn, Colonel P. F. "Vosstanie v Iaroslavle v 1918." Iaroslavskoe vosstanie, 1918, Belye o Iaroslavskom vosstanii, document no. 3, *Fond Aleksandra N. Yakovleva*. Accessed September 5, 2020 <http://www .alexanderyakovlev.org/fond/issues-doc/64702>.

Zubarev, Dmitrii. "Boris Savinkov: Chelovek, kotoryi khotel rasshirit' chelovecheskuiu svobodu. K 70-i letiiu so dnia gibeli." *Nezavisimaia gazeta*, May 23, 1995, 3.

NOTES

ABBREVIATIONS:

BVS   Boris Viktorovich Savinkov (except in bibliographic references)

VGS   Vera Glebovna Savinkova

CHAPTER ONE

1–3   **Police raid:** Savinkova, "Gody," 215, 217-218. **Family:** Zubarev; Khairetdinov, 112; Figner, 163; Chaikovskii.

3–5   **Russo-Polish relations:** Dabrowski, 262–263, 281–288, 303, 306–308, 311–312, 315–316, 334–337, 343. **Monument in Vilnius:** Weeks. **Student reaction:** Khairetdinov, 112–113.

5–9   **BVS' family:** Spence, *Savinkov*, 8, 379 n. 7; Chuikina, 310 n. 3, 313 n. 7., 314. **Victor Mikhailovich:** Savinkova, "Gody," 215, 218. **Sofia Alexandrovna:** Chaikovskii; AN, Sûreté report, "Savinkoff, Boris," April 28, 1922, 1. **School:** Spence, *Savinkov*, 9–10; photograph of BVS and schoolmates, "Moi trud ne prineset," 18; Savinkov, "Shkol'nye vospominaniia." **Kalyaev:** "O vyiasnenii sviazei I. P. Kaliaeva"; Chaikovskii; Chernov, 183–185; Savinkov, "Iz vospominanii," 120. **Young BVS:** Figner, 163–164; Spence, *Savinkov*, 7–8. **Yaroshenko:** "Nikolai Iaroshenko." **Zasulich:** Riasanovsky, 425. **Trip to Caucasus:** Dan, 55; Spence, *Savinkov,* 9. **Visitors to BVS home:** Spence, *Savinkov*, 9; Prutskov, 99 (Uspensky as model for "The Prisoner"). **Young BVS vegetarian:** Voloshin, *Izbrannoe*, 367–368.

9–11   **Warsaw:** Baedeker, *Russia*, xv, xiii, 12; Savinkov, "Rossiia i Pol'sha," 29. **After arrest:** Khairetdinov, 113; Zubarev; Savinkova, "Gody," 219.

11–13   **Alexander's arrest, Sofia in Saint Petersburg:** Savinkova, "Gody," 219–226; Baedeker, *Russia*, 99–101.

13–15   **Student protests:** Kassow, 104. **BVS's passion:** Gorbunov, part 1, 183–185. **Vera:** Figner, 148. **Police repression:** Savinkova, "Gody," 225; Morrissey, 62. **BVS's expulsion:** Kassow, 91–92, 110, 120; Savinkova, "Na volos," 249; "Autobiography of Boris Savinkov," IISH. **Wedding:** Zubarev. Early 1899 on the assumption that they would have waited for marriage and their daughter was born on April 26, 1900; nine months before that would be July 1899. BVS was even willing to submit to the military draft in 1900, but was judged unfit for service (Gorodnitskii, *Boevaia*, 186).

16–17   **Family relations:** VGS to BVS, May 11, 1901, GARF, d. 178, l. 2; "Uspenskii, Gleb Ivanovich." **BVS in Europe:** Police report, March 19, 1903, Hoover, Index No. XVIIi, Folder 2; Spence, *Savinkov,* 16–17; "Spravka," Hoover, Index No. XVIIi, Folder 2, no. 18. **BVS and revolutionaries:** Dan, 474 n. 8; Spence, *Savinkov*, 16–17; "Autobiography of Boris Savinkov," IISH; Police report, March 19, 1903, Hoover, Index No. XVIIi, Folder 2.

17–20   **Evno Azef:** Geifman, *Entangled*, 11–40, 46–47, 69–70; *Pis'ma Azefa*, 14–16.

20–21   **BVS becomes a revolutionary:** Police report, March 19, 1903, Hoover, Index No. XVIIi, Folder 2. **Situation in Russia:** Pushkarev, 429–433; Riasanovsky, 441, 472, 474; Judge, 8; Pipes, *Revolution*, 78–80; Bushkovitch, 294. **Moscow:** Il'in, 34, 86, 88.

22–23   **BVS's Marxism:** Gorbunov, part 1, 168–169, 183. **Early family life:** VGS to BVS, 31 [Thursday, no month] 1901, GARF, d. 178, l. 365; however, another one of their three children died at a young age, Gorodnitskii, *Boevaia*, 186. **Born conspirator:** Broido, 16. **First publication:** B-v. [BVS], "Peterburgskoe dvizhenie." **Lenin:** the title of Lenin's brochure had already been used for a novel by the radical nineteenth-century writer Nikolai Chernyshevskii that became highly influential among Russian revolutionary youth; Gorbunov, part 1, 169.

23–25   **Arrest:** "Moi trud ne prineset," 6 n. 2; "Vedomost' VGZhU o rozyske," n. 2, 3; Savinkova, "Gody," 225; Savinkova, "Na volos," 249. **Rejects violence:** Gorodnitskii, *Boevaia*, 186. **Vera's letters:** VGS to BVS, approximately April, 1901, GARF, d. 178, ll. 365, 366; photograph of Tanya, "Moi trud ne prineset," 10; VGS to BVS, September 1, 1901, GARF, d. 178, ll. 3, 8. **"Vitya":** VGS to BVS, October 26, 1901, GARF, d. 178, l. 11.

25–28   **Vologda:** Savinkov, *Vospominaniia*, 11; Savinkova, "Gody," 226; "Vedomost' VGZhU o rozyske"; "Moi trud ne prineset," 11; Lu're, *Khraniteli*, 32; "Vologodskaia ssylka"; Fediuk, 125, 130; Remizov, *Iveren'*, 444, 477; "Vologda"; Zhukov, 33. **Employment:** "Vedomost' VGZhU o rozyske," n. 1; Fediuk, 125–126. **Writing:** Savinkov, Anonymous reviews; Remizov, *Iveren'*, 453–456; Kanin.

28–29   **Athens of the North:** Remizov, *Iveren'*, 438, 441, 476, 484; *Istoriia vologodskogo kraia*, 27–30; "Iz politicheskogo obzora VGZhU za 1904 g."; Lunacharskii, *Byvshie liudi*, 15. **BVS to funeral:** Fediuk, 130; "Vedomost' VGZhU o rozyske," n. 4. **Mother and brother visit:** Savinkova, "Gody," 238.

29–32   **BVS contra Marxism:** Pipes, *Revolution*, 360; Zenzinov, 178; Pipes, *Russia*, 167–169; Kelly, 294. **SRs:** e.g., "Ko vsemu russkomu krest'ianstvu," 154; Erofeev, 8. These were the defining features of the SRs throughout their history, although, like all political parties everywhere, they did not remain ideologically monolithic and developed factions and splinter groups with various "left" and "right" inclinations. **Central terror:** e.g., "Ko vsem grazhdanam tsivilizovannogo mira," 157. **Bolsheviks contra SRs:** Morozov, *Partiia*, 7, 10; Zenzinov, 178–179; Gusev, 12.

32–34   **"Moral" terror:** Zenzinov, 272–275. **Babushka:** *Hidden Springs*, xiii, 278–279, and frontispiece photograph; Gusev, 11; Remizov, *Iveren'*, 484; Savinkov, *Vospominaniia*, 11; Spence, *Savinkov*, 24. **Babushka's manner:** Chernov, 309; Knight, 142–143; *The Little Grandmother*, 120. **17,000 killed by terrorists:** Geifman, *Thou Shalt Kill*, 20–21.

34–36   **Moiseyenko:** Remizov, *Iveren'*, 480. **Balmashov:** Gorodnitskii, *Boevaia*, 41–42; Chernov, 162. **Gershuni:** Gorodnitskii, *Boevaia*, 33, 72; Savinkov, *Vospominaniia*, 11; Geifman, *Entangled*, 51. **"temperament":** Savinkov, *Vospominaniia*, 11; Dan, 141. **BVS escapes:** Savinkova, "Gody," 239; "Spravka," [n.d.], Hoover, Index No. XVIIi, Folder 2, doc. 18/69; Savinkova, "Na volos," 249; "Vedomost' VGZhU o rozyske"; Savinkov, *Vospominaniia*, 11–12; Baedeker, *Russia*, xviii–xix.

36–39   **Alexander's sentence:** Savinkova, "Gody," 239. **BVS to Geneva:** Savinkov, *Vospominaniia*, 11–12; "Spravka," [n.d.], Hoover, Index No. XVIIi, Folder 2, doc. 18/69; Chernov, 170. **Gots:** Gorodnitskii, *Boevaia*, 58; "Gots, Mikhail"; Chernov, 150–151, 172; Zenzinov, 110; Savinkov, *Vospominaniia*, 12. **Our Benjamin:** Zenzinov, 134. **Geneva:** Baedeker, *Switzerland*, 250. **Moiseyenko:** Savinkov, *Vospominaniia*, 13.

39–42   **Babushka:** Zenzinov, 134. **BVS's manner:** Zenzinov, 134. **Chernov on BVS:** Chernov, 185. **BVS, Volsky and poetry:** Valentinov, 266–267. **"In Twilight":** B. S-t. **Azef:** Savinkov, *Vospominaniia*, 13; Chernov, 174; Popova, part 2, 47; Ivanovskaia, 69; Gorodnitskii, *Boevaia*, 87.

42–44   **Azef's reputation:** Chernov, 172, 174–175; Zenzinov, 103. **Suspicions:** Popova, part 2, 48. Savinkov, *Vospominaniia*, 14–15; Gorodnitskii, *Boevaia*, 65. **Azef's plan against Plehve:** Geifman, *Entangled*, 19; Savinkov, *Vospominaniia*, 13–14.

44–47   **Plot against Plehve:** Savinkov, *Vospominaniia*, 14–16. **Azef's agenda and letters:** *Pis'ma Azefa*, 90–95, 85. **Okhrana archive:** Hingley, 79; Agafonov 17–19; Fischer. **Structure of SR Party:** Gorodnitskii, *Boevaia*, 37; "Iz pokazanii S. N. Sletova," 148.

CHAPTER TWO

48–51   **Von Plehve:** Judge, 2–3, 12–32, 38, 93–101, 218, 222, 233 (quotes on 95–96); Pipes, *Revolution*, 9–12; Zenzinov, 133; Geifman, *Entangled*, 49. **Amateur days:** Savinkov, *Vospominaniia*, 15–16, 21, 133.

51–53   **Sankt-Peterburg:** Baedeker, *Russia*, 102, 116; Nabokov, *Speak Memory*, 190; Riasanovsky, 356–357; Pushkarev, 384–386.

53–55   **Police pursuit and escape:** Savinkov, *Vospominaniia*, 17–19, 61. **BVS regroups:** Savinkov, *Vospominaniia*, 19–21. **Azef's dark affairs:** *Pis'ma Azefa*, 96.

55–58   **War with Japan:** Alexandrov, 66–68. **SR response:** "Ko vsemu russkomu krest'ianstvu," 155. **BVS's team:** Savinkov, *Vospominaniia*, 21–23; Baedeker, *Russia*, 271; Popova, part 1, 62; Levitskii, "A. D. Pokotilov,"158–159, 170, 171; Chernov, 171; Geifman, *Entangled*, 60; Gorodnitskii, *Boevaia*, 187. **Soldiers' connections:** Gal, 149; Department of the Army, 51; Eberle, 30.

58–61   **March 18, 1904:** Savinkov, *Vospominaniia*, 22–28. The name of Tsepnoy Bridge was changed to Panteleymonovsky in 1908.

61–63   **Azef's designs:** Geifman, *Entangled*, 39, 41–42, 67, 69–70; Aldanov; Pavlov, 4; Shchegolev, 7; *Pis'ma Azefa*, 4 n. 1; Gorodnitskii, *Boevaia*, 167, 169–171; Argunov, 43.

63–66   **Regrouping:** Savinkov, *Vospominaniia*, 29–32, 36; Levitskii, "A. D. Pokotilov," 171; Zavarzin, 442; *Pis'ma Azefa*, no. 117, p. 98. **Azef the savior:** Savinkov, *Vospominaniia*, 31–32, 36; Gorodnitskii, *Boevaia*, 96–97.

66–68   **Azef contra Plehve:** Rataev, 153; *Pis'ma Azefa*, 97–101; Savinkov, *Vospominaniia*, 33. **Female recruit:** Knight, 139, 141–143, 145, 149; Gorodnitskii, *Boevaia*, 235; Levitskii, *Za chetvert' veka*, 86; Savinkov, *Vospominaniia*, 33; Savinkov, "Revoliutsionnye siluety. Dora Brilliant," 10.

68–72   **Azef's theatrical plot:** Savinkov, *Vospominaniia*, 36–39, 42; Ivanovskaia, 55–58; *Pis'ma Azefa*, 57; Levitskii, *Za chetvert' veka*, 86.

72–74   **Kalyaev:** Savinkov, *Vospominaniia*, 33–34, 40–41; Zenzinov, 275–276. **Brilliant:** Ivanovskaia, 92; Savinkov, *Vospominaniia*, 44–45. **Sikorsky:** Ivanovskaia, 89; Savinkov, *Vospominaniia*, 46–47, 59–60.

74–78   **A stumble:** *Pis'ma Azefa*, 103; Savinkov, *Vospominaniia*, 48–49. **First blood:** Savinkov, *Vospominaniia*, 51–55; Sazonov, 9–10.

78–81   **Sazonov's experience:** Sazonov, 9–10; Savinkov, *Vospominaniia*, 56, 58; "Iz sekretnykh," 52–57, 62–63; Chernov, 178–179. In *Pamiati Viacheslava Konstantinovicha Pleve*, 53, a half-dozen other victims are mentioned, including the coachman, grandmother and little girl, and a detective on a bicycle who supposedly knocked Sazonov down. **Reaction to Plehve's assassination in Warsaw:** Ivanovskaia, 93, 94; Gorodnitskii, *Boevaia*, 100–101. **Reactions elsewhere:** Zenzinov, 132; Judge, 238; Davydov, 5; Savinkova, "Gody," 244.

81–84   **Bomb's echoes:** Pipes, *Revolution*, 16–17, 19; Savinkova, "Gody," 242, 246; Spiridovich, 184. **Sazonov's trial:** Judge, 239; Savinkov, *Vospominaniia*, 44 (italics his); 60; Sazonov, 98–100. **On leave:** Savinkov, *Vospominaniia*, 62–64, 67–69; Gorodnitskii, *Boevaia*, 99; Popova, part 1, 62; part 2, 62.

84–85   **Azef's warmth:** Popova, part 2, 48–49; Argunov, 47–48; Ivanovskaia, 111–114; *Pis'ma Azefa*, 124.

CHAPTER THREE

86–87   **Three governors general:** Savinkov, *Vospominaniia*, 71. **Azef's deceptions:** *Pis'ma Azefa*, 104–106, 109, 262 n. 284; Gorodnitskii, "Tri stilia," 57. **Grand Duke Sergey as target:** Gorodnitskii, *Boevaia*, 101–102. However, M. E. Bakay, a man who worked for the police, later claimed that although the police had learned about the plot against Grand Duke Sergey and BVS's involvement in it from an informant, they still could not prevent it. The police also initiated a close surveillance of BVS's family, who were in Warsaw at the time (Savinkov, *Vospominaniia*, 304).

87–88   **Grand Duke Sergey's sins and character:** Goldovskii, 153; Van Der Kiste, 137; Warwick, 98–99, 187–189; Kassow, 191–194; Pipes, *Revolution*, 20; Vitte; *A Lifelong Passion*, 266–267; *Nikolai i Aleksandra*, 268–269.

88–91   **First steps:** Savinkov, *Vospominaniia*, 69, 73–75, 77, 80, 81. **Aloof "Britisher":** Zenzinov, 141–143; Gorodnitskii, *Boevaia*, 124–125. **BVS's swagger:** Savinkov, *Vospominaniia*, 85; police reports, June 20 and July 17, 1904, Hoover, Index No. XVIIi, Folder 1; Valentinov, 267. Savinkov's quotation at length (*Vospominaniia*, 87–88) from a letter dated January 22, 1905, which Kalyaev wrote to Vera, implies that Savinkov may have gotten it from her.

91–92   **Most Russian city:** Baedeker, *Russia*, 276–277; Alexandrov, 57; Savinkov, "Dnevnik," April 24, 1925, 187.

92–94   **Surveillance of Sergey:** Warwick, 216; Savinkov, *Vospominaniia*, 76–77, 80. **Sergey moves, "Bloody Sunday":** Riasanovsky, 446; Savinkov, *Vospominaniia*, 80–81; Zenzinov, 148, 176; Pipes, *Revolution*, 25–26. **BVS haggard:** Ivanovskaia, 120.

94–97   **BVS's chance:** Savinkov, *Vospominaniia*, 88; Warwick, 216; Baedeker, *Russia*, 270, 297. **BVS and Kalyaev:** Savinkov, "Iz vospominanii ob Ivane Kaliaeve," 127; Savinkov, *Vospominaniia*, 87–88.

Kalyaev's attack: Savinkov, *Vospominaniia*, 88–89; Warwick, 216–217, claims that Sergey's carriage was accompanied by a Cossack escort "as always at night." Although this would have seemed prudent, the fact that Kalyaev was not seen or seized by anyone suggests that there was no escort or that it failed spectacularly in its duty. Savinkov, "Iz vospominanii ob Ivane Kaliaeve," 127–128.

97–99 **The children:** Savinkov, *Vospominaniia*, 89; *A Lifelong Passion*, 258; Savinkov, "Iz vospominanii ob Ivane Kaliaeve," 127–128; Van Der Kiste, 125, 167. **Aftermath:** Savinkov, *Vospominaniia*, 89–91; "Iz vospominanii ob Ivane Kaliaeve," 127–128.

99–101 **Attack on Sergey resumed:** Savinkov, *Vospominaniia*, 91–94. Contrary to what Savinkov recalls, the corner to which the picture was attached must have been on the Historical Museum or the Kazansky Chapel or the Upper Trading Row; Nikolsky Tower is not visible from the Iberian Chapel. **Monument to Alexander II:** Baedeker, *Russia*, 280 (it was destroyed by the Soviets); Savinkov, *Vospominaniia*, 93. **Sergey and Ella:** Spiridovich, 180; Warwick, 217–218; *A Lifelong Passion*, 263; *Nikolai i Aleksandra*, 265.

101–104 **Sergey's death:** Savinkov, *Vospominaniia*, 93–96; Warwick, 218; *Nikolai i Aleksandra*, 263–264; *A Lifelong Passion*, 260. **Maria's and Ella's recollections:** *A Lifelong Passion*, 262, 267; *Nikolai i Aleksandra*, 264; Warwick, 220; Van Der Kiste, 173.

104–108 **Reactions to Sergey's death:** Zenzinov, 153. **Ella's life with Sergey:** Warwick, 130–34, 141, 148; Van Der Kiste, 137, 161, 196; *A Lifelong Passion*, 264–265. **Ella after Sergey's death:** Warwick, 222–224. **Ella visits Kalyaev:** *Nikolai i Aleksandra*, 271–272; Savinkov, *Vospominaniia*, 96–100; *Lifelong Passion*, 269–270; Warwick, 224. **Kalyaev's sense of victory:** Savinkov, *Vospominaniia*, 96–97.

108–110 **Two mortals:** Savinkov, *Vospominaniia*, 97–100; Kaliaev; *A Lifelong Passion*, 277. A less gruesome version of Kalyaev's execution is reported in "Poslednii den' Kaliaeva," 190, and Savinkov, *Vospominaniia*, 106. **Ella's fate:** Warwick, 228, 246, 259–260, 304–305, 312.

110–111 **Terror's aftermath:** BVS is reported to have reworked his memoir as many as a dozen times because of Socialist Revolutionary Party demands (Mogil'ner, 106). Gorbunov, part 3, 170, who was BVS's political opponent, points out supposed inaccuracies in BVS's description of the preparations for the assassination of Grand Duke Sergey. By contrast, Gorodnitskii, *Boevaia*, 88–92, who relies on archival evidence, concludes that the memoir is very accurate. Savinkov, *Vospominaniia*, 107–108; Geifman, *Entangled*, 73. **Azef:** Gorodnitskii, *Boevaia*, 127; Savinkov, *Vospominaniia*, 110; *Pis'ma Azefa*, no. 147, 117.

CHAPTER FOUR

112–114 **Shveytser:** Ivanovskaia, 123, 129–131; Savinkov, *Vospominaniia*, 108. **An accident:** Popova, part 1, 63; Savinkov, *Vospominaniia*, 110, 116–117, 119; Nabokov, *Speak, Memory*, 184; *Journal de Genève*, Sunday, March 12, 1905, 2nd edition, 2. **BVS inadvertently saved:** Savinkov, *Vospominaniia*, 114. **The rout:** Ivanovskaia, 133–134; Savinkov, *Vospominaniia*, 120, 122.

114–117 **Guilt by association:** Savinkova, "Gody," 247–252. **Victor Mikhailovich's despondency and death, Alexander's suicide:** Savinkova, "Gody," 252–254.

117–118 **BVS's life choice:** Savinkov, "Dnevnik," May 2, 1925, 193. **VGS's life and letters:** VGS to BVS, n.d. [April 27, 1905, based on internal evidence: daughter's fifth birthday "yesterday"], GARF, d. 178, ll. 356–357; VGS to BVS, n.d. [spring 1905, based on internal evidence—apparent references to Alexander's recent suicide and BVS's wanting to know details about it, and Vera's apparent remark that he needs to write to his father] GARF, d. 178, ll. 26–27; BVS to VGS, May 8, 1905, Gorodnitskii, *Boevaia*, 188; Goncharova, 19.

118–121 **Rank amateurs:** Savinkov, *Vospominaniia*, 125–131; Lebedev, "Konets,"164; Shkol'nik, 573, 578–579, 583. **Tsushima and political tensions:** Pipes, *Revolution*, 30–33. **Kiev fiasco:** Savinkov, *Vospominaniia*, 132; Shkol'nik, 592.

121–124 **Betrayals:** Savinkov, *Vospominaniia*, 121–122, 135–140; Zenzinov, 194; "Tatarov"; Kara-Murza. **Azef's betrayal:** Gorodnitskii, *Boevaia*, 128; Popova, part 3, 56; Police reports, June 19 and July 15, 1905, Hoover, Index No. XVIIi, Folder 1; *Pis'ma Azefa*, 124, 132.

124–126 **Party suspicions:** Savinkov, *Vospominaniia*, 141–147, 154–155, 208. **Strikes and reforms:** Pipes, *Revolution*, 35–44; Engelstein, 12–14.

126–128 **Reactions among revolutionaries:** Savinkov, *Vospominaniia*, 158–159; Martynov, 105. **Terrorism inadmissible:** Savinkov, *Vospominaniia*, 159–163; Pipes, *Revolution*, 44, 153, points out that there was no formal "constitution" in the manifesto, that the word was avoided subsequently, and that "Fundamental Laws" was used instead. Geifman, *Entangled*, 85–86; Gorodnitskii, *Boevaia*, 189.

128–130 **Turmoil and revolution:** Pipes, *Revolution*, 41, 46, 48–50; Kassow, 273–274; Riasanovsky, 452; Alexandrov, 69.

130–133 **BVS's twilight existence, failures, Dora Brilliant's arrest:** Savinkov, *Vospominaniia*, 167–168, 172–174. **Resurrection of terror:** Savinkov, *Vospominaniia*, 174–181, 183–185, 188–189; Popova, part 1, 61–62, 65–66 (she gives a different version of Savinkov's argument with Azef over the female technician).

133–134 **Repeated failures and Azef:** Savinkov, *Vospominaniia*, 189–199, 218; Popova, part 1, 64. **Benevskaya:** Savinkov, *Vospominaniia*, 183, 196–198, 232; Zenzinov, 312; Popova, part 1, 64–65.

134–135 **Azef's close calls:** Savinkov, *Vospominaniia*, 208–215, 223–229. **Azef and the imperial police:** Burtsev, "Azef i Gen. Gerasimov," 209 (Burtsev's April 10 is more plausible than Gerasimov's April 15); Gerasimov, 210–213; "Protokoly sionskikh mudretsov"; Geifman, *Entangled*, 93–94.

135–140 **Gerasimov and Azef:** "Protokoly sionskikh mudretsov"; Gerasimov, 214–215, 227–229; Geifman, *Entangled*, 94. **BVS to Sevastopol:** Savinkov, *Vospominaniia*, 232–233, 235–38; Remizov, *Iveren'*, 505–506; Savinkova, "Na volos," 256, gives a different version of what happened. **I am no less a gentleman:** Maugham, *A Writer's*, 176; Maugham, *A Traveler*, 227.

140–142 **BVS's team betrayed:** Gererasimov, 227. **Rush to trial:** Savinkov, *Vospominaniia*, 237–240. **BVS's family to Sevastopol:** Savinkov, *Vospominaniia*, 239, 241–242; Savinkova, "Na volos," 247–249, 252; Viktor Savinkov to BVS, June 30, 1906, "Moi trud ne prineset," 7–8. **Zilberberg and VGS:** Savinkov, *Vospominaniia*, 241–242; Argunov, 65.

142–146 **Sevastopol prison:** Savinkov, *Vospominaniia*, 242–244; Savinkova, "Na volos," 252. **Escape:** Savinkov, *Vospominaniia*, 245–246 (July 31 on p. 245 is probably a typo), 248–250. **Stahlberg:** Savinkov, *Vospominaniia*, 250–251.

146–148 **To Romania:** Savinkov, *Vospominaniia*, 252–256; Savinkova, "Na volos," 270.

CHAPTER FIVE

149–151 **Gots:** Savinkov, *Vospominaniia*, 114, 257. **Duma dissolved and Stolypin:** Zenzinov, 338–339; Pipes, *Revolution*, 164–171; Engelstein, 18–19. **Attempt on Stolypin:** Pipes, *Revolution*, 169; Savinkov, *Vospominaniia*, 256–257; Figner, 145. **Leontyeva:** Ivanovskaia, 173; Okhrana "Spravka" about Savinkov, no date [but after February, 1908], Hoover, Index No. XVIIi, Folder 2, no. 18, sheet 69.

152–153 **No attack on Stolypin, Azef and Savinkov relieved of duties:** Gorodnitskii, *Boevaia*, 108–110; Savinkov, *Vospominaniia*, 258–259, 262–263. **BVS and VGS:** BVS to VGS, August 20, 1906, "Moi trud ne prineset," 8–9. **Sofia:** Viktor Savinkov to BVS, June 30, 1906, "Moi trud ne prineset," 6–8; Sofia Savinkova [unsigned, based on internal evidence] to BVS, no date, GARF, d. 178, ll. 212, 332. **VGS and Sofia to France:** VGS to BVS, no dates, GARF, d. 178, ll. 332, 352, 363; Police Report, October 13, 1906, Hoover, Index No. XVIIi, Folder 2, no. 309. (The report says that it was Savinkov's "mother and sister" who visited him, but the latter is a mistake, as other evidence indicates, Goncharova, 14 n. 26.)

154–158 **Terrorist in repose:** *Pis'ma Azefa*, e.g., July 15, 1907 (p. 142), in which Savinkov is offered a regular pension; Figner, 154, 157–158, 164. **Figner:** Geifman, *Entangled*, 107; "Uspenskii, Gleb Ivanovich"; Figner, 148; photograph of Figner in 1906, accessed May 20, 2019 <https://commons.wikimedia.org/wiki/File:Vera_Figner_1906.jpg>. **Figner on BVS:** Figner, 149, 152–153, 155, 157, 163, 171. **Figner on Azef:** Figner, 146–147, 155–156. **Figner on BVS's poetry and ideas:** Figner, 154–155, 159–160; "Pis'mo B. V. Savinkova V. N. Figner," 196.

159–161 **Bukhalo bomber:** Savinkov, *Vospominaniia*, 264–265. **History of flight:** Bilstein; "Airplane. History"; "Blériot XI"; "Flight Airspeed Record." **BVS's dream of flying:** *Pis'ma Azefa*, 138–139; Savinkov, *Vospominaniia*, 265–266; Figner, 156. **Okhrana monitors flying:** Ruud, 70; Morozov, *Partiia*, 424. **Airplane unfinished:** Savinkov, *Vospominaniia*, 273–275; *Pis'ma Azefa*, 145–146; Gorodnitskii, *Boevaia*, 226; Geifman, *Entangled*, 135.

161–165   **Azef's sabotage:** *Pis'ma Azefa*, 124–125; Gorodnitskii, *Boevaia*, 137–138; Goncharova, 24–25 n.
59; Savinkov, *Vospominaniia*, 280. **Suspicions about Azef:** Geifman, *Entangled*, 106–107. **Burtsev:**
Geifman, *Entangled*, 107–108; "Burtsev, Vladimir L'vovich." **Burtsev's suspicions:** Burtsev, "Kak ia
razoblachil Azefa," 175, 184, 189–190, 193–196. **Azef betrays Zilberberg:** Gorodnitskii, *Boevaia*,
133; Savinkov, *Vospominaniia*, 289–290; Figner, 217; Bunin, 522. **Azef fights back:** Burtsev, "Kak ia
razoblachil Azefa," 196–197, 202.

165–168   **BVS on writing:** Sofia Savinkova [inference based on internal evidence and handwriting; no
signature; no dates] to BVS, GARF, d. 178, ll. 332, 333; Goncharova, 35; BVS to VGS, May 8,
1905, Gorodnitskii, 191–192. **Zinaida and two Dmitrys:** Goncharova, 8–11; Matich, 205; "Dmitrii
Merezhkovskii. Biografiia"; "Dmitry Merezhkovsky." **BVS and the Merezhkovskys:** Goncharova,
12–13; "Fondaminskii, Il'ia Isidorovich"; BVS to Sofia Petit, November 22, 1907, BDIC, F delta Rés
571 (4) (3), Carton 4, Chemise 3, "Lezhnev Veniamin, Lezhnev Pavel" (psevdonimy Borisa Savinkova).
Zinaida Gippius on BVS and "bombers": Goncharova, 13–19, 22–23.

168–172   **Merezhkovsky's lecture and influence on BVS:** Goncharova, 16–18, 22–26, 30–31; "Pis'mo B. V.
Savinkova V. N. Figner." **New Love:** Police *fileur* report, January 16, 1908, Hoover, Index No. XVIIi,
folder 2; Ianovskii, 172, 175; Bunin, 522; Gippius, *Dmitrii Merezhkovskii*, part 2, chap. 6; VGS to BVS
and vice versa, Gorodnitskii, *Boevaia*, 192; anonymous letter [Evgeniia Somova-Zil'berberg, inference
based on internal evidence] to BVS, and related Police report, January 16/29, 1908, no. 36, Hoover,
Index No. XVIIi, folder 2.

172–174   **BVS family's turmoil:** Maid [Mme Le Hon (?)] to Sofia Petit, December 24, 1907, BDIC, F delta Res
571 (5) (1) (2). **Evgeniya:** Police Reports, January 16/29, no. 36, and February 18/March 12, 1908, no. 68,
Hoover, Index No. XVIIi, folder 2; Police report, February 8/21, 1911, no. 194, Hoover, Index No. XVIIi,
folder 3b, sheet 27; Gorodnitskii, *Boevaia*, 193. **VGS's letters:** VGS to BVS, no dates [probable date based on
context and internal evidence], GARF, d. 178, l. 42; VGS to BVS, February 25, 1908, GARF, d. 178, l. 46;
VGS to BVS, March 7, 1908 [inferred date based on context and internal evidence], GARF, d. 178, l. 48.

174–176   **Regicide:** Gorodnitskii, *Boevaia*, 139–141, 192; Goncharova, 35; Chernov, 283. *Ryurik*: Savinkov,
Vospominaniia, 280–287; Burtsev, "Azef i Gen. Gerasimov," 213–214 (Burtsev speculates the sailors
could have been stopped by the local revolutionary committee, which had plans for an uprising that
would have been disrupted); Gorodnitskii, *Boevaia*, 144–146.

176–179   **Burtsev strikes:** Savinkov, *Vospominaniia*, 296, 299–302, 308, 313; Amfiteatrov, 165–167; Figner, 271.
Court of honor: Amfiteatrov, 165; Savinkov, *Vospominaniia*, 303–310, 316–319; Figner, 251–254.

179–181   **Lopukhin's evidence:** Gorodnitskii, *Boevaia*, 149–151; "Lopukhin, Alexey Alexandrovich"; Figner,
260; Savinkov, *Vospominaniia*, 311, 313–319; *Pis'ma Azefa*, 154–161, 164–165 (between October 10 and
December 21, 1908); Gerasimov, 276–278, 280.

182–185   **Azef exposed:** Savinkov, *Vospominaniia*, 322–330; Geifman, *Entangled*, 115. **Azef escapes:** Geifman,
Entangled, 144–146, 156, 160–162, 165; quotes from Shchegolev, 10–11; Nicolaievsky, 274, 277, 279.
Most brazen letter: Figner, 267.

185–187   **Blast waves:** Savinkov, *Vospominaniia*, 330–339; Geifman, *Entangled*, 128, 131–132; Iskhakova;
Burtsev, "Azef i Gen. Gerasimov," 206–208, 211–212, 218, 221; Gerasimov, 286–287. **Lopukhin's fate:**
Geifman, *Entangled*, 123, 126–128. **SR reactions:** Zenzinov, 414; Chernov, 279; Geifman, *Entangled*,
134, 137; Savinkov, *Vospominaniia*, 347.

187–188   **BVS's pain:** Savinkov, "Terror i delo Azefa," 10. **Relations with VGS:** VGS to BVS, February 9,
19[09?], GARF, d. 178, l. 102; BVS to VGS, February 11, 1909, "Moi trud ne prineset," 13; VGS to
BVS, n.d [summer 1909? based on internal evidence], GARF, d. 178, l. 295; BVS to VGS, November 9,
1909, "Moi trud ne prineset," 13; VGS to BVS, October 21 to December 23, [1908?] GARF, d. 178, l.
77, 83, 89, 95, 97, 271; VGS to BVS, May 3, [1909?] GARF, d. 178, l. 58; VGS to BVS, April 30, 1909,
"Moi trud ne prineset," 14 n.

188–192   *The Pale Horse*: Goncharova, 38, 35; Savinkov, *Kon' blednyi*, 7, 77. **Dostoyevsky allusions:** Savinkov,
Kon' blednyi, 33, 32, 125. **Nabokov:** Nabokov, *Strong Opinions*, 19. Figner may well have projected some
of her later impressions of *The Pale Horse*, which would be published in 1909, onto her recollections of
her dealings with BVS in 1907. In what he said to her on the Riviera, BVS may also have been echoing

not only Dostoyevsky but Friedrich Nietzsche, whose ideas about "the will to power," "the overman," life "beyond good and evil," and the "death of god" had acquired an almost hypnotic grip on the imaginations of many Europeans and Russians at the beginning of the twentieth century. Similar ideas can also be found in Max Stirner, another German thinker whom many linked to Nietzsche at the time (Spence, *Savinkov*, 17, 41–42).

192–193   **Gippius on *The Pale Horse*:** Gippius to Sofia Petit, June 10 [?], 1909, BDIC, F Delta Res 571 (2) (5), p. 4. **BVS's dissatisfaction:** BVS to Sofia Petit, September 3, 1908, BDIC, F Delta Res 571 (4) (3), p. 3. **Publication, reactions to *The Pale Horse*:** Goncharova, 36, 37; Gippius to BVS, February 6, 1909, Goncharova, 156–158; BVS to Sofia Petit, February 14, 1909, BDIC, F delta Res 571 (4) (3); Merezhkovsky's review "Kon' blednyi" is reprinted in Goncharova, 347–363; quotes from 349, 352. **Bryusov and Tolstoy:** Goncharova, 158 n. 1; Viktor Savinkov to BVS, October 7, 1923, GARF, d. 177, l. 56. Viktor Savinkov claimed that he was told by Tolstoy's former secretary, Valentin Bulgakov, that some of the remarks were positive, some were editorial, and none were as negative as those Tolstoy made about Gorky's works. Tolstoy had recently condemned the imperial regime for doing more evil than the terrorists with their assassinations (Goncharova, 42–43).

193–194   **Revolutionaries' outrage, fame and notoriety:** "Amfiteatrov i Savinkov," 125; Morozov, "Poiski otvetov," n. 83. BVS started by publishing sketches of Kalyaev and other members of the Combat Organization in the historical and revolutionary journal *Byloe* in 1908 (Lur'e, 204–205). His mother had already published the story of her two eldest sons' travails in *Byloe*, including BVS's notorious escape from prison in Sevastopol, even earlier, starting in 1906. **Call of honor:** Gorodnitskii, *Boevaia*, 184–234. **New "Combat Group":** Morozov, "B. V. Savinkov," 244–245, 248–249; Gorodnitskii, *Boevaia*, 202–203, 227–228; Savinkov, *Vospominaniia*, 346–347; Lebedev, "Konets," 166.

194–196   **Things go wrong:** Morozov, "B. V. Savinkov," 251, 254, 260, 264, 301, 312–313 n. 7; Gorodnitskii, "B. V. Savinkov," 228; Morozov, *Partiia*, 430–432. **BVS loses hope:** Gorodnitskii, *Boevaia*, 228, 231–232; Morozov, "B. V. Savinkov," 244, 301; Morozov, *Partiia*, 431; Goncharova, 58; Police report, May 6/April 23, 1911, no. 567, Hoover, Index No. XVIIi, Folder 3B.

CHAPTER SIX

197–199   **BVS out of the fight:** Police report, March 3/April 5 no. 277/278, Hoover, Index No. XVIIi, Folder 1. **Okhrana still watches:** Police report, May 6/April 23, 1911, no. 567, Hoover, Index No. XVIIi, Folder 3B; French *fileur* reports about losing Savinkov at a train station, February 1, 1912, Hoover, Index No. XVIIi, Folder 1; French *fileur* reports on Savinkov's movements and his awareness that he is being followed, February 2, 1912, Hoover, Index No. XVIIi, Folder 1. **Elaborate charade, moments of discovery:** Police report, April 19/May 2, 1911, no. 544, Hoover, Index No. XVIIi, Folder 3B; Police report, November 30/December 13, 1910, no. 1105, Hoover, Index No. XVIIi, Folder 2; Russian police reports quoting texts by Sofia Savinkova, February 21 (no. 106617) and March 10, 1910 (no. 107520), Hoover, Index No. XVIIi, Folder 2.

199–202   **Writing:** BVS to Sofia Petit, May 11, 1909, BDIC, 571 (4) (3); Gorodnitskii, *Boevaia*, 229. **Poetry:** Ropshin, *Kniga stikhov*, 4, 6, 7, 13, 15, 17. ***What Never Happened*:** "Primechaniia," Ropshin, *To, chego ne bylo*, 716; Police Report, December 13, 1912/January 13, 1913, no. 1730, Hoover, Index No. XVIIi, Folder 4. Although established legally in 1912, *Zavety* encountered difficulties with censorship from the start and was shut down by the government in 1914, "Zavety (zhurnal)." **Provokator executed:** Ropshin, *To, chego ne bylo*, 448.

202–205   ***War and Peace*, "Man proposes, God disposes":** Tolstoy, 971. The echoes of *War and Peace* in *What Never Happened* include much else beyond Tolstoyan fatalism, including narrative techniques, plot turns, symbols, and depictions of human consciousness. But despite the importance of Tolstoy's novel for BVS, his characters and the experiences they have ultimately owe more to his own past than to his great predecessor. **Echoes of *War and Peace*:** Ropshin, *To, chego ne bylo*, 258, 318, 320, 324, 420, 421. **True SR believers, concluding paean:** Ropshin, *To, chego ne bylo*, 334, 504. **Critics:** Police Report, December 31, 1912/January 13, 1913, no. 1730, Hoover, Index No. XVIIi, Folder 4; Morozov, "Poiski otvetov," before n. 90 (no pagination in internet publication). **Lenin ridicules:** Zhukov, 47;

Police report, November 9/22, 1912, no. 1463, Hoover, Index No. XVIIi, Folder 1; Police Report, December 31, 1912/January 13, 1913, no. 1730, Hoover, Index No. XVIIi, Folder 4; *Russkaia literature kontsa XIX–nachala XX v.*, 527–528, 547. **Gippius and others:** *Russkaia literatura kontsa XIX–nachala XX v.*, 528; Goncharova, 226 n. 9, 228–230. **BVS's reactions:** BVS to VGS, August 6/19, 1912, "Moi trud ne prineset," 14; BVS to VGS, March 20, 1913, "Moi trud ne prineset," 16.

205–206 **Money:** Goncharova, 260 n. 6; BVS to Iakov Osipovich [no surname], November 16, 1913, draft of letter purloined by French fileurs, and BVS to Viktor Chernov, July 31, 1911, copy of letters, Hoover, Index No. XVIIi, Folder 3C; BVS to Il'ia Fondaminskii, December 12, 1913, draft of letter, and BVS to editor of *Zavety*, May 3/16, 1914, Hoover, Index No. XVIIi, Folder 3C. *Petersburg*: Dolgopolov, 230ff, discusses the novel's connections to BVS and other Socialist Revolutionaries, as well as many additional sources; Goncharova, 274; Police report including drafts of letters purloined from BVS [to Zinaida Gippius] about Belyi's novel *Petersburg*, January 28/February 10, 1914, Hoover, Index No. XVIIi, Folder 3D. **Other writing:** Goncharova, 266, 272–273, 275; Viktor Savinkov to BVS, March 1, 1913, GARF, d. 177, l.1; d. 177, l. 1; Police report with BVS's purloined letter drafts, August 17/30, 1911, no. 1074, Hoover, Index No. XVIIi, Folder 3B; Police report with transcript of BVS's purloined letter, August 8/31, 1912, no. 1052, Hoover, Index No. XVIIi, Folder 1; BVS to Sofia Petit, May 11, 1909, BDIC 571 (4) (3). **Loans and pawning:** Police report, September 17, 1911, no. 1191, Hoover, Index No. XVIIi, Folder 1; Goncharova, 262 n. 2; Morozov, *Partiia*, 431; Morozov, "B. V. Savinkov," 305; BVS to Sergei Nikolaevich [no surname], May 18, 1914, Hoover, Index No. XVIIi, Folder 3C.

206–209 **Gambling:** French *fileur* reports, November 26, 1912, January 11, 1913, Hoover, Index No. XVIIi, Folder 3D; Alexandrov, 45; Morozov, *Partiia*, 431, 435; Police report, April 28/May 11, 1911, no. 588, Hoover, Index No. XVIIi, Folder 1; French *fileur* report, April 28, 1911, Hoover, Index No. XVIIi, Folder 3C. *Fileur* **close surveillance:** French *fileur* report, February 3, 1913, Hoover, Index No. XVIIi, Folder 3D; French *fileur* report, December 27, 1910, Hoover, Index No. XVIIi, Folder 3A; French *fileur* report, February 8/21, 1911, Hoover, Index No. XVIIi, Folder 3B; Goncharova, 177 n. 4; French *fileur* report, February 11, 1911, Hoover, Index No. XVIIi, Folder 3C; French *fileur* report, November 25, 1912, Hoover, Index No. XVIIi, Folder 3D. **Son and family:** Goncharova, 58, 248 n. 15, 284–285; French *fileur* report, November 28, 1912, Hoover, Index No. XVIIi, Folder 3D; Savinkov, "Dnevnik," 189. **Exercise and social events:** French *fileur* reports, January 1, 1910, March 22, 1911, Folder 3B, June 22, 1913, Folder 3D, Hoover, Index No. XVIIi; Police report, December 28, 1913/January 9, 1914, no. 2019, with letters purloined from Savinkov, Hoover, Index No. XVIIi, Folder 3D; Amfiteatrov, 168. **Prokofyeva:** "Prokof'eva, Mariia Alekseevna"; Gorodnitskii, *Boevaia*, 194; Spiridonova, 482–483; Goncharova, 188 n. 11. **BVS, "vomited blood":** French *fileur* reports, September 6, 1911, Folder 3C, November 30, 1912, January 21, 1913, Folder 3D, Hoover, Index No. XVIIi; French *fileur* reports, April 28, 1911, Folder 1, May 15, May 17, June 2, 1911, Folder 3C, Hoover, Index No. XVIIi. The Italian police tracked BVS and members of his circle as well: Reports by Prefect of Genoa and Porto Maurizio to Minister of Interior, Rome, Fondo A11, 1911, b. 6, Nervi Colonia Russa. **Prokofyeva not of this world:** Goncharova, 257; Gippius, *Dmitrii Merezhkovskii*; Savinkov, "Dnevnik," 190; French *fileur* report July 31, 1913, Hoover, Index No. XVIIi, Folder 3D.

209–213 **War:** Alexandrov, 109–110; Lebedev, *Iz riadov*, 3–5, 78. **Zimmerwald Movement:** Pipes, *Revolution*, 382–383; "Zimmerwald Conference." **BVS seeks a role:** Goncharova, 295, 306–307 n. 3 (as this note explains, at times he had to support nine people, including Evgeniya's sister-in-law with her daughter and her mother); Lebedev, *Iz riadov*, 75, 167; Savinkov, *Vo frantsii*, 218. **BVS against Prussian militarism:** BVS to Plekhanov, September 18, 1914, Goncharova, 303–304 n. 5; "Autobiography of Boris Savinkov," IISH; Chernov, 300. **War correspondent:** Goncharova, 303 n. 4; "Boris Viktorovich Savinkov" (photograph and note); document about Belgian regulations pertaining to war correspondents, March 3, 1915, "Vu du Front"; purloined letter, Evgeniia Savinkova to Sofia Savinkova, September 12, 1914, Hoover, Index No. XVIIi, Folder 1. *In France During the War*: the full title is *Vo frantsii vo vremia voiny: sentiabr' 1914—iiun' 1915*, with the date range September 1914–June 1915, which is not completely accurate since some of the pieces date from the beginning of 1916; BVS to VGS, October 26, 1914, "Moi trud ne prineset," 17.

213–216 *In France During the War*: BVS acknowledges censorship in his letter to VGS, October 26, 1914, "Moi trud ne prineset," 17. BVS's later, negative comments about the sketches (Savinkov, "Dnevnik," 187) may well have been influenced by his being in the Lubyanka Prison and the hands of the OGPU. Savinkov, *Vo frantsii:* Apocalyptic terms: e.g., 52, 94, 187; bayoneted German: 101–102; first-hand impressions: 90, 189; the British: 70, 104–107; French landscapes and Russian soldiers: 62, 64, 127, 166, 218, 259; self-sacrifice and John 12:24: 115, 207; universality of human nature: 207; democratic relations: 121–123, 241, 228, 330ff.

216–220 BVS on the war in Russia: BVS to Voloshin, July 26, 1915, Frezenskii, 23; BVS to Voloshin, July 19, 1915, Frezenskii, 22. Progress of the war in Russia: Alexandrov, 116–117, 120–121, 126, 128–129, 131–133; Pipes, *Revolution*, 238–239. BVS's allusions to the war in Russia: Savinkov, *Vo frantsii*, 101, 194–195, 220, 279, 308. Russian soldiers will fight for freedom: 321, 347. War and rebirth: Savinkov, *Vo frantsii*, 298, 303, 319.

220–222 Lies about the war: Goncharova, 306 n. 1; Savinkov, *Vo frantsii*, 76–77. Tsetlin: "Tsetlin, Mikhail"; Frezinskii, 16; Erenburg, *Liudi*, 144. Voloshin: Frezinskii, 15; "Voloshin [Maksimilian Aleksandrovich]"; Voloshin, *Izbrannoe*, Introduction; Vorobëv, 136–137. Ehrenburg: Frezinskii, 47; "Ilya Ehrenburg"; "Erenburg, Il'ia Grigor'evich." Ehrenburg on BVS: Frezinskii, 15, 18, 55, 35; Vorobëv, 134; Erenburg, *Liudi*, 193–194.

222–225 La Rotonde: Erenburg, *Liudi*, 158; Vorobëv, 120–121; Bromberger. Rivera and Modigliani: Erenburg, *Liudi*, 198; Fifield, 252–253; Vorobëv, 157; "With $170.4 Million Sale at Auction, Modigliani Work Joins Rarefied Nine-Figure Club," *The New York Times*, November 10, 2015, Section A, 20; Vorobëv, 137. Marevna: Erenburg, *Liudi*, 159, 195; Frezinskii, 16, 40, 42. Marevna and BVS: Vorobëv, 137 (she mistakenly refers to "Grand Duke Michael" instead of "Sergey" as BVS's target), 138; Frezinskii, 15, 32, 36, 94. Zadkine and Picasso: Vorobëv, 138, 180.

225–228 Romantic entanglements: Frezinskii, 22–24, 42, 48; Marnham, 121; Vorobëv, 193. Evgeniya and Marevna: Frezinskii, 58; Vorobëv, 236–237, 241. BVS's financial difficulties: Frezinskii, 30, 40. BVS and VGS: BVS to VGS, September 20, 1916, "Moi trud ne prineset," 22; Frezinskii, 76–77; BVS to VGS, March 14, 1915, September 3, 1915, "Moi trud ne prineset," 19, 21; BVS to VGS, February 15, 1915, February 3/18, 1915, "Moi trud ne prineset," 18–19; BVS to VGS, November 24, 1916, "Moi trud ne prineset," 22; Tatyana Savinkova to BVS, n.d. [summer 1909?], and April 15, [no year, 1910?], GARF, d. 178, l. 288; l. 191. Tanya: Tatyana Savinkova to BVS, October 13 [no year, 1917?], GARF, d. 178, l. 386.

228–231 BVS's sense of purposelessness: Frezinskii, 40–41, 48, 53, 55. Revolution in Russia: Alexandrov, 133–134, 136–137; Rappaport, 130; Pipes, *Revolution*, 296. Hardly a whimper: Riasanovsky, 505–508; Saul, 95. Monarchy's collapse greeted with elation: Rappaport, 141; Alexandrov, 137. Sense of liberty: Rappaport, 143–144, 146–148. Crime: Alexandrov, 138.

231–234 News of Revolution arrives in France: Viktor Savinkov to BVS, March 22, 1917, GARF, d. 177, l.5; d. 177, l. 5; BVS to G. V. Plekhanov, March 23, 1917, Goncharova, 76 n. 191; Pipes, *Revolution*, 400; Chernov, 318; Frezenskii, 77. Returning home: Chernov, 304; Pipes, *Revolution*, 298; Nabokoff, 94–95, 97, 99, 100–101; Spence, *Savinkov*, 103. Reception in Petrograd: "Autobiography of Boris Savinkov," IISH; Spence, *Savinkov*, 108, 407 n. 14; Chernov, 304–306; Annenkov, 259.

234–236 Chernov and the Soviet: Chernov, 307; Pipes, *Revolution*, 296, 304; Alexandrov, 138. Germans and Lenin: Pipes, *Revolution*, 380–381, 386, 391–392; Churchill, *Churchill by Himself*, 553. Lenin on February Revolution: Pipes, *Revolution*, 387, 389, 392–393.

236–238 Petrograd after February: Rappaport, 18–19. Army's collapse accelerates, Dardanelles: Alexandrov, 138. BVS as commissar: BVS wrote that he was appointed commissar in April 1917 (Savinkov, *K delu Kornilova*, 3). Since Kerensky became the new minister of war on May 2, 1917 (Kerensky, *Russia and History's*, 269), this implies that Savinkov was appointed by Guchkov before he resigned as the Provisional Government's first minister of war. Pipes, *Revolution*, 413. Seventh Army: estimate based on data in "Brusilovskii proryv"; "Iz zhurnala zasedaniia Vremennogo pravitel'stva No. 132"; "Autobiography of Boris Savinkov," IISH. BVS to Gippius: April 17, 1917, Goncharova, 309.

CHAPTER SEVEN

239–242 **BVS to the front:** Ropshin, "Iz deistvuiushchei armii," 192; Savinkov, *K delu Kornilova*, 4. **Stepun:** "Fyodor Stepun"; Stepun, 365. **BVS's behavior as commissar:** Stepun, 365–366; Lebedev, "Konets Savinkova," 170; Woytinsky, 334. **Belkovich on BVS:** Vandervelde, 162–163.

242–245 **BVS at the front:** BVS to Gippius, July 2, 1917, Goncharova, 311–312; Anonymous memoir [Viktor Savinkov], IISH, 97; Wędziagolski, 22; Stepun, 366, 368–370. **BVS and rebellions at front:** Vandervelde, 152, 158–159; Ropshin, "Iz deistvuiushchei armii," 214; Kerensky, *Russia and History's*, 275; Stankevich, 191; Savinkov, "General Kornilov," 200–201; Anonymous memoir [Viktor Savinkov], IISH, 91. **BVS, radicalized soldier, Bolshevik agitation:** Stepun, 367; BVS to Sofia Savinkova, June 3, 1917, *Boris Savinkov na Lubianke*, 561; Anonymous memoir [Viktor Savinkov], IISH, 96.

245–248 **Wędziagolski:** Photographs, accessed September 12, 2020 <http://naszczas2002.tripod.com/056/czas .html>; Wędziagolski, 3, 145; Vendziagol'skii, part 1, 191. **BVS and resolute commanders:** Ropshin, "Iz deistvuiushchei armii," 193; Vendziagol'skii, part 1, 192–193; Wędziagolski, 4–6. **BVS and Kornilov:** Vendziagol'skii, part 1, 193–194, 205–206; Pipes, *Revolution*, 440; Wędziagolski, 7, 26–27.

248–251 **Change in Provisional Government:** Pipes, *Revolution*, 402–406. **Kerensky:** Stepun, 363–364; Pipes, *Revolution*, 413. **BVS's efforts and promotion:** BVS to Sofia Savinkova, June 3, 1917, *Boris Savinkov na Lubianke*, 561; Savinkov, "General Kornilov," 193. **Kerensky offensive:** Pipes, *Revolution*, 417–418; Savinkov, "General Kornilov," 194; BVS to Sofia Savinkova, June 26, 1917, *Boris Savinkov na Lubianke*, 562; Kerensky, *Russia and History's*, 281; Wędziagolski, 4–6.

251–254 *From the Active Army:* Ropshin, "Iz deistvuiushchei armii," 191, 195, 198, 206, 214; Wędziagolski, 18–19; Vendziagol'skii, part 1, 200; BVS to Sofia Savinkova, June 26, 1917, *Boris Savinkov na Lubianke*, 562; BVS to Gippius, July 2, 1917, Goncharova, 311. **Peasant soldiers:** Wędziagolski, 15; Bushnell, 65; Ropshin, "Iz deistvuiushchei armii," 198, 206. **Assault Battalion of Death:** Ropshin, "Iz deistvuiushchei armii," 217–218. **Women's Death Battalion:** Rappaport, 193–201.

254–256 **Soldiers dispirited, ill-supplied:** Ropshin, "Iz deistvuiushchei armii," 210; Bushnell, 65. **Soldiers' backwardness:** Ropshin, "Iz deistvuiushchei armii," 200; Wędziagolski, 15. **BVS and family:** BVS to Sofia Savinkova, June 3 and 26, 1917, *Boris Savinkov na Lubianke*, 561, 562; Spence, *Savinkov*, 109, 408 n. 21; Anonymous memoir [Viktor Savinkov], IISH, 35, 64; Viktor Savinkov to BVS, April 14, May 6, May 29, 1914, GARF, d. 177, ll. 12, 13, 19; Viktor Savinkov to BVS, February 10, 1917, "Moi trud ne prineset," 22.

256–259 **Bolshevik view of Revolution:** Pipes, *Revolution*, 407–408; Rappaport, 209; Kotkin, 231. **"July Days":** Pipes, *Revolution*, 419, 425–433, 435–438; Riasanovksy, 509; Engelstein, 154–157. **Governmental crisis:** Pipes, *Revolution*, 437; Knox, 672.

259–261 **Mutinous soldiers:** *Revoliutsionnoe dvizhenie*, 182, 212–213, 288. **BVS and Kornilov:** Savinkov, "General Kornilov," 194–196; Kerensky, *Delo Kornilova*, 66. **BVS on need for discipline and death penalty:** Savinkov, "O 'Soglashateliakh'," 43; *Revoliutsionnoe dvizhenie*, 194; "Quelle Mémoire pour les fusillés de 1914–1918?"; Savinkov, "General Kornilov," 199. **BVS and Kornilov, warning and collaboration:** Savinkov, "General Kornilov," 196–197; Savinkov, *K delu Kornilova*, 6–7 (the account of the telegram in Savinkov, "General Kornilov," 196–198, differs in several details).

261–263 **BVS, Kornilov, dictatorship:** Ratkovskii, "Vosstanovlenie," 48–53; Savinkov to Commissars on the South-Western Front [telegram], July 9, 1917, *Revoliutsionnoe dvizhenie*, 197; Stankevich, 191, 193; Military dispatches, July 20, 23, 28, 1917, *Revoliutsionnoe dvizhenie*, 231, 268, 277.

263–265 **BVS at military conference:** "Prizrak Stavki na staroi ploshchadi"; Denikin, "Soveshchanie v Stavke 16 iulia"; Savinkov, "General Kornilov," 202; Savinkov, *K delu Kornilova*, 7–8. **BVS in Kerensky's confidence:** Savinkov, *K delu Kornilova*, 9–10; Gourko, 389–390; Savinkov, "General Kornilov," 202.

265–267 **Kerensky's resolve fades:** Savinkov, *K delu Kornilova*, 9–10; Knox, 674; Sir George Buchanan to Lord Hardinge, August 15, 1917, NAK, FO 371/2998, no. 172561. **BVS Director of Ministry of War:** Savinkov, *K delu Kornilova*, 10–11, 29; "Iz zhurnala zasedaniia Vremennogo pravitel'stva No. 139," n. 1. **Reactions to BVS's appointment:** Anonymous memoir [Viktor Savinkov], IISH, 69–70, 73; Oberuchev, 317; Sir George Buchanan to Lord Hardinge, August 15, 1917, NAK, FO 371/2998, no. 172561; Noulens, 198–199.

267–271   **BVS's energy:** Oberuchev, 319–320; Erenburg, *Liudi*, 230; Savinkov, *K delu Kornilova*, 17. **BVS's new prominence:** Woytinsky, 351; Lebedev, "Konets Savinkova," 170, 173; Erenburg, *Liudi*, 229. **Private motorcar:** "Spisok lits." **Petrograd's decline:** Erenburg, *Liudi*, 229; Gippius, *Dnevniki*, vol. 1, 535; Rappaport, 229, 234–236. **Writers and Masons:** Remizov, *Vzvikhrennaia Rus'*, 265; Gippius, *Dnevniki*, vol. 1, 540; Startsev, 47, 179–185, 198, 265, 277 n. 64; "Protokol doprosa [Borisa Savinkova]," 73.

271–274   **BVS and Kornilov:** Savinkov, *K delu Kornilova*, 12; Savinkov, "General Kornilov," 203. **BVS and restructuring government:** Gippius, vol. 1, 525–527. **BVS and Kerensky:** Savinkov, *K delu Kornilova*, 13–15; Savinkov, "General Kornilov," 202–204; Pipes, *Revolution*, 446. **Kerensky's fears:** Gippius, *Dnevniki*, vol. 1, 531–533. (Gippius's and BVS's accounts differ in a number of ways, but because she was writing a daily diary, I accept her dates.) Pipes, *Revolution*, 437–438.

274–277   **Kerensky's plot:** Pipes, *Revolution*, 446–449 and 447 note; Kerensky, *Delo Kornilova*, 66; Gippius, *Dnevniki*, vol. 1, 539; Savinkov, *K delu Kornilova*, 19. **German advance, Bolshevik threat:** Pipes, *Revolution*, 448. **Kerensky and new statutes:** Savinkov, *K delu Kornilova*, 12–13, 19; Pipes, *Revolution*, 442–443, 450. **Kerensky vacillates:** Savinkov, *K delu Kornilova*, 15, 21, 23–24; Savinkov, "General Kornilov," 205; Gippius, *Dnevniki*, vol. 1, 543; Pipes, *Revolution*, 442–443.

277–280   **Meeting in Malachite Hall:** photograph of Malachite Hall, accessed September 12, 2020 <http ://spbfoto.spb.ru/foto/details.php?image_id=915&mode=search>; photograph of Nicholas II's library, accessed September 12, 2020 <http://spbfoto.spb.ru/foto/details.php?image_id=1022>; Savinkov, *K delu Kornilova*, 24; Gippius, *Dnevniki*, vol. 1, 551 (differs from BVS). **Lvov's list:** Pipes, *Revolution*, 454–455; Savinkov, *K delu Kornilova*, 24. **BVS attempts to salvage situation:** Savinkov, *K delu Kornilova*, 25–26; Savinkov, "General Kornilov," 206, 208, 210; Pipes, *Revolution*, 458–459. **August 27:** Miliukov, part 2, chap. VII, "'Ugovor' prevrashchaetsia v 'zagovor'"; Pipes, *Revolution*, 457, 459; Savinkov, *K delu Kornilova*, 26–27; Savinkov, "General Kornilov," 210; Gippius, *Dnevniki*, vol. 1, 552–553, 562; Savinkov, *Bor'ba*, 155–156; Rappaport, 272.

280–281   **Kornilov in Mogilyov:** Miliukov, part 2, chap. VIII, "Kornilov vystupaet protiv pravitel'stva"; Pipes, *Revolution*, 459–460. **Kerensky's use of Lvov:** Pipes, *Revolution*, 451–456, 463; Kerensky, *Delo Kornilova*, 100, 105–106 (Pipes, *Revolution*, 454 n., mentions that Miliukov was another source of information in addition to Kerensky because he talked to Lvov immediately before and after the meeting; see Miliukov, part 2, chap. VII, "'Ugovor' prevrashchaetsia v 'zagovor.'"); Gippius, *Dnevniki*, vol. 1, 580–581.

281–283   **BVS and defense of Petrograd:** Kerensky, *Delo Kornilova*, 33, 96; Pipes, *Revolution*, 460–461; Stepun, 438–439. **Why BVS turned on Kornilov:** Savinkov, *K delu Kornilova*, 27–28; Savinkov, "General Kornilov," 210; Gippius, *Dnevniki*, vol. 1, 531–533; Miliukov, part 2, chap. VIII, "Kornilov vystupaet protiv pravitel'stva"; Pipes, *Revolution*, 461, 463. **BVS's "stupid honesty":** Savinkov, "Dnevnik," 191; Anonymous memoir [Viktor Savinkov], IISH, 102.

284–287   **Bolsheviks armed:** Pipes, *Revolution*, 461, 466–467; Gippius, *Dnevniki*, vol. 1, 553–554; Savinkov, *K delu Kornilova*, 28. **Tragicomedy:** Gippius, *Dnevniki*, vol. 1, 555–556, 563; Pipes, *Revolution*, 461–462; Miliukov, part 2, chap. IX, "Neudacha i likvidatsiia vystupleniia Kornilova"; Savinkov, *K delu Kornilova*, 28–29. **Aftermath of Kornilov affair:** Savinkov, "General Kornilov," 210; Pipes, *Revolution*, 462–463; Anonymous memoir [Viktor Savinkov], IISH, 106; Savinkov, *K delu Kornilova*, 29; Gippius, *Dnevniki*, vol. 1, 564–566; Miliukov, part 2, chap. IX, "Neudacha i likvidatsiia vystupleniia Kornilova"; Stepun, 441; Kerensky, *Delo Kornilova*, 168. **Savinkov expelled by SRs:** Savinkov, *K delu Kornilova*, 29.

287–291   **BVS, Native Division, and Cossacks:** Stepun, 442; Gippius, *Dnevniki*, vol. 1, 569, 571. **British agent:** Jeffreys-Jones, 91–92; Rappaport, 267–269; Maugham, *A Writer's*, 172–173; Meyers, 35, 125. **Maugham on BVS:** Maugham, *A Traveler*, 227. **Shared views:** Jeffreys-Jones, 98; Maugham, *A Writer's*, 182; Maugham, *A Traveler*, 228. **The most extraordinary man:** Meyers, 123, 125, 126–128; Maugham, *A Traveler*, 228; Maugham, *A Writer's*, 184–186.

291–293   **October 1917:** Riasanovksy, 511; Pipes, *Revolution*, 471–474, 476–477, 485; Engelstein, 182; Bushkovitch, 301. **Bolsheviks' force, Kerensky's weakness:** Pipes, *Revolution*, 485–486, 488–489. **BVS and Cossacks:** Gippius, *Dnevniki*, vol. 1, 576, 579; Pipes, *Revolution*, 477; Savinkov, "K vystupleniiu bol'shevikov"; Kerenskii, "Gatchina." **Lenin returns from hiding:** Pipes, *Revolution*,

482. **BVS seeks help:** Savinkov, "K vystupleniiu bol'shevikov," 2; Gippius, *Dnevniki*, vol. 1, 581, 585; Savinkov, *Bor'ba*, 151.

293–296 **The coup:** Gippius, *Dnevniki*, vol. 1, 587; Pipes, *Revolution*, 491–493; Kerensky, *Russia and History's*, 439; "Pogoda istoricheskikh dat"; Rappaport, 287. **Kerensky seeks help:** Pipes, *Revolution*, 493–494. **BVS attempts to organize resistance, "storming" of Winter Palace:** Savinkov, "K vystupleniiu bol'shevikov"; Pipes, *Revolution*, 494–496; Gippius, *Dnevniki*, vol. 1, 589, 593; Trotskii, vol. 2, chap. XXIV, "V Petrograde."

296–298 **BVS tries to organize resistance:** Savinkov, "K vystupleniiu bol'shevikov," 2; Savinkov, *Bor'ba*, 151–155; Woytinski, 383; Wędziagolski, 46. **"Military council":** Savinkov, "K vystupleniiu bol'shevikov," 2–3; Savinkov, *Bor'ba*, 154–157 (BVS also refers to two Finnish divisions).

299–301 **Saving a grand duke:** "Savinkov" [Vladimir Burtsev's summary of Flegont Klepikov's recollections of BVS after the October Bolshevik coup], Hoover, Nicolas A. de Basily Papers, Box 25, Burtsev/Savinkov File, p. 4; Wędziagolski, 47. **Final struggle:** *Bor'ba*, 156–158; Kerenskii, "Gatchina"; Kerensky, *Russia and History's*, 446–447 (Kerensky says he left openly, but in disguise); Savinkov, "K vystupleniiu bol'shevikov"; Wędziagolski, 53–54. **October in Moscow:** Pipes, *Revolution*, 501–504; Alexandrov, 144.

CHAPTER EIGHT

302–305 **Petrograd reeling:** Gippius, *Dnevniki*, vol. 1, 596–598; Savinkov, *Bor'ba*, 158; Wędziagolski, 54. **Rising on the Don:** Savinkov, *Bor'ba*, 158; Wędziagolski, 58; Vendziagol'skii, part 2, 150. **BVS wanted, escapes to south:** Anonymous memoir [Viktor Savinkov], IISH, 110; Gippius, *Dnevniki*, vol. 2, 22; Savinkov, *Bor'ba*, 158; Wędziagolski, 58, 60–63. **The Don:** Savinkov, *Bor'ba*, 158–160; Wędziagolski, 65–72; Anonymous memoir [Viktor Savinkov], IISH, 126, 137.

305–308 **The Volunteer Army:** Savinkov, *Bor'ba*, 160–162; Wędziagolski, 78–92 (his account of the failed assassination attempt against BVS differs in many details, but the essence of the story is the same); Vendziagol'skii, part 2, 165. **Conflict in the Volunteer Army:** Denikin, "'Moskovskii tsentr'"; Goncharova, 313–315; *Boris Savinkov pered voennoi kollegiei*, 34; Savinkov, *Bor'ba*, 160. **BVS will work with anyone:** BVS to Gippius, January 4, 1918, Goncharova, 313–315.

308–309 **BVS to Petrograd:** *Boris Savinkov pered voennoi kollegiei*, 33, 39; Wędziagolski, 111. **Tatyana and Evgeniya:** BVS to Tatyana Uspenskaia, late December, 1917, "Moi trud ne prineset," 23; Fonds de Moscou, AN, Box 20010216/0238, delo no. 68, Rapport, May 31, 1918, "Hoffman, Emile." (The French Sûreté Nationale, or National Police, had kept an eye on Evgeniya after Savinkov left for Russia and carried out an investigation when they found out about the money she received. It determined that the Ministry sent the money to an agent in Paris who sent the sum to Evgeniya at the villa Belvédère in Théoule, on the Riviera, where she had lived with Savinkov before he returned to Russia.) **Cheka:** Alexandrov, 151; Savinkov, *Bor'ba*, 162.

309–312 **Bolsheviks choose tyranny:** Chernov, 346–349; Riasanovsky, 528; Alexandrov, 151; *Boris Savinkov pered voennoi kollegiei*, 39–40. **"Ice March":** Savinkov, *Bor'ba*, 162. **Going it alone:** Savinkov, *Bor'ba*, 162; Pipes, *Revolution*, 593–594. **Bolsheviks dismantle institutions, robberies, confiscation:** Alexandrov, 151–153; Shapovalova; Sergeev.

312–315 **Brest-Litovsk:** Pipes, *Revolution*, 593–594; Riasanovsky, 529; Combs, 66. **Foreign intervention:** Pipes, *Revolution*, 608 (estimates of numbers of transferred German troops vary); Riasanovsky, 535–536. **BVS's "Union":** Savinkov, *Bor'ba*, 162–163; Klement'ev, 72; Perkhurov, 5–7, Shentalinskii, "Svoi sredi svoikh," part 1. **Nonpartisan membership:** Klement'ev, 155; Savinkov, *Bor'ba*, 163.

315–317 **Dikgof-Derental, Lyubov Efimovna:** Perkhurov, 9; Klement'ev, 153; "Dikgof-Derental', Aleksandr Arkad'evich"; Dikgof-Derental', "Opiat' na rodine!" IISH, doc. 257; "Dikgof, Liubov' Efimovna"; Iarutskii; Dikgof-Derental', "Vospominaniia chlena Soiuza," IISH, 3; Zhukov, 79. **Underground army:** Savinkov, *Bor'ba*, 163–164; *Boris Savinkov pered voennoi kollegiei*, 47, 49; Klement'ev, 114, 156, 158–160, 162, 188; Perkhurov, 8. **BVS's plans:** Savinkov, *Bor'ba*, 163–164; Pipes, *Revolution*, 649; Perkhurov, 10; Klement'ev, 153–154.

317–320 **Foreign money:** Pipes, *Revolution*, 624–628; Masaryk, 198–199; Zhukov, 77; *Delo Borisa Savinkova*, 41; Perkhurov, 8; Klement'ev, 160. **British connection:** Hughes; Sergeev; Lockhart, *Memoirs*, 182;

R. H. B. Lockhart to Lord Balfour, November 7, 1918, NAK, FO 371/3337, no. 185499, 7 (Lockhart's report refers to the French disbursing money "even before I did."); Lockhart dispatch on Russia, May 17, 1918, NAK, FO 371/3332, no. 92708; Denikin, "Smert' Generala Kornilova." **French help:** Lockhart dispatch on Russia, May 17, 1918, NAK, FO 371/3332, no. 92708; *Boris Savinkov pered voennoi kollegiei*, 56–60; R. H. B. Lockhart to Lord Balfour, November 7, 1918, NAK, FO 371/3337, 7–8 (In his memoirs, Noulens, 110–111, does not mention any such promises, but this may have been out of later political considerations); Perkhurov, 11; Gopper. **Lockhart on intervention:** Occleshaw, 179–180; Lockhart dispatch on Russia, May 17, 1918, NAK, FO 371/3332, no. 92708; Milton, 114–115; Pipes, *Revolution*, 647, 650.

320–322   **Foreign intervention:** Pipes, *Revolution*, 599, 614; Alexandrov, xii; Kennan, 426. **Reilly:** Milton, 26–28, 33, 94–99; Sergeev; Spence, *Trust No One*, 91, 92, 213; Cook, 10–12, 60–61, 68 (Cook debunks various stories about Reilly, including that he stole German plans); "Sidney Reilly: Russian Spy"; Robin Lockhart, *Ace*, 74.

322–324   **Bolshevik police state:** Savinkov, *Bor'ba*, 164. **BVS's bravado:** Gul'; Lockhart, *Memoirs*, 182; Stepun, 463–464; Savinkov, "S dorogi!"; Dikgof-Derental', "Vospominaniia chlena Soiuza," IISH; Sergeev. **Cheka's arrests:** Savinkov, *Bor'ba*, 165–166; Klement'ev, 192; Gul'; Pipes, *Revolution*, 649; Dikgof-Derental', "Vospominaniia chlena Soiuza," IISH.

325–327   **Uprisings on the Volga:** Perkhurov, 10; Savinkov, *Bor'ba*, 166–167; Pipes, *Revolution*, 627–629. **Rybinsk and Yaroslavl:** Kidiarov, "Rybinskoe," 29–30; Savinkov, *Bor'ba*, 167–168; Baedeker, *Russia*, 330; Perkhurov, 13. **Klepikov and Lyubov Efimovna:** Klepikov to Boris Savinkov, September 27, 1921, 3–4, Hoover, General N. N. Golovin Papers, box no. 14.

328–332   **Battle for Yaroslavl:** Perkhurov, 14, 19, 21–22; Dikgof-Derental', "Vospominaniia chlena Soiuza," IISH; Pipes, *Revolution*, 651; "Vozzvanie k zhiteliam goroda Iaroslavlia"; Zlunitsyn; Kidiarov, "Iaroslavskii miatezh"; Gopper; "Stenograficheskii otchet o protsesse nad rukovoditelem Iaroslavskogo vosstaniia"; "Zapis' vospominanii V. A. Davatsa." **Foreign Bolshevik troops and artillery:** Dikgof-Derental', "Vospominaniia chlena Soiuza," IISH; Pipes, *Revolution*, 652. **BVS delays and betrayal:** Dikgof-Derental', "Iz perevernutykh stranits. Otryvki vospominanii," IISH, doc. 261, 2; Kidiarov, "Rybinskoe"; Savinkov, *Borba s bol'shevikami*, 168; Dikgof-Derental', "Vospominaniia chlena Soiuza," IISH. **Yaroslavl and the French:** Kidiarov, "Rybinskoe"; Savinkov, *Bor'ba*, 168–169; Dikgof-Derental', "Iz perevernutykh stranits. Otryvki vospominanii," IISH, doc. 261, 3; Perkhurov, 23, 29. **French officers:** There are conflicting descriptions of this crucial meeting, including two by Perkhurov that differ in some details (Perkhurov, *Ispoved' prigovorennogo* and "Stenograficheskii otchet o protsesse nad rukovoditelem Iaroslavskogo vosstaniia") and one by Gopper ("Iz vospominanii Tveritskogo uchastka oborony Iaroslavlia generala K. Goppera 'Chetyre katastrofy'"), which questions whether the Frenchmen were really officers connected with the planned intervention and suggests they were Bolsheviks carrying out a deception. **Dikgof-Derental and General Lavergne:** "Pokazaniia A. A. Dikgof-Derentalia," 387. In his memoirs, Noulens, 109–110, does not mention French involvement in Savinkov's uprising. Pipes, *Revolution*, 648, 650, states there is no archival evidence of French plans to help Savinkov militarily, and that Savinkov invented the French intervention in retrospect after he was arrested by the OGPU in 1924 because the Soviets wanted to blame everything on foreigners. However, Lockhart's report to London on May 28, 1918, that he had been told that the French were going to provide military assistance to Savinkov (more than a month before the uprisings) suggests that the promise had been made. Perkhurov's records of encountering two French billeting officers during the rising in Yaroslavl, as well as the consistency of Dikgof-Derental's and Savinkov's memoirs, also support the idea that the French promised military help.

332–336   **Bolshevik vengeance, BVS's evaluation:** Kidiarov, "Rybinskoe," 31; Pipes, *Revolution*, 652; "Iaroslavskoe vosstanie. Material'nyi ushcherb"; Boris, *Bor'ba*, 168–169; Denikin, "'Moskovskii tsentr'"; Ermolin; Riazantsev. **Bolsheviks under attack:** Pipes, *Revolution*, 636, 638, 641, 644; Engelstein, 266–268. **Execution of Romanovs:** Pipes, *Revolution*, 745–786, provides a detailed history of the murder of the Romanovs; "live banner," Pipes, *Revolution*, 787; see above, Chapter

Three, "Terror's Aftermath." **SR Combat Organization, Kaplan's attempt on Lenin:** Pipes, *Revolution*, 807, 809–812; Savinkov, *Bor'ba*, 166; *Boris Savinkov pered voennoi kollegiei*, 53–55.

336–339 **Red Terror:** Pipes, *Revolution*, 820; Engelstein, 270–271. **Ambassadors' Plot:** Pipes, *Revolution*, 656, 658; Occleshaw, 200, 214, 228, 237–238; Sergeev; Spence, "The Tragic Fate of Kalamatiano"; Milton, 183–184; Saul, 16–17, 300, 419. **Kalamatiano's fate, Reilly:** Milton, 166; Spence, "The Tragic Fate of Kalamatiano"; Cook, 170, 174, 188; Sergeev.

339–344 **BVS's typhus and Petrograd:** Klepikov to BVS, September 27, 1921, 4, Hoover, General N. N. Golovin Papers, box no. 14; Savinkov, *Bor'ba*, 169. **To Kazan:** Savinkov, *Bor'ba*, 170–171. **Czech Legion, Komuch:** Pipes, *Revolution*, 630, 659; Savinkov, *Bor'ba*, 172. **Kazan:** Vyrypaev, chap. 5, "Na Kazan'," chap. 6, "Na Moskvu!"; Pipes, *Revolution*, 659; Perkhurov, 26–30; Savinkov, *Bor'ba*, 172; Bushkovitch, 307; *Boris Savinkov pered voennoi kollegiei*, 73. **BVS rebuffed:** *Boris Savinkov pered voennoi kollegiei*, 73; Lebedev, "Konets Savinkova," 182.

344–347 **BVS as soldier:** Lebedev belittles Savinkov in "Konets Savinkova," 183, but Vyrypaev's description is more plausible: chap. 6, "Na Moskvu!"; Trotskii, vol. II, chap. XXXIII, "Mesiats v Sviiazhske"; Savinkov, *Bor'ba*, 173; *Boris Savinkov pered voennoi kollegiei*, 73; Ratkovskii, *Khronika*, 507–510, 449–465.

347–349 **Komuch defeated, retreat to the east:** Savinkov, *Bor'ba*, 174–175; Tsvetkov; Boldyrev, 25. **"Omsk Directory":** Borisov; Pipes, *Revolution*, 444; Boldyrev, 67, 82–83; Knox to Clerke, Wiseman, Vesey, and House, October 24, 1918, IISH, doc. 27; Simkin.

349–351 **BVS to Paris:** *Boris Savinkov pered voennoi kollegiei*, 80; Accounts of Boris Savinkov's mission to Paris, IISH, doc. 30; Odintsov passport, IISH, doc. 31; Boldyrev, 67, 521 n. 58; Accounts of salary paid to Savinkov, IISH, doc. 29. **Aims of BVS's mission:** Secret instructions to BVS for mission to Paris, IISH, doc. 26. **Ship to Europe:** Boldyrev, 83; Journal of correspondence received and sent by the Special military mission during its trip to Paris, BVS to Boldyrev, October 15 [*sic*, other evidence suggests correct date closer to November 17] 1918, 5–6, and Dikgof-Derental's copy of BVS's telegram, IISH, doc. 28; "Le Paul Lecat"; Newall, 53.

351–352 **The *Lecat*'s voyage:** "Russian Mission on Way to France: Kerensky's Former War Minister Says Army of 250,000 Needs Help." *New-York Tribune*, November 13, 1918, 7; Savinkov, "Dnevnik," 193; "Raport V. I. Speranskogo," 171.

CHAPTER NINE

353–355 **BVS seeks role in Paris:** BVS to Boldyrev, October 15 [*sic*, other evidence suggests correct date closer to November 17] 1918; Journal of the correspondence received and sent by the Special military mission during its trip to Paris, IISH, doc. 28; *Boris Savinkov pered voennoi kollegiei*, 82; BVS to Maklakov, December 21, 1918, Hoover, Vasilii Maklakov Papers, box 13; "United Russia Seen in Coup of Kolchak: Admiral Becomes Virtual Dictator of New Government in Omsk. Hope for Success Lies with America. Change Accepted by Troops Without Disorder; Allies Approve." *New-York Tribune*, November 22, 1918, 3; Boldyrev, 117; *Dopros Kolchaka*, 6-go fevralia 1920 g., 181; Lebedev, "Konets Savinkova," 184. **Kolchak:** Khandorin, "Pod poliarnym nebom," "Voina—zvezdnoe vremia Kolchaka," "Na rasput'e. Rossiia v ogne," "Voennyi perevorot i prikhod k vlasti," "Pervye shagi"; *Dopros Kolchaka*, 30-go ianvaria 1920 g., 140–141; Smirnov, 167–168; see photograph: "Kolchak, Aleksandr Vasil'evich," accessed September 14, 2020 <https://ru.wikipedia.org/wiki/Колчак,_Александр_Васильевич>.

355–358 **Family matters:** Gippius, "Savinkov," 88; Foreign Office memoranda, August 29, September 2, 3, 14, 1918, docs. 148345, 151966, 157503, 130–38, FO 371/3340, NAK; "Imperial and Foreign News Items." *The Times* (London, England), December 30, 1918, 7. **Paris after the war:** Merriman, 1061; MacMillan, 26–27; Nabokov, *The Real Life of Sebastian Knight*, 74. **The people:** MacMillan, 26–27; "Geules cassées." **BVS's life:** BVS to Sofia Petit, January 28, 1919, BDIC, F Delta res 571 (5) (1) (1); Wędziagolski, 127–128; Vendziagol'ski, part 3, 138; Rolland, 295.

358–360 **Representing Russia:** BVS to Maklakov, December 21, 1918, Hoover, Vasilii Maklakov Papers, box 13; "Chaikovskii, Nikolai Vasil'evich"; Denikin, "Vneshniaia politika pravitel'stva Iuga." **Sazonov:** Kenez, *Civil War in South Russia, 1918*, 262–263; Nabokoff, 284–285; Denikin, "Vneshniaia politika pravitel'stva Iuga"; *Boris Savinkov pered voennoi kollegiei*, 49; Lebedev, "Konets Savinkova," 184; BVS to

Boldyrev, October 15 [*sic*, other evidence suggests correct date closer to November 17], 1918, Journal of the correspondence received and sent by the Special military mission during its trip to Paris, IISH, doc. 28. **BVS as propagandist:** Interview with Savinkov, *The Times* (London), January 11, 1919, 8; Pipes, *Revolution*, 662–666, 670; "Le Calvaire de la Russie. Conférence de M. Boris Savinkoff." February 15, 1919, Hoover, Boris Gerua Papers, Box 9; "Russian Mission on Way to France. Kerensky's Former War Minister Says Army of 250,000 Needs Help." *New-York Tribune*, November 13, 1918, 7. **General Savinkov:** Lebedev, "Konets Savinkova,"185–186.

361–363 **Propaganda office:** "Telegram from Omsk with press dispatches," May 30, 1919, IISH, doc. 79; "Letter to Georgij Evgen'evič L'vov" and attachments, January 1920, IISH, doc. 47; "Telegram to the 'Président section Union nationale. Omsk'" with texts by Savinkov and Dikgof-Derental, August 1919, IISH, doc. 48; French Sûreté report "'Union' Agence télégraphique russe," March 27, 1919, AN, Fonds de Moscou, Box 20010216/284; Detailed report on "Union"'s activities, November 1919, IISH, doc. 44. **Russian war losses:** Bushkovitch, 297; MacMillan, 63. **Allies and Russia:** Nabokoff, 284; MacMillan, 67, 70, 73. **French debacle in Odessa:** Alexandrov, xv–xix, 159–160. **Prinkipo Conference:** MacMillan, 76–77; "Telegram to the 'Président section Union nationale. Omsk'" with texts by BVS and Dikgof-Derental, August 1919, IISH, doc. 48; *Delo Borisa Savinkova*, 57, 53.

363–365 **Persuading Kolchak:** BVS to Kolchak, March 9, 1919, IISH, doc. 9; "German Time Limit." *The Times* (London), May 22, 1919, 12; Basily to BVS, November 20, 1919, IISH, doc. 2; Notes about Savinkov's reputation enhancing Kolchak's, IISH, doc. 33; "Telegram to the 'Président section Union nationale. Omsk'" with texts by BVS and Dikgof-Derental, August 1919, IISH, doc. 48; *Delo Borisa Savinkova*, 51. **Allied recognition of Kolchak:** Khandorin, "Na poliakh srazhenii," "Soiuzniki i bor'ba za priznanie"; "New Russian Policy. Koltchak Regime Recognized." *The Times* (London), May 27, 1919, 14; "Admiral Koltchak's Reply to Allies." *The Times* (London), June 7, 1919, 11.

366–367 **BVS seeks Kolchak's recognition:** MacMillan, 459, 463, 473; Maklakov to Vologodskii, May 6, 1919, Hoover, Vasilii Maklakov Papers, Box 13, doc. 1207. **Peace treaty signed:** MacMillan, 474, 478, 485. **BVS persists:** BVS to Kolchak, July 1919, IISH, doc. 10; BVS to Maklakov, July 13, 1919, Hoover, Vasily Maklakov Papers, box 13; Kolchak to BVS, August 19, 1919, IISH, doc. 11; *Le Figaro*, August 23, 1919, 3.

367–368 **Changing fortunes:** Khandorin, "Slova i dela"; BVS, et al., to Kolchak, September 1919, IISH, doc. 13; Kolchak to Russian Paris Delegation, October 8, 1919, IISH, doc. 14; *Boris Savinkov pered voennoi kollegiei*, 84. **BVS's struggle with Whites:** "Amfiteatrov i Savinkov," 107.

368–371 **BVS's bitterness, his success:** *Boris Savinkov pered voennoi kollegiei*, 83, 86; MacMillan, 69. **BVS and Churchill:** Stafford, 112–114, 121; Lockhart, *Ace*, 87–88; Jones; "Situation in Soviet Russia. Interview with Mr. Keeling," February 10, 1919, "Conditions in Russia. Interview with Mr. Roberts," March 11, 1919, NAK, FO 608/196, file no. 602/1/4; Weidhorn, 29; Nicholas. **Karsh's photograph:** "Winston Churchill," Yousuf Karsh, Master Photographer of the 20th Century, accessed September 14, 2020 <https://karsh.org/photographs/winston-churchill/>; Lancaster.

371–374 **Churchill on BVS:** *Boris Savinkov pered voennoi kollegiei*, 84, 88; Churchill, *Great Contemporaries*, 103–104. **BVS, Churchill, and the Whites:** Tashlykov; *Boris Savinkov pered voennoi kollegiei*, 86; "Memorandum sur le voyage à Londres de M. Boris Savinkoff," October 6, 1919, IISH, doc. 36; "Zapiska o severo-zapadnom russkom pravitel'stve," n.d., IISH, doc. 37; "The Old War Office"; "World War I Casualties"; Denikin, "Nastuplenie VSIuR letom i osen'iu 1919 goda"; Kenez, *Civil War in South Russia, 1919–1920*, 150–154, 163–167; Press dispatches in Russian, November–December 1919, IISH, doc. 80.

374–376 **BVS and Churchill agree:** "Memorandum sur le voyage à Londres de M. Boris Savinkoff," October 6, 1919, IISH, doc. 36; "Iudenich, Nikolai Nikolaevich"; Khandorin, "Katastrofa"; "Note présentée à Mr. Winston Churchill," by BVS and Nikolay Chaikovsky, December 1919, IISH, doc. 15; BVS to Churchill, December 19, 1919, IISH, doc. 4; Winston S. Churchill, "M. Savinkov and Russian Policy. Memorandum by the Secretary of State for War," November 18/27, 1919, NAK, catalogue reference CAB/24/94.

376–378 **Polish connection:** Wędziagolski, 127–129; Vendziagol'skii, part 3, 138–139; BVS to Vrangel', July 3, 1920, IISH, doc. 122. **BVS tries to democratize Whites:** "Interview with Messrs. Savinkov and

Chaikovski," December 1, 1919, Political Intelligence Department, NAK, FO 371/4382, no. 676, file no. 453, 407–409; "Note présentée à Mr. Winston Churchill," by BVS and Nikolay Chaikovsky, December 1919, IISH, doc. 15; BVS to Churchill, December 19, 1919, IISH, doc. 4; BVS to Denikin, Dec. 1919, "Moi trud ne prineset," 23–24 (also drafts: BVS to Denikin, January 1920, IISH, doc. 7). **BVS procures help for Whites:** "Court mémorandum sur les nouvelles perspectives de la lutte contre les bolchéviks" [about events between November 1919 and January 1920], IISH, doc. 222; *Delo Borisa Savinkova*, 56.

378–381   **Poland beckons:** Wędziagolski, 129–154; Vendziagol'skii, part 3, 142–143; Gippius, "Savinkov," 88. **Warsaw:** Wędziagolski, 156; Dabrowski, 379; Blobaum, 2, 3, 4, 8, 11, 24, 232, 235. **BVS and Piłsudski:** It is possible that BVS and Piłsudski spent time in the same place in exile, as suggested by a historical marker commemorating Piłsudski's visit on La Passeggiate Anita Garibaldi, in Nervi, Liguria, Italy; this town was a favorite of Russian exiles. The idea that BVS and Piłsudski knew each other from school, which is often repeated in writings about BVS, is implausible because Piłsudski was twelve years older than BVS, went to the Russian gymnasium in Vilnius (not Warsaw like BVS), studied in Kharkov (not Saint Petersburg and Germany), and was exiled to Siberia after his arrest, not Vologda. Wędziagolski's description of their first meeting (156) also does not indicate that they already knew each other. MacMillan, 208; Dabrowski, 364–383; BVS to L'vov, January 17, 1920, IISH, doc. 107. **Piłsudski's proposals:** BVS to Vrangel', June 26, 1920, IISH, doc. 122. **Kolchak executed:** Khandorin, "Katastrofa," "Admiral ukhodit v poslednee plavanie."

381–383   **BVS's efforts on behalf of a Polish-Russian alliance:** BVS to Prince-Regent Alexander of Serbia, January 26, 1920, IISH, doc. 105; BVS to Piłsudski, February 13 and 14, 1920, IISH, doc. 112; BVS to Piłsudski, March 11, 1920, IISH, doc. 114; BVS to Chaikovskii, March 1, 1920, Hoover, Sergei P. Mel'gunov Papers, box 13, folder 13–5; BVS to Vrangel', June 26, 1920, IISH, doc. 122; BVS to Piłsudski, January 31 and February 8, 1920, IISH, docs. 110 and 111. **BVS's disappointments and pain:** BVS to Chaikovskii, March 1, 1920, Hoover, Sergei P. Mel'gunov Papers, box 13, folder 13–5.

383–386   **Polish-Soviet War:** BVS to L'vov, January 17, 1920, IISH, doc. 107; BVS to Vrangel', June 26, 1920, IISH, doc. 122; Dabrowski, 388. **BVS's agreement with Piłsudski:** BVS to Vrangel', June 26 and July 3, 1920, IISH, doc. 122. **Polish-Soviet war ties up Red troops:** Alexandrov, 182; Kenez, *Civil War in South Russia, 1919–1920*, 255, 259, 265–266, 273, 280–282, 292–293, 300–302; BVS to Vrangel', June 26 and July 3, 1920, IISH, doc. 122. **BVS's political committee in Warsaw:** Baedeker, *Russia*, 9; Wędziagolski, 157; "Politicheskaia gruppa B. V. Savinkova i ee deiatel'nost v Pol'she za period vremeni s 1-go iunia 1920 g. po 25-oe sentiabria 1921 goda," n.d. Hoover, Boris I. Nicolaevsky Papers, Folder 11–3; Fleishman, 155–156; Penson, 163.

386–389   **Savinkov's army:** BVS to Vrangel', July 3, 1920, IISH, doc. 122; "Politicheskaia gruppa B. V. Savinkova i ee deiatel'nost v Pol'she za period vremeni s 1-go iunia 1920 g. po 25-oe sentiabria 1921 goda," n.d. Hoover, Boris I. Nicolaevsky Papers, folder 11–3; "The People's Voluntary Army and the Russian Political Committee in Poland," November 14, 1920, NAK, FO 371/5439, no. 3857; BVS to Vrangel', June 26, 1920, IISH, doc. 122. **Bulak-Balakhovich:** Alekseev, 253–256; "The People's Voluntary Army and the Russian Political Committee in Poland," November 14, 1920, NAK, FO 371/5439, no. 3857; "New Army to Fight the Reds." *The Times* (London), October 15, 1920, 9; BVS to Piłsudski, July 21, 1920, IISH, doc. 117. **BVS and Wrangel:** "Politicheskaia gruppa B. V. Savinkova i ee deiatel'nost v Pol'she za period vremeni s 1-go iunia 1920 g. po 25-oe sentiabria 1921 goda," n.d. Hoover, Boris I. Nicolaevsky Papers, folder 11–3; BVS to Vrangel', June 26, 1920, IISH, doc. 122; BVS to Piłsudski, August 23, 1920, Hoover, Boris I. Nicolaevsky Papers, series no. 114, folder 182–33.

389–392   **BVS and Gippius, and Lyubov Efimovna:** Gippius, "Savinkov," 83–85, 88–90; Gippius to BVS, October 1920, Goncharova, 316–318.

393–395   **Polish-Soviet War:** Szumiło; Secret Political Report, "The People's Voluntary Army and the Russian Political Committee in Poland," November 29, 1920, NAK, FO 371/5439, no. 3857, 8–9; Dabrowski, 390. **Ground shifts under BVS's army:** Dabrowski, 389–390; Secret Political Report, "A Cabinet Meeting at Moscow," October 21, 1920, NAK, FO 371/5423, no. 928; Alekseev, 258–259; BVS to Vrangel', October 15, 1920, BDIC, F Delta res 571 (6) (2) (5); Savinkov, "Russkaia narodnaia," 449; BVS to Gippius, October 18, 1920, Goncharova, 320. **BVS and Bulak-Balakhovich:** Goncharova, 81–82, 320.

395–397 **BVS joins campaign:** Savinkov, "Russkaia narodnaia," 430; *Russkaia voennaia emigratsiia,*
333–334; Cook 247–248, 208, 210; Lockhart, *Ace,* 109. **Character of troops, "Green" movement
and new warfare:** Alekseev, 258; Savinkov, "Russkaia narodnaia," 429, 433–434, 438; "The
People's Voluntary Army and the Russian Political Committee in Poland," November 14, 1920,
NAK, FO 371/5439, no. 3857. **BVS brigade:** "Russkaia brigada imeni Borisa Savinkova," n.d.,
IISH, doc. 193.

397–400 **Invasion of Belarus:** Alekseev, 257–259, 261–262; "The People's Voluntary Army and the Russian
Political Committee in Poland," November 14, 1920, NAK, FO 371/5439, no. 3857; "Komitet gruppy
russkikh sotsialistov-revoliutsionerov v Pol'she" to Paris Committee, September 30, 1921, Hoover,
Boris I. Nicolaevsky Papers, folder 11–3. **Maklakov on BVS and Bulak-Balakhovich:** Maklakov to
Bakhmetev, October 21, 1920, Al'manakh "Rossiia. XX Vek," "Russkaia Vandeia" Na Puti k Gibeli,
doc. no. 2, Arkhiv Aleksandra N. Iakovleva, accessed September 15, 2020 <http://www
.alexanderyakovlev.org/almanah/inside/almanah-doc/58531>. **Mozyr:** "The People's Voluntary Army
and the Russian Political Committee in Poland," November 14, 1920, NAK, FO 371/5439, no. 3857;
"Komitet gruppy russkikh sotsialistov-revoliutsionerov v Pol'she" to Paris Committee, September 30,
1921, Hoover, Boris I. Nicolaevsky Papers, folder 11–3. **Wrangel evacuates:** Kenez, *Civil War in
South Russia, 1919–1920,* 302, 307; Alekseev, 274. **Bulak-Balakhovich defeated, pogroms:** Alekseev,
263–264; Goncharova, 377 n. 2; Savinkov, "Russkaia narodnaia," 443–445, 451; BVS to Evgenii Petit,
November 17, 1920, BDIC, F del res 571 (6) (2) (6); Loraine report, November 23, 1920, NAK, FO
371/5438, no. 3123.

400–402 **Regrouping:** Loraine report, November 23, 1920, NAK, FO 371/5438, no. 3123; "Politicheskaia
gruppa B. V. Savinkova i ee deiatel'nost v Pol'she za period vremeni s 1-go iunia 1920 g. po 25-oe
sentiabria 1921 goda," n.d. Hoover, Boris I. Nicolaevsky Papers, folder 11–3; *Russkaia voennaia
emigratsiia,* 343–344, 350, 353, 356, 364, 369. **New popular revolution:** *Russkaia voennaia emigratsiia,*
333; Secret Intelligence Report on Savinkov, May 5, 1921, NAK, FO 371/6910, no. 5593, 30;
Conquest, 47–49, 51–52. **"War Communism":** Pipes, *Revolution,* 671–713; Secret Intelligence Report,
Appeal of Peasants to Savinkov, May 5, 1921, NAK, FO 371/6910, no. 5482.

403–404 **Desertions and rebellions in the Red Army:** Hosking, 91; Radzinsii, 135; Conquest, 53. **BVS's
"Information Bureau":** "Politicheskaia gruppa B. V. Savinkova i ee deiatel'nost v Pol'she za period
vremeni s 1-go iunia 1920 g. po 25-oe sentiabria 1921 goda," n.d. Hoover, Boris I. Nicolaevsky Papers,
folder 11–3; Secret Intelligence Report on Savinkov, May 5, 1921, NAK, FO 371/6910, no. 5593, 35;
BVS to Barthou, French Minister for War, January 22, 1921, BDIC, del res 571 (6) (3), 2, 5; Document
about the Russian Evacuation Committee, n.d. BDIC, del res 571 (6) (3); *Russkaia voennaia emigratsiia,*
364, 366; BVS to Maklakov, August 10, 1921, nos. 4273 and 132/A; BVS to Bakhmetev, August 24,
1921; Maklakov to BVS, August 17, 1921; box 13, Vasilii Maklakov Papers, Hoover; Permykin to
Vrangel', August 14, 1921, Hoover, Evgenii Miller Papers, box 14.

404–407 **New blows:** Vladimir Korostovich [*sic?*] to Maklakov, March 18, 1921, Hoover, Vasilii Maklakov
Papers, box 13; Fleishman, 23, 36–40; Gladkov, 79–83; Safonov; Conquest, 51; Radzinskii, 185.
Family problem: Evgeniia Savinkova to BVS, March 3, 1921, IISH, doc. 23; Remizov, *Iveren',* 502;
Chuikina, 320–322. **NEP:** Conquest, 53–55; Riasanovsky, 541–542; Radzinskii, 186–187; Fitzpatrick,
96; Bushkovitch, 318–319. **NEP a setback and opportunity for BVS:** Fitzpatrick, 97–98, 100;
Radzinskii, 187; "Lenin's Admission. Communism the Cause of Collapse." *The Observer* (London),
November 6, 1921, 15.

407–409 **BVS thorn in Soviets' side:** "Trotzky Preparing to Fight Rumania." *Philadelphia Inquirer,* September 22,
1921, 5; American Chargé d'Affaires ad interim, Prague [signature illegible] to the Secretary of State,
November 17, 1921, forwarding report on BVS by Sidney Reilly, NARA II, National Archives Microfilm,
Roll 46, Records of the Department of State Relating to Internal Affairs of Russia and the Soviet Union,
1910–29, 861.00/9065-9159, item no. 607 (quotation about money for Savinkov's expulsion on p. 5). **BVS
expelled from Poland:** BVS to Piłsudski, October 30, 1921, Filosofov to BVS, October 8, 1921, BVS to
Lukasevich, n.d., Filosofov to Skirmunt, October 10, 1921, BVS to (unnamed) Minister, October 28,
1921, BVS's note about expulsion, October 30, 1921, Filosofov to Petit, October 31, 1921, BDIC, F del res

571 (6) (3); Chicherin to Skirmunt about Russo-Polish relations, n.d., Hoover, Vasilii Maklakov Papers, box 21, file 21–17. **Whites lose Civil War:** Riasanovsky, 538–539.

CHAPTER TEN

410–414　**BVS in Prague:** In his novel about BVS, Ardamatskii, 51–53, includes FSB archival documents about Masaryk's meetings with Savinkov in Moscow and his financial support, e.g., BVS to Masaryk, November 29, 1921; Raeff, 62–64, 86–87; Cook, 209; Lockhart, *Ace*, 105; Andreev and Savický, 58. **Churchill and BVS:** Stafford, 115–117; Kettle, 103; Cook, 211; Heller, 65. **BVS and Krasin:** Liberman; Heller, 66. **Meetings of Churchill, BVS and Lloyd George:** "Weather." *The Times* (London), December 17, 1921, 12; Heller, 66–67; Stafford, 118–119; Kettle, 103. **Lloyd George backs out:** "The Premier's Bombshell." *The Times* (London), January 7, 1922, 10; Makhrov to Miller, March 4/13, 1922, Hoover, Vrangel' Papers, box 93, folder 16; Vinogradov and Safonov, 16; Pipes, *Revolution*, 578 n.

414–418　**Family matters:** Evgeniia Savinkova to BVS, December 20, 1921, "Moi trud ne prineset," 25–26; Sûreté report, "Savinkoff, Boris," April 22, 1922, AN, Fonds de Moscou, no. 1492; Savinkov, "Dnevnik," 183; Zhukov, 89; Chuikina, 310, 311; Viktor Savinkov to BVS, March 27, 1922, GARF, d. 177, l. 21; d. 177, l. 21; information about Baron Maidel, under "Savinkov Anatolii Ivanovich," accessed September 9, 2020 <http://baza.vgdru.com/1/29916/>. **Mussolini:** "Mussolini, Benito"; Lyttelton, 35–63. **film of Mussolini speaking:** accessed September 15, 2020 <https://www.youtube .com/watch?v=CfS8AulsYRk>. **Mussolini admired:** Tooze; Kaplan, 21, 26, 151–152. **BVS and Mussolini:** Savinkov to TsK NSZRiS (Moskva), May 5, 1924, *Boris Savinkov na Lubianke*, 353.

418–419　**BVS and Mussolini meet:** "Benito Mussolini s'exprime en français sur les relations franco-italiennes et sur ses intentions pacifiques. 30 avril 1931," accessed December 24, 2018 <https://www.youtube.com /watch?v=258bJqeVdlA>; Vinogradov and Safonov, 17–18. **Secret exposed:** Vinogradov and Safonov, 17–18, 27 n. 39; "Edinyi banditsko-chernosotennyi front." *Izvestiia*, March 21, 1922; *Baltimore Sun*, March 23, 1922, 11; "Plot to Waylay Soviet Genoa Envoys Charged." *Minneapolis Morning Tribune*, March 23, 1922, 1; "Garantii lichnoi bezopasnosti." *Nakanune* [Berlin], March 28, 1922, 1; "Russians and Genoa: Assassination Feared." *Manchester Guardian*, March 30, 1922, 7; "Oslozhneniia s poezdkoi sovetskikh delegatov v Genuiu." *Rul'* [Berlin], March 28, 1922, 1.

419–421　**Terror in Berlin:** Kichkasov, 11–14, 17–19; "Gives Bolsheviki Berlin Embassy." *New York Times*, April 4, 1922, 1; Orlov, 245–246 (the names of the Soviets that Orlov and Kichkasov report differ from other sources); "Soviet Delegates Arrive in Berlin." *New York Times*, April 2, 1922, 24; "Berlin Takes Elaborate Measures to Guard Reds. Savinkov, Who Plotted Death of Lenin, in City. Delegates to be Lavishly Entertained." *New York Tribune*, April 3, 1922, 4.

421–423　**Genoa:** "Genoa Conference (1922)"; Boris Savinkov, "'Recognising' The Bolshevists." *The Times* [London], April 7, 1922, 6; Mackenzie to British Passport Control Office, Rome, April 7, 1922. **GPU and BVS's plan in Genoa:** Vinogradov and Safonov, 15, 19; "Svodka Inostrannogo otdela GPU . . . 'Savinkov podgotovliaet vosstaniia,'" *Russkaia voennaia emigratsiia*, 249–251; Litvin and Mogil'ner, 42–43; "Genoa Police Arrest 1,400 to Insure Safety of Delegates." *Baltimore Sun*, April 8, 1922, 1; "Gathering at Genoa." *Manchester Guardian*, April 8, 1922, 11; "Allies Duped at Genoa." *Daily Mail*, April 18, 1922, 9; "Zashchita russkoi delegatsii v Genue." *Nakanune*, March 31, 1922, 1; "Soviet Delegates Nervous at Genoa." *New York Times*, April 7, 1922, 15; "Russians and Genoa: Assassination Feared." *Manchester Guardian*, March 30, 1922, 7; "Chicherin i Litvinov v Genue." *Rul'*, April 1, 1922, 3; "Zaiavleniia Chicherina i Litvinova." *Nakanune*, April 1, 1922, 1. **Saloon car:** "Genuezskie vpechatleniia." *Nakanune*, April 28, 1922, 4.

423–427　**Security in Genoa:** "Genuezskie vpechatleniia." *Nakanune*, April 28, 1922, 4; "The 'Circus.'" *Daily Mail*, April 7, 1922, 9. **Gulenko:** Vinogradov and Safonov, 19; Prefettura di Genova to Senatore Vigliani, report on "Gvozdavo-Golenko," April 14, 1922, no. 127/3, registry code 10245a5 [*sic?*]; Regia Questura to Ministero dell'Interno, report on "Gvozdavo-Golenko," April 18, 1922, no. 4199, registry code 10431as [*sic?*]; Prefettura di Genova to Ministero dell'Interno, report on Golenko's interrogations, April 26, 1922, no. 7906, registry code 11615.a5; Prefettura di Genova to Ministero dell'Interno, report about Golenko and that his photograph not recognized as BVS, May 2, 1922; Ministero degli

Affari Esteri to Ministero dell'Interno, report on Golenko, June 7, 1922, no. 32754, registry no. 15188.
a5; Ministero dell'Interno, Archivio Centrale dello Stato, Rome. **BVS and Gulenko:** "Kerensky's
Minister Arrested in Genoa." *Minnesota Daily Star*, April 22, 1922, 1; "Russ Disturber Held at Genoa."
Des Moines Capital, April 23, 1922, 10; "Un Complot à Gênes contre les Bolcheviks." *La croix*, April 25,
1922, 2. **Photograph and confusion about identity:** Vinogradov and Safonov, 19. The GPU agents'
confusion about who was who is evidenced by a photograph of Gulenko that is misidentified as one
of Savinkov taken in Genoa, and that is included in *Boris Savinkov in the Lubyanka* (*Savinkov na
Lubianke*, fifth page, reverse, illustrations inserted between pages 288 and 289; the volume consists
of documents from the KGB archives). **Gulenko arrested:** Prefettura di Genova to Senatore Vigliani,
about BVS and Gulenko's arrest, April 18, 1922, no. 169=2/II, registry code 10806.as [*sic*?]; Prefettura
di Genova to Ministero dell'Interno, report on Gulenko's interrogations, April 26, 1922, no. 7906,
registry code 11615.a5; Gulenko's fingerprints and signature, April 18, 1922; Ministero dell'Interno,
Archivio Centrale dello Stato, Rome. **Full face Gulenko does not resemble BVS closely:** Ministère
des Affaires étrangères to Ministero dell'Interno, June 6, 1922; police photographs of Gulenko
and Savinkov; Ministero dell'Interno, Rome. **Russians and others consulted about Gulenko's
photograph:** Prefettura di Genova to Senatore Vigliani, report on "Gvozdavo-Golenko," April 14,
1922, no. 127/3, registry code 10245as [*sic*?]; Prefettura di Genova to Ministero dell'Interno, report on
Golenko's interrogations, April 26, 1922, no. 7906, registry code 11615.a5; Prefettura di Genova to
Ministero dell'Interno, report about Golenko and that his photograph not recognized as BVS, May 2,
1922; Ministero dell'Interno, Archivio Centrale dello Stato, Rome. **BVS's confederates arrested, GPU
seeks extradition:** "Savinkoff Seized In Genoa." *New York Times*, April 27, 1922, 4; Vinogradov and
Safonov, 19, have April 18, as the date of arrest; "Un Complot à Gênes contre les Bolcheviks." *La croix*,
April 25, 1922, 2; Litvin and Mogil'ner, 38. **BVS and Gulenko released:** Ministero degli Affari Esteri,
report about Gulenko, May 18, 1922, registry code 13734a5; Poggi to Ministero dell'Interno, May 12,
1922, telegram no. 10841; Prefettura di Genova to Senatore Vigliani, report on "Gvozdavo-Golenko,"
May 12, 1922, no. 3460, registry code 13100.a5; Prefettura di Genova to Ministero dell'Interno, July 1,
1922, no. 37440, registry code18455.a5; Ministero dell'Interno, Archivio Centrale dello Stato, Rome.

427–429 **GPU declares war:** Gladkov, 15, 19, 20, 66, 72, 74, 85–86, 101–103, 107–110, 121–122, 124–128;
Litvin and Mogil'ner, 36; Vinogradov and Safonov, 31.

429–433 **Famine, attack on church, labor unrest:** Werth, 123, 125; Borisova, 192, 247–248. **Suppression of
political opposition:** Werth, 126–127; Borisova, 252–253. **Smaller, dirtier war:** "Protokol doprosa
Pavlovskogo," 336, 342 (BVS later denied seeking money from Ford during his trial; but he also
misrepresented his past in various other ways: *Boris Savinkov pered voennoi kollegiei*, 136); "Protokol
doprosa," 70; "Obvinitel'noe zakliuchenie," 86–87. **BVS's raiders:** "Obvinitel'noe zakliuchenie," 84–85;
Vinogradov and Safonov, 13. **Pavlovsky:** Gladkov, 136; "Protokol doprosa Pavlovskogo," 333–339;
Borisova, 164; "S. Pavlovskii rasskazyvaet," 314–323; "Obvinitel'noe zakliuchenie," 86.

433–439 **Artuzov's plot:** Gladkov, 128–130; Vinogradov and Safonov, 30 n. 54, 31 n. 58, n. 59. **Artuzov begins:**
Gladkov, 103–104, 130–132. **Writer's itch, selling intelligence:** "Amfiteatrov i Savinkov," 118; Mozokhin
and Gladkov, 193; "Protokol doprosa Pavlovskogo," 340; BVS to Maklakov, October 25, November 4 and 16,
1922, Hoover, Vasilii Maklakov Papers, Box 13. **Bodyguards, clothing, books:** Reilly, 114; Mozokhin and
Gladkov, 202. *The Black Horse:* "Amfiteatrov i Savinkov," 118; "Iz pokazanii polkovnika S. Pavlovskogo,"
284–286. **Novel's main character agent of Whites:** *Kon' voronoi*, 151, 154, 199. **Dark view of anti-
Bolshevik struggle:** *Kon' voronoi*, 137, 142, 152, 144, 154, 172. **Love for Russia, hatred for Bolsheviks:** *Kon'
voronoi*, 133, 137, 214. **Publishing** *The Black Horse:* "Amfiteatrov i Savinkov," 118, 120 n. 1, 123, 124 n. 3,
125, 130 n. 3, 148; Viktor Savinkov to BVS, October 7, 1923, GARF, d. 177, l. 56.

439–441 **GPU agent to Poland:** Mozokhin and Gladkov, 193, 195–196; Gladkov, 132; "Amfiteatrov i
Savinkov," 114 n. 4. **Artuzov and Fomichyov:** Mozokhin and Gladkov, 198–199; *Boris Savinkov na
Lubianke*, 349 n. 5. **Lenin's health:** Kotkin, 412, 483, 492–493; "Lenin's Illness Brings Debate on
New Leader." *Chicago Daily Tribune*, June 10, 1922, 5; "Trotzky, Ambitious to Succeed Lenine, Keeps
Peace for Sake of 'Cause' and Awaits Chance." *St. Louis Post-Dispatch*, July 11, 1923, 16; "Amfiteatrov
i Savinkov," 125–126 n. 3.

442–445   **Amfiteatrov to BVS about attack on Petrograd:** "Daniil Aleksandrovič Amfiteatrov"; "Amfiteatrov i
              Savinkov," 81–82, 83 (n. 1, 2), 84; Cassels, 187. **Mukhin to Paris:** Mozokhin and Gladkov, 201–203;
              Gladkov, 132, 136 (his timing of visit by Mukhin differs from Mozokhin's and Gladkov's); "Protokol
              doprosa Pavlovskogo," 338. **Mukhin returns to Moscow:** Mozokhin and Gladkov, 206.
445–448   **BVS about Mukhin:** BVS to Vera Miagkova, August 31, 1924, *Boris Savinkov na Lubianke*, 98; "Protokol
              doprosa Pavlovskogo," 338; "Amfiteatrov i Savinkov," 114 n. 4. **Italian interest ends, Reilly ends
              support for BVS:** "Amfiteatrov i Savinkov," 95–97 n. 1; Lockhart, *Ace*, 105–106, 114–116; Golinkov,
              105–106; "$28,473 Paid for Literary Relics of Great Napoleon." *New-York-Tribune*, May 6, 1921, 10;
              Advertisement for auction, *New York Times*, May 3, 1921, 6; Cook, 209–210, 212. **Pavlovsky mission to
              Moscow:** Gladkov, 137–138; Mozokhin and Gladkov, 208–209 (their description differs from Gladkov's).
              Pavlovsky's letters: Mozokhin and Gladkov, 209; Gladkov, 139. **Savinkov elected, Mukhin's trips:**
              Fedorov (Mukhin) to Savinkov, October 29, 1923, *Boris Savinkov na Lubianke*, 362; Gladkov, 133
              n.; Mozokhin and Gladkov, 216, 219. "Doklad A. P. Fedorova o 8-i," 373; "Doklad A. P. Fedorova o
              desiatoi," 383.
448–451   **BVS resolves to go to Moscow:** Mozokhin and Gladkov, 214–215, are inconsistent here and say later
              that Savinkov announced his plan to return after July 12; **BVS tries to meet Mussolini, to contact
              Pavlovsky:** Reilly, 144; BVS to Fedorov (Mukhin), April 18, 1924, BVS to Pavlovskii, May 5, 1924,
              Boris Savinkov na Lubianke, 352; "Protokol doprosa," 73 n. 63. **Artuzov, Pavlovsky's performance,
              Fomichyov:** Mozokhin and Gladkov, 217–218, 224–225; Gladkov, 140–142. **BVS prepares for
              Moscow:** Mozokhin and Gladkov, 226; "Doklad A. P. Fedorova o 8-oi," 373; Zhukov, 106; "Doklad
              A. P. Fedorova o desiatoi," 381; Chaikovskii; Gladkov, 143; "Zaveshchanie B. V. Savinkova," 56–57
              (Savinkov's archive in Prague was brought to the Soviet Union after World War II); Rolland, 295;
              Savinkov, "Dnevnik," 185. **BVS and son Lev:** "Amfiteatrov i Savinkov," 144 n. 5; Rolland, 295. **BVS
              and Reilly:** Reilly, 117, 145, 148; Cook, 216–220; Reilly to Miagkov, August 8, 1924, "Tri nedeli," 278.
451–453   **BVS's confession to Burtsev:** Burtsev, "Pechal'nyi konets," 44–45. **BVS's varying doubts:** BVS to
              Reilly, October 7, 1924, *Boris Savinkov na Lubianke*, 114. BVS to V. Miagkova, October 24, 1924, *Boris
              Savinkov na Lubianke*, 132; "Protokol doprosa," 67. **BVS plans to assassinate one leading Bolshevik:**
              Burtsev, "Pechal'nyi konets," 45–48.
453–455   **BVS leaves for Moscow:** "Doklad A. P. Fedorova o desiatoi," 382–383; Mozokhin and Gladkov,
              227; **BVS and Artsybashev:** "M. P. Artsybashev," 58–59, 61. **BVS and companions travel to border:**
              "Doklad A. P. Fedorova o desiatoi," 383; Dikgof-Derental', L. E., 198. **OGPU agents in position:**
              Mozokhin and Gladkov, 227–228; Gladkov, 143.

CHAPTER ELEVEN

456–459   **Friday, August 15, 1924:** *Boris Savinkov pered voennoi kollegiei*, 5; Mozokhin and Gladkov, 228. My
              account of the border crossing is a collation of several sources, all of which differ to varying degrees:
              "Dnevnik L. E. Dikgof-Derental'," 197ff.; Gladkov, 143ff.; Mozokhin and Gladkov, 227–228; and
              other documents in *Boris Savinkov na Lubianke*. I have mostly followed Lyubov Efimovna's account
              because she was a participant and recorded her recollections shortly after the events. In all cases, for
              the sake of clarity and simplicity, I use the OGPU agents' aliases, which are the only names by which
              Boris and his group knew them, at least initially. **Lyubov Efimovna amused by the men's disguises:**
              "Dnevnik L. E. Dikgof-Derental'," 198–199; Gladkov, 143–144. **Lyubov Efimovna about Andrey
              Petrovich's mocking expression:** Gladkov, 144; "Dnevnik L. E. Dikgof-Derental'," 199. **Groups
              split up in Minsk:** Mozokhin and Gladkov, 228; Gladkov, 144. **Fomichyov arrested and later shot:**
              Vinogradov and Safonov, 27 n. 33.
460–464   **BVS and others in OGPU apartment, arrest:** "Dnevnik L. E. Dikgof-Derental'," 200–202; "Pilliar,
              Roman Aleksandrovich." **Lyubov Efimovna searched, trip to prison in Moscow:** "Dnevnik L. E.
              Dikgof-Derental'," 202–203. **Treatment in the Lubyanka:** "Dnevnik L. E. Dikgof-Derental'," 203–204.
464–467   **BVS and Lyubov Efimovna in prison:** "Dnevnik L. E. Dikgof-Derental'," 210–211, 213. **Change in
              BVS:** "Dnevnik L. E. Dikgof-Derental'," 214, 216. **Enigma of BVS's change:** Litvin and Mogil'ner,
              42–43; "Dnevnik L. E. Dikgof-Derental'," 197, 219 n.; Shentalinskii, "Svoi sredi svoikh," part 1,

"Nomer shestidesiatyi," "Ul'timatum." **BVS's letter to Dzerzhinsky:** May 5, 1925, *Boris Savinkov na Lubianke*, 168–169; Shentalinskii, "Svoi sredi svoikh," part 1, "Ul'timatum."

467–471   **BVS's show trial:** Mozokhin and Gladkov, 229–230; "Dom Soiuzov"; Averbakh. **Duranty:** Duranty, "Death Penalty"; Duranty, "Soviet Spares." **Indictment:** Duranty, "Soviet Spares," 2; *Boris Savinkov pered voennoi kollegiei*, 14–27. **The trial:** "Savinkov v Moskve." *Poslednie novosti*, September 2, 1924, 1; *Boris Savinkov pered voennoi kollegiei*, 29, 53, 57, 64, 69, 103, 108, 113, 138, 143, 144. **BVS acknowledges Soviet regime:** *Boris Savinkov pered voennoi kollegiei*, 144. **BVS's ambiguous appeal:** *Boris Savinkov pered voennoi kollegiei*, 139–144; Duranty, "Soviet Spares," 2. **Radek on BVS:** Duranty, "Soviet Spares," 2. **Verdict, appeal, Duranty on BVS's reaction, commutation:** *Boris Savinkov pered voennoi kollegiei*, 149–150; Duranty, "Soviet Spares," 2.

472–474   **Hypotheses about BVS's deal with the Soviet regime:** e.g., Besedovskii, 209–210; Bazhanov, 214–215; Spence, *Savinkov*, 349–350, 355–357, 480 n. 124 (For a summary and critique of Spence's hypotheses, see Litvin and Mogil'ner, 38–40. Parts of Spence's scenario are not supported by the documents to which he refers, and what he proposes is unpersuasive even hypothetically because of infighting in the Politburo.) **Burtsev's version:** Burtsev, "Pechal'nyi konets," 45, 51–53, 55; Kotkin, 516, 520. **Burtsev's hypothesis, Lyubov Efimovna's interview with KGB:** Litvin and Mogil'ner, 40–41. **Differences in BVS's statements:** "Protokol doprosa," 65, 67; *Boris Savinkov pered voennoi kollegiei*, 137. **BVS initially refused to accept Soviet regime:** *Boris Savinkov na Lubianke*, 168–169; "Protokol doprosa," 165.

474–476   **Discrepancies between BVS's testimony and activities:** Litvin and Mogil'ner, 44. In addition to Italy, Fascism, and Mussolini, there were other discrepancies as well, both big and small—including that there is a need for popular support for terrorism (132), which BVS did not mention to Burtsev when he said he would show how one can die alone for Russia; and that BVS never got help from England (29), whereas he had boasted that he had gotten millions. BVS also exaggerates greatly how quickly Kolchak appointed him to the Paris delegation (80); claims that the Siberian Directory did not give him money for Paris (82), whereas it did; says that Piłsudski was waging war against Russia not the Bolsheviks (99), which is not how BVS saw it at the time. BVS further claims that he was squeezed by the Poles and French to work with Bulak-Balakhovich (103), and that the Green movement was pointless from the start (132). Both contradict his original, earlier views. **BVS denies Genoa plot:** *Boris Savinkov pered voennoi kollegiei*, 132, 134; Cassels, 192. **BVS on Fascism and Mussolini:** "Protokol doprosa," 73 n. 63; *Boris Savinkov pered voennoi kollegiei*, 132; "Amfiteatrov i Savinkov," 83–84, 148; "Savinkov o Fashizme i Kommunizme, Vyderzhki iz pisem Borisa Viktorovicha Savinkova k Mikhailu Petrovichu Artsybashevu," Hoover, Nicolas A. de Basily Papers, Burtsev File, Savinkov, Boris V., Box 25; "B. Savinkov—TsK NSZRiS (Moskva)," May 5, 1924, *Boris Savinkov na Lubianke*, 353–355.

476–477   **Evidence that BVS lied about going over to the Soviets:** "Doklad A. P. Fedorova o 8-i," "Dokladnaia zapiska A. P. Fedorova S. V. Puzitskomu," *Boris Savinkov na Lubianke*, 369–370, 384–385; "Protokol doprosa," 74 n. 81. In his prison diary, which he knew the OGPU would read, Savinkov also lied about his "confessional" meeting with Burtsev, claiming that he told Burtsev he was certain he would be arrested when he crossed the border and that Burtsev dismissed his fears: Savinkov, "Dnevnik," 189. **News released:** "Arest Borisa Savinkova." *Pravda*, August 29, 1924, 1; "Savinkoff Given Death-Sentence at Moscow Trial." *St. Louis Post-Dispatch*, August 29, 1924, 1; "Leading Anti-Bolshevik." *Times of India*, September 1, 1924, 9; "Revolutionary Turned Reactionary." *The Scotsman*, August 30, 1924, 10; "Russian Terrorist Cheats Death Again." *The New York Times*, September 7, 1924, XX6; "Gleanings from Moscow." *Christian Science Monitor*, December 12, 1924, 20; "Death Penalty for Savinkoff." *Los Angeles Times*, August 30, 1924, 4; "Noted Anti-Bolshevik Sentenced to Death." *North-China Herald and Supreme Court and Consular Gazette*, September 6, 1924, 391; "M. Boris Savinkov est gracié." *Le Figaro*, September 1, 1924, 3. **Russian diaspora reaction:** Polian; "Savinkov." *Rul'*, August 31, 1924, 5; "Novaia avatara Savinkova." *Poslednie novosti*, September 5, 1924, 1.

477–479   **BVS's "Why I recognized the Soviet Regime," NEP:** "Pochemu ia priznal sovetskuiu vlast'," *Boris Savinkov na Lubianke*, 102–107; Radzinskii, 187. **"Nepmen," peasants, workers:** e.g., "Soviet Policy Creates New Bourgeoisie." *New York-Tribune*, January 30, 1923, 1; Borisova, 179–180; Fitzpatrick, 112,

131; Kotkin, 548–549; Conquest, 69–71, 75; Werth, 132–133. **Prefigurations of police state:** Werth, 138, 140, 141, 142, 143, 159, 167, 190.

479–481   **BVS writes to friends:** Litvin and Mogil'ner, 45; "B. Savinkov—D. V. Filosofovu," "B. Savinkov—V. Burtsevu," "B. Savinkov—S. Reili," *Boris Savinkov na Lubianke,* 100–101, 107–109, 113–118. **BVS to Burtsev:** "B. Savinkov—V. Burtsevu. Otkrytoe pis'mo," September 1924, "B. Savinkov—V. Burtsevu," October 31, 1924, "B. Savinkov—V. Burtsevu," December 20, 1924, *Boris Savinkov na Lubianke,* 107, 121, 142; Burtsev, "Nyneshnim zashchitnikam Savinkova"; Burtsev, "Pechal'nyi konets," 54–55. It is of course also possible that BVS did not mean to hint anything in his letter to Burtsev, but without countervailing evidence it remains a possibility that he did. **Filosofov:** "Tri nedeli," 306 n. 3; Savinkov to Filosofov, December 20, 1924, March 31, 1925, *Boris Savinkov na Lubianke,* 143, 157. **Reilly, Churchill:** "Tri nedeli," 289, 291–292, 297, 303; Lockhart, *Ace,* 118–123.

481–484   **BVS in Lubyanka prison:** Reswick, 7–10; Gladkov, 149. **Yagoda:** Reswick, 10–11. **OGPU rivalry with Artuzov:** Kotkin, 461. **Allegations against Lyubov Efimovna:** "Amfiteatrov i Savinkov," 107 n. 8. **BVS's cell, living conditions, and Lyubov Efimovna:** Vinogradov and Safonov, 22; Savinkov, "Dnevnik," 182; "Zapiska B. V. Savinkova S. V. Puzitskomu s perechisleniem neobkhodimykh emu i suprugam Dikgof-Derental' uslug v tiur'me," *Boris Savinkov na Lubianke,* 147–148; Gladkov, 150; Litvin and Mogil'ner, 41, 155.

485–486   **BVS writes and is published:** "Poslednie pomeshchiki," about the empty lives of philistine Russian émigrés in the south of France; "Nedorazumenie," about the absurdity of opponents of the Soviet regime in Russia and their monarchist fantasies; "V tiur'me," in which an ex-tsarist officer in a Soviet prison kills his interrogator but fails to escape and demonstrates his moral failings. According to Shentalinskii, "Svoi sredi svoikh," part 2, drafts of the last story show that it was heavily censored before publication to soften its portrayal of the prison; in the original, the main character was shot, whereas in the published version he was supposed to be released. Shentalinskii also says that in the original story (and another one that was never published) BVS included the autobiographical theme of feigning cooperation with the OGPU in order to be able to escape. Litvin and Mogil'ner, 41, 42; BVS to Vera Miagkova, November 29, 1924, *Boris Savinkov na Lubianke,* 137; "Predsedatel' Pravleniia Proletkino." **BVS earns money:** BVS to Viktor Uspenskii [son], March 20, 1925, "Moi trud ne prineset," 26; "B. Savinkov—I. Sosnovskomu," "B. Savinkov—S. Puzitskomu," *Boris Savinkov na Lubianke,* 159, 161–162. **BVS "rich," sends and spends money:** BVS to Vera Miagkova, November 29, 1924, "Zaveshchanie B. V. Savinkova," *Boris Savinkov na Lubianke,* 137, 55–57. **Family visits:** Litvin and Mogil'ner, 47 n. 15, "B. Savinkov—V. Miagkovoi," November 29, 1924, January 4, 1925, *Boris Savinkov na Lubianke,* 134, 150; BVS to Viktor Uspenskii [son], March 20, April 15, May 5, 1925, "Moi trud ne prineset," 26, 28, 30. **Grandfather, Vera, money:** "B. Savinkov—V. Miagkovoi," November 29, 1924, *Boris Savinkov na Lubianke,* 137; BVS to Viktor Uspenskii [son], March 20, April 15, May 5, 1925, "Moi trud ne prineset," 28, 29, 31.

486–487   **BVS, sister, younger siblings:** "B. Savinkov—V. Miagkovoi," August 31, 1924, October 24, 1924, November 21, 1924, January 4, 1925, *Boris Savinkov na Lubianke,* 99, 130, 134, 149. **BVS and son:** "B. Savinkov—V. Miagkovoi," January 4, 1925, *Boris Savinkov na Lubianke,* 148; "B. Savinkov—L. Savinkovu," November 4 and December 20, 1924, *Boris Savinkov na Lubianke,* 123, 144. **BVS's diary:** Savinkov, "Dnevnik," 179, 182, 185.

487–489   **BVS and the Politburo:** *Politbiuro TsK RKP (b),* 325, 327, 328. **Dzerzhinsky's decree about BVS:** "Postanovlenie Politburo TsK RPP (b) 'O Savinkove.'" **BVS's hopes of being freed:** "B. Savinkov—A. Artuzovu," March 16, 1925, "Raport V. I. Speranskogo S. V. Puzitskomu," May 5, 1925, *Boris Savinkov na Lubianke,* 156, 166; Savinkov, "Dnevnik," 188. **Small frustrations, Dikgof-Derental released, Lyubov Efimovna:** "B. Savinkov—I. Sosnovskomu," January 6 and 12, February 23, March 6 and 31, 1925, *Boris Savinkov na Lubianke,* 151, 154, 156, 158. "B. Savinkov—S. Puzitskomu," April 1, 2, 3, 1925, *Boris Savinkov na Lubianke,* 160–163; Savinkov, "Dnevnik," 179–181.

489–490   **BVS's petitions:** BVS to Artuzov, March 16, 1925, *Boris Savinkov na Lubianke,* 156; "Raport V. I. Speranskogo," *Boris Savinkov na Lubianke,* 163–164; Savinkov, "Dnevnik," 193. **BVS's mood darkens:** Savinkov, "Dnevnik," 195; "Raport V. I. Speranskogo," "Pokazaniia V. I. Speranskogo v sviazi s samoubiistvom B. V. Savinkova," *Boris Savinkov na Lubianke*, 166, 173. **BVS's requests for a different cell and an outing:** "Raport V. I. Speranskogo," *Boris Savinkov na Lubianke*, 166–168.

490–492 **BVS's letter to Dzerzhinsky:** Savinkov, "Dnevnik," 195; "B. Savinkov—F. Dzerzhinskomu," May 7, 1925, *Boris Savinkov na Lubianke*, 168. **BVS asks OGPU guards about letter to Dzerzhinsky:** "Pokazaniia S. V. Puzitskogo po delu o samoubiistve Borisa Savinkova," "Pokazaniia V. I. Speranskogo v sviazi s samoubiistvom B. V. Savinkova," *Boris Savinkov na Lubianke*, 172–173, 174, 175. **Tsaritsyno:** "Raport V. I. Speranskogo," "Pokazaniia V. I. Speranskogo v sviazi s samoubiistvom B. V. Savinkova," "Pokazaniia S. V. Puzitskogo po delu o samoubiistve Borisa Savinkova," *Boris Savinkov na Lubianke*, 163, 172, 175. **BVS back in KRO office:** "Pokazaniia V. I. Speranskogo v sviazi s samoubiistvom B. V. Savinkova," "Pokazaniia S. V. Puzitskogo po delu o samoubiistve Borisa Savinkova," "Zakliuchenie V. Fel'dmana po faktu samoubiistva B. V. Savinkova," *Boris Savinkov na Lubianke*, 173, 175–76, 177. **BVS's suicide:** "Pokazaniia V. I. Speranskogo po delu o samoubiistve srochnogo zakliuchennogo Borisa Savinkova," "Pokazaniia V. I. Speranskogo v sviazi s samoubiistvom B. V. Savinkova," "Pokazaniia S. V. Puzitskogo po delu o samoubiistve Borisa Savinkova," "Pokazaniia G. S. Syroezhkina po povodu samoubiistva arestov[annogo] B. V. Savinkova," *Boris Savinkov na Lubianke*, 171–172, 172–173, 174, 175–176. Shentalinskii, "Svoi sredi svoikh," part 2, provides other details about May 7, including Lyubov Efimovna's visit to Savinkov's cell, his behavior during the outing, and his suicide; see also Gladkov, 155.

492–495 **Commission, inquest:** "Pokazaniia V. I. Speranskogo v sviazi s samoubiistvom B. V. Savinkova," "Akt o smerti B. Savinkova," "Raport S. V. Puzitskogo o smerti B. Savinkova," "Zakliuchenie V. Fel'dmana po faktu samoubiistva B. V. Savinkova," *Boris Savinkov na Lubianke*, 172, 169–170, 170–171, 177, Vinogradov and Safonov, 23. **No grave, BVS's possessions:** Uspenskaia to Peshkova, 2 [explanatory addendum]. **News of death kept secret, *Pravda*:** Vinogradov and Safonov, 23; "Samoubiistvo B. V. Savinkova." *Pravda*, May 13, 1925, 4; *Politbiuro TsK RKP (b)*, 381. **Lyubov Efimovna disbelieves official story:** Litvin and Mogil'ner, 35. **Foreign press:** "Gen. Boris Savinkoff Ends Life in Prison; Soviet Had Just Refused to Release Him." *The New York Times*, May 13, 1925, 1; "Anti-Bolshevik's Suicide: Belated Recantation." *Times of India* (Mumbai), May 14, 1925, 4; "Savinkoff Ends Life, Hated by Soviet He Aided." *New-York Herald*, May 17, 1925, A1 (with mistakes, e.g., "fired a bullet into his brain"). **Evgeniya and Vera:** "Mystery of Boris Savinkoff." *The Scotsman*, May 20, 1925, 7; "Boris Savinkoff s'est-il réellement suicidé? Sa veuve et ses amis en doutent." *Le Petit Parisien*, May 19, 1925, 1; Litvin and Mogil'ner, 32 n. 60; "K samoubiistvu Savinkova." *Poslednie novosti*, May 21, 1925, 1. **Rumors that BVS was killed:** "Konets Savinkova." *Poslednie novosti*, May 15, 1925, 1; "Pravda o Savinkove." *Poslednie novosti*, June 11, 1925, 1. **Solzhenitsyn, Shalamov:** Litvin and Mogil'ner, 41; Zhukov, 118. **Rumors that BVS did not die:** Remizov, *Iveren'*, 499–500. **OGPU needs BVS's captive soul:** Shentalinskii, "Svoi sredi svoikh," part 2.

EPILOGUE

497–499 **Dikgof-Derental's fate:** Vinogradov and Safonov, 31–32 no. 60; "B. Savinkov—S. Puzitskomu," April 1, 1925, *Boris Savinkov na Lubianke*, 161; "Dikgof, Liubov' Efimovna"; Iarutskii. **Lyubov Efimovna:** Vinogradov and Safonov, 31–32 no. 60; "B. Savinkov—S. Puzitskomu," April 1, 1925, *Boris Savinkov na Lubianke*, 161; "Dikgof, Liubov' Efimovna"; Iarutskii. **Victor Savinkov (son):** Uspenskaia to Peshkova, 3, 4. **Vera (first wife):** Uspenskaia to Peshkova, 2, 3, 5–8. **Tatyana:** Uspenskaia to Peshkova, 8. **Reilly:** Gladkov, 85–86, 121–122, 127; Cook, 240, 242, 244–251, 257–258. **Evgeniya:** Ianovskii, 172–175; "Iurii Alekseevich Shirinskii-Shikhmatov." **Lev:** "Tri nedeli," 305 n. 2; Ianovskii, 174; Gladkov, 146 n.; Roland, 314–315; Erenburg, *Liudi*, 194–195. Some details about other descendants are in Savinkov, Sergei.

499–500 **Fates of Puzitsky, Pilyar, Sheshenya, Fyodorov (Mukhin), Syroezhkin, Dzerzhinsky, Menzhinsky, Yagoda:** Vinogradov and Safonov, 29 nn. 50, 51; 30 nn. 54, 55; 31 n. 58. Shentalinskii, "Svoi sredi svoikh," part 2. **Artuzov's fate:** Vinogradov and Safonov, 29 n. 49; Shentalinskii, "Svoi sredi svoikh," part 2; Gladkov, photographs between 320–321.

501–503 **Judgment of BVS by Lunacharsky, Radek, SRs:** Lunacharskii, "Artist avantiury"; Radek, 105; "V. Klement'ev—B. Savinkovu," November 6, 1924, *Boris Savinkov na Lubianke*, 123–125; "Ia. Akimov—B. Savinkovu," November 10 and 14, 1924, *Boris Savinkov na Lubianke*, 125–130. **BVS in**

popular memory and culture: "Savinkov, Boris Viktorovich," accessed February 8, 2021
<https://ru.wikipedia.org/wiki/Савинков,_Борис_Викторович>. **New scholarship on BVS:**
R. Gorodnitskii; K. Morozov; K. Morozov and A. Morozova. See also information about a roundtable
discussion of Savinkov in Moscow in 2015, "Boris Savinkov v istoricheskom i v sovremennom
obshchestvenno-politicheskom diskursakh" ("Boris Savinkov in historical and contemporary
socio-political discourse"): accessed March 27, 2021 <https://volistob.ru/post/videomaterialy
-kruglogo-stola-boris-savinkov-v-istoricheskom-i-v-sovremennom-obshchestvenno> and the recording
of the roundtable: <https://www.youtube.com/watch?v=g0JrE2tezOg&feature=youtu.be>.

INDEX

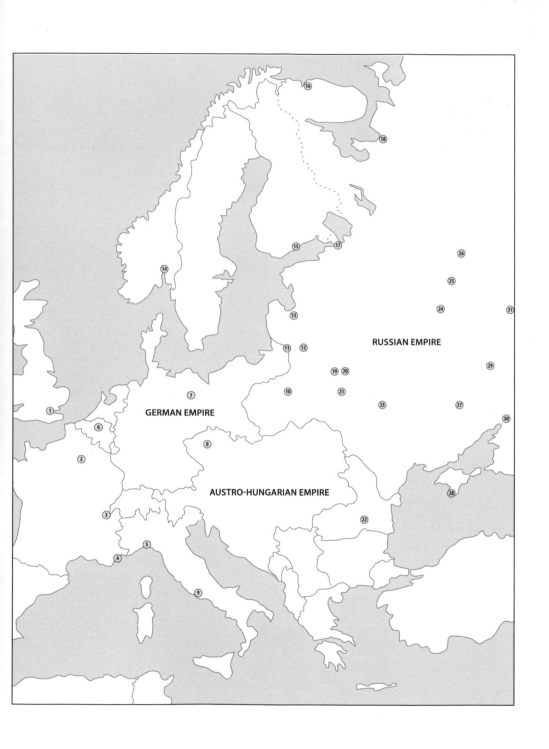